STRONG VOICES, WEAK HISTORY

STRONG VOICES, *Weak History*

Early Women Writers & Canons in England, France, & Italy

PAMELA JOSEPH BENSON &
VICTORIA KIRKHAM
Editors

THE UNIVERSITY OF MICHIGAN PRESS
ANN ARBOR

Published in the United States of America by
The University of Michigan Press
Manufactured in the United States of America
♾ Printed on acid-free paper

2008 2007 2006 2005 4 3 2 1

A CIP catalog record for this book is available from the British Library.

Library of Congress Cataloging-in-Publication Data

Strong voices, weak history : early women writers and canons in England, France, and Italy / Pamela Joseph Benson and Victoria Kirkham, editors.
p. cm.
Results of a conference held at the University of Pennsylvania in March 2000.
Includes index.
ISBN 0-472-09881-0 (cloth : alk. paper)—ISBN 0-472-06881-4 (pbk. : alk. paper) 1. European literature—Renaissance, 1450–1600—History and criticism—Congresses. 2. European literature—Women authors—History and criticism—Congresses. 3. Literature, Medieval—Women authors—History and criticism—Congresses. I. Benson, Pamela. II. Kirkham, Victoria.
PN715.S76 2004
809'.89287'09409031—dc22 2004020171

Acknowledgments

This volume originated in the proceedings of an interdisciplinary conference co-organized by the editors and held at the University of Pennsylvania in March 2000 entitled "Strong Voices, Weak History? Medieval and Renaissance Women in Their National Literary Canons." We are profoundly indebted to the participants, those in the audience, and all who made the occasion such a stimulating success.

Stuart Curran, director of the University of Pennsylvania Center for Italian Studies, provided fundamental assistance by lending us his most able assistant, Nicola Gentili; giving a major portion of the conference funding; and offering the encouragement of his enthusiasm. For additional financial support, we thank the Department of Romance Languages, the Women's Studies Program, and the School of Arts and Sciences at the University of Pennsylvania, along with its associate dean for humanities, Rebecca Bushnell, who graciously inaugurated the conference. Liliane Weissberg, director of the Comparative Literature Program at Penn, donated useful preliminary advice, and she coordinated graduate student help during conference registration. A special word of thanks goes to Richard R. Weiner, dean of arts and sciences at Rhode Island College, and to John J. Salesses, vice president for academic affairs at the college, for their willingness to make the leap of faith that sent significant shared funding to a conference co-organized by one of their faculty members but held afar at another university in another state.

Our greatest practical debt for the conference that made this volume possible is to a silent third partner, Nicola Gentili. In his capacity as assistant to the director of the Center for Italian Studies at Penn, he was responsible for the countless logistical arrangements that made our three-day gathering flow so smoothly. We planned it as a workshop, allowing ample segments of time to discussion, almost all of which Dottor Gentile was able to capture on tape with his traveling microphone. For a printout of those recorded discussions, 114 typescript pages, we are grateful to Pamela Benson's son, Thomas Benson, who arranged for and assisted with the work of transcribing. Preserving animated conversation that would otherwise have been ephemeral, the transcripts conveyed many insights that we have woven into our introduction to this volume, wherever possible with attributions to individual speakers.

The collected essays and the many fragments of dialogue that have passed from the transcripts into our introduction cannot adequately credit other friends in the community of scholars whose presence was essential in giving our conference its memorable identity. Mary Weitzel Gibbons, Sara S. Poor, and Diana Robin contributed thoughtfully to our dialogue by chairing sessions as respondents and discussion moderators. The participants in our final roundtable, "The Modern Creation of a New Canon," reported on projects of their own or other recent work that makes newly available texts and studies on medieval and early modern women writers. David Wallace described the volume he and Carolyn Dinshaw coedited in his presentation, "Designing Companiate Women, viz., The Cambridge Companion to Medieval Women's Writing" (Cambridge: Cambridge University Press, 2003). Albert Rabil Jr. announced that as of March 2000 the translation series he and Margaret King codirect for the University of Chicago Press, "The Other Voice in Early Modern Europe," had grown to twenty-seven volumes in print and in production. Since then, as he informed us, another forty-one titles have been approved for publication, making a total of sixty volumes by women and eight by men, translated from Italian, French, Spanish, German, and Latin. Susanne Woods elucidated the theory behind the Brown University Women Writers Project's compilation of its huge database of texts, discussed the potential effect of this resource on canons, and made the audience aware that the project had joined with Oxford University Press to publish a few volumes. Dennis McAuliffe announced his hopes of creating an ambitious database, "A Bio-bibliographic Handbook of Italian Women Writers 1200–1600." Georgianna Ziegler delivered the closing words of the conference, carrying us into the new millennium with a magisterial compilation of Web sites, "Early-Modern Women Online."

The task of transforming the conference proceedings into a coherent volume was greatly assisted by the comments of William Kennedy and an anonymous reader who read the manuscript for the University of Michigan Press and by our editor, Collin Ganio. In the many conversations that went into the planning of the conference and the book, we each as coeditors experienced firsthand the riches yielded by the exchange of information about the differing cultures of medieval and Renaissance Europe. We hope that this volume will benefit others as our joint labor has benefitted us.

Contents

Illustrations

Introduction

The title of this volume, *Strong Voices, Weak History*, asserts a dual premise. First, during the Middle Ages and Renaissance in the three countries visited here, contrary to Aristotelian and biblical injunction, women did not keep an obedient, humble silence. Instead, a good number of them became authors of secular poetry, classical dialogues, pious translations, public letters, and private diaries, winning recognition and respect from contemporaries of both sexes. Second, such admiration tended to be short-lived. Women's presence in national literary histories, generally speaking, has been less stable than men's, their niches more shallow or precarious, their memory more quickly occluded by time.[1]

Our anthology probes this premise, as its subtitle declares, by exploring the relationship of women writers to canons in the English, French, and Italian traditions. Its comparative structure raises to a new level the recovery of their largely forgotten history, opened to view by recent editions, translations, and monographic studies of works often previously accessible only in manuscript or in rare early imprints. These fifteen essays, which collectively document a wide range of choices made by women depending on their place of origin, nationality, and social class, reveal how they negotiated the structures of their particular cultures by concentrating their efforts in certain kinds of writing, why genres that were open to them in one country were closed in another, and how the reputation of their works endured over time. Pointing to an unexpected complexity of social context, our transnational perspective displays the nuances of local difference and the commonalities of European culture as single nation studies cannot.

This volume's focus on canons fits the period. During the Middle Ages and the Renaissance in Italy, France, and England, there was a lively sense that many different kinds of vernacular and Latin canons were in the process of formation. Authors competed for inclusion and announced their ambitions by imitating already accepted works in the subjects they chose and in the genres, language, and lexicon they adopted. Theorists and arbiters of taste compiled lists of famous poets. Editors and publishers promoted their authors by praising them as successors to the classics. Patrons put their money and power behind their favored candidates. Readers affirmed the place of authors on the lists by buying their books, translating their texts, copying them into commonplace books along with the works of established authors, and imitating them in their turn.

In its most basic sense, the term *canon* derives from ecclesiastical usage, where it originally referred to the officially sanctioned books of Scripture, a "closed list" that evolved through successive openings. The Hebrew Bible, which took form in phases that connected the Pentateuch, the prophets, and other writings, was joined with the New Testament, itself the product of compilation that linked the Gospels, Acts, the letters, and prophecy. The Christian Bible, canonized in the Vulgate version of St. Jerome, proved in turn vulnerable to revision when challenged by Luther and other reformers during the early modern period. Meanwhile, the word *canon* came to describe other more open official lists formulated by the Church, such as proclamations of ecumenical councils, the legal statutes of the Church (canon law), and "rules about patterns of life" (monastic rules), the subject of E. Ann Matter's essay in this volume. Candidates for admission to these lists were tested by conformity to "agreed-upon habits [of conduct] or codes of reading." These two notions borrowed from biblical studies—the closed but always open list and the determination of canonicity on the basis of social or stylistic criteria—are essential to this volume.

We explore three kinds of canons: first, those composed of earlier texts and authors considered authoritative and worthy of imitation during the Middle Ages and Renaissance; second, those made up of medieval and Renaissance texts and authors elevated to a similar status by contemporary readers; and third, those composed of works and authors considered by succeeding generations to be the best and most representative of the period. We chose to explore the notion of "canon" rather than the concept of "tradition" or "the classic" because like "classic" it acknowledges the identification of certain texts and certain authors as stars that guide and influence other authors and provoke a sense of reverence in them, but like "tradition" it suggests that these texts and authors are connected one to the other and to the social context that favored them. Unlike both "classic" and "tradition," "canon" focuses attention on a question of particular interest to our own age:

how these specific authors and works came to be singled out for special reverence, how it happened that others were not chosen, who was doing the choosing, and how the list changed over time—the topic of canon formation. The authors of the essays in this volume do not suppose that the final decision on inclusion emanates from an absolute authority at the top of the system, that the canon is closed and fixed for all time, or that texts are admitted on the disinterested basis of perennial truth, which in literary terms would be an elusive ideal of absolute aesthetic merit that transcends the tastes and social exigencies of any particular period. Rather, they assume a dynamic interaction between writers, texts, and readers that has resulted over time in manifold, fluid canons.[2]

Much like their masculine counterparts, early women writers in Europe aspired to join canons by imitating male-authored precedent. They, too, connected with classics by writing in the canonized genres: for example, Olympia Morata composed Latin dialogues in the Ciceronian manner (essay by Smarr); and lyric poets in Italy practiced the Petrarchan sonnet (essays by Cox; Finotti; Kirkham; Shemek; Curran; and Jones). Women confronted the most challenging intellectual and rhetorical forms: both Christine de Pizan and Isotta Nogarola, attending to such church fathers as Augustine, explored the philosophical paradox (essay by Fenster); Helisenne de Crenne adopted the "unfeminine" mode of the invective (essay by Smarr); and Mary Sidney experimented with meter (essay by Benson). They imitated a venerable national treasure, as when Christine de Pizan or Helisenne placed herself in the tradition descended from the *Romance of the Rose* (essays by Smarr and Brownlee). They wrote commentary on canonical texts, as did Laura Terracina on Ariosto's *Orlando furioso* (essay by Shemek); Laura Battiferra on the Psalms (essay by Kirkham); and Maria Domitilla Galluzzi on St. Claire's adaptation of the Franciscan *Rule* (essay by Matter). Highly educated and ambitious in their art, they could lay claim to whole genealogies spanning the centuries, as Kevin Brownlee shows in his essay that Christine de Pizan did when she shaped a "personal" canon that stretches from Ovid and Boethius to Dante, Boccaccio, and Jean de Meun.

Women influenced canons even when they did not write. One well-recognized way they did so was through patronage, but Fabio Finotti in his essay offers a still broader understanding of the role that women played in canon formation in Italy that provides a model for exploring their role elsewhere. He argues that the great flowering of women writers during the sixteenth century, a phenomenon that makes Italy unique in all Europe, resulted from their participation on the "stage" of the country's many courts, where, at least a generation before they began to write, women shaped the mode of Petrarchism and became essential to its success. Their activity as a group changed the course of Italian literary history, opening pathways not only to a new generation of female religious mystics but also to the style that was to predominate during the Catholic Reformation and to the most authoritative of that era's poets, Torquato Tasso. A similar argument could be made for the effect of the submerged presence of English women on the Protestant canon that culminates in Milton's *Paradise Lost*. The women, so to speak, went underground when their names and writings were forgotten, but they nonetheless had a shaping influence on canons that from our retrospective position look to be overwhelmingly male.

For the first time in the Western literary tradition, in this period women took inspiration from living or near-contemporary authors of their own sex, either through open citation or implicitly through allusive borrowing. They modeled what they wrote on antecedents along "memory chains."[3] When living in a certain proximity, chronologically and geographically, they formed writing communities. An important French example of this phenomenon is discussed by Janet Smarr, who demonstrates that genre sharing and intertextuality define a succession of dialogue writers from Helisenne de Crenne to Louise Labé to the mother-daughter team of Madeleine and Caterine des Roches to Marie Le Gendre. Salonlike gatherings of men and women at one of these households resulted in a "witty exchange of poems" in Latin, French, and Greek on the subject of a flea, published as *La Puce de Madame des Roches* in 1582.[4] Mary Sidney, the sister of Sir Philip Sidney and aunt of Lady Mary Wroth, was at the center of an English coterie, which in this case overlapped with a family canon. Pamela Joseph Benson shows in her essay that the English poet Aemilia Lanyer, who was on the outer fringes of this circle, used allusions to Mary Sidney's translation of Petrarch's *Triumph of Death* to inscribe herself into the canonical list that ran from Petrarch through Sidney. In Italy communities of religious gave rise to a separate canon of female mystics whose numbers grew after the Council of Trent and its decrees forced nuns into claustration (essay by Maggi). The aristocratic widow Vittoria Colonna crafted a version of *Petrarchismo* that canonized her, metaphorically speaking, as the "founding mother" for a feminine literary posterity that flourished well beyond Italy. Virginia Cox, in her essay, shows us that Colonna's remarkable following carried through successive generations of women poets, proving readily adaptable to the middle classes and even to the purposes of a seventeenth-century feminist nun.

By the sixteenth century, the notion of the woman writer as a member of a single-sex canon that began with Sappho had become a commonplace, regularly invoked by male promoters. The conclusion of Francis Meres's "Comparative Discourse of our English Poets, with the Greeke, Latine, and Italian

Poets" (1598) asserts the similarity to Sappho of Mary Sidney, countess of Pembroke (essay by Benson). After the humanist Piero Vettori declared Laura Battiferra to be Sappho's equal artistically (and her superior morally) in a letter of 1565, the association continues, along a line traced by Victoria Kirkham in her essay, in expressions of admiration by others, among them Battiferra's Urbino compatriot Bernardino Baldi, who in the seventeenth century wrote a history of the city's marvels that naturally included Laura; still as late as the 1800s, in vignettes transmitted by literary scholars, the pairing remained integral to her iconography.

When male authors, editors, and anthologizers canonized women writers by inscribing them into catalogs of female worthies, sometimes they used the connection with classical figures as did Christine de Pizan, to make a single modern example stand out in an otherwise ancient canon. Alternatively, their aim might be to buttress an argument that the moderns are the equals of ancients. In this case, the canon associated contemporary women with one another and created the impression of writing as a field crowded with modern examples. Such lists could be international in scope, as is shown by two that Pamela Joseph Benson discusses, one in Harington's translation of the *Orlando furioso* (1591) and one in Thomas Heywood's *Gunaikeion, Nine Books of Various Histories Concerning Women* (1624). These boost the English women to canonical status by comparing them with Vittoria Colonna, whose works along with those of Franco and d'Aragona were known to at least a few English readers. The first printed catalog of the Bodleian Library at Oxford (1605) includes volumes by Vittoria Colonna and Tullia d'Aragona, and Veronica Franco's name appears on Florio's list of the books he consulted in writing his entries for his Italian-English dictionary, *A Worlde of Wordes* (1598).[5]

Two anthologies compiled by men, one published in Italy and one in England, created virtual assemblies exclusively of women. Deanna Shemek in her essay characterizes the 1559 collection—Europe's first—edited by Lodovico Domenichi as a "curiosity cabinet" akin to the *Wunderkammer*, or chamber of marvels, popular among Renaissance connoisseurs, who collected everything from paintings to proverbs. John N. King in his essay discusses the near-contemporary English counterpart, Thomas Bentley's *The Monument of Matrons*, a lavish multivolume work fashioned to celebrate Queen Elizabeth's virginity. Two large volumes of this set, political in its motivation, assemble spiritual writings by women. One produces a newly conceived canon of exclusively biblical authors—including Hagar, Miriam, Naomi, Hannah, Abigail, Sara (the wife of Tobit), Judith, Esther, Susanna, Deborah, and the Virgin Mary. The other gathers devotional works by learned English Protestant women.

In spite of the excitement these two early modern female anthologies generate among students of women's history today, they did not inaugurate a new taste for all-female anthologies, and unlike the general category of poetry anthology to which they belonged, they exercised no canonizing influence. In Italy, and to a lesser extent in France, mixed-sex anthologies had a substantial influence on the canon in their day and afterward. Many Italian anthologies include substantial numbers of poems by women, and some of those who were most famous among their contemporaries first found their way into print in them. In France, anthologies regularly included established women writers, though as a rule each published only one or two poems by one or two women.[6] In England, by contrast, although poetry anthologies were just as popular, before the late seventeenth century women's works were conspicuously absent; only one anthology identified only one poem as being by a woman (essay by Benson). Frequently republished and mined by later anthologizers, the Italian and French collections preserved the women poets, at least in "sprinklings," through the centuries, and the absence of women poets from English print anthologies is a cause of their far lesser representation in canons of succeeding generations.

Single-author volumes were as important as anthologies for the survival of women's names and literary writing, especially in Italy and France. In Italy, the country that assimilated the most women into print,[7] it became fashionable for these books to include sonnet exchanges that often connected women with men in poetic dialogue. For example, Pietro Bembo's highly influential *Rime* [Rhymes], in the editions of 1535 and 1548, appends to more than 150 of his own lyrics 5 such poems by others, including two women—the noble widows Vittoria Colonna and Veronica Gambara—launched and thereafter often linked thanks to their appearance together in a book by such an important arbitor of taste (essays by Finotti and Kirkham). Giolito in Venice printed Tullia d'Aragona's *Rime* (1547), and the following year the same press issued the first of nine surviving volumes of verse by Laura Terracina (essay by Shemek). Upon the death of Gaspara Stampa, her sister Cassandra and the editor Giorgio Benzone together brought out her verse (1554) (essay by Jones).[8] Vittoria Colonna's poetry, the first to be sanctioned by male-authored commentary (essay by Cox), appeared at Venice with the apparatus by Rinaldo Corso in Girolamo Ruscelli's edition of 1558. Giunti of Florence printed Laura Battiferra's *First Book of Tuscan Works* (1560) and her *Penitential Psalms* (1564) (essay by Kirkham).

With regard to printing, England was at the opposite extreme from Italy. There, considerations of class propriety made manuscript circulation an important and influential mode of publication for both sexes well into the seventeenth century, and for women it was the dominant mode of publication. English authors could find an audience and substantial fame in literary circles without going into print, although for women the fame achieved by this means of circulation rarely lived more than one generation beyond the author (essay by Benson).

In France and Italy, being published greatly increased the chances that a work by a woman would attract the attention necessary to make it survive and even become part of a canon, but it certainly did not guarantee it. Susan Broomhall has documented that works by eighty-five women were printed in France between 1488 and 1599. Very few of those published works were noticed, however, by the influential bibliographer François La Croix Du Maine; in 1584 of the forty-six women authors that he recorded, only fifteen had appeared in print.[9] For Christine de Pizan, who wrote in the early fifteenth century, not even publication, popularity, and association with other well-known authors overcame the barriers posed by changes in taste and language. Although *The City of Ladies,* now her most famous work, received only manuscript publication in France, many of her works were printed and reprinted through 1549, but after that date the texts that were printed did not have an edge on the one that remained in manuscript. They all fell out of favor, probably because their genres and language were perceived as old-fashioned.[10]

Christine's eclipse in France raises the issue of women's reception more generally. How do voices that were once "strong" fade and become "weak"? One of the most vexed areas of female writing in this regard is mystical and devotional literature. This has tended to drop out of literary canons except for the few cases in which it has also been perceived as high art. Thus Mary Sidney's translations of the Psalms and Vittoria Colonna's *Rime spirituali* have survived, but among the writers in Bentley's *Monument of Matrons*, discussed by John N. King, only Queen Elizabeth continued in the canon, for obvious reasons, even though works by her stepmother, Queen Catherine Parr, were popular in the sixteenth century, as their repeated republication shows. For their character and deeds, writers like Catherine of Siena, an Italian Catholic saint, and Anne Askew, an English Protestant martyr, won canonization or its equivalent within their respective churches, but they have been read mostly by the devout for their content, while their literary value has been all but ignored (essays by Maggi and Beilin).

Literary historians of the modern secular state are partly responsible for the weakened voices of the Italian female mystics because, according to Armando Maggi in his essay, they relegated spiritual writers to a separate canon, of interest only to students of religion. Equally responsible are the mystics themselves, he believes, who disavow authorship and distance themselves from any esthetic intent by claiming that what they wrote was not their own creation, rather an inspired text dictated by God. Their own stance encouraged earlier generations of critics to sidestep their work. Modern scholars, however, are looking beyond these disclaimers and devising new methods of reading mystics, asking, as Sara Poor has put it, if these writings "are not expressions of a distinct and independent subjectivity, then how can we hope to use them to define . . . a female kind of spirituality?"[11] E. Ann Matter's essay on the seventeenth-century Capuchin Maria Domitilla Galluzzi, the first woman to write a commentary on a monastic rule for women, confronts the paradox. She demonstrates that Sister Maria Domitilla, who claimed to be only the amanuensis of her "visions," actually wrote a good deal of herself into her commentary on the Franciscan *Rule*. Within a strict tradition, she managed to assert her own voice. This problem of an apparent absence of subjectivity also occurs in the English tradition. Writers like Anne Cooke Bacon, who translated sermons and Protestant polemical texts, appear to have no personal voice, yet they do express their own interpretations in their translations, many of which, like Bacon's, were important in their day (essay by Benson).

Relegating religious writers like Catherine of Siena, Maria Maddalena de' Pazzi, Maria Domitilla, Anne Askew, Julian of Norwich, Anne Bacon, and those in the *Monument of Matrons* to a separate category distorts our perception of women's genre choices in Italy and leaves us with a paucity of female writers in England. Because comparatively few English women chose nonsacred subject matter and genres, their voice has seemed weak, and because Italian authors have been identified above all with the playground of Petrarchism, their preferred forms were assumed to be secular. When we combine the sacred and secular canons, a richer picture emerges for each country, running a gamut from high literary art to carefully crafted devotional texts and inspired writings. The conventional great divide between Italy and England narrows. The range of the two literatures is similar.

If the literary canon has rejected mystical texts and biblical translations for containing too little of their writers' selves, it has ironically suppressed other kinds of writing precisely on grounds of sincerity. Like Chaucer's Wife of Bath, women writers are thought to be talking about their real experience and writing about what they really believe. Fabio Finotti shows in his essay how Sperone Speroni, in an early-sixteenth-century dialogue, stages the contemporary courtesan Tullia d'Aragona, an accomplished and published writer, as a woman who cares more about passion than poetry, unlike her poet-lover Bernardo Tasso, with just the reverse priorities. Assuming that sincerity varies inversely with art has meant that we fail to realize how wittily women use canonical authorities to build a position or create an authorial persona. Some women challenged tradition, asserting their own new voice by constructing philosophical debates that redefined their anticipated gender role. Thelma S. Fenster shows in her essay how Isotta Nogarola uses canonical arguments drawn from Scripture and the church fathers to prove that Eve's intelligence was inferior to Adam's, paradoxically demonstrating women's rational capacity even as she argues against it. Janet Smarr describes how Helisenne de Crenne makes a misogynist husband a spokesman for Sensuality, while the wife argues for Reason. Elaine V. Beilin powerfully demonstrates in her essay this pairing of sincerity and art in the Protestant martyr Anne Askew, read—or most recently seen in a television documentary—for her heroic resistance to persecution for her faith. She only now is being taken seriously as a writer in control of her own voice.

The assumption of artless sincerity that kept Askew in view at the expense of her authentic voice also provided an entry into later canons for other writers. This was the case with the works of the courtesans whose late Romantic afterlife Ann Rosalind Jones reconstructs in her essay. Although scholars were willing to recognize Tullia d'Aragona and Gaspara Stampa as worthy of canonization in new editions, they read the poetry as genuinely autobiographical and ignored the ways in which those authors, interacting with contemporary male poets, shaped their personae in response to conventional male poses. Moralistic editorial strategies better suited to personal, confessional narrative than the highly stylized and public Petrarchan lyric skewed the reputation these poets handed on to posterity, turning them from free-spirited writers into tearful Magdalenes.

In the twentieth century, Fascist ideology colored the editorial agenda of Jolanda De Blasi. As Lina Insana's essay teaches, De Blasi put her party's own spin on the compendious twin-volume anthology and history of women writers that she assembled (1930). In one half she collected the poetry of fifteenth- and sixteenth-century women writers; in the other, paradoxically, she denigrated it because its authors did not conform to Fascist models of womanhood. Still for all its antifeminist faults, De Blasi's resource remains a classic in the modern canon of Italy's women writers. Her anthology, like the nineteenth-century editions, at least has the virtue of preserving the names of women we might otherwise have forgotten and of saving some snippets of what they wrote.

English literary history, however, presents a very different case for the reception of women authors. The cultural setting that contained their work in private domestic coteries and mitigated against going into print made their work far less durable. Preserved only in manuscripts and extremely rare printed editions, it was not easily available to later editors. By the time that George Ballard wrote his *Memoirs of Several Ladies of Great Britain* in 1752, he could lament that "there may yet be some learned women of those times whose characters I am an entire stranger to, so there are others whom I well know to have been persons of distinguished parts and learning, but have been able to collect very little else relating to them."[12] Included on his list of women whose works (both print publications) were believed lost are two who are now recognized as among the most skillful: Lady Mary Wroth and Aemilia Lanyer. By the nineteenth century, the works of sixteenth- and seventeenth-century women persisted only in a few brief fragments in general anthologies of female writers, and they had so faded from sight by the early twentieth century that Virginia Woolf could eloquently and picturesquely say, "One has only to think of the Elizabethan tombstones with all those children kneeling with clasped hands; and their early deaths; and to see their houses with their dark, cramped rooms, to realize that no woman could have written poetry then."[13] Woolf's friend Vita Sackville-West was one of the first to recognize that many important contributions by English women writers were in so-called nonliterary genres like family letter writing and diaries—what Anne Larsen speaks of with reference to the history of women writers in France as "para-literary genres."[14] Sackville-West began to remedy this situation and redraw the image of English women's writing with her publication of *The Diary of the Lady Anne Clifford* (New York: George H. Doran [nd]).

Even those women whose work has survived represent only a fraction of the population that once upon a time flourished. To see how many have faded from "strong" to "weak," it is enough to pick up the Domenichi anthology (1559) or page through *The Monument of Matrons* (1582). Similarly telling is Luisa Bergalli's *Poetical Compositions of the Most Illustrious Women Versifiers of Every Century* (1726) with 114 authors up to the year 1575. This feminist project, of which Stuart Curran elegantly takes the measure in his essay, preserves not just sonnets but other lesser known metrical types, such as Laura Terracina's sapphics. As literary ideals changed, so did the anthologies that mirror tastes, narrowing the range of examples that have transmitted the women's work and shrinking our memory of how venturesome they were in formal experimentations. Tullia d'Aragona's identity as a lyric poet has prevailed even though she wrote in the dialogue and epic, too. Likewise, thematic breadth tends to shrink, reducing the prolific Laura Battiferra from an erudite author of occasional poetry both secular and spiritual to a supposedly confessional poet, surviving only through a handful of "pastoral" sonnets. Still remembered in the eighteenth century in Bergalli's and Ballard's books, many of these women were erased from history in all three countries during the nineteenth century, when a new canon of scholars, such men as Walter Pater, John Addington Symonds, and Jacob Burckhardt, emphasized a more masculine kind of humanism in their reconstructions of the Renaissance.[15]

This near silence effected by editors, critics, and time has been broken dramatically in recent decades through the efforts of scholars who have rediscovered countless forgotten women, more than we could have imagined ever existed. In France, two important modern presses are issuing critical editions of texts by women.[16] For English speakers, three major series have opened this territory. The Women Writers Project based at Brown University, of which Susanne Woods and Stuart Curran were founding forces, has made hundreds of texts by early modern Englishwomen available on-line, and Oxford University Press issued several of these titles. "The Other Voice," a series coedited by Albert Rabil and Margaret King at the University of Chicago Press, is publishing translations of dozens of continental texts written by women in the early modern period (and a few fundamental protofeminist texts by men). Dozens of texts have been reproduced by Ashgate in the series *The Early Modern Englishwoman: A Facsmile Library of Essential Works*.

With this embarrassment of riches, the present has come to resemble the past; it is a moment of canon formation like the Renaissance, when authors and their sponsors jostled to gain a place for their works. Now instructors, scholars, and presses promote their candidates, and as Georgianna Ziegler has pointed out, the on-line presence of texts even makes it possible to create with ease a personal canon in an individual anthology, much as a Renaissance reader put together a commonplace book.[17] As participants in this open and formative moment, the essays in *Strong Voices, Weak History* explore the theoretical and ideological underpinnings of past canons and, by returning to the period itself, demonstrate that women were not the wanderers in some anticanonical no-man's land that succeeding generations had made them seem. Committed to the principle of inclusiveness, our collective effort offers a multicanon model of European medieval and Renaissance writing that can serve the future as strong history worthy of strong women's voices from the past.

✻ ✻ ✻

NOTES

Much of the information in the introduction not tied to a volume contributor acknowledged in a footnote has been generated by the editors from the transcription of the "Strong Voices, Weak History" conference discussion sessions.

1. Karen L. Kilcup speaks of "soft canons" to describe an analogous phenomenon in American literature. See the volume she edited, *Soft Canons: American Women Writers and Masculine Tradition* (Iowa City: University of Iowa Press, 1999).

2. In this sense, consider also Harold Bloom's concept of the canon "as the rela-

tion of an individual reader and writer to what has been preserved out of what has been written," in *The Western Canon: The Books and School of the Ages* (New York: Riverhead Books, 1994), 17.

3. Nadia Cannata Salamone speaks of the "memory chain," a concept similar to that of the canon adapted from Armando Petrucci's discussion of how writing was transmitted in the Middle Ages, in her essay "Women and the Making of the Italian Literary Canon," in *Women in Italian Renaissance Culture and Society*, ed. Letizia Panizza (Oxford: Legenda, European Humanities Research Center, 2000), 498–512.

4. Georgianna Ziegler, remarks presented at the concluding roundtable of the conference "Strong Voices, Weak History."

5. John L. Lievsay, *The Englishman's Italian Books: 1550–1770* (Philadelphia: University of Pennsylvania Press, 1969), 36, 38, 34.

6. For the titles of French anthologies and publication information and lists of authors whose works were included in them, see Frédéric Lachévre, *Bibliographie des recueils collectives de poésies du XVIe siécle* (Paris: Librairie Ancienne Honoré Champion, 1922).

7. It is worth noting that one of the first printing presses in Italy was run by the nuns of San Jacopo a Ripoli, whose house was in Florence. See Elissa Weaver, *Convent Theater in Early Modern Italy: Spiritual Fun and Learning for Women* (Cambridge: Cambridge University Press, 2002), 27. Even in Italy, however, despite women writers' easier access to print, some of their work only circulated in manuscript. The same was true of male authors, for example, Bronzino. See Deborah Parker's remarks on his little studied lyric anthology, still lacking a reliable printed edition and almost entirely left in manuscript until the nineteenth century, in *Agnolo Bronzino: The Painter as Poet* (Cambridge: Cambridge University Press, 2000), 40–41.

8. Fiora Bassanese, "Gaspara Stampa," in *Italian Women Writers: A Bio-Bibliographical Sourcebook*, ed. Rindaldina Russell (Westport, Conn.: Greenwood Press, 1994), 406.

9. See Anne R. Larson's excellent review essay, "French Women and the Early Modern Canon: Recent Conferences, Editions, Monographs, and Translations," *Renaissance Quarterly* 53, no. 4 (2000): 1183–97, esp. 1184.

10. Kevin Brownlee suggested this reason for Christine's eclipse during the conference discussion. Charity Cannon Willard endorses it in her account of Christine's publication history, chap. 11 of *Christine de Pizan: Her Life and Works* (New York: Persea Books, 1984), from which the details here cited are taken. As Willard notes, Christine's works were well known and influential not only in France but also in England. There, two translations were published by Caxton very early in the history of English printing, and various others were printed through the first third of the sixteenth century. Christine is an outstanding example of an early woman writer with an international reputation.

11. Quoted from Poor's statement as respondent in the session she chaired at the conference. See further Sara S. Poor, "Historicizing Canonicity: Tradition and the Invisible Talent of Mechthild von Magdeburg," *Women in German Yearbook* 15 (2000): 49–72.

12. George Ballard, *Memoirs of Several Ladies of Great Britain*, ed. Ruth Perry (1752; Detroit: Wayne State University Press, 1985), 66.

13. Quoted in Margaret J. M. Ezell, *Writing Women's Literary History* (Baltimore: Johns Hopkins University Press, 1993), 66.

14. Larson, "French Women and the Early Modern Canon," 1185.

15. For some contemporary critical perspectives on this humanistic canon, which excluded not only women but also "minor" male authors, see Marilyn Migiel and Juliana Schiesari, eds., *Refiguring Woman: Perspectives on Gender and the Italian Renaissance* (Ithaca: Cornell University Press, 1991).

16. Larson, "French Women and the Early Modern Canon," 1197.

17. Georgianna Ziegler, remarks presented at the concluding roundtable of the conference "Strong Voices, Weak History." See also Ziegler's "Lost in the Archives? Searching for Records of Early Modern Women," in *Teaching Tudor and Stuart Women Writers*, ed. Margaret Hannay and Susanne Woods (New York: Modern Language Association, 2000), 315–47. The kind of personal commonplace book envisioned by Ziegler, generated from Web sources, will be much less unwieldy than the printed "blockbuster," which, as Marjorie Perloff has argued in a witty review of the new *Norton Anthology of American Literature*, makes "the very notion of canonicity absurd." See her article, "Why Big Anthologies Make Bad Textbooks," *Chronicle of Higher Education*, April 16, 1999, B6–B7.

Women Writers & the Canon in Sixteenth-Century Italy

THE CASE OF VITTORIA COLONNA

Virginia Cox

Donna ammirabile! Possa il luminoso tuo esempio servir di sprone a quei felici, ma timidi ingegni, che slanciarsi non osano nel bel cammin della gloria!

[Most admirable lady! May your shining example serve as a spur to those gifted but timorous minds that have not yet dared to launch themselves upon the sweet road to glory!]

A distinctive feature of the Italian literary tradition—shared only, perhaps, to some extent, by the French—is its precocious and definitive acceptance into the canon of a number of early modern women writers. Within a tradition like the English, the women writers of this period most widely studied today are for the most part recent critical rediscoveries, having either been little known in their lifetime or subsequently suffered periods of critical neglect. In Italy, by contrast, there are instances from this period of women recognized in their lifetimes as leading literary figures and whose critical reputation has tranquilly endured to this day. The most clear-cut case of this is the subject of this essay, Vittoria Colonna (1490–1547). Colonna was the object, in her day, of unchallenged popular and critical acclaim: as well as being one of the most-published poets of the sixteenth century, she was a staple figure in anthologies and listings of notable literary figures of the period and, remarkably, was the first vernacular poet other than Petrarch to receive the tribute of a published commentary on her work.[1] Her reputation, firmly established in her lifetime, has never been seriously contested in successive centuries: to cite the terms of the title of the present volume, Colonna represents an interesting case of a strong female voice coupled with a uniformly (or almost uniformly) strong history.[2]

The principal object of the present essay is to examine the implications for later-sixteenth-century Italian women writers of Colonna's rapid and definitive acceptance into the canon. Before this problem may be addressed directly, however, it will be as well to consider the motives of Colonna's "canonization" and to remark on the significance that her name came to assume within the literary culture of the day. Prime among the reasons for the success of Colonna's poetry in her own time was, of course, the high quality of her writing and, perhaps particularly, her impeccable mastery of the technical skills so prized in lyric poetry at this time. A faultless stylist and a faithful adherent to the canons of Petrarchist imitation elaborated by Pietro Bembo (1470–1547), Colonna is the antithesis of the untutored and spontaneous model of expression that so many schools of criticism, whether hostile or admiring, have regarded as characterizing the feminine poetic voice.[3] That this has been a factor in making her writing so historically assimilable within the male canon is borne out by a stream of prestigious testimonials, from Bembo's early discovery in her verse of a "gravity" he would not have expected in a woman[4] to Burckhardt's appreciation of her verses as "so far removed from the dilettantism which we commonly find in the poetry of women that we should not hesitate to attribute them to male authors if we had not clear external evidence to the contrary."[5] Beyond its stylistic rigor and control, a further factor contributing to this traditional perception of Colonna's verse as "virile" is likely to have been the ethical tone of the authorial persona she crafted for herself, characterized by a stoicism and austerity more easily readable as "masculine" than as "feminine" within her culture.[6] This, along with her high social status and the intellectual and spiritual authority she had accrued by the end of her life, must have contributed to Michelangelo's occasional casting of her in his writings as male: "un grande amico" [a very great friend (of the masculine gender)] as he addresses her in one letter, or "un uomo in una donna" [a man within a woman].[7]

In part, then, Colonna owed her easy assimilation within a male-dominated literary culture to her perceived masculine qualities as poet and cultural protagonist. At the same time, however, any threat that might be evoked by this transexually "virile" element in her persona was conveniently offset by her adherence in other respects to a reassuringly conventional ideal of femininity. Although she had written poetry from a relatively early age—a single verse epistle survives from the time of her marriage—Colonna's national fame as a poet dated from the period following the death of her husband in 1525, and the poems that won her fame were those devoted to celebrating his virtues and expressing her inconsolability at his loss.[8] Later in her life, from the late 1530s to the 1540s, the thematic emphasis of her poetry shifted, increasingly expressing the religious concerns that dominated the latter part of her life. The grieving widow, devoting her poetic talents to the cult of her dead husband, and the saintly older woman, properly turning in her declining years toward an exclusive focus on spiritual salvation: these were not unpalatable or difficult images for sixteenth-century literary culture to swallow. If one contrasts Colonna's eminently "digestible" moral and poetic persona with that of, say, Gaspara Stampa (1523–54), whose poetry recounts in turn the poet's turbulent and undisguisedly sexual affair with Collaltino da Collalto, its unhappy ending, and the beginnings of a further love story with Bartolomeo Zen, it is not difficult to explain why the former became one of the most acclaimed and published poets of the century, while the latter's renown proved barely capable of transcending the faintly libertine Venetian circles in which Stampa had moved in her lifetime.[9]

Up to this point, I have been looking at the qualities in Colonna's poetry that made it sufficiently palatable to the male literary establishment of her day to ensure her canonization. But a final, and more fundamental, factor must be taken into account in gauging the reasons for Colonna's success as a poet: the fact that, at the time of her "discovery" around 1530, elite literary culture in Italy was in a phase of its history peculiarly propitious to a discovery of precisely this kind. Without disparaging Colonna's very genuine poetic talent, one might say that a cultural space had created itself at this moment for a great woman poet and that part of Colonna's genius lay in her ability to craft herself persuasively and unthreateningly as the right candidate to step into that space. The principal developments in Italian literary history in the first three decades of the sixteenth century had been the diffusion of printing and the subsequent, gradual displacement of Latin by the vernacular: a process symbolically sealed by the publication of Bembo's *Prose della volgar lingua* [Writings on the vernacular] in 1525. More specifically, Bembo's influential treatise signaled the triumph of one particular brand of vernacular literary culture: polite, urbane, self-consciously courtly in its values and diction and purged of the air of provincialism that had dogged vernacular poetry in the previous century. Gallantry and chivalry toward women—typically courtly attitudes as they were—were among the distinguishing features of the new poetic culture, which may be further characterized as "feminized" in its thematic emphasis on love and its stylistic privileging of refinement and formal polish. An affirmative attitude to women thus became a badge of appurtenance to the new culture, a point well illustrated by the two most notable literary works published in these years, Castiglione's *Libro del cortegiano* [Book of the courtier] (1528) and Ariosto's *Orlando furioso* (1532).[10]

Within this context, it should be clear why a woman poet of indubitable quality such as Colonna should have been greeted with such enthusiasm by her male peers when she emerged in the late 1520s. A key factor to note in this connection is Colonna's exalted social background as a member of the highest Italian aristocracy, a status she shared with Veronica Gambara (1485–1550), the only other woman poet of her generation to rival her in fame.[11] Women like Colonna and Gambara were thus socially well suited to act as figureheads for the new literary culture, the novelty of their profile, moreover, equipping them to express metonymically the novelty of the values represented by that culture. It cannot surprise us that these women's male contemporaries competed to shower praises on the "divine" marchioness of Pescara and the equally "divine" countess of Correggio, when this allowed them to position themselves simultaneously as part of a cultural avant-garde and a social elite.

These points may be developed by looking at an important document of this early phase of Colonna's "canonization": the proem to Canto 37 of Ariosto's *Orlando furioso*, which the poet added during his painstaking revision of the poem for its third and final edition in 1532.[12] The passage signals the emergence of women writers as an important contemporary cultural phenomenon and isolates Colonna for particular notice as the most distinguished representative of this development. This prominent mention in a work of such popular diffusion and critical prestige was a key factor in the establishment of Colonna's reputation, sealing her status, never subsequently challenged, as the supreme female cultural luminary of her age. At the same time, the terms of Ariosto's praise would help to crystallize a particular, and strongly gendered, biographical image of Colonna, which would powerfully shape the reception of her poetry both in her lifetime and in ages to come.

The passage in question, which extends for a full twenty-one stanzas, may be divided into three sections. In the first (stanzas 1–6), the poet laments the gender bias that has led male writers throughout history to disparage women's virtues and suggests that the only antidote to this malign cultural dynamic will come about when women begin to write for themselves. The second section (stanzas 7–13), mitigating this pessimism, calls attention to the change in attitude to women apparent in numerous contemporary male writers who have eschewed the misogyny of the "ancients" in favor of a more affirmative stance. Following this, at stanza 14, the poet turns back to the question of women's writing, introduced at the outset as a pure desideratum, and reveals it rather as a phenomenon already beginning to manifest itself in practice. Many women, he states, leaving their conventional domestic arts, are devoting themselves to the cultivation of the muses. It is at this point that he introduces Colonna as the supreme living exponent of this trend.

A feature of this *proemio* worth noting in particular is that the phenomenon of women's gaining access to the means of self-expression is initially introduced by Ariosto in the context of a hostile and agonistic representation of the relation between the sexes (stanzas 1–6). Men are seen to have abused their historical monopoly on literary expression to perpetuate false perceptions of women as inferior, and it is assumed that women's first act on achieving literary empowerment will be to vindicate the honor of their sex. The faint anxiety that one might detect here attending on the prospect of women's becoming culturally "vocal" is distinctly amplified by the passage's narrative context. Canto 37 of the *Furioso* recounts the overturning by the female warriors Marfisa and Bradamante of the misogynistic regime of the tyrant Marganorre and their setting up in its place a gynocracy promising a compensatory oppression of men.[13] The tone of the episode is uncharacteristically dark, with great emphasis placed on the answering cruelty a tyrant's excesses elicit in his victims. In this context, the female *virtù* whose suppression from history the poet laments in his *proemio* is accompanied by threatening associations with sexual vendetta. Behind the proem's earnest auguries for a future in which women will be empowered to speak for themselves, it is not difficult to detect a distinct unease in the surrounding text about what use they will make of this power.

This context needs to be borne in mind when considering Ariosto's subsequent invocation of the example of Colonna, whose function appears in part that of defusing the sexual anxieties just noted. Certainly, as an image of the articulate woman, nothing could be further than Ariosto's gracefully self-effacing Colonna from the specter he originally conjures of the emasculatory virago bent on revenge for the oppression of her sex. One notable feature of Ariosto's encomium of Colonna is its moral, rather than literary, emphasis. While he warmly commends the unrivaled "sweetness" of her poetic style, the burden of Ariosto's praise for Colonna falls on her devotion to the memory of her husband, the late marquis of Pescara: tellingly, seeking classical antecedents for her virtue, it is to exemplary widows such as Artemisia and Brutus's Portia, rather than to Sappho or Corinna, that he turns (stanzas 18–19). The reassurance offered by this strategy of representation is reinforced by the imagery of the passage, as when Colonna's superiority to other women poets is expressed through an analogy with the moon, which shines more brightly than other planets because it receives more of the rays of the sun (stanza 17). The logic of the image relies, of course, on the dual identity of Apollo as sun-god and the god of poetry; the image of the sun's reflected rays could thus come to signify poetic inspiration, in a reference to the ultimately platonic notion of artistic creativity as divinely inspired. Though there is nothing innately gendered in this very conventional imagery, its effect in context is certainly to confirm the impression of Colonna as passive and reactive: a jealous custodian and reflector of her husband's glory rather than an agent of her own. This is reinforced when, echoing an image frequently used by Colonna herself, Ariosto presents Pescara himself as a *sole*, leaving Colonna playing moon not only to Apollo but also, implicitly, to her husband (stanza 17, l.8).

To summarize my argument to this point, it seems clear that Colonna's acceptance into the canon was considerably facilitated by her adherence to social ideals of femininity, which offset the potential challenge represented by her incursion into masculine territory in her writing. In her person, a powerful literary voice coincided with a decorously feminine authorial ethos, the latter serving to domesticate the former and to banish the anxieties it might potentially generate. While I have been presenting Colonna's image up to this point as an expression of the agendas of her numerous male promoters, it would be misleading to present her as in any way passive in this process; rather, her letters and other writings reveal an astute and self-conscious orchestration of her public persona.[14] The "myth" thus collaboratively created performed a function of great significance for the history of women's writing in Italy, serving, along with the parallel and reinforcing myth of Gambara, to legitimize the figure of the woman writer. In particular, as women who combined literary protagonism with an unimpeachable reputation for chastity, Colonna and Gambara helped counteract the endemic tendency in this period to associate public articulacy in women with looseness of morals. Emblematic in this respect is the role the two play in a text like Lodovico Dolce's *Dialogo della institution delle donne* [Dialogue on the education of women] (1545), where they are cited, precisely, as examples of how learning and eloquence can coexist in women with chastity and religion.[15]

These considerations need to be borne in mind when we turn to consider the theme that will occupy the remainder of this essay: Colonna's role as an exemplar and aspirational model for subsequent Italian women writers. The generations that followed hers saw the practice of women's writing filtering down from the aristocratic circles in which it had originated down to the less exalted strata of the minor provincial nobility and the elites of the remaining city republics. The extent of this diffusion is well illustrated by Lodovico

Domenichi's 1559 anthology of "poetry by noble and virtuous ladies," which, without pretending to comprehensiveness, gathers verse by no fewer than fifty women poets.[16] For these later women writers, Gambara and, especially, Colonna became crucially important literary role models, providing as they did a model of Petrarchist poetic discourse inflected to a feminine ethos and invested, moreover, with the incomparable social prestige and moral capital associated with their names. The extent of Colonna's stylistic influence on later women writers has recently been revealed through the painstaking researches of Giovanna Rabitti, who has traced echoes of her voice not only, as one might expect, in women poets of the decades immediately following her death but even, though more faintly, in chronologically and culturally remote figures such as Veronica Franco (1546–91) and Isabella Andreini (1562–1604).[17]

Besides the more or less implicit tributes to Colonna's pioneering role constituted by this practice of imitative *pietas*, we also encounter more explicit acknowledgments of it, again over a substantial arc of time. This process started, in fact, during Colonna's lifetime, with a sonnet by Veronica Gambara, which, after praising Colonna for her wisdom, grace, and virtue, presents her as deserving in particular of the reverence of women, who should by rights erect a temple to her "as in ancient times to Pallas or Apollo," in recognition of the honor she has brought to her sex.[18] Similar emphases are found in a sonnet by a later, and lesser, poet, Lucia Bertani dell'Oro (1521–67), which praises Colonna and Gambara together as the Sappho and Corinna of their age and cites them as the inspiration for her own attempt to seek glory through literary endeavor.[19] Bertani's sonnet is interesting for its staging of the author's self-identification with a distinctive tradition of women's writing stretching back to antiquity and capable of "authorizing" her quest for literary protagonism seemingly independently of any male precedent. Traces of the same stance are not difficult to find in subsequent Italian women writers, down to the Venetian nun Arcangela Tarabotti (1604–52), who, in her attack on the practice of enforced claustration, *La semplicità ingannata* [Innocence deceived], evokes a tradition of women's writing running from Colonna and Gambara down to her contemporary Lucrezia Marinella as evidence of "quite how radiant are the beams of divinity with which the feminine intelligence is crowned."[20]

That Colonna and Gambara should be cited in this way, in an incendiary tract denouncing the oppression of women, is particularly interesting in view of what was argued earlier about these poets' role within the male literary-historical discourse of the period as icons of conventional feminine virtue. The moral construction of Colonna as devoted wife and widow we saw crystallized in Ariosto was anything but forgotten when Tarabotti was writing: it forms the basis, for example, of the substantial entry dedicated to Colonna in Francesco della Chiesa's *Theatro delle donne letterate* [Theater of literary ladies] (1620).[21] As we have seen, though, this seemingly did not inhibit Tarabotti from appropriating her name, along with that of the similarly exemplary Gambara, to lend the authority of tradition to her eminently untraditional writings. There is a certain irony here, when we recall the context of Ariosto's original construction of Colonna as the "acceptable face" of women's literary protagonism, in that Tarabotti's outspoken onslaught on women's oppression and on the misogynistic cultural traditions that sustain it may be seen as incarnating precisely the threat of a politicized and "vengeful" female voice that Ariosto's evocation of Colonna in the *Furioso* was intended to exorcise.

A further instance of a later woman writer co-opting Colonna's prestige to an end very different from those countenanced by the latter's male admirers occurs in a little-known text of the late sixteenth century, Maddalena Campiglia's pastoral drama *Flori* (1588).[22] The interest of this unjustly neglected work largely centers on its portrayal of its protagonist, the nymph Flori, whose successive loves for her dead companion, Amaranta, and for the bereaved shepherd, Alessi, provide the psychological focus of the play. Both loves are "irregular" within the conventions of pastoral: that for Amaranta, obviously, because of its same-sex object and that for Alessi, because of its resolutely platonic, desexualized character, which contrasts with the "natural," though virtuously disciplined, models of love characteristic in pastoral fiction. The perversity of Flori's amorous choices is underlined throughout the play by the normalizing figure of her companion Licori, who identifies both loves as ultimately stemming from a "yearning towards the impossible," which initially manifested itself in Flori's ambition to reject her "natural" destiny of marriage and childbirth in the pursuit of literary immortality.[23]

There is much of interest in Campiglia's ambiguous figuration in the *Flori* of the position in her society of the intellectually aspirant woman. Within the context of this essay, however, the key point to call attention to is the role played by Vittoria Colonna as an inspirational model for the transgressive ambitions fictionally embodied in the figure of Flori. Campiglia's mention of Colonna occurs in a speech by Licori toward the beginning of the drama, in which she makes a connection between Flori's doomed passion for Amaranta and her rejection of traditional female roles.

> Perhaps it is a heaven-sent punishment that condemns you to wander raving in folly for the love of a woman; for you always despised the sex, saying "Oh what name is more despised than that of a woman?" How often you would say, "Licori, come set yourself like me on that

> path on which one sole immortal woman has ventured, the most VICTORIOUS [*vittoriosa*] and DIVINE among all those of our sex who have attained fame and glory! The Mincio and the Tiber can well attest to it, whose waters were arrested in their course at the sweet singing of she who outdid all the worthiest shepherds of her day.[24]

Campiglia's tribute to Colonna in the *Flori* is richly suggestive both of the legendary status that the latter had achieved half a century after the publication of her *Rime*[25] and of the polyvalence of her image, which here escapes entirely its conventional, morally normalizing construction. The examples we have been looking at so far of this kind of "revisionist" citation of Colonna—Campiglia and Tarabotti—date from the late sixteenth and seventeenth centuries, at a time when social attitudes to gender division appear to have been hardening and a resurgence of misogynist discourses is apparent.[26] Similar examples are, however, found to some extent from around the middle years of the sixteenth century, when the courtly model of the woman poet began to filter down to strata of society in which gender roles were more rigidly defined.

This brings me to an important general point. The early modern Italian tradition of women's writing has at its heart a curious social anomaly: that its founding figures, Colonna and Gambara, though widely adopted as role models by later women writers, were in many ways almost as unrealistic as models of conduct for women not of their class as that archetypically inimitable female role model, the Virgin Mary. Colonna's and Gambara's exceptional social position conferred a degree of freedom on them in their social and cultural intercourse with men unimaginable for women outside the highest circles of the Italian aristocracy. Their social eminence also, undoubtedly, conditioned the reception that their writings received. As was argued earlier, Colonna's and Gambara's illustrious example served to legitimize literary activity on the part of women and enabled the diffusion of the practice of women writing to lower strata of society. But this could hardly be a seamless process, given the different social mores of the classes into which this courtly model was transplanted. Vivid testimony to the resulting tensions is offered by the letter appended to Chiara Matraini's *Rime* of 1555, in which the author defends her right to literary self-expression against critics who have argued that poetry is an inappropriate activity for women not "descended from the highest lineage and born and bred in the most sumptuous palaces."[27] Nor is this simply the expression of an initial phase of prejudice, later superseded; the biography of Moderata Fonte, written shortly after her death in 1592, tells the same story as Matraini's letters of the 1560s: of the difficulty for "respectable" women living outside the exceptional ambience of the princely courts in fulfilling their literary vocation in the face of entrenched social prejudices that would limit women's social sphere to the household and their activity to traditional domestic pursuits.[28]

Largely, one suspects, as a result of this social dynamic, in women writers of Matraini's generation onward, literary activity tends to be figured as in tension with conventional feminine roles. Writing is increasingly portrayed by Italian women writers in this period as emancipatory, as a means of escape from the tyranny of "spindle and distaff" and a bid to transgress the domestic sphere to which women had traditionally been confined.[29] This politicized conception of women's literary empowerment is already apparent in a text such as Laura Terracina's 1548 rewriting of Ariosto's proem to Canto 37 of the *Furioso,* in her *Discorso sui primi canti d'Orlando Furioso* [Discussions of the proems of the *Orlando Furioso*] (1549).[30] Terracina's version of this proem gives voice to precisely those implications of women's accession to literary self-expression that Ariosto's original is intent on suppressing: writing is here explicitly presented as a means for women to escape from their "servitude" to men. In this new context, Terracina's citing of Veronica Gambara as a model of the woman writer has nothing of the socially normalizing function of Ariosto's original invocation of Colonna. Rather, Gambara becomes here for Terracina a figurehead for a conception of the woman writer as gender warrior,[31] just as Colonna is later co-opted by Campiglia as a model for the woman intellectual as gender transgressive.

To conclude on a more general note, the material presented in this essay serves as an interesting reminder of the complexity and "negotiability" of the currency of literary reputation. This is an important point to bear in mind when considering the question of women writers' relation to the canon. Surveying the cases of Colonna and Gambara, it would be easy on a superficial overview of the evidence to conclude that these writers' relatively painless acceptance into the canon was largely the result of their assimilability to conventional gender expectations and that their canonization thus had the "conservative" effect of delimiting the emergent figure of the woman writer within socially acceptable bounds. While there is evidently some truth in this, a scrutiny of the ways in which these "founding mothers" concretely figure within the texts of subsequent Italian women writers suggests the need for a more nuanced and dynamic analysis of their role. However powerful the moral construction placed on the figures of Colonna and Gambara within the dominant, male literary-historical discourse of the period, the evidence examined here suggests that these writers' cultural prestige was still available to be appropriated and mobilized for alternative ends. Ariosto may cast Colonna as the recipient of Apollo's rays and as a feminine figure ultimately valorized by her relationship to a man. As we have seen, however, this does not stop Veronica Gambara from promoting Colonna herself to the status of Apollo, nor Maddalena Campiglia—improbable though this may seem—from adopting her as a transgressive icon of female autonomy.

✲ ✲ ✲

NOTES

The quotation that begins this essay is from Isabella Teotochi Albrizzi, *Vita di Vittoria Colonna*, in *Ritratti scritti da Isabella Teotochi Albrizzi*, 4th ed. (Pisa: Niccolò Capurro, 1826), 192, cited in Adriana Chemello, "La biografia come rispecchiamento: *La vita di Vittoria Colonna* di Isabella Teotochi Albrizzi," in *Geografie e genealogie letterarie: Erudite, biografe, croniste, narratrici, "épistolières," utopiste tra Settecento e Ottocento*, ed. Adriana Chemello and Luisa Ricaldone (Padua: Il Poligrafo, 2000), 130. Unless otherwise stated, all translations in this essay are my own.

1. For a list of sixteenth-century editions of Colonna's writings, see Alan Bullock's critical edition of her *Rime* (Bari: Laterza, 1982, 258–70); Axel Erdmann, *My Gracious Silence: Women in the Mirror of Sixteenth-Century Printing in Western Europe* (Lucerne: Gilhofer and Rauschberg, 1999), 211. On her appearances in printed literary anthologies of the period, see *Rime*, cit., 28–85; Erdmann, *My Gracious Silence*, cit., 221–23; for discussion, Luciana Borsetto, "Narciso ed Eco. Figura e scrittura nella lirica femminile del Cinquecento: esemplificazioni ed appunti," in *Nel cerchio della luna. Figure di donna in alcuni testi del XVI secolo*, ed. Marina Zancan (Venice: Marsilio, 1983), 181–84; Adriana Chemello, "Il codice epistolare femminile. Lettere, libri di lettere,' letterate nel Cinquecento," in *Per lettera. La scrittura epistolare femminile tra archivio e tipografia, secoli XV–XVII*, ed. Gabriella Zarri (Rome: Viella, 1999), 33–38. On her appearances in manuscript anthologies, see Giovanna Rabitti, "Vittoria Colonna, Bembo e Firenze: Un caso di ricezione e qualche postilla," *Studi e problemi di critica testuale* 44 (1992): 127–55. On Rinaldo Corso's two commentaries on, respectively, Colonna's *Rime spirituali* (1548) and her complete collected verse (1558), see Monica Bianco, "Le due redazioni del commento di Rinaldo Corso alle rime di Vittoria Colonna," *Studi di filologia italiana* 56 (1998): 271–95, and "Rinaldo Corso e il 'canzoniere' di Vittoria Colonna," *Italique* 1 (1998): 35–45; Chiara Cinquini, "Rinaldo Corso editore e commentatore delle *Rime* di Vittoria Colonna," *Aevum* 73 (1999): 669–96. More generally, on Colonna's critical fortunes, see Carlo Dionisotti, "Appunti sul Bembo e su Vittoria Colonna," in *Miscellanea Augusto Campana*, ed. R. Avesani et al. (Padua: Antenore, 1981), 1:257–86; Nuccio Ordine, "Vittoria Colonna nell'*Orlando Furioso*," *Studi e problemi di critica testuale* 42 (1991): 55–92, esp. 55–66, 82–92; Mirella Scala, "Encomi e dediche nelle prime relazioni culturali di Vittoria Colonna," *Periodico della Società Storica Comense* 54 (1990): 95–112; Carlo Vecce, "Paolo Giovio e Vittoria Colonna," ibid., 67–93; Suzanne Thérault, *Un cenacle humaniste de la Renaissance autour de Vittoria Colonna chatelaine d'Ischia* (Florence: Sansoni, 1968), pt. 3, chaps. 1 and 2; Michel Plaisance, "La diffusione a Firenze delle *Rime* di Vittoria Colonna," in *L'Accademia e il suo principe: Cultura e politica a Firenze nel tempo di Cosimo I e Francesco I de' Medici* (Rome: Vecchiarelli, 2004), 281–89 and "Vittoria Colonna et L'Académie Florentine: un commentaire en forme d'oraison funèbre," in *L'Accademia e il suo principe*, 291–309.

2. A temporary occlusion of Colonna's critical fortunes might be noted in the decades following her death in 1547, plausibly as a result of the change in the religious climate in Italy brought about by the Counter-Reformation (see Bianco, "Le due redazioni," 278–80, who notes that Colonna's reformist sympathies may have clouded her reputation at this time). Even during this period, however, Colonna continued to be honored as an important writer, and it would certainly be exaggerated to speak of anything like a period of oblivion. On her modern critical fortunes in Italy, as testified by the evidence of anthologies, see Amedeo Quondam, *Petrarchismo mediato: per una critica della forma "antologia"* (Rome: Bulzoni, 1974), 133–53.

3. On Bembo's advocacy of a classicizing model of lyric poetry, based on a close stylistic imitation of Petrarch, see Gordon Braden, *Petrarchan Love and the Continental Renaissance* (New Haven and London: Yale University Press, 1999), 86–101. On Colonna's relationship with the tradition initiated by Bembo, see Dennis J. McAuliffe, "Vittoria Colonna and Renaissance Poetics, Convention, and Society," in *Il Rinascimento: Aspetti e problemi attuali,* ed. Vittore Branca et al. (Florence: Olschki, 1982), 531–41.

4. The phrase is contained in a letter to Vettore Soranzo of April 9, 1530: "Ebbi il Sonetto della Marchesa di Pesc[ara]. [. . .] Di vero egli è bello e ingenioso e grave più che da donna non pare sia richiesto: ha superato la espettation mia d'assai" [I received the Marchioness of Pescara's sonnet. . . . In truth, it is a fine and an intelligent piece, and more weighty than one might expect of a woman; she has far exceeded my expectations]. For the text of the letter, see Bembo, *Lettere*, ed. Ernesto Travi (Bologna: Commissione per i testi di lingua, 1987–93), 4 vols, 3, 126 (no. 1078); for discussion of its context see Dionisotti, "Appunti sul Bembo," 261–63; Rabitti, "Vittoria Colonna, Bembo e Firenze," cit., 147–48.

5. Jacob Burckhardt, *The Civilisation of the Renaissance in Italy*, trans. S. G. C. Middlemore (Harmondsworth, England: Penguin, 1990), 251.

6. As an example of the stoic coloring of Colonna's self-presentation, see the emblem devised for her by Paolo Giovio of an unyielding storm-battered rock, with the device *Conantia frangere frangunt*, "quasi volesse dire che gli scogli della sua fermissima virtù ribattevano indietro le furie del mare con romperle e risolverle in schiuma" [as if to say that the rocks of her unyielding virtue resisted the raging of the sea, breaking the waves and reducing them to harmless spray]. *Dialogo delle imprese* (1555), ed. Maria Luisa Doglio (Rome: Bulzoni, 1978), 110–11.

7. See James M. Saslow, *The Poetry of Michelangelo: An Annotated Translation* (New Haven and London: Yale University Press, 1991), 50–51, 398 n.

8. A useful introductory study of Colonna's poetry is Fiora A. Bassanese, "Vittoria Colonna," in *Italian Women Writers,* ed. Rinaldina Russell (Westport, Conn., and London: Greenwood Press, 1994), 84–94; see also Giovanna Rabitti, "Lyric Poetry, 1500–1650," in *A History of Women's Writing in Italy*, ed. Letizia Panizza and Sharon Wood (Cambridge: Cambridge University Press, 2000), 37–40. Further bibliography is cited in note 1 above and note 14 below.

9. On Stampa (whose critical rediscovery dates, significantly, mainly from the romantic period), see Fiora A. Bassanese, "Gaspara Stampa," in *Italian Women Writers*, ed. Russell, 404–13, and the bibliography cited there; see also Rabitti, "Lyric Poetry," 42–43.

10. The question of the significance to be attached to the pro-feminist attitudes displayed in these texts has been the subject of keen critical debate in recent years. For

recent bibliography on these issues, see, for Castiglione, Virginia Cox, "Seen but Not Heard: Women Speakers in Cinquecento Dialogue," in *Women in Italian Renaissance Culture and Society*, ed. Letizia Panizza (Oxford: Legenda, European Humanities Research Centre, 2000), 388 n. 2; for Ariosto, Deanna Shemek, *Ladies Errant: Wayward Women and Social Order in Early Modern Italy* (Durham and London: Duke University Press, 1998), 222 n. 36; 223–24 nn. 45–46.

11. Colonna was descended on her father's side from the great Roman baronial family of the Colonna and on her mother's side from the Montefeltro of Urbino. Through her marriage to Ferrante d'Avalos, she became Marchioness of Pescara. Veronica Gambara was descended from a noble Brescian family and became countess of Correggio through marriage. On Gambara, see the entry by Rinaldina Russell in *Italian Women Writers*, 145–53 and the bibliography cited there; Rabitti, "Lyric Poetry," 40–42.

12. For critical discussion of this passage, see Ordine, "Vittoria Colonna," 60–66; Pamela J. Benson, *The Invention of the Renaissance Woman: The Challenge of Female Independence in the Literature and Thought of Italy and England* (University Park: Pennsylvania State University Press, 1992), 134–39. On the context of Ariosto's 1532 revision of the poem and his likely motives for including the passage in praise of Colonna, see Tobia R. Toscano, "Due 'allievi' di Vittoria Colonna: Luigi Tansillo e Alfonso d'Avalos (con un sonetto inedito della Marchesa di Pescara)," *Critica letteraria* 16 (1988): 762–64.

13. For critical discussion of this episode see Benson, *Invention*, 139–48; Deanna Shemek, "Of Women, Knights, Arms, and Love: The *Querelle des Femmes* in Ariosto's poem," *Modern Language Notes* 104 (1989): 95–97; C. P. Brand, "From the Second to the Third Edition of the *Orlando Furioso:* The Marganorre Canto," in *Book Production and Letters in the Western European Renaissance*, ed. Anna Laura Lepschy, Dennis E. Rhodes, and J. F. Took (London: MHRA, 1986), 32–46.

14. This has been stressed in recent studies by Sara M. Adler, "Strong Mothers, Strong Daughters: The Representation of Female Identity in Vittoria Colonna's *Rime* and *Carteggio*," *Italica* 77 (2000): 311–30, and Abigail Brundin, "Vittoria Colonna and the Virgin Mary," *Modern Language Review* 96 (2001): 61–81, esp. 62–63.

15. Lodovico Dolce, *Dialogo della institution delle donne*, 3d ed. (Venice: Giolito, 1553); see esp. 15v, where Colonna and Gambara are described as "ambedue dotte nelle humane e nelle divine lettere, e ambedue essemplari di religione e di castità parimente" [both well versed in both secular and religious literature, and both equally exemplary in their faith and chastity], also 73r and 80v. Also of interest in this regard is the treatment given to Colonna and Gambara in Giuseppe Betussi's translation and updating of Boccaccio's *De mulieribus claris*, *Libro di Messer Giovanni Boccaccio delle donne illustri, tradotto per Messer Giuseppe Betussi con una additione fatta dal medesimo delle donne famose dal tempo di Messer Giovanni fino a i giorni nostri e alcune altre state per inanzi* (Venice: Comin di Trino, 1545), 213r–214v and 230r–232v.

16. Ludovico Domenichi, ed., *Rime diverse di alcune nobilissime e virtuosissime donne* (Lucca: Busdraghi, 1559). A list of the poets included can be found in Erdmann, *My Gracious Silence*, 223. See also Shemek's essay in this volume.

17. See Rabitti, "Vittoria Colonna, Bembo, e Firenze," 149–55, and "Vittoria Colonna as Role Model for Cinquecento Women Poets," in Panizza and Wood, ed., *Women, Culture, and Society*, 478–97. See also Maria Antonietta Grignani, "Introduzione," in Isabella Morra, *Rime*, ed. Grignani (Rome: Salerno, 2000), 26–27. For

Colonna's continuing importance as a model for Italian women writers in later centuries, see Elisabetta Graziosi, "Arcadia femminile: presenze e modelli," *Filologia e critica*, 17 (1992), 339; Luisa Ricaldone, "Il secolo XVIII come laboratorio della modernità," in Chemello and Ricaldone, *Geografie e genealogie*, 32.

18. For the text of the sonnet, "O della nostra etade unica gloria" [O unique glory of our present age!], see Veronica Gambara, *Le rime*, ed. Alan Bullock (Florence: Olschki, 1995), 103 (no. 42); for an English translation, cfr. Laura Anna Stortoni, ed., *Women Poets of the Italian Renaissance: Courtly Ladies and Courtesans*, trans. Laura Anna Stortoni and Beatrice Prentice Lillie (New York: Italica Press, 1997), 29. Along with another sonnet addressed to Colonna (*Mentre da vaghi e giovenili pensieri*), this headed the selection of Gambara's verse found in Lodovico Domenichi's 1559 anthology of women's poetry, cit. above, n. 16; see Gambara, *Rime*, 45). Gambara also seems to have been behind the initiative of Rinaldo Corso's commentary on Colonna's poetry (on which see note 1); see Bianco, "Le due redazioni," 271–73.

19. For the text of Bertani's sonnet, see Stortoni, ed., *Women Poets*, 132. For discussion of this (and of Gambara's sonnet to Colonna), see Ann Rosalind Jones, *The Currency of Eros: Women's Love Lyric in Europe, 1540–1620* (Bloomington and Indianapolis: Indiana University Press, 1990), 34.

20. Cited in Patricia H. Labalme, "Venetian Women on Women: Three Early Modern Feminists," *Archivio veneto*, 5th ser., 177 (1981): 107. The other women writers cited in this passage are Maddalena Salvetti, Margherita Sarrocchi, Isabella Andreini, and Laura Terracina. Elsewhere, Tarabotti also cites Moderata Fonte; see Tarabotti, *Che le donne siano della specie degli uomini: Women Are No Less Rational than Men*, ed. Letizia Panizza (London: Institute of Romance Studies, 1994), 95. In general the degree of mutual citation among Italian women writers is much higher than is often recognized (see Jones, *Currency of Eros*, 33).

21. *Theatro delle donne letterate, con un breve discorso della preminenza e perfettione del sesso donnesco* [The theatre of literary ladies, with a brief discourse on the pre-eminence and perfection of the female sex] (Mondovì: Giovanni Tommaso Rossi, 1620), 296–98.

22. The edition of this text, edited by Lisa Sampson and Virginia Cox with English translation, *Flori, a Pastoral Drama* (Chicago: University of Chicago Press, 2004) was published too late to be cited. For discussion, see Virginia Cox, "Fiction, 1560–1650," in *A History of Women's Writing in Italy*, 55–57, and for further bibliography, 289–90.

23. See, esp., *Flori, favola boschereccia* (Vicenza: Heirs of Perin Libraro and Tommaso Brunelli, 1588), 56v (V, 5), where Licori recalls Flori rejecting marriage and motherhood with the words "Sian nostri figli le cose create / dal divin nostro pelegrino ingegno, / né serva ad'huomo Angelica fattura" [May our offspring be the products of our divine and wondrous intellect; and let not angelic creations such as we ever be the servants of men]. For Licori's criticism of Flori's tendency to "correr dietro a l'impossibil sempre," see 51r (V, 1).

24. Ibid., 2v (I, 1). "Forse è del ciel castigo, che per donna / tu vada errando folle; poi che sempre / Le solevi sprezzar, dicendo quale / Di questo nome donna è più vil nome? / O quante volte ella dicea, Licori, / Tenta meco poggiar per quel sentiero / ove donna immortal sola sen gio / VITTORIOSA, e DIVA tra mai quante / del sesso nostro fur chiare, e illustri. / Ben sallo il Mincio, e 'l Tebro, / ch'arrestaro il lor corso al dolce canto / di lei che vinse a prova / i più degni Pastor di quell'etate." Of the geographical

coordinates given in this passage—the Rivers Tiber and Mincio, respectively indicative of Rome and Mantua—the latter is perplexing in the light of Colonna's biography. Rather than a connection with the city itself, it may well serve to commemorate Colonna's connections with Mantua's ruling dynasty, the Gonzaga, with whom Campiglia was herself connected by marriage. On Colonna's connections with the Gonzaga, see Marjorie Och, "Vittoria Colonna and the Commission for a *Mary Magdalene* by Titian," in *Beyond Isabella: Secular Women Patrons of Art in Renaissance Italy*, ed. Sheryl E. Reiss and David G. Wilkins (Kirksville, Mo.: Truman State University Press, 2001), 197; on Campiglia's connections with the Gonzaga, see Giovanni Mantese, "Per un profilo storico della poetessa vicentina Maddalena Campiglia: aggiunte e rettifiche," *Archivio veneto* 81 (1967): 97.

25. Further evidence of Campiglia's admiration for Colonna is found in a letter of February 1588, in which she replies to her correspondent's request for a portrait by suggesting that "[he] would be better advised instead to conserve with due love and reverence the images of the Nogarola sisters, [Veronica] Gambara, and the divine Victoria." [Ben sarebbe conveniente, gentilissimo Signore, ch'Egli facesse dolce et honorata conserva delle immagini delle Nogarole, della Gambara, e della divina Vittoria.]; see Bernardo Morsolin, *Maddalena Campiglia, poetessa vicentina: Episodio biografico* (Vicenza: Paroni, 1882), 61.

26. On gender attitudes in Italian literary culture in this period, see Emilia Biga, *Una polemica antifemminista del '600: La "Maschera scoperta" di Angelico Aprosio* (Ventimiglia: Civica Biblioteca Aprosiana, 1989). The reasons for the cultural shift referred to here—often simplistically and misleadingly attributed to the influence of the Counter-Reformation—deserve further investigation.

27. Giovanna Rabitti, "Le lettere di Chiara Matraini tra privato e pubblico," in *Per lettera. La scrittura epistolare femminile tra archivio e tipografia, secoli XV–XVII*, ed. Gabriella Zarri (Rome: Viella, 1999), 213–14.

28. See Giovanni Niccolò Doglioni, *Vita della Signora Modesta Pozzo de' Zorzi nominata Moderata Fonte*, in Moderata Fonte, *Il merito delle donne*, ed. Adriana Chemello (Venice: Eidos, 1988), esp. 9, where it is stated that Fonte gave preference to her domestic duties over her writing after marriage in deference to "l'abuso, che corre oggidì in questa città, che non si vol veder donna virtuosa in altro, che nel governo della casa" [the false notion, so widespread in our city today, that women should excel in nothing but the running of the household]. See also Rabitti, "Le lettere," 231, for Matraini's protest against the widespread view that "quella Donna solamente merita d'esser lodata, i cui fatti e le cui lodi non escon dalle mura della sua casa" [the only woman worthy of praise is she whose deeds and praise are entirely confined within the walls of her house].

29. A similar thirst for cultural recognition is apparent in the artist Irene di Spilimbergo, in the account of her contemporary biographer, Dionigi Atanagi; see Anne Jacobsen Schutte, "Irene di Spilimbergo: The Image of a Creative Woman in Late Renaissance Italy," *Renaissance Quarterly* 44 (1991): 51–52.

30. An edition of this work edited by Michael Sherberg is forthcoming from the University of Chicago Press series *The Other Voice in Early Modern Europe*. For discussion, see Shemek, *Ladies Errant*, 126–57; see also Virginia Cox, "Women as Readers and Writers of Chivalric Fiction in Early Modern Italy," in *Sguardi sull'Italia: Miscellanea dedicata a Francesco Villari*, ed. Gino Bedani et al. (London: Society for Italian Studies, 1997), 136–37.

31. She is praised, for example, for having used her literary skills to confound the "cruel and murderous slanders" men have directed toward women; see Cox, "Women as Readers," 137.

BIBLIOGRAPHY

Adler, Sara. "Strong Mothers, Strong Daughters: The Representation of Female Identity in Vittoria Colonna's *Rime* and *Carteggio*." 77 (2000): 311–30.

Bassanese, Fiora A. "Gaspara Stampa." In *Italian Women Writers*, ed. Rinaldina Russell, 404–13. Westport, Conn., and London: Greenwood Press, 1994.

———. "Vittoria Colonna." In *Italian Women Writers*, ed. Rinaldina Russell, 84–94. Westport, Conn., and London: Greenwood Press, 1994.

Bembo, Pietro. *Lettere*, ed. Ernesto Travi. 4 vols. Bologna: Commissione per i testi di lingua, 1987–93.

Benson, Pamela J. *The Invention of the Renaissance Woman: The Challenge of Female Independence in the Literature and Thought of Italy and England*. University Park: Pennsylvania State University Press, 1992.

Betussi, Giuseppe. *Libro di Messer Giovanni Boccaccio delle donne illustri, tradotto per Messer Giuseppe Betussi con una additione fatta dal medesimo delle donne famose dal tempo di Messer Giovanni fino a i giorni nostri e alcune altre state per inanzi*. Venice: Comin di Trino, 1545.

Bianco, Monica. "Le due redazioni del commento di Rinaldo Corso alle rime di Vittoria Colonna." *Studi di filologia italiana* 56 (1998): 271–95.

———. "Rinaldo Corso e il 'canzoniere' di Vittoria Colonna." *Italique* 1 (1998): 35–45.

Biga, Emilia. *Una polemica antifemminista del '600: La "Maschera scoperta" di Angelico Aprosio*. Ventimiglia: Civica Biblioteca Aprosiana, 1989.

Borsetto, Luciana. "Narciso ed Eco. Figura e scrittura nella lirica femminile del Cinquecento: esemplificazioni ed appunti." In *Nel cerchio della luna. Figure di donna in alcuni testi del XVI secolo*, ed. Marina Zancan, 171–233. Venice: Marsilio, 1983.

Braden, Gordon. *Petrarchan Love and the Continental Renaissance*. New Haven and London: Yale University Press, 1999.

Brand, C. P. "From the Second to the Third Edition of the *Orlando Furioso*: The Marganorre Canto." In *Book Production and Letters in the Western European Renaissance*, ed. Anna Laura Lepschy, Dennis E. Rhodes, and J. F. Took, 32–46. London: MHRA, 1986.

Brundin, Abigail. "Vittoria Colonna and the Virgin Mary." *Modern Language Review* 96 (2001): 61–81.

Burckhardt, Jacob. *The Civilisation of the Renaissance in Italy*. Trans. S. G. C. Middlemore, with an introduction by Peter Burke and notes by Peter Murray. Harmondsworth, England: Penguin, 1990.

Campiglia, Maddalena. Flori, a Pastoral Drama. Ed. Lisa Sampson and Virginia Cox. Trans. Virginia Cox. The Other Voice in Early Modern Europe. Chicago: University of Chicago Press, 2004.

———. *Flori, favola boschereccia*. Vicenza: Heirs of Perin Libraro and Tommaso Brunelli, 1588.

Chemello, Adriana. "Il codice epistolare femminile. Lettere, 'libri di lettere,' letterate nel Cinquecento." In *Per lettera. La scrittura epistolare femminile tra archivio e tipografia, secoli XV–XVII*, ed. Gabriella Zarri, 3–42. Rome: Viella, 1999.

———. "La biografia come rispecchiamento: *La vita di Vittoria Colonna* di Isabella Teotochi Albrizzi." In *Geografie e genealogie letterarie: Erudite, biografe, croniste, narratrici, "épistolières," utopiste tra Settecento e Ottocento*, ed. Adriana Chemello and Luisa Ricaldone, 115–35. Padua: Il Poligrafo, 2000.

Cinquini, Chiara. "Rinaldo Corso editore e commentatore delle *Rime* di Vittoria Colonna." *Aevum* 73 (1999): 669–96.

Colonna, Vittoria. *Rime*, ed. Alan Bullock. Bari: Laterza, 1982.

Cox, Virginia. "Women as Readers and Writers of Chivalric Fiction in Early Modern Italy." In *Sguardi sull'Italia: Miscellanea dedicata a Francesco Villari*, ed. Gino Bedani et al., 134–45. London: Society for Italian Studies, 1997.

———. "Fiction, 1560–1650." In *A History of Italian Women's Writing in Italy*, ed. Letizia Panizza and Sharon Wood, 52–64. Cambridge: Cambridge University Press, 2000.

———. "Seen but Not Heard: Women Speakers in Cinquecento Dialogue." In *Women in Italian Renaissance Culture and Society*, ed. Letizia Panizza, 385–400. Oxford: Modern Humanities Research Association, 2000.

Della Chiesa, Francesco. *Theatro delle donne letterate, con un breve discorso della preminenza e perfettione del sesso donnesco*. Mondovì: Giovanni Tommaso Rossi, 1620.

Dionisotti, Carlo. "Appunti sul Bembo e su Vittoria Colonna." In *Miscellanea Augusto Campana*, ed. R. Avesani et al., 1:257–86. 2 vols. Padua: Antenore, 1981.

Doglioni, Giovanni Niccolò. *Vita della Signora Modesta Pozzo de' Zorzi nominata Moderata Fonte*. In Moderata Fonte, *Il merito delle donne*, ed. Adriana Chemello, 3–10. Venice: Eidos, 1988.

Dolce, Lodovico. *Dialogo della institution delle donne*. 3d ed. Venice: Giolito, 1553.

Domenichi, Ludovico, ed. *Rime diverse di alcune nobilissime e virtuosissime donne*. Lucca: Busdraghi, 1559.

Erdmann, Axel. *My Gracious Silence: Women in the Mirror of Sixteenth-Century Printing in Western Europe*. Lucerne: Gilhofer and Rauschberg, 1999.

Gambara, Veronica. *Le rime*, ed. Alan Bullock. Florence: Olschki, 1995.

Giovio, Paolo. *Dialogo delle imprese*. Ed. Maria Luisa Doglio. Rome: Bulzoni, 1978.

Graziosi, Elisabetta. "Arcadia femminile: presenze e modelli." *Filologia e critica* 17 (1992): 321–58.

Grignani, Maria Antonietta. "Introduzione." In Isabella Morra, *Rime*, ed. Maria Antonietta Grignani, 11–38. Rome: Salerno, 2000.

Jacobsen Schutte, Anne. "Irene di Spilimbergo: The Image of a Creative Women in Late Renaissance Italy." *Renaissance Quarterly* 44 (1991): 42–61.

Jones, Ann Rosalind. *The Currency of Eros: Women's Love Lyric in Europe, 1540–1620*. Bloomington and Indianapolis: Indiana University Press, 1990.

Labalme, Patricia H. "Venetian Women on Women: Three Early Modern Feminists." *Archivio veneto*, 5th series, 177 (1981): 81–109.

Mantese, Giovanni. "Per un profilo storico della poetessa vicentina Maddalena Campiglia: aggiunte e rettifiche." *Archivio veneto* 81 (1967): 89–123.

McAuliffe, Dennis J. "Vittoria Colonna and Renaissance Poetics, Convention, and Society." In *Il Rinascimento: Aspetti e problemi attuali*, ed. Vittore Branca et al., 531–41. Florence: Olschki, 1982.

Morsolin, Bernardo. *Maddalena Campiglia, poetessa vicentina: Episodio biografico*. Vicenza: Paroni, 1882.

Och, Marjorie. "Vittoria Colonna and the Commission for a *Mary Magdalene* by Titian." In *Beyond Isabella: Secular Women Patrons of Art in Renaissance Italy*, ed. Sheryl E. Reiss and David G. Wilkins, 193–223. Sixteenth Century Essays & Studies, vol. 54. Kirksville, Mo.: Truman State University Press, 2001.

Ordine, Nuccio. "Vittoria Colonna nell *Orlando Furioso*." *Studi e problemi di critica testuale* 42 (1991): 55–92.

Plaisance, Michel. *L'Accademia e il suo principe: Cultura e politica a Firenze nel tempo di Cosimo I e Francesco I de' Medici*. Rome: Vecchiarelli, 2004.

Quondam, Amedeo. *Petrarchism mediato: Per una critica della forma "antologia."* Rome: Bulzoni, 1974.

Rabitti, Giovanna. "Vittoria Colonna, Bembo e Firenze: Un caso di ricezione e qualche postilla." *Studi e problemi di critica testuale* 44 (1992): 127–55.

———. "Le lettere di Chiara Matraini tra privato e pubblico." In *Per lettera. La scrittura epistolare femminile tra archivio e tipografia, secoli XV–XVII*, ed. Gabriella Zarri, 209–34. Rome: Viella, 1999.

———. "Lyric Poetry, 1500–1650." In *A History of Women's Writing in Italy*, ed. Letizia Panizza and Sharon Wood, 37–51. Cambridge: Cambridge University Press, 2000.

———. "Vittoria Colonna as Role Model for Cinquecento Women Poets." In *Women, Culture, and Society*, ed. Letizia Panizza, 478–97. Oxford: Legenda, European Humanities Research Centre, 2000.

Ricaldone, Luisa. "Il secolo XVIII come laboratorio della modernità." In *Geografie e genealogie letterarie: Erudite, biografie, croniste, narratrici, épistolières, utopiste tra Settecento e Ottocento*, ed. Adriana Chemello and Luisa Ricaldone, 11–45. Padua: Il Poligrafo, 2000.

Russell, Rinaldina. "Veronica Gambara." In *Italian Women Writers*, ed. Rinaldina Russell, 145–53. Westport, Conn., and London: Greenwood Press, 1994.

Saslow, James M. *The Poetry of Michelangelo: An Annotated Translation*. New Haven and London: Yale University Press, 1991.

Scala, Mirella. "Encomi e dediche nelle prime relazioni culturali di Vittoria Colonna." *Periodico della Società Storica Comense* 54 (1990): 95–112.

Schutte, Anne Jacobsen. "Irene di Spilimbergo: The Image of a Creative Woman in Late Renaissance Italy." *Renaissance Quarterly* 44 (1991): 51–52.

Shemek, Deanna. *Ladies Errant: Wayward Women and Social Order in Early Modern Italy*. Durham and London: Duke University Press, 1998.

———. "Of Women, Knights, Arms, and Love: The *Querelle des Femmes* in Ariosto's Poem." *Modern Language Notes* 104 (1989): 68–97.

Stortoni, Laura Anna, ed. *Women Poets of the Italian Renaissance: Courtly Ladies and Courtesans*. Trans. Laura Anna Stortoni and Beatrice Prentice Lillie. New York: Italica Press, 1997.

Tarabotti, Arcangela. *Che le donne siano della specie degli uomini: Women Are No Less Rational than Men*. Ed. Letizia Panizza. Romance Texts. London: Institute of Romance Studies, 1994.

Thérault, Suzanne. *Un cenacle humaniste de la Renaissance autour de Vittoria Colonna chatelaine d'Ischia*. Florence: Sansoni, 1968.

Toscano, Tobia R. "Due 'allievi' di Vittoria Colonna: Luigi Tansillo e Alfonso d'Avalos (con un sonetto inedito della Marchesa di Pescara)." *Critica letteraria* 16 (1988): 762–64.

Vecce, Carlo. "Paolo Giovio e Vittoria Colonna." *Periodico della Società Storica Comense* 54 (1990): 67–93.

A Female Tradition?

WOMEN'S DIALOGUE WRITING IN SIXTEENTH-CENTURY FRANCE

Janet Levarie Smarr

During the Renaissance hundreds of men published dialogues on all sorts of topics. Most of these dialogues did not contain female speakers, except for a few examples, chiefly concerned with discussions about love or female beauty. Women, however, also wrote their own dialogues during this time, and several of them were aware of each other's work. While Italian women tended to imitate the mainstream Ciceronian model of dialogue, a reported conversation among historically identifiable or at least plausibly real people, often including the author herself,[1] French women, despite their humanist education, frequently turned to a different and more medieval model, the *débat* between allegorical figures.

The influence of Lucian was better suited than was that of Cicero to this "debate" model. As in Lucian's writings, the use of clearly fictional characters, including both humans and gods, facilitated a reconception of the dialogue in a more dramatic mode, with imagined scenes. If Lucian did provide a model for these women, however, he remains completely unacknowledged in their dialogues. Even among French male dialogue authors, Bonaventure des Periers was perhaps unique in taking up this more dramatic and unrealistic style for his *Cymbalum mundi*, which, like Lucian, he casts entirely with male speakers. Most other male dialogue writers in France followed the Ciceronian form, including often long speeches among the learned. A desire to forge a French culture distinct from mere imitation of the Italians might have encouraged des Periers's attention to the Greek Lucian, but his compatriot women found a different home-grown model. As Italians had sought a classical Italian ancestor in Cicero, so French women turned to French medieval literature such as the *Roman de la Rose*, with its combination of humans, personifications, and classical gods, engaged during a series of scenes in conversations and debates of satirical wit and learning, and speaking for the qualities they represent rather than for the author or other known persons directly.

Since the French women who engaged in these projects were—in some cases definitely, in others quite possibly—aware of each other's writings, the similar features and direction of development for the women's exercises in this genre can be considered to form a French female tradition of dialogue writing, which I would like to trace here. By tradition, I mean simply the chain of direct influences from one writer to the next, which suggests that women were knowingly developing a certain kind of dialogue rather than happening by chance to share certain techniques and concerns. One of the women also acknowledges an Italian woman as a partial model or influence, but we shall see that this Italian influence produced merely a digression from the French direction of development. In sum, there are two connected theses here: that French female writers took the dialogue in a direction unlike that of their Italian counterparts and that they did so with an awareness of each other's work.

In this essay I will discuss a series of four French women: Helisenne de Crenne, Louise Labé, Catherine des Roches, and Marie Le Gendre. Their publications span from 1540 to 1595. The first author is the most loosely connected to the others; but from there on, the influence of each one on the next is quite evident. Signs of possible influence from Helisenne and Labé on Marie Le Gendre will also be indicated. We shall see too that some of these dialogues explicitly value supportive relations among learned women.

First is Helisenne de Crenne (1500/1515?–1552?), the pen name of a well-educated, Latin-reading, provincial woman of Picardie, author of a famous romance, *Les Angoysses douloureuses qui procedent d'amours* (1538), and a set of *Epistres familieres et invectives* (1539), both of which she proudly arranged to have published in Paris. In 1540 and 1541 Helisenne published another work entitled *Songe*, which was reprinted repeatedly with her complete *Oeuvres*.[2] "Songe," as its title indicates, picks up the medieval genre of lover's dream vision. Helisenne's *Angoysses* had already demonstrated her familiarity with the *Roman de la Rose*. As in the *Roman*, so in this new *Songe* moral abstractions and symbolic pagan deities argue for the allegiance of human lovers. Disarmingly, Helisenne's text refers at the start to a humanistic model: Cicero's *Dream of Scipio,* "en la lecture duquel on peut veoir plusieurs disputations" [in the reading of which one can see several disputations]. Thus the form of a dream containing debates or disputations is presented as classical, even Ciceronian, just as her previous humanist letters had been. Cicero, however, would not at all have recognized his mode of writing in this new work.

Introduced as "Le Songe de ma Dame Helisenne, la consideration duquel est apte à instiguer toutes personnes de s'aliener de vice, & s'approcher de vertu" [The Dream of my Lady Helisenne, the consideration of which is apt to provoke all persons to withdraw from vice and approach virtue], the dream stages itself as Helisenne's persuasion of the reader, represented through the persuasion of the human characters in the dream. The dream is like a theater show with the dreamer as its audience and with several separate scenes. Helisenne opens with a long description of the setting and includes stage directions as the text progresses (the youth lies down, the lady enters, etc.). The whole piece ends with a splendid pageant, which would be a suitable conclusion for either a medieval morality play or a humanist masque.

Within the dream are three pairs of speakers: first two humans, Lady and Lover; then two classical goddesses, Venus and Pallas, who address the male lover; and finally two abstractions, Sensuality and Reason, who address the lady. The dialogues form a nested series, for the goddesses and abstractions directly address the human characters, who become the audiences and judges of their debates. We have thus a structure with a pair of abstract debates at its center, set within the framing scenes of a human situation and the outcome that results from human choices. This entire drama is then presented to the dreamer, who in turn presents it to us. The lady, whose turn to virtue and faith is celebrated by the final pageant, is the special object of persuasion; her audience, the dreamer-author, is also female. Since the male lover is part of the audience but disappears halfway through the work, and since the main and final lesson addresses women, by implication the anticipated readership includes both sexes but with an emphasis on the female. Apparently Helisenne expected to have female readers.

The lady who is the dream's main character has fallen vehemently in love with a youth and lives under suspicion from her jealous and even violent husband. The first dispute is within the lady: whether to choose the satisfaction of her desire along with perpetual infamy or sexual frustration along with chastity and honor. Supporting the side of honor is the fear that if she yields to love she will be abandoned by her lover. Yet she concludes by confessing that she is so overwhelmed by desire that she is willing to be utterly reckless.

The second dispute is between the lady, who declares this reckless desire to her beloved, and the young man, who argues for restraint out of fear that her husband may destroy them both. This perfectly human conversation includes expressions of joy at meeting, complaints about the husband's jealousy and a warning about the peril of sending letters, considerations of whether they might be able to get away with their crime, and ultimately the decision to think it over and defer action. Although there is disagreement and discussion, this feels more like a scene from a romance or play than an abstract disputation. It ends with the laments of the lover that love's service is too cruel and unhappy, so that he wishes he could free himself from love.

This exclamation of despair provokes the next layer of debate, as Venus appears suddenly in order to prevent rebellion in her ranks, while Pallas enters in order to seize the opportunity to persuade the young man back into her camp. Although we might expect Pallas to represent Reason, just as Venus is to be identified with Sensuality, her speech actually identifies her more specifically with Learning. This debate between goddesses focuses on the persuasion of the young man, who, as a student, must choose between his sexual urges and his studies, each presented as female objects of possible desire. Pallas, a more masculine female and appealing to the auditor's manhood, contrasts the virility of arduous study with the effeminacy of sensual yielding. It is only the youth who feels the opposite tugging of these two goddesses, who lay into each other with a relish reminiscent of Helisenne's *Invective Letters*.

Even though the lady is, understandably, not interested in Pallas's speech, the rhetorical strategies of both goddesses make us aware of the learnedness and eloquence of the author herself and of her humanist interest in the genre of orations. The sheer playful delight in eloquence supports Pallas's argument against the claims of Venus that the choice of study is a choice of dreariness instead of pleasure, for Pallas clearly has her pleasures too.

Pallas's victory is aided by the theatrical entrance of two menacing symbolic figures in strange garb, whose identities she explains. One is the hideous *Inconvenient* (Trouble) and the other a *Renomée* (Reputation) based on Vergil's Fama, covered in feathers, tongues, and ears.[3] These entrances would certainly liven up a performance, even though Helisenne creates a performance for the reader's mind and not for the stage. The youth flees from their threatening approaches, convinced to leave his horrified lady for his books. Her fears of male mutability have come true in a way that she had not expected.

To comfort her protégé and punish her deserter, Venus now reverses the situation: the lady is cured of her love, while the youth is inflicted with renewed passion. This time the lady is the object of persuasion, for Sensuality tries to persuade her to find another better lover, while Reason seizes the opportunity of removing her from such dangerous desires altogether. Although in one sense the two sets of debate are simply parallel arguments, one addressed to a male and the other to a female, Helisenne has made the effort to link them causally into a dramatic plot. The influence of the *Roman de la Rose*, with its series of dialogues linked into a story, clearly takes precedence here over the separate satirical scenes of Lucian or des Periers or the many male dialogues with separate "days" of discussion.

Unlike Pallas, who as a pagan refers to human studies as a path to virtue, liberty, and tranquility, Reason at once refers to God, sin, repentance, and grace. The argument for the male was a rational choice, threatened by the menacing figures of Trouble and Reputation—both of which are worldly concerns. For the lady the argument becomes religious, even though it is Reason who presents religion's teachings. Sin is equated with adultery against God, who is the only "*parfait amy*" [perfect friend].

At this point a feminist argument creeps in, and we find an odd mingling of frame and content. Sensuality protests:

> O Raison: parquoy t'esforce tu tant de dominer en ce sexe muliebre? Ne sces tu, que selon nature, ton domicille est plustost au sexe viril? Car vulgairement la femme se regit & gouverne plus selon moy, & a sa fantaisie que ne faict l'homme. Et comme chacun scet, la femme fut cause premierement de peché. (T, viii)[4]
>
> *[O Reason, why do you try so hard to dominate within this female sex? Don't you know that, according to nature, your domicile is rather the virile sex? For commonly women rule and govern themselves more according to me, and to her fantasy, than does a man. And as everyone knows, a woman was the first cause of sin.]*

Here the dreamer exclaims that the words of Sensuality so irritated her,

> de ce que nostre condition feminine tant vituperoit: & pource stimulee d'un excessif courroux, ne fis difficulté d'interrompre leurs propos: & m'aprochant de raison, avec instantes prières luy requis, que la vertu de ceste chose voulust exprimer (T, viii).
>
> *[in that she so vituperated our female condition, and therefore stimulated by extreme anger, I did not hesitate to interrupt their talk; and drawing near to Reason, with insistent prayers I requested her to explain the virtue of this matter.]*

The narrative has been presenting the debaters as self-motivated; but now we see the dreamer entering the dream and explicitly requesting Reason to discourse on a particular topic, a topic that readers of Helisenne's previous works would recognize at once as dear to the author's heart. Yet instead of speaking in her own voice, she presents her case as that of Reason itself. Thematic links with her *Epistres* suggest an identification of Sensuality with the misogynist Husband of the invective letters and of Reason with the Wife, a reversal of the usual gender stereotypes.[5] As there, so here the reversal serves as a defense of women's rationality and morality.

Summoning a battery of church fathers and doctors (Reason names Augustine, Thomas Aquinas, Hugh of St. Victor, Gregory the Great, and Cassiodorus) to counteract Sensuality's "low opinion" [*petite estime*] of women, Reason argues that although women are physically weaker, both sexes are equally the image of God, an image based on their faculty of understanding and capacity for salvation. She concludes,

> pourquoy ne m'efforceray-ie nonobstant la fragilité, d'avoir domination en elle, & la corroborer de vertu? Certainement en ma force tant ie me confie, que de toy Sensualité sucumberas. (V, v)
>
> [*why shouldn't I try to achieve domination within her, notwithstanding her fragility, and to strengthen her with virtue? Certainly I am so confident in my power that you, Sensuality, will yield of your own accord.*]

Indeed, Sensuality at once submits. The implication of this argument is that a negative view of women makes it more likely that they will sin, whereas the view that women are rational and at least mentally strong can help them preserve their virtue. This argument in the dream is addressed beyond the text to both men and women and bolstered by Reason's use of the male tradition of patristic writers.

Nonetheless, the most important worldly concern for a woman is her chastity, and the lady summons Truth to declare that she is indeed still chaste.

> e porta tesmoignage, que nonobstant les detractions des langues pestiferes, si n'avoit la dame Chasteté corrompue: car de ce, la clemence divine par grace especialle l'avoit preservee. (X, iii–iiij)
>
> [*and (Truth) bore witness that, notwithstanding the detractions of pestiferous tongues, the lady had not corrupted her Chastity: for divine mercy had saved her from this with special grace.*]

Certainly this is a view of chastity based not on the heart's intent but only on effective actions. Truth vouches for the lady's chastity; yet Reason calls her a repentant sinner.

The lessons of this piece are ambiguous. On one hand, the obvious message is, as Pallas puts it, "si par fantasie en amour tu es entré, par sapience tu en peux issir" (S, iiij) [If you have entered into love through fantasy, you can exit from it through wisdom]. Yet Pallas's success with the youth is very short-lived, for the irate Venus swiftly makes him worse than ever. So too Reason cannot even make itself heard to the lady until she has already begun to withdraw her love from the youth, again a situation brought about by Venus. The forces of unreason are the most powerful, even though the advocates of reason seem to win. Finally, what reason was unable to prevent, God's mercy has ultimately succeeded in preventing. Unlike the youth—and the author herself—women are urged not to study but to pray.

As the dreamer awakes and writes down her dream, she makes no judgment of her own. The pageant-like triumph of virtues and heavenly Peace that end the dream are a clear enough conclusion. The unresolvable conflicts created by love render it a wretched condition from which, as the youth had proclaimed, one can long only to free oneself or die. Peace is the final goal of the dream, and the pageant of heavenly peace is its ending. The dream ends with that theatrical vision.

I have described this work at some length because it is mainly unknown these days; but that was not the case in the sixteenth century. Helisenne's volume of works was published early and repeatedly: in 1543, 1551, 1553, 1555, and 1560.[6] François de Billon, in the *Fort Inexpugnable de l'Honneur du Sexe Feminin* [Indestructible fortress of the honor of the female sex] (1555), claims that Helisenne has brought honor to Picardie. "Les Compositions de laquelle sont si souvent es mains des François se delectans de Prose, qu'il n'est besoin en faire autre discours" [Her compositions are so often in the hands of Frenchmen who enjoy prose that there is no need to say anything further about them].[7] As I have mentioned, Helisenne clearly expected women among her readers. Was her work of "*disputations*" known to the female dialogue-writers of the following decades, Louise Labé, Catherine des Roches, and Marie le Gendre? Quite possibly; for although they do not mention her, there are some suggestive connections. Marie de Romieu, in her versified defense of women—"*Brief discours: Que l'excellence de la femme surpasse celle de l'homme*" [Brief discourse: That the excellence of woman surpasses that of man]—published with her *Oeuvres* in 1581, names "Elisenes" and "Des Roches de Poictiers" side by side as well-known examples of intellectual literary women (vv. 307–8).[8] If women did continue to read Helisenne for decades, what signs of that reading might we find in their work?

Louise Labé (1515/1524?–1566), like Helisenne, had surprising education and ambition for her social position. The daughter and wife of prosperous rope makers in Lyon, she learned Latin and Italian, possibly also some Greek, and was friends with some of the most famous poets of her day, for example, Maurice Scève, Olivier de Magny, and Pontus de Tyard.[9] The preface to her *Oeuvres Complètes* published in Lyon in 1555 dedicated the volume to a noblewoman of Lyon and urged other women to take up the pen. Her *Débat de Folie et d'Amour*, which is now much better known than Helisenne's "Songe," was published as part of this volume. It had a rich context of sources for its creation; yet Enzo Giudici calls it "one of the most original works of the sixteenth century."[10] The title again suggests a medieval genre (*débat*); yet Giudici denies the importance of medieval debate poems for Labé's work because those are more schematic and lack her subtlety and psychological insight (106). Certainly her writing feels much more Renaissance than medieval.

The use of Apollo and Mercury, who take up the debate between Love and Folly, has suggested to some Lucian or possibly des Periers as models for a dialogue among gods, but Labé's topic is quite different from theirs, and she connects her several scenes into an ongoing plot. Pietro Bembo's *Asolani* with its praise and dispraise of love and Erasmus's *Praise of Folly* with its deification and defense of Folly may have contributed importantly to the contents of Labé's debate.[11] The Renaissance fashion for paradoxical encomia more broadly may have formed part of Labé's inspiration. Nonetheless, her particular theme and the mixed manner in which she carries it out—partly dramatic with a series of scenes, partly forensic debate with advocates pleading on behalf of their clients before a divine judge, the whole introduced briefly by a narrative summary—are with good reason declared by Giudici to be uniquely her own.[12]

Without denying the relevance of a wide set of male-authored texts for Labé's creation, I would like to suggest the possibility that a female-authored model is part of the mix. Indeed, the opening of the *Débat* stages a challenge for precedence between a male and a female. Since Helisenne's works were still in enough demand to be reprinted twice in the early 1550s, it is quite likely that Labé, with her keen interest in women's writing, was aware of Helisenne's *Songe*. We find an initial confrontation between two characters leading into orations by pagan deities who champion opposite sides, and we relish the writer's delight in the strategies of competing orations. In both works there are sets of paired speakers, each with their own dramatic scene. Labé's decision to shift this dialogue toward a dramatic form may be connected to the theatrical qualities of Helisenne's piece. But whether or not Labé knew Helisenne's work, both gave to the tradition of *débat* a theatrical form.

The *Débat* begins with a direct confrontation between the young male Love and the older female Folly, who insult each other while each proclaiming superior importance. Attacked by Love, Folly causes his blindness. They decide to refer their case to Jupiter, and each selects an advocate for his or her cause. The consequence at stake is whether Love and Folly shall be compelled to go about together, Folly leading the blind archer, or whether Love shall be allowed to go free of Folly and regain his sight. Although officially Jupiter postpones his decision, he orders in the meantime that Folly and the still blinded Love stay together, thus handing Folly a temporary victory. The argument used to win Folly's case is the need of these two beings for each other. Without folly, no one would love; without love, folly would not seem so sweet and desirable. The possibility of a wise or rational love is rendered remote, and Labé has no interest in offering religious love as a solution.[13]

Was it part of Labé's wit to reverse a didactic debate between love and reason into an officially unresolved dispute between love and folly—even into a tentative victory of folly?[14] To accomplish this, Labé had to drop all reference to Christian religion. The absence of such reference, the unified presentation of a world of classical gods, and the relative openness of the ending all result in bringing Labé's dialogue out of the Middle Ages and fully into the classical mode of the Renaissance. Yet at the same time, the work remains a *débat,* linked by its title and by its central conflict of personified abstractions to medieval roots.

Just as Helisenne had shaped a loosely linked series of scenes into a drama of the mind, so Labé presented this debate as a series of five "*discours*" or scenes of an action covering two days. On the first day the confrontation of Folly and Love is followed by the dialogue of Love with his mother, Venus; the third scene, in the presence of the assembled gods, arranges for the judicial contest before Jupiter. The second day offers a conversation between Jupiter and Love on how to make oneself loved and then the long public debate between the two advocates, Apollo (for Love) and Mercury (for Folly). Thus, although the piece does not end with a pageant, each day closes with a scene involving the full assembly of gods. The text ends with Jupiter's suspended judgment. While not including a long introductory description of the setting such as we find in Helisenne's piece, Labé does share with Helisenne the indication of stage actions: Folly and Love shove each other, Folly bandages Love's eyes, Venus tries in vain to remove the bandage, and so forth. We have no evidence that this text was performed in Labé's home or in the salons of Lyon, but it could have been done easily and amusingly. Its liveliness has made it one of the famous writings of the French Renaissance.

Labé's dialogue was certainly known to the des Roches, for Madeleine des

Roches had published her first poems in a 1578 volume containing also Labé's *Débat.*[15] The des Roches mother and daughter were a celebrated pair of intellectual hostesses in the town of Poitiers. Catherine (1542–87), the daughter, learned in the classical languages as well as in French, astonished her contemporaries by refusing all offers of marriage, asserting her desire to devote her life to her mother and her studies. It was a life she not only enjoyed but also wished for other women, as her writings make clear. Mother and daughter published their writings together in two volumes, containing dedicatory letters to each other, poetry in various forms, verse narrative, prose dialogues, and a religious play.[16] Both volumes contain sets of dialogues by Catherine, but their form changes notably from one volume to the next as Catherine responded to different female models. The dialogues in the first volume of the des Roches *Oeuvres* (1579) clearly borrow from Labé's and also share some features with Helisenne's.

As with Helisenne and Labé, a convergence of medieval and humanist traditions informed Catherine's set of six dialogues, which shift between personifications and human lovers as speakers in a series of parallel debates. The dialogue of Old Age and Youth is most closely related to the medieval debate poem. The argument of Hand and Foot, however, clearly derives from another tradition: the famous Roman anecdote recounted by Livy.[17] The conversation of Fortune and Virtue draws its topic from another humanist favorite: Plutarch's moral essays on whether virtue or fortune is more responsible for Greek and Roman greatness. Catherine's dialogue of Beauty and Love introduces a pair of speakers readily identifiable with the human pair Charite and Sincero, whose exchange directly follows. Thus, besides finding a mix of classical and medieval sources, we are led through abstractions into human characters. The debates do not form a plot but are linked by thematic connections.

Although Catherine is generally explicitly Christian in a manner quite unlike Labé, the entire set of dialogues offers a series of formal and thematic variations on a basic pattern drawn from Labé's *Débat.* They tend to begin with an aggressive confrontation between their two disputants, who sometimes allow a third party to adjudicate their dispute. In most cases, the resolution is precisely that the two need each other and thus must go together willy-nilly. The dialogues tend in this way to explore the nature of the relation between concepts that are not necessarily in simple contradiction. For example, Virtue seeks to combine with Fortune, who refuses to alter her proper character in order to become a predictable follower of Virtue. The issue is, as in Labé's debate, whether these two should work together or remain separate. The mutual insult and complaint of Hand and Foot, and their listing of necessary services performed by each, gets referred to a third party, Mouth, who points out to the disputants how necessary they are to each other and persuades them to work in concord. Poverty and Hunger are similarly a necessary pair; although each blames the other for her own bad reputation, they have been chained together by fate.

In the dialogue of Poverty and Hunger, the classical setting contributes to bringing the piece closer than ever to Labé's model. Like Labé's Folly, so des Roches's Poverty and Hunger are deities on a par with Venus, Mercury, and Apollo. Both Labé's and des Roches's dialogues begin with a very similar opening line, in which the elderly female, Folly or Poverty, expresses her desire to attend a party being thrown by Jupiter. Both goddesses are impeded right away by an encounter with a hostile and belligerent Cupid, who refuses to recognize what he owes to her.[18] The closeness of these openings, calling us to see the two dialogues in relation to each other, induces our awareness of how Labé's light-hearted theme of foolish love has become the much grimmer theme of the poverty and hunger affecting war-torn regions of France.

Both women's dialogues also offer near the end a set of satirical portraits. Labé's Mercury demonstrates Folly's power over kings and courtiers, philosophers and astronomers, military men, lawyers and judges, and all the rest of the world who admire such fools. Similarly des Roches's Hunger describes courtiers, bankers, judges, lawyers, and merchants in brief but biting terms as she considers where she might get a meal. Both writers see their particular topic as a way of addressing at the same time much broader social concerns.

The insertion of a feminist criticism against men who think that women lack reason is Catherine's addition to a topic (hunger and poverty) that might seem remote from this gender issue. However, both her dialogue and Labé's emphasize the gender of the speakers. Poverty, like Labé's Folly, is an older woman scorned by the young male Love. When Poverty explains as rational her decision not to challenge Love's hostility, Hunger responds, "Si dict-on communément que les femmes abondent en parolles, et manquent de raison" [Yet it is said that generally women are abundant in words and lacking in reason]. Poverty replies, "Qui dict ce propos sinon des hommes lourds et grossiers?" [Who says such a thing except for gross and uncultivated men?] and launches into a tirade against such misogynists (230–31). Did Catherine here have in mind Helisenne's digression in defense of the rationality of women? The gendering of Poverty and Love suggests an identification of the male with sensuality and excess, of the female with prudence and restraint, associations counter to traditional gendering. Whether or not Catherine knew the work of Helisenne, they are playing a similar game.

As the dialogue between Poverty and Hunger most clearly shows her use of Labé's text, so the subsequent dialogue between Love and Beauty became influential in its turn on another woman writer, as we shall see. Catherine's dialogue of Love and Beauty is once again about whether the two characters must be coupled or whether Beauty can find a refuge free from the importunities of Love. Physis or Nature orders them to stay together as they need each other, for neither is honored without the other. The opening with its emphasis on Love's bandaged eyes reinforces the link with Labé's text. Although this image was certainly common, Beauty's question (247)—"Pourquoy donc portez-vous ce bandeau sinon pour cacher l'imperfection de vos yeux?" [Why then do you wear this blindfold if not to hide the imperfection of your eyes?]—brings it more specifically into connection with Labé's scene, where Folly bandages Love's eyes after having injured them. So does Beauty's insistence, like Folly's, that all of Love's force derives from her.

As in the previous dialogue on hunger and poverty, Catherine's personal feminist concerns are again given voice. Beauty in the end gains one place of respite, not in the convent (explicitly rejected) but with Pallas and among her books, "mon temple de franchise" [my temple of freedom] (250). Perhaps because the judge, Nature, is a female (both disputants call her "ma mere"), she aids Beauty's request in clear response to the critics of Catherine who considered her rejection of marriage unnatural. This mother is undoubtedly also a reference to Catherine's own mother, praised in two of the preceding dialogues,[19] and to the maternal support that has enabled Catherine to live as she wishes. Love addresses Nature the way a suitor would address the parent of his beloved, asking for Beauty's hand, while Beauty begs her mother not to grant his request. The solution is for Beauty to be offered a refuge where she can be free from Love, who waits hoping that she will eventually emerge.

Whereas Labé presented folly and love as necessarily companions, Catherine des Roches declares her own consequent rejection of love on behalf of wisdom. If this was intentionally a response to Labé's text, which Catherine had indeed evoked, we might have a series of women rewriting each other's conclusions in debates concerning love: Labé turning Helisenne's victory of reason over sensual love into a victory of folly joined with love, while Catherine returns to the celebration of a wisdom that flees from love.

Catherine, wittingly or unwittingly, shares with Helisenne the combination of human and inhuman speakers in a linked series of disputes. Helisenne begins with two human lovers and then shifts to more abstract debaters. Catherine's series of dialogues begins with personifications and ends with two flirting humans, Charite and Sincero. Sincero is explicitly presented as an ideal lover created from Catherine's imagination by analogy with Castiglione's perfect courtier. Charite's name evokes three meanings: as a partial anagram of Catherine, as one of the classical Graces, and as the Christian *caritas* opposed to *cupiditas* or lust. Thus it sums up Catherine's mingling of historical, classical, and medieval frames of reference. The relationship of Sincero and Charite largely parallels that of Love and Beauty in the preceding dialogue: he woos, she deflates his rhetoric and points out the contradictions in his claims. Finally the dialogue of Sincero and Charite overflows into the sonnets and songs that continue their wooing and response through poems addressed to each other. These two characters, whose combined names come close to an anagram of "Catherine Roches," form a transition between the clearly fictional speakers of the previous dialogues and the poems in the volume that are presented in Catherine's own acknowledged voice. They thus connect the dialogues fluidly to the rest of her volume rather than allowing us to see them as a neatly separate piece.

Like Labé's debate, Catherine's dialogues are presented in dramatic form without any narrative frame. Thus the author never speaks in her own voice. Perhaps, given the quickness of men to read women's writing as autobiographical, the dehumanizing of speakers by the use of personifications or mythical figures was a way to distance the work from the historical author and to allow ideas to speak as if on their own.

Yet Catherine continually teases us by evoking herself and her mother through these figures. It is therefore not surprising that she soon found herself drawn to a more Italianate mode. Catherine's break, in her second volume of works, from personification dialogues to a more fully human and realistic (i.e., more Ciceronian) type followed from her acquaintance with the work of another dialogue-writing woman, this time the Italian Olympia Morata, whose name she mentions with praise and whose posthumous volume of works she obviously knew. Olympia (1526–55) had been educated by her humanist father and his scholarly, reform-minded friends in Ferrara and had spent a number of years in her youth as a study companion of the duke's daughter Anne. At the ducal court of Ferrara she had become friends with a somewhat older and much nobler married woman, Lavinia della Rovere Orsini, who supported her enthusiasm for learning. Lavinia and Olympia became the interlocutors in Olympia's two Latin dialogues. Expelled from the court for the reformist leanings of her father and teachers, Olympia began for the first time to consider seriously their religious views, married a German Protestant, and moved with him to Germany. The first dialogue, written still in Ferrara in 1550, discusses the value of learning for women, despite the criticisms of those who think that a woman should care only for her good looks; but Lavinia also urges Olympia to turn her studies in a more religious direction. The second dialogue, written in a letter to Lavinia after Olympia had left for Germany, offers spiritual advice to the friend she left behind. After her early death, her mostly Greek and Latin writings, made up of letters, poems, essays, translations (of two *Decameron* stories into Latin and of several Psalms into Greek), and dialogues, were collected by an old family friend, Celio Secondo Curione, and printed four times as her *Opera omnia* in Basel, in 1558, 1562, 1570, and 1580, with dedications to women who supported religious reform: Isabella of Brisegna and Queen Elizabeth.[20]

The first dialogue in Catherine's second volume, a dialogue between two fathers, indicates Catherine's awareness of Morata. One of the fathers gives examples of learned women whose learning increased their virtue; and the modern examples include Sigea, Laura Terracina, Hippolyta Taurella, and Olympia Morata.[21] Although the dialogue in which this list occurs is a conversation in the vernacular between men, one of whom is blatantly ignorant, Catherine's list emphasizes classically educated women who wrote in Latin. The combination of the last two names indicates that Catherine was acquainted with the volume of Morata's works, which oddly included at the end the epistolary poem of Taurella to her husband specifically mentioned in Catherine's dialogue.[22] Even though the des Roches were solid Catholics, Catherine was open to Morata's influence in the matter of reconceiving the dialogue genre. Morata's writings offered Catherine the model of a woman's humanist dialogue between contemporary female speakers.[23] While des Roches remains more witty and worldly than Morata and, furthermore, continues to refuse the historical identification of her speakers, her acquaintance with Morata's work supported her own already incipient transition from a debate among personifications to speakers who are more human and natural.

It is particularly the first of Morata's dialogues—where, in a discussion between two female friends, the superior value of a life of study to the usual female life of frivolity is advocated—that seems to have provided a model for Catherine's own.[24] It opens with the image of Olympia studious among her books, the very self-image dear to Catherine. It defends and justifies this activity for women on several grounds. It also notes the resistance to it from both men and other women and their concern that the learned woman will turn away possible suitors. At this point in her life, Olympia had just married a man who admired her learning, so she could triumphantly dismiss such fears, happy to have attracted the right sort of man and not one of those who would prefer, as her critics kept arguing, a wealthy woman to a learned one. Not only the topic but also the model of a dialogue in which two female friends converse on subjects of interest to Catherine must have shown her how a version of the dialogue genre both more Ciceronian and more modern could be put to use to further her agenda.

Like the connected series of dialogues in Catherine's first volume, the two dialogues in the second volume, "Dialogue de Placide et Severe" and "Dialogue d'Iris et Pasithée" are again clearly linked with each other, this time both by theme and speakers, for the two girls who converse in the second are the daughters of the two men who argue in the first. How girls should be raised and how they should spend their time is the theme of both encounters. Just as Olympia introduces herself as busy with her books, so Pasithée is introduced by her father in Catherine's first dialogue as sitting alone in her room with "les belles sentences de Plutarque et de Seneque" (192) [the fine sayings of Plutarch and Seneca]. As Olympia had recalled the recurrent criticisms of her studies by both men and women, so both the father and mother of Iris resist the notion of allowing their daughter to read: the father because he thinks her incapable and, if not, fears it will make her rebellious against men; the mother because she sees no need for her daughter to have an education that she herself never received. Placide defends the education of his daughter Pasithée as a virtuous occupation of idle time and a morally good influence. Yet Catherine's more worldly concerns relative to Morata become evident not only in the omission of reference to God but also in the practical nature of the learning that Placide advocates: besides moral essays and scripture, a smattering of law and medicine for their needed applications in a woman's life. Catherine's mother was involved in a lengthy lawsuit; hence Catherine realized the usefulness of some knowledge of law.

The question of how education will affect a woman's marriage is raised by both the fathers and the daughters, as it was in Morata's dialogue, but the two generations express slightly different aspects of the problem. Severe, the father of Iris, does not question whether learning will drive away suitors, for he views marriage as something that he will arrange rather than something that the youngsters will choose for themselves. His worry is that learning will make a woman into a proud and ornery wife. Placide's counterargument is therefore that a learned woman such as his daughter Pasithée will make a better, more obedient, reasonable, and loving wife. Iris's concern, unlike her father's, is not whether she will become a better wife but whether she will attract a husband at all, since the men she knows mock learned women. Pasithée therefore argues to Iris not that learning will produce a better wife but that it will attract a different and better type of husband, one more serious, respectful, and faithfully affectionate. Where the woman has been properly educated, suggests Catherine, both she and the sort of man attracted to her are likely to be better people and the marriage therefore more likely to be a happy one.

Morata and des Roches shared a clear sense of the importance of bonds of support and encouragement among women. Catherine's dialogue between the daughters resembles Morata's in its setting: a conversation between two friendly women at the home of one of them and an argument that, for women as well as for men, attention to the mind is better than attention merely to physical and material goods. As Lavinia seeks to encourage and influence Olympia, so Pasithée seeks to encourage and influence Iris. Catherine knew from her own experience with her mother how important female support could be for a woman interested in education. What a delight it must have been for Catherine to discover the dialogues of other women—and not just an isolated example but two very different writers, Labé and Morata. Given the wide range of forms and genres that she attempted, it is not surprising that she wanted to try out her own versions of both these models. Morata's influence, however, drew des Roches away from the line of development that would be picked up from her first volume by another French woman.

Catherine's early dialogues, and probably Labé's and possibly Helisenne's as well, inspired Marie Le Gendre, Dame de Rivery, whose *Dialogue des chastes amours d'Eros et de Kalisti* [Dialogue of the chaste loves of Eros and Kalisti] was published together with some poems and her *L'exercice de l'âme vertueuse* [Exercise of the virtuous soul] in Paris in 1596 and again by a different printer in 1597.[25] Almost nothing is known about the life of this noblewoman, other than that her husband died in 1595, an event she laments in her poetry.

The first edition of the *Dialogue des chastes amours* was dedicated to François Le Poulchre, Sieur de La Motte-Messeme, a nobleman, retired military captain, and staunch royalist, who, to pass the time since his retirement, had composed and dedicated to the king a long history of the recent French civil wars in execrable verse. A later work of his entitled *Le Passe-Temps* is full of moral, political, and scientific reflections, along with references to the classical gods and philosophers. Marie Le Gendre refers to Le Poulchre's "*doctes oeuvres*" [learned works] and calls him "*mon père*" [my father]. The name Kalisti in Le Gendre's dialogue (from the Greek *kallos* or beauty) is obviously in part a play on Le Poulchre's name (*pulcher* being the Latin word for beautiful). Curiously, this identifies him with the female beloved rather than with the male. It implies that Le Gendre herself is the male Eros attracted by his Beauty. But this flattering identity has little bearing once we are within the text.

Like the *Songe* of Helisenne and the *Débat* of Labé, Le Gendre's *Dialogue* is presented in a series of dramatic scenes that form a play. Like Helisenne, Le Gendre intertwines this play with narrative interjections by the author, making it a play for the mind rather than for the stage. The narrator opens the text with general observations about love. She makes the traditional Aristotelian distinction between three objects of love, the honorable, the useful, and the beautiful; but for her all three are good, and love of beauty the best.[26] The story that follows this introduction develops Catherine des Roches's dialogue of Love and Beauty into a more elaborated dramatic form.

The two title characters, Eros and Kalisti, are clearly an imitation of Catherine des Roches's Amour and Beauté. Le Poulchre had been present in Poitiers during the Huguenot siege of 1569 and was personally acquainted with the des Roches, including them in his *Passe-Temps* in a list of contemporary women whose knowledge he admired.[27] Most likely, therefore, it was through Le Poulchre that Le Gendre became acquainted with the volumes of the des Roches. That might be a reason for her having dedicated this dialogue to him.

The influence of des Roches's work on Le Gendre's is undeniable, for the storyline is essentially the same. Like Catherine's Love, Eros woos his beloved; and as Catherine's Beauty had fled from her suitor to Minerva's temple, so Kalisti flees to the palace of her mother, Sophie (Wisdom), and the school of her mother's friend Minerva. As Love appealed for help to Nature, who is partly suggestive of Catherine's own mother, so Eros appeals to Sophie (Wisdom), who is Kalisti's mother. However, where des Roches left her Beauty unwed, Le Gendre ends her dialogue with the wedding of Eros and Kalisti, to which the gods are invited. Apparently, having herself been married,[28] she does not see marriage and learning as incompatible activities for a woman. Indeed, married love becomes for her the ideal love that can combine all three kinds enumerated at the start: the honorable, useful, and delightful.

Le Gendre defends learning for women partly on the basis that they are capable of it and partly on the basis that it will actually protect them from falling into error and vice. Moreover, like Helisenne and Labé, Le Gendre adds pleasure as a goal of learning that is not to be disdained. After the initial scenes in which Eros makes his love known to Kalisti and her mother, Sophie advises her daughter to avoid Eros by staying at home and entertaining herself with the activities and company of Sophie and Minerva. Lured out by Curiosity, represented as a woman intervening on Eros's behalf, Kalisti finds Eros lying in wait for her, just as Catherine's Love planned to lie in wait for Beauty to emerge from her temple of studies. However, when Kalisti flees at once to her mother, Sophie surprisingly offers to accompany her daughter back along with Curiosity; for in the company of Wisdom, Curiosity cannot do harm and can lead us to learn things that are pleasing: "d'assez agreable accez et conduict à la cognoissance de choses qui plaisent" (154). As Sophie says to her daughter, without Sophie and Minerva (or Wisdom and Learning) Kalisti is in grave danger, but together they are invincible (137, 145, 147).

Much of Sophie's advice is plain maternal advice to an adolescent daughter. In some very human scenes, Sophie scolds her daughter for fixing her hair and showing signs of interest in Eros, warning her daughter that Eros is not to be trusted even when he claims to be seeking an honest marriage. With affectionate obedience Kalisti, like Catherine, praises her mother as her best instructor and example. The double sense throughout the action that we are witnessing humans and abstractions simultaneously reminds us of des Roches's shift from the dialogue of Love and Beauty to that of Sincero and Charite with their obvious parallels and of her evocation through abstract debates of her own and her mother's real situation.

In other scenes Sophie evokes not Catherine's mother but Labé's Folly, for she bandages Eros's eyes so tightly that he cannot see. It may seem odd that Wisdom should have the same effect on love as Folly, but her blindfolding is less permanent. Sophie is testing Eros, who comically begins in his blindness to reveal his true feelings and to give the lie to his former expressions of good intentions, complaining of Sophie's obstructions to his desires. As Kalisti comments: "Vous ne parliez pas d'elle, voyant clair, comme vous faites maintenant que vous estes aveuglé" (140) [You were not speaking about her when you saw clearly the way you are speaking now that you are blinded]. The allegorical intent is only too clear; but the presence of Labé's text also seems evident in this bit of stage action as Sophie, a mature woman like Folly, ties the bandage tightly around young Eros's eyes only to have him complain bitterly about her.[29]

A number of other elements suggest that Marie Le Gendre was influenced by Labé as well as by des Roches, although none of these particulars proves the matter decisively. Among the possible signs of Labé's influence, Berriot-Salvadore cites the humorous undercutting of Neoplatonic notions that beauty will automatically inspire a wise love, the combination of allegorical and realistic qualities in the speakers, the natural quality of the dialogue, the dramatic framing of the dialogue, and the presence of the gods as witness to the relationship between the two main characters. Winn indicates echoes of Labé's writing in Le Gendre's lyric poetry and proposes that Kalisti's comments about Eros draw from Apollo's speech on love in Labé's *Débat*.[30]

Le Gendre seems to have been aware of a number of previous dialogues by women and to have combined elements from all of them. Labé or Helisenne, rather than des Roches, presents a model for the theatrical quality of this piece with its series of scenes interspersed (as by Helisenne) with narrative comments. The narrative as well as theatrical qualities of Le Gendre's *Dialogue* follow the patterns established by Helisenne and Labé but go beyond either in the construction of a unified and concluded plot. We see Eros speaking to Kalisti, lamenting alone after her departure, seeking out her mother, talking again to Kalisti while blindfolded, trying to see her when she ventures outside, and finally accompanying mother and daughter to the house of Minerva for the wedding. In between we see Sophie watching her daughter for signs of love, scolding her, warning her, helping her, offering to accompany and chaperone her, and ultimately happily accepting for her daughter a suitor whose intentions have become honest. Even the narrative sections frequently function either as stage directions and setting descriptions or as dumb show interludes accompanied by song.

Like Helisenne's *Songe* the dialogue of Eros and Kalisti addresses both sexes but primarily females. This is clear from the message that ends the work: that girls should imitate Kalisti in order to triumph over passion and win honor and glory. Le Gendre's ending with its explicit moralizing resembles the end of Helisenne's *Songe* more than the dialogues of either Labé or des Roches. Like Labé rather than Helisenne, however, Le Gendre avoids any Christian reference, leaving her message thoroughly within a context of classical gods.

I have tried to suggest that there is in France a female dialogue tradition by women aware of each other's writing. It is certain that Marie Le Gendre was influenced by the dialogues of Catherine des Roches, probably also by Louise Labé's, and possibly by Helisenne de Crenne's. Catherine des Roches herself certainly knew and drew from Labé's *Débat*, whose satiric wit she imitated happily along with formal patterns and verbal details. She also knew and was influenced later by the dialogues of the Italian Olympia Morata, whom she mentions explicitly; the list of learned, writing women in her second volume indicates clearly her search for female models to corroborate her own intellectual aims. It is quite possible that any or all of these later French women knew the work of Helisenne, with whom they share the theatrical tendencies of their dialogue writing. These French women writers are much more interconnected as a group than are the Italian women who wrote in the dialogue genre, who seem unaware of each other's work.

The French writers openly aimed at and expected female as well as male readers. The signs of their influence by and on other women show that those expectations of a female readership were fulfilled.

They share a certain feminist agenda: the defense of women's intellectual and moral equality with men and the advocacy of women's education. This appears in the dreamer's unhappy request to Reason and in Reason's reply in Helisenne's *Songe*. It reappears in the diatribe of Catherine des Roches's Poverty against misogynists who consider women irrational, and in Beauty's preference for studies over love. The issue returns once again in Le Gendre's text, both through the significant presence of the female characters Sophie and Minerva and through a reference to Minerva's school, where boys and girls are educated together according to their abilities. While love is a recurring topic of these writings, their authors insist on the possibility for women to be rational, and they encourage women's study both as an aid to moral wisdom and as a pleasure.

They share also the combination of speaker types across a series of connected disputations. For Helisenne, humans converse and then are addressed by paired gods and by paired personifications. For Labé, two gods similarly perform as advocates in parallel with a conflict between personifications. For Catherine des Roches, disputes between personifications shift into a human conversation in parallel dialogues; already in the dialogue of Love and Beauty we sense the presence of Catherine and her mother behind the personifications of Beauty and Nature. Similarly with Marie Le Gendre we find ourselves watching classical gods and abstractions that feel at the same time very much like human characters. The increased realism of the speakers in the later dialogues of Catherine under Italian influence serves to highlight the relatively dehumanized speakers of the dialogues in France. But the distancing made possible by the avoidance of historical persons also encouraged the envisioning of these conversations and disputes as dramatic scenes with a plot and a theatrical finale: a pageant of celestial virtues, a judgment before the assembly of gods, and a wedding in the presence of gods and graces.

All four women present a series of dialogues or scenes within a larger unifying format. Helisenne, Labé, and Le Gendre unify the discussions via a dramatic plotline, more rudimentary in Helisenne and Labé, more fully elaborated by Le Gendre. Thematic and formal parallels among discourses in a series also provide unity for Helisenne and des Roches. Furthermore, for all these writers, dialogue is set into a volume with other texts with which it is thematically linked. Thus not only do speaker types shift, but form itself changes in a formal variation on recurring themes that overflow into or from letters, essays, romance, and poetry. The very fluidity of the dialogue genre is here repeatedly on display. These French women were experimenting with the form and its possible connections to other genres, such as a masque or morality drama. Certainly des Roches and Le Gendre—possibly also Labé—were doing this with an awareness that it was something in which other women had recently been similarly engaged.

NOTES

1. Examples include the dialogic writings of Isotta Nogarola, Olympia Morata, Tullia d'Aragona, and Chiara Matraini; I am preparing a longer work on the topic of women's dialogue writing in Italy and France.

2. Helisenne's *Epistres familieres et invectives* have been edited by Jean-Philippe Beaulieu with Hannah Fournier (Montreal: Les Presses de l'Université de Montréal,

1995) and by Jerry Nash (Paris: Honoré Champion, 1996); they have been translated as *A Renaissance Woman: Helisenne's Personal and Invective Letters* by Marianna Mustacchi and Paul Archambault (Syracuse: Syracuse University Press, 1986). *Les Angoysses douloureuses qui precedent d'amours* has been edited by Christine de Buzon (Paris: Honoré Champion, 1997) and translated as *The Torments of Love* by Lisa Neal and Steven Rendall (Minneapolis: University of Minnesota Press, 1996). *Le songe de madame Hélisenne* was edited by Jean-Philippe Beaulieu (Paris: Indigo and Côté-femmes Éditions, 1995), with modernized punctuation and some modernized spellings. It has been translated by Lisa Neal in *Writings by Pre-Revolutionary French Women*, ed. Anne Larsen and Colette Winn (New York: Garland, 2000). Translations of a small portion of her romance and some of her letters, along with an essay by Kittye Delle Robbins-Herring, appear also in *Women Writers of the Renaissance and Reformation*, ed. Katharina Wilson (Athens, Ga.: University of Georgia Press, 1987). The introductions to these editions and translations contain much useful information and further bibliography about Helisenne, whose real name was Marguerite Briet. The 1560 Groulleau edition of Helisenne's *Oeuvres* has been reprinted by Slatkine Reprints (Geneva, 1977). My quotations are taken from that edition. While there is a growing body of criticism about Helisenne's romance and letters, her *Songe* remains almost completely neglected.

3. *Aeneid* 4.173–88.

4. The 1560 edition does not use page numbers but does assign a letter to each set of sixteen pages, followed by a Roman numeral for the combined front and back of the page. The translations are my own.

5. Jerry Nash, "Exerçant oeuvres viriles': Feminine Anger and Feminist (Re)Writing in Helisenne de Crenne," *L'Esprit Créateur* 30, no. 4 (winter 1990): 38–48, and Deborah Losse, "Women Addressing Women: The Differentiated Text," in *Renaissance Women Writers: French Texts / American Contexts*, ed. Anne Larsen and Colette Winn (Detroit: Wayne State University Press, 1994), 31, both point out how Helisenne's letters and romance reverse the characteristics of male and female, making the female rational and the male irrational.

6. *Les Oeuvres de ma dame Hélisenne* (Paris: Charles Langelier, 1543; Paris: Grouleau, 1560).

7. Cited by Christine de Buzon in her edition of Helisenne's *Angoysses*, 9.

8. Marie de Romieu, *Les Premières Oeuvres Poétiques*, ed. André Winandy (Geneva: Librairie Droz, 1972).

9. For information on her life, see Dorothy O'Connor, *Louise Labé: Sa vie et son oeuvre* (1926; reprint, Geneva: Slatkine Reprints, 1972); Albert Champdor, *Louise Labé, son Oeuvre et son Temps* (Trevoux: Editions de Trevoux, 1981); and Jeanne Prine, "Louise Labé: Poet of Lyon," in *Women Writers of the Renaissance and Reformation*, 132–48. The French text of her *Débat de Folie et d'Amour* has been published in her *Oeuvres Complètes*, ed. Enzo Giudici (Geneva: Droz, 1981), and has been translated into English by Edith Farrell, *Louise Labé's Complete Works* (Troy, N.Y.: Whitson, 1986); see also *Debate of Folly and Love*, French text with English translation by Anne-Marie Bourbon (New York: Peter Lang, 2000), which has an excellent bibliography of editions, translations, and criticism. The *Débat* has received considerable critical attention. Robert Greene made an incomplete translation as early as 1584, an indication that the work was soon known even in England.

10. Enzo Giudici, *Amore e Follia nell'Opera della "Belle Cordière"* (Napoli: Liguori Editore, 1965), 105.

11. On the availability of Erasmus's *Praise of Folly* to Labé in numerous editions, Latin, French, or Italian, see François Rigolot, *Louise Labé Lyonnaise ou La Renaissance au Féminin* (Paris: Honoré Champion, 1997), 202.

12. Giudici, in Labé's *Oeuvres complètes*, 87–90, 108, mentions these suggestions but hastens to add that des Periers's subject matter and tone are totally different from Labé's. He seems to me a very unlikely source. Lucian is much more likely; however, Giudici's claim that especially Lucian's "Toxaris" comes closest to Labé's dialogue (106 n. 57) frankly puzzles me, as the two texts have absolutely nothing in common that I can see.

13. Marie Claude Malenfant, "L'Ambiguité finale du *Débat de Folie et de l'Amour* de Louise Labé," in *L'Ecriture des Femmes à la Renaissance Française*, ed. Diane Desrosiers-Bonin, special issue, *Littérature* 18 (1998): 107: Labé "fait montre de sa capacité à argumenter dans des sens opposés sans chercher à conclure de façon dogmatique."

14. On Labé's reference to the traditional Pallas versus Love binary, and Mercury's rejection of its use because of Pallas's equal enmity to Folly, see Rigolot, *Louise Labé Lyonnaise*, 117–26.

15. Anne Larsen has demonstrated this connection in "Catherine des Roches (1542–1587): Humanism and the Learned Woman," *Journal of the Rocky Mountain Medieval and Renaissance Association* 8 (1987): 103, 115 n. 24.

16. *Les Oeuvres* (Paris: Abel l'Angelier, 1578) and *Les Secondes Oeuvres* (Poitiers: Nicolas Courtoys, 1583) have been republished in modern editions by Anne Larsen (Geneva: Droz, 1993 and 1998). The introductions, notes, and bibliographies of these modern volumes are excellent sources of further information. See also George Diller, *Les Dames des Roches. Étude sur la vie littéraire à Poitiers dans la deuxième moitié du XVIe siècle* (Paris: Droz, 1936). A translation of selected writings, including the dialogue of Iris and Pasithée, appears in *Women Writers of the Renaissance and Reformation*; a translation of Catherine's *Bergerie* is included in *Writings by Pre-Revolutionary French Women*.

17. Livy, *The Early History of Rome*, 2:32.

18. Anne Larsen in her notes to the edition of the des Roches' *Oeuvres*, 223, affirms for this dialogue in particular the clear influence of Labé's *Débat*. All quotations are from this edition. For further discussion of Catherine des Roches's debt to Labé see Evelyne Berriot-Salvadore, "Les Héritières de Louise Labé," in *Louise Labé: Les voix du lyrisme*, ed. Guy Demerson (Paris: Editions du CNRS, 1990), 93–106.

19. Oblique but readily recognizable references to her mother occur in the dialogues of Virtue and Fortune and of Hunger and Poverty.

20. The 1558 edition is less complete and does not include the dialogues; Curione added additional materials in the 1562 edition. Olympia's *Opere* have been edited into two volumes by Lanfranco Caretti (R. Deputazione di Storia Patria per l'Emilia e la Romagna, sezione di Ferrara. Ferrara: Tipografia Sociale, 1940 and 1954). Her work has recently been translated by Holt N. Parker as *The Complete Writings of an Italian Heretic* (Chicago: University of Chicago Press, 2003); however, the translations in this essay are mine. The most thorough account of her life, besides her own letters, is Jules Bonnet, *Vie d'Olympia Morata, épisode de la renaissance et de la réforme en Italie* (3d ed., rev.

Paris: Charles Meyrueis, 1856). See also Roland Bainton, *Women of the Reformation in Germany and Italy* (Minneapolis: Augsburg, 1971). Morata has generally been discussed in the context of Reformation studies. For a more literary focus and some translated passages, see my essay, "Olympia Morata: From Classicist to Reformer," forthcoming in *Phaethon's Children: The Este Court and Its Culture in Early Modern Ferrara*, ed. Dennis Looney and Deanna Shemek (Tempe, AZ: Medieval and Renaissance Texts and Studies, 2004).

21. Sigea is Luisa Sigea, famed for her exchange of polyglot letters with the pope and mentioned by des Roches as the author of the Latin poem "Syntra" published in Paris in 1566. The des Roches probably could not have known that Sigea, companion of the Portuguese princess, had also written ca. 1552 a dialogue between two women, which remained unpublished until its modern edition and translation, *Dialogue de deux jeunes filles sur la vie de la cour et la vie de retraite* [Dialogue of two young girls on life at court and life in retreat], ed. and trans. Odette Sauvage (Paris: Presses Universitaires de France, 1970). Laura Terracina was a Neapolitan noblewoman, who published eight volumes of poetry between 1548 and 1561 (a ninth remained in manuscript) and was associated with the Neapolitan Academy of the Incogniti. Her most famous work is the *Discorso sopra tutti i primi canti di Orlando Furioso* [Discourse on all the first cantos of Orlando Furioso]. Terracina is the only woman in Catherine's list who wrote in Italian rather than Latin. Hippolyta Taurella married Baldassare Castiglione in 1516 and died three years later in childbirth. Scholars now attribute the Latin elegy on her husband's absence to Castiglione himself.

22. "Mais que diray-je de cete Morata, qui receut meritamment du ciel le nom d'Olympe? Et comment representerai-je la reverence que je porte à la memoire de la belle, gentille et vertueuse Hippolyte Taurelle, de qui les plaintives Elegies, donnoient tant de plaisir et de peine à son mari absent?" *Les Secondes Oeuvres*, ed. Anne Larsen, 219. Larsen in her notes to this passage and in her introduction, 52–53, suggests that the des Roches may have known of Morata's work through Agrippa d'Aubigné, who attended their salon and in a letter to his own daughters mentions possessing Morata's volume.

23. Referring to one of Catherine's dialogues from the second volume, Larsen comments in her introduction to the des Roches' *Secondes Oeuvres*, 50: "La nouveauté de ce "Dialogue d'Iris, et Pasithae" réside dans l'importance qu'il accorde à la voix feminine." This is precisely what Morata's example offered.

24. Morata's first dialogue is untitled but is headed, either by herself or by Curione, "Lavinia Ruverensis Ursina & Olympia Morata colloquuntur."

25. See the bibliographies by Alexandre Cioranesco, *Bibliographie de la littérature du seizième siècle* (Geneva: Slatkine Reprints, 1975), and by Romeo Arbour, *L'Ère Baroque en France* (Geneva: Droz, 1975). The *Dialogue* and *Exercice* were published together by Jean Le Blanc and then by Claude Micard and Gilles Robinot. Since the time this essay was presented as a conference paper, an edition of her complete work, including a history of its publication, has appeared: *L'exercice de l'âme vertueuse*, ed. Colette Winn, *Textes de la Renaissance* 38 (Paris: Honoré Champion, 2001); my quotations are now from this edition. Marie Le Gendre's work is mentioned briefly in Evelyne Berriot-Salvadore, *Les Femmes dans la société française de la Renaissance*. Histoire des idées et critique littéraire, vol. 285 (Geneva: Droz, 1990), 462, 545.

The *Cabinet des saines affections*, a frequently reprinted collection of brief moral essays intended for practical use, was sometimes attributed to her as well and sometimes to another woman; the latter now seems more likely. On the vexed attribution of the *Cabinet* see Colette Winn's introduction to her edition, *Cabinet des saines affections*, attributed to Madeleine de l'Aubespine, *Textes de la Renaissance* 39 (Paris: Honoré Champion, 2001).

26. Her positive evaluation of all three kinds of love is quite remarkable given the historical background of this topic. Aristotle's *Ethics* 8.2–4, without being initially negative about a love or friendship based on utility or on pleasure, nonetheless considers them impermanent (because focused on accidentals) and thus inferior to one based on the goodness of the person loved. Evil men love only for some gain to themselves and are thus incapable of the best love. Aristotle's discussion thus drives an ever wider moral wedge between the two "ignoble" kinds of love and the one true and enduring kind. Boccaccio's *Filocolo* 4.43–46, in an argument based on this passage from Aristotle but transferred into the setting of a romance, praises only the honest love of friends unequivocally; the pursuit of utility is condemned harshly right away by both speakers, and the delightful love of pleasure and beauty is reluctantly dismissed as dangerously deluding and destructive. The scene of love questions from the *Filocolo*, which contains this discussion, had been translated into French as *Treize elegantes demandes d'amour* and published in Paris in 1530 and again in 1541; a French translation of the whole *Filocolo* appeared as *Le Philocope* in 1542 and was printed eight times. See Victoria Kirkham, *Fabulous Vernacular: Boccaccio's Filocolo and the Art of Medieval Fiction* (Ann Arbor: University of Michigan Press, 2001), 16. Thus Boccaccio's discussion would have been available to Le Gendre. Le Gendre follows up Aristotle's notion that one can love with two kinds of love at once by introducing the new notion that a combination of all three is actually the best.

27. Léo Mouton, "Le capitaine François Le Poulchre de la Motte-Messemé," *Revue d'Histoire Littéraire de la France* 38 (1931): 279.

28. See Berriot-Salvadore, *Les Femmes dans la société française*, 462, and the poems (in Winn's edition) in which Le Gendre laments her husband's death.

29. Berriot-Salvadore, "Les Héritières de Louise Labé," 99–105, inquiring about the possible influence of Labé on later women writers, finds this scene a suggestive link but concludes that the evidence for Labé's influence remains uncertain.

30. Winn, *L'exercice de l'âme vertueuse*, 99, 106, 141.

BIBLIOGRAPHY

Arbour, Romeo. *L'Ère Baroque en France*. Geneva: Droz, 1975.

Bainton, Roland. *Women of the Reformation in Germany and Italy*. Minneapolis: Augsburg, 1971.

Berriot-Salvadore, Evelyne. *Les Femmes dans la société française de la Renaissance*. Histoire des idées et critique littéraire, vol. 285. Geneva: Droz, 1990.

———. "Les Héritières de Louise Labé." In *Louise Labé: Les voix du lyrisme*, ed. Guy Demerson, 93–106. Paris: Editions du CNRS, 1990.

Bonnet, Jules. *Vie d'Olympia Morata, épisode de la renaissance et de la réforme en Italie*. 3d ed., rev. Paris: Charles Meyrueis, 1856.

Champdor, Albert. *Louise Labé, son Oeuvre et son Temps*. Trevoux: Editions de Trevoux, 1981.

Cioranesco, Alexandre. *Bibliographie de la littérature du seizième siècle*. Geneva: Slatkine Reprints, 1975.

Crenne, Hélisenne de. *Les oeuvres de ma dame Hélisenne de Crenne*. 1560. Reprint, Geneva: Slatkine Reprints, 1977.

———. *Le songe de madame Hélisenne de Crenne*. 1541. Reprint, ed. Jean-Philippe Beaulieu. Paris: Indigo and Côté-femmes Éditions, 1995.

———. *Epistres familieres et invectives*. Ed. Jean-Philippe Beaulieu with Hannah Fournier. Montreal: Les Presses de l'Université de Montréal, 1995.

———. *Epistres familieres et invectives*. Ed Jerry Nash. Paris: Honoré Champion, 1996.

———. *The Torments of Love*. Trans. Lisa Neal and Steven Rendall. Minneapolis: University of Minnesota Press, 1996.

———. *Les Angoysses douloureuses qui precedent d'amours*. Ed. Christine de Buzon. Paris: Honoré Champion, 1997.

———. *Lady Helisenne's Dream*. Trans. Lisa Neal. In *Writings by Pre-Revolutionary French Women*, ed. Anne Larsen and Colette Winn, 63–105. New York: Garland, 2000.

des Roches, Madeleine and Catherine. *Les Oeuvres*. Ed. Anne Larsen. Geneva: Droz, 1993.

———. *Les Secondes Oeuvres*. Ed. Anne Larsen. Geneva: Droz, 1998.

Desrosiers-Bonin, Diane, ed. *L'Ecriture des Femmes à la Renaissance Française*. Special issue. *Littérature* 18 (1998).

Diller, George. *Les Dames des Roches. Étude sur la vie littéraire à Poitiers dans la deuxième moitié du XVIe siècle*. Paris: Droz, 1936.

Giudici, Enzo. *Amore e Follia nell'Opera della "Belle Cordière."* Napoli: Liguori Editore, 1965.

Kirkham, Victoria. *Fabulous Vernacular: Boccaccio's Filocolo and the Art of Medieval Fiction*. Ann Arbor: University of Michigan Press, 2001.

Labé, Louise. *Oeuvres Complètes*. Ed. Enzo Giudici. Geneva: Droz, 1981.

———. *Complete Works*. Trans. Edith Farrell. Troy, N.Y.: Whitson, 1986.

———. *Debate of Folly and Love*. Trans. Anne-Marie Bourbon. New York: Peter Lang, 2000.

Larsen, Anne. "Catherine des Roches (1542–1587): Humanism and the Learned Woman." *Journal of the Rocky Mountain Medieval and Renaissance Association* 8 (1987): 97–117.

Larsen, Anne, and Colette Winn, eds. *Renaissance Women Writers: French Texts / American Contexts*. Detroit: Wayne State University Press, 1994.

———. *Writings by Pre-Revolutionary French Women: From Marie de France to Elizabeth Vigée-Le Brun*. New York: Garland, 2000.

L'Aubespine, Madeleine de. *Cabinet des saines affections*. Ed. Colette Winn. Textes de la Renaissance, 39. (Paris: Honoré Champion, 2001).

Le Gendre, Marie. *L'exercice de l'âme vertueuse*. Ed. Colette Winn. Paris: Honoré Champion, 2001.

Losse, Deborah. "Women Addressing Women: The Differentiated Text." In *Renaissance Women Writers: French Texts/American Contests*, ed. Anne Larsen and Colette Winn 23–37. Detroit: Wayne State University Press, 1994.

Morata, Olympia. *Opere*. Ed. Lanfranco Caretti. R. Deputazione di Storia Patria per l'Emilia e la Romagna, sezione di Ferrara. Ferrara: Tipografia Sociale, 1940 and 1954.

Morata, Olympia. *The Complete Writings of an Italian Heretic*. Ed. and trans. Holt N. Parker. Chicago: University of Chicago Press, 2003.

Mouton, Léo. "Le capitaine François Le Poulchre de la Motte-Messemé." *Revue d'Histoire Littéraire de la France* 38 (1931): 262–82.

Mustacchi, Marianna, and Paul Archambault. A *Renaissance Woman: Helisenne's Personal and Invective Letters*. Syracuse: Syracuse University Press, 1986.

Nash, Jerry. "'Exerçant oeuvres viriles': Feminine Anger and Feminist (Re)Writing in Helisenne de Crenne." *L'Esprit Créateur* 30, no. 4 (winter 1990): 38–48.

O'Connor, Dorothy. *Louise Labé: Sa vie et son oeuvre*. 1926. Reprint, Geneva: Slatkine Reprints, 1972.

Prine, Jeanne. "Louise Labé: Poet of Lyon." In *Women Writers of the Renaissance and Reformation*, ed. Katharina Wilson, 132–48. Athens, GA: University of Georgia Press, 1987.

Rigolot, François. *Louise Labé Lyonnaise ou La Renaissance au Féminin*. Paris: Honoré Champion, 1997.

Romieu, Marie de. *Les Premières Oeuvres Poétiques*. Ed. André Winandy. Geneva: Librairie Droz, 1972.

Sigea, Luisa. *Duarum virginum colloquium. Dialogue de deux jeunes filles sur la vie de la cour et la vie de retraite*. Ed. and trans. Odette Sauvage. Paris: Presses Universitaires de France, 1970.

Wilson, Katharina, ed. *Women Writers of the Renaissance and Reformation*. Athens, Ga.: University of Georgia Press, 1987.

Strong Voices, Weak Minds?

THE DEFENSES OF EVE BY ISOTTA NOGAROLA AND CHRISTINE DE PIZAN, WHO FOUND THEMSELVES IN SIMONE DE BEAUVOIR'S SITUATION

Thelma S. Fenster

At the midpoint of the fifteenth century, Isotta Nogarola (1418–66), a humanist living in Verona and corresponding in Latin with educated contemporaries, undertook a discussion by letter with her frequent correspondent, the well-known diplomat and humanist Ludovico Foscarini, to determine whether Adam and Eve had sinned in equal measure. Humanist practice, of course, nurtured letter writing as a form of publication, and the debate became part of Isotta's permanent legacy. With encouragement from Ludovico, Isotta recopied the epistolary exchange as a dialogue, and it appears today as part of her collected letters on varying subjects, some addressed to well-known figures of her day.[1]

The two debated the Augustinian proposition that "They [Adam and Eve] sinned unequally according to sex, but equally according to pride."[2] This meant entering into issues of Adam and Eve's relative strengths and weaknesses and the nature of the pride that each displayed in disobeying God. The heart of Isotta's defense of Eve lies in the paradox that Eve's ignorance and weak-mindedness made her less sinful than Adam. Eve's *imperfection,* that is, explains her naïveté in the face of the snake's beguilement, whereas Adam's *perfection* makes his eating of the forbidden fruit a far greater sin. Ludovico does not so much defend Adam as condemn Eve. He argues that ignorance is not an excuse and that Eve had enough God-given sense, in any case, not to have acted as she did. In Ludovico's opinion, her sin was therefore worse than Adam's.

Isotta's paradoxical reading of Eve's error, a version of the strength-in-weakness paradox, was scarcely new in the fifteenth century.[3] The Italian-born Parisian Christine de Pizan (1365–1430?) also knew and used the idea in her writing. As the two women's lives overlapped chronologically, they offer a valuable occasion for comparison at a time when such opportunities are indeed rare. My interest in this study is Isotta, but Christine's example will help to suggest how each woman's personal reach overcame imposed limitations. Although over the last quarter of the twentieth century a few of Christine's works have become canonical themselves, Isotta's writing and her defense of Eve, dazzling in its command of authoritative male sources, have received surprisingly little attention from medieval or Renaissance scholars, feminist or otherwise.[4] Yet the debate with Ludovico marks a signal event in the history of writing by women, in literary history generally, and in intellectual history. At the very least, both women participated prominently in Western culture's long history of recorded discussions about the "nature of woman" in which women themselves, in their own voices, were heard.

It is perhaps not surprising that Isotta and Christine shared not only a knowledge of that paradoxical view of Eve but also a perception that they themselves, because of their personal dispositions toward learning and writing, were anomalous, paradoxical men-women. Although that personal quandary is not explicitly addressed in Isotta's dialogue with Ludovico, it is certainly hinted at elsewhere in her writing. Then, too, it is ineluctably though silently present as the paradoxical frame for her defense of Eve, for Isotta herself offers the spectacle of an educated and intelligent woman promoting Eve's cause on the grounds of woman's inherent weak-mindedness. Over the long view, moreover, Isotta's dilemma appears to feed into Western culture's discursively varied, centuries-old discussion over sameness versus difference, and with it essentialism versus constructionism, a binary model whose disadvantages are today notorious. To some, it may appear that Isotta lost the debate because she argued her case within the limits of male canonical, theological views. On the contrary, given that those views supplied the only anthropology available, Isotta rather triumphed by "speaking male voices," but with a difference. Isotta (and, as we shall see, Christine) managed to hold the irreconcilables of her life in tension, in a two-dimensional conceptualization that defied binaries and enabled her to pursue the life she had chosen.

The particular Augustinian context for the debate between Isotta and Ludovico can be found in *The Literal Meaning of Genesis*, 11.35:48, on "The excuses of Adam and Eve": "Then the Lord God said to the woman, '*What is this that you have done?' And she replied, 'The serpent beguiled me, and I ate.'* She too fails to confess her sin. She shifts the blame to another, and although her sex is different from Adam's, her pride is the same."[5] Eve's seduction by the snake, her "beguiling," led, first, to the conclusion that she sinned out of ignorance, whereas Adam knew that he was sinning, and, second, that he who is better or who should be better fails more significantly when he sins. In that view Eve, more malleable, more suggestible than Adam, was also less sinful than Adam. This is the position that Isotta defends.

What follows here is a necessarily abbreviated synopsis of the debate between the two friends, limited to key points. Ludovico begins with three points that show Eve's greater sin: Eve's punishment was harsher than Adam's; she thought she was made more like God (Eve's pride); she was the cause of Adam's sin, but he was not the cause of hers.[6]

Isotta retorts by arguing that, where there is less reason and constancy, the sin is also smaller. Eve ate the apple because of her weakness, and pride was never at issue. The serpent led Eve into sin not through bold assertion but by asking her why God instructed her not to eat of the tree of paradise. When God placed the couple in paradise, he told Adam about the tree, thus bestowing responsibility on the man. Eve ate the apple because she was more likely to indulge in pleasure, not because she wanted to rival God. If Adam had not eaten the apple, moreover, Eve's sin would have been without consequence for the human race, for she would have harmed only herself, whereas Adam brought sin upon all humanity. Isotta claims that Adam's punishment—hard labor and death—was worse than Eve's, because when God uttered that punishment, he was addressing Adam (146–47).

Ludovico, answering that had he not been born a man he might well have been persuaded by Isotta, states that he will "assault" Isotta's "fortress" with her own "weapons." He begins, therefore, with a refutation of Isotta's arguments. Ignorance is not an excuse, he says, especially when it is borne of negligence and arrogance. Her intellect, created by God, is not to be faulted, for she appeared clever enough to the snake that he approached her by indirection (with a question). Inconstancy is an evil in itself. Pride, not frailty, was the cause of Eve's sin. She believed the snake only because she was overcome by love for her own power. The way that Eve sinned suggests that, like the demons, she did not merit redemption, whereas Adam's sin can be regarded as fortunate, given that it produced the redeemer, Jesus Christ. Woman experiences all the pains that man does, and in addition she suffers the pain of childbirth. Then Ludovico adds some points of his own. Eve, he states, is responsible for all of Adam's faults because, as Aristotle says (in *Posterior Analytics*), "the cause of a cause is the cause of that which is caused."

Eve deceived her husband, vulnerable because he loved her. Eve was both the "cause" and the "example" of sin and thus was guiltier. Moreover, the longer the sin lasts, the worse it is, and Eve sinned first (147–50).

Isotta now says that she had contemplated not continuing the debate because Ludovico was in fact assaulting her fortress with her own weapons, so that even learned men would have had difficulty retorting; however, she goes on, stating that it was God who made Eve ignorant. Acts that come from innate inconstancy are not sins. The greater the gifts given by God, the greater the responsibility. God created man perfect, "and the powers of his soul perfect, and gave him a greater understanding and knowledge of truth as well as a greater depth of wisdom." Eve, on the other hand, was created to be Adam's helper.

Eve desired not to equal God, Isotta states, but to have knowledge of good and evil, which is less of a sin than to disobey divine commandment, as Adam did. Eve was redeemed along with Adam, and if it seems otherwise, that is no doubt because God himself thought her sin negligible. Adam's sin was greater than Eve's because it became general in all men and because it had to be redeemed by Christ's most shameful and most horrible sort of death.

In response to Ludovico's citation of Aristotle on causes, Isotta says that Eve could not have led Adam into sin, for she was inferior to him and could not have constrained his will. Supposing that Adam had free will, he would have been guiltier than Eve; if he did not, Eve did not take it away from him, God did. Finally, Isotta takes up the issue of temporality, saying that the fact of having sinned before Adam in time, and thus for longer, doesn't make Eve worse, given her greater weakness (150–56).

Ludovico claims that Eve's inconstancy was not given by nature but arose from habit. God created her to comfort Adam, but she brought him sorrow. Adam may have transgressed against God's commandments, but so did Eve. Isotta "pushes too far Aristotle's views on first causes," and, in any event, Ludovico says, he does not believe that Adam's sin "was entirely and in every way" caused by Eve. Women are deceitful, and nothing could be worse than an "intimate enemy." Ludovico now bids Isotta farewell, saying that he was "ordered not to exceed the paper" she sent him and that he does not wish to presume to guide someone as brilliant as Isotta (156–58).[7]

As a display of learning from theological sources, the debate is comprehensive and focused.[8] Both debaters draw heavily upon Genesis itself and upon commentary, often naming their authorities. Isotta's sources tend to be primarily the Bible and Christian commentators: Peter Lombard's *Sentences*, Augustine's *On Nature and Grace*, Ambrose's *On Paradise* and *Expositio in Lucam;* Gregory's *Morals on the Book of Job*, Bernard on free will (perhaps in his *On Grace and Free Choice*), as well as Ecclesiasticus, John, Mark, Matthew, Luke, and Romans. She paraphrases the first line of Aristotle's *Metaphysics* (that "All men by nature desire to know"), and she responds to Ludovico's arguments from Aristotle's *Posterior Analytics*. She incorrectly attributes a comment on the Trinity to Isidore. For his part, Ludovico also calls upon Genesis and Ecclesiasticus, as well as patristic writing, citing Augustine's *Literal Commentary on Genesis* and his letters to Orosius, as well as St. Gregory. He quotes from Aristotle's *Posterior Analytics*. Unnamed texts or authors that he uses include Aristotle's *Nicomachean Ethics*, 1 Corinthians, Boethius's *Consolation of Philosophy*, Sallust, and Cicero.[9]

The format allows Ludovico to begin the dialogue and to end it. There is no "logical" conclusion to the contest, conducted of course on theological grounds. At its end, Ludovico states: "Though I have spoken, you may not hear. You may spurn and disdain [my words because of] Augustine's conclusion that they were equally guilty."[10] It is noteworthy that Ludovico leaves room for Isotta to disagree, recognizing their diverse readings both of the creation portion of Genesis and of Augustine.

In spite of having the *either/or* appearance of medieval dialectic, that play of opinion calls to mind the practice of medieval exegesis, especially as Catherine Brown has defined it. In her analysis of scriptural contradiction, Brown observes that the Bible may teach one doctrine, but it does so in many ways, and exegesis therefore proceeds by "endlessly unpacking and remaking the single doctrine and multiple teachings embodied in Scripture."[11] And indeed, some of the most powerful hermeneutic pronouncements "teach exegetes to read scriptural opposition not primarily through the disambiguating division of *either/or* but through the sacramentally multiple *both-and*."[12] The dazzle in the debate, then, owes a great deal to its enmeshment in multiple readings in and of the creation story: how Eve and Adam each read God's word; the serpent's competing reading of God's instructions; how commentary read the creation story; and how Isotta and Ludovico read and evaluated the creation story itself, inescapably through the mediation of commentary.

Brown recalls the famous formula according to which there could be no *adverse* statements, only *diverse* ones; apparent "logical incoherence" was in reality "a harmonious and congruent showing of divine generosity"; however, the debate's apparently "harmonious" conclusion may be due not so much to generosity as it is to the real extratextual lack of true multiple possibilities. As Jesse Gellrich has put it, "The writing that composed the Book of culture is preoccupied with foreground; questioning, contradiction, and uncertainty cannot disturb the authority of traditional meanings."[13] To put it another way, the medieval church never really wished to reconsider women's subordination, as Ann Matter has emphasized.[14] At the end, Ludovico can perhaps afford to be generous when he anticipates that Isotta will not agree with what he has said, for his own masculine privilege will remain.

The exchange between Isotta and Ludovico remains one of the most densely argued of its kind on woman's nature, especially when compared with earlier vernacular courtly literature in which comments upon woman's nature had become fashionable. Ideas about woman that had begun their life in biblical commentary had, in the period between the twelfth and the fourteenth centuries, stimulated renewed interest.[15] Diverse material, containing views from numerous sources including the writing of the Greek fathers, silted into the vernacular languages. Eric Jager, discussing the processes by which dissemination of these ideas in the vernacular occurred, notes that medieval commentators routinely incorporated earlier commentary into their own writing,[16] just as Isotta and Ludovico did. Then too, as preaching orders took up the oral instruction of the unlettered, their teaching on creation made its way into sermons and out into open, public spaces. The subject of woman became the stuff of, or was inserted into, courtly *dits* and other short narrative pieces, such as those in the blame of women and praise of women series.[17] It could be said that by the time Isotta and Ludovico began to write to one another, they were at once continuing an older Latin tradition as well as, in a sense, "translating" back into Latin some points that had already circulated in the vernacular tongues.

Given that the worth of woman topoi informed medieval literature written overwhelmingly by men who often sought to entertain their audiences through irony or suggestiveness, the "sincerity" of masculine defenses of woman has frequently been found wanting. Possibly nothing could raise that warning more than the Renaissance genre of the literary paradox, relevant here because many medieval ideas in defense of woman made their way into the paradox. Paradox is, in Rosalie Colie's words, a "formal defense, organized along the lines of traditional *encomia,* of an unexpected, unworthy or indefensible subject."[18] Related to it is the "defense of a proposition officially disapproved in public opinion."[19] To take but one example: Ortensio Lando's witty *Paradossi,* first published in Lyon in 1543, thus almost a hundred years after Isotta debated with Ludovico.[20] Items in Lando's collection purport to prove, for example, that poverty is better than wealth, ignorance better than learning, or war better than peace. Boccaccio's writing, it is argued, is not worthy of being read, and Aristotle was not only ignorant but also the most evil man of his age. Among such seemingly frivolous subjects, manifestly designed to test the paradoxist's abilities, is Lando's "Paradosso XXV, Che la donna è di maggior eccelenza che l'uomo" [that woman is more excellent than man]. There, familiar arguments make an appearance; however, as Colie points out, the paradox doesn't really commit itself to a position, nor does the paradoxist, for "all paradoxes . . . are self-enclosed statements with no external reference point from which to take a bearing on the paradox itself."[21] As is typical of Renaissance paradox when it courts the subject of woman, Lando's seems to bring the entire issue of woman's worth to a *reductio ad absurdum*, and it puts in relief an ironic strain already present in earlier literature.

In a deliberate referencing of earlier literature that poked fun at women or otherwise maligned them, Christine de Pizan (1365–1430?) deployed her wit to defend women and poke fun at men. Her first such defense was conducted in the octosyllabic rhymed couplets of her *Letter of the God of Love*, her first narrative poem (1399).[22] Cupid protests men's deceitfulness and vanity, a topic that elsewhere could have passed for conventional courtly material. At about the halfway point, however, Christine takes up, and attempts to refute, the extant body of antiwoman opinion. The subject of women's smaller guilt based upon Eve's weak-mindedness, though not a centerpiece of Christine's defense as it is of Isotta's, links Eve's lesser lights with another known and admired concept, that of simplicity. Cupid urges that Eve's lack of rationality and intellectual will should be understood as *simplece*, a Christian ideal of guilelessness and trust. It was because of her *simplece* that Eve thought the snake was loyal and true; only in good faith did she approach Adam with the apple. In other words, Eve did not beguile Adam in the way that the snake beguiled her. Eve had no hidden malice, and her intention was pure; she did not know how to deceive.[23] Later, in Christine's *Advision*, a more mature and autobiographical work, Christine links the special frailty of woman with the frailty of human beings in general, so that embodied woman comes to represent humanity.[24] In the third, most autobiographical part of the *Advision*, Lady Philosophy says that Christine is indeed a "tender, fragile woman, not able to withstand adversity."[25] Most significantly, Philosophy addresses man/mankind, saying: "Alas, man, and if you look at your body, you will not find anything weaker, for the bite of a dog or of a fly, if it gets inside you, kills you!"[26] Christine does not exactly argue for the equality of the female with the male body but rather just the other way around: in the end, it is the male who is equal to the female—no stronger, no more worthy, just as mortal.

For both women, the act of writing had *ad feminam*, and certainly not always pleasant, consequences. Isotta had shunned both marriage and the convent to spend her days in reading, learning, and writing. Trained by tutors engaged by her mother, Isotta probably did not receive a formal education to equal that of her male contemporaries. For men, humanist training was designed to lead to public service, but Isotta's public orations surely struck many as unusual.[27] The extent to which her situation sometimes left her open to ridicule can be inferred from the accusation that she had committed incest with her brother; that forced her to leave Verona for two years.[28] She was also advised by her male contemporaries that she would have to become a man in order to write. Furthermore, in a letter to the famous Latin teacher Guarino of Verona she says that she has pondered often of what value women might be, since they were scorned by men in word and in deed. She bemoans her own fortune in having been born a woman.[29] Elsewhere, she looks for antecedents, adducing the examples of two women in antiquity, Lastheneia of Mantinea and Axiothea of Phlius, who were said to have been among Plato's students; the latter, Isotta said in a letter to Antonio Borromeo, "wore men's clothing in order to study with him."[30]

As for Christine, she was largely self-taught—interestingly, she laments that she had to defy her mother, who wanted her to learn women's tasks—but she had her father's learning as an example (he was Tommaso da Pizzano, astrologer to Charles V) and a substantial library at hand. She does not seem to have suffered as much as Isotta from character defamation, perhaps in part because she had fulfilled her womanly obligation to be a mother. Christine, too, in her *Book of the City of Ladies*, broods upon the problem of her female birth. She says that for a long time she had accepted that women were weak, because so many learned men said so. But having mulled over their pronouncements, she wonders how it could be that God had gone wrong in creating woman. She asks God why he did not allow her to be born as a man and thus "as perfect as a man is said to be."[31]

In the *Mutation of Fortune* Christine announces her gender change, following the death of her husband.

> I will tell you who I am who is speaking,
> Who from female became male
> Through Fortune, who wanted it thus;
> She changed me in body and in face
> Into a perfect, natural man;
> And formerly I was a woman, in fact
> I am a man, I do not lie.[32]

In the *Advision*, too, Lady Philosophy reminds Christine that "your weak and feminine body was changed into [that of] a man in order for you to be changed in your condition."[33]

In an important sense, when those statements are lifted out of their context, something of a misrepresentation can occur. For it was *in the act of writ-*

ing (and in the reading and learning that accompanied it) that Isotta and Christine took on the quality of "men." When Isotta perfected her Latin, clearly she was entering upon terrain considered masculine, although she was hardly the only Italian woman of her time to do so.[34] As for French, as a vernacular it had been considered traditionally a "feminine" adjunct to masculine Latin.[35] King Charles V's large-scale translation program of canonical Latin works, however, undertaken during Christine's own formative years, showed that French, too, could be a language of learning. Paradoxically once more, at the moment when Christine, a woman, began to write, the language in which she wrote had undergone an elevation of status: a virilization. Finally, it was in masculine writing that Isotta and Christine found not only the words that condemned woman but also those in support of woman.

Although what each wrote in defense of woman already existed in various male writings, which authorized it, it would be inappropriate to say that they were women who wrote exclusively in male voices, just as it would be a mistake to presume that they could, in any sense, shuttle back and forth between mutually exclusive, binary categories. What their own comments suggest is that they were metaphorically women *and* men, more suitably represented by the "bothness" of exegesis, not the *either/or* of dialectic. At the risk of anachronism, I suggest that Olympe de Gouges, a Frenchwoman famous for publishing her *Declaration of the Rights of Woman and Citizen* in 1791, in the wake of the French Revolution, explained her situation through the use of a rhetorical trope that we may apply as well to Isotta and Christine. She said: "I am neither man nor woman. I have all the courage of the one and, sometimes, the weaknesses of the other."[36] Though at a remove of more than three hundred years, Olympe's words seek a discursively viable position that recalls the cases of Isotta and Christine: Olympe may be using the vocabulary of binaries, but her point is a refusal of *either/or*.

The bothness of the sex-gender dilemma, the female and male, came from each woman's personal experience, but it could also be traced to Augustine. My intention is not to defend or criticize Augustine but simply to note that his explanation of man and woman in *The Literal Meaning of Genesis*, which had become a foundational text, a "true anthropological treatise,"[37] also authorized some women to claim a masculine quality for themselves. Troubled by the contradictory versions of creation in Genesis (Genesis 1.26–27 says that God created woman and man in his image, but in Genesis 2.21–23 woman is said to be derived from man, which meant that only man had been made in the image of God), Augustine proposed a Neoplatonic schema according to which both man and woman possess a rational soul and are called *homo*, human being, but that description applies only at the level of the *homo interior*. As *homo exterior*, or *femina*, woman did not reflect the image of God, although man, whose *homo exterior* is captured in the word *vir*, does reflect the *imago Dei*.[38] What this implies, as Kari Børresen has pointed out, is that for man, the *homo interior* harmonizes with the *homo exterior*, whereas for woman a dissonance arises between the two.[39] This need not be stated as a duality of exclusive categories, however, given that in Augustine's formulation the human being is always composed of *exterior* and *interior*; and no human can be one *or* the other. The result is that woman can "be" both woman and man, but man is always man. Augustine's formulation "provided both the theological underpinnings and the justification for the roles of women in the medieval church. Women were categorically excluded from sacramental leadership in the church."[40] With the same stroke, however, Augustine had created the theoretical environment in which Isotta and Christine could feel authorized to strive beyond their femininity and, I would argue, invoke the bothness of man-woman that Augustine's interpretation of Genesis—and that notion of diverse readings so crucial to exegesis more generally—had made available. After all, had Augustine himself not already done so in his praise of the strong-mindedness of saints Perpetua and Felicity, whose souls became "assuredly more virile" for not having given in to female fragility?[41]

That same model can be invoked to explain how Isotta and Christine reconciled Eve's purported ignorance and weak-mindedness with their own clear intellectual resolve and considerable learning. In a conceptualization that may speak for both women, Christine, I suggest, would not have thought impossible the reconciling of *simplece* with learnedness, and perhaps in the same way that Augustine's *interior* and *exterior* harmonized. More than that, there is reason to believe that she would have seen it as especially possible in the case of a woman. It is well known that she reproached certain men for using their learning to deceive (Jean de Meun, for example, in his *Roman de la Rose*), but she does not seem to have made any *necessary* link between learning and a penchant for duplicity. Ludovico's praise of Isotta for her complete devotion to Christ and her "admirable and incredible humanity, by which [she yields] to all" suggests that he in no way thought Isotta's learning detracted from her modesty (he may of course have wanted to emphasize that very point, for the sake of Isotta's reputation). On the other hand, he was not eager to believe that women in general could be clever: the woman he saw as his interlocutor was an exception to the general run of women, whose "burden" of "weakness" she bore.[42]

It has been argued over the centuries that women were worthy either because they were like men or because they had their own intrinsic value, of a kind not given to men—the matter of sameness, or equality, versus difference. Some recent scholarship has called attention to feminism's long—too long—meditation on that conundrum, which, because of the way in which it is stated, inevitably leads to one of only two possible conclusions, neither one satisfactory. Joan Wallach Scott, historian of modern France and feminist theorist, regards the difference and equality positions as paradoxes because of "the discursive practices of democratic politics [following the French Revolution] that have equated individuality with masculinity."[43] That is, the dominant masculine position that women seek to join or dissent from never changes, and women never cease to take it as the standard. The paradox that Scott writes about lies in "the need both to accept *and* to refuse 'sexual difference.'" She believes that the question "cannot be resolved as it has been posed."[44] What Scott says emphasizes that, however much the discursive surface of the woman's worth question may differ from period to period (for the postrevolutionary era it is the discourse of "democratic politics"), its core—what comes first and what the surface discourse is meant to validate—is the same: a hierarchy according to which man is valued more highly than woman.

Implicated in the argument over sameness versus difference is the one between essentialism and constructionism. Notable twentieth-century "difference" feminists, such as the French writer Hélène Cixoús and French philosopher Luce Irigaray, stand accused of essentialism. Yet the idea that "gender" denotes something that has been socially constructed—presented once more as the opposite position in a binary formulation—can be equally troubling. The credit, or blame, for inspiring late-twentieth-century constructionism is generally given to French philosopher Simone de Beauvoir. But a recent substantial analysis of *The Second Sex* by Toril Moi, currently perhaps Beauvoir's staunchest explicator, argues that English-language feminism has misunderstood Beauvoir's philosophy. According to Moi, Beauvoir never posited a free-floating constructionism. For Beauvoir the "body both is a situation *and* is placed within other situations."[45] Moi points out that, whereas "most feminist theories today rely on a universalized and reified concept of 'femininity,'" Beauvoir herself had written that, "Surely woman is, like man, a human being, but such a declaration is abstract. The fact is that every concrete human being is always in a specific situation."[46] Like Scott, Moi laments that the "amount of time feminists have spent worrying about women's 'equality' or 'difference' is a symptom of the success of this ideological trap." She argues that a "genuinely feminist position would refuse either option, and insist, rather, that women should not have to choose between calling themselves women and calling themselves writers (or intellectuals, or painters, or composers). To put this differently: it does not go without saying that what a woman does or says is always expressive of the 'woman in her.'"[47]

Studies of Christine de Pizan have repeatedly pointed to her emphasis upon the common human essence of man and woman.[48] I agree with that characterization but have argued elsewhere that Christine did not do so to the exclusion of the body.[49] I suggest that Beauvoir's formulation, that the "body both is a situation *and* is placed within other situations," can afford a useful way of looking at the "situations" of both Isotta and Christine as sexed bodies. It is not feasible, in this space, to interpret fully either woman's writing in that light, although I would like to offer a few observations. As I touched upon earlier, in much modern writing about medieval defenses of woman, it appears implicit that when men defended women, they were insincere (because men), but when women wrote defenses, they must have been sincere (because women). For either assumption to be true, however, we must risk falling once again into the essentialism trap. That is, it is the *authorial body*, seen as essentially male or female, that determines whether the defense is sincere or insincere. It depends on the premise, as Moi puts it, that "what a woman does or says is always expressive of the 'woman in her.'"

With respect to Isotta and Christine as women writing, I suggest that in offering their critiques from the *subject* position, they were in Beauvoir's "specific situation," the human being in situ. That both were "subject of" and "subject to"[50] medieval discourse about woman may correspond in part to Beauvoir's "body as situation" and "body as background." The body as situation is "agency in the subject"; it is the body that interacts with others, "the body as experienced by a human subject, the body as interwoven with the projects of that subject"—Isotta and Christine as the "subject of" their words. The body as background, on the other hand, "precedes and enables perception and experience."[51] The body in situation is—for example—each woman in the act of writing. That heightened awareness of situation is, to my mind, what Christine expresses when she explains her gender change in the *Mutation of Fortune*, referred to earlier, by saying, "I will tell you who I am, who is speaking." It is foreground, not background.

The body as background can also be the woman behind the text as perceived by readers. Sometimes it corresponds to the position of the woman "subject to." For example, when Ludovico surmised that Isotta would not "hear" him, it was in part because he thought that, as an embodied woman, she would continue to uphold Eve's innocence. Isotta's material existence prejudged the conclusion just as much as Ludovico's being an embodied man had prevented him from subscribing to Isotta's defense, as he himself said. With these concepts of situation (foreground) and background, Beauvoir "avoids implying that women's words can be reduced to their bodies."[52] Moreover, "the individual woman in the foreground cannot be reduced to the general historical situation which is her background."[53] To sum up, Moi says, "What is admirable about Beauvoir's understanding of what a woman is, is precisely her capacity to convey this doubleness without reducing it to one or the other of its components, without acquiescing in it, and also without choosing one of the two equally unsatisfactory theories of what a woman is ('a woman is just a human being' *versus* 'a woman is always just a woman')."[54] In situation—reading, writing, learning—Isotta and Christine also exist as backgrounded and foregrounded bodies. They know the experience of doubleness.

Articulate and educated women like Isotta and Christine lived out deeply individual experiences at a moment long before a feminist movement of women, joining in community, would grapple with issues of sex and gender. It is all the more remarkable that two women, writing centuries ago, isolated from each other, and leading relatively solitary existences, each came to similar conclusions about their situation. For both women, doubleness, or bothness, was enabling, for it alone gave to each the complex framework within which to pursue the writing life, a pursuit that a male canon and its dispute about woman's responsibility for the fall thought to inhibit, even as it unwittingly cleared the way for some clever women to justify their own intellectual achievements.

❧ ❧ ❧

NOTES

1. Isotta Nogarola, "De pari aut impari Evae atque Adae peccato," in *Isotae Nogarolae Veronensis opera quae supersunt omnia; accedunt Angelae et Zeneverae Nogarolae epistolae et carmina,* ed. E. Abel (Budapest: Magyar Tudomanyos Akademia, 1885), 2:187–216. I wish to thank Fr. Martin Chase, S.J., and Fr. Christopher Cullen, S.J., for helpful pointers as I was writing this article. Catharine Randall and Jocelyn-Wogan-Browne read the manuscript and offered valuable observations and information. Finally, my special thanks go to Pamela Benson, whose probing questions made this a better essay.

2. "De pari aut impari," in *Opera* 2:187. Augustine: "*Et dixit Dominus Deus mulieri, Quid hoc fecisti? Et dixit mulier, Serpens seduxit me, et manducavi*. Nec ista confitetur peccatum, sed in alterum refert, impari sexu, pari fastu" (*De Genesi ad Literam* 11.48, in *Patrologia latina Cursus completus* 34:449 translated in *The Literal Meaning of Genesis*, trans. John Hammond Taylor, Ancient Christian Writers, vols. 41, 42 [New York: Newman Press, 1982], 42:168–69).

3. Alcuin Blamires states that Peter Abelard founded his profeminine treatise on the strength-in-weakness paradox, and indeed, variants of this approach remained prominent in the case for women throughout the Middle Ages (*The Case for Women in Medieval Culture* [Oxford: Clarendon, 1997], 136). Hildegard of Bingen (1098–179) interpreted the strength-in-weakness paradox in favor of woman almost three hundred years earlier. The notion that weakness has value is said to have originated with St. Paul (1 Cor. 1.27–29); see Barbara Newman, "Divine Power Made Perfect in Weakness: St. Hildegard on the Frail Sex," in *Peaceweavers*, vol. 2 of *Medieval Religious*

Women, ed. Lillian Thomas Shank and John A. Nichols (Kalamazoo, Mich.: Cistercian Publications, 1987), 103–22; "A Pauline paradox" at 103.

4. Margaret L. King is an exception. See her "The Religious Retreat of Isotta Nogarola (1418–1466): Sexism and Its Consequences in the Fifteenth Century," *Signs* 3 (1978): 807–22; "Book-Lined Cells: Women and Humanism in the Early Italian Renaissance," in *Beyond Their Sex: Learned Women of the European Past*, ed. Patricia H. Labalme (New York: New York University Press, 1980), 66–90; and "Thwarted Ambitions: Six Learned Women of the Early Italian Renaissance," *Soundings* 59 (1976): 280–304. Earlier articles include Percy Gothein, "L'amicitia fra Ludovico Foscarini et l'umanista Isotta Nogarola," *La Rinascita* 6 (1943): 391–413; and D. M. Robathan, "A Fifteenth-Century Bluestocking," *Mediaevalia et Humanistica*, fasc. 2 (1944): 106–11.

5. Augustine, *Literal Meaning of Genesis*, 42:168–69.

6. The dialogue is translated as "Of the Equal or Unequal Sin of Adam and Eve: Verona, 1451," in *Isotta Nogarola, Complete Writings: Letterbook, Dialogue on Adam and Eve, Orations*, ed. and trans. Margaret L. King and Diana Robin. The Other Voice in Early Modern Europe (Chicago and London: University of Chicago Press, 2004), 145–58. All references are to this translation; here, 146. An earlier translation appears in *Her Immaculate Hand: Selected Works by and about the Women Humanists of Quattrocento Italy*, ed. and trans. Margaret L. King and Albert Rabil, Jr. (Binghamton, N.Y.: Center for Medieval and Renaissance Studies, 1983), 57–69. See also Cecil H. Clough, "The Cult of Antiquity: Letters and Letter Collections," in *Cultural Aspects of the Italian Renaissance: Essays in Honor of Paul Oskar Kristeller*, ed. Cecil H. Clough (Manchester: Manchester University Press; New York: Alfred F. Zambelli, 1976), 33–67.

7. The absence here of any reference to Thomas Aquinas is striking, not only because he treated the same question, in his *Summa Theologiae*, in very similar terms, but also because of the characteristic pro and con format he employed, through which he took up opposing points in Augustine's thinking on responsibility for the Fall. King and Robin conclude that the "Great Gender Debate" was rather a form of the Renaissance dialogue (140–41). In 2a2ae.163.4, Thomas asks, which sin was the graver, Adam's or Eve's? (*utrum peccatum Adae fuerit gravius quam peccatum Evae*). He begins characteristically by listing three objections, whose content argues in favor of Eve: 1. Adam sinned knowingly, whereas Eve did so out of ignorance; Adam is thus the guiltier. 2. Adam ought to have done better but did not; he is therefore the guiltier. 3. Adam sinned counting on God's mercy; such a presumption makes him guiltier than Eve. "On the other hand," Thomas states, the punishment fits the crime, and according to Genesis, Eve's punishment was harsher. Thomas then quotes the Augustinian formulation that provided the subject of Isotta's debate with Ludovico, and he sets out to explain, refining Augustine's thinking through Aristotelian categories, how there was "parity of pride" but "disparity of sex." As to "the generic kind of wrong," each sinned equally, out of pride. But as to the kind of pride, the woman sinned more grievously, because she believed the serpent's affirmation that by eating the fruit, she would become like God. Pride caused her to defy God's will; man, who did not believe the serpent, instead exhibited pride by willing to reach a likeness of God through his own efforts. Eve's wrong was committed against God and against Adam. Again quoting Augustine, Thomas declares that Adam consented out of "a certain friendly goodwill." These show that Eve's error was worse than Adam's, (*Summa Theologiae*, vol. 44: *Well-Tempered Passion* [*2a2æ.* 155–70], ed. and trans. Thomas Gilby O.P. Blackfriars; New York: McGraw-Hill; London: Eyre and Spottiswoode, 1972, 158–63). That brief sum-

mary shows that Isotta's arguments parallel two of Thomas's objections, which he "defeats" by his replies, and that parts of Ludovico's rebuttal can be found in those replies. Gilby comments in a note that the "discussion, abstract to the point of attenuation, may be treated as a quaint period-piece" (159 n). In spite of Gilby's somewhat condescending tone, the fact that many of these points made their way into vernacular courtly literature, as I will discuss further on in this essay, may offer some support for his view.

8. For discussion of the circumstances of Isotta's scholarly formation and her mother's important role in it, see King and Robin, 2–9.

9. See the translators' notes, King and Rabil, ed., *Her Immaculate Hand*, 137–38.

10. King and Robin, 157.

11. Catherine Brown, *Contrary Things: Exegesis, Dialectic, and the Poetics of Didacticism* (Stanford, Calif.: Stanford University Press, 1998), 15. The Augustinian doctrine in question is charity.

12. Ibid., 17.

13. As quoted by Brown, 29.

14. E. Ann Matter, "The Undebated Debate: Gender and the Image of God in Medieval Theology," in *Gender in Debate from the Early Middle Ages to the Renaissance*, ed. Thelma S. Fenster and Clare A. Lees (New York: Palgrave, 2002), 41–55.

15. For the example of Alexander of Hales's *De corpore humano*, see Maaike van der Lugt, "Pourquoi Dieu a-t-il créé la femme? Différence sexuelle et théologie médiévale," in *Eve et Pandora: La Création de la première femme*, ed. Jean-Claude Schmitt (Paris: Gallimard, 2001), 91. Hales's work raised again a number of questions that had been asked before: Why did God create woman? Is it good for humankind to be composed of males and females? Was woman created in the image of God, as man was? Was woman already under masculine domination in paradise, or did that occur as a result of the fall? Did woman give birth in pain in paradise? Did Eve sin more than Adam?

16. There were two other, principal reasons, according to Jager. First, the *pecia* system of reproducing patristic writings that accompanied the rise of universities in the thirteenth century increased availability of such texts. Second, medieval bibles were generously glossed, especially, according to Jager, with Augustine's views on the serpent, on Eve, and on Adam. *The Tempter's Voice: Language and the Fall in Medieval Literature* (Ithaca and London: Cornell University Press, 1993), 15–16.

17. See, for example, the translations and editions of *La Contenance des Fames*, *Le Bien des Fames*, and *Le Blasme des Fames*, in *Three Medieval Views on Women*, ed. and trans. Gloria K. Fiero, Wendy Pfeffer, and Mathé Allain (New Haven, Conn.: Yale University Press, 1989).

18. Rosalie Colie, *Paradoxia Epidemica* (Princeton: Princeton University Press, 1966), 3.

19. Ibid., 10. For the paradox, see also A. M. Tomarken, *The Smile of Truth: The French Satirical Eulogy and Its Antecedents* (Princeton: Princeton University Press, 1990); M. T. Jones-Davies, ed., *Le paradoxe au temps de la Renaissance*, Centre de Recherches sur la Renaissance, 7 (Paris: J. Touzot, 1982); A. E. Malloch, "The Technique and Function of the Renaissance Paradox," *Studies in Philology* 3 (1956): 191–203. On Lando see N. N. Condeescu, "Le paradoxe bernesque dans la littérature française de la Renaissance," *Beiträge zur romanischen Philologie* 2 (1963): 27–51. I thank Pamela Benson who, some time ago, brought the Renaissance paradox to my attention as relevant to Isotta's debate with Ludovico.

20. The full text of the *Paradossi*, edited by Antonio Corsaro, may be accessed at <http://www.meri.unifi.it/n-rinasc/pub/homepage.htm>.

21. Rosalie Colie, *Paradoxia Epidemica*, 38. Lando's popular collection was quickly followed by additional editions before being translated into French in 1553 by Charles Estienne.

22. In *Poems of Cupid, God of Love: Christine de Pizan*'s Letter of the God of Love *and* Tale of the Rose; *Thomas Hoccleve*'s The Letter of Cupid; *with George Sewell*'s The Proclamation of Cupid, ed. Thelma Fenster and Mary Carpenter Erler (Leiden: Brill, 1990). Christine wrote at least four further works about woman—the *Tale of the Rose* (another courtly poem, 1402); the letters in the Debate of the *Rose* (1401–4), the *Book of the Three Virtues* (1403), and the *Book of the City of Ladies* (1405)—in which she repeated her thoughts on the value of woman from multiple perspectives.

23. I first presented this observation in "*Simplece et sagesse:* Christine de Pizan et Isotta Nogarola sur la culpabilité d'Eve," in *Une femme de lettres au Moyen Age: Etudes autour de Christine de Pizan*, ed. Liliane Dulac and Bernard Ribémont (Orleans: Paradigme, 1995), 483–84.

24. I have argued this point in "Possible Odds: Christine de Pizan and the Paradoxes of Woman," in *Contexts and Continuities: Proceedings of the IVth International Colloquium on Christine de Pizan (Glagow 21–27 July 2000), Published in Honour of Liliane Dulac*, ed. Angus J. Kennedy, 3 vols. (Glasgow: University of Glasgow Press, 2002), 2:355–66.

25. "femme tendre, fraile et pou souffrant" (Christine de Pizan, *Le livre de l'advision Cristine*, ed. Christine M. Reno and Liliane Dulac [Paris: Honoré Champion, 2001], 118).

26. "Helas! homme, et se tu regardes ton cours, tu ne trouveras pas plus foible chose, car le mors d'un chien ou une mousche, se elle entre dedens toy, t'occist aucune fois" (ibid., 134).

27. For discussion of Isotta's orations, see King and Robin, 14.

28. King and Rabil, ed., *Her Immaculate Hand*, 17.

29. King and Robin, 53.

30. King and Robin, 38. Diogenes Laertius says that two women, Lasthenia of Mantinea and Axiothea of Phlius, were among Plato's students, and Axiothea garbed herself in men's clothing. Later the two women are said to have attended the lectures of Speusippus of Athens, who succeeded Plato. (Diogenes Laertius, *Lives of Eminent Philosophers*, trans. R. D. Hicks, Loeb Classical Library [Cambridge, Mass.: Harvard University Press; London: Heinemann, 1972] Chaps. 3:46, 4.2.)

31. "de si grant perfeccion comme homme masle se dit estre" (Christine de Pizan, *La Città delle Dame*, trans. [into modern Italian] Patrizia Caraffi, ed. E. Jeffrey Richards [Milan: Luni, 1998], 44–45). In English, *The Book of the City of Ladies*, trans. E. Jeffrey Richards (New York: Persea, 1982), 4–5.

32.

Vous diray qui je suis, qui parle,
Qui de femelle devins masle
Par Fortune, qu'ainsy le voult;
Si me mua et corps et voult
En homme naturel parfaict;
Et jadis fus femme, de fait
Homme suis, je ne ment pas.

(Christine de Pizan, ll. 141–47; *Le Livre de la Mutacion de Fortune*, ed. Suzanne Solente, SATF [Paris: Picard, 1959–66], 1:12.)

33. "fust mesmes converti ton corps foible et femmenin en homme pour estre transmuee de condicion" (Christine de Pizan, *Le livre de l'advision Cristine*, 129.)

34. A number of Italian women were trained in Latin letters in the period before and after Isotta wrote: Maddalena Scrovegni (1356–1429); Battista da Montefeltro Malatesta (1383–1450); Costanza Barbaro (b. after 1419); Cecilia Gonzaga (1425–51); Costanza Varano (1428–47); and Caterina Caldiera (d. 1463). See King and Rabil, *Her Immaculate Hand*, and *Women Writing Latin from Roman Antiquity to Early Modern Europe*, eds. Laurie J. Churchill, Phyllis R. Brown, and Jane E. Jeffrey. 3 vols. (New York and London: Routledge, 2002); vol. 3 contains Holt N. Parker, "Angela Nogarola (ca. 1400) and Isotta Nogarola (1418–66): Thieves of Language," 11–30, and Parker's "Costanza Varano (1426–47): Latin as an Instrument of State," 31–54; Diana Robin's "Cassandra Fedele (1465–1558)," 55–82, and Robin's "Laura Cereta (1469–99)," 83–108.

35. See Serge Lusignan, *Parler vulgairement* (Paris: Vrin; Montreal: Presses de l'Université de Montréal, 1987).

36. Olympe de Gouges, *Réponse à la justification de Maximilien Robespierre, addressée à Jérome Pétion* (Paris, 1792), 10; quoted in Joan Wallach Scott, *Only Paradoxes to Offer: French Feminists and the Rights of Man* (Cambridge: Harvard University Press, 1996), 23, 182.

37. van der Lugt, "Pourquoi Dieu a-t-il créé la femme?" 90.

38. Augustine's solution had important ramifications for salvation theology. See the discussion by E. Ann Matter, "The Undebated Debate," 43–44.

39. "La dualité est nette entre son *homo interior*, qui participe à la supériorité de l'âme de l'homme, et son *homo exterior*, qui lui reste inférieure en tant qu'auxiliaire. . . . Malgré l'identité et l'asexualité de l'âme rationnelle chez l'homme et chez la femme, il existe une sorte de conformité entre le corps masculin et l'âme asexuée. Ainsi le *vir* n'éprouve pas, comme la *femina*, de dualité entre les deux éléments de son être." [The duality is clear between her *homo interior*, which shares in the superiority of man's soul, and her *homo exterior*, which remains inferior inasmuch as it is auxiliary. . . . In spite of the identicalness and asexuality of the rational soul in man and woman, there is a kind of conformity between the masculine body and the asexual soul. Thus the *vir* does not experience, as does the *femina*, a duality between the two elements of its being.] Kari Elisabeth Børresen, *Subordination et équivalence: Nature et rôle de la femme d'après Augustin et Thomas d'Aquin* (Oslo: Universitetsforlaget; Paris: Mame, 1968), 38.

40. Matter, "The Undebated Debate," 45.

41. Augustine, Sermon 281, *PL* 38.1284; as cited in Blamires, *The Case for Women*, 133, and n. 26.

42. As Ludovico said to Isotta in a letter that was not part of the debate; see King and Rabil, 118.

43. Scott, *Only Paradoxes to Offer*, 1.

44. Ibid., 4.

45. Toril Moi, *What Is a Woman? And Other Essays* (New York: Oxford University Press, 2000), 65.

46. Ibid., 8.

47. Ibid., 206.

48. See, most recently, Rosalind Brown-Grant, in her reading of Christine's *Epistre*

Othea, who has stated that Christine "allegorized . . . certain female characters as the human soul itself, which . . . has no sex." *Christine de Pizan and the Moral Defence of Women: Reading beyond Gender* (Cambridge: Cambridge University Press, 1999), 85. See further Brown-Grant, "Christine de Pizan: A Feminist *avant la lettre?*" in *Christine de Pizan 2000: Studies on Christine de Pizan in Honor of Angus J. Kennedy*, ed. John Campbell and Nadia Margolis (Amsterdam: Rodopi, 2000), 65–76.

49. Fenster, "Possible Odds: Christine de Pizan and the Paradoxes of Woman."

50. I have borrowed this term from Clare Lees and Gillian Overing, who use it in "The Clerics and the Critics: Misogyny and the Social Symbolic in Anglo-Saxon England," in *Gender in Debate from the Early Middle Ages to the Renaissance*, ed. Thelma S. Fenster and Clare A. Lees (New York: Palgrave, 2002), 35.

51. Moi, *What Is a Woman?* 197.

52. Ibid., 196.

53. Ibid., 199.

54. Ibid., 206.

BIBLIOGRAPHY

Angliviel de la Baumelle, Laurent. "Eve à l'épreuve des Pères." In *Eve et Pandora: La Création de la première femme*, ed. Jean-Claude Schmitt, 69–87. Paris: Gallimard, 2001.

Aquinas, Thomas. *Well-Tempered Passion*. Vol. 44 of *Summa Theologiae*, ed. and trans. Thomas Gilby, O.P. Blackfriars. New York: McGraw-Hill; London: Eyre and Spottiswoode, 1972.

Augustine. *The Literal Meaning of Genesis*. Trans. John Hammond Taylor. Ancient Christian Writers, vols. 41, 42. New York: Newman Press, 1982.

Blamires, Alcuin. *The Case for Women in Medieval Culture*. Oxford: Clarendon, 1997.

Børresen, Kari Elisabeth. *Subordination et équivalence: Nature et rôle de la femme d'après Augustin et Thomas d'Aquin*. Oslo: Universitetsforlaget; Paris: Mame, 1968.

Brown, Catherine. *Contrary Things: Exegesis, Dialectic, and the Poetics of Didacticism*. Stanford, Calif.: Stanford University Press, 1998.

Brown-Grant, Rosalind. *Christine de Pizan and the Moral Defence of Women: Reading beyond Gender*. Cambridge: Cambridge University Press, 1999.

———. "Christine de Pizan: A Feminist *avant la lettre?*" In *Christine de Pizan 2000: Studies on Christine de Pizan in Honor of Angus J. Kennedy*, ed. John Campbell and Nadia Margolis, 65–76. Amsterdam: Rodopi, 2000.

Christine de Pizan. *Le Livre de la Mutacion de Fortune*. Ed. Suzanne Solente. 4 vols. SATF. Paris: Picard, 1959–66.

———. *The Book of the City of Ladies*. Trans. E. Jeffrey Richards. New York: Persea, 1982.

———. *La Città delle Dame*. Trans. Patrizia Caraffi. Ed. E. Jeffrey Richards. Milan: Luni, 1998.

———. *Le livre de l'advision Cristine*. Ed. Christine M. Reno and Liliane Dulac. Paris: Honoré Champion, 2001.

Churchill, Laurie J., Phyllis R. Brown, and Jane E. Jeffrey, eds. *Women Writing Latin from Roman Antiquity to Early Modern Europe*. 3 vols. New York and London: Routledge, 2002.

Clough, Cecil H. "The Cult of Antiquity: Letters and Letter Collections." In *Cultural*

Aspects of the Italian Renaissance: Essays in Honor of Paul Oskar Kristeller, ed. Cecil H. Clough, 33–67. Manchester: Manchester University Press; New York: Alfred F. Zambelli, 1976.

Colie, Rosalie. *Paradoxia Epidemica*. Princeton: Princeton University Press, 1966.

Condeescu, N. N. "Le paradoxe bernesque dans la littérature française de la Renaissance." *Beiträge zur romanischen Philologie* 2 (1963): 27–51.

De Gouges, Olympe. *Réponse à la justification de Maximilien Robespierre, addressée à Jérome Pétion*. Paris, 1792.

Diogenes Laertius, *Lives of Eminent Philosophers*. Trans. R. D. Hicks. Loeb Classical Library. Cambridge, Mass.: Harvard University Press; London: Heinemann, 1972.

Fenster, Thelma S. "*Simplece et sagesse:* Christine de Pizan et Isotta Nogarola sur la culpabilité d'Eve." In *Une femme de lettres au Moyen Age: Etudes autour de Christine de Pizan*, ed. Liliane Dulac and Bernard Ribémont. Orleans: Paradigme, 1995.

———. "Possible Odds: Christine de Pizan and the Paradoxes of Woman." In *Contexts and Continuities: Proceedings of the IVth International Colloquium on Christine de Pizan (Glasgow 21–27 July 2000), Published in Honour of Liliane Dulac*, ed. Angus J. Kennedy, 2:355–66. Glasgow: University of Glasgow Press, 2002.

Fenster, Thelma S., and Mary Carpenter Erler, eds. *Poems of Cupid, God of Love: Christine de Pizan's* Letter of the God of Love *and* Tale of the Rose; *Thomas Hoccleve's* The Letter of Cupid; *with George Sewell's* The Proclamation of Cupid. Leiden: Brill, 1990.

Fenster, Thelma S., and Clare A. Lees, eds. and trans. *Gender in Debate from the Early Middle Ages to the Renaissance*. New York: Palgrave, 2002.

Fiero, Gloria K., Wendy Pfeffer, and Mathé Allain, eds. and trans. *Three Medieval Views on Women*. New Haven, Conn.: Yale University Press, 1989.

Gothein, Percy. "L'amicitia fra Ludovico Foscarini et l'umanista Isotta Nogarola." *La Rinascita* 6 (1943): 391–413.

Jager, Eric. *The Tempter's Voice: Language and the Fall in Medieval Literature*. Ithaca, N.Y., and London: Cornell University Press, 1993.

Jones-Davies, M. T., ed. *Le paradoxe au temps de la Renaissance*. Centre de Recherches sur la Renaissance, 7. Paris: J. Touzot, 1982.

King, Margaret L. "Thwarted Ambitions: Six Learned Women of the Early Italian Renaissance." *Soundings* 59 (1976): 280–304.

———. "The Religious Retreat of Isotta Nogarola (1418–1466): Sexism and Its Consequences in the Fifteenth Century." *Signs* 3 (1978): 807–22.

———. "Book-Lined Cells: Women and Humanism in the Early Italian Renaissance." In *Beyond Their Sex: Learned Women of the European Past*, ed. Patricia H. Labalme, 66–90. New York: New York University Press, 1980.

King, Margaret L., and Albert Rabil Jr., eds. and trans. *Her Immaculate Hand: Selected Works by and about the Women Humanists of Quattrocento Italy*. Medieval and Renaissance Texts and Studies, vol. 20. Binghamton, N.Y.: Center for Medieval and Renaissance Texts and Studies, 1983.

King, Margaret L., and Diana Robin, eds. and trans. *Isotta Nogarola, Complete Writings: Letterbook, Dialogue on Adam and Eve, Orations*. The Other Voice in Early Modern Europe. Chicago and London: University of Chicago Press, 2004.

Lando, Ortensio. *Paradossi*. Ed. Antonio Corsaro. Available at <http://www.meri.unifi.it/n-rinasc/pub/homepage.htm>.

Lees, Clare, and Gillian Overing. "The Clerics and the Critics: Misogyny and the

Social Symbolic in Anglo-Saxon England." In *Gender in Debate from the Early Middle Ages to the Renaissance*, ed. Thelma S. Fenster and Clare A. Lees, 19–39. New York: Palgrave, 2002.

Lusignan, Serge. *Parler vulgairement*. Paris: Vrin; Montreal: Presses de l'Université de Montréal, 1987.

Malloch, A. E. "The Technique and Function of the Renaissance Paradox." *Studies in Philology* 3 (1956): 191–203.

Matter, E. Ann. "The Undebated Debate: Gender and the Image of God in Medieval Theology." In *Gender in Debate from the Early Middle Ages to the Renaissance*, ed. Thelma S. Fenster and Clare Lees, 41–55. New York: Palgrave, 2002.

Moi, Toril. *What Is a Woman? And Other Essays*. New York: Oxford University Press, 2000.

Newman, Barbara. "Divine Power Made Perfect in Weakness: St. Hildegard on the Frail Sex." In *Peaceweavers*, 103–22. Vol. 2 of *Medieval Religious Women*, ed. Lillian Thomas Shank and John A. Nichols. Kalamazoo, Mich.: Cistercian, 1987.

Nogarola, Isotta. "De pari aut impari Evae atque Adae peccato." In *Isotae Nogarolae Veronensis opera quae supersunt omnia; accedunt Angelae et Zeneverae Nogarolae epistolae et carmina*, ed. E. Abel, 2:187–216. Budapest: Magyar Tudomanyos Akademia, 1885; republished in *History of Women*. New Haven, Conn.: Research Publications, 1976. Microfilm reel 472, no. 3527.

———. "Of the Equal or Unequal Sin of Adam and Eve." In *Her Immaculate Hand: Selected Works by and about the Women Humanists of Quattrocento Italy*, trans. and ed. Margaret L. King and Albert Rabil Jr., 57–69. Medieval and Renaissance Texts and Studies, vol. 20. Binghamton, N.Y.: Center for Medieval and Renaissance Texts and Studies, 1983.

Robathan, D. M. "A Fifteenth-Century Bluestocking." *Mediaevalia et Humanistica* 2 (1944): 106–11.

Scott, Joan Wallach. *Only Paradoxes to Offer: French Feminists and the Rights of Man*. Cambridge, Mass.: Harvard University Press, 1996.

Tomarken, A. M. *The Smile of Truth: The French Satirical Eulogy and Its Antecedents*. Princeton: Princeton University Press, 1990.

van der Lugt, Maaike. "Pourquoi Dieu a-t-il créé la femme?" In *Eve et Pandora: La création de la première femme*, ed. Jean-Claude Schmitt, 89–113. Paris: Gallimard, 2001.

The Canon of Religious Life

MARIA DOMITILLA GALLUZZI AND THE *RULE* OF ST. CLARE OF ASSISI

E. Ann Matter

The idea of canon, an officially recognized closed list, is obviously very influential in traditional Christianity. The canon of Scripture, a collection that included the Greek version of the Jewish scriptures and the important Christian writings that claimed authoritative authorship, was one of the earliest points of debate at the church councils of the fourth and fifth centuries.[1] The resulting "closed canon" of Scripture, from which all the other literary canons of Western culture take their inspiration, was not debated from the close of the fifth century until the Protestant Reformation of the sixteenth century.[2] The biblical canon was presented as a starting place, and medieval manuscripts of the Gospels often included copies of the "canon list" compiled by Eusebius in the fourth century, by which a reader could find the same stories in different Gospels.[3]

From this primarily textual meaning, there developed a broader idea of canon as an official list, used in various ways. For example, the proclamations of the ecumenical councils of the classical period of Christian doctrinal formation were known and promulgated as the "canons" of Nicaea, Ephesus, and Chalcedon.[4] In this way, canon came to be understood as a sort of rule and even took on a legal context. By the twelfth century, there had developed a code of Church law, replete with a tradition of elaborate commentary, known as "Canon Law."[5] The shape of this development suggests that, in the language of medieval Christianity, canonicity was as much a concept of rules about patterns of life as it was agreed-upon habits or codes of reading. In this essay, I will explore one aspect of the semantic field suggested by canonicity in medieval and early modern Christianity to offer some context for the literary debates about canon addressed by many of the other contributions to this volume.

I will focus on the way the term *canon* was extended to religious life, especially religious life as it was understood for women's communities. I will investigate some aspects of "canonical life" for women with particular reference to the early modern communities of women in the Capuchin order. Before turning to this specific example, though, I would like to consider the relative roles of canonical rules of life for men and women in some earlier monastic traditions.

From the period of the councils, certain forms of monastic discipline were thought of as "canonical," such as that outlined by the *Rule* of Augustine, the rule still followed by Augustinian canons and canonesses, the term that designates those who live by this canonical rule.[6] The *Rule* of Augustine can be traced to the writings of the great Bishop of Hippo; it is widely accepted that in a letter to his sister, the head of a community of religious women in fifth-century North Africa, Augustine created a version of this life appropriate for women. What is disputed, and hotly, is the possibility that the *Rule* for Augustinian canonesses was the original version of Augustine's vision of canonical life, a possibility based on manuscript studies and suggested as early as the sixteenth century by no less a figure than Erasmus of Rotterdam.[7] The important difference here is whether the Augustinian *Rule* for women is understood as an adaptation of a rule written for men (which is the normal and expected state of affairs) or vice versa.

If the Augustinian *Rule* was indeed first written for women and then adapted for men, it is an exception to (so to speak) a general rule about such developments. The growth of the monastic movement of the Western Middle Ages is marked by the formulation of various rules of religious life in community, each reflecting the specific spiritual ideals of the founder.[8] When viewed from the perspective of gender, these rules very often follow a familiar pattern: a male founder of an order creates a vision of communal life for men; this vision is later adapted for the use of women. The paradigm is set by the most influential monastic rule of the West, the *Rule* of St. Benedict.[9] As related by Pope Gregory I, Benedict and his sister, St. Scholastica, together worked out an adaptation of his *Rule* for the women under her spiritual care.[10] Just what was involved in this feminization can be seen from the extant manuscripts of communities of Benedictine women, such as the twelfth-century "House Book" of Notre Dame de Saintes now in Yale's Beinecke Library.[11] Here, items of dress have been changed to suit women, but the liturgical life of prayer remains substantially the same.

Adaptations of monastic rules for nuns are usually revealing of the way the adapter thought about women. For example, the rules for women's monasteries written by Caesarius of Arles in sixth-century Gaul are obsessively concerned with the enclosure and sexual purity of the nuns, leading to a sort of demonization of women and female nature; this misogyny is refreshingly missing from the Benedictine tradition.[12] But, even though Caesarius is an extreme example of the need to contain women, rules for nuns, even in more positive environments, habitually had to adapt the ideal of a canonical life in community to a context in which autonomy and physical freedom were extremely limited, to the situation, that is, of premodern women.

Not all religious women were always locked up, of course. Over the course of the Middle Ages there developed a tradition of religious women in the world, such as the Beguines of Northern Europe or the Pizzochere of the Italian cities.[13] These women were enormously influential in some times and places, yet their alternative form of religious life must have been seen as dangerous, since it was prohibited by the last sessions of the Council of Trent in 1563, which imposed strict monastic enclosure for religious women.[14] For several centuries, including the century most specifically addressed in this essay, the seventeenth, and especially in Italy, where the dictates of Trent were carried out most enthusiastically, the imposition of *clausura* was strictly enforced for congregations of nuns.

Against this historical background of the development of female monasticism, the women of the Franciscan orders, of which the Capuchins were a variety based on strict observance, articulated their unique form of life. Franciscan spirituality was always based on the charismatic ideals of poverty, preaching, and repentance espoused by Francis of Assisi; in some ways, especially in the abhorrence of possessions and glorification of poverty, it was an antimonastic type of life. Yet Francis was deeply committed to obtaining papal sanction for his *Rule*, and he traveled to Rome for this purpose twice, obtaining approval from Pope Innocent III in 1221 and Pope Honorius III in 1223.[15] This shows the official nature of canonical rules for religious life. Franciscan legends tell us that his fellow friars were uneasy about Francis's zeal for poverty; one account even says that a delegation of friars complained that Francis's new *Rule* would be too severe and that they did not wish to be bound to it. They said: "Let him make it for himself and not for us."[16] Then Francis heard the voice of Christ saying: "Francis, there is nothing of yours in the *Rule*, but all which is there is mine. I want the *Rule* to be observed as it is to the letter, to the letter, to the letter, and without gloss, and without gloss, and without gloss" [sic obseruetur ad litteram, ad litteram, ad litteram, et sine glossa, et sine glossa, et sine glossa].[17]

A worthy ideal, no doubt. But how could such a life possibly be observed "ad litteram et sine glossa" by women? Could women have no stable house, no possessions? Could women beg directly for their food and wander the world preaching the virtues of poverty and repentance? Certainly not in thirteenth-century Italy! Nevertheless, the zeal for evangelical poverty so inflamed the heart of Francis's follower Clare of Assisi that she became the leader of a group of Poor Ladies (later known as Poor Clares or Clarisse, the Second Order of St. Francis) committed to finding some accommodation of this ideal to women's existence. Thomas of Celano, Francis's first biographer, said about the Poor Ladies: "they have all become so conspicuous by the title of the highest poverty that their food and clothing hardly at all or never come together to satisfy extreme necessity."[18]

The *Rule* of St. Clare of Assisi is, then, the adaptation of a canonical ideal of strictest poverty, an ideal that Franciscan legendaries celebrate as obtained by St. Francis right from the mouth of God, to the circumstances of women's lives in thirteenth-century Italy. Yet, in spite of the legends surrounding it, we have no textual evidence that Clare actually wrote this form of life. The earliest extant copy of the *Rule* is actually also the vehicle of its formal approval: the bull *Solet annuere* proclaimed by Pope Innocent IV on August 9, 1253, just in time for Clare to see the official document on her deathbed two days later.[19] This papal bull is the *prima exemplar* of Clare's *Rule*. There is no extant copy of the document she sent to Rome for approval, nor any surviving draft from Clare's own hand or community; nevertheless, there is no doubt that this adaptation was the lifelong goal of the female founder of the congregation of Poor Ladies, Clare herself.[20] Nevertheless, the *Rule* of St. Clare is, in a certain way, the first example in all of Christian history of a canonical life for women written by a woman.

The bull of Innocent IV is not divided into chapters, but very early on in the manuscript history the *Rule* of Clare took the form of twelve chapters, in congruence with the Second *Rule* of St. Francis and because of the strong biblical allusions of the number twelve.[21] Chapter headings soon became a part of the received text; they describe the twelve chapters and are comparable to the twelve chapters of Francis's *Rule* as shown in the first two columns of chart 1.

The influence of Francis's vision on the *Rule* for Franciscan sisters is obvious: both rules start with a comment on "the life" (chapter 1), immediately turn to the question of just who should be following this life (chapter 2), and then turn to the Divine Office and fasting (chapter 3). But chapter 3 also points to the enormous differences between the Franciscan life in its male and female versions: the friars "should go about the world," while the sisters should concentrate on confession and communion. This underlines the major difference of life between the male Franciscans, an itinerant congregation, and the female Franciscans, a cloistered community. Two other chapters of the *Rule* of Francis—chapter 9, "the preachers," and chapter 12, about those who "wish to go among the Saracens and other nonbelievers"—point to the same contrast and have no parallels in the *Rule* of Clare. In fact, it is not in any way surprising to realize that thirteenth-century women could not preach or convert Saracens, even if they were Franciscans. Whereas Franciscan friars became famous for preaching and traveling the world (and, indeed, are still the keepers of most Christian shrines in the Holy Land under Roman Catholic control), the Franciscan women had to find some other model for a life of evangelical poverty.

Because of this, the *Rule* of Clare is largely concerned with the internal functioning of the monastery. Chapter 4 is dedicated to the elected leaders of the community, an abbess, a chapter of officials (with whom the abbess is to consult every week), and the "discreets," the most trusted members of the community, to whom she should turn for advice. The interiorized, isolated nature of the Franciscan life for women is emphasized by chapter 5, which prescribes long hours of silence and the limited contact nuns could have with the outside world through a grille in formal visiting parlors. There is, obviously, nothing quite like this in the *Rule* of Francis. In the men's *Rule*, chapter 8 (on the election of officials) is dedicated to the order as a whole and the need to elect a minister general in the place of Francis himself. Franciscan women's houses were, in contrast, self-contained entities.

Having made these differences clear, the *Rule* of Clare returns to the model of the *Rule* of Francis. Both friars and sisters are forbidden to own anything personally (F4, C6), both types of Franciscans must work (F5, C7), both communities must pay attention to seeking alms and caring for their own sick (F6, C8), both communities must impose penance on members who sin (F7, C9), and both communities must see to the admonition and correction of their members (F10, C10). The eleventh chapter of both *Rules* stresses that the sisters of St. Clare live in strict enclosure (*clausura*), into which the friars are forbidden to venture.

From the very beginning, then, the Franciscan ideal of strictest poverty meant very different things for men and women. The friars literally flung themselves into the teeming world of late medieval Europe, whereas the sisters had to find a way to be just as dedicated to extreme poverty within the closed walls of the cloister. This has remained the main historical difference between the First and Second Orders of St. Francis. Most Franciscan sisters in the twenty-first century are actually part of congregations founded within the broad outlines of the Third Order, the "Tertiaries," who by definition live in the world and teach, nurse, or administer in many institutions, although there are still enclosed houses of Franciscan nuns, such as the famous Monastery of Santa Chiara in Assisi, where the original document of Clare's *Rule* is kept to this day.

Throughout the centuries, the Second Order of Franciscans, the Sisters of St. Clare, have struggled to maintain the goals of the foundress, even as the friars have had a series of reforms bent on modeling their lives more faithfully on Francis. The Spiritual Franciscans and the fanatical "Fraticelli" are both examples of friars striving to be more like Francis, but neither of these had a parallel movement among women's communities.[22] The one Franciscan reform movement that also had implications for the women of the Second Order was the Franciscan reform of the early modern period, that of the Capuchins.

The Capuchin reform is a result of the struggles between the Franciscan Conventuals and Observants (or *Zoccolanti*) in the Marches. The founder, Matteo di Bassi, an Observant Franciscan from Fermo, wanted to secure papal approval for a strict interpretation of the *Rule* of Francis. In 1525, Clement VII authorized the new community, marked by the wearing of a hooded garment, from which the order took its name.[23] The Capuchin legends portray di Bassi in the role of Francis: giving his cloak to a beggar, and, while in prayer, hearing a command to observe the *Rule* "to the letter."[24]

Within a decade, the Capuchins had become the most zealous of the Franciscan communities. They were famous as preachers and "home missionaries," such as the uncompromising fra Cristoforo of Manzoni's *I promessi sposi*,[25] and had by the early seventeenth century founded missions in Asia, Africa, and the Americas.[26] The Capuchins, like the Jesuits, have been since the early modern period the shock troops of Catholic orthodoxy. Their profile is considerably less intellectual and more devotional than the Jesuits, though: they are still the custodians of the shrine of the Holy House of Loreto; and the most famous stigmatist of the twentieth century, the recently canonized Padre Pio, was a Capuchin.[27]

The female version of the Capuchins was founded in Naples in 1538 by the Venerable Maria Laurentia Longo. Longo, a Franciscan Tertiary, founded a hospital and a home for fallen women. She wanted to take a pilgrimage to the Holy Land but was told in prayer that she should instead found a monastery for women and call it Santa Maria in Gerusalemme.[28] This community was first directed by priests of the Theatine order, who soon turned the enterprise over to the Capuchin friars. Clare's *Rule* was used by the women Capuchins, and each house developed constitutions, that is, additional directions for the common life drawn up by each community and based on those of the Capuchin friars' houses. Within a generation, there were communities of Cappuccine all over Italy. Most were founded by wealthy women patrons, and most were supervised by diocesan clergy, especially the canons of the local cathedral.

In 1587, two noblewomen of the Lombard city of Pavia—Giovanna Mezzabarba (wife of Count Galeazzo Beccaria) and Giovanna Veggi (wife of Francesco Beccaria)—expressed their intention to found a house of Cappucine in Pavia. They bought a monastic building that had housed the venerable Benedictine/Cistercian community of Santa Maria delle Pertice and had been empty for seven years. With the help of the canons of the Cathedral of Pavia, they found twelve women, six Pavese and six *forastiere*, or "outsiders," to become the first Cappucine of Pavia. These twelve solemnly received the habit of religious life from Fabio Bottigella, a canon of the cathedral, on February 24, 1589.[29] It was in this house, a textbook example of early modern Catholic piety, that Maria Domitilla Galluzzi wrote a commentary on the *Rule* of St. Clare; she may also have been the author of the specific constitutions of her monastic house.

Maria Domitilla was born Severetta Galluzzi on May 26, 1595. In her autobiography, she calls attention to the fact that (among other signs and wonders attending her birth) this was the very day of the Heavenly Birthday (i.e., the death) of St. Philip Neri, a leader in the Catholic reforms of the sixteenth century.[30] Her parents, who were involved in lay confraternities in their Piedmontese city of Acqui, and her aunt Domitilla, a young widow described as a model of piety, brought her up to want to be a nun.[31] In 1615, at the age of twenty, she entered the monastery of Cappucine at Pavia, where she took the name Domitilla out of respect for her aunt.[32]

I have described elsewhere how Maria Domitilla gradually gained her own voice as a spiritual writer, producing over the next three decades an autobiography, two books of spiritual devotions, many letters, and, most interesting for our purposes here, a commentary on the *Rule* of St. Clare, her first written work.[33] In brief, soon after her entrance into religious life, Maria Domitilla began to have visions of St. Peter and the Trinity and to fight with the Devil.[34] During Lent of 1618, she began to have revelations of the proper way the Capuchin life should be lived. A few years later, probably in 1621–22, she wrote *Vero lume del modo d'osservare l'antica regola di Santa Chiara* [True light on the way to observe the ancient *Rule* of St. Clare], a chapter-by-chapter commentary on an Italian version of Clare's *Rule*.[35] This is an important book, a first in the Christian tradition: the first commentary by a woman on a rule of religious life for women written by a woman.[36]

This was also an important book in the life and literary career of Maria Domitilla Galluzzi, the work that transformed a young nun barely out of the novitiate into one of the most famous figures of seventeenth-century Catholic piety, widely consulted by lay and religious leaders from Lithuania to Madrid to Vienna.[37] This work was never published in a printed edition, but it circulated in a number of manuscripts and seems to have been read by lay people (who owned some of the copies) as well as monastic communities.[38]

The *Lume* is presented as a series of revelations: nearly every paragraph begins "Vidi" [I saw], "Conobbi" [I knew], "Intesi" [I understood]. Not surprisingly, she quotes (in Latin) the famous phrase of Franciscan legends, that the *Rule* should be followed "ad litteram, sine glossa."[39] Maria Domitilla's claim, of course, is that her commentary on Clare's *Rule* shows the way to observe this form of life "to the letter, and without gloss." But the guide does not come from a young religious of twenty-six, someone who, by her own admission, had difficulty fitting in to the community of Cappucine at Pavia,[40] but right from the mouth of God.

Nevertheless, as I have pointed out elsewhere, there is a fair amount of Maria Domitilla in the *Lume*, especially in the details of the particular customs of her community (clothing, food, devotion).[41] That is to say, her own experiences as a member of the community of Capuchins in Pavia strongly influenced her interpretation of the life of the community. Perhaps even her own experience as a problematically scrupulous novice, always seeking more mortification and not afraid to correct the Mistress of Novices from time to time, is also evident in the propensity to go *beyond* the letter, for example, in strict fasting of a daily Lent, but always with an eye to the Devil, who sometimes introduces pride into observance (chapter 3), and in the long descriptions of the (literal) nuts and bolts of the enclosure (chapter 11). On the guidelines for the acceptance of novices (chapter 2), Maria Domitilla perhaps shows a certain lack of self-awareness by interpreting Clare's stipulation that "a majority" [la maggior parte] of the sisters accepts the candidate with the following comment.

> I knew that a majority can follow from only one vote more, but in those early days the majority was two parts out of three, and that it was so ordained so that the sisters, in accepting the new sister, can see more clearly the effects of the Divine Will, the communal good, and the peace of the monastery. The majority is mistaken with difficulty, since it moves correctly through God, who takes care that no one be received who could abandon the perfect observance of the Holy Rule.[42]

This is a dramatic statement from someone who was, as she herself tells us, not exactly the most popular person in her community, since it insists on more rather than less consensus from the community. It does, however, give us a glimpse of the remarkable self-confidence and certainty about her mission that runs through all of Maria Domitilla Galluzzi's works.

As important as the *Lume* was, it was not the last treatise by Maria Domitilla about the life of her community. In 1648, when she was fifty-three years old and had written several other large works, she was at least the scribe (and I would argue, in some way, the author) of the new *Constitutiones* of the Capuchins of Pavia. The document written for the Capuchin women of Pavia in 1648 superseded the *Constitutiones* of 1610, and the two documents were bound into the same codex. Each version had been signed by all of the sisters living in the house at the time it was written (1610 and 1648); therefore, the *Constitutiones* of 1648 includes Maria Domitilla's signature.[43] The tradition of specific constitutions for each house had been introduced into the life of female Capuchins from their male model. The function of these documents was to give more specific information about the functioning of the community. In this sense, it was meant as a supplement to the *Rule*.

For example, the *Rule* of Clare says (chapter 4), "in the election of the Abbess the sisters are bound to observe the canonical form [formam canonicam]," but only in the *Constitutiones* of 1648 is it specified that the abbess is to be elected by secret ballot beginning with the sister who is eldest in religion (i.e., has been there the longest) and can be won by even one vote. In the case of a tie, the abbess shall be selected by lot.[44] Similarly, the *Rule* says (chapter 8) that the sisters should own nothing, but "let them send confidently for alms" [mittant pro eleemosyna confidenter], yet nowhere does it explain how this could be done by enclosed nuns.[45] The *Constitutiones* of 1648, though, end with a description of the life of the "Fratelli Cercanti," a sort of mini-rule for the men who made their living seeking alms for the Capuchin sisters. Without these "Seeking Brothers," the sisters faced a more severe life than even they had bargained for, as is evident from a letter Maria Domitilla wrote in 1644 to Father Anselmo Casabianca of the famous (and famously wealthy) monastery of la Certosa di Pavia asking for a few eggs and some butter.[46]

As the third column of chart 1 shows, part 1 of the *Constitutiones* of 1648 shares some characteristics of the written text of Clare's *Rule*, at least insofar as it is in twelve chapters and deals with some of the same issues, such as poverty, obedience, the entry into the Capuchin life, and the Divine Office. Yet there are some striking differences, such as the inclusion of a chapter on mental prayer (chapter 3). This is a sure sign of Maria Domitilla's hand, since mental prayer, a concept she took largely from Teresa of Avila, and Carmelite and Jesuit spirituality in general, does not appear at all in Clare's writings. Clare probably knew nothing about this intense form of individual meditation because, at least in the form Maria Domitilla propounded it, it had not yet been invented.[47] But by the mid-seventeenth century, especially for a religious virtuoso like Maria Domitilla Galluzzi, *oratione mentale* was one of the first things a Capuchin neophyte needed to learn, right after the Divine Office (chapter 2). Part 2 of the 1648 *Constitutiones* continues this move toward specificity, spelling out the exact duties of every office in the monastery (chart 2).

The two identifiable works of Maria Domitilla Galluzzi on the canonical Franciscan life—the *Vero lume del modo d'osservare l'antica regola di Santa Chiara*, revealed and written between 1618 and 1622, and the *Constitutiones* of her community written down and signed by all the sisters in 1648—show a certain progress in Maria Domitilla's spiritual and literary voice. The *Lume* in particular looks a lot like traditional Christian biblical commentary in that it is a point-by-point analysis of a venerated text that claims to be giving the true meaning of the text while actually manifesting a good deal about the particular circumstances of the author. The *Constitutiones* goes even further by introducing elements that were never a part of Clare's experience of the Franciscan canonical life.

What makes these texts particularly interesting, especially in relation to the investigation of women and canons that is the subject of this book, is that they share medieval and early modern women's subversive relationship to canons of all sorts. Here we have three female-authored texts (Clare's rule, Maria Domitilla's commentary, and the *Constitutions* of her house), each of which reshapes a male-written rule for women's use. Yet, Maria Domitilla's commentary presents this as a direct rather than a mediated text: Clare's true meaning comes from God's mouth to nuns' lives and is presented by Maria Domitilla as the way the Cappucine of Pavia live the canonical Franciscan life—or at least the way they should live it. But at the same time, even as she is commenting on this life, and precisely because of and through this canonical authority, Maria Domitilla Galluzzi shares with her readers her own understanding and vision of the religious life.

It is intriguing to wonder if this example can be extrapolated into a broader statement about the role of Franciscan women in reshaping the canons of their lives. Close study of the writings of later Franciscan women such as Veronica Giuliani (1660–1727) might help us to better articulate such a female Franciscan movement.[48]

❧ ❧ ❧

NOTES

1. Henry Chadwick, *The Early Church*, vol. 1 of *The Pelican History of the Church* (Harmondsworth, Middlesex: Penguin Books, 1967), 40–44, 81–82; G. W. Anderson, "Canonical and Non-Canonical," in *From the Beginnings to Jerome*, ed. P. R. Ackroyd and C. F. Evans, vol. 1 of *The Cambridge History of the Bible* (Cambridge: Cambridge University Press, 1970), 113–59; R. M. Grant, "The New Testament Canon," in *The Cambridge History of the Bible*, vol. 1, *From the Beginnings to Jerome*, ed. P. R. Ackroyd and C. F. Evans, 284–308. It is important to note that the canon of the Greek Bible (the "Septuagint") is not same as the Hebrew Masoretic text that is now the standard text of Judaism because it includes additional texts known only in Greek.

2. O. Chadwick, *The Reformation*, vol. 3 of *The Pelican History of the Church* (Harmondsworth, Middlesex: Penguin Books, 1967), 57–58, 223–25, 276–77; Roland H. Bainton, "The Bible in the Reformation," in *The West from the Reformation to the Present Day*, ed. S. L. Greenslade vol. 3 of *The Cambridge History of the Bible* (Cambridge: Cambridge University Press, 1963), 1–37; F. J. Crehan, "The Bible in the Roman Catholic Church from Trent to the Present Day," in *The West from the Reformation to the Present Day*, vol. 3 of *The Cambridge History of the Bible* (Cambridge: Cambridge University Press, 1963), 199–237.

3. Modern Bibles include extensive cross-listing in notes to show parallel texts in the Gospels but have lost this tradition of canon lists, which was found in some of the most beautifully illustrated early medieval bibles. Important manuscripts with canon tables include the Book of Durrow, seventh century, now in Trinity College, Dublin (see Bernard Meehan, *The Book of Durrow: A Medieval Masterpiece at Trinity College, Dublin* [Dublin: Town House and Country House, 1996], 24, 27); the Lindisfarne Gospels, seventh century, now in the British Library, London (see Janet Blackhouse, *The Lindisfarne Gospels: A Masterpiece of Book Painting* [London: British Library, n.d.], 11); the Book of Kells, ninth century, now in Trinity College, Dublin (see Bernard Meehan, *The Book of Kells* [London: Thames and Hudson, 1994], 6–7); and *The Golden Gospel Book of Echternach*, eleventh century, now in Germanisches Nationalmuseum Nürnberg (see Rainer Kahsnitz, Ursula Mende, and Elisabeth Rücker, *Die Goldene Evangelienbuch von Echternach: Eine Prunkhandscrift des 11. Jahrhunderts* [Frankfurt am Main: S. Fischer Verlag, 1982], tables 8–9).

4. For the canons of the ecumenical councils of the early Church, see Giovan Domenico Mansi, *Sacrorum conciliorum nova et amplissima collectio* (1759; reprint, Graz: Akademische Druck-u. Verlagsanstalt, 1960–62).

5. The literature on Canon Law is vast and notably self-referential, but a good place to start to learn about the tradition is Gratian, *The Treatise on Laws (Decretum DD. 1–20)*, trans. Augustine Thompson, O.P., with *The Ordinary Gloss*, trans. James Gordley with an introduction by Katherine Christensen (Washington, D.C.: Catholic University Press of America, 1993).

6. Caroline Walker Bynum, "The Spirituality of Regular Canons in the Twelfth Century," in *Jesus as Mother: Studies in the Spirituality of the High Middle Ages* (Berkeley: University of California Press, 1982).

7. L. Verheijen, ed., *La Règle de Saint Augustine*, vol. 1, *Tradition Manuscrite*, and vol. 2, *Recherches Historiques* (Paris: Études augustiniennes, 1967); on this topic, see also A. Zumkeller, *Augustine's Rule: A Commentary*, trans. M. J. O'Connell, ed. J. E.

Rotelle (Villanova, Pa.: Augustinian Press, 1987); and G. Lawless, *Augustine of Hippo and His Monastic Rule* (Oxford: Oxford University Press, 1987).

8. C. H. Lawrence, *Medieval Monasticism: Forms of Religious Life in Western Europe in the Middle Ages*, 2d ed. (London and New York: Longman, 1989).

9. There are two critical editions of Benedict's *Rule: Benedicti regula*, ed. Rudolphus Hanslik, Corpus scriptorum ecclesiasticorum Latinorum, vol. 75 (Vienna: Hoelder-Pichler-Tempsky, 1960); and *La règle de Saint Benoît*, ed. Jean Neufville, trans. Adalbert de Vogüé, Sources chrétiennes 181–86 (Paris: Éditions du Cerf, 1971–77). A good English translation is *The Rule of Saint Benedict*, trans. Anthony C. Meisel and M. L. del Mastro (New York: Doubleday Image, 1975).

10. Gregory the Great, *Dialogi de vita*, Sources chrétiennes 260 (Paris: Éditions du Cerf, 1978–80). The English translation is *Saint Benedict*, trans. Myra L. Uhlfelder, book 2 of *The Dialogues of Gregory the Great* (Indianapolis: Bobbs-Merrill, 1967).

11. Yale University, Beinecke Library, MS. Marston 25. See also Penelope D. Johnson, *Equal in Monastic Profession: Religious Women in Medieval France* (Chicago: University of Chicago Press, 1991).

12. Caesarius of Arles, *Regula sanctarum virginum* in *Oeuvres monastiques*, Sources chrétiennes 345, 398 (Paris: Éditions du Cerf, 1988). The English translation is *The Rule for Nuns of St. Caesarius of Arles*, trans. Maria Caritas McCarthy (Washington, D.C.: Catholic University Press, 1960).

13. Brenda Bolton, "Mulieres Sanctae," in *Women in Medieval Society*, ed. Susan Mosher Stuard (Philadelphia: University of Pennsylvania Press, 1976), 141–58; Florence Koorn, "Women Without Vows: The Case of the Beguines and the Sisters of the Common Life in the Northern Netherlands," trans. Anne MacLachlan, in *Women and Men in Spiritual Culture, XIV–XVII Centuries*, ed. Elisja Schulte van Kessel (The Hague: Netherlands Government Publications Office, 1986), 135–49; Katherine Gill, "Open Monasteries for Women in Late Medieval and Early Modern Italy: Two Roman Examples," in *The Crannied Wall: Women, Religion, and the Arts in Early Modern Europe*, ed. Craig Monson (Ann Arbor: University of Michigan Press, 1992), 15–47.

14. December 3, 1563, "Decree on the Reform of the Friars, especially number 5, which demands strict enclosure for religious women." See Paolo Sarpi, *Istoria del Concilio Tridentino* (Turin: Einaudi, 1974), 2:1244. See also Raymond Creytens, "La riforma dei monasteri femminili," in *Il concilio di Trento e la riforma tridentina* (Rome: Herder, 1963), 1:62–77. Important studies of the open and enclosed religious life of women in the later Middle Ages are Katherine Gill, "Open Monasteries for Women," 15–47, and Maiju Lehmijoki-Gardner, *Worldly Saints: Social Interaction of Dominican Penitent Women in Italy, 1200–1500* (Helsinki: Suomen Historiallinen Seura, 1999).

15. The complete corpus of Francis's works is found in *Écrits/François d'Assise*, ed. Théophile Desbonnets et al., Sources chrétiennes (Paris: Editions du Cerf, 1981). The *Rules* of 1221 and 1223 are found in English in *St. Francis of Assisi, Writings and Early Biographies: English Omnibus of the Sources for the Life of St. Francis*, ed. Marion A. Habig (Chicago: Franciscan Herald Press, 1983), 31–66 (hereafter, *Omnibus*), and in the translation of Regis J. Armstrong and Ignatius C. Brady in *Francis and Clare: The Complete Works* (New York: Paulist Press, 1982), 107–45. See also the biographical accounts of Thomas of Celano, *The First Life of St. Francis*, and Bonaventure, *Major Life of St. Francis*, both in *Omnibus*.

16. *Scripta Leonis, Rufini et Angeli Sociorum S. Francesci: The Writings of Leo, Rufino*

and Angelo Companions of St. Francis, ed. and trans. Rosalind B. Brooke (Oxford: Clarendon, 1970; repr. 1990), 284–85.

17. Ibid., 286–87.

18. Celano, *First Life*, in *Omnibus*, 245.

19. Marie-France Becker, Jean-François Godet, Thaddée Matura, eds., introduction to *Écrits*, by Clare of Assisi, Sources Chrétiennes 325 (Paris: Les Éditions du Cerf, 1985), 19–20. The original is still kept at the Monastery of St. Clare in Assisi.

20. Cf. Margaret Carney, O.S.F., *The First Franciscan Woman: Clare of Assisi and Her Form of Life* (Quincy, Ill.: Franciscan Press, 1993).

21. Marie-France Becker, Jean-François Godet, Thaddée Matura, eds., introduction to *Écrits*, 21.

22. Gordon Leff, *Heresy in the Later Middle Ages*, vol. 1, pt. 1 (New York: Barnes and Noble, 1967); D. Douie, *The Nature and Effect of the Heresy of the Fraticelli* (Manchester: Manchester University Press, 1932); and the English translations of Franciscan Spirituals in Bernard McGinn, ed., *Apocalyptic Spirituality* (New York: Paulist Press, 1979).

23. See the description by Father Cuthbert in *The Catholic Encyclopedia*, vol. 3 (New York: Robert Appleton, 1908), and Z. Boverio, *Annal. Ord. S. Fr. Cap* (Lyons, 1632). For the history of the order see Thaddeus MacVicar, *The Franciscan Spirituals and the Capuchin Reform* (St. Bonaventure, N.Y.: Franciscan Institute, 1986), and Father Cuthbert, *The Capuchins: A Contribution to the History of the Counter-Reformation* (New York: Longmans, Green, 1929).

24. Father Cuthbert, *Catholic Encyclopedia*.

25. A work rewritten no fewer than three times, leading to the definitive edition of 1840 entitled *I promessi sposi: Storia milanese del secolo XVII scoperta e rifatta* (Milan: Tipografia Guglielmini e Redaelli, 1840). The English translation is Alessandro Manzoni, *The Bethrothed: 'I Promessi Sposi' a Tale of XVII Century Milan*, trans. Archibald Colquhoun (London: Dent, 1983). For the earlier versions, see Alessandro Manzoni, *Fermo e Lucia*, ed. Sergio Romagnoli and Luca Toschi (Florence: Sansoni Editore, 1985).

26. Rocco Cocchia (Rocco da Cesinale), *Storia delle missione dei Cappucini* (Paris: P. Lethielleux, 1867).

27. Guiseppe Santarelli, *Guida del Santuario di Loreto* (Ancona: Edizioni Aniballi, 1998). For Padre Pio, see the three-volume historical novel of Renzo Allegri, *La Vita e I Miracoli di Padre Pio* (Milan: Mondadori, 1999); see also Felice Rosetti, *Padre Pio* (Ravenna: Faenza, 1999); and Francis Mary Kalvelage, *Padre Pio: The Wonder Worker* (New Bedford, Mass.: Franciscan Friars of the Immaculate, 1999).

28. The secondary literature on female Capuchins is scant, Francesco Saverio da Brusciano Toppi, *Maria Lorenza Longo: Donna della Napoli* de '500 (Pompei [Naples]: Pontificio Santuario di Pompei, 1997).

29. Rodolfo Maiocchi, *Le Chiese di Pavia, Notizie* (Pavia: Tipografia Artigianelli, 1903), 2:31–43.

30. Maria Domitilla Galluzzi, *Vita*, 1.1–2. This autobiography is available only in manuscript. I have located the following six copies: Milano, Biblioteca Ambrosiana D.77 sussidio to 1622 Lent; Milano, Biblioteca Ambrosiana H.47 sussidio; Milano, Biblioteca Ambrosiana I. 41 sussidio copied 1672; Milano, Biblioteca Ambrosiana A. 276 sussidio; Milano, Biblioteca Ambrosiana G. 97 sussidio to 1635; and Milano, Bib-

lioteca Ambrosiana H. 91 sussidio Books 4–5. I will be quoting from Milano, Biblioteca Ambrosiana G. 97 sussidio. All translations from this source are my own.

31. Ibid., 1.3–19.

32. Ibid., 1.20–21.

33. E. Ann Matter, "Discourses of Desire: Sexuality and Christian Women's Visionary Narratives," *Journal of Homosexuality* 18 (1990): 119–31; also published in *Homosexuality and Religion*, ed. Richard Hasbany (New York: Hawthorne, 1989), 119–31; and with Antonio Riccardi, "Per la morte di Suor Maria Domitilla Galluzzi, Un inedito anonimo del seicento pavese," *Poesia: Mensile di cultura poetica* 2, no. 12 (1989): 11–14; see also "The Personal and the Paradigm: The Book of Maria Domitilla Galluzzi," in *The Crannied Wall*, ed. Craig Monson, 87–103; "Interior Maps of an Eternal External: The Spiritual Rhetoric of Maria Domitilla Galluzzi d'Acqui," in *Maps of Flesh and Light: The Religious Experience of Medieval Women Mystics*, ed. Ulrike Wiethaus (Syracuse, N.Y.: Syracuse University Press, 1993), 60–73; "The Commentary of the Rule of Clare of Assisi by Maria Domitilla Galluzzi," in *Creative Women in Medieval and Early Modern Italy: A Religious and Artistic Renaissance* ed. E. Ann Matter and John Coakley (Philadelphia: University of Pennsylvania Press, 1994), 201–11.

34. Maria Domitilla Galluzzi, *Vita*, 1.23–30, 5.4–5.

35. The *Vero lume* is also available only in manuscript. I have located the following three copies:

Pavia, Biblioteca Universitaria MS Aldini 306/1(u); Pavia, Biblioteca Civica "Bonetta" MS I,11(B); and Milan, Archivio Storico Civico e Biblioteca Trivulziana MS 491(T). None of the manuscripts gives the date of composition, although the narrative of the *Vita* (1.46, 54) dates it to "age 26, in the fifth year of my profession." All translations from this source are my own. The *Rule* had been available in Italian as early as the fifteenth century (the Urbino manuscript, cf. Marie-France Becker, Jean-François Godet, Thaddée Matura, eds., introduction to *Écrits*, 26).

36. An earlier Franciscan woman, Colette of Corbie, had also promulgated a strict adherence to Clare's *Rule*, although she does not seem to have written a line-by-line commentary like Maria Domitilla's. See Elisabeth Lopez, *Culture et sainteté: Colette de Corbie, 1381–1447* ([Saint-Etienne]: Publications de l'Université de Saint-Etienne, 1994). Colette of Corbie's works have not been published for the most part.

37. The *Carteggio* preserved in Pavia (Biblioteca Universitaria Aldini 306/3) is a bound collection of original letters to Maria Domitilla. There evidently was another volume no longer extant; many of these letters have been copied into manuscripts of the *Vita* and the *Passione*. All translations from this source are my own.

38. The first manuscript: Pavia, Biblioteca Universitaria Aldini 306/1 from The Capuchins of Pavia; Pavia, Biblioteca Civica "Bonetta" I also from a monastic community of Pavia (perhaps also her own house); and Milano, Biblioteca Trivulziana 491, belonged to the noble Milan Belgioioso family.

39. The phrase appears twice in the commentary on chapter 2 of the *Lume*: U = f. 6v, 7r; B = 4r, 5R; T is unfoliated.

40. Maria Domitilla Galluzzi, *Vita* 1.23, 5.5.

41. E. Ann Matter, "The Commentary of the Rule of Clare of Assisi," 201–11.

42. "Conobbi che la maggior parte può seguire con un solo voto di più, ma che in quei primi tempi la maggior parte era delle tre parti le due, et che ciò fù ordinato accioche concorrendo la maggior parte delle sorelle nel riccevere la nuova sorella più

chiaramente si vedesse l'effetto della Divina Volontà, la commune utilità, et pace del monastero, essendo che difficilmente la maggior parte può errare pur che rettamente si muova per Dio, il qual ha poi cura che non si ricceva alcuna che fosse per rilasciare la perfetta osservanza di tal Santa Regola." *Lume* 2.2 U= f. 11r, B = f. 8v.

43. Pavia, Biblioteca Universitaria MS Aldini 502 f. 34 r of the 1648 document. Each version, and parts 1 and 2 of the 1648 version, is foliated separately.

44. "L'elettione dell'Abbadessa si farà a voti secreti con quest'ordine, la sorella più antica di religione sarà la prima che dia il suo voto, seguiranno poi le altre per ordine sino all'ultima vocale, e quella che haverà più della metà de' voti ancorche fosse d'un voto solo sarà l'Abbadessa canonicamente eletta. Quando saranno nello scrutinio elette due con voti pari, si ritorni à nova scrutinio dei boletini <biglietti> i nomi d'ambidue, e posti in un vaso si cavi a sorte e la prima ch'esca <uscirà> sia l'Abbadessa eletta." Pavia, Biblioteca Universitaria MS Aldini 502 (1648) parte 2, f. 1r.

45. Clare of Assisi, *Écrits*, ed. Marie-France Becker, Jean-François Godet, and Thaddée Matura, Sources Chrétiennes 325 (Paris: Les Éditions du Cerf, 1985), 146.

46. "e siamo senza li soliti fratelli cercanti, che tutti se ne sono andati ad altro ordine, in tepo si tanti nostri bisogni, per il che se il Reverendissimo Padre Priore ne potrà far carità di un poco d'ova, e butino, meteremo quest'obligo con li molti altri nel Signore." Milan, Archivio Storico Civico e Biblioteca Trivulziana, Fondo autografi, cartella 2, pacco 3, fasicolo 14 b.

47. Teresa's theory of prayer is found passim in her autobiography: Teresa of Avila, *Libro de la vida*, ed. Dámaso Chicharro (Madrid: Ediciones Catedra, 1993); the English translation is *The Life of Saint Teresa of Avila by Herself*, trans. J. M. Cohen (London: Penguin, 1957). For knowledge of Teresa in seventeenth-century Italy, see Elisabetta Marchetti, *Gli scritti e le prime traduzioni italiane delle opere di Teresa di Gesù, nel quadro dell'impegno papale post-tridentino*, Dottorato di Ricerca in Storia religiosa—X Ciclo, Università degli Studi di Torino, Anno Accademico 1998–99. "Oratione Mentale" is found in other works of Maria Domitilla Galluzzi, especially the *Passione*, which appears in some manuscripts as part two of the *Vita* and in some by itself, and *Quarant' hore de meditatione mentale*, which I have found only in one copy.

48. Veronica Giuliani's works in print include *Visioni*, ed. Massimo Baldini. (Florence: Nardini, 1991). Armando Maggi is currently working on Giuliani's visions.

BIBLIOGRAPHY

Works by Maria Domitilla Galluzzi

Vero lume

Pavia. Biblioteca Universitaria. Ms Aldini 306, vol. 1.
Pavia. Biblioteca Civica "Bonetta." MS I, 11.
Milan. Archivio Storico Civico e Biblioteca Trivulziana. MS 491.

Vita

Milan. Biblioteca Ambrosiana. D. 77 sussidio 468 ff. to 1622 Lent.
Milan. Biblioteca Ambrosiana. H. 47 sussidio 191 ff.
Milan. Biblioteca Ambrosiana. I. 41 sussidio 64 ff. (copied 1672).
Milan. Biblioteca Ambrosiana. A. 276 sussidio 260 ff.

Milan. Biblioteca Ambrosiana. G. 97 sussidio 431 ff. to 1635.
Milan. Biblioteca Ambrosiana. H. 91 sussidio 271 ff. Books 4–5.

Other texts

Pavia. Biblioteca Universitaria. Ms Aldini 502. *Consitutiones*.
Milan. Archivio Storico Civico e Biblioteca Trivulziana. Fondo autografi, cartella 2, pacco 3, fasicolo 14 b.

Other Manuscript

Pavia. Biblioteca Universitaria Aldini. 306 vol. 3. *Carteggio*.
Yale University. Beinecke Library. MS. Marston 25. "House Book" of Notre Dame de Saintes.

Primary References

Anderson, G. W. "Canonical and Non-Canonical." In *From the Beginnings to Jerome*, ed. P. R. Ackroyd and C. F. Evans. Vol. 1 of *The Cambridge History of the Bible*. Cambridge: Cambridge University Press, 1970.

Annali de frati minori Cappuccini, ed. Zaccaria Boverio da Saluzzo, e tradotti in volgare dal padre f. Benedetto Sanbenedetti, da Milano. Venice: Giunti, 1643–45.

Augustine of Hippo. *La Règle de Saint Augustine*. Vol. 1, *Tradition Manuscrite*. Vol. 2, *Recherches Historiques*. Ed. Luc Verheijen. Paris: Études augustiniennes, 1967.

Bainton, Roland H. "The Bible in the Reformation." In *The West from the Reformation to the Present Day*. Ed. S. L. Greenslade Vol. 3 of *The Cambridge History of the Bible*. Cambridge: Cambridge University Press, 1963.

Benedict of Nursia, *Benedicti regula*. Ed. Rudolphus Hanslik. Corpus scriptorum ecclesiasticorum Latinorum, vol. 75. Vienna: Hoelder-Pichler-Tempsky, 1960.

———. *La règle de Saint Benoît*. Ed. Jean Neufville. Trans. Adalbert de Vogüé. Sources Chrétiennes 181–86. Paris: Éditions du Cerf, 1971–77.

———. *The Rule of Saint Benedict*. Trans. Anthony C. Meisel and M. L. del Mastro. New York: Doubleday Image, 1975.

Blackhouse, Janet. *The Lindisfarne Gospels: A Masterpiece of Book Painting*. London: British Library, n.d.

Bolton, Brenda. "Mulieres Sanctae." In *Women in Medieval Society*, ed. Susan Mosher Stuard, 141–58. Philadelphia: University of Pennsylvania Press, 1976.

Bonaventure. *Major Life of St. Francis*. In *St. Francis of Assisi, Writings and Early Biographies: English Omnibus of the Sources for the Life of St. Francis*, ed. Marion A. Habig. Chicago: Franciscan Herald Press, 1983.

Bynum, Caroline Walker. "The Spirituality of Regular Canons in the Twelfth Century." In *Jesus as Mother: Studies in the Spirituality of the High Middle Ages*. Berkeley: University of California Press, 1982.

Caesarius of Arles. *The Rule for Nuns of St. Caesarius of Arles*. Trans. Maria Caritas McCarthy. Washington, D.C.: Catholic University Press, 1960.

———. *Regula sanctarum virginum*. In *Oeuvres monastiques*. Sources chrétiennes 345, 398. Paris: Éditions du Cerf, 1988.

Carney, Margaret, O.S.F. *The First Franciscan Woman: Clare of Assisi and Her Form of Life*. Quincy, Ill.: Franciscan Press, 1993.

Chadwick, Henry. *The Early Church.* Vol. 1 of *The Pelican History of the Church.* Harmondsworth, Middlesex: Penguin Books, 1967.

Chadwick, O. *The Reformation.* Vol. 3 of *The Pelican History of the Church* Harmondsworth, Middlesex: Penguin Books, 1967.

Clare of Assisi. *Francis and Clare: The Complete Works.* Trans. Regis J. Armstrong and Ignatius C. Brady. New York: Paulist Press, 1982.

———. *Écrits.* Ed. Marie-France Becker, Jean-François Godet, and Thaddée Matura. Sources Chrétiennes 325. Paris: Les Éditions du Cerf, 1985.

Cocchia, Rocco (Rocco da Cesinale). *Storia delle missione dei Cappuccini.* Paris: P. Lethielleux, 1867.

Crehan, F. J. "The Bible in the Roman Catholic Church from Trent to the Present Day." In *The West from the Reformation to the Present Day.* Ed. S. L. Greenslade Vol. 3 of *The Cambridge History of the Bible.* Cambridge: Cambridge University Press, 1963.

Creytens, Raymond. "La riforma dei monasteri femminili." In *Il concilio di Trento e la riforma tridentina.* Rome: Herder, 1963.

Douie, D. *The Nature and Effect of the Heresy of the Fraticelli.* Manchester: Manchester University Press, 1932.

Francis of Assisi. *Ecrits/François d'Assise.* Ed. Théophile Desbonnets et al. Sources chrétiennes 285. Paris: Editions du Cerf, 1981.

———. *Francis and Clare: The Complete Works.* Trans. Regis J. Armstrong and Ignatius C. Brady. New York: Paulist Press, 1982.

———. *Rules.* In *St. Francis of Assisi, Writings and Early Biographies: English Omnibus of the Sources for the Life of St. Francis.* Ed. Marion A. Habig. Chicago: Franciscan Herald Press, 1938.

Gill, Katherine. "Open Monasteries for Women in Late Medieval and Early Modern Italy: Two Roman Examples." In *The Crannied Wall: Women, Religion, and the Arts in Early Modern Europe,* ed. Craig Monson, 15–47. Ann Arbor: University of Michigan Press, 1992.

Giuliani, Veronica. *Visioni.* Ed. Massimo Baldini. Florence: Nardini, 1991.

Grant, R. M. "The New Testament Canon." In *From the Beginnings to Jerome,* ed. P. R. Ackroyd and C. F. Evans. Vol. 1 of *The Cambridge History of the Bible.* Cambridge: Cambridge University Press, 1970.

Gratian. *The Treatise on Laws (Decretum DD. 1–20).* Trans. Augustine Thompson, O.P. With *The Ordinary Gloss,* trans. James Gordley. With an introduction by Katherine Christensen. Washington, D.C.: Catholic University Press of America, 1993.

Gregory the Great. *The Dialogues of Gregory the Great.* Book 2, *Saint Benedict.* Trans. Myra L. Uhlfelder. Indianapolis: Bobbs-Merrill, 1967.

———. *Dialogi de vita.* Sources chrétiennes 260. Paris: Éditions du Cerf, 1978–80.

Johnson, Penelope D. *Equal in Monastic Profession: Religious Women in Medieval France.* Chicago: University of Chicago Press, 1991.

Kahsnitz, Rainer, Ursula Mende, and Elisabeth Rücker. *Die Goldene Evangelienbuch von Echternach: Eine Prunkhandscrift des 11. Jahrhunderts.* Frankfurt am Main: S. Fischer Verlag, 1982.

Koorn, Florence. "Women Without Vows. The Case of the Beguines and the Sisters of the Common Life in the Northern Netherlands." Trans. Anne MacLachlan. In *Women and Men in Spiritual Culture, XIV–XVII Centuries,* ed. Elisja Schulte van Kessel, 135–49. The Hague: Netherlands Government Publications Office, 1986.

Lawless, G. *Augustine of Hippo and His Monastic Rule*. Oxford: Oxford University Press, 1987.

Lawrence, C. H. *Medieval Monasticism: Forms of Religious Life in Western Europe in the Middle Ages*. 2d ed. London and New York: Longman, 1989.

Leff, Gordon. *Heresy in the Later Middle Ages*. New York: Barnes and Noble, 1967.

Lehmijoki-Gardner, Maiju. *Worldly Saints: Social Interaction of Dominican Penitent Women in Italy, 1200–1500*. Helsinki: Suomen Historiallinen Seura, 1999.

Lopez, Elisabeth. *Culture et sainteté: Colette de Corbie, 1381–1447*. [Saint-Etienne]: Publications de l'Université de Saint-Etienne, 1994.

MacVicar, Thaddeus. *The Franciscan Spirituals and the Capuchin Reform*. St. Bonaventure, N.Y.: Franciscan Institute, 1986.

Maiocchi, Rodolfo. *Le Chiese di Pavia, Notizie*. Vol. 2. Pavia: Tipografia Artigianelli, 1903.

Mansi, Giovan Domenico. *Sacrorum conciliorum nova et amplissima collectio*. 1759. Reprint, Graz: Akademische Druck-u. Verlagsanstalt, 1960–62.

Manzoni, Alessandro. *I promessi sposi: Storia milanese del secolo XVII scoperta e rifatta*. Milan: Tipografia Guglielmini e Redaelli, 1840.

———. *The Bethrothed: 'I Promessi Sposi' a Tale of XVII Century Milan*. Trans. Archibald Colquhoun. London: Dent, 1983.

———. *Fermo e Lucia*. Ed. Sergio Romagnoli and Luca Toschi. Florence: Sansoni Editore, 1985.

Marchetti, Elisabetta. *Gli scritti e le prime traduzioni italiane delle opere di Teresa di Gesù, nel quadro dell'impegno papale post-tridentino*. Dottorato di Ricerca in Storia religiosa—X Ciclo, Università degli Studi di Torino, 1998–99.

Matter, E. Ann. "Discourses of Desire: Sexuality and Christian Women's Visionary Narratives," *Journal of Homosexuality* 18 (1990): 119–31; also published in *Homosexuality and Religion*, ed. Richard Hasbany, 119–31. New York: Hawthorne Press, 1989.

———. "The Personal and the Paradigm: The Book of Maria Domitilla Galluzzi." In *The Crannied Wall*, ed. Craig Monson, 87–103. Ann Arbor: University of Michigan Press, 1992.

———. "Interior Maps of an Eternal External: The Spiritual Rhetoric of Maria Domitilla Galluzzi d'Acqui." In *Maps of Flesh and Light: The Religious Experience of Medieval Women Mystics*, ed. Ulrike Wiethaus, 60–73. Syracuse, N.Y.: Syracuse University Press, 1993.

———. "The Commentary of the Rule of Clare of Assisi by Maria Domitilla Galluzzi." In *Creative Women in Medieval and Early Modern Italy: A Religious and Artistic Renaissance*, ed. E. Ann Matter and John Coakley, 201–11. Philadelphia: University of Pennsylvania Press, 1994.

Matter, E. Ann, and Antonio Riccardi. "Per la morte di Suor Maria Domitilla Galluzzi, Un inedito anonimo del seicento pavese." *Poesia: Mensile di cultura poetica* 2, no. 12 (1989) 11–14.

McGinn, Bernard, ed. *Apocalyptic Spirituality*. New York: Paulist Press, 1979.

Meehan, Bernard. *The Book of Kells*. London: Thames and Hudson, 1994.

———. *The Book of Durrow: A Medieval Masterpiece at Trinity College, Dublin*. Dublin: Town House and Country House, 1996.

Sarpi, Paolo. *Istoria del Concilio Tridentino*. Turin: Einaudi, 1974.
Scripta Leonis, Rufini et Angeli Sociorum S. Francesci: The Writings of Leo, Rufino and Angelo Companions of St. Francis. Ed. and trans. Rosalind B. Brooke. Oxford: Clarendon, 1970/1990.
Teresa of Avila. *The Life of Saint Teresa of Avila by Herself*. Trans. J. M. Cohen. London: Penguin, 1957.
———. *Libro de la vida*. Ed. Dámaso Chicharro. Madrid: Ediciones Catedra, 1993.
Thomas of Celano. *The First Life of St. Francis*. In *St. Francis of Assisi, Writings and Early Biographies: English Omnibus of the Sources for the Life of St. Francis*, ed. Marion A. Habig. Chicago: Franciscan Herald Press, 1983.
Toppi, Francesco Saverio da Brusciano, OFM Cap. "Maria Lorenzo Longo e l'opera del Divino Amore a Napoli." *Collectanea Francescana* 23 (1953): 166–226.
———. *Maria Lorenza Longo: Donna della Napoli de '500*. Pompei (Naplesi): Pontificio Santuario di Pompei, 1997.
Zumkeller, A. *Augustine's Rule: A Commentary*. Trans. M. J. O'Connell. Ed. J. E. Rotelle. Villanova, Penn.: Augustinian Press, 1987.

Further Reading

Matter, E. Ann, and John Coakley, eds. *Creative Women in Medieval and Early Modern Italy: A Religious and Artistic Renaissance*. Philadelphia: University of Pennsylvania Press, 1994.
Monson, Craig, ed. *The Crannied Wall: Women, Religion, and the Arts in Early Modern Europe*. Ann Arbor: University of Michigan Press, 1992.
Scaraffia, Lucetta, and Gabriella Zarri, eds. *Women and Faith: Catholic Religious Life in Italy from Late Antiquity to the Present*. Cambridge, Mass.: Harvard University Press, 1999.

CHART 1. The Franciscan Canonical Life—Three Models

Francis of Assisi (1223) (Monumenta Ordinis Minorum)	Clare of Assisi (1253) (Sources Chrétiennes 325)	Maria Domitilla Galluzzi Constitutiones (1648) (Pavia, Bib.Univ. MS Aldini 502)
1. The Life of the Friars Minor.	1. Form of the Life of the Poor Sisters.	1. Accepting novices and their exercises.
2. Those who wish to take up this life, and how they are to be received.	2. Those who wish to receive this life, and how they are to be received.	2. The Divine Office.
3. The Divine Office and fasting, and how the Friars should go about the world.	3. The Divine Office and fasting, of Confession and Communion.	3. On Mental Prayer.
4. The Friars are forbidden to accept money.	4. The Election of the Office of the Abbess, of the Chapter, of the Officials and the Discreets.	4. Confession and Examination of Conscience.
5. The manner of working.	5. Of Silence, and of the Parlor, and the Grille.	5. Of Most Holy Communion.
6. The Friars are to appropriate nothing for themselves; on seeking alms; and on the sick Friars.	6. The lack of possessions.	6. The Chapter of Fault, and the discipline.
7. The penance to be imposed on Friars who fall into sin.	7. The manner of work.	7. Of the Refectory, and Fasting.
8. The election of the Minister General of the Order and the Pentecost Chapter.	8. The Sisters shall not acquire anything as their own; begging alms; the sick sisters.	8. Of Silence and Seclusion.
9. The preachers.	9. The penance imposed on Sisters who sin; the Sisters who serve outside of the monastery.	9. Of Obedience.
10. The admonition and correction of the Friars.	10. The admonition and correction of the Sisters.	10. Of Poverty.
11. The Friars are forbidden to enter the monasteries of nuns.	11. The custody of the enclosure (*clausura*).	11. Of Admission to the enclosure (*clausura*).
12. Those who wish to go among the Saracens and other non-believers.	12. The Visitator, the Chaplain, and their Cardinal Protector.	12. Of the sick, dying and deceased.

CHART 2. Maria Domitilla Galluzzi, *Constitutiones* (1648) (Pavia, Bib.Univ. MS Aldini 502) (trans. E. Ann Matter)

1. Of the election of the Abbess and the Vicaress.
2. Of the election of the Officials.
3. Of the Office of the Abbess.
4. Of the Office of the Mother Vicaria.
5. Of the Office of the Discreets.
6. Of the Mistress of Novices.
7. Of the Office of the Sacristan.
8. Of the Porter.
9. Of the Second Porter.
10. Of the Infermarian.
11. Of the Cook.
12. Of the Cancellaria (writes letters).
13. Of the Pagniera (gives out linens).
14. Of the Vestiaria (makes and gives out clothes).
    (new hand after 2 blank folios)

Chapter on defects and their penances.
On light fault.
On medium fault.
On grave fault.
On the most grave fault.
On the Seeking Brothers ("Fratelli Cercanti").
Signatures of the 1610 *Constitutiones* (copy).
Signatures of the 1648 *Constitutiones* (originals).
Signatures of Canons of the Cathedral of Pavia.
Signature and seal of Bishop Laurentius Bigonus.

Christine de Pizan

GENDER AND THE NEW VERNACULAR CANON

Kevin Brownlee

Throughout her long literary career, Christine de Pizan was deeply concerned with the interrelated questions of gender and the literary canon, which were essential to her own claim to "canonical" status as a female writer in the vernacular. Indeed, these issues of gendered writerly identity and authority were fundamental to her innovative self-presentation as the first French woman writer whose status as a woman constituted a fundamental, explicit, and elaborate part of her authorial persona.

Christine was born in Italy circa 1364, moved to Paris when quite young, and was bilingual in Italian and French. She was married at fifteen and widowed at twenty-five (1390), left with three children and a widowed mother to care for. In many important ways, her literary career emerged from her widowhood. Over the course of the first ten years of this literary career (1395–1405), Christine developed a series of strategies that enabled her to achieve success as a dominant presence in the Parisian literary establishment. After starting from a position of complete professional obscurity, by the year 1405 she was writing for the most prestigious patrons in France: the king, the queen, and the royal princes and princesses.[1] She remained in this successful professional situation for an additional decade, writing prose treatises as well as poetry and giving political advice to the key members of the French ruling class as the threat of the renewed Hundred Years War constantly increased. With the decisive French defeat by the English at the battle of Azincourt in 1415, and the ensuing Anglo-Burgundian capture of Paris in 1418, Christine was obliged to seek shelter in the Abbey of Poissy, where she remained in virtual silence as a writer for over a decade. It was Joan of Arc's triumphant arrival in the first half of 1429 to lead the French troops under Charles VII to (temporary) victory that prompted Christine to write her final work, a militant poem in praise of the Maid of Orleans. Medieval France's greatest woman writer thus concluded her long career by composing the first vernacular literary treatment of medieval France's greatest woman hero.[2]

In the present essay I will focus on the formative first decade of this literary career (1395–1405) in order to explore how Christine's initial commercial and professional success involved a tripartite strategy for presenting herself as a canonical woman writer. Various manipulations of complex notions of gender and of the vernacular are at issue.

The first of these strategies involves Christine's establishment of a new sort of literary canon into which she ultimately inserts herself. This progressive project of self-authorization is effected by a series of aggressive self-presentations as reader and as writer—the elaboration, in other words, of an autobiographical fable recounting her progressive empowerment in a literary career that appears as a sacred vocation. This autobiography is articulated in a set of first-person works composed between 1402 and 1405, by far the single most productive period of Christine's writerly life. The set begins with the dossier of the *Débat sur le "Roman de la Rose"* [Debate on the "Romance of the Rose"] (1402), continues with the *Chemin de longue estude* [Path of long study] (1402–3) and the *Livre de la Mutacion de Fortune* [Book of fortune's transformation] (1403), and culminates in the *Livre de la Cité des Dames* [Book of the city of ladies] (1404–5), the *Livre des Trois Vertus* [Book of the three Virtues] (1405), and *Le Livre de l'advision Christine* [Christine's vision] (1405).[3]

In each of these works, Christine's autobiographical enterprise is directly linked to—even articulated in terms of—a set of encounters with a privileged group of model authors who, for Christine, constituted a kind of personal canon: Jean de Meun, Dante, Ovid, Boccaccio, and Boethius. In these works, Christine engages quite polemically with each of her authorities in turn, rewriting these *auctores* in accord with the requirements of her ongoing and self-authorizing autobiographical project. At the same time, she establishes her own status as a member of the new multilingual canon—French, Italian, Latin—that she has set into place as such.

In the chronological order determined by Christine's literary production, her first, most overt and most aggressive literary engagement with a canonical work is her confrontation with the *Romance of the Rose*.[4] What emerges over the course of the *Débat* dossier is Christine's strategic displacement of Jean de Meun, the single most important author figure in the French vernacular canon. The minor Ovid (the term the Middle Ages used to designate Ovid's love poetry as opposed to his *Metamorphoses*) is subsumed into Jean de Meun's *Rose* and similarly undermined. At the same time, Christine presents the public debate on the *Roman de la Rose* (the first such debate in French literary history) as above all an event in her own, ongoing autobiography. Next, in her *Chemin de longue estude*, Christine utilizes the *Divine Comedy* to recount an autobiographical narrative that presents her as a new regendered Dante, writing in French.[5] In effect, she reads the Italian Dante against the French Jean de Meun in order to construct for herself an empowering bilingual vernacular literary genealogy. Third, in her *Mutacion de Fortune*, Christine innovatively uses Ovid's *Metamorphoses* to represent both the onset of her widowhood and the beginning of her literary career. What results in Christine's text is an Ovidian narrative of gender transformation—from woman to man—that Christine employs to authorize herself for the first time as a woman historian. Within Christine's autobiographical fable, this allegorical metamorphosis—this sex change from woman to man—figures her response to her husband's death, to her shift in status from married women to widow.[6] Fourth, in the *Cité des Dames*, which I view as a "revisionist" text in a number of complementary ways, Christine radically and visibly rewrites her Boccaccian model, the *De mulieribus claris* [On illustrious women], in such a way as to present herself as a "corrected" Boccaccio figure, regendered, vernacularized, and writing in the first person. Boccaccio's third-person, male-authored Latin treatise on women is rewritten as Christine's French autobiography. At the same time, the *Cité des Dames* definitively rejects the construct of gender change that had served as a kind of provisional solution to the problem of self-representation in the *Mutacion*. Within the context of Christine's Boccaccian polemic, the auctorial figures of Ovid and Jean de Meun are also remotivated, and the *Cité* emerges as, in part, a positive, "feminist" rewriting of the *Rose*. Finally, the *Livre des Trois Vertus* effects the culmination of this process of dynamic canon formation. Here, Christine utilizes auto-citation to cast *herself* as an *auctor*, authoritative enough to be worthy of citing. With this work, Christine's strategy of self-authorization by means of citing and rewriting her personal canon of *auctores* culminates in her self-presentation as a member of this very canon. In this sense, her autobiographical narrative, which had proceeded by means of her encounters with various model authors, concludes with a kind of dramatic self-confrontation in which she "discovers" that her own earlier works have become canonical, requiring her present writing self to come to terms with them as such. In the *Trois Vertus*, Christine presents herself as having successfully arrived at the writerly status of vernacular canonical author to which she had begun to aspire at the fragmentary beginning of her literary career a decade earlier. This newly canonical Christine then plays out fully her relationship with her last canonical male author, Boethius, in part 3 of the *Avision*. Having opened her literary engagement with Boethius at the beginning of the *Chemin*, and elaborated it over the course of the *Cité*, Christine stages herself in the concluding section of the *Avision* as a regendered Boethius, instructed by the self-identified "same" Lady Philosophy who had dialogically instructed her "earlier" pupil in the *Consolation*. At the same time, Christine is presented as the legitimate descendent—as autobiographical subject, as writer, and as thinker—of her "canonical" predecessor.[7]

The first of Christine's strategies for establishing herself as a new kind of "canonical" female writer involved a powerful and systematic self-presentation as the only female member of a privileged male writerly canon, which she simultaneously continues, corrects, and completes, in large part because of her unique gendered status as the only woman author. At the same time, she expands this male canon not only with regard to gender but also with regard to time: she keeps this canon "alive" by bringing it into the contemporary fifteenth century. In addition, this construct involves a new status for vernacular authors as "canonical," as well as a newly Franco-Italian vernacular hybridity.[8]

Christine's second, and complementary, strategy for presenting herself as a canonical woman writer involves the construction of various all-female canons of intellectual achievement. These are invariably situated in the distant classical (even mythographic) past and most often involve points of intellectual origin. Such female canons are to be found most systematically and pointedly elaborated in the *Cité des Dames*.

Particularly relevant is the first and most overtly literary canon of this sort, found in *Cité* 1.28–30 and involving a trio of exemplary women writers, exemplary in "grant science et de haut entendement" [deep learning and of high understanding]: Cornificia, Proba, and Sappho, each of whom is explicitly presented as having been praised by Boccaccio, in the first three references in the entire *Cité* to the canonical male author whom Christine herself is rewriting.[9] Cornificia (*Cité* 1.28), through a combination of native talent and exceptionally hard study, becomes a master poet ("celle fillette par merveilleux engin tant frequenta les letres . . . qu'elle *fu souveraine poete*"). Excelling in "clergie" [learning, erudition], she writes a number of very famous books and poems ["livres et dictiez"] that receive much public approbation during the time of St. Gregory (ca. 540–604), who mentions them himself. Proba (*Cité* 1.29), a Roman Christian, is also a "*souveraine poete*" [master poet] and a master Virgilian. Her life's work is to Christianize the Virgilian corpus by combining the Old and New Testaments with the *Eclogues*, the *Georgics*, and the *Aeneid*. She effects a corrective rewriting of the arch-canonical Latin poet from a Christian, female perspective that makes the Virgilian text "better": "someone who knew only Proba's book would have thought that Virgil had been both a prophet and evangelist." Proba thus authorizes (among other things) Christine's own enterprise of rewriting male canonical authors. Her works were known in Christine's time, the two most famous both being named *Cento*.[10] Finally, Proba's rewritings of the Homeric poetic corpus (as well as her perfect knowledge of Greek literature in general) are affirmed.

Sappho (*Cité* 1.30) is perhaps the most elaborately treated of the female classical authors in Christine's canon. Like her fellow female authorial exemplars, Sappho possesses the key defining characteristics of "science" and "hault entendement." Her literary innovation and productivity receive special stress: "d'elle mesmes trouva maintes choses nouvelles et fist plusieurs *livres et dictiez*" [she discovered many new things herself and wrote many *books and poems*]. The superlative testimonies to her literary achievements begin in the classical world and continue to the present, including their difficulty for learnèd male readers: "the profundity of both her understanding and of her learnèd books can only be known and understood by men of great perception and learning, according to the testimony of the ancients and right up to today."[11] Sappho's exceptional status as a functioning canonical woman author is further emphasized both by the contemporary accessibility of her writings and by their exemplary pedagogic quality.

> Her writings and poems ["escrips et dictiez"] still survive, most remarkably constructed and composed, and they serve as illumination and models ["lumiere et exemple"] of consummate poetic craft and composition ["de parfaictement dictier et faire"] to those who have come after her. She invented different genres of lyric and poetry, short narratives, tearful laments and strange lamentations about love and other emotions, and these were so well made and so well ordered that they were named "Sapphic" after her. (67–68)

It is with a final articulation of Sappho's canonical status that the chapter closes: "thus was this lady placed and counted among the greatest and most famous poets" [si fu celle dame mise et comptee entre les grans poetes renommez] (68).

In addition to this classical female literary canon within which Christine implicitly situates (and authorizes) herself, two other exemplary ancient women play a complementary role as inventors of writing. Carmenta[12] (*Cité* 1.33), a "grant clergece" [great learnèd woman] possessed of "merveilleux engin" [marvelous intelligence] and "especiaulx dons de savoir" [exceptional gifts of knowledge], having been exiled from her native Greece to Italy,[13] proceeded to invent the Latin alphabet: "she worked and studied so hard that she invented her own letters, which were completely different from those of other nations, that is, she established the Latin alphabet and syntax, spelling, the difference between vowels and consonants, as well as a complete introduction to the science of grammar" (72). The motif of comparative superiority to corresponding male achievement (present in each of Christine's female canon members in the *Cité*) reaches a culmination with Carmenta: "one can say that nothing more worthy in the world was ever invented. . . . The Italians not only deemed this woman to be greater than any man, but considered her to be a goddess" (72). Finally, poems in Latin were named *carmen* after this lady's name: "De ceste dame Carmentis furent nommez dictiez *carmen* en latin."[14]

Minerva (*Cité* 1.34) complements Carmenta in that she was a Greek maiden taken for a goddess who remained in her native land. Again, Christine employs euhemerism to stress the literal historicity of the exemplary members of her canonical female intellectuals. Minerva "through her ingenuity ["soubtiveté"] invented a shorthand Greek script called *caracteres* in which a long written narrative could be transcribed with far fewer letters [en l'espace de bien pou de letres et de brieve escripture], and which is still used by the Greeks today, a fine invention whose discovery demanded great subtlety" (73).[15]

The second of Christine's strategies for establishing herself as a new kind of "canonical" woman writer involves her presentation of an all-female literary and writerly canon firmly situated in the temporal remoteness of the classical world. The fifteenth-century Christine is authorized by the example of this canon but remains distant from it. There are no direct links. Female gender solidarity is tempered by linguistic difference and chronological distance. In Christine's works there are no female contemporaries or near-contemporaries writing in the vernacular who figure as part of an emerging new female literary canon within which Christine situates herself.

The third strategy by which Christine presents herself as a canonical contemporary woman writer involves her attempt to establish a "genealogical" link to the line of dominant fourteenth- and fifteenth-century French poets, who are beginning to constitute (and to be perceived as) a new kind of vernacular literary canon, developing diachronically. The single most import document in which Christine engages in this kind of claim for a position in the emerging contemporary French canon is her letter to her most distinguished living poetic predecessor, Eustache Deschamps (ca. 1346–ca. 1406;

also called Morel). This is the "Epistre a Eustace Mourel,"[16] dated February 10, 1403, when Christine was writing the Dantean *Chemin de longue estude*. In this epistle, she sets up a hierarchical, genealogical relationship with Deschamps. After explicitly naming him as a distinguished poet in the salutation—"A trés expert, en scens apris, / Eustace Mourel . . . / Orateur de maint vers notable" (vv. 1–4) [To Eustache Morel, highly skilled and learnèd orator of many notable poems]—Christine addresses him twice as her *maistre* [teacher] (vv. 6, 51). She concludes the epistle by naming herself, thus effecting an onomostic frame at the same time as she casts herself as the *disciple* of the older poet:

> Escript seullette en m'estude,
> Le dixsiesme jour par estude
> De Fevrier l'An Mil quatre cens
> Et trois en deliberé scens.
>
> *Christine de Pizan*, ancelle
>
> De Science, que cest an celle
> Occuppacion tint vaillant,
> *Ta disciple* et ta bienveillant.
>
> (vv. 205–12; emphasis added)[17]

The single most important aspect of Christine's epistle to Deschamps from the perspective of her enterprise to claim canonical status for herself is the epistle's implicit participation in a series of disciple-to-master exchanges going back to a famous set of ballades addressed by Deschamps to his master, Guillaume de Machaut.[18] The two most famous of these are Deschamps's pair of lamentation ballades (123 and 124) on the death of Machaut in 1377, with the refrain "La mort Machaut le noble rethorique" [The death of Machaut, the noble rhetorician]. In these two commemorative ballades, as in ballade 447 to "dame Peronne, après la mort Machault" [Lady Peronne, after the death of Machaut], Deschamps represents himself as Machaut's "disciple," who, after the master poet's death, will step into his prestigious predecessor's position, authorized by a privileged relationship to him. Deschamps's staging of his disciple status vis-à-vis Machaut goes back at least to 1364 and ballade 127, which praises the success of Machaut's masterpiece, the *Voir-Dit,* which Deschamps presents himself as performing. In her epistle to Deschamps of 1403, Christine implicitly claims a relation to Deschamps analogous to that claimed by Deschamps to Machaut. A French, vernacular, canonical poetic genealogy is thus suggested in which Christine is the current (and, again, the uniquely female) member.

Deschamps's ballade 1242 (4.251–52) responds to Christine's epistle with a series of epithets bestowing canonical status upon her as a woman writer, while at the same time stressing her uniqueness in this regard. She does not figure as a member of a female canon, but as the only female member of a male canon, as the ballade's refrain makes clear: Christine is addressed as "seule en tes faiz ou royaume de France" [your accomplishments are unique in the kingdom of France]. Several high prestige associations deriving from Christine's *Chemin de longue estude* are redeployed by Deschamps to valorize the woman writer in canonical terms, beginning with the ballade's opening line: "Muse eloquent entre les .IX., Christine" [eloquent muse among the nine, Christine]. The biographical Christine (named in the emphatic rhyme position) is here figured as one of the Muses, whom Christine-protagonist had merely observed in *Chemin* vv. 989–96. Second, she is associated with the special vocabulary that constitutes the semantic field of the canonical author: *sens, doctrine, philosophie, sçavoir, estude, clergie* [intelligence, erudition, philosophy, knowledge, study, learning]. Third, as in *Chemin* vv. 1045–48, she is valorized by the high intellectual status of her father, the "bon maistre" Thomas de Pizan, "docteur d'astronomie." This feature, it seems to me, also serves as a gender marking: the canonical woman writer requires, as it were, an extra family credential deriving from her male parent. Fourth, Deschamps compares Christine in the envoy to the solitary exiled Boethius, that member of her "personal canon" whose presence had opened the *Chemin* (vv. 202–305)—and closed her earlier *Cent Ballades* (ballade 97).

Finally, an onomastic frame linking the two interlocutors is established in Deschamps's ballade as it had been in Christine's epistle: the ballade's first line names "*Christine*" in the vocative; the envoy opens with the speaker naming himself: "O douce suer, *je, Eustace*, te prie" (v. 31; emphasis added). At the same time, Deschamps's designation of Christine as his "sweet sister" picks up and confirms her earlier designation of him as "dear brother" (vv. 137, 163). This stylized fraternal/sororal relationship between the two writers reinforces and complements their dominant master/disciple relationship, as staged by Christine as a prolongation of that between Deschamps and Machaut.

I would like to conclude with a brief consideration of the single most important treatment of Christine as a canonical writer in the decade or so immediately following her death: Martin Le Franc's *Champion de Dames* (1440–42). Second and finally, I will consider the issue of the new vernacular canon in René d'Anjou's *Livre du Cuer d'Amours espris* (1457).

Martin Le Franc's defense of women in 24,384 verses is in part a kind of anti–*Roman de la Rose* that utilizes Christine's *Cité des Dames* as a polemical and structural model. The presence of Christine's own *Cité des Dames* is most visible in book 4 of the *Champion*, where Carmenta, Sappho, Proba, and Cornificia are treated in sequence as members of the female canon of Antiquity, before the Champion (the poem's "profeminist" protagonist) introduces as the single and illustrious example of a canonical French women writer "Dame Christine, dont la renommee est tres fresche et tres clere" [Lady Christine, whose renown is quite fresh and clear].[19] Christine is explicitly presented as the equal in learning ("de clergie tres*or*," v. 18940, rhyming with *or* = now and *or* = gold; vv. 18938, 18941) of the canonical women of Antiquity, with a fame equal to theirs: she thus extends (through a version of the *translatio studii* and as the unique example) the "national" honor of female canonicity into fifteenth-century France. The first "proof" of this status for "dame Christine" (18942) is her post mortem fame: "De laquelle a trompe et a cor / Le nom par tout va et ne fine" (18943–44) [whose name is proclaimed by trumpet and horn and is everywhere known and does not die]. Next, her various works are listed as a further demonstration and celebration. We start with two *cas limites*: on the one hand, her rhetorical prowess in the vernacular is shown by her love poems, "les beaux dictiers longs et cours / fait . . . en langage poly" (vv. 18951–52) [the beautiful poems both long and short, composed in polished language]; on the other hand, her (in fact apocryphal) Latin works are evoked in order to figure her erudition: "la vaillant Cris*tine*" shows her *vertu* [power] "en lettre et en langue la*tine*" (vv. 18954–56) [the valliant Christine . . . in Latin letters and language]; note the rhyme that suggests a semantic link between Christine's name and her Latinate learning. Finally, the binomial "ses euvres et ses dis" (v. 18958) [her learnèd books and her elegant poems] serves to summarize the totality of her *œuvre*, which will guarantee her immortality: her name will last forever ("son nom dure toudis," v. 18960).

In the stanza that immediately follows, Martin Le Franc's *Champion des Dames* explicitly presents Christine as the single female member of the vernacular French canonical line of poets that has come into being, beginning with Machaut and continuing through the early 1440s (see appendix 2 for the text and translation; see also appendix 3). In rough chronological sequence we have, first, Guillaume de Machaut (d. 1377). At the same time "Eustache Deschamps" (d. ca. 1406), though not explicitly named, is *implicitly* present through the octosyllabic evocation in v. 18963 ("La mort Machaut grand rethorique") of the decasyllabic refrain line of Deschamps's two ballades commemorating Machaut's death ("La mort Machaut le noble rethorique"). Thus Martin, in effect, cites Machaut as canonical by simultaneously (and implicitly) citing Deschamps's earlier "canonization" of Machaut. The ongoing process of the new genealogy of vernacular canonical authors is thus foregrounded as such. The second and third explicitly named canonical vernacular authors are Jean Froissart (d. after 1404) and Alain Chartier (d. 1430). Fourth comes Jean Castel (d. 1425/1476), a conflation of Christine's son (d. 1425; sole surviving work: *Le Pin*) and her grandson of the same name (fl. from 1439; d. 1476).[20] The fifth and sixth are Pierre de Nesson (d. before 1442–43) and Eustache Mercadé (d. 1440).[21]

This stanza (2371) and the following one constitute a single rhetorical figure. First Christine is implicitly inducted as the only woman member of a now established (and expanded) lineage of canonical French writers. This involves an extraordinary *amplificatio* of Christine's own earlier strategy for self-insertion into the French vernacular canon effected by means of her epistle to Deschamps and that older poet's response. Next (in *Champion* stanza 2372), Christine's unique, even superior, place within this canon is emphatically affirmed. Her "unique" status as *female* canonical writer is doubled by special links to two key classical writerly models, which provide her with a kind of supplementary prestige at the same time as they highlight her own exemplary characteristics as a writerly model in her own right, with regard both to form and to content: *eloquence and wisdom.* Quite significantly, these exemplary features derive from Christine's own self-presentations as canonical writer in various works composed and published during her lifetime. Also important is the witty concluding hendiadys used to articulate her final triumph over Jean de Meun, the canonical French poet whom Christine's polemical "feminist" self-creation most needed to suppress in order to succeed on its own newly gendered terms. Her status as a new (female-gendered) Cicero is figured by her taking the prize in eloquence that is nothing other than a witty, alternative, corrective taking of the *Rose,* which, implicitly, Jean de Meun (and his misogynistic poetics) does not win. Christine de Pizan, twelve years after her death and forty years after the *Débat sur le "Roman de la Rose"* that she had initiated, wins the rosebud ("la rose et le bouton," v. 18976) of eloquence. Martin Le Franc's *Champion des Dames* thus reads the *Rose* on Christine's polemical, negative terms, a strategy that culminates in the *Champion*'s presentation of Christine as the single—but glorious and triumphant—*female* member of the new French literary canon that she had herself earlier expanded and regendered by a strategic act of self-inclusion.

For Martin as for Christine, Jean de Meun's *Rose* functions as a negative model and point of departure—as *the* French canonical text, which must be resisted, corrected, rewritten. The *Rose* of Jean de Meun is named at least twenty-eight times in the *Champion,* always in negative, polemical terms, always as a threat to be overcome. The minor Ovid is consistently treated in the same way, linked to Jean de Meun as it had been in Christine's various works. What is "missing" from Martin's innovative version of Christine's new vernacular canon is the hybrid—that is, Franco-Italian—aspect that was so crucial to Christine's "canonical" self-presentation as "simultaneously" Italian and French.

It is in René d'Anjou's *Livre du Cuer d'Amours épris* [Book of the love-smitten heart](1457) that this bilingual aspect of Christine's new vernacular canon is extended and monumentalized. In the famous *Cimetière d'Amour* [Cemetery of love] sequence of the *Livre du Cuer*, the most prestigious space is reserved for the memorial tombs of six canonical love poets (354–69): Ovid, Guillaume de Machaut, Boccaccio, Jean de Meun, Petrarch, and Alain Chartier.[22] On the one hand, this is a linguistically hybrid canon, presented at the formal level with a carefully crafted tessellation. After the opening, "foundational" Latin *auctor* we have French-Italian-French-Italian-French. On the other hand, this is a canon of "courtly" love poets. The minor Ovid thus appears as fundamental, recalling his place in the literary genealogy at the approximate midpoint of the conjoined *Rose* text (vv. 10508–503, ed. Langlois).[23] At the same time, Jean de Meun himself is reinstated into the vernacular canon, but qua love poet—subsuming Guillaume de Lorris. Indeed, later in René's *Livre du Cuer*, the *Rose* will function—at the level of the plot—both as doctrine and as a material object: the book on which the allegorical protagonist Cuer takes his oath of loyalty to the God of Love's service (448–53). René's reinscription of this *Rose*-based, courtly poetic ideology, while allowing and valorizing the key Franco-Italian component of Christine's new vernacular canon, excludes her even more innovative gender component. It excludes Christine herself.

❧ ❧ ❧

APPENDIX ONE

Eustache Deschamps, Ballade1242 ("Réponse à une épitre de Christine de Pisan"), trans. Renate Blumenfeld-Kosinski; selectively modified.

Muse eloquent entre les .IX., Christine,	Christine, eloquent muse among the nine,
Nompareille que je saiche au jour d'ui,	beyond comparison in present times,
En sens acquis et en toute doctrine,	accomplished in wisdom and in all learning,
Tu as de Dieu science et non d'autruy;	your knowledge comes from God, not from man;
Tes epistres et livres, que je luy	your letters and great philosophical books,

En pluseurs lieux, de grant philosophie,
Et ce que tu m'as escript une fie,
Me font certain de la grant habondance
De ton sçavoir qui tousjours monteplie,
Seule en tes faiz ou royaume de France.

which I have frequently read,
and that which you have now written to me,
make me certain of the great wealth
of your knowledge which always increases,
unique through your accomplishments in the kingdom of France.

Dieu t'a donné de Salemon le signe,
Cuer ensaignant qu'il demanda de lui;
A l'estude es, ou tu ensuis la ligne
Du bon maistre Thomas, que je congnuy,
De Boulongne, Pizain, recors en suy:
Ton pere fut docteur d'astronomie;
Charles le Quint, roy, ne l'oublia mie,
Mais le manda pour sa grant souffisance,
Et tu l'ensuis es .VII. ars de clergie,
Seule en tes faiz ou royaume de France.

God has given you the sign of Salomon,
the teaching heart He required of him;
You are devoted to study, thus continuing the lineage
of good Master Thomas de Pisan of Bologna,
whom I knew. I remember his life:
your father was doctor of astronomy;
the king Charles V did not forget him,
but sent for him because of his great achievements,
and you follow his example in the Seven Liberal Arts,
unique through your accomplishments in the kingdom of France.

Ha! quelle honeur entre les femmes digne
Et les hommes! Pour aprandre a toy fuy,
Qui trop te plains de la fausse racine
Dont le fruit fait a tout le monde ennuy;
Par t'espitre le voy, que je reçuy
Benignement, dont cent foiz te mercie;
Mais plus a plain sçaras de ma partie,
Qui en tous cas te faiz obeissance,

Ah! what a worthy honor among women
and among men! I am coming to you to learn, you
who complain so much over the deceptive root
whose fruit troubles everyone. I can see it by
your letter, which I received with great joy, and
for which I thank you a hundred times.
But you will learn more about my opinions
which agree with you in all things.

Le remede de ta grief maladie,
Seule en tes faiz ou royaume de France.

May your painful malady find a remedy,
unique through your accomplishments in the kingdom of France.

O douce suer, je, Eustace, te prie,
Comme ton serf, d'estre en ta compaignie
Pour bien avoir d'estude congnoissance;
Mieulx en vaudray tous les temps de ma vie,
Car je te voy, com Boece a Pavie,
Seule en tes faiz ou royaume de France.

Oh, sweetest sister, I, Eustache, beg you to be
allowed to be in your company, as serf,
to learn about your studies.
I could spend my life on nothing better,
for I look to you as to Boethius in Pavia,
unique through your accomplishments in the kingdom of France.

APPENDIX TWO

Martin Le Franc, *Le Champion des Dames* (1440–42), ed. Robert Deschaux, trans. Kevin Brownlee.

Aux estrangiers pouons la feste vaillant
Faire de *la vaillant Cristine*
Dont la vertu est manifest
En lettre et en langue latine
Et ne debvons pas soubs courtine
Mettre ses euvres et ses dis,
Affin que se mort encourtine
Le corps son nom dure toudis.
(vv. 18953–60)

Before all foreigners we can celebrate the valiant
Christine, whose power is clear in writing and in
the Latin language. And we should not hide her
writings and her poems, so that if Death
hides her body, her name will last forever.

Froissart sçavoit bien le pratique
De bien dicter, ou ilz me mentent;
La mort *Machaut* grand rethorique
Les facteurs amoureux lamentent;
Les aultres d'*Alain* se dement
Car il a le mieulx baladé;
Aultres pour *Castel* se desmentent,

Froissart well understood the techniques of
composing poetry, unless people have lied to
me; the death of the great rhetorician Machaut
caused love poets to lament; others grieve over
Alain, because they think he composed the best
ballades; others regret Castel,

Pour *Nesson* et pour *Mercadé*. (vv. 18961–68; emphasis added)	Nesson and Mercadé.
De baladans et de rimans, D'ungs et d'aultres parler peut on, Le langage amoureux limans Et polissans comme letton. Mais elle fut Tulle et Cathon: Tulle, car en toute eloquence Elle eust la rose et le bouton, Cathon aussy en sapience. (vv. 18969–76)	People can speak of how one poet or another makes ballades or rhymes, refining the language of love, polishing it highly. But she [=Christine] was a Cicero and a Cato. A Cicero, because she won the rose and the bud of all eloquence; a Cato as well, in wisdom.

APPENDIX THREE

Chronology of Works Cited (in terms of representations of the "new vernacular canon")

1. Christine de Pizan (1364–ca. 1429): "Epistre a Eustace Mourel," dated February 10, 1403.
2. Eustache Deschamps (ca. 1346–1406/7):
   (a) "Muse eloquent entre les .IX., Christine," written in 1403 (Ballade 1242: "Réponse à une épitre de Christine de Pisan"; refrain: "Seule en tes faiz ou royaume de France").
   (b) The two ballades on the death of Guillaume de Machaut (ca. 1300–1377), dated 1377: "Armes, Amours, Dames, Chevalerie"; refrain: "La mort Machaut le noble rethorique" (Ballade 123 [1:243–44], *Balade pour Machautt*, "Sur la mort de Guillaume de Machaut," 1377); "O fleur des fleurs de toute melodie"; refrain: "La mort Machaut, le noble rethorique" (Ballade 124 [1:245–46], *Autre Balade*, "Sur le même sujet avec les mêmes rimes").
   (c) Other relevant Machaut ballades by or about Deschamps: 127 (1:248–49), dated 1364, "A Guillaume de Machaut sur le *Voir Dit*"; 1372 (5:53–54), addressed to Deschamps by an unnamed poet who claims that after the death of Machaut and Philippe de Vitry (ca.1290–1361), no one other than Eustache Deschamps is "si grant faiseur ne si grant poete" (refrain); 447 "A dame Péronne, après la mort de Machault." See also 2:202; 3:259; 8:43, 178.
3. Christine de Pizan: *Le Livre de la Cité des Dames* (1405): part 1, chapters 28 (Cornificia), 29 (Proba), 30 (Sappho), 33 (Carmenta), and 34 (Minerva).
4. Martin Le Franc (ca. 1410–61): *Le Champion des Dames* (written 1440–42):
   (a) Book 4, part 6 (vv. 18201–19624), esp. vv. 18890–992, the chapter where the Champion "parle de dame Cristine dont la renommee est tres fresche et tres clere." Christine is presented as the new, female Cicero and Cato in a vernacular canon that also involves Jehan Froissart, ca. 1337–after 1404 (see also v.

12121); Machaut (see also vv. 6918, 12738, 12840); Deschamps (through an evocation of the refrains from his ballades 123 and 124); Alain Chartier, ca. 1390–1430 (see also vv. 12586: "lise souvent le *Breviaire* / Du doulx poete Alain Chartier"); Jean Castel, a conflation of Christine's son (ca.1385– ca.1425; only surviving text: *Le Pin*) and grandson (d. 1476; chronicler of France; author of the moral-spiritual *Specule des pecheurs* [1468]) of the same name; Pierre de Nesson, 1383–before 1442 (his major works include *Lai de Guerre* [ca. 1424]; *Vigiles des Morts*; and *Oraison à Notre Dame*); Eustache Mercadé, ca.1390–1440 (his major works include *Mystère de la Vengeance de Notre Seigneur* and *Mystère de la Passion d'Arras?*).

(b) Other vernacular authors or works mentioned in the *Champion* as "canonical" include the following:

(1) Jean de Meun (d. ca. 1305?) is mentioned by name twenty-two times, virtually always negatively (see Deschaux's index), while [Jean] Clopinel (an alternate name for Jean de Meun) is mentioned negatively six times (see Deschaux's index). The *Rose*'s first author, Guillaume de Lorris (fl. 1225–30), is mentioned in v. 11762.

(2) Charles d'Orléans (1394–1465) is mentioned four times, positively.

(3) Oton de Grandson (ca. 1345–97), v. 14126.

(4) Dante (1265–1321), v. 1409 ("Le florentin poete Dante")

(5) Boccaccio (1313–75) is treated as an authority by the Champion in v. 10864 in his argument with the Adversaire in favor of exculpating Cleopatra: "Je voy le point a toy mater / A l'ayde de Jehan Bocasse."

5. René d'Anjou (1409–80): *Le Livre du cuer d'amours épris* (1457). A culmination of the hybrid vernacular canon is represented by the memorial tombs of six canonical poets in the Cemetery of Love (ed. Bouchet 354–69): Ovid; Guillaume de Machaut; Boccaccio, Jean de Meun; Petrarch (1304–74); and Alain Chartier. Christine is not present. Nor are the aristocratic poets René d'Anjou and Charles d'Orléans, who have their tombs among the "canonical" lovers (rather than love poets), from antiquity to the contemporary Anglo-Italo-French courtly world.

6. *Instructif de seconde rhétorique*, Renaud Le Queux? (ca. 1480). The chapter entitled "De tredecimo colore rethorice, de servantaisio" gives a list of exemplary French authors in what amounts to a vernacular canon: Alain Chartier; Arnoul Greban (ca. 1425–ca 1495); Christine de Pizan and her son Jean Castel; Pierre de Hurion and (Jean?) Vaillant (two poets from the circle of René d'Anjou); and Georges Chastellain (1405–75), great poet and official chronicler (*indiciare*) of the court of Burgundy.

NOTES

1. See Charity Cannon Willard, *Christine de Pizan: Her Life and Works* (New York: Persea, 1984), esp. 155–71; James C. Laidlaw, "Christine de Pizan: An Author's Progress," *Modern Language Review* 78 (1983): 532–50; James C. Laidlaw, "Christine de Pizan: A Publisher's Progress," *Modern Language Review* 82 (1987): 35–75; and Daniel Poirion, *Le Poète et le prince: l'évolution du lyrisme courtois de Guillaume de Machaut à Charles d'Orléans* (Paris: PUF, 1965), 237–59.

2. For Christine's life in the context of her literary production, see Charity Cannon

Willard, *Christine de Pizan;* and Daniel Poirion, *Le Poète et le prince.* See also *The Selected Writings of Christine de Pizan: A Norton Critical Edition*, ed. Renate Blumenfeld-Kosinski, trans. Renate Blumenfeld-Kosinski and Kevin Brownlee (New York: Norton, 1997); and *The Writings of Christine de Pizan*, selected and ed. Charity Cannon Willard (New York: Persea, 1994). For a good sense of recent scholarship on Christine, see the following collections of essays: Margarete Zimmermann and Dina De Rentiis, eds., *The City of Scholars: New Approaches to Christine de Pizan* (Berlin and New York: de Gruyter, 1994); Liliane Dulac and Bernard Ribémont, eds., *Une Femme de Lettres au Moyen Age: Études autour de Christine de Pizan* (Orléans: Paradigme, 1995); Marilynn Desmond, ed., *Christine de Pizan and the Categories of Difference* (Minneapolis: University of Minnesota Press, 1998); and Eric Hicks, ed., *Au champ des escriptures* (Paris: Champion, 2000). For Christine's last work, see Angus J. Kennedy and Kenneth Varty, eds. and trans., *Ditié de Jehanne d'Arc* (Oxford: Medium Aevum, 1977), and Renate Blumenfeld-Kosinski's translation, "The Tale of Joan of Arc," in *The Selected Writings of Christine de Pizan: A Norton Critical Edition*, ed. R. Blumenfeld-Kosinski, 252–62.

3. Within the text of the present essay, these works will be referred to by their French titles. All citations from and references to them are from the following editions. *Le Débat sur le «Roman de la Rose»*, ed. Eric Hicks (Paris: Champion, 1977); *Le Chemin de longue étude*, ed. and trans. Andrea Tarnowski (Paris: Livre de Poche, 2000); *Le Livre de la mutacion de Fortune*, ed. Suzanne Solente, 4 vols., (Paris: Picard, 1959–66); *La Cité des Dames*, ed. Earl Jeffrey Richards in *La Città delle Dame*, a cura di Patrizia Caraffi (Milan: Luni, 1997); *Le Livre des Trois Vertus*, ed. Charity Cannon Willard and Eric Hicks (Paris: Champion, 1989); *Le Livre de l'advision Christine*, ed. Christine Reno and Liliane Dulac (Paris: Champion, 2001). Complete English translations of these works of Christine may be found in *"La Querelle de la Rose": Letters and Documents*, trans. Joseph L. Baird and John R. Kane (Chapel Hill: North Carolina Studies in the Romance Languages and Literatures, 1978); *The Book of the City of Ladies*, trans. Earl Jeffrey Richards (New York: Persea, 1982; rev. ed. 1998); *The Treasure of the City of Ladies or The Book of the Three Virtues*, trans. Sarah Lawson (Harmondsworth, England: Penguin, 1985); *Christine's Vision*, trans. Glenda McLeod (New York: Garland, 1993). For English translations of the key autobiographical passages from *The Path of Long Study* and *The Book of Fortune's Transformation* (as well as from *The Book of the City of Ladies*, *The Book of the Three Virtues*, and *Christine's Vision*), see *The Selected Writings of Christine de Pizan: A Norton Critical Edition*, ed. Renate Blumenfeld-Kosinski, trans. Renate Blumenfeld-Kosinski and Kevin Brownlee. While all citations to the *Cité* in the present essay come from Richards's edition, I have also profited from Maureen C. Curnow, ed., "The Livre de la Cité des Dames' of Christine de Pizan: A Critical Edition," 2 vols. (Ph.D. diss., Vanderbilt University, 1975). The *Cité* is cited from Richard's edition of the French text by book and chapter numbers (e.g., 1.28); English translations of the *Cité* are indicated by page number from Richards, with selective emendations.

4. The *Romance of the Rose*, the single most widely disseminated vernacular work in the French Middle Ages, was written by two different authors: Guillaume de Lorris completed the first, "courtly" part (ca. 4,000 lines) roughly between 1225 and 1230; Jean de Meun composed his "clerkly" continuation and completion of the *Rose* (ca. 17,000 lines) between ca. 1269 and ca. 1278. Virtually from the moment it was finished by Jean de Meun, the *Rose* became *the* canonical vernacular French literary work par excellence, dominating the French literary scene for over two centuries. The

Debate on the *Romance of the Rose* (1401–3) pitted the work's supporters (a group of Parisian intellectuals led by Jean de Montreuil, provost of Lille; Pierre Col, canon of Paris and Tournay; and his brother, Gontier Col, secretary to the king) against Christine de Pizan and her key ally, Jean Gerson (the celebrated chancellor of the University of Paris), who condemned the *Rose* on moral as well as literary grounds. In her dossier of the *Debate*, Christine presents herself as making a book out of the public dispute, a book of which she is the "author." The reference editions of the *Rose* for this essay are Guillaume de Lorris and Jean de Meun, *Le Roman de la Rose*, ed. Ernest Langlois, 5 vols. (Paris: Picard, 1914–24); and *Le Roman de la Rose*, ed. Félix Lecoy, 3 vols. (Paris: Champion, 1965–75). A good English translation is *The Romance of the Rose*, trans. Charles Dahlberg (Princeton: Princeton University Press, 1971).

5. See Kevin Brownlee, "Le moi «lyrique» et la généalogie littéraire: Christine de Pizan et Dante," in *«Musique naturele»: Interpretationen zur französische Lyrik des Spätmittellalters*, ed. Wolf-Dieter Stemple (München: Fink, 1995), 105–39.

6. See Nadia Margolis, "Christine de Pizan: The Poetess as Historian," *Journal of the History of Ideas* 47 (1986): 361–75; Kevin Brownlee, "Ovide et le moi poétique «moderne» à la fin du moyen âge: Jean Froissart et Christine de Pizan," in *Modernité au moyen âge: Le défi du passé*, ed. Brigitte Cazelles and Charles Méla (Genève: Droz, 1990), 153–73; and Renate Blumenfeld-Kosinski, "Christine de Pizan and Classical Mythology: Some Examples from the *Mutacion de Fortune*," in *The City of Scholars*, ed. Zimmermann and De Rentiis, 3–14.

7. See Kevin Brownlee, "Widowhood, Sexuality, and Gender in Christine de Pizan," *Romanic Review* 85 (1995): 341–55. Boethius's (ca. 480–524) masterpiece, *The Consolation of Philosophy*, was written in 524 during his incarceration in Pavia by the Ostrogothic king Theodoric (493–526) on trumped up charges of treason. The work is an extended dialogue between the first-person protagonist and Lady Philosophy, a personification allegory who instructs her initially naive charge in true philosophical wisdom.

8. See David Wallace, "Chaucer's Inheritance: The Early Poems and *Troilus and Criseyde*," in *The Cambridge Chaucer Companion*, ed. Piero Boitani and Jill Mann (Cambridge: Cambridge University Press, 1986), 19–37. See esp. 29–30, where Wallace discusses the "sixth of six topos" in terms of personal canons in which the present writer figures as the final member: Jean de Meun's *Rose* vv. 10477–644 (ed. Lecoy); Dante's *Inferno* 4.80–102; Boccaccio's *Filocolo* 5.97.4–6; Chaucer's *Troilus* 5.1786–92. Canon formation is here used polemically to raise the vernacular writer to canonical status, in each case a base of classical *auctores* to which are added one or two vernacular writers in a single vernacular language.

9. See Kevin Brownlee, "Il *Decameron* di Boccaccio e la *Cité des Dames* di Christine de Pizan: Modelli e contro-modelli," in *Boccaccio 1990: The Poet and His Renaissance Reception*, ed. Kevin Brownlee and Victoria Kirkham, *Studi sul Boccaccio* 20 (1991–92): 233–51.

10. *Cité*, trans. Richards, 66. In her fine English translation of Boccaccio's *De mulieribus claris*, *Famous Women* (Cambridge, Mass.: Harvard University Press, 2001), Virginia Brown emphasizes two key points made by Vittorio Zaccaria (546) in his authoritative edition (with Italian translation) of Boccaccio's Latin text (Milan: Mondadori, 1967; 2d ed. 1970): (1) the text of Proba's *Cento* as it appears in the *Patrologia latina* (vol. 19) and the *Corpus scriptorum ecclesiasticorum latinorum* (vol. 16.1) ends at the feast of the Ascension, not on Pentecost Sunday, as Boccaccio had claimed; and (2) the existence of a second, Homeric *Cento* by Proba appears doubtful (500).

11. *Cité*, trans. Richards, 67: "La parfondeur de son entendement et les livres qu'elle fist de si profondes sciences [are such] que les sentences en sont fortes a savoir et entendre meismes aux hommes de grand engin et estudes, selon le tesmoing des anciens et jusques aujourd'huy" (*Cité*, ed. Richards, 160).

12. See Jacqueline Cerquiglini-Toulet, "Cadmus ou Carmenta: Réflexion sur le concept d'invention à la fin du moyen âge," in *What Is Literature? 1100–1600*, ed. Douglas Kelly and Ulrich Langer (Lexington, Ky.: French Forum, 1993): 211–30.

13. This embodiment of the *translatio studii* topos is highly relevant to Christine's self-empowering conception (and portrayal) of her own life as involving her *translatio* from Italy to France.

14. "Tant fist et tant estudia que elle trouva propres letres, du tout differenciees des autres nacions, c'est assavoir l'a.b.c. et l'ordenance du latin, l'assemblee d'icelles, et la difference des voyeux et des muets et toute l'entrée de la science de grammaire. . . . On peut dire que oncques chose plus digne ne fut trouvee au monde . . . les Ytaliens . . . ne reputerent mie seulement ceste femme plus que homme, mais deesse" (168). Curnow notes that Carmenta's invention of the Latin alphabet is itself an invention of Christine, found in none of her sources.

15. Curnow (1072) notes that Minerva as inventor of Greek writing is also an invention of Christine, not found in her sources—thus stressing the parallel with Carmenta for Latin.

16. See Lori Walters, "Fathers and Daughters: Christine de Pizan as Reader of the Male Tradition of *Clergie* in the *Dit de la Rose*," in *Reinterpreting Christine de Pizan*, ed. Earl Jeffrey Richards (Athens: University of Georgia Press, 1992), 63–76, esp., 64–70 on the Machaut/Deschamps–Deschamps/Pizan parallel link. See also E. Jeffrey Richards, "The Lady Wants to Talk: Christine de Pizan's *Epistre a Eustace Morel*," in *Eustache Deschamps, French Courtier-Poet: His Work and His World*, ed. Deborah M. Sinnreich-Levi (New York: AMS, 1984), 109–22 and Nadia Margolis, "'The Cry of the Chameleon': Evolving Voices in the Epistles of Christine de Pizan," *Disputatio* 1 (1996): 37–70. Citations are from Eustache Deschamps, *Œuvres complètes*, 11 vols., ed. Marquis de Queux de Saint-Hilaire and Guy Raynaud (Paris: Didot, 1878–1903). Translations are mine unless otherwise noted.

17. "Written all alone in my study on the tenth day of February of the year one thousand four hundred and three, out of my learning and in carefully considered terms. [Signed,] Christine de Pizan, the handmaiden of Learning, who stoutly holds to this calling, your disciple and your well-wisher." Text from Maurice Roy, ed., *Œuvres poétiques de Christine de Pisan*, vol. 2 (Paris: Didot, 1891).

18. For these ballades, see the magisterial article by Jean-Claude Mülethaler, "Un poète et son art face à la posterité: Lecture des deux ballades de Deschamps pour la mort de Machaut," *Studi Francesi* 99 (1989): 387–410. In addition to analyzing the entire Deschamps/Machaut relationship, Mülethaler's study treats the broader question of vernacular literary authority in fourteenth- and fifteenth-century France.

19. All citations of the *Champion des Dames* are from the recent five-volume edition by Robert Deschaux, the first modern edition of the complete text (Paris: Champion, 1999). The citation here indicated is the rubric introducing section six of book 4 (4:176).

20. This seems analogous to Deschamps's earlier evocation of Christine's prestigious father as somehow essential to his valorization of Christine herself as writer in his ballade. What appears to be at issue here is the necessity felt by male fifteenth-century supporters of Christine qua woman writer to supplement her status by evoking her male

blood relatives as a kind of required final authorization for her. This female gender marking in the context of vernacular canonicity simultaneously reconfirms Christine's status as an exemplary female role model with regard to the family: in Deschamps's ballade her role as *daughter* is foregrounded; in Martin's *Champion,* her role as *mother* is foregrounded. Is this a kind of *apologia* for Christine's unique status? A way of neutralizing anticipated criticism of her as a woman writer? The presentation of Christine-writer as Christine-mother will occur again in the *Instructif de seconde rhétorique* (ca. 1480, an anonymous rhetorical treatise that was widely disseminated; see appendix 3), where she is named as the only woman on the list of exemplary French writers but explicitly linked to her son Jean Castel, who is accorded the same canonical status. They here form a privileged pair, a binomial—analogous, however, to the pair of named male writers that follows them in the list. But compare also what can be seen as the construct of misogynist denigration of Christine as writer through assigning her works to her son qua male writer by the Adversaire in the *Champion des Dames* (vv. 18977–84). This is analogous to an a priori denial of the very possibility of a canonical woman writer.

21. It is interesting to note that in terms of direct naming—since Deschamps is evoked rather than explicitly identified—there are six vernacular writers named here, a "canonical" number, as David Wallace has shown (see note 8). In a (perhaps self-conscious) variation on what Wallace has identified as the "sixth of six" topos, Christine would here be number seven, a privileged numerological position with important Christian poetic overtones. See Victoria Kirkham, "Reckoning with Boccaccio's *Questioni d'Amore,*" *Modern Language Notes* 89 (1974): 51–53; and Charles S. Singleton, "The Poet's Number at the Center," *Modern Language Notes* 80 (1965):1–10.

22. References are to the excellent new edition with modern French translation by Florence Bouchet, *Le Livre du Coeur d'amour épris* (Paris: Livre de Poche, 2003), based on the Paris ms., B.N. Fr. 24399. See also *The Book of the Love-Smitten Heart (Le Livre du Cuers d'Amour Espris)*, ed. with English translation by Stephanie Viereck Gibbs and Kathryn Karczewska (New York and London: Routledge, 2001), based on the Vienna ms., Österreichische National Bibliothek, Codex Vindobonensis 2597.

23. It is significant to note Jean de Meun's use in this passage of *Amores* 3.9, the lament on the death of Tibullus, in which Ovid invites Gallus and Catullus to welcome Tibullus's shade to the underworld. A Latin canon of lyric poets culminating in Ovid is already present in Jean's Ovidian model text. Also relevant is Guillaume de Lorris's opening self-presentation as a new Ovid by characterizing his French vernacular work as "the Romance of the Rose in which the Art of Love is entirely enclosed" [li Romanz de la Rose, / Ou l'Art d'Amors est toute enclose] (vv. 37–38), thus conflating it with the Ovidian *Ars amatoria*.

BIBLIOGRAPHY

Primary References

Boccaccio, Giovanni. *Famous Women*. Ed. and trans. Virginia Brown. Cambridge, Mass.: Harvard University Press, 2001.

Deschamps, Eustache. *Œuvres complètes*. Ed. Marquis de Queux de Saint-Hilaire and Guy Raynaud. 11 vols. Paris: Didot, 1878–1903.

Le Franc, Martin. *Le Champion des Dames*. Ed. Robert Deschaux. 5 vols. Paris: Champion, 1999.

Guillaume de Lorris and Jean de Meun. *Le Roman de la Rose*. Ed. Ernest Langlois. 5 vols. Paris: Didot, 1914–24.

———. *Le Roman de la Rose*. Ed. Félix Lecoy. 3 vols. Paris: Champion, 1965–75.

———. *The Romance of the Rose*. Trans. Charles Dahlberg. Princeton: Princeton University Press, 1971.

Pizan, Christine de. *The Book of the City of Ladies*. Trans. E. Jeffrey Richards. New York: Persea, 1982; rev. ed. 1998.

———. *Le Chemin de longue étude*. Ed. and trans. Andrea Tarnowski. Paris: Livre de Poche, 2000.

———. *Christine's Vision*. Trans. Glenda McLeod. New York: Garland, 1993.

———. *Le Débat sur le «Roman de la Rose»*. Ed. Eric Hicks. Paris: Champion, 1977.

———. *Ditié de Jehanne d'Arc*. Ed. and trans. Angus J. Kennedy and Kenneth Varty. Oxford: Medium Aevum, 1977.

———. *Le Livre de L'Advision Cristine*. Ed. Christine Reno and Liliane Dulac. Paris: Champion, 2000.

———. "The 'Livre de la Cité des Dames' of Christine de Pizan: A Critical Edition." Ed. Maureen C. Curnow. 2 vols. Ph.D. diss., Vanderbilt University, 1975.

———. *Le Livre de la Cité des Dames*. Ed. E. Jeffrey Richards in *La Città delle Dame*, ed. Patrizia Caraffi. Milan: Luni, 1997.

———. *Le Livre de la mutacion de Fortune*. 4 vols. Ed. Suzanne Solente. Paris: Picard, 1959–66.

———. *Le Livre des Trois Vertus*. Ed. Charity Cannon Willard and Eric Hicks. Paris: Champion, 1989.

———. *Œuvres poétiques de Christine de Pisan*. 3 vols. Ed. Maurice Roy. Paris: Didot, 1886–96.

———. *"La Querelle de la Rose": Letters and Documents*. Trans. Joseph L. Baird and John R. Kane. Chapel Hill: North Carolina Studies in the Romance Languages and Literatures, 1978.

———. *The Selected Writings of Christine de Pizan: A Norton Critical Edition*. Ed. Renate Blumenfeld-Kosinski. Trans. Renate Blumenfeld-Kosinski and Kevin Brownlee. New York: Norton, 1997.

———. *The Treasure of the City of Ladies or The Book of the Three Virtues*. Trans. Sarah Lawson. Harmondsworth, England: Penguin, 1985.

———. *The Writings of Christine de Pizan*. Selected and ed. Charity Cannon Willard. New York: Persea, 1994.

René d'Anjou. *Le Livre du Cuer d'amours espris*. Ed. Florence Bouchet. Paris: Livre de Poche, 2003.

———. *The Book of the Love-Smitten Heart (Le Livre du Cuers d'Amours Espris)*. Ed. and trans. Stephanie Viereck Gibbs and Kathryn Karczewska. New York and London: Routledge, 2001.

Secondary References

Blumenfield-Kosinski, Renate. "Christine de Pizan and Classical Mythology: Some Examples from the *Mutacion de Fortune*." In *The City of Scholars: New Approaches to Christine de Pizan*, ed. Margarete Zimmerman and Dina De Rentiis, 3–14. Berlin: De Gruyter, 1994.

Brownlee, Kevin. "Ovide et le moi poétique «moderne» à la fin du moyen âge: Jean Froissart et Christine de Pizan." In *Modernité au moyen âge: Le défi du passé*, ed. Brigitte Cazelles and Charles Méla, 153–73. Genève: Droz, 1990.

———. "Il *Decameron* di Boccaccio e la *Cité des Dames* di Christine de Pizan: Modelli e contro-modelli." In *Boccaccio 1990: The Poet and His Renaissance Reception*, ed. Kevin Brownlee and Victoria Kirkham, *Studi sul Boccaccio* 20 (1991–92): 233–51.

———. "Le moi «lyrique» et la généalogie littéraire: Christine de Pizan et Dante." In *«Musique naturele»: Interpretationen zur französische Lyrik des Spätmittelalters*, ed. Wolf-Dieter Stempel, 105–39. München: Wilhelm Fink-Verlag, 1995.

———. "Rewriting Romance: Courtly Discourse and Auto-Citation in Christine de Pizan." In *Gender and Text in the Middle Ages*, ed. Jane Chance, 172–94. Gainesville: University of Florida Press, 1995.

———. "Widowhood, Sexuality, and Gender in Christine de Pizan." *Romanic Review* 85 (1995): 341–55.

———. "Le projet «autobiographique» de Christine de Pizan: Histoires et fables du moi." In *Au Champ des escriptures*, ed. Eric Hicks et al., 5–24. Paris: Champion, 2000.

Cerquiglini-Toulet, Jacqueline. "Cadmus ou Carmenta: Réflexion sur le concept d'invention à la fin du moyen âge." In *What Is Literature? 1100–1600*, ed. Douglas Kelly and Ulrich Langer, 211–30. Lexington, Ky.: French Forum, 1993.

Desmond, Marilynn, ed. *Christine de Pizan and the Categories of Difference*. Minneapolis: University of Minnesota Press, 1998.

Dulac, Liliane, and Bernard Ribément, eds. *Une Femme de Lettres au Moyen Age: Études autour de Christine de Pizan*. Orléans: Paradigme, 1995.

Hicks, Eric, ed., *Au champ des escriptures*. Paris: Champion, 2000.

Kirkham, Victoria. "Reckoning with Boccaccio's *Questioni d'Amore*." *Modern Language Notes* 89 (1974): 47–59.

Laidlaw, James C. "Christine de Pizan: An Author's Progress." *Modern Language Review* 78 (1983): 532–50.

———. "Christine de Pizan: A Publisher's Progress." *Modern Language Review* 82 (1987): 35–75.

Margolis, Nadia. "Christine de Pizan: The Poetess as Historian." *Journal of the History of Ideas* 47 (1986): 361–75.

———. "'The Cry of the Chameleon': Evolving Voices in the Epistles of Christine de Pizan," *Disputatio* 1 (1996): 37–70.

Mühlethaler, Jean-Claude. "Un poète et son art face à la posterité: Lecture des deux ballades de Deschamps pour la mort de Machaut." *Studi Francesi* 99 (1989): 387–410.

Poirion, Daniel. *Le Poète et le prince: L'évolution du lyrisme courtois de Guillaume de Machaut à Charles d'Orléans*. Paris: PUF, 1965.

Richards, E. Jeffrey. "The Lady Wants to Talk: Christine de Pizan's *Epistre a Eustace Mourel*." In *Eustache Deschamps. French Courtier-Poet: His Work and His World*, ed. Deborah M. Sinnreich-Levi, 109–22. New York: AMS, 1984.

Singleton, Charles S. "The Poet's Number at the Center." *Modern Language Notes* 80 (1965):1–10.

Wallace, David. "Chaucer's Inheritance: The Early Poems and *Troilus and Criseyde*." In *The Cambridge Chaucer Companion*, ed. Piero Boitani and Jill Mann, 19–37. Cambridge: Cambridge University Press, 1986.

Walters, Lori. "Fathers and Daughters: Christine de Pizan as Reader of the Male Tradition of *Clergie* in the *Dit de la Rose*." In *Reinterpretating Christine de Pizan*, ed. E. Jeffrey Richards et al., 63–76. Athens: University of Georgia Press, 1992.

Willard, Charity Cannon. *Christine de Pizan: Her Life and Works*. New York: Persea, 1984.

Zimmermann, Margarete, and Dina De Rentiis, eds., *The City of Scholars: New Approaches to Christine de Pizan*. Berlin: De Gruyter, 1994.

Women Writers in Renaissance Italy

COURTLY ORIGINS OF NEW LITERARY CANONS

Fabio Finotti

Writing women, who flourished in Italy by the 1550s, had already emerged as a phenomenon a half century earlier, attested in the works of such authors as Vincenzo Calmeta, Pietro Bembo, Baldassare Castiglione, and Matteo Bandello. The stage on which women made their entry into public literary life was the Italian court, where a taste for spectacle encouraged them to display their wit, first as connoisseurs, then as creators of poetry. Women's move from the performance of male-authored poetry to the production of their own verse was facilitated by Neoplatonic idealization of "poetic passion," born in the soul. The notion that lyric could spring from such inner inspiration freed women, many of whom did not have an education in the classics, to write in the vernacular. Developing Petrarchism in their own directions, they practiced a "rhetoric of the truth," featuring a new style at once melancholy and sensual. Tullia d'Aragona, Gaspara Stampa, and Veronica Franco were among the women who invented a new poetic voice that would prove fundamental to the psychology and rhetoric of such later major writers as Torquato Tasso.

Between the end of the fifteenth century and the beginning of the sixteenth, the bourgeois, domestic model of womanhood that Leon Battista Alberti had outlined in his treatise *On the Family* yields to a new image, shaped in the Italian court.[1] Not just a place of social life, Renaissance courts were above all a theater. Count Baldassare Castiglione's *Book of the Courtier* (1528) clarifies that at court success is not a matter of being or knowing but of being able to represent what one is and what one knows. Even military activity becomes a performance.

> [W]henever the Courtier chances to be engaged in a skirmish or an action or a battle in the field, or the like, he should discreetly withdraw from the crowds, and do the outstanding and daring things that he has to do in as small a company as possible and in the sight of all the noblest and most respected men in the army, and especially in the presence of and, if possible, before the very eyes of his king or the prince he is serving; for it is well indeed to make all one can of things well done.[2]

The good courtier is not just a person but a "persona." He must capture attention. He must exploit the rhetoric of gesture and word to transform the other courtiers into spectators. His life becomes art, and he must have the capacity to arouse interest, approval, and admiration.

In these courts women acquire a new freedom. To be sure, it is not a process without difficulties. In the dedications to prominent court personalities that precede his *Novelle*, Matteo Bandello (1485–1561) evokes jealous husbands, unable to accept the worldly ways of their learned wives who have become accustomed to participating in a gallant and sparkling social life. Women, too, are now protagonists in the court "theater." If one essential aspect of this social refined scene is literary competence, then the true court lady does not limit herself to consuming poetry, stories, and moral discussions.[3] She will want to translate her own personal culture into a character and play the part of the learned woman who calls poets to her feet, who inspires their works, and, above all, who transforms herself into an actress capable of staging poetry. Isabella d'Este Gonzaga in her court at Mantua does not limit herself simply to collecting manuscripts and gathering around her men of letters. She recites and sings the new lyrics of Petrarch's sixteenth-century heir, Pietro Bembo.[4]

Between the fifteenth and sixteenth centuries, the shift from poetry in Latin to poetry in the vernacular is spurred by a more and more active female world with increasing influence on the direction of culture. The splendid, pictorial interpretation of Petrarch's *Canzoniere* and *Trionfi* in the Querini incunabulum now at Brescia is most probably undertaken for Beatrice d'Este.[5] To this same lady Gasparo Visconti dedicates a Petrarchesque collection of lyrics preserved in a Milanese codex made of the most precious materials, pages of parchment dyed purple and inked in silver and gold.[6] Vincenzo Calmeta (1460–1508), a historian and poet who wrote a treatise on questions of vernacular style, offers his commentary on the *Canzoniere* to Isabella d'Este.[7] In growing measure, the courtly Renaissance recognizes women as the staid bastions of its civility. Calmeta devotes the first eleven books of his chronicles to the gloomy shadow of arms, looting, battles, and the betrayal of contemporary Italy. The last book, however, is dedicated to a collection of the most famous ladies of the time, women in whose name civilization seems to defend and vindicate itself.[8] Castiglione's *Courtier* will likewise turn in its final pages to the ideal lady of court.

Although the twentieth-century Italian literary critic Carlo Dionisotti believed that women writers didn't become a phenomenon until after 1530,[9] Calmeta reveals how much women had already become protagonists of literary life beginning as early as the turn of the century. On the daily stage of their theatrical courts, ladies give rise to the figure of the *precieuse*, as Calmeta ironically depicts it. In his chapter "On Ostentation," he observes that now even ladies of "dull" intelligence exhibit literary taste, that "to flaunt their ability to enjoy and judge literature, they dedicate their attention to every jotting and defend some *true, true poets* that only they know."[10]

Here, too, on a more elevated level of intelligence and beauty, we find the charming Giulia Farnese and Cecilia Gallerani, the former favored by Pope Alexander VI and the latter by Ludovico il Moro, duke of Milan.[11] Calmeta depicts Giulia Farnese as she attracts and "caresses" poets in order to win the social prestige that comes from their fame. For Cecilia Gallerani, literature becomes a daily study and exercise that permits her to judge poetry in public. This is one more decisive step toward the achievement and display of complete competence that culminates in the court lady's step up from the performance of literature to its production. The dedicatory letters that Bandello writes for each of the short stories in his *Novelle* will offer several examples of this phenomenon.

Two dominant features of early-sixteenth-century rhetoric permit the woman of letters to mature into the woman writer. First, Platonic culture insists on a *poetic enthusiasm* that is borne of a "divine rapture" of the soul.[12] Even those who do not have a thorough knowledge of ancient literature are authorized to become creators of poetry, given that the performances as inspired poets count for more than any classical reference. Many dilettantes, women included, acquire the right to declaim their vernacular lyrics, even without the erudition required by former humanists in the fifteenth century. Attesting to lively interest in the subject at court, Calmeta writes:

> we recalled the case of some intellects endowed with passion and poetic vein who, without being learned, expressed in their verses wonderful things worthy of praise. And so as the discussion continued, someone asked me if a vernacular poet could achieve some degree of perfection without a knowledge of Latin literature. To this question I replied thusly, "The ancient philosophers, in particular Pythagoras, Plato, and Aristotle, believed that poetry is a divine passion infused in the mind, and that the poet has much in common with the prophet. . . . For this reason, and by this authority, it could almost be affirmed that a vernacular poet can attain some part of perfection in the poetic profession, as long as he is endowed by nature with a poetic vein and is moved by divine passion."[13]

Second, if the court itself is performance, the tendency to crystallize behavior as a rite and to codify manners is balanced by an impulse to break with tradition through variety and originality, singularity and astonishment. In a theater of reasoning that up until then had been the male domain, feminine conquest of the word is a novelty that gives rise to an almost histrionic taste for representing the new *woman of wit.* Calmeta writes:

> There are some other women who may have wit. But if they are called upon to talk about something, first they arrange their mouth in the mirror and make gestures with their eyes and shoulders, just to suggest to you that they want to say something important or original. They are also so pleased with their talk that they stretch it out to the point of leaving you more annoyed by their prolixity than admiring of their ingenuity.[14]

On this horizon the so-called universal woman makes her appearance. She is amazing for her capacity to practice activities reserved until then for men, not only writing but also arms. Her sharp dagger will shine during the course of the Renaissance through the many poetic images of women warriors, from Pulci to Ariosto, from Tasso to Veronica Franco.[15] The background is always court society with its taste for exhibition and stagy protagonism.

> [W]omen even more than men stumble into this ostentation, this silly vanity. . . . Today in Milan there is a very beautiful young woman, born of noble parents and married into an illustrious household, named Bianca Lucia. She has many praiseworthy attributes, each of which alone would make any other woman seem special. She can play

> any instrument, knows all types of song, is affable with everyone, chaste and unfailingly faithful to her husband. Some admirers, however, have made her head swollen, convincing her that she is the most universal woman in the world. Prompted by this vain arrogance, she has taken up fencing, dancing the galliard, wearing a dagger at her side and a cloak like the bravoes . . . inebriated by the silly idea of being the world's leading lady.[16]

Calmeta finds the same ostentation in the behavior of many women who write and go into print. The creation of literary texts comes to dovetail with the creation of a persona.

> If they are at a party or in church, they assume a thousand positions, one moment sitting very straight, the next arranging their clothes below, then the veil on their head, just to be seen and to remind everyone that they are in that place, not at home. Dianora da Correggio is one of these sorts, for whom it is not enough just to print her writings, but in church or any other public place she is seen talking at one moment to the person on her right and the next to the person on her left. You will never see her sit still, not even for the length of an *Ave Maria,* and all of this for vain ambition, to show off courtly and witty manners.[17]

No doubt there is some male disrespect in these words. Still, as Calmeta bears witness, women writers with a capacity and determination to dominate the court scene had made their appearance well before the years to which Dionisotti restricted their activity. Before the 1530s, this development is evident in the revolution brought by the new medium of print. Calmeta, in his usual caustic vein, writes:

> [I]n our present age, thanks to the great convenience offered by printers, arrogant ambition triumphs to the point that . . . when one has composed something, it is hustled off to the printer immediately, all to get a name. . . . Ah! Why shouldn't I be indignant if I see poetry almost always in the hands of either uncouth courtiers or vain women?[18]

In the first half of the sixteenth century, courtly civilization confirms the woman of letters as a new protagonist of the social stage and a privileged interlocutor for the masters of Renaissance literature. Pietro Bembo engages in poetic correspondence with Veronica Gambara and Vittoria Colonna. In his *Rime* [Rhymes] he calls female writing a "wonder" that contributes to the glory of the century, and he points to women's ability to seduce with words: "When has human life ever had such a wonder / that an unseen beauty burns the heart / and in unheard harmony injures it?"[19] Women more and more often animate literary dialogues and contribute to converting the former academies of male humanists into worldly gatherings. Bembo's *Asolani* of 1505 are set in Caterina Cornaro's female court.[20] Similarly, Castiglione's *Book of the Courtier,* although not published until 1528, harks back nostalgically to the court of Urbino in 1507, when it was dominated by Elisabetta Gonzaga and Emilia Pio.

On a theoretical level, too, these writers defend women's intellectual ambitions. Bembo dedicates the opening of the third book of his *Asolani* to supporting the thesis that women can devote themselves to the search for truth and hence pursue philosophical studies. Castiglione sketches the ideal qualities of the noble woman, whose fundamental competencies include the gift of the sparkling word.[21] In the *Book of the Courtier* the court lady is a mistress of conversation (3.5); she must know how to make her own speech flexible, so that it can be molded for each type of interlocutor (3.6), and she must be literate (3.9). Finally, when it comes to writing, women are shown respect equal to men. Classicism provides the last piece in this evolution. According to Castiglione, the ancient models of Corinna and Sappho live again in the modern character of the woman writer (3.13, 3.18).

Matteo Bandello[22] is another defender of the learned woman, the perfect incarnation of a new ideal that moves beyond humanistic erudition and fuses beauty and culture, passion for letters and courtly elegance, virtue and art.[23] In Bandello's tales (1554) women are able to build an exiting universe, in which the production and discussion of texts are no longer carried out by the humanist closeted in his *studiolo* but have become an all-female performance, offered to a silenced and admiring court. Thus Bandello writes to Ippolita Sforza Bentivoglio in the general dedication of his *Novelle:*

> It is a wonder to see with what depth and subtlety you penetrate, explain, and interpret certain passages by the writers, one word and one meaning at a time, such that you clarify them to all those listening. . . . Whoever could have heard you the day that the learned scholar and sweetest poet Niccolò Amanio came to present you his homage, when two sonnets were read, one by the lady Cecilia Bergamina, Countess of San Giovanni in Croce [Cecilia Gallerani], and the other by the lady Camilla Scarampa, and how wisely you discussed the art of the poet, and what is required of those who wish to

> compose verses in Latin or the vernacular, and how acutely you clarified the doubts that were put to you, with what abundance of pure and proper words, and how finely you ordered all your remarks, would have truly said that it was not a women talking, but that the speaker was one of the more learned and well spoken and most eloquent men living today. . . . those who had the fortune to hear you were left so full of admiration that they didn't know what to say.[24]

Here, in Bandello's vignette, a woman comments on the texts of other women. At this point female writing places itself at center stage, a mixture of the courtly and the literary, among scholarly men dedicated to the service of the court.[25] For this reason Bandello is able to evoke a society already suggested by Calmeta, but from a very different perspective of absolute support. Expressing enchanted admiration, he exalts the new women writers and warriors in a splendid dedication to Giovanna Sanseverina.

> How mistaken some men are, deprived of every good and sound judgment, who do not want women to be capable in letters and arms in any way at all! This is so easy to demonstrate that it seems to me superfluous to take the trouble because when we read ancient and modern history, no matter what language, you will find many women worthy of honored and immortal memory in both one activity and the other. And certainly if fathers wanted to permit some of their daughters to pursue literary studies and arms, too, many would rise to great excellence, as in the past. But in order not to roam Europe, for now we shall not go beyond Milan, leaving aside Penthesilea, Camilla, Tomyris, Hippolita, Zenobia, Sappho, Themistoclea, Proba, Polla, Argentaria and many other women scholars and warriors, we shall remember only the marvelous heroine, that lady Ippolita Sforza Bentivoglia, whom we hear every day discuss learnedly the most difficult passages of Latin literature. How could I forget the modern Sappho, the lady Cecilia Gallerana, Countess Bergamina, who so gracefully composes verses in Italian as well as in Latin? Who does not by now know the lady Camilla Scarampa Guidobona whose cultured verses are so valued? . . . And there is also the noble and courageous Lucia Stanga who with sword in hand strikes fear in many bravoes.[26]

At this point our inquiry should address another question: To what degree do women transform the personality of the Petrarchist writer who appears at the beginning of the sixteenth century? What is their relationship with courtly theater and its literary canon? When they present themselves, do the women writers conform to the ideology of the dominant rhetoric, or are they able to change? Are they able to create a new model of poetic identity, modifying the stage they finally entered as protagonists? Let us answer these questions by looking at the lyrical scene, where we shall see whether the female personality, as performed by Italian Renaissance women, corresponds to the voices of sixteenth-century Petrarchism.

Italian poets introduce three new formal and thematic features with respect to Petrarch's lyric model, the *Canzoniere*. All of these changes are closely tied to a flourishing court theater and are destined to influence pan-European Petrarchism.

First, a plurality of loves replaces the unity of a single love. In contrast to Petrarch, a solitary soul enshrouded in his life-long obsession of Laura, the courtier is gallantly sociable, passing from one relationship to the next. Already in Bembo's *Rime,* the first edition of which is published in 1530 and then in Giovanni Della Casa's *Rime* (1558), there is a sense of amazement that love can keep returning for different women, even in old age. Love, the subject's main impulse, becomes capable of projecting itself on many objects rather than taking the form of an absolute passion, centered once and for all on a single person.[27]

Second, unlike Petrarch's unreciprocated love, Petrarchist love unfolds against a background of mature sensuality. Poetry features love stories that have already reached the erotic rather than remaining perennially suspended in an ideal sphere. As lyric narratives describe the fulfillment in love, new themes enter, unknown to Petrarch: weariness of the senses, betrayal, the abandonment and reconciliation of lovers. It is a sentimental life that makes amorous discourse more real, interweaving matters of the heart with callings of the flesh, the yearnings of Petrarch's *Rerum vulgarium fragmenta* with the earthy affairs of Boccaccio's pastoral comedy, *Ameto,* or his sad romance, *The Elegy of Madonna Fiammetta.* The lyric becomes a love comedy responding to a courtly taste for romantic adventures like those evoked by the interlocutors of Bembo's *Asolani.* As it listens to the new poets' stories, the sixteenth-century court wants to suffer and delight with them.

Third, *Petrarchismo* tends to replace Petrarch's attempts at sublimating love in the service of higher moral values with another kind of sublimation that is purely literary. The real aim of Petrarch's imitators is not for the spirit to dominate the flesh. The real goal is now, at a lower level, to transform passion into an elegant and seductive language. Pietro Aretino comments ironically on this in his comedies and dialogues. At a higher level, the aim is to achieve glory thanks to one's love-inspired lyrics. Bembo writes in the opening sonnet of his *Rime,* speaking to the Muses: "Muses . . . wont to deceive death, give life to this style, born of my suffering, when I am dead and buried."[28] The medieval ideal of an eternal life of the spirit is replaced by the classical concept of a survival after death through "fame."

Considering these three cardinal points of the Petrarchist canon, we shall be able to see the measure in which women writers, obeying or renewing them, construct their own poetic personalities.

All the major sixteenth-century Petrarchists in Italy depart from their model on the second point in their narratives of mature sensual love. Transferred to the female sphere, this explains the ambiguity of personalities like Gaspara Stampa, Tullia d'Aragona, and Veronica Franco, suspended between poetess and courtesan. Yet biographical experience does not count for so much as a new rhetoric of amorous discourse in producing the more open-minded, more passionate female voice. Even if the poetess has a spotless moral reputation, as was true of Veronica Gambara and Vittoria Colonna, she still describes a requited love, transforming it into conjugal love, a theme absolutely new with respect to Petrarch. From this full-blown language of love fulfilled there will open a path to female mysticism, which passes from union with a man to fusion with God, interweaving spirituality and sensuality as ecstasy.[29]

As for the two remaining characteristics of *Petrarchismo*, the plurality of loves and the tendency to sublimate it in a literary style, women writers react more to the latter. This is a point of crucial importance, for it explains why women do not limit themselves simply to participating in the Petrarchist canon of the sixteenth century. Instead, with their presence they stimulate its transformation.

How the female stance contrasts with the male attitude emerges clearly in Sperone Speroni's *Dialogo d'Amore* [Dialogue on love],[30] which compares a celebrated courtisane poetess, Tullia d'Aragona, with Bernardo Tasso, father of the more famous epic poet, Torquato, and a courtier of high social standing. Speroni, obedient to a poetics of the dialogue that approaches play acting,[31] gives a most lively rendering of the difference between male and female rhetoric in matters of life and its translation into poetry. Tullia and Bernardo both are lovers and poets, but they represent two conflicting existential as well as literary perspectives.

Bernardo Tasso is about to leave. Court obligations force him to abandon Tullia d'Aragona. Writing, however, will shorten the distance between them. That distance will therefore be positive, giving him the chance literally to develop and ennoble passion, to transform imperfect reality into perfect lyrical accomplishments. For Tasso and for the moderator of the dialogue, Grazia, the two levels are distinct. Reality is associated with a kind of sensuality that does not suffer from excessive nostalgia, does not complicate sentiments too much, but is gratified by the occasional outburst. Literary fiction, in contrast, conceives life as raw material, dignifies it, resolves it rhetorically. The more it succeeds, the more love becomes imagery rather than reality, falling under the poet's absolute artistic control.

Man, as Speroni will have it, is like a centaur, in that he represents not a unity but a juxtaposition of parts. On the one hand, there is the mind, which exalts love in literature, and it can do so only from a distance. On the other hand, there is the body, which lives love from close quarters. Seeking to convince Tullia to let her lover leave without too much drama, Grazia tells her:

> When our Mother Reason considers this matter . . . she judges it opportune for the lover, turning from the senses to the intellect and from the present to the future, to live far from the beloved for months and even years. During that time, in a noble spirit every amorous operation, happy and sad alike, once remembered and examined by reason, will become a thing such that Apollo and Minerva will not refuse to behold it. . . . The present and future ages, my dear Tullia, most rightly will grieve too much for Tasso, too much for you; and he would lose too much, and so would you, if he, postponing virtue in favor of your presence, were to exchange eternal and unwavering glory, won for the two of you by his studies, for brief and fugitive pleasure. . . . Be happy that once every two years he comes to see you, and mindful that he was born a centaur, lingers to satisfy the part of his life that makes him mortal, as we all are.[32]

Tullia is very different from Tasso and Grazia. She does not make do with the occasional fling; neither does this woman writer accept fictitious fires of passion. Rather, she defends the fulfillment of a love both poetic and real.

> GRAZIA: In the rhymes of Tasso . . . you will be the relic in a tabernacle. Your name, your merits, your virtues will be adored devoutly by Love's faithful.
>
> TULLIA: They will adore not the relics but the tabernacle. . . . your words of praise will be for me what the songs are for the dead that accompany them to burial.[33]

Continually reacting to her lover's rhetoric, Tullia resists reducing amorous discourse to a dimension that is merely staged and deceitful. She doubts that even now, in his dialogue with her, Tasso is talking to his lady. She supposes instead that he is transforming the conversation with his lover into an occasion for literary invention, listening with satisfaction to himself like a Spanish gentleman filled with hollow phrases. "It's just as well for you this time," Tullia tells him, "that I love you. If I loved you just a little less, I could believe you a quick-witted Spaniard, rather than a real lover."[34] And while Tasso exalts and dissolves her reality through literary transfiguration, Tullia exclaims, with a pained but lucid sense of her status as a courtesan, "It is very true that, loving me as you say you do, you deceive yourself, for I know who I am, and I know that I should be different to deserve your words."[35]

The model poet and man, represented by Bernardo Tasso, turns the woman into an object of sensual pleasure or dissolves her into a nominal identity. In both cases the male perspective in Petrarchism is not to create a relationship but to explore the narcissistic satisfaction of pleasure in the word. Tasso says to Tullia d'Aragona:

> My lady, it is not your job to love, but to be loved. . . . It is true that you, not content to be loved by me, give of yourself generously (or rather lavishly) to me, exceeding the limits of your gender; you come to meet my love so much so that it must seem that you do not receive it, you anticipate it. But this cannot be, for otherwise you would pervert the natural order of things.[36]

It is, in fact, a scandal that woman insists on loving, rejecting her conventional role as a sheer phantasm of male desire.[37]

From the beginning, a breath of melancholy pervades Sperone's dialogue. The presence of women on the scene promotes a return of Ovidian rhetoric, which is both interlaced and at war with the Petrarchist code, unmasking its tendency for formalism and reacting against its ideal woman. These self-confident sixteenth-century women writers are far from the mournful heroine Boccaccio had brought to life two centuries earlier in his *Elegy of Madonna Fiammetta,* but Ovid's *Heroides*[38] echo through their voices, expressing a new sense of painful abandon and solitude that recognizes how useless it is to claim totality in a relationship. Their rhymes will have an elegiac note, generated not by indifference but by the excessive praise, the affected eloquence of the lover. Gaspara Stampa writes:

> A che vergar, signor, carte ed inchiostro
> in lodar me, se non ho cosa degna,
> onde tant'alto onor mi si convegna;
> e, se ho pur niente, è tutto vostro?
> . . . .

Ma voi cercate con sì dolce canto,
lassa, oltra quel che fa vostra bellezza,
d'accrescermi più foco e maggior pianto.

[Why do you waste, my lord, paper and ink
In praising me, since I have nothing worthy
Of such high honor as you pay to me,
Or, if have, it is all due to you?
. . . .
But now, alas, you seek in lovely songs,
Beyond what you accomplish with your beauty,
To add fire to my flame, to cause more tears.][39]

Even more explicitly the courtesan Veronica Franco asks her lovers for fewer words on the one hand and stronger reciprocal sentiments on the other.

e da parole e da vezzi delusa,
tutti i lor vani indizi lascio a tergo
. . . .
ma s'avete di favole desio
mentre anderete voi favoleggiando
favoloso sarà l'accento mio;
e di favole stanco e sazio, quando
l'amor mi mostrerete con effetto,
non men del mio v'andrò certificando
. . . .
Io bramo aver cagion vera d'amarvi.

[and, disappointed by words and charm
I leave behind all their misleading lures
. . . .
but if instead you long for fictions,
as long as you persist in spinning out tales,
my welcome to you will be just as false;
and, when, fatigued and annoyed by fictions,
you show me your love in deeds,
I will assure you of mine in the same way.
. . . .
I long to have a real reason to love you.][40]

This reason, which will open the doors of Franco's heart as well as her bed, is spiritual virtue: "My heart falls in love with virtues."[41] Veronica Franco aspires to a union not only of bodies but also of souls—a complete relationship, fusing in literature as in life the two aspects of the "centaur" and its two images of women: as a fantasy of desire and a sensual courtesan. Thus follow rebukes to the poet, who feels confident that he has captured her in the web of rhetorical seduction and who would like to pass immediately from literary exaltation to the crude consummation of love: "E poi da me volete farvi amare? / quasi credendo che così d'un salto, / di voi mi debba a un tratto innamorare?" [And do you then hope to make me love, / as if you believed that with one single leap / I should suddenly fall in love with you?].[42]

Certainly, the insistence of many women, beginning with Gaspara Stampa, on their lack of literary quality, on the immediateness of their own work, does not allude so much to insufficiency of expressive means as to the self-consciousness of rhetorical fiction in Petrarchist discourse. Nevertheless, in women writers the theme of solitude takes on new tones, mingling with a diffidence toward the kind of writing that masks relationships lacking in real, memorable consistency. Gaspara Stampa laments:

o carte invan vergate e da vergarse
per lodar quegli ardenti amati giri,
o speranze ministre de' disiri,
a cui premio più degno dovea darse,
tutte ad un tratto ve ne porta il vento.
poi che da l'empio mio segnore stesso
con queste proprie orecchie dir mi sento
che tanto pensa a me, quanto m'è presso
e, partendo, si parte in un momento
ogni membranza del mio amor da esso.[43]

[Oh pages vainly written today or tomorrow
to praise those beloved burning rounds!
Oh hopes, servants of my desires,
to whom a greater reward should have been given!
Suddenly the wind carries you away,
since from the impious lord himself
with these my own ears, I hear it said to me
that my lord thinks of me as long as he is near,
and when he departs, there departs in a moment
all memory of my love from him.]

Something new resonates here, both sensual and sentimental, a melancholy of the body and the spirit that makes even poetic discourse more moving, more expressive and musical. The female voice provides a foundation for the new psychology and new melancholy and sensual rhetoric of Torquato Tasso, in turn a model for Italian and European poetry of the seventeenth century.[44] A tendency develops for the woman writer courageously to enclose herself within a total passion from which she does not want to escape, a passion no longer sublimated. Thus the woman knows how to shake herself free of the usual Petrarchan and Petrarchist laments over the bond of love. Veronica Gambara writes:

> Libra non son, né mai libra esser spero
> dal crudel laccio ove già fui legata,
> . . . .
> Né libra mai sarò da un sol pensiero,
> nel qual dì e notte sempre isto occupata,
> che la mia libertà, qual t'ho donata,
> non sprezzi, ahimè! tuo cor superbo e fiero.[45]
>
> *[I am not free, nor do I hope to be free,*
> *from the painful noose that once bound me,*
> . . . .
> *nor will I ever be free from a single worry,*
> *in which day and night I am always occupied,*
> *that my liberty, as I gave it to you,*
> *not be scorned by your prideful, fierce heart.]*

This sentimental resonance becomes even more intense when it refuses all images and is carried out in pure alternating movements of the heart, in secret intimate palpitations of a loving memory almost inebriated with itself, as she keeps repeating his name. Again Veronica Gambara writes,

> Poiché Fortuna volse farmi priva
> di te, Signor mio car, deh! tolto almeno
> m'avesse la memoria . . .
> . . . .
> La memoria mantienmi e mi disface:
> la memoria mi fa lieta e scontenta;
> ne la memoria il ben e 'l mal mio tace.

La memoria m'allegra e mi tormenta;
dunque da la memoria ho guerra e pace
e in tal variar lei sola mi contenta.[46]

[Since Fortune decided to deprive me
of you, my dear Lord, would that at least
it had effaced your memory
. . . .
Memory keeps me alive and undoes me,
Memory makes me happy and discontent,
in Memory my well being and my pain rest,
Memory cheers me and torments me,
thus from Memory I have war and peace
and in this alternation, she alone contents me].

This is the line that reaches its expressive height in Vittoria Colonna's *Rime amorose*. Colonna remaps the canonical route laid out in Petrarch's *Canzoniere*, which had distinguished between the verses written during the life of the lady and those written after her death, replacing it with a route that departs immediately from death of the beloved, her husband.[47] It is a brilliant stroke of intuition, a choice springing from her sense of poetry, one that collects all the characteristics of Renaissance female writing into a thematic unity. The desire of which Colonna speaks is requited; desire is accomplished in marriage, but it is also a total, absolute love. Death defends it from the snares of time and immediately moves it into a dimension that is only interior, where the deceitfulness of rhetoric is no longer possible between two lovers. The theater of the soul has replaced the theater of the court.

It is there, in this land of soul, that the image of the man Colonna loves returns in ecstatic epiphanies that seem to annul all reality and almost consciousness itself.[48] Woman once and for ever exits the scene of the very court theater that gave her words. Both ardent and lofty, like a lady in a portrait painted by Bronzino, she withdraws in concentration to an interior scene.[49] She wins total autonomy in life and in poetry. We can understand why women, and Vittoria Colonna in particular, open the door toward the transition from Petrarchism to religious poetry and modern mysticism. The sublime truth is there, beyond the words, in a secret thunderbolt, nourished only by itself: "my divine ardor thrives on itself."[50] It is a new dawning. There, announces Vittoria Colonna, is the "internal aurora"[51] of a new poetry that no longer wears the empty mask of courtiers.

❧ ❧ ❧

NOTES

This essay in its present form owes much to the unstinting editorial assistance of Victoria Kirkham, whom I would like to thank most warmly for her collegial generosity. Unless otherwise noted, all translations are my own.

1. The brilliant and versatile Leon Battista Alberti (1404–72), a Florentine architect, art theorist, inventor, and humanist, composed the books of his dialogue *Della famiglia* during the 1430s and 1440s. Rooted in Aristotelian principles of hierarchy and order, his ideal family conceives of its women as obedient wives and fertile breeders whose role is to assure continuity of the male line. See *I libri della famiglia,* ed. Ruggiero Romano and Alberto Tenenti (Turin: Einaudi, 1972); and *The Albertis of Florence: Leon Battista Alberti's Della Famiglia,* trans. Guido A. Guarino (Lewisburg, Pa.: Bucknell University Press, 1971). On the Italian Renaissance woman see Maria Ludovica Lenzi, *Donne e madonne: L'educazione femminile nel primo Rinascimento italiano* (Torino: Loescher, 1982); Ottavia Niccoli, ed., *Rinascimento al femminile* (Bari: Laterza, 1991); Pamela Benson, *The Invention of the Renaissance Woman* (University Park, Pa.: Pennsylvania State University Press, 1992); and Letizia Panizza, ed., *Women in Italian Renaissance Culture and Society* (Oxford: European Humanities Research Centre, 2000).

2. Baldesar Castiglione, *The Book of the Courtier,* trans. Charles S. Singleton (Garden City, N.Y.: Anchor Books, 1959), 99 (bk. 2.8). See Castiglione, *Il libro del Cortegiano,* ed. Bruno Maier (Turin: UTET, 1964), 200–201: "ritrovandosi il cortegiano nella scaramuzza o fatto d'arme o battaglia di terra o in altre cose tali, dee discretamente procurar di appartarsi dalla moltitudine e quelle cose segnalate ed ardite che ha da fare, farle con minor compagnia che po ed al conspetto de tutti i piu nobili ed estimati omini che siano nell'esercito, e massimamente alla presenzia e, se possibil è, inanzi agli occhi proprii del suo re o di quel signore a cui serve; perchè in vero è ben conveniente valersi delle cose ben fatte."

3. For images of women reading in the fifteenth century, see *Women and the Book: Assessing the Visual Evidence,* ed. Jane H. M. Taylor and Lesley Smith (London: British Library, 1997).

4. Mauda Bregoli Russo, *Teatro dei Gonzaga al tempo di Isabella d'Este* (New York: Peter Lang, 1997), 7–22; Iain Fenlon, "Gender and Generation: Patterns of Music Patronage among the Este, 1471–1539," in *La Corte di Ferrara e il suo mecenatismo,* ed. Marianne Pade, Lene Waage Petersen, and Daniela Quarta (Modena: Panini, 1990), 213–32.

5. The first edition of Francis Petrarch's *Rerum vulgarium fragmenta* and his *Trionfi* appeared in Venice in 1470, printed by Vindelino da Spira. The Queriniana Library in Brescia holds in its collection a copy unrivaled in the originality and richness of its illumination. See the facsimile reproduction in Francesco Petrarca, *Il canzoniere, I trionfi: Edizione anastatica dell'Incunabolo queriniano* G.V.15 *(Venice, Vindelino da Spira, 1470),* ed. Ennio Sandal and Pietro Gibellini (Brescia: Grafo, 1995). A recent joint study devoted to this copy has discovered the unknown author of the side notes and illustrated commentary to be Antonio Grifo, a poet who read and commentated on the works of Dante and Petrarch at the Milanese court of Ludovico Sforza and Beatrice d'Este: see Giuseppe Frasso, Giordana Mariani Canova, and Ennio Sandal, *Illustrazione libraria, filologia e esegesi petrarchesca tra Quattrocento e Cinquecento: Antonio Grifo e l'incunabolo questriniano* GV15 (Padua: Antenore, 1990). Petrarch's *Canzoniere* has been

known by various titles: *Rerum vulgarium fragmenta* [Fragments of things in the vernacular], which was the title Petrarch himself gave his 366 lyric poems; *Rime sparse* [Scattered rhymes], an implicit title in the first verse of the first sonnet; and *Canzoniere* [Song book], this being the classic Italian lyric collection par excellence. For texts in Italian and English, see *Petrarch's Lyric Poems*, ed. and trans. Robert M. Durling (Cambridge, Mass.: Harvard University Press, 1976).

6. This is the *Purpureo codex* (cod. 2157) of the Trivulziana Library in Milan. See Gasparo Visconti, *I canzonieri per Beatrice d'Este e per Bianca Maria Sforza*, ed. Paolo Bongrani (Milano: Fondazione Arnoldo e Alberto Mondadori, 1979), xi–xxiv; Paolo Bongrani, "La poesia lirica alla corte di Ludovico il Moro," in *Lingua e letteratura a Milano nell'età sforzesca* (Parma: Università degli Studi, 1986), 53.

7. Vincenzo Calmeta, *Prose e lettere edite e inedite*, ed. Cecil Grayson (Bologna: Commissione per i Testi di Lingua, 1959), 87–89.

8. Ibid., 118–22.

9. See Carlo Dionisotti, *Geografia e storia della letteratura italiana* (Torino: Einaudi, 1967), 237: "Soltanto nella letteratura del medio Cinquecento le donne fanno gruppo. Non prima né poi." The lasting influence of Dionisotti's discussion can be found even in such recent work as Giovanna Rabitti, "Lyric Poetry, 1500–1650," in *A History of Women's Writing in Italy*, ed. Letizia Panizza and Sharon Wood (Cambridge: Cambridge University Press, 2000), 37–51. The first woman writer discussed by Rabitti is Vittoria Colonna, whose verse was first published (without her permission) in 1538!

10. Calmeta, *Prose e lettere*, 44: "altre, che d'ingegno sono un poco tondette . . . per mostrar ancor esse aver circa le vertù dilettazione e giudizio, d'ogni scartabello fanno monizione, difendendo alcuni poetissimi che da nessun altro eccetto che da loro sono conosciuti."

11. Ibid., 26–31.

12. See Cristoforo Landino, "Proemio al commento dantesco (1481)," in *Scritti critici e teorici*, ed. Roberto Cardini (Roma: Bulzoni, 1974), 1:141–42: "E che dal furore divino proceda la facultà poetica efficacemente lo pruova Platone nel libro che lui intitola Ion, per tre segni: primo, perché gl'uomini non imparano una dell'altre arti se non dopo lungo tempo sanza el divino furore, ma e' veri poeti, quali lui afferma essere Orfeo, Omero, Esiodo, Pindaro, ne' suoi poemi pongono certi indizi di tutte l'arti e segni che loro le 'ntesono; el secondo è che, infuriati, molte cose stupende cantano, le quali dipoi, cessato el furore, appena essi medesimi le 'ntendono, come se non loro l'abbino pronunziate, ma Idio per la bocca loro; terzio, che non e' più prudenti uomini né da' teneri anni più eruditi son quegli che divengono miglior poeti, ma quegli che sono spinti da furore, come Platone scrive essere intervenuto a Ione e Tinnico calcidense e ad Esiodo. E aggiugne tanto filosofo che le Muse alcuna volta inspirano questo divino spirito a uomini inettissimi, perché vuole la divina providenzia dimostrarci che e' preclari poemi non sono invenzione di filosofi, ma sono doni di Dio." [And Plato, in the book he entitled *Ion*, proves efficaciously by three signs that the poetic faculty proceeds from divine furor: first, because without divine furor men take a long time to learn even one of the arts, but true poets, whom he affirms are such as Orpheus, Homer, Hesiod, and Pindar, place in their poems certain indications of all the arts and signs of understanding them; the second is that while in this furor, they sing many stupendous things, which afterward, when the furor has ceased, they themselves hardly understand, as if they hadn't pronounced them, but God through their mouth; third, that those who become the best poets are not the wisest men educated from their most tender years, but those who are

pushed by furor, as Plato writes happened to Ion and Tynnichus of Chalcis and Hesiod. And this great philosopher adds that the Muses sometimes inspire this divine spirit in the most inept men because divine providence wants to show us that distinguished poems are not the invention of philosophers, but they are gifts from God.]

13. Calmeta, *Prose e lettere*, 7–9: "venimmo in menzione di alcuni ingegni che, dotati dalla natura di furore e vena poetica, senza aver lettere, cose mirabili e di laude degne ne' loro poemi esprimevano. E così in tal ragionamento perseverando, fui domandato se senza lettere latine poteva un poeta volgare ad alcun grado di perfezione aggiungere. Alla qual domanda in questo modo risposi: 'Vogliono gli antichi filosofi, massimamente Pitagora, Platone e Aristotile, che la poesia sia un furor divino nella mente infuso, e tra 'l poeta e 'l profeta esser molta conformità. . . . Per la qual ragione e auttorità par quasi poter affermare che senza lettere un poeta volgare possa a qualche parte di perfezione nella profession poetica aggiungere, purché da natura sia di poetica vena dotato e da divino furor mosso.'"

14. Ibid., 42: "Alcune altre sono che averanno ingegno, ma se le occorrerà di ragionar qualche cosa, prima s'acconciano la bocca allo specchio, o faranno alcuni gesti d'occhi o di spalla, solo per volerti accennare che voglian dir cose che siano di sustanza, o che abbian del rimoto; poi vagheggiandosi nel parlar loro procederanno tanto in lungo che prenderai poi più fastidio della prolissità che ammirazione dell'ingegno."

15. See such characters as Meredianа in Pulci's *Morgante*, Bradamante in Ariosto's *Orlando Furioso*, and Clorinda in Tasso's *Gerusalemme Liberata*. See especially Veronica Franco, *Terze rime*, XVI, in Franco, *Rime*, ed. Stefano Bianchi (Milan: Mursia, 1995), 106–11. For Franco's texts in English see Veronica Franco, *Poems and Selected Letters*, ed. and trans. Ann Rosalind Jones and Margaret F. Rosenthal (Chicago: University of Chicago Press, 1998).

16. Calmeta, *Prose e lettere*, 40–41: "in questa vana ostentazione e bestial fumo incappano non meno le donne che gli uomini, anzi più. . . . In Milano oggidì è una giovene di competente bellezza, nata di nobili parenti e in casa assai illustre maritata, che Bianca Lucia si nomina. Costei ha in sé molte parti laudabili, che ciascuna da per sé fariano qual si voglia donna tener singulare: musica d'ogni natura d'instrumento e d'arte di canto, affabile con ciascuno, casta del corpo e al coniugale amore ossequientissima. Ma, persuasa da alcuni adulatori che l'hanno sollevata con metterle in capo ch'ella è la più universal donna del mondo, s'è data per questa vana boriosità a schermire, ballar la gagliarda, portar pugnale a canto, un mantello alla brava. . . . inebriata di questo bestial fumo d'esser la prima donna del mondo."

17. Ibid., 41–42: "se saranno in festa o in chiesa, faranno mille mutazioni, or di sedere alto, or di racconciarsi i panni sotto, ora il velo in testa, solo per esser viste e ricordare a' circostanti che sono in quel luogo e non a casa. Di questa sorte è Dianora da Correggio, la quale non sol le basta avere i detti atti in stampa, ma in chiesa o in festa o in altro luogo publico dove si trova, or parlando con chi l'è a destra, or con chi l'è da sinistra, mai per uno spazio d'Avemaria la vedrai star salda; e tutto questo per una vana ambizione, per mostrar d'aver del cortigiano e del faceto."

18. Ibid., 3–5: "nella presente nostra età, per la commodità grande degli stampatori, tanto regna la boriosa ambizione che . . . quando uno ha fatto qualche composizione, subito la fa stampare, acciocché possa qualche nome vendicarsi. . . . Deh! perché non mi debbo io sdegnare, se il più delle volte veggio le rime in arbitrio o de' grossieri cortigiani, o di vane donne?"

19. Pietro Bembo, *Rime*, 64.9–11, in *Prose della volgar lingua. Gli Asolani. Rime*, ed.

Carlo Dionisotti. Milan: TEA, 1989: "Quando ebbe più tal mostro umana vita: / bellezze non vedute arder un core, / e 'mpiagarlo armonia non anco udita?" See Giorgio Dilemmi, "'Ne videatur strepere anser inter olores': Le relazioni della Gambara con il Bembo," in *Veronica Gambara e la poesia del suo tempo nell'Italia settentrionale*, ed. Cesare Bozzetti, Pietro Gibellini, and Ennio Sandal (Florence: Olschki, 1989), 24–35; Guglielmo Gorni, "Veronica e le altre: Emblemi e cifre onomastiche nelle rime del Bembo," in *Veronica Gambara e la poesia del suo tempo nell'Italia settentrionale*, ed. Bozzetti, Gibellini, and Sandal, 37–57.

20. See Margaret L. King, *Women of the Renaissance* (Chicago: University of Chicago Press, 1991), 162–63: "When Cornaro was tempted by a marriage into the Neapolitan royal house, Venice exerted its authority mightily to force her to abdicate the Cypriot throne. . . . Cornaro left her rich island kingdom for the miniature one at Asolo. In that court she reigned as queen over a coterie of *letterati:* not the least of them Pietro Bembo, who memorialized the activities over which Cornaro presided in the . . . dialogue *Gli Asolani*. . . . Cornaro's court as described by Bembo prefigures the one in Urbino which Castiglione described. There two women—the Duchess, Elisabetta Gonzaga, and her companion, Emilia Pia—guided and inspired the discussions of proper behaviour for both sexes that made up the age's principal handbook of aristocratic values, circulated in some hundred editions and translated into all the major vernaculars: *The Book of the Courtier (Il libro del Cortegiano)*."

21. Marina Zancan, "La donna nel *Cortegiano* di B. Castiglione: Le funzioni del femminile nell'immagine di corte," in *Nel cerchio della luna: Figura di donna in alcuni testi del XVI secolo* (Venice: Marsilio, 1983), 13–56; Antonio Sole, "L'amore e la corte: La concezione dell'amore nel Cortegiano, fra esemplarità petrarchesca e attualità cortigiana," in *Il gentiluomo-cortigiano nel segno del Petrarca* (Palermo: Palumbo, 1992), 7–39.

22. Matteo Bandello, *Novelle*, ed. Gioachino Brognoligo (Bari: Laterza, 1910–12). The first edition of Bandello's tales was published in 1554, but the *Novelle* are strongly connected to the courtly life of the earlier decades of the century. See Adelin Charles Fiorato, *Bandello entre l'Histoire et l'Ecriture* (Florence: Olschki, 1979), 197: "On remarque en effet qu'un nombre appréciable de dédicaces milanaises, qui peuvent être théoriquement datées, se réfèrent aux années qui vont de 1513 à 1516."

23. Bandello, *Novelle*, 1:232: "Essendomi paruta l'istoria degna d'eterna memoria, l'ho descritta, come vederete, ed al nome vostro dedicata. E come poteva io meglio collocarla, che un generoso atto d'una magnanima vergine ad un'altra vergine non meno onesta e magnanima, qual voi sète, donare? Attendete pur e perseverate, seguendo il cammino che principiato avete, ché ogni giorno più s'accrescerà in voi *il desio de la vertù e de le buone lettere, le quali, usandole in bene, come già fate, saranno cagione di rendervi ai futuri secoli immortale*" (emphasis added). [Since this story seemed to me worthy of eternal memory, I have written it down and, as you will see, dedicated it to your name. And how could I better place it than by giving this, the generous act of one magnanimous virgin toward another virgin, no less honest and magnanimous that you are? Attend to the path on which you have embarked and persevere, for each day there will grow in you *the desire for virtue and fine letters, which, used for good, as you are already doing, will be the reason for your immortality in future centuries*.] On this topic see also André Rochon, ed., *Images de la femme dans la littérature italienne de la Renaissance; préjugés misogynes et aspirations nouvelles. Castiglione, Piccolomini, Bandello* (Paris: Université de la Sorbonne Nouvelle, 1980).

24. Bandello, *Novelle*, 1:5–6: "Meravigliosa cosa certo è quanto profondamente e

con sottigliezza grandissima talora certi passi degli scrittori cribriate, ventiliate e a parola per parola e senso per senso andiate di maniera interpretando, che ogni persona che vi sente ne rendete capace. . . . Ora, chi udita v'avesse quel giorno che il dotto dottore e poeta soavissimo messer Niccolò Amanio venne a farvi riverenza, e che furono letti i dui sonetti, uno de la signora Cecilia Bergamina, contessa di San Giovanni in Croce [Cecilia Gallerani], e l'altro de la signora Camilla Scarampa, quanto accomodatamente disputaste de l'ufficio del poeta e de le parti che deve avere chi vuol versi latini o volgari comporre, e quanto acutamente faceste chiari i dubi che proposti vi furono, e con quanta copia di parole pure e proprie, e con quanto bell'ordine il tutto dichiaraste, avrebbe egli nel vero detto che non donna era quella che parlava, ma che alcuno dei più dotti e facondi uomini ed eloquentissimi che oggi vivano fosse stato il dicitore. . . . quelli che ebbero grazia d'udirvi restarono tutti sì pieni d'ammirazione, che non sapevano che dirsi." On Cecilia Gallerani and Camilla Scarampa, see Fiorato, *Bandello entre l'Histoire et l'Ecriture*, 231–36. Fiorato does not, however, mention Calmeta's beautiful portrait of Gallerani.

25. Bandello, *Novelle*, 1:13: "tra uomini dotti ed al servigio delle corti dedicati."

26. Ibid., 5:229–30: "Quanto errino alcuni buoni uomini privi di ogni buono e sano giudicio, li quali non vogliono che in modo veruno le donne siano atte a le lettere e a l'armi, è tanto facile a provare che soverchio parmi il volervisi affaticare; perchè leggendo le istorie antiche e moderne, di quale lingua si sia, si troveranno molte donne in l'una e l'altra facoltà degne di onorata e immortale memoria. E certamente se li padri volessero permettere alcune de le figliuole darsi agli studi litterali e anco a l'armi, molte riusceriano eccellentissime, come fu per lo passato. Ma per non discorrere per l'Europa, non usciremo per ora fora di Milano, lasciando Pentesilea, Camilla, Tomiri, Ippolita, Zenobia, Saffo, Temistoclea, Proba, Polla, Argentaria e molte altre dotte e bellicose, e diremo solamente de la mirabile eroina la signora Ippolita Sforza e Bentivoglia, che tutto il dì si vede di passi reconditi de la lingua latina dottamente disputare. Ma come posso tacere la moderna Saffo, la signora Cecilia Gallerana contessa Bergamina, che oltre alla lingua latina, così leggiadramente versi in idioma italiano compone? Chi oramai non conosce la signora Camilla Scarampa e Guidobona, le cui colte rime sono in tanto prezzo? . . . Ci è ancora la nobile e valorosa signora Luzia Stanga, che con la spada in mano fa paura a molti bravi."

27. See Bembo, *Rime*, 587–88 (no. 98, vv. 1–8), referring to his withdrawal from the stress of the court of Rome to the peace of his home in Padua, founded according to legend by the Trojan exile Antenor: "In poca libertà con molti affanni, / di là 'v'io fui gran tempo, al dolce piano, / che cesse in parte al buon seme Troiano, / venni già grave di pensieri e d'anni; // e posimi dal fasto e dagl'inganni / e dagli occhi del vulgo assai lontano: / ma che mi valse, Amor, s'a mano a mano / tu pur a lagrimar mi ricondanni?" [In little freedom with many struggles, / from there where I was for a long time to the sweet plain / that yielded in part to the good Trojan seed, / I came heavy with thoughts and years; // and I set myself very far from the display and deceits / and from the eyes of the vulgar mob; / but what did it avail me, Love, if hand-in-hand / you still recondemn me to weep?]; 588–89 (no. 99, vv. 5–14.): "Così molt'anni ho già varcato; e, quando / mancar devea la fiamma del tuo strale, / Amor, che questo incarco stanco e frale / tutto dentro e di fuor si va lentando, // sento un novo piacer possente e forte / giugner ne l'alma al grave antico foco, / tal ch'a doppio ardo e par che non m'incresca. // Lasso, ben son vicino a la mia morte: / ché pote omai l'infermo durar poco, / in cui scema virtù, febre rinfresca." [Thus many years have I pressed on, and when / the flame of your arrow should have failed, / Love, for this tired and frail burden / is all slowing

down inside and out, // I feel a new pleasure powerful and strong / join to my soul the heavy old flame, / such that I burn doubly, and it seems not to trouble me. // Alas, I am indeed near my death, / for the infirm man can little endure / in whom virtue shrinks, fever grows.]

28. Ibid., 507 (no. 1, vv. 5–8): "Dive, per cui s'apre Elicona e serra, / use far a la morte illustri inganni, / date a lo stil, che nacque de' miei danni, / viver, quand'io sarò spento e sotterra." [Goddesses, for whom Helicon opens and locks, / wont to deal illustrious tricks to death, / let my style, which is born of my woes, / live when I shall be spent and underground.]

29. See Vittoria Colonna, *Rime spirituali,* in *Rime*, ed. Alan Bullock (Bari: Laterza, 1982), 121 (no. 73, vv. 1–6): "Tira su l'alma al Ciel col Suo d'amore / laccio attorto il gran Padre, e stringe il nodo / per man del caro Figlio, e sì bel modo / non men che l'opra stessa appaga il core, // tal ch'io sento sottil vivace ardore / penetrar dentro, sì ch'ardendo godo." [The great Father pulls the soul to heaven with his love / a twisted noose, and he tightens the knot / with the hand of his dear Son, and such a fine way / no less than the work itself, satisfies the heart, // so that I feel a subtle lively ardor / penetrate within, and thus burning I delight.]

30. Sperone Speroni, *Dialogo d'amore*, in *Trattatisti del Cinquecento*, ed. Mario Pozzi (Milano: Ricciardi, 1978), 511–63. The first edition of Sperone's *Dialogi* was published in 1542 (Venice: Manuzio).

31. Speroni, *Apologia dei dialoghi*, in *Trattatisti del Cinquecento*, ed. Mario Pozzi, 683–724.

32. Speroni, *Dialogo d'amore*, 560–62: "La qual cosa fra sé medesima considerando la nostra madre ragione . . . giudica essere ben fatto che l'amante, da' sensi all'intelletto e dal presente al futuro rivolto, mesi e anni viva lontano dalla cosa amata. Nel qual tempo in un animo nobile ogn'amorosa operazione, così lieta come dolente, ricordata e esaminata dalla ragione, tale e sì fatta cosa diventa ch'Apollo e Minerva non si sdegna di riguardarla. . . . Troppo del Tasso, troppo di voi, signora Tullia mia cara, l'età presente e la futura con gran ragion si dorrebbe e egli troppo, e troppo voi perdereste se, posposta la vertù sua alla vostra presenzia, una eterna e stabil gloria ch'ad ambidue voi partoriranno i suoi studii, a brieve e fugitivo piacere sì legermente si cambiasse. . . . Siavi assai che ogni dui anni una volta, sostando sua maggior cura, egli venga a vedervi e, ricordandosi d'esser nato centauro, alquanto a quella parte della sua vita compiaccia che 'l fa mortale, come noi siamo."

33. Ibid., 554–55: "GRAZIA. Nelle rime del Tasso . . . come reliquia in un tabernacolo, il nome, le laude e le virtù vostre saranno divotamente adorate da' fedeli d'Amore. / TULLIA. Adoreran quei tali non la reliquia ma il tabernacolo. . . . tali a me saranno le vostre parole, quali a' morti sono quei canti che li accompagnano alla sepoltura."

34. Ibid., 541: "Pur vi gioverà egli una volta il troppo amor ch'io vi porto, che poco men ch'io vi amassi, più tosto vi crederei uno acuto Spagnolo ch'innamorato verace."

35. Ibid., 542: "egli è ben vero che, amandomi voi come voi dite, io vedo ingannate voi stesso, ch'io so chi io sono e chi bisognerebbe ch'io fossi per meritarlo."

36. Ibid., 549: "Signora mia, egli non è vostro officio l'amare, ma l'essere amata. . . . Bene è vero che voi mi siete così cortese (per non dire prodiga) di voi stessa che, non contenta di lasciarvi amare da me (uscendo d'i vostri termini) vi fate incontra 'l mio amore intanto ch'egli vi par di precorrerlo, non che di riceverlo. E ei non è così, altramente voi pervertireste la condizione delle cose."

37. This attitude finds confirmation in Tullia d'Aragona's *Dialogo della infinità di*

amore [Dialogue on the infinity of love] of 1547, even if she aims there to erase the courtesan character portrayed by Speroni in his *Dialogo d'amore*. See the introduction by Rinaldina Russell to Tullia's *Dialogue on the Infinity of Love*, ed. and trans. Rinaldina Russell and Bruce Merry (Chicago: University of Chicago Press, 1997), 36: "Such a character would have found a tolerant public in the moral climate of earlier times . . . in the 1530's. In 1547, however, the increasingly censorial mood of officialdom had changed society, and Aragona saw fit to disavow the personality and values of Speroni's courtesan." Nevertheless, in the *Dialogue on the Infinity of Love*, "by advocating a kind of love that partakes of the intellectual and the sensual faculties of both lovers, Aragona implicitly argues for women's capacity for intellectual discourse and for their equal participation in the joyous life of the senses."

38. Renaissance rereadings of Ovid's *Heroides* are confirmed by translations into the vernacular. A beautiful and celebrated translation was published in 1554 by Nannini. See Remigio Nannini, *Epistole d'Ovidio*, ed. Domenico Chiodo (Turin: RES, 1992). On the first decades of the century see Silvia Longhi, "Lettere a Ippolito e a Teseo: La voce femminile nell'elegia," in *Veronica Gambara e la poesia del suo tempo nell'Italia settentrionale*, ed. Bozzetti, Gibellini, and Sandal, 385–98.

39. See Gaspara Stampa and Veronica Franco, *Rime*, ed. Abdelkader Salza (Bari: Laterza, 1913), 67 (no. 117); Gaspara Stampa, *Selected Poems*, ed. and trans. Laura Anna Stortoni and Mary Prentice Lillie (New York: Italica Press, 1994), 94 (no. 117).

40. See Franco, *Terze rime*, 56–61 (no. 2, vv. 23–187); Veronica Franco, *Poems in Terza Rima*, in *Poems and Selected Letters*, 60–70 (no. 1, vv. 23–187).

41. Franco, *Poems in Terza Rima*, 64 (no. 2, v. 106). See Franco, *Terze rime*, 58 (no. 2, v. 106): "De le virtuti il mio cor s'innamora."

42. Franco, *Terze rime*, 59 (no. 2,. vv. 127–29); Franco, *Poems in Terza Rima*, 66 (no. 2, vv. 127–29).

43. Stampa, *Rime*, 70 (no. 123, vv. 5–14).

44. Maria Luisa Doglio, "Il Tasso e le donne," in Torquato Tasso, *Discorso della virtù feminile e donnesca*, ed. M. L. Doglio (Palermo: Sellerio 1997), 7–39.

45. Veronica Gambara, *Le rime*, ed. Alan Bullock (Florence: Olschki, 1995), 62 (no. 6, vv. 1–8).

46. Ibid., 70–71 (no. 14).

47. Colonna, *Rime amorose*, in *Rime*, 2.9–11.

48. Ibid., 3.12: "veggio il fulgorar del chiaro lampo."

49. Ibid., 7.1–2: "Di così nobil fiamma Amor mi cinse / ch'essendo morta *in me* vive l'ardore." See Maria Luisa Doglio, "L'Occhio interiore' e la scrittura nelle lettere spirituali di Vittoria Colonna," in *Lettera e donna: Scrittura epistolare al femminile tra Quattro e Cinquecento* (Rome: Bulzoni, 1993), 17–31.

50. Ibid., 23.12: "vive in se stesso il mio divino ardore."

51. Colonna, *Rime spirituali*, 7.13–14: "mostrami i segni, *quasi interna aurora*, / del venir del mio Sol chiaro e beato."

BIBLIOGRAPHY

Alberti, Leon Battista. *The Albertis of Florence: Leon Battista Alberti's Della Famiglia*. Trans. Guido A. Guarino. Lewisburg, Pa.: Bucknell University Press, 1971.

———. *I libri della famiglia*. Ed. Ruggiero Romano and Alberto Tenenti. Turin: Einaudi, 1972.

Aragona, Tullia d'. *Dialogo della infinità di amore*. In *Trattati d'amore del Cinquecento*, ed. Mario Pozzi, 185–248. Bari: Laterza, 1980.

———. *Dialogue on the Infinity of Love*. Edited and trans. Rinaldina Russell and Bruce Merry. Chicago: University of Chicago Press, 1997.

Bandello, Matteo. *Novelle*. Ed. Gioachino Brognoligo. 3 vols. Bari: Laterza, 1910–12.

Bembo, Pietro. *Prose della volgar lingua. Gli Asolani. Rime*. Ed. Carlo Dionisotti. Milan: TEA, 1989.

Benson, Pamela. *The Invention of the Renaissance Woman*. University Park, Pa.: Pennsylvania State University Press, 1992.

Bongrani, Paolo. *Lingua e letteratura a Milano nell'età sforzesca*. Parma: Università degli Studi, 1986.

Bozzetti, Cesare, Pietro Gibellini, and Ennio Sandal, eds. *Veronica Gambara e la poesia del suo tempo nell'Italia settentrionale*. Florence: Olschki, 1989.

Bregoli Russo, Mauda. *Teatro dei Gonzaga al tempo di Isabella d'Este*. New York: Peter Lang, 1997.

Calmeta, Vincenzo. *Prose e lettere edite e inedite*. Ed. Cecil Grayson. Bologna: Commissione per i Testi di Lingua, 1959.

Castiglione, Baldesar. *The Book of the Courtier*. Trans. Charles S. Singleton. Garden City, N.Y.: Anchor Books, 1959.

———. *Il libro del Cortegiano*. Ed. Bruno Maier. Turin: UTET, 1964.

Colonna, Vittoria. *Rime*. Ed. Alan Bullock. Bari: Laterza, 1982.

Dilemmi, Giorgio. "'Ne videatur strepere anser inter olores': Le relazioni della Gambara con il Bembo." In *Veronica Gambara e la poesia del suo tempo nell'Italia settentrionale*, ed. Cesare Bozzetti, Pietro Gibellini, and Ennio Sandal, 24–35. Florence: Olschki, 1989.

Dionisotti, Carlo. *Geografia e storia della letteratura italiana*. Turin: Einaudi, 1967.

Doglio, Maria Luisa. *Lettera e donna: Scrittura epistolare al femminile tra Quattro e Cinquecento*. Rome: Bulzoni, 1993.

Fenlon, Iain. "Gender and Generation: Patterns of Music Patronage among the Este, 1471–1539." In *La Corte di Ferrara e il suo mecenatismo*, ed. Marianne Pade, Lene Waage Petersen, and Daniela Quarta, 213–32. Modena: Panini, 1990.

Fiorato, Adelin Charles. *Bandello entre l'Histoire et l'Ecriture*. Florence: Olschki, 1979.

Franco, Veronica. *Rime*. Ed. Stefano Bianchi. Milan: Mursia, 1995.

———. *Poems and Selected Letters*. Ed. and trans. Ann Rosalind Jones and Margaret F. Rosenthal. Chicago: University of Chicago Press, 1998.

Frasso, Giuseppe, Giordana Mariani Canova, and Ennio Sandal. *Illustrazione libraria, filologia e esegesi petrarchesca tra Quattrocento e Cinquecento: Antonio Grifo e l'incunabolo questriniano GV15*. Padua: Antenore, 1990.

Gambara, Veronica. *Le rime*. Ed. Alan Bullock. Florence: Olschki, 1995.

Gorni, Guglielmo. "Veronica e le altre: Emblemi e cifre onomastiche nelle rime del Bembo." In *Veronica Gambara e la poesia del suo tempo nell'Italia settentrionale*, ed. Cesare Bozzetti, Pietro Gibellini, and Ennio Sandal, 37–57. Florence: Olschki, 1989.

King, Margaret L. *Women of the Renaissance*. Chicago: University of Chicago Press, 1991.

Landino, Cristoforo. *Scritti critici e teorici*. Ed. Roberto Cardini. Vol. 1. Rome: Bulzoni, 1974.

Lenzi, Maria Ludovica. *Donne e madonne: l'educazione femminile nel primo Rinascimento italiano*. Turin: Loescher, 1982.

Longhi, Silvia. "Lettere a Ippolito e a Teseo: La voce femminile nell'elegia." In *Veronica Gambara e la poesia del suo tempo nell'Italia settentrionale*, ed. Cesare Bozzetti, Pietro Gibellini, and Ennio Sandal, 385–98. Florence: Olschki, 1989.

Nannini, Remigio. *Epistole d'Ovidio*. Ed. Domenico Chiodo. Turin: RES, 1992.

Niccolia, Ottavia, ed. *Rinascimento al femminile*. Bari: Laterza, 1991.

Pade, Marianne, Lene Waage Petersen, and Daniela Quarta, eds. *La Corte di Ferrara e il suo mecenatismo*. Modena: Panini, 1990.

Panizza, Letizia, ed. *Women in Italian Renaissance Culture and Society*. Oxford: European Humanities Research Centre, 2000.

Panizza, Letizia, and Sharon Wood, eds. *A History of Women's Writing in Italy*. Cambridge: Cambridge University Press, 2000.

Petrarca, Francesco. *Il canzoniere, I trionfi. Edizione anastatica dell'Incunabolo queriniano G.V.15 (Venice, Vindelino da Spira, 1470)*. Ed. Ennio Sandal and Pietro Gibellini. Brescia: Grafo, 1995.

———. *Lyric Poems*. Ed. and trans. Robert M. Durling. Cambridge, Mass.: Harvard University Press, 1976.

Pozzi, Mario, ed. *Trattatisti del Cinquecento*. Milan: Ricciardi, 1978.

Rabitti, Giovanna. "Lyric Poetry, 1500–1650." In *A History of Women's Writing in Italy*, ed. Letizia Panizza and Sharon Wood, 37–51. Cambridge: Cambridge University Press, 2000.

Rochon, André, ed. *Images de la femme dans la littérature italienne de la Renaissance; préjugés misogynes et aspirations nouvelles. Castiglione, Piccolomini, Bandello*. Paris: Université de la Sorbonne Nouvelle, 1980.

Rosenthal, Margaret. *The Honest Courtesan: Veronica Franco Citizen and Writer in Sixteenth Century Venice*. Chicago: University of Chicago Press, 1992.

Speroni, Sperone. *I dialogi*. Venice: In casa de' figliuoli di Aldo, 1542.

Sole, Antonino. *Il gentiluomo-cortigiano nel segno del Petrarca*. Palermo: Palumbo, 1992.

Stampa, Gaspara. *Rime*. In Gaspara Stampa and Veronica Franco, *Rime*, ed. Abdelkader Salza. Bari: Laterza, 1913.

———. *Selected Poems*. Ed. and trans. Laura Anna Stortoni and Mary Prentice Lillie. New York: Italica Press, 1994.

Tasso, Torquato. *Discorso della virtù feminile e donnesca*. Ed. Maria Luisa Doglio. Palermo: Sellerio 1997.

Taylor, Jane H. M., and Lesley Smith. *Women and the Book: Assessing the Visual Evidence*. London: British Library, 1997.

Visconti, Gasparo, *I canzonieri per Beatrice d'Este e per Bianca Maria Sforza*, ed. Paolo Bongrani. Milan: Fondazione Arnoldo e Alberto Mondadori, 1979.

Zancan, Marina. *Nel cerchio della luna: Figura di donna in alcuni testi del XVI secolo*. Venice: Marsilio, 1983.

Further Reading

Albonico, Simone. *Il ruginoso stile: Poeti e poesia in volgare a Milano nella prima metà del Cinquecento*. Milan: Franco Angeli, 1990.

Aretino, Pietro. *Sei giornate*. Ed. Giovanni Aquilecchia. Bari: Laterza, 1969.

———. *Teatro*. Ed. Giorgio Petrocchi. Milan: Mondadori, 1971.

Baldacci, Luigi. *Il petrarchismo italiano nel Cinquecento*. 2d ed. Padua: Liviana, 1974.

———., ed. *Lirici del Cinquecento*. Florence: Salani, 1957.

Baldan, Paolo. *Marfisa: Nascita e carriera di una reina amazzone*. In *L'intrigo e l'avventura*, 72–83. Alessandria, Italy: Edizioni dell'Orso, 1990.

Bandello, Matteo. *Canti XI composti dal Bandello de le lodi de la signora Lucrezia Gonzaga di Gazuolo e del vero amore col tempio di Pudicizia e con altre cose per entro poeticamente descritte; Le Tre Parche da esso Bandello cantate ne la natività del signor Giano primogenito del Signor Giano primogenito del Signor Cesare Fregoso e de la Signora Gostanza Rangona sua consorte* [1545]. In Bandello, *Tutte le opere*, ed. Francesco Flora, 2 vols., 2:831–1102. Milan: Mondadori, 1934–35.

Bianco, Monica, and Elena Strada, eds. *"I più vaghi e i più soavi fiori": Studi sulle antologie di lirica del Cinquecento*. Alessandria, Italy: Edizioni dell'Orso, 2001.

Della Casa, Giovanni. *Rime*. Ed. Roberto Fedi. Rome: Salerno, 1978.

De Maio, Romeo. *Donna e Rinascimento: l'inizio della rivoluzione*. Naples: Edizioni Scientifiche Italiane, 1987.

Domenichi, Lodovico, ed. *Rime diverse d'alcune nobilissime, et virtuosissime donne, raccolte per m. Lodovico Domenichi, et intitolate al signor Giannoto Castiglione gentil'huomo milanese*. Lucca: Vincenzo Busdrago, 1559.

Fedi, Roberto. *La memoria della poesia: Canzonieri, lirici e libri di rime nel Rinascimento*. Rome: Salerno, 1990.

Forni, Giorgio. "Rassegna di studi sulla lirica del Cinquecento (1989–1999): Dal Bembo al Casa." *Lettere Italiane* 52 (2000): 100–140.

Franco, Veronica. *Lettere*. Ed. Stefano Bianchi. Rome: Salerno, 1998.

Kirkham, Victoria. "Laura Battiferra degli Ammannati's 'First Book' of Poetry." *Rinascimento* 35 (1996): 351–91.

———. "Laura Battiferra degli Ammannati benefattrice dei gesuiti fiorentini." *Quaderni Storici* 104, no. 2 (2000): 331–54.

Quondam, Amedeo, *Il naso di Laura: Lingua e poesia lirica nella tradizione del Classicismo*. Modena: Panini, 1991.

Santagata, Marco, and Stefano Carrai. *La lirica di corte nell'Italia del Quattrocento*. Milan: Angeli, 1993.

Santagata, Marco, and Amedeo Quondam, eds. *Il libro di poesia dal copista al tipografo*. Ferrara-Modena: Istituto di Studi sul Rinascimento-Panini, 1989.

Stampa, Gaspara. *Rime*. Ed. Maria Bellonci. Milan: BUR, 1994.

The Stigma of Italy Undone

AEMILIA LANYER'S CANONIZATION OF LADY MARY SIDNEY

Pamela Joseph Benson

The works of English women writers provide a striking contrast to the cult of Italian literature that prevailed among men in England during the sixteenth and early seventeenth centuries. With rare—and remarkable—exceptions, they display no awareness of Italian authors and literary genres. Very few women attempted direct imitations of Petrarchan and Ariostan texts or wrote in the Italian genres of sonnet and chivalric epic, Boccaccesque fiction, or pastoral romance and drama, as did Thomas Wyatt, Edmund Spenser, Philip Sidney, and countless other men.[1] As a result, the literary writings of most English women are conspicuously different in genre and content from those of most English men.

English women's isolation from the Italian canon was, at least in part, due to what might be called the "stigma of Italy."[2] This is the term that I use to refer to the common English conviction that contact with things Italian would result in moral and religious corruption for both men and women. This belief developed in concert with the English fascination with Italy so that, at the same time that the models of high art were primarily Italian, suspicion of Italy, Italians, Italian texts, and Italian religion ran high. Ascham's influential *Schoolmaster* of 1571 is the classic text; in it the author warns against the moral and religious corruption of travel to Italy, and, arguing that such corruption occurs from reading as much as from traveling, he complains of the recent rash of published translations from the Italian.[3] Ascham's is but one of many expressions of an enduring italophobia. For English women, whose conduct was already constrained by the generally held assumption that women were more at risk from immoral influences than were men, the stigma of Italy was especially forceful. Imitating the Italians meant imitating texts—consorting with foreigners—that were reputed to corrupt minds and souls, and so, by staying clear of the Italians, women writers could better maintain their good reputations.

In this context two women stand out for their lack of concern about publicly showing their knowledge of secular Italian culture: Lady Mary Sidney and Aemilia Lanyer.[4] Sidney was above the stigma of Italy. She was born a member of the gentry, became countess of Pembroke on her marriage, and for many years was the most powerful woman patron in the country, after the queen. Lanyer was born with the stigma of Italy. Not only was she the daughter of an immigrant Italian musician, Baptista Bassano, but she grew up in a community of Italian immigrants.[5] Yet, these two women, so different in every other aspect of their lives, are linked by their public display of their unusual knowledge of a single Italian author, Petrarch. Sidney translated Petrarch's "Trionfo della morte" [Triumph of death] and circulated it in manuscript, and Aemilia Lanyer published an original triumph in the Petrarchan mode, "The Authors Dreame to the Ladie Marie, the Countesse Dowager of Pembrooke," in her volume *Salve Deus Rex Judeorum*.[6] These works bring Sidney and Lanyer close to conventional male sixteenth-century practice. For them, as for their male contemporaries, the imitation of Italians offered an opportunity for competition and the display of their own skills.

That Sidney and Lanyer had Petrarch in common was not a coincidence. Lanyer's poem "The Authors Dreame" is a response to Sidney as a fellow Italianist and an encomium of her as a fellow poet. In it she uses explicit imitation of the language and structure of Sidney's "Triumph of Death," and she celebrates Sidney's poetry as already eternally famous; then, in the concluding section of her poem, she submits her "unlearned lines" to Sidney, the great, learned author, for approval.[7] In "The Authors Dreame," Lanyer uses a poem by Petrarch, the most canonical of Italian authors, to establish a canon of English women writers; Sidney is the first woman in the canon, and, if all goes as Lanyer hopes, Lanyer herself will be the second.

Mary Sidney and Italian Literature

Mary Sidney was unusual among contemporary female writers for a number of reasons in addition to her interest in Italian literature. She was a patron, an author, and an editor. Her marriage to William Herbert, earl of Pembroke, made her a member of one of the most important and wealthiest families in England, so she had means and influence, which she exercised in part through patronage.[8] She gathered writers around her and encouraged them in various projects; so influential was she on some that Samuel Daniel nostalgically spoke of her country seat at Wilton as a "school."[9] She was the recipient of a great many dedications, especially in the period 1586–1601, and was frequently praised for her writing.[10] Frances Meres included her on an early canon list of English women in his collection of aphorisms and literary notes, *Palladis Tamia* (1598). After citing Queen Elizabeth I, who excels in ode, elegy, epigram or any other kind of poem "heroicke or lyricke," he states that "learned Mary, the honorable Countesse of Pembrook, the noble sister of immortall sir Philip Sidney, is very liberall unto Poets; besides shee is a most delicat Poet, of whome I may say, as Antipater Sidonius writeth of Sappho: Dulcia Mnemosyne demirans carmina Sapphus, Quaesiuit decima Pieris unde foret" [Wondering at the sweet songs of Sappho, Mnemosyne asked where the tenth Muse was from].[11]

Sidney produced a wide variety of literary works. She was and is best known and admired for the translation of the Psalms that she continued after her brother's death; he paraphrased 1–43, and she 44–150. The Psalms circulated in manuscript but were well known, and their influence can be seen in the work of numerous later poets.[12] In 1592 two of Sidney's translations from French were published, Philippe de Mornay's *Discourse of Life and Death* and Robert Garnier's *Antonius*.[13] Several other authors, stimulated by her interest in Garnier, wrote original plays in his style; one of these was Elizabeth Cary, whose *Mariam* has become part of the modern teaching canon of seventeenth-century literature. Two of Mary Sidney's poems appeared in contemporary collections. "The Lay of Clorinda," an elegy for Philip in Spenser's *Colin Clouts Come Home Againe*, is attributed to her by most modern scholars because a head note suggests it to be by Sidney's sister, though her name is not printed as author. The other, "A Dialogue between two shepheardes," in praise of Queen Elizabeth, was explicitly attributed to "the excellent Lady, the Lady Mary Countesse of Pembrook" by the editor Francis Davison in *A Poetical Rapsodie* (1602).[14] The inclusion of these poems in anthologies, with at least one clear indication of her authorship, makes Sidney unique among English women writers of her day. Commonplace in Italy, the publication of a woman's verse in an anthology was unprecedented in England.[15]

Mary Sidney's choice of Petrarch's *Trionfi* as a text to translate was part of a long-standing family commitment to Italian literature that she kept up after her brother Philip's death in 1586. She not only sponsored the publication of his *Arcadia*, in which the debt to Italian literature was conspicuous, but she put her name on the title page—it is *The Countess of Pembrooke's Arcadia*—and the dedicatory letter by the publisher makes it "clear that Mary Sidney bears the ultimate responsibility for the form of the 1593 *Arcadia* ('most by her doing; all by her directing')." She also was responsible for the publication of her brother's love sonnet sequence, *Astrophil and Stella*, and his *Defence of Poetry*, in which he holds Italian literature up as a standard that English authors need to match if they are to be taken seriously.[16]

Sidney chose wisely when she selected the "Trionfo della morte" to translate. It carried less potential for harm to her reputation than most Italian works.[17] Unlike the Petrarch of the sonnets, who was seen as a love poet, the Petrarch of the *Trionfi* was generally seen as a moral poet. Most Renaissance Italian editions of the latter included annotations that asserted their philosophical substance, as did the previous English translation by Henry Parker, Lord Morley (ca.1553–56). Morley states:

> [T]here be a nomber of that sorte, that percase when they shall eyther heare redde, or them selfe reade this excellent tryumphes, of this famous clercke Petrarcha, shall lytle set by them, and peradventure caste it from them, desyrynge rather to have a tale prynted of Robyn Hoode, or some other dongehyll matter then of this, whiche I dare affirme, yea, and the Italians do the same, that the devine workes set aparte, there was never in any vulgar speche or language, so notable a worke, so clerckely done as this his worke. And albeit that he setteth forth these syxte wonderfull made triumphes all to the laude of hys Ladye Laura, by whome he made so many a swete sonnet, that never yet no poete nor gentleman could amend, nor make the lyke, yet who that doth understande them, shall se in them comprehended al morall vertue, all Phylosophy, all storyall matters, and briefely manye devyne sentences theologicall secretes declared.[18]

As Morley suggests here, the *Trionfi* are particularly open to theological interpretation, and, although Petrarch was Roman Catholic, his pre-Reformation philosophical works do not carry the negative connotations of later Catholic Reformation texts.[19] Because they generally were seen as ethical and theologically correct, the *Trionfi* offered Mary Sidney the unusual opportunity to work with a canonical Italian author, perhaps The Canonical Italian Author, without invoking the "stigma of Italy."

The *Trionfi* also escaped the "stigma of Italy" because they were open to Protestant political applications. Kenneth Barlett has argued that Morley himself was advancing the cause of nationalistic English Protestantism when he published during the reign of Catholic Queen Mary a translation of the

Trionfi that he had presented in manuscript to Protestant Henry VIII—with the addition of a new dedication to a possible husband for the Protestant Princess Elizabeth. Sidney's "Triumph" has also been seen as advancing a Protestant agenda. Danielle Clarke persuasively argues that in her "Triumph" the countess wrote a "radical Protestant" panegyric of the aging queen. "[O]n the one hand, [she views] the conventional registers of praise for Elizabeth as inappropriate, and on the other, [she suggests] that the proper form of praise is to stress the divine and eternal in relation to the Queen."[20] Others have read the "Triumph" as one of the group of poems Sidney wrote after her brother's death to mourn him and to establish his reputation as poet and hero of the Protestant cause.[21]

Canonizing Mary Sidney

Lanyer was by no means the first author to recognize Sidney's interest in Italian literature or to assert Sidney's membership in a canon of women writers, although she was the first woman to do so and the first author to advance her own literary reputation by doing so. Twice the countess was compared with specific Italian near-contemporaries who were her equals in rank. In 1592 Nicholas Breton, a prolific author who dedicated a number of religious works to Mary Sidney, praised her capacity to gather authors around her and to stimulate their intellectual pursuits. He paralleled her with Duchess Elisabetta Gonzaga, who was celebrated by Castiglione in his *Cortegiano*, which was enormously popular in England after its translation and publication as *The Courtier* in 1561.[22]

> [W]ho hath redde of the Duchesse of Vrbina, may saie, the Italians wrote wel : but who knowes the Countesse of Penbrooke, I thinke hath cause to write better : and if she had many followers? haue not you mo seruants? and if they were so mindfull of their fauours : shall we be forgetfull of our dueties? no, I am assured, that some are not ignorant of your worth, which will not be idle in your seruice : that will make a title but a tittle, where a line shall put downe a letter : and if shee haue receiued her right in remembrance, you must not haue wrong in being forgotten : if shee were the honour of witte, you are the comfort of discretion, if shee were the fauourer of learning, you are the mainteiner of Arte, and if she had the beauty of Nature, you beautifie Nature, with the blessing of the spirite: and in summe, if she had any true perfection to be spoken of, you haue many mo truly to be written of.[23]

Although the comparison with Gonzaga celebrates Sidney as a patron, a second dedicatory letter that immediately follows this one makes it clear that the text being introduced by these letters was written in order to call Sidney's Psalms to the readers' attention. Together these letters assert Sidney's primacy over the Italian duchess as a patron, as an author, and as a Christian.[24]

The second Italian noblewoman with whom Sidney was compared is the illustrious poet Vittoria Colonna. Comparison with her raises Sidney to membership in an international canon of women writers. It occurs in Thomas Heywood's substantial *Gunaikeion, or Nine Books of Various Histories Concerning Women,* which was published in 1624, three years after Sidney's death. In a section labeled "Of Women Poets," after discussing classical women writers, Heywood makes Sidney the culminating name in a canon list of "poetesses." He names Elizabeth I, Lady Jane Gray, Lady Arabella Stuart, the four daughters of Sir Anthony Cooke, "the author of the Urania," and "Vittoria Colonna with whom I may ranke (if in the comparison I underpraise not the beautiful and learned Ladie Mary, Countesse of Penbrooke, the worthie sister to her unmatchable brother Sir Philip Sydney)."[25] The comparison with Vittoria Colonna raises Sidney above her British colleagues. Because Colonna's name stood for absolute excellence in writing and morals, it shields Sidney from any stigma that might attach to association with an Italian, but the pairing is also apt, perhaps more apt than Heywood knew.[26] Both women wrote works—Colonna's *Rime* and Sidney's lyric Psalms—that shared the distinction of being the only works by women to become part of the nonce canon (that is, accorded respect like that given to classic texts in their own day) in their respective countries. Both were very interested in reformed theology, although Colonna remained within the Roman Church. Both used their skill at writing to make the men closest to them famous—Sidney her brother, Colonna her husband. Finally, both were important formative influences on other writers in their day, especially women.[27] For both, it could be said that, though there were women writers before them, their example authorized those who came after them to speak with stronger voices.

Though Heywood does not directly refer to Sidney's liberating example, he tacitly recognizes Sidney's empowerment of other women writers with his inclusion in his list of "the author of the Urania." This was Lady Mary Wroth, Sidney's niece. Her debt to her aunt (and long deceased uncle) is clear in her choice to write in Italianate genres: pastoral romance and drama and a sonnet sequence, the very genres sponsored by Mary Sidney when she had Philip's works printed. Wroth acknowledges her debt to her aunt explicitly on the title page of *Urania,* where she identifies herself as "Neece to the ever famous, and renowned Sir Phillips [*sic*] Sidney knight. And to the most excellent Lady Mary Countess of Pembroke late deceased."[28] With this family and poetic genealogy, she makes herself the heir of the Sidney tradition (they are "deceased," while she is alive); she creates a family canon and designates herself its representative in the present generation. She also celebrates Sidney as an example to women writers in the text of the *Urania,* but obliquely because it is a roman à clef. In it, according to Josephine Roberts, editor of the definitive edition of the text, she figures her aunt as the queen of Naples, a poet who gathers others around her, as did Sidney, but the poetry that Wroth writes for this character does not resemble any of Sidney's surviving poetry.[29] The title "queen of Naples" may be another flattering analogy between Sidney and Vittoria Colonna, since Colonna was marchesa of Pescara, near Naples, and lived in and near Naples during her marriage.

Aemilia Bassano Lanyer's Italianate Career

Aemilia Lanyer was another of the writers influenced by Sidney who celebrated her, yet she could not claim descent from Sidney by birth as could Wroth, nor could she, a middle-class woman, have hoped to be associated with her in Heywood's canon list of writers from the gentry and nobility. No material link between her and the countess has been discovered. No record of a payment, no stray reference in the countess's correspondence testifies to their acquaintance. If Lanyer was to have a writerly relationship to Sidney, she had to rely on her own inventions, and she did so. In her poem "The Authors Dreame" she forged a link with Sidney by showing her familiarity with the countess's translation of the Psalms and by imitating her "Triumph of Death," and she also attempted to create a more personal connection through a direct poet-to-poet appeal for encouragement of her own poetic endeavors.

Lanyer's detailed allusions to the text of Sidney's unpublished poetry raise the question of access. How could a woman of her social class have been able to read the Psalms and "Triumph of Death," both works that only circulated in manuscript form? Her knowledge of the first is not so surprising; it seems to have been widely diffused, and some of the Psalms quickly were set to music, so the text was probably available in the musical circles in which Lanyer moved because she was the daughter of a musician. Her knowledge of the "Triumph" is more tantalizing. This text does not seem to have circulated widely, and there is no reason to think that it was seen by musicians. The only surviving copy was sent by Sir John Harington to Lucy, countess of Bedford.[30] Yet, Lanyer's detailed allusions demonstrate firsthand knowledge of Sidney's poem. The only likely way that she could have seen this poem was by participating in a manuscript circle that had access to the more private texts by the countess of Pembroke.[31]

Lanyer's own testimony suggests an answer to this puzzle. According to the notes that Simon Forman, the astrologer, kept of her consultations with him, she claimed that during the 1590s, the period when the Sidney manuscripts began to circulate, "She hath bin favored moch of her mati [Majesty] and of mani noblemen, & hath had gret gifte & bin moch made of. and a nobleman that is ded hath loved her well & kept her and did maintain her long." This nobleman was Henry Cary, the Lord Chamberlain. In another interview, she explained that "being with child [by Cary] she was for collour maried to a minstrell"; that is, her marriage with court musician Alfonso Lanyer was arranged to cover up her pregnancy by Cary.[32] If, as is likely, part of Lanyer's charm was due to her exotic origins among Italians and musicians, then it can be said that in her personal life she turned the stigma of Italy into the allure of Italy.

Yet, even if we accept Lanyer's claims as true, being the mistress of a courtier did not usually result in favor at court and connection with literary circles. Considered altogether, however, the evidence suggests an Italian solution to the mystery of Aemilia Lanyer: her affair with the Lord Chamberlain, her having "bin favored moch" at court, her familiarity with courtly manuscript poetry, and her appeal for recognition to a woman poet and potential patron who was far above her in rank and to whom she was unconnected by birth or employment fit an Italian pattern of behavior, that of the *cortegiana onesta* [honest courtesan], a mode of female behavior of which her upbringing in the Italian musical community in London might have made her aware. It was probably as an honest courtesan that she participated in court society. As Margaret Rosenthal explains in her book on the life of the Venetian poet Veronica Franco, "The honest courtesan offered social and intellectual refinement in return for patronage. Playing music, singing, composing poetry, and presenting a sophisticated figure were the courtesan's necessary, marketable skills. Much like the courtier, [her] texts were appeals for social connection and public recognition."[33] The surviving documentary and poetic evidence shows that Lanyer behaved like an honest courtesan. She was known at court; was the mistress of Henry Cary, the Lord Chamberlain; was a member of a manuscript circle; wrote poetry; appealed for patronage at the highest levels; and, in addition, was probably a musician.[34]

By the time she published her meditation on the Passion, *Salve Deus Rex Judeorum*, Lanyer certainly was not calling attention to her past sexual practices, but in many other aspects of her self-presentation in that volume she seems more like an Italian woman writer, honest courtesan, or even honest woman, than an English one.[35] Her name is on the title page, common enough in Italy but rare in England, where women frequently took advantage of the well-established publishing practice of placing only the author's initials on the title page.[36] She addresses nine of her dedicatory epistles to noble potential patrons to whom she is not related or, in most cases, connected by service, whereas English women dedicated their works to family members and those in whose households they had served or with whom they had some previous connection. Italian women dedicated their works to noblemen and noblewomen with whom they had no family connection with good success; both respectable, married Laura Battiferra and *cortegiana onesta* Tullia d'Aragona did.[37] Lanyer also writes to another woman as a fellow poet, a unique appeal in the England of her day. Italian women authors wrote poems to and about each other, and they especially frequently cited Vittoria Colonna and Veronica Gambara as precedents for their literary endeavors.[38]

Aemilia Bassano Lanyer's Canonization of Mary Sidney (and Herself)

Lanyer's extraordinary Italianate appeal to the countess across class lines, poet to poet, was not addressed to the countess personally in a letter or privately circulated manuscript. "The Authors Dreame" was published in multiple copies in print.[39] As Lanyer says clearly and repeatedly in this poem, her goal is not just to persuade Sidney of her appreciation of her poetry but also to make Sidney famous and, she says more subtly, to make her own poetry known by doing so. Even though Lanyer may not have succeeded in making Sidney famous among her contemporaries—Sidney did a fairly good job of doing that on her own, and there is no evidence that Lanyer's poem was at all widely read—as a piece of rhetoric "The Authors Dreame" marks a major moment in the development of a canon of English women writers. Lanyer was the first woman writer to pay explicit tribute to an English woman poet predecessor, the first to imitate a poem by another English woman, and the first to appeal to another English woman for literary judgment. In sum, she was the first woman to attempt to add a woman author to the canon of major English authors and her works to the canon of major literary texts, and, beyond this, she was the first to attempt to forward her own career by doing so. She advanced her double project by asserting Sidney's fame and by representing Sidney's Psalms as satisfying three essential criteria for elevation to canonical status: they are judged to be excellent by esteemed authorities, they have the capacity to continue to be admired forever, and, along with the "Triumph of Death," they have a powerful influence on other authors, namely, Lanyer herself.[40] Having exalted Sidney to canonical status, she made room for herself to be considered among the best of the poets who were still in competition.[41]

The genre in which Lanyer cast her tribute to Sidney was an essential part of her canonizing strategy. "The Authors Dreame" is a triumph, a form particularly well suited to Lanyer's project of creating fame for Sidney and attributing canonical status to her works, not only because Sidney herself wrote one but also because it is traditionally used to give recognition to supreme excellence. In its simplest form, the triumph—whether written, pictorial, or enacted—presents a victory parade in which the victor, such as a Roman general or a medieval or Renaissance ruler or an embodied abstraction such as love or fame or Miss Connecticut, rides on a float or triumphal car accompanied by a parade of those over whom he or she triumphed—victims or supporters or runners-up, depending on the nature of the conqueror.

Unlike graphic representations and real parades, literary triumphs sometimes describe abstract, emotional, and spiritual victories without processions. For example, the first part of "Triumph of Death" begins with a highly visualized account of Laura's formal triumphal return from her conquest of Love (in the preceding poem) at the head of a squadron of chaste women, but the second part is devoted to the dreaming poet's interview with Laura. There is no physical movement at all; he and she are seated in a pastoral setting, and she explains how she has succeeded in not being dead despite the death of her body. Her triumph lies in her transit from one state of being to a higher one, from life to afterlife.[42]

The triumph as Petrarch, Sidney, and Lanyer use it is a visionary genre. We readers are told about what the narrating poet was privileged to see and hear and are given a glimpse of eternal truth that lies beyond waking humans' everyday powers of perception.[43] In "Triumph of Death," Petrarch sees and then talks with Laura's spirit; in "The Authors Dreame," Lanyer first "sees" Sidney celebrated in a mysterious and magical visionary procession accompanied by the Graces, Muses, and goddesses. And then, still dreaming, she receives a clear explanation of the truth revealed by what she has seen. She learns that Sidney already has been accepted in heaven as a great author because of the beauty of her Psalm translations, and yet, because she is still alive, she is available on earth to help struggling mortals. This paradox of a person alive in heaven and on earth makes it clear that Sidney has satisfied two of the criteria for canonization: definitive authorities have judged her and her works. Because Lanyer's phrasing of this idea is imitated from "Triumph of Death," she also satisfies the third criterion: that another poet treat her works as classics by imitating them. Finally, waking up, Lanyer acts on what she has learned and petitions Mary Sidney, the poet, to be her audience.

The opening stanzas of the poem create a powerful sense of Sidney's exalted stature by embedding her in a group of figures symbolic of her selection as a famous poet. In her mind's eye, Lanyer sees "a Lady whom Minerva chose"

> Fast ti'd unto them [the Graces] in a golden Chaine,
> They stood, but she was set in Honors chaire.
>
> And nine faire Virgins sate upon the ground,
> With Harps and Vialls in their lilly hands;
> Whose harmony had all my sences drown'd,
> But that before mine eyes an object stands,
>
> Whose Beauty shin'd like *Titons* cleerest raies,
> She blew a brasen Trumpet, which did sound
> Throgh al the world that worthy Ladies praise,
> And by Eternall Fame I saw her crown'd.
>
> (7–16)

Although there is an action in this scene—Fame crowns the lady—the description of the enthroned lady, surrounded by the Muses playing their instruments and by the Graces, to whom she is linked by golden chains, is static. The crowning seems like a scene on a float. It is an eternally repeated action that is displayed in front of ever-changing audiences.

Lanyer's description of the many goddesses and nymphs arriving one by one, attracted by the lady's fame, exalts Sidney by echoing elements in Spenser's famous pastoral panegyric of Queen Elizabeth from the "Aprill" eclogue in *The Shepheardes Calender*, which also resembles a triumph.[44] In "Aprill," a shepherd-poet, Spenser's alter ego Colin, invites the Muses to help him sing the praises of "Eliza" (Queen Elizabeth) and then describes her, seated on a "grassie greene," and stanza by stanza tells the responses of the various gods—Phoebus, Cynthia, Calliope, the Graces, nymphs—who come to admire her, much as Lanyer depicts the centrally seated lady and the ever-increasing crowd around her, which includes the moon and Calliope.[45] By invoking "Aprill" Lanyer applies one of the best-known pieces of contemporary literature to Sidney's praise; she draws a flattering analogy between her and the former queen (d.1603) and between her encomiast (Lanyer) and Spenser, the most famous poet of the previous generation.

Within this overall framework of resemblance, however, Lanyer adapts the text in ways that differentiate Sidney's admirers from the queen's admirers and Sidney herself from the queen. As a result, Sidney is made glamorous by being described in a text that is imitated from one that was used to praise the queen, but her own particular virtues and situation are defined. For example, Lanyer alludes to Sidney's position as mentor and patron by changing the attitude of the admiring crowd. Awe at Eliza's beauty characterizes Spenser's group, whereas Lanyer's deities competitively jostle for the prime position in her favor. Spenser's Phoebus "blusht to see another Sunne belowe," a blush indicating his shame at being outdone by Eliza's beauty (77). Thus, if even the sun god admits his inferiority, Elizabeth truly is without compare. Lanyer's Aurora blushes too, but because she feels envy when she sees that the lady (Sidney) has welcomed Phoebe, the goddess of the moon, into her entourage.

> *Aurora* rising from her rosie bedde,
> First blusht, then wept, to see faire *Phoebe* grac'd,
> And unto Lady *Maie* these wordes shee sed,
> Come, let us goe, we will not be out-fac'd.
>
> I will unto *Apolloes* Waggoner,
> A bidde him bring his Master presently,
> That his bright beames may all her Beauty marre,
> Gracing us with the luster of his eie.
>
> (61–68)

Aurora thinks of the others who are joining the lady as rivals. Unlike Spenser's vignette, which diminishes a god to make the queen bright, Lanyer's diminishes a goddess to make Sidney desirable. Aurora and the other goddesses are like girls competing with each other for the attention of the head girl or like poets competing for the attention of their poet mentor and patron who, though she turns none away, can be persuaded to change the hierarchy of those she has received into her favor if she is presented with works of greater beauty.

Lanyer calls attention to Sidney's poetic powers by changing what happens at the end of the scene. Colin, Spenser's poet, says that Eliza is so lovely that she could be a Grace and join them in their dance and "reigne with the rest in heaven" (117), but this is just hyperbole; we do not see it happen. Eliza merely rises and the others depart. By contrast, Lanyer's lady joins the Graces, Muses, and other goddesses, goes to a sacred spring with them, judges an art contest—"the antient quarrell" between Art and Nature (83)—and sings with them. In Lanyer's vision Sidney bests the former queen. She reigns in heaven with the Graces and Muses.

By giving Sidney the prize for lifetime achievement—a place in the canon—and making her a judge, Lanyer has put her out of the competition among poets and made room for herself, the new poet, who replaces Spenser as the greatest English encomiast, as Sidney has replaced Elizabeth as woman most worthy of celebration. This strategy is also indebted to "Aprill." The eclogue is the fourth in Spenser's series and by its position evokes Virgil's messianic fourth eclogue "with its prophecy of an ideal reign and so lays claim to the role of Virgil's English successor" for Spenser.[46] Thus, Lanyer's imitation of "Aprill" advances both strands of her project; it helps her to represent Sidney's canonical status, and it helps her to represent herself as a poet worthy of serious attention.

Sidney's canonization is completed in the third scene of the processional section. Having resolved the quarrel between Art and Nature, the "Worthies" begin to sing, and the text they choose is Mary Sidney's Psalms or "holy sonnets." This scene represents Sidney's art as already well established in the canon of divine literature because the authorities who have so honored it are both the divine sponsors of art who participated in the procession and the "saints." Lanyer makes this clear in her description of the singing of the Psalms.[47]

> Those holy Sonnets they [the deities] did all agree,
> With this most lovely Lady here to sing;
> That by her noble breasts sweet harmony,
> Their musicke might in eares of Angels ring.
>
> While saints like Swans about this silver brook
> Should *Hallalu-iah* sing continually,
> Writing her praises in th'eternal booke
> Of endlesse honour, true fames memorie.
>
> (121–28)

For a Protestant, the term *saint* referred not to a person whose special virtue and miraculous powers were recognized by the earthly church but rather to the elect, those chosen for salvation by God at the beginning of time. So, in this complex scene, Sidney's Psalms, sung by a chorus of pagan deities, reach heaven (the ears of the angels) and move the elect to sing "Hallalu-iah." That Sidney and her art will endure the test of time, a prerequisite for canonical status, is made clear in the phrase "writing her praises in th'eternal booke / of endlesse honour." The line can mean either that the saints will write her Psalms (the psalms are praises) in the book or that they will write praise of her in the book, but in practice, the two actions have the same result. In either case, Sidney is famous, and she is famous through a combination of her own efforts in writing the Psalm translations and the efforts of the saints, who have recognized the merit of her work.

At this point in the poem, it would seem that the canonization of Mary

Sidney has resulted from celestial recognition of the sublime merit of her work and that Aemilia Lanyer's efforts are not needed, but the second phase of the poem demonstrates what Lanyer can contribute to Sidney's canonization: imitation. By imitating Sidney's work, Lanyer places it in the category of a classic text, like Spenser's *Shepherd's Calendar*, which she has just finished imitating and which Sidney's brother Philip included on his short list of English texts "worthy the reading" in his *A Defence of Poetry*.[48]

Imitation of classic texts was fundamental to poetic practice in the early seventeenth century. Lanyer's contemporary Ben Jonson explains,

> The third requisite in our *Poet*, or Maker, is *Imitation*, to be able to convert the substance, or Riches of an other *Poet*, to his own use . . . as a Creature . . . that . . . hath a Stomach to concoct, divide, and turn all into nourishment. Not, to imitate servilely, as *Horace* saith . . . but, to draw forth out of the best, and choicest flowers, with the Bee, and turn all into Honey. . . . [O]bserve, how the best writers have imitated, and follow them. How *Virgil*, and Statius have imitated *Homer*.[49]

Lanyer follows Jonson's advice. She converts Sidney's substance or "Riches" to her own use in this second part of "The Authors Dreame." The text of Sidney's that Lanyer imitates is not the Psalms (although she continues to praise them) but "Triumph of Death," and the use to which she puts it is to persuade her reader that Sidney "farre before him [her brother] is to be esteemd / For virtue, wisedome, learning, dignity" (151–52). She uses the poem that many scholars have read as being one of Sidney's many tributes to her brother to elevate Mary Sidney above him.

Lanyer's manner of imitating Sidney's "Triumph of Death" suggests that she, like the modern critics, read the poem as an oblique celebration of Philip. When the sleeping Lanyer asks her guide Morpheus the name of the lady whom she has just seen and heard celebrated, he identifies Mary Sidney by name and by reference to her deceased brother. He attributes Philip's fame to his battlefield death and his Christian faith: his "dying wounds restor'd him life agen" (144). The passage of "Triumph of Death" that Lanyer imitates is a crucial point in the poem—the moment when Laura discloses that she is still alive, in heaven, as Morpheus has just said that Philip Sidney is. Petrarch asks,

> My Goddesse, who me did, and doeth revive,
> Can I but knowe? . . .
> But art thow dead? Ah speake, or yett alive?
> [and Laura answers,]

Alive am I: and thow as yett art dead,
And as thow art shalt so continue still
Till by thy ending hower, thow hence be led.[50]

Paradoxically, Laura is alive because she is dead. What we call life is death to her, and poor Petrarch, not she, is dead. In "The Authors Dream," by contrast, Morpheus uses similar lines to startle Lanyer, to whom he is speaking, with the paradox that Mary Sidney is alive in heaven while she is still alive on earth. Morpheus, calling her "a faire earthly goddess" (143), tells Lanyer that,

[Her] beauteous soule hath gain'd a double life,
Both here on earth, and in the heav'ns above,
Till dissolution end all worldly strife:
Her blessed spirit remaines, of holy love,

Directing all by her immortall light,
In this huge sea of sorrowes, griefes, and feares;
With contemplation of Gods powrefull might,
She fils the eies, the hearts, the tongues, the eares

Of after-comming ages, which shall reade
Her love, her zeale, her faith, and pietie;
The faire impression of whose worthy deed,
Seales her pure soule unto the Deitie.

That both in Heav'n and Earth it may remaine,
Crownd with her Makers glory and his love.

(153–66)

Lanyer's imitation of Sidney here "convert[s] its substance," as Jonson suggests. Like Petrarch in the original and in Sidney's translation, she refers to the lady as a goddess, a term that seems a bit odd in the highly Christian context but that fits the allegorical mode; both so embody virtue that they have become heavenly beings. Also, like Laura, Mary Sidney is alive when the context might have suggested that she was dead. But, of course, Laura, like Philip Sidney, is only alive in Christ, whereas Mary Sidney has "a double life." Her soul lives in heaven because of her intense contemplation of God in her Psalms, but it also lives in her body on earth. She is still physically alive, and the "dissolution [that will] end all worldly strife" is still ahead of her, whereas in "Triumph of Death" Laura is dead in earthly terms and Petrarch feels his continued bodily existence to be a hard sentence when he learns that "as thow art shalt so continue still / Till by thy ending hower, thow hence be led" (chap. 2, 23–24). That Petrarch is still alive is, at least according to Laura, a cause for lament; that Mary Sidney is still alive is a cause for rejoicing.

Lanyer's second allusion to "Triumph of Death" is a response to the silencing of Laura's voice in death. Petrarch and Sidney show us a group of women gathered around Laura's deathbed and attribute a lament to these female mourners. In Mary Sidney's translation this reads:

> Vertue is dead; and dead is beawtie too,
> And dead is curtesie, in mornefull plight,
> The ladies saide: And now, what shall we doe?
>
> Never againe such grace shall blesse or sight;
> Never lyke witt, shall we from woman heare
> And voice, repleate with Angell-lyke delight.
>
> (chap. 1, 145–50)

Lanyer gives us Mary Sidney's angel-pleasing songs rather than the voice that even while in this world resembled an otherworldly angel's. Her Psalms' "musicke might in eares of Angels ring" (124).

Because of her poetry, Mary Sidney differs from Laura not just in her "double life" but also in the way she achieves it. Though the mourning ladies lament Laura's silenced voice, Laura never had any literary voice of her own because she only spoke through Petrarch. Mary Sidney achieves her "double life" by means of her own voice in the "Triumph of Death," which transformed Petrarch's voice into her own, and in her Psalms, which made David's voice hers. Sidney will not just conquer death when she dies, as any blessed spirit does; she conquers it now and forever by means of her Psalm translations, which will be read by "after-coming ages" whose "eies, . . . hearts, . . . tongues, . . . ears" will be filled by her contemplation of God.[51] Mary Sidney is not only a better Sidney, she is a better Laura—better because she has written verse that will speak forever, verse that has become part of the English canon of spiritual poetry. Lanyer's praise of the Psalms and her imitation of the "Triumph of Death" play a role in Sidney's eternal presence because they stimulate a hunger to read Sidney's work, and this hunger and its satisfaction will help to keep her poetry and reputation alive.[52]

This change from dead-but-eternally-living woman at the center of the poem to living-and-eternally-living woman radically redirects "The Authors Dreame" away from the melancholy close of the "Triumph of Death," where we see Petrarch looking forward to his "meeting day" with Laura—the day of his own death. Lanyer wakes from her dream and, in a final section of the poem that has no parallel in "Triumph of Death," looks forward to her meeting day with Sidney in this life. She imagines herself, book of verses in hand, approaching the great poet humbly but with confidence, "these unlearned lines beeing my best, / Of her great wisedom can no whit be blam'd" (203–4).

One of the duties of an established author is the mentoring of those still perfecting their art, and it is to this aspect of Sidney that Lanyer appeals in this concluding section. Lanyer represents Sidney as the older poet, elevated, refined, abstracted, a bit out of touch with this world. She continues to praise her poetry but without the passion and detail that animated the earlier portions of the poem in which she describes the procession and the psalm singing in company with the goddesses. She speaks of Sidney's style as "higher." She says, "my cleare reason sees her by that streame, / Where her rare virtues daily are increast," but she does not show her doing anything. Sidney's "faire mind on worthier workes is plac'd / On workes that are more deepe, and more profound" (202, 207–8, 215–16). She is *hors de concours*. The focus subtly shifts to Lanyer's poetry, its quality, what Sidney can do for it by reading it, and what it can do for Sidney's spirit. Sidney becomes the reader and beneficiary of Lanyer's book.

To describe the value of her own work Lanyer uses the classical commonplace that a good poet is like a bee. She digests the many texts on which she draws and makes honey from them, a simile that also appears in the passage quoted earlier from Jonson's *Timber, or Discoveries*.

> For to this lady now I will repaire,
> Presenting her the fruits of idle houres;
> Thogh many Books she writes that are more rare,
> Yet there is hony in the meanest flowres:
>
> Which is both wholesome, and delights the taste:
> Though sugar be more finer, higher priz'd,
> Yet is the painefull Bee no whit disgrac'd,
> Nor her faire wax, or hony more despiz'd.
>
> (193–200)

Even while Lanyer uses it in apparently humble apology for her rough style and lower social class (sugar is "finer" than honey), the reference to the theory of imitation suggests the special excellence of Lanyer's poetry. Sidney's highly refined poetry comes from single sources, the *Trionfi* or the Psalms, whereas Sidney's sugar is just one of the elements in Lanyer's honey, though it is a "choicest flower." Without disparaging Sidney's works, Lanyer shows the value of her own.[53]

In this last section of the poem, Lanyer calls attention to herself as a writer by repeatedly asking Sidney to receive and read her poems, six times in the final eight stanzas (ll. 193–94, 205–6, 210, 213–16, 217–20, 221–24). Although she also urges the other dedicatees to read her poem in the letters addressed to them, in all the other cases, reading is presented as beneficial to the reader. She extensively lauds the spiritual benefits each one will gain by reading the *Salve Deus* poem about Christ's Passion, and she does not ask any of them to form a critical opinion of the poetic merits of the dedicatory epistle itself. Yet, that is exactly what she does here, where she speaks far more about Sidney's reading of "The Authors Dreame," a mere dedicatory epistle, than she does about her reading of the spiritually instructive *Salve Deus*. Lanyer even gives priority to the epistle when she imagines hand-delivering the volume of poems to Sidney, saying, "And therefore, first I here present my Dreame, / And next, invite her Honour to my feast" (the feast is her metaphor for the *Salve Deus* poem) (205–206). Even when, in the last two stanzas of the entire epistle, she finally addresses the topic that provides the whole content for most of the other dedicatory letters—the spiritual benefits of reading about Christ—she draws as much attention to her own agency as the author of the account of Christ as she does to His power. She speaks of her *Salve Deus* poem as a portrait of Christ ("him") made by her hand. Only in the very last two lines does she speak of Christ's saving power.

> Receive him here by my unworthy hand,
> And reade his paths of faire humility;
> Who though our sinnes in number passe the sand,
> They all are purg'd by his Divinity.
>
> (221–24)

All that Lanyer asks from Sidney is that she read her work. Perhaps she thought that the patronage, which she must surely have hoped for, would follow naturally if only she could persuade the great woman to receive and read her book.

Why Canonize a Woman Poet?

That Lanyer canonizes Mary Sidney can be seen clearly in her poem, as can the various strategies she uses to do so—the representation of the election of the texts to canonical status by arbiters of taste and the use of imitation of them as a demonstration of their canonical status. Yet, while a desire to persuade her contemporary Sidney to read her works and true admiration for the countess can explain why Lanyer represents Sidney's poetry in such a positive light and even why she removes her to a zone beyond competition, the treatment of her predecessor also raises two larger questions: How could an early-seventeenth-century English woman have conceived of raising a fellow woman poet to canonical status and what does her having done so signify?

If my initial hypothesis that Lanyer was exposed to Italian ideas about women writers and even to writings by Italian women and that part of Sidney's appeal to her as an author lay in her appreciation of Italian literature is accepted, then a possible explanation for her ability to conceive of the project in the first place suggests itself. By 1611, Italy offered an example of an established canon of women writers. It could be observed in individual volumes of women's works, in poetry anthologies, and in the praise given to women writers and the praise they gave each other in their poetry. Lanyer's "The Authors Dreame" is an application of her knowledge of Italian literary behavior to the English scene in which she found herself. She could conceive of a canon of women writers, a canon open to the addition of her name as well as Sidney's because such a multiclass canon already existed in Italy. The "stigma of Italy" with which she was branded by birth and upbringing not only freed her to write, it freed her to attempt to change the literary landscape in England.

Part of the answer to the second question, what her having added Sidney to the canon signifies, is certainly that it created a precedent for herself as a poet. Where Sidney, a woman of her own time, place, and language had gone, so might she go, too. But a less self-interested explanation is also possible. Two important themes in Lanyer's *Salve Deus* volume are the need for fellowship among women and the importance of showing women in a good light, and this social theory underlies her advocacy of canonical status for Sidney, a woman poet, in "The Authors Dreame."

The extent to which Lanyer's poem expresses her ambition, her awareness of class differences and antagonisms, and her advocacy of women's fellowship is one of the pivotal points of discussion in recent criticism of Lanyer's work. Almost everyone who has written about her has taken a stand, from those who argue that Lanyer shows herself to be dedicated to creating communities of women and to building bonds between women to those who find her far less utopian.[54] My reading of her canonization of Sidney and of her imitation of a famous predecessor offers confirmation of Lanyer's interest in the cause of women, even as it also recognizes that she is a practical woman seeking recognition in a competitive world; the two do not exclude one another. Lanyer is a protofeminist, like Rachel Speght, another commoner, who published her *A Mouzell for Melastomus*, a tract in defense of women, a few years later (1617),[55] but she achieves her defense through art and not logic. It is precisely as an artist that she appreciates Sidney's work and claims fellowship with her in this poem.

Lanyer's often quoted final dedicatory letter, which is addressed "To the Vertuous Reader," is especially vocal about the necessity for women to band together and to speak well of one another in order to undo the damage done by men and, even worse, by women who have denigrated women. She explains,

> Often have I heard, that it is the property of some women, not only to emulate the virtues and perfections of the rest, but also by all their powers of ill speaking, to ecclipse the brightnes of their deserved fame: now contrary to this custome, . . . I have written this small volume, or little booke, for the generall use of all virtuous Ladies and Gentlewomen of this kingdome; and in commendation of some particular persons of our owne sexe, such as for the most part, are so well knowne to my selfe, and others, that I dare undertake Fame dares not to call any better. And this have I done, to make knowne to the world, that all women deserve not to be blamed though some forgetting they are women themselves, and in danger to be condemned by the words of their owne mouthes, fall into so great an errour, as to speake unadvisedly against the rest of their sexe. (48)

Mary Sidney is one of the "particular persons of our owne sexe" whose fame Lanyer martials to assist in her defense of womankind. Her imitation of Sidney, which is part of her strategy of canonization because it demonstrates that Sidney is an author of a status to be "emulated," shows Sidney's "virtues and perfections" and also Lanyer's own. Her description of the competitive goddesses who gather around Sidney shows that she knows all too well how competition among women can work, but her handling of Sidney's poetry shows that an author can "emulate the virtues and perfections" of a fellow woman, without eclipsing "the brightnes of their deserved fame." In her hands, imitation is not necessarily a means for the imitator to triumph over the imitated, as it so often was in the highly competitive world of male poets, though her treatment of Spenser shows that she can compete when she wants to.[56] Her strategy of attributing eternal status to Sidney, which appears so self-serving, actually contributes to the success of her protofeminist agenda because it means that Lanyer is not setting herself up in competition with Sidney. Readers can read Sidney and they can read Lanyer. It is pleasing to see that in recent years, after so much neglect, Fame has taken up Aemilia Bassano Lanyer's cause as well as Mary Sidney's. As a glance at any anthology shows, she has been added to the canon not just of women writers but of English writers of the seventeenth century.

NOTES

Unless otherwise noted, all translations are my own.

1. A single author, Lady Mary Wroth, accounts for English women's entries in the categories of love sonnet sequence, pastoral romance, and pastoral drama. *The Countess of Montgomeries Urania,* Part I (London: John Marriott and John Grismand, 1621) includes the sonnet sequence *Pamphilia to Amphilanthus.* Part II of *Urania* and *Love's Victories,* a pastoral play, were not published in Wroth's lifetime.

2. My invention of the term "the stigma of Italy" is indebted to the term "the stigma of print," which I adapt from J. W. Saunders, "The Stigma of Print: A Note on the Social Bases of Tudor Poetry," *Essays in Criticism* 1 (1951): 139–64. The force of the "stigma of Italy" for aristocratic women writers was increased by its coincidence with the "stigma of print." Felt by authors who wrote high art—poetry, fiction, drama—according to Saunders, who first identified the phenomenon among male writers, it inhibited "the leading Court poets, those who set the pattern of the times," from publishing because they perceived publication to be socially degrading and because they achieved the purposes for which they wrote through manuscript circulation. On women and print, see Wendy Wall, *The Imprint of Gender* (Ithaca: Cornell University Press, 1993). On lyric poets and print, see Arthur F. Marotti, *Manuscript, Print, and the English Renaissance Lyric* (Ithaca: Cornell University Press, 1995).

3. Roger Ascham, *The Scholemaster,* in *English Works,* ed. William Aldis Wright (Cambridge: Cambridge University Press, 1904), 229, 230, 231.

4. One English writer had earlier publicly demonstrated her knowledge of Italian. In about 1551, Lady Anne Bacon published a translation of sermons by Bernardino Ochino, an Italian Cappuchin who had become a Lutheran and had preached in England, but the clerical source, the didactic genre, and the religious subject matter put Bacon's translation in a different category from the works by Sidney and Lanyer that I am discussing. A.C. [Anne Cooke Bacon], trans., *Fourtene Sermons of Barnardine Ochyne* (London: John Day and William Seres [1551]). Lady Mary Wroth, mentioned in note 1, was another exception; she can be accounted for by her origins in the Sidney family.

5. Her father and his brothers had come from Italy in 1539 or 1540 at the invitation of Henry VIII to form a recorder consort at court. All the brothers kept up close ties with their homeland, and, after her father's death, when Aemilia was seven, she and her mother lived near their Italian relatives, so she almost certainly learned Italian and without doubt would have retained the aura of an Italian to the ethnically sensitive English. For more on the Bassano family, see David Lasocki and Roger Prior, *The Bassanos: Venetian Musicians and Instrument Makers in England, 1531–1665* (Aldershot, Hants: Scholar Press; Brookfield, Vt.: Ashgate, 1995).

6. Translation was considered a form of imitation in the Renaissance. On this topic with regard to Mary Sidney's Psalms, see Louise Schleiner, *Tudor and Stuart Women Writers* (Bloomington: Indiana University Press, 1994), 55–58. For an extended discussion of "The Triumph of Death" as a "deeply nuanced" (283) literary

work in its own right, see Danielle Clarke, "'Lover's Songs Shall Turne to Holy Psalmes': Mary Sidney and the Transformation of Petrarch," *Modern Language Review* 92 (1997): 282–94.

7. "The Authors Dreame," in *The Poems of Aemilia Lanyer: Salve Deus Rex Judeorum*, ed. Susanne Woods (New York: Oxford University Press, 1993), l. 203. All citations of Lanyer's poetry are from this edition.

8. For complete biographical information on Sidney and a discussion of all her works in their domestic, social, and cultural context, see Margaret P. Hannay, *Philip's Phoenix: Mary Sidney, Countess of Pembroke* (New York: Oxford University Press, 1990).

9. In the dedication of his *A Defence of Ryme* to William Herbert, the countess's son, Daniel said, "Having beene first incourag'd or fram'd thereunto by your most Worthy and Honourable Mother, receiuing the first notion for the formall ordering of those compositions at Wilton, which I must euer acknowledge to haue beene my best Schoole, and therefore alwayes am to hold a feeling and gratefull Memory." Samuel Daniel, *A Defence of Ryme*, ed. G. B. Harrison, The Bodley Head Quartos (London: John Lane The Bodley Head; New York: E. P. Dutton, 1925). Louise Schleiner eloquently describes Mary Sidney's gathering of intellectuals. Schleiner, *Tudor and Stuart*, 61.

10. The former year marks the date of the death of her famous brother, Sir Philip Sidney; at that time, authors who had addressed themselves to her brother turned to her for support. Her husband died in the latter year, and after that "the Dowager Countess did not enjoy the prestige, the money or the power that had made her a prime patron of literature." Hannay, *Philip's Phoenix*, 184.

11. Frances Meres, *Palladis Tamia* (London: Cuthbert Burbie, 1598), 284 verso. Thanks to Sara Johnson and Christine Cooper for help with the translation.

12. For a thorough discussion of the influence of Sidney's works, see Margaret P. Hannay, Noel J. Kinnamon, and Michael G. Brennan, eds., *The Collected Works of Mary Sidney Herbert*, 2 vols. (Oxford: Clarendon Press, 1998), 1:21–55. In her elegantly argued, "Spectres and Sisters: Mary Sidney and the 'Perennial Puzzle' of Renaissance Women's Writing," Suzanne Trill makes a strong case for the "pivitol significance of the *Psalms* for Mary Sidney's contemporary reputation" (201) and uses "The Authors Dreame" as one of the pieces of evidence for her case. *See Voicing Women: Gender and Sexuality in Early Modern Writing*, eds. Kate Chedgzov, Melanie Hansen, and Suzanne Trill, 191–211 (Pittsburgh, Pa.: Duquesne University Press, 1997).

13. *A Discourse of Life and Death. Written in French by Ph. Mornay. Antonius, A Tragodie Written also in French by Ro. Garnier. Both done in English by the Countesse of Pembroke* (London: William Ponsonby, 1592).

14. For a discussion of the attribution of "Clorinda" to Sidney, see Hannay, Kinnamon, and Brennan, eds. *Collected Works*, 1:119–32; Hyder Edward Rollins, ed., *A Poetical Rhapsody (1602–21)* (Cambridge, Mass.: Harvard University Press, 1931), 1:15. The poem is on B5 in the 1602 edition.

15. The exception to the omission of English women writers from anthologies is one volume of the multivolume *Monument of Matrons*, but the texts included in it are devotional, not secular, as are Mary Sidney's anthologized works. For more on the *Monument*, see John King's essay in this volume. The absence of English women writers from poetry collections contrasts markedly with the frequent publication of Italian

women writers in the enormously popular Petrarchist anthologies that appeared in the sixteenth century. Publication in these made Italian women part of the Petrarchist canon. For example, Lodovico Dolce's *Rime di diversi signori napolitani, e d'altri* (Venice: Gabriel Giolito de Ferrari, e fratelli, 1556) includes twenty-six authors of whom four were women, and the number of poems by the women is substantial. Of the volume's 290 pages, 86 pages are devoted to the poetry of Chiara Matraini; the entire first edition of her poems is reproduced. For more information on the Italian sixteenth-century anthologies, see the essays by Finotti, Shemek, Kirkham, and Cox in this volume.

16. Hannay, *Philip's Phoenix*, 70, 69.

17. In the dedication to *Silkewormes and their flies* (1599), Thomas Moffett put Sidney's Psalms and "Triumph of Death" on an equal footing when he cautioned her not to exhaust herself by working too hard at her translations: "Let Petrarke sleep, giue rest to Sacred Writte," quoted in Hannay, *Philip's Phoenix*, 107.

18. Henry Parker, Lord Morley, *Tryumphes of Fraunces Petrarcke*, ed. D. D. Carnicelli (Cambridge, Mass.: Harvard University Press, 1971), 77.

19. Despite the general approval of the *Trionfi*, Ascham, whose suspicion of Italian literature I cited earlier (see note 3), thought they were appreciated by readers who "scornefullie mocke his [God's] worde. . . . they haue in more reuerence, the triumphes of Petrarche: than the Genesis of Moses." Ascham, *The Scholemaster*, 232.

20. Kenneth R. Bartlett, "The Occasion of Lord Morley's Translations of the *Trionfi:* The Triumph of Chastity over Politics," in *Petrarch's Triumphs: Allegory and Spectacle*, ed. Konrad Eisenbichler and Amilcare A. Iannucci (Ottawa: Dovehouse, 1990), 325–34. For a discussion of Italian Protestant annotations of Petrarch, see William J. Kennedy, *Authorizing Petrarch* (Ithaca: Cornell University Press, 1994), 67–81. Clark points out that the "Triumph of Death" "sets forth the fundamental elements of Petrarchan poetics (mainly in 'The first chapter') then undermines them and replaces them with another register of praise dependent upon eternity and mutability. Ultimately, it can be seen to reverse Petrarchan conventions, as the poet is criticized for his concern with earthly things, erotic desire and superficiality, while Laura speaks from a position of authority about the transitory nature of earthly values, and the durability of the divine. The poet is abandoned to a legacy of loss and longing until he can renounce worldly passions." Danielle Clarke, ed., "Introduction" in *Isabella Whitney, Mary Sidney, and Aemilia Lanyer: Renaissance Women Poets* (Harmondsworth, Middlesex: Penguin, 2000), xxviii–xxix.

21. See, for example, Mary Lamb, *Gender and Authorship in the Sidney Circle* (Madison: University of Wisconsin Press, 1990).

22. Thomas Hoby, trans., *The Book of the Courtier* by Count Baldassare Castiglione, ed. Virginia Cox (London: J. M. Dent; Rutland, Vt.: Charles E. Tuttle, 1994).

23. Nicholas Breton, "*To the Right Honourable . . . Ladie, the Ladie Mary Countesse of Penbrooke*" (dedicatory letter to "*The Pilgrimage to Paradise, ioyned with the Countesse of Penbrookes loue*"), in *The Works in Verse and Prose of Nicholas Breton*, ed. Alexander B. Grosart (1879; New York: AMS Press, 1966), 1:b.4. According to Grosart, Breton knew Italian. Grosart, "Memorial Introduction," in *Works in Verse and Prose of Nicholas Breton*, 1:xx.

24. "To the Gentlemen studients and Scholers of Oxforde" praises her writing. Breton states that "the occasion, that made me first enter into this action, was to acquaint the honest mindes of vertuous dispositions, with the heavenly Meditations, of an honourable Lady"—the "heavenly Meditations" are Sidney's Psalms. *Works in Verse and Prose of Nicholas Breton*, ed. Grosart, 1:b.4.

25. Thomas Heywood, *Gunaikeion or Nine Books of Various Histories Concerning Women* (London: Adam Islip, 1624).

26. It is possible that Colonna was acceptable to Protestants because she was known to have been attracted to the party of reform in Italy. She was very interested in Ochino, who had preached in London, and her close association with him led to her being called before the Inquisition. Colonna would have been familiar to English readers of Ariosto's *Orlando Furioso*, where she is praised in Canto 37. John Harington in his 1591 translation of the *Furioso* used Ariosto's praise of Colonna as a pretext for praising the four daughters of Sir Anthony Cooke, who also appear on Heywood's list, so Sidney is not the first English woman to be compared with Colonna. But having introduced the Cooke sisters because one of them wrote epitaphs on her husband and, thus, resembled Colonna, who wrote poetry about her deceased husband, Harington stresses the domestic, private nature of the writing done by the Cooke sisters. He does not mention the publication by one of them, Anne Cooke Bacon, of a translation from the Italian of Bernardino Ochino's sermons (see note 4). John Harington, *Ludovico Ariosto's Orlando Furioso, Translated into English Heroical Verse by Sir John Harington (1591)*, ed. Robert McNulty (Oxford: Clarendon Press, 1972), 434.

27. Sidney influenced her niece, Lady Mary Wroth; Elizabeth Cary (mentioned in this essay in the context of Sidney's translation of Garnier); and Lanyer. For Colonna's influence, see the essay by Virginia Cox in this volume.

28. Josephine A. Roberts, ed., *The First Part of the Countess of Montgomery's Urania by Lady Mary Wroth* (Binghamton, N.Y.: Medieval and Renaissance Texts and Studies, 1995), civ.

29. Roberts, ed., *Urania*, lxxxiv–lxxxv.

30. On the manuscript of "Triumph of Death," see Hannay et al., *Collected Works*, 315–16.

31. On manuscript circles and Mary Sidney, see Lamb, *Gender and Authorship*.

32. Oxford, Bodleian Library, Ashmole 226, fol. 201recto (September 2, 1597); ibid, fol. 95verso (May 17, 1597). Forman's records of Lanyer's visits were first discussed by A. L. Rowse, *Sex and Society in Shakespeare's Age: Simon Forman the Astrologer* (London: Weidenfeld and Nicolson, 1974), and in his edition of *Salve Deus: The Poems of Shakespeare's Dark Lady* (London: Jonathan Cape, 1978). As the title of the latter book indicates, Rowse was convinced that Lanyer was the Dark Lady of Shakespeare's sonnets, but most scholars have not accepted his conclusions. For a refutation of his view, see Lorna Hutson, "Why the Lady's Eyes are Nothing Like the Sun," in *New Feminist Discourses: Critical Essays on Theories and Texts*, ed. Isobel Armstrong (London: Routledge, 1992), 154–75. For a reinterpretation of what Forman's texts tell about Lanyer's life, as well as an all-round study of Lanyer in her English literary context, see Susanne Woods, *Lanyer: A Renaissance Woman Poet* (New York: Oxford University Press, 1999). See also Pamela Joseph Benson, "To Play the Man: Aemilia Lanyer and the Acquisition of Patronage," in *Opening the Borders*, ed. Peter C. Herman (Newark, N. J.: University of Delaware Press; London: Associated University Presses, 1999), 243–64.

33. Margaret F. Rosenthal, *The Honest Courtesan: Veronica Franco, Citizen and Writer in Sixteenth-Century Venice* (Chicago: University of Chicago Press, 1992), 6.

34. For a thorough discussion of the evidence that Lanyer was a musician and an honest courtesan, see Benson, "To Play the Man."

35. In sharing so many qualities with Italian women writers, as in her Italian origins, Aemilia Lanyer was unique in early-seventeenth-century England. Although several male Italian intellectuals were active in London at the time—John Florio, author

of a dictionary and language instruction texts, is the obvious example—she is the only instance of a writing woman with firsthand knowledge of Italian culture.

36. Examples of texts identified only by the woman author's initials on the title page are Margaret Tyler, trans., *The Mirrour of Princely Deedes and Knighthood,* by Diego Ortunez de Calahorra (London: Thomas East, 1578); Anne Lock, trans., *Sermons of John Calvin* (London: John Day, 1560); and Elizabeth Cary, *The Tragedie of Mariam* (London: Richard Hawkins, 1613). There are several modern editions of Cary's play, for example, *The Tragedy of Mariam, the Fair Queen of Jewry with the Lady Falkland: Her Life by One of Her Daughters,* ed. Barry Weller and Margaret W. Ferguson (Berkeley: University of California Press, 1994).

37. For example, of the women listed in the previous note, Tyler dedicated to Lord Thomas Howard, with whose parents' household, she says, she had a connection; Lock dedicated to several important noblewomen with whom she was connected in Calvinist circles; Cary dedicated to a sister-in-law. On Lock's connections with her dedicatees, see Susan M. Felch, ed., *The Collected Works of Anne Vaughan Lock* (Tempe: Arizona Center for Medieval and Renaissance Studies with Renaissance English Text Society, 1999), xv–lxviii passim. On Battiferra's and Aragona's dedications to the Medici duchess Eleonora de Toledo, see Victoria Kirkham's essay in this volume.

38. See Virginia Cox's essay in this volume.

39. There are nine copies of Lanyer's *Salve Deus* volume extant. Six of them include all the dedicatory letters; the others include various combinations of them. On the contents of the editions, see Susanne Woods, ed., "Textual Introduction," in *The Poems of Aemilia Lanyer* (New York: Oxford University Press, 1993), xlvii–li.

40. I derived this practical definition of canonical from M. H. Abrams, *A Glossary of Literary Terms,* 5th ed. (Fort Worth, Tex.: Holt, Rinehart and Winston, 1988), 20.

41. In an exciting and provocative essay, Keri Boyd McBride also discusses "The Authors Dreame" as a poem in which Lanyer figures herself as a poet in succession after Mary Sidney, though she finds Lanyer to be interested in displacing Sidney, whereas I argue that Lanyer is interested in joining or succeeding Sidney. One of the causes of our differing readings is the genres or modes that we identify at work in the poem. I discuss McBride's essay at more length in note 52. Kari Boyd McBride, "Remembering Orpheus in the Poems of Aemilia Lanyer," *Studies in English Literature* 38 (1998): 87–108. Debra Rienstra also engages with McBride's argument and explores Lanyer's "The Authors Dreame" as a response to and representation of Mary Sidney's performance of the role of poet. Her particular focus is on Sidney as Lanyer's mentor in "writing of divinest things." Debra Rienstra, "Dreaming Authorship: Aemilia Lanyer and the Countess of Pembroke," in *Discovering and (Re)Covering the Seventeenth Century Religious Lyric,* ed. Eugene R. Cunner and Jeffrey Johnson (Pittsburgh: Duquesne University Press, 2001), 80–103.

42. This highly visual form was generally familiar during the Renaissance in dramatic and pictorial forms as well as the written one popularized by Petrarch. The entries of monarchs into cities often imitated ancient Roman triumphs, and throughout Europe many tapestries, murals, and even domestic objects such as the chests made for the bedrooms of Florentine brides depicted historical and allegorical triumphs. Henry VIII owned numerous *Trionfi* tapestries. For information on these and on the *Trionfi* and English literature, see Robert Coogan, "Petrarch's 'Trionfi' and the English Renaissance," *Studies in Philology* 67 (1970): 306–27. For more on triumphs, see Alas-

tair Fowler, *Triumphal Forms: Structural Patterns in Elizabethan Poetry* (Cambridge: Cambridge University Press, 1970); and Konrad Eisenbichler and Amilcare A. Iannucci, eds., *Petrarch's Triumphs: Allegory and Spectacle* (Ottowa: Dovehouse, 1990).

43. Like so many poetic dreamers who wander through a beautiful landscape in search of something, Lanyer finds herself walking through "th'Edalyan Groves" in search of "a Lady whom Minerva chose" (2–3), but she immediately realizes that she does not need to look for the Lady. She already knows where the Lady is—she can see her in her thoughts with her "eye of Reason." This change of the dream from something perceived by the outward eye to something perceived by the inward "eye of Reason" makes it seem true. Like Philip Sidney looking at the image of Stella in his heart in the first poem in *Astrophel and Stella*, Lanyer needs only to describe what can be apprehended by her reason. The vision of Mary Sidney's triumph is not fancy; it is true.

44. Lisa Schnell also identifies Spenser as an influence on the opening scene of the poem. She usefully cites "the famous episode in [*Faerie Queene*] Book VI in which Sir Calidore stumbles upon 'a troupe of Ladies dauncing'" and quotes the stanza that describes these Ladies and the Graces dancing around "[a]nother Damzell." Schnell's essay is on patronage and the "gift-exchange relationship," and she incorporates the echo of this scene into her argument about Lanyer's handling of this relationship. The first part of the poem presents a "utopian vision of courtesy," but "we are never quite allowed to forget that the vision is just an illusion," and "Lanyer sets the earthly institution of patronage beside its heavenly prototype constructing a situation in which the countess is obliged, if she is indeed the latter-day David that Lanyer has depicted her as, to form a relationship with the poet." Lisa Schnell, "Breaking 'The Rule of Cortezia': Aemilia Lanyer's Dedications to *Salve Deus Rex Judaeorum*," *Journal of Medieval and Early Modern Studies* 27 (1997): 87, 91.

45. Edmund Spenser, "Aprill," in *The Yale Edition of the Shorter Poems of Edmund Spenser*, ed. William A. Oram et al. (New Haven and London: Yale University Press, 1989), l. 55. All quotations from "Aprill" are from this edition.

46. Thomas H. Cain, introduction to "Aprill," in *Shorter Poems*, ed. Oram et al., 67.

47. In my essay, "To Play the Man," I speculated that Lanyer herself was skilled at accompanying psalm singing on the lute. Her celebration of the psalms as music here shows an appreciation of their musical qualities. Might it also refer to her own settings of Sidney's Psalms or at least to her musicianship?

48. Philip Sidney, *Sidney*, A *Defence of Poetry*, ed. Jan Van Dorsten (Oxford: Oxford University Press, 1966), 64.

49. Ben Jonson, *Timber or Discoveries*, in *Ben Jonson's Literary Criticism*, ed. James D. Redwine (Lincoln: University of Nebraska Press, 1970), 31–32. I have quoted Jonson here even though *Timber or Discoveries* was only a manuscript collection of fragments, because this passage is the classic expression of this notion of imitation in English. On Jonson's theory and practice of imitation, see Richard S. Peterson, *Imitation and Praise in the Poems of Ben Jonson* (New Haven: Yale University Press, 1981). On Lanyer and Jonson, see Woods, *Lanyer: A Renaissance Woman Poet*, chap. 4.

50. Mary Sidney, "Triumph of Death," in *Collected Works*, vol. 1, ed. Hannay, Kinnamon, and Brennan (Oxford: Clarendon Press, 1998), chap 2, ll. 19–24. All quotations from Sidney are from this edition. Sidney's poems are also available in *The Triumph of Death and Other Unpublished and Uncollected Poems by Mary Sidney, Countess of*

Pembroke (1561–1621), ed. G. F. Waller (Salzburg: Institut für Englische Sprache und Literatur, Universität Salzburg, 1977).

51. This is an allusion to I Corinthians 2.9–10. "Eye hath not seen, nor ear heard, neither have entered into the heart of man, the things which God hath prepared for them that love him. But God hath revealed them unto us by his Spirit." Though Sidney's Psalms originate in the Hebrew Bible, they serve a Christian function.

52. While I speak of Lanyer's canonization of Sidney as blazing a trail for Lanyer, Keri McBride interprets moving Sidney into the canon as silencing her. "Her great work, her translation of the psalms is finished, and Sidney herself, as an inhabitant of heaven . . . can produce nothing more—nothing that could challenge the primacy of Lanyer, the poet who means to replace Sidney even as she writes in praise of her," and again, "[b]y the end of the poem, praise has turned to eulogy and Mary Sidney is a corpse/corpus, a fixed and finished work, a closed book, whose silencing creates the space in which Lanyer can speak." I suggest that Lanyer's praise makes readers want to read Sidney's works, thus prolonging her life. The differing conclusions that McBride and I come to are, in part, due to the difference in the genre or mode that we find dominant in the poem. Whereas I find it to be a triumph with definite allusions to Sidney's "Triumph of Death" and to Spenser's "Aprill," she sees it, along with the entire *Salve Deus*, to be "in the pastoral mode, the literary form that had traditionally signaled a poet's debut in the world of serious literature through its invocation of Orpheus, the mythic father of poetry." She finds the entire volume's Spenserian poetic predecessor to be the *Epithalamion*, because Spenser figures himself as Orpheus in that work, and she also finds it linked to elegy. McBride's conclusions about Lanyer's positioning of herself with regard to Sidney are appropriate to the Orphic vision of pastoral, as mine are to the triumph, because death is central to the former and continuity to the latter. "Lanyer, like other poet-initiates, was faced with the problem of creating a requisite corpse upon which to construct the poetic self, celebrating the death of one's (supposedly greater) predecessor in order to create a space for one's own voice." According to McBride, Sidney provided Lanyer with that corpse. McBride, "Remembering Orpheus," 95, 97, 87, 90.

53. Lanyer's use of the bee and its digestive production of honey may be indebted to Jonson's formulation of the trope because his critical ideas were influential even though unpublished, but the apian figure was such a commonplace by the time she wrote that it is impossible to identify her source. On the apian simile, see further Thomas M. Greene, *The Light in Troy: Imitation and Discovery in Renaissance Poetry* (New Haven: Yale University Press, 1982), 72–75. Lanyer's contrast of honey with sugar seems to me to be original.

54. One of the earliest and most eloquent proponents of Lanyer's attempt to build a female community is Barbara Kiefer Lewalski. See one of her many publications on Lanyer, "Imagining Female Community: Aemilia Lanyer's Poems," in *Writing Women in Jacobean England* (Cambridge, Mass.: Harvard University Press, 1993), 213–41.

55. Rachel Speght, *A Mouzell for Melastomus*, in *The Polemics and Poems of Rachel Speght*, ed. Barbara Kiefer Lewalski (New York and Oxford: Oxford University Press, 1996), 1–27.

56. An example is Ben Jonson, whose practice, according to Richard Peterson, shows that "to imitate in the true sense is to assimilate and remake in a spirit of admiration that inevitably shades over into active emulation and rivalry." Peterson, *Imitation and Praise*, 6.

BIBLIOGRAPHY

Abrams, M. H. *A Glossary of Literary Terms*. 5th ed. Fort Worth, Tex.: Holt, Rinehart, and Winston, 1988.

Ascham, Roger. *The Scholemaster*. In *English Works*, ed. William Aldis Wright. Cambridge: Cambridge University Press, 1904.

Bacon, Anne Cooke [A.C.], trans. *Fourtene Sermons of Barnardine Ochyne*. London: John Day and Wylliam Seres [1551].

Bartlett, Kenneth R. "The Occasion of Lord Morley's Translations of the *Trionfi*: The Triumph of Chastity over Politics." In *Petrarch's Triumphs: Allegory and Spectacle*, ed. Konrad Eisenbichler and Amilcare A. Iannucci, 325–34. Ottawa: Dovehouse, 1990.

Benson, Pamela Joseph. "To Play the Man: Aemilia Lanyer and the Acquisition of Patronage." In *Opening the Borders: Inclusivity in Early Modern Studies, Essays in Honor of James V. Mirollo*, ed. Peter C. Herman, 243–64. Newark, N. J.: University of Delaware Press; London: Associated University Presses, 1999.

Breton, Nicholas. *The Works in Verse and Prose of Nicholas Breton*. Ed. Alexander B. Grosart. 2 vols. 1879; Reprint, New York: AMS Press, 1966.

Cain, Thomas H. Introduction to "Aprill." In *The Yale Edition of the Shorter Poems of Edmund Spenser*, ed. William A. Oram et al. New Haven: Yale University Press, 1989.

Cary, Elizabeth. *The Tragedie of Mariam*. London: Richard Hawkins, 1613.

———. *The Tragedy of Mariam the Fair Queen of Jewry with the Lady Falkland: Her Life by one of her daughters*. Ed. Barry Weller and Margaret W. Ferguson. Berkeley: University of California Press, 1994.

Clarke, Danielle. "'Lover's Songs Shall Turne to Holy Psalmes': Mary Sidney and the Transformation of Petrarch." *Modern Language Review* 92 (1997): 282–94.

———, ed. "Introduction." *Isabella Whitney, Mary Sidney and Aemilia Lanyer: Renaissance Women Poets*. Harmondsworth, Middlesex: Penguin Books, 2000.

Coogan, Robert. "Petrarch's 'Trionfi' and the English Renaissance." *Studies in Philology* 67 (1970): 306–27.

Daniel, Samuel. *A Defence of Ryme*. Ed. G. B. Harrison. The Bodley Head Quartos. London: John Lane The Bodley Head; New York: E. P. Dutton, 1925.

Dolce, Lodovico, ed. *Rime di diversi signori napolitani, e d'altri*. Venice: Gabriel Giolito de' Ferrari, e fratelli, 1556.

Eisenbichler, Konrad, and Amilcare A. Iannucci, eds. *Petrarch's Triumphs: Allegory and Spectacle*. University of Toronto Italian Studies 4. Ottowa: Dovehouse, 1990.

Felch, Susan M., ed. *The Collected Works of Anne Vaughan Lock*. Tempe: Arizona Center for Medieval and Renaissance Studies with Renaissance English Text Society, 1999.

Forman, Simon. Notebooks. Oxford, Bodleian Library, Ashmole 226.

Fowler, Alastair. *Triumphal Forms: Structural Patterns in Elizabethan Poetry*. Cambridge: Cambridge University Press, 1970.

Greene, Thomas M. *The Light in Troy: Imitation and Discovery in Renaissance Poetry*. New Haven: Yale University Press, 1982.

Hannay, Margaret P. *Philip's Phoenix: Mary Sidney, Countess of Pembroke*. New York: Oxford University Press, 1990.

Harington, John. *Ludovico Ariosto's Orlando Furioso, Translated into English Heroical*

Verse by Sir John Harington (1591). Ed. Robert McNulty. Oxford: Clarendon Press, 1972.

Heywood, Thomas. *Gunaikeion, or Nine Books of Various Histories Concerning Women*. London: Adam Islip, 1624.

Hoby, Thomas, trans. *The Book of the Courtier* by Count Baldassare Castiglione. Ed. Virginia Cox. London: J. M. Dent; Rutland, Vt.: Charles E. Tuttle, 1994.

Hutson, Lorna. "Why the Lady's Eyes Are Nothing Like the Sun." In *New Feminist Discourses: Critical Essays on Theories and Texts*, ed. Isobel Armstrong, 154–75. London: Routledge, 1992.

Jonson, Ben. *Timber or Discoveries*. In *Ben Jonson's Literary Criticism*, ed. James D. Redwine. Regents Critics Series. Lincoln: University of Nebraska Press, 1970.

Kennedy, William J. *Authorizing Petrarch*. Ithaca: Cornell University Press, 1994.

Lamb, Mary Ellen. *Gender and Authorship in the Sidney Circle*. Madison: University of Wisconsin Press, 1990.

Lanyer, Aemilia. *The Poems of Aemilia Lanyer: Salve Deus Rex Judaeorum*, ed. Susanne Woods. New York: Oxford University Press, 1993.

Lasocki, David, and Roger Prior. *The Basssanos: Venetian Musicians and Instrument Makers in England, 1531–1665*. Aldershot, Hants: Scholar Press; Brookfield, Vt., 1995.

Lewalski, Barbara Kiefer. "Imagining Female Community: Aemilia Lanyer's Poems." In *Writing Women in Jacobean England*. Cambridge, Mass.: Harvard University Press, 1993.

Lock, Anne, trans. *Sermons of John Calvin*. London: John Day, 1560.

Marotti, Arthur F. *Manuscript, Print, and the English Renaissance Lyric*. Ithaca: Cornell University Press, 1995.

McBride, Kari Boyd. "Remembering Orpheus in the Poems of Aemilia Lanyer," *Studies in English Literature* 38 (1998): 87–108.

Meres, Frances. *Palladis Tamia*. London: Cuthbert Burbie, 1598.

Parker, Henry [Lord Morley]. *Tryumphes of Fraunces Petrarchke: The First English Translation of the* Trionfi. Ed. D. D. Carnicelli. Cambridge, Mass.: Harvard University Press, 1971.

Peterson, Richard S. *Imitation and Praise in the Poems of Ben Jonson*. New Haven: Yale University Press, 1981.

Rienstra, Debra. "Dreaming Authorship: Aemilia Lanyer and the Countess of Pembroke." In *Discovering and (Re)Covering the Seventeenth Century Religious Lyric*, ed. Eugene R. Cunner and Jeffrey Johnson, 80–103. Pittsburgh: Duquesne University Press, 2001.

Rollins, Hyder Edward, ed. A *Poetical Rhapsody (1602–21)*. Cambridge, Mass.: Harvard University Press, 1931.

Rosenthal, Margaret F. *The Honest Courtesan: Veronica Franco, Citizen and Writer in Sixteenth-Century Venice*. Chicago: University of Chicago Press, 1992.

Rowse, A. L. *Sex and Society in Shakespeare's Age: Simon Forman the Astrologer*. London: Weidenfeld and Nicolson, 1974.

———. ed. *The Poems of Shakespeare's Dark Lady*. London: Jonathan Cape, 1978.

Saunders, J. W. "The Stigma of Print: A Note on the Social Bases of Tudor Poetry." *Essays in Criticism* 1 (1951): 139–64.

Schleiner, Louise. *Tudor and Stuart Women Writers*. Bloomington: Indiana University Press, 1994.

Schnell, Lisa. "Breaking 'The Rule of Cortezia': Aemilia Lanyer's Dedications to *Salve Deus Rex Judaeorum*." *Journal of Medieval and Early Modern Studies* 27 (1997): 77–101.

Sidney, Mary. *A Discourse of Life and Death. Written in French by Ph. Mornay. Antonius, A Tragodie Written also in French by Ro. Garnier. Both done in English by the Countess of Pembroke*. London: William Ponsonby, 1592.

———. *The Triumph of Death and Other Unpublished and Uncollected Poems by Mary Sidney, Countess of Pembroke (1561–1621)*. Ed. G. F. Waller. Salzburg: Institut für Englische Sprache und Literatur, Universität Salzburg, 1977.

———. *The Collected Works of Mary Sidney Herbert*. Vol. 1, *Poems, Translations, and Correspondence*. Vol. 2, *The Psalmes of David*. Ed. Margaret P. Hannay, Noel J. Kinnamon, and Michael G. Brennan. Oxford: Clarendon Press, 1998.

Sidney, Philip. *Sidney, A Defence of Poetry*. Ed. Jan Van Dorsten. Oxford: Oxford University Press, 1966.

Speght, Rachel. *A Mouzell for Melastomus*. In *The Polemics and Poems of Rachel Speght*, ed. Barbara Kiefer Lewalski, 1–27. New York: Oxford University Press, 1996.

Spenser, Edmund. "Aprill." In *The Yale Edition of the Shorter Poems of Edmund Spenser*, ed. William A. Oram et al. New Haven: Yale University Press, 1989.

Trill, Suzanne. "Specters and Sisters: Mary Sidney and the 'Perennial Puzzle' of Renaissance Women's Writing." In *Voicing Women: Gender and Sexuality in Early Modern Women's Writing*. Eds. Kate Chedgzoy, Melanie Hansen, and Suzanne Trill. Pittsburgh, PA: Duquesne University Press, 1997. 191–211.

Tyler, Margaret, trans. *The Mirrour of Princely Deedes and Knighthood* by Diego Ortunez de Calahorra. Book 1. London: Thomas East, 1578.

Wall, Wendy. *The Imprint of Gender: Authorship and Publication in the English Renaissance*. Ithaca: Cornell University Press, 1993.

Woods, Susanne. *Lanyer: A Renaissance Woman Poet*. New York: Oxford University Press, 1999.

Wroth, [Lady] Mary. *The First Part of The Countess of Montgomery's Urania by Lady Mary Wroth*. Ed. Josephine A. Roberts. Binghamton, N.Y.: Medieval and Renaissance Texts and Studies, 1995.

Additional Reading

Ballard, George. *Memoirs of Several Ladies of Great Britain*. Ed. Ruth Perry. 1752. Reprint, Detroit: Wayne State University Press, 1985.

Beilin, Elaine V. *Redeeming Eve: Women Writers of the English Renaissance*. Princeton, N.J.: Princeton University Press, 1987.

Grossman, Marshall, ed. *Aemilia Lanyer: Gender, Genre, and the Canon*. Lexington: University Press of Kentucky, 1998.

Walker, Kim. *Women Writers of the English Renaissance*. New York: Twayne; London: Prentice Hall International, 1996.

Woods, Susanne, and Margaret P. Hannay. *Teaching Tudor and Stuart Women Writers*. New York: Modern Language Association, 2000.

Sappho on the Arno

THE BRIEF FAME OF LAURA BATTIFERRA

Victoria Kirkham

A poet celebrated by her contemporaries, Laura Battiferra degli Ammannati suffered the fate of many women writers, soon falling into obscurity. During her lifetime (b.1523, Urbino–d. 1589, Florence), male peers embraced her in their literary communities and canonized her in cycles of the world's most famous women. In comparisons with Sappho, the ancient paradigm for all women writers, Battiferra was held not only equal but superior, admired as a female of both marvelous talent and spotless moral character. Yet by the time Francesco De Sanctis published the first literary history of a newly united modern Italy (1871), she had altogether disappeared from the national annals. What caused her eclipse? Ironically, the qualities for which the sixteenth century most praised her have distanced her from our cultural universe—classical learning, a Mannerist style of wit, versatility as an occasional poet, and Catholic-Reformation religious values.

One measure of her celebrity survives in the beautifully turned account of an event that took place shortly before Christmas 1565, when Florentine men of learning gathered in the venerable monastery of Santa Maria degli Angeli for the funeral of their leader, Benedetto Varchi. Several weeks later, the famed humanist Piero Vettori would write of that occasion in a Latin epistle to his patrician friend Mario Colonna, a Medici court diplomat and amateur poet. Sad though the day had been, the memory of Varchi's many uplifting contributions had buoyed him to a sense of happiness.

> And then, my gladness waxed greater—this too it pleases me to remember now—when I saw that there was also a lady present, standing as close as she could get. Yet it did not move me to amazement, for why should a woman not want to share in a celebration of poetic virtue and industry, especially one herself afire with that same learning, one whom the Muses favor over all other women and whom they assist in writing comely, graceful verse? As a matter of fact, you must remember what I told you then, how we deplored, and rightly so, the rules of the place that excluded and segregated her, forcing her to watch from the rear, as if from behind a curtain. I reckoned that out of respect for her great intellect and her talent for composing beautiful verse, she ought not to be counted as a woman but truly taken for a man.[1]

To Vettori, chaired professor of Greek and Latin at the nearby University of Pisa, her outrageous treatment suggests a parallel from antiquity. Although Dionysius the tyrant had decreed that the first citizen of Athens to set foot on the island of Egina should be summarily put to death, his judges made an exception for Plato, arguing that he should be called not an Athenian but a philosopher. Surely no one will reproach me, Vettori asserts, if I compare a woman to Plato, "font of all knowledge," and plead for her the same privilege as was accorded him. "For I deem that we should not so much have regard merely for her species and sex as we should consider her intellect and culture." To buttress his position, Vettori can turn to another thinker from his arsenal of examples, Maximus of Tyre, who in the second century A.D. "demonstrated how the poetess Sappho was in her life and in her studies equal to Socrates" and how many parallel experiences linked the two. Only after Piero Vettori has constructed this rhetorical platform, setting his mystery woman on a par with Plato, Sappho, and Socrates, does he finally break the suspense and reveal her identity.

> And I know very well that you know that this woman of ours—and would to God I were permitted to say truly ours, because she was not born here, rather she is an outlander and noble plant transported from other terrain into ours, where she has already put down roots together with her consort, he too an excellent artist, and as it were, a new Phidias—you know, I say, that she was Madonna Laura Battiferra. . . . in her gifts of spirit and in her powers of composing she is not a whit

> inferior to Sappho; in fact, she has far and away outstripped and surpassed her in her life and in her morals.

Before he names her, the humanist compliments her husband, the sculptor and architect Bartolomeo Ammannati, the new Phidias. Laura, too, has a classical counterpart. With an unassailable argument, Vettori has pushed his compliments to the limit for this "outlander," a native of Urbino who in 1555 had moved with her husband to Florence. Not only is Laura Battiferra the equal of the greatest of the ancient female poets for her lyrics, she is superior to the woman Plato himself, no less, called "divine" because her life is not tainted with the unsavory reputation that surrounded Sappho, whose biographers from earliest times reported her indulgence in the homosexual love described in some of her verse.[2]

As it happens, Vettori's letter of January 1565 (1566 modern style) is not the only account of this poignant moment at the great male religious house of Santa Maria degli Angeli. Founded in 1295, that monastery formerly flourished at the very heart of Florence, next to Brunelleschi's rotunda, between the Duomo and the Foundling Hospital in Piazza Santissima Annunziata, in a structure that today houses the Department of Literature and Philosophy at the university. An eighteenth-century *History of the Monastery of the Angeli* records that Laura Battiferra Ammannati saw Varchi's last rites there "from a locked window in the little Ladies' Oratory."[3] The chronicler deems it noteworthy to record both her presence and her confinement to a matroneum, behind a small opening in the wall probably covered by an iron grate. Laura must have been standing with her face pressed against it, clutching the bars.

Laura Battiferra's isolation at Benedetto Varchi's funeral was a mighty irony. If anyone should have been among the front ranks of mourners, it was she, as well Vettori knew. The letters and sonnets they sent each other, a correspondence that spans the last decade of Varchi's life, give evidence of how, after the Ammannati settled in Florence, Laura's acquaintance with the literary lion king there ripened to mutual friendship and professional parity. Gestures of generosity, small and large, sprang from the affection that bound them. Concern for the health of Varchi, twenty years older than Laura and slipping into physical decline, often prompts her to ask in her letters how he fares, to worry if he is indisposed, or to send solicitous advice—for a headache, "see if it is coming from the stomach and think about doing some purgations." In November 1557, she writes with thanks for Benedetto's gift of apples and chestnuts, delivered to her at the Ammannati country home in Maiano by Girolamo Razzi, another writer in their circle who was soon to join the Camaldulensions and would later become the abbot of

Santa Maria degli Angeli; a month after, she informs the bachelor Varchi that she has found him a place to live in the country, one she is certain will please him for "the beautiful view." Writing on July 21, 1561, she shares her pleasure in the company that had come calling just the day before: "Yesterday, which was Sunday, Messer Pier Vettorio and the humanist from Pisa came here to the house, led by Messer Baccio Valori, to whom I am much obliged because he did me the greatest favor, since I much desired to see those two great men, whom I had not yet met." At the end of the note, she alludes to a fine point of wording in one of her sonnets that she has discussed with Agnolo Bronzino, the Medici court painter to whom she sat for a splendid portrait. She copies out the relevant verses, a quatrain from one of her sonnets, so Varchi can weigh in with his opinion.[4] The ruling she requests from Varchi on her debate with Bronzino, another older male friend and catalyst in her career, reflects Battiferra's main purpose in the correspondence, her eagerness to excel as a poet. In time, she and Varchi published each other's poetry and collaborated on occasional anthologies; after he died Laura assisted behind the scenes as a silent editor, helping to gather sonnets for a commemorative volume of bereavement poetry.[5]

By 1565, when Varchi passed away, Laura Battiferra degli Ammannati was at the height of her fame, admired as a phenomenal female, accepted by her male colleagues as a peer among peers. In 1560, she had published her first book of poetry, *The First Book of Tuscan Works*, a Petrarchan anthology dedicated to the Medici duchess that won laudatory responses from poets across Italy and made her a celebrity at home. That publication must have been the occasion for her portrait by the Medici court artist Bronzino, who depicts her Dante-like in a profile bust, displaying a manuscript of sonnets by Petrarch. The pose assimilates her to the canon of Italy's vernacular classics, inspirational models for the cultural circle around Duke Cosimo de' Medici's Accademia Fiorentina.[6]

Even before her *First Book of Tuscan Works* appeared, she had won an international reputation as poet of culture and talent. Three years earlier, in 1557, word reached her in Florence that her poetry was being read at the court of King Philip II in Madrid. Friends urged her to acknowledge the good news and honor Duke Cosimo's most powerful ally in her *canzoniere* of 1560, which she did by dedicating a pair of sonnets to Philip and his wife, Queen Maria—"Bloody Mary" of England. Battiferra continued to be esteemed in Spain, as evidenced by translation of her verse there after her death. The painter-poet Francisco Pacheco, father-in-law of Velasquez, rendered into his own language one of her poems on the death of Michelangelo.[7]

Closer to home, she was sought after for membership in several academies, a singular honor for a woman. A letter from her husband to the secretary of Cosimo de' Medici dated November 3, 1559, reports the news from Siena, where he was working on ducal assignment.

> My wife, Laura Battiferra of Urbino, a woman gifted as a poet, has come here and been much courted and caressed by these Academicians, who want her to be in one of their academies, whichever one she likes of the three—that is, The Intronati [The dazed], The Rozzi [The clods], and the Desiosi [The wishful]. I think she'll choose the Intronati, and some of their fine minds have already made up some good sonnets. And that is how we are spending our time.

In 1560 Laura would accept the most prestigious, the Intronati, winning the distinction of being the first woman ever admitted to an Italian academy. This one, so named because members conceived it as a retreat from the noise of the world, which left them "dazed," claimed the honor of being the first academy to have an *impresa,* their mock heraldic emblem being a pumpkin with two pestles crossed above it and the motto "Meliora latent" [The best things are hidden] (a reference to the Tuscan custom of using pumpkins that had been hollowed out and dried in the sun as salt cellars). Seasoned with the salt of wit, the Intronati also pioneered the practice of having each member adopt a humorous, antiphrastic pseudonym. Laura's was "la Sgraziata" [the graceless], corroboration of the talent Piero Vettori had complimented when he wrote of her "graceful verse" in his letter describing Varchi's funeral.[8]

Even before Vettori declared Battiferra the new, and improved, Sappho, the comparison occurs in a note that was transmitted to posterity by Dionigi Atanagi in his *De le rime di diversi nobili poeti toscani* [Rhymes by diverse noble Tuscan poets] of 1565. Like Laura a native of the duchy of Urbino, Dionigi had earlier published a funerary anthology for the female prodigy Irene di Spillimbergo (1561). As was appropriate for the person he honors, his volume features more female poets than usually found in such polyvocal collections. Alongside Laura Terracina, Lucia Bertana, and Olimpia Malipiero, Laura Battiferra takes her place, represented by her sonnet on the death of Irene from the *First Book of Tuscan Works*. Her inclusion in the poetry that Atanagi gathered to mourn Irene marks a significant—and very early—stage in Battiferra's canonization.[9]

Her second book, *The Seven Penitential Psalms . . . with some Spiritual Sonnets* (1564), dedicated to the duchess of Urbino, would prove her success as a biblical translator and exegete, areas of endeavor normally reserved in Italy for men. Her prefatory letter to the duchess signals this new phase in her career, a step up from secular to sacred literature.[10]

> Perhaps I shall be reproached, Most Illustrious and most Excellent Lady, by all those who may perchance know how I, who have always for the most part looked to human letters, should now have dared to translate David's Penitential Psalms, so divine and mysterious, without having expert knowledge of the Holy Scriptures, especially since he had the authority of the blessed Jerome. . . . Yet why should I not be, if not praised, surely excused, for wanting to dwell no longer with the poets and with the philosophers (even though we find in their books no end of things that are useful and helpful for good living), because I wished with sincerity of heart to begin asking for grace from the Lord God with the same prayers as the most holy Hebrew poet? . . . As we can see, neither Achilles in Homer nor Aeneas in Virgil has armor like that of this most prudent warrior, who with the helmet of salvation, with the shield of faith, and with the sword of the spirit, which is the word of God, always accomplished his so many just and honored victories.

To justify her project, embellished by dedicatory letters to cloistered nuns for each Psalm with an explanation of its meaning and application to the recipients life, Laura boldly places herself in two canons of poets. Dominant, as suits her context, is the biblical confraternity of David, his Latin translator Jerome, and St. Paul, whose letters in the New Testament counterpoise the Old Testament king's Psalms. Secondary, as models that she has now superceded are the classical epic poets Homer and Virgil. A successor to St. Jerome, the church father responsible for the "authorized" Latin Bible, she appropriates the language of St. Paul (Ephesians 6.13–17) to declare her pious Christian mission. Sometime after she published her Tuscan version of the Penitential Psalms, in her later years, she embarked on a work that would fuse these two families of poets by composing a sacred epic. Unfortunately, only the first eighteen stanzas survive, but they are enough to reveal her intentions of telling a story whose heroes were the early Hebrew kings.[11] Meanwhile, many of the faithful in the period immediately following the Council of Trent must have profited from her book of 1564, which was reprinted separately in 1566 and again in 1568, 1570, and 1572 as part of a small pocket anthology, *Penitential Psalms by Diverse Excellent Authors*.[12]

Whenever members of the Florentine artistic community came together for a great public event—to celebrate a wedding, a birth, a battle victory, or, more often, to mourn—Laura participated by contributing occasional poetry, almost always as the sole woman. She voiced her grief in major funeral anthologies of 1561 for Luca Martini, an early Dantista and patron of the arts; in 1562 for the Duchess Eleonora de Toledo and the two young

Medici princes who died suddenly of malarial fever; and in 1564 for Michelangelo, a reader of hers who kept her poetry in his notebooks. Ammannati was her link to other leading artists as well, with whom she exchanged sonnets. Bronzino became her good friend, and Benvenuto Cellini contributed a sonnet to her *First Book of Tuscan Works*. Battiferra's correspondents, both in sonnet exchanges and letters, are the leading literary figures of the day—Annibal Caro, the Roman courtier who was secretary to Cardinal Alessandro Farnese, remembered for his plays, letters, and translation of the *Aeneid;* Antonfrancesco Grazzini, known as Il Lasca [the roach fish] in the Accademia degli Umidi [The academy of the soggy] and author of novellas, comedies, jocose, and lyric verse; Bernardo Tasso, who published his gigantic chivalric epic *Amadigi* the same year as Laura brought out her lyric anthology; and Lodovico Domenichi, competent as a poet but most memorable as an editor who indefatigably turned out volume after volume of contemporary verse, among them the first European collection of female poetry (Lucca, 1559). Later in her career, apparently beginning in the early 1570s, Battiferra became a patron of the Jesuits, entering into correspondence with the general of their order. When the German painter Hans van Aachen visited Florence in 1582–83, he painted the Medici duke, by then Cosimo's son Francesco, and he elected to do a portrait as well of Laura, that people north of the Alps might know this amazing Italian lady.[13]

While still a living poet, she was canonized by her contemporaries. First to so enshrine her was Bernardo Tasso. His masterpiece, *Amagidi,* after the fashion of Ariosto, integrates a catalog of famous people at its finale. Caterina de' Medici, the queen of France, leads off the female line; later comes Vittoria Colonna, and afterward Laura too marches through Bernardo's stanzas, making a flattering cameo appearance as "honor of Urbino." In 1561, the Benedictine monk Pietro Calzolari bows to her and her husband in his fat *Historia monastica*. With a structure that copies the *Decameron* and a purpose that recalls *The Book of the Courtier*, Calzolari's book stages the five-day dialogue of a group in Padua gathered to create conversationally a gallery of pious notables. From popes to saints, their survey progresses on day three to "Empresses, Queens, and Other Illustrious and Holy Ladies who have been Nuns." One interlocutor asks rhetorically, remembering the colossal *Hercules* that Bartolomeo Ammannati had sculpted for the Paduan jurist Marco Mantua Benavides:

> Has this age of ours any cause to envy the ancient and learned Sappho, since we have had our Vittoria Colonnas, Veronica Gambaras, and many others, famous indeed for their poetry in Italy and beyond Italy? And we had them not only in past years, but there lives today,

> to the infinite glory of women, the most learned and never adequately celebrated Madonna Laura Battifferra de gl'Amannati, wife of that Most excellent Messer Bartolomeo, who made, not many years ago, the very beautiful and big statue we see today in Padua.[14]

The second edition of Giorgio Vasari's *Lives of the Artists* (1568) similarly pays Battiferra tribute in a female canon. Vasari 's cycle, ranged historically from antiquity to the present, launches his life of Properzia de' Rossi, the only woman to whom he devotes an entire *vita*. As a tally makes clear, Vasari was thinking of them by categories, canons within the canon. The first are twelve Amazons, starting with Camilla; next follow ten ancient poets, beginning with Corinna and Sappho; then eleven more ancients who excelled in various fields—philosophy, oratory, grammar, and prophecy (Cassandra and Manto); and finally "women of our age who have acquired great fame": Vittoria Colonna, Veronica Gambara, Caterina Anguissola, la Schioppa, la Nogarola, Laura Battiferra, "and others."[15]

In 1586, three years before her death, Battiferra was admitted into an encyclopedia of marvels by Tomaso Garzoni, a learned canon at St. John of the Lateran in Rome: *Lives of Illustrious Women of Sacred Scripture. With the addition of the lives of the obscure and ugly women of both Testaments. And a Discourse at the end on the nobility of women*. In his closing peroration, citing Plato's *Republic*, Garzoni argues that men and women are equals in their capacity for learning and literary achievement. As ancient examples, he names such figures as Corinna and Aspasia; among the moderns, some from the fifteenth century (Isotta Nogarola is one); and then he continues, "Should I be silent on those who are the lights of our era: Vittoria Colonna, Laura Terracina, Laura Battiferra, Tarquinia Molza, and a thousand others who with their fame fill the whole universe?"[16]

Internationally famous in her day, how was Laura Battiferra later remembered? Her compatriot Bernardino Baldi, born in the next generation (1553–1617) and author of *Memories Concerning the City of Urbino*, calls her another "Corinna, another Sappho—nay better because if they wrote things lascivious and profane, she to her great credit treated of sacred matters." Baldi of Urbino, quoted word for word, enters the great Enlightenment *History of Vernacular Poetry* by Giovan Maria Crescimbeni (1730), who portrays Battiferra in the most laudatory terms, emphasizing her constant commitment to learning and literature, especially in the Italian language. As examples, Crescimbeni lists her translation into terza rima of Jeremiah's oration, her free verse rendering of Saint Augustine's hymn on Paradise (both included in her first published volume), and her Penitential Psalms, cast in the form of *canzoni*. Her writings, he asserts, were among the best published in her age, "shaped with excellent taste and worthy of praise from the century's first rank of *litterati*"—Annibal Caro, Benedetto Varchi, Bernardo Tasso, Lodovico Domenichi, and Pietro Calzolai, "who says there lives today, to the infinite glory of women, the most learned and never adequately celebrated Madonna Laura Battiferra." She was "such a visible lady," Crescimbeni rightly avows, that her virtue was known in all Italy.[17]

At midcentury, Giammaria Mazzuchelli in turn invokes Crescimbeni's authority for his *Writers of Italy* (1753–63), and Mazzuchelli's words pass into the monumental *History of Italian Literature* by Girolamo Tiraboschi (1782–86), polymath of Modena. Important for his Illuminist encyclopedias, Tiraboschi merits citation on Battiferra.

> [S]he was a most worthy poetess, and in keeping with the rare piety that was her adornment, she exercised her skills chiefly in sacred subjects. The Cavaliere Mazzuchelli speaks of her, and he recalls what high praises she receives from Caro, Varchi, and others besides. To these we can add the even more lavish praise of her that comes from Piero Vettori in a letter of his to Mario Colonna that tells how Laura too attended Lionardo Salviati's funeral oration for Varchi, "for why should a woman not want to share in a celebration of poetic virtue and industry, especially one herself afire with that same learning, one whom the Muses favor over all other women and whom they assist in writing comely, graceful verse?" And Vettori continues, praising Laura highly, and he affirms among other things that as she is not inferior in art and elegance to the ancient Sappho, so she rises far above her in the purity of her morals.[18]

Linking her to the most authoritative male poets of her age, Tiraboschi speaks of "praise she receives from Caro, Varchi, and others." He must have in mind letters Laura wrote to Varchi and received from Caro (in both cases, only one side survives). The cumulative chain of transmission that leads from Baldi to Tiraboschi suggests that, as time went by, the establishment was not reading Battiferra so much as the men who had something to say about her.

Battiferra's epithet as the new Sappho was to travel in the stream of memory that flowed from the early 1560s, Laura's most public years as a Petrarchista, into the twentieth century, at least in a few small rivulets. Indicative of the tradition that reached the nineteenth century is a book by the educator Eugenio Comba, who in the 1880s authored several pedagogical texts for the first generation of students in the new public school system of the United Italy. For the girls now benefiting from universal instruction, he wrote a pearl of a manual, *Illustrious Italian Women Proposed as Examples for Young Ladies*. A relative of the etiquette books that were beginning to be produced for the new middle class, this mirror of maids and matrons begins in the tenth century with Cinzica de' Sismondi of Pisa, who saved her fellow citizens from Saracen invaders. Comba continues chronologically with other heroines such as St. Catherine of Siena; the artists Properzia de' Rossi, Sofonisba Anguissola, and Artemisia Gentileschi; and the poets Veronica Gambara, Vittoria Colonna, and Tullia d'Aragona. As a late addition in an appendix, Laura Battiferra receives mention: "She rose through her poems to the greatest fame, and she was celebrated by the most learned men of her time. Annibale Caro, who called her a 'new Sappho,' in a letter to Piero Bonaventura proposed her as a guide in Poetry; Bernardo Tasso in the one hundredth canto of his epic *Amadigi* called her 'honor of Urbino'; Varchi held her in consummate esteem, and the Academy of Siena inscribed her among its members." Although Comba's information is quite accurate, he tacks it on after the main body of his biographical sketches, suggesting that it came to him belatedly, through sources less powerful than those that had assured the mainstream reputations of Gambara and Colonna, privileged because of their moral status as chaste widows and early inducted into a poetic hall of fame by the influential Pietro Bembo, who published a sonnet exchange with each of them in his *Rime* (1535, 1548).[19]

Comba is proof that a biographical tradition on Battiferra, laudatory if peripheral and intermittent, continued in the nineteenth century. Francesco De Sanctis, on the other hand, attests to that tradition's fragility. His *Storia della letteratura italiana* of 1871, foundational for the new United Italy, does not even mention Battiferra's name. The coup de grace for Italy's sixteenth-century women poets came where we should least expect it, from another woman, Iolanda De Blasi, who authored a history and anthology of Italian women writers in twin volumes of 1930. Merciless in her blanket condemnation of these "hothouse songstresses" and their sugary, frozen rhymes, she manages to suggest that Battiferra was not as bad as the rest because she was a faithful wife, completely under the influence of her husband, esthetically as well as domestically.[20]

A countering voice to the disdainful Blasi came from Benedetto Croce, the first major critic of the twentieth century to resurrect the female Petrarchists of the Renaissance. His interest is not surprising, given his esthetic preference for sentiment over "cold" reason, an opposition that allowed him to distinguish, in the broadest sense, "poetry" from "nonpoetry." Writing in 1933, he states his position: "Let no one be amazed that I am dwelling on these female rhymes: when we are looking for an effusion of sentiment in literature, it very often happens that we have to say, for better or for worse, 'I went looking for the man, and I found the woman—Quaesivi hominem et inveni foeminam!'"[21] Battiferra does figure, although briefly with a single sonnet, in Croce's positive reassessment of an entirely female literary family.

Whether one reads Comba, De Blasi, or Croce, one point is constant: The ladies are segregated, as Laura had once been at Varchi's funeral. Yet that tendency is not new. It begins in the Renaissance and within her lifetime, in the all-female canons proposed by Calzolari, Vasari, and Garzoni. In the Renaissance, however, the male community integrated Laura in other ways—by admitting her into the Accademia degli Intronati, by exchanging sonnets with her, and by incorporating sonnets by her in their collected *Rime*—as, for example, Varchi, Caro, Bronzino, and Mario Colonna all did.

Over time, the poems by which Battiferra has been remembered have shrunk from an imposing corpus of five hundred to just a handful. Her impressive thematic and metrical ranges have likewise largely been forgotten. What survives, skewing and diminishing her artistic identity, is one narrow family of sonnets with personal meditations in beloved landscape settings. Her favorite natural environs are near Maiano, the village northeast of Florence where Laura and Bartolomeo had a country home. Characterized as "pastoral," these limpid lyrics—among her most beautiful, to be sure—reflect preferences of the Romantics and their late epigone, Croce. Questions of taste aside, they have surely also survived because they can still be appreciated, even if the circumstances that prompted them are long forgotten.[22]

Typically, Battiferra's verse is occasional. How highly contingent, how learned, and how intellectually sophisticated her production was can be seen in the sonnet she dedicated to Pope Paul III (1534–49). Convener of the Council of Trent in 1545, this long-lived and shrewdly political pontiff had favored Laura's family. Giovan'Antonio Battiferri, the wealthy cleric who was Laura's father, enjoyed privileges in an inner Vatican circle as a "familiar" of Paul III. The connection is documented in a brief of 1543, signed by that pope, which legitimizes all three of Giovan'Antonio's children.[23] His daughter, whose loyalties in the religious conflicts of the sixteenth century were militantly Catholic, addresses their papal benefactor with flattery and piety. Written when she was still only in her twenties, the poem hints at biblical erudition that would later surface openly in her translation and exegesis of the Penitential Psalms.

A un volger d'occhio, a un picciol cenno vostro
Paolo, beato, eccelso, almo pastore,
umil s'inchina ogni mondan valore,
s'apre il ciel, trema il tenebroso chiostro;

e mentre de' più saggi il chiaro inchiostro
vi sacra eterno alla fama, all'onore,
v'apparecchia nel ciel pregio maggiore
Quel che vi scelse al gran governo nostro.
Così la Parca a gli anni vostri aggiunga
quei del buon PIERO, o del gran re, ch'insieme
con l'ombra, l'ore e 'l tempo indietro volse,
come spera con voi tranquilla e lunga
vita goder di vostra greggia il seme,
e con voi ritornare onde si tolse.[24]

[At a flick of your eye, at your slightest sign, Paul, blessed exalted bountiful shepherd, every worldly value humbly kneels, heaven opens, the tenebrous cloister trembles;

and while the lustrous ink of the wisest consecrates you eternal to fame, to honor, He who chose you for our great government readies for you a finer prize in heaven.

Thus may the Fate add to your years those of good PETER, *or of the great king, who together with the shadow turned back the hours and time,*

just as the seed of your flock hopes to enjoy long and tranquil life with you, and return with you whence it arose.]

Addressed to the still living pope, this sonnet could have been written as early as 1543 as an occasional piece of thanks for his papal brief of legitimation, but a later date seems more likely. It could well belong to the end of 1549, after Battiferra had left Urbino to rejoin her father in Rome following the death of her first husband, which probably befell in January of that year. While admirably suited to a frail old pontiff, the message may relate more specifically to his last illness. Some ten years later, as she was shaping her pro-Medicean *First Book of Tuscan Works*, Laura excluded this youthful effort, less because Paul was now dead than because of his politics. He was an antagonist of Duke Cosimo de' Medici in the struggle for Siena, a trophy that the pope wanted for himself in order to augment the Farnese family territories in northern and central Italy.

The poem envisions Pope Paul in his seat of power, like a cosmic emperor. At his slightest glance or nod all people drop to their knees, shunning material values. He is the Good Shepherd who opens for his followers a door to salvation in Paradise. In Hell the damned quake for fear of his righteousness and justice, which thunders even to the depths. Among men, his memory will live forever because here on earth the most prudent poets will assure his unending renown. After death, an eternal spiritual life awaits him, for God, who sent him to preside over the Church, is preparing his heavenly reward. But before he dies, when he will enter the halls of fame in this world and pass on in the next to his celestial prize, he should enjoy prolonged life, a boon with biblical precedents in two miracles wrought through a "shadow." The first comes from a passage in the New Testament, which relates how the "good Peter" (his name in capital letters to underline Paul's authority as his heir on the chair of St. Peter) added years to people's lives when he walked past the infirm, healing with his shadow. It happened as the apostles were gathered at Jerusalem in Solomon's Portico: "more than ever believers were added to the Lord, multitudes both of men and women, so that they even carried out the sick into the streets, and laid them on beds and pallets, that as Peter came by at least his shadow might fall on some of them" (Acts 5.14–15). In the second, more obscure allusion, to "the great king, who together with the shadow turned back the hours and time," Laura touches eruditely on Old Testament verse. After the prophet Isaiah told King Hezekiah to put his house in order for he was soon to die, the ailing ruler prayed for a reprieve from the Lord, who granted his faithful servant fifteen more years of life.

> And Hezekiah said to Isaiah, "What shall be the sign that the Lord will heal me, and that I shall go up to the house of the Lord on the third day?" And Isaiah said, "This is the sign to you from the Lord, that the Lord will do the thing that he has promised: shall the shadow go forward ten steps, or go back ten steps?" And Hezekiah answered, "It is an easy thing for the shadow to lengthen ten steps; rather let the shadow go back ten steps." And Isaiah the prophet cried to the Lord; and he brought the shadow back ten steps, by which the sun had declined on the dial of Ahaz. (2 Kings 20.8–11)

A compromise candidate already well along in years when the College of Cardinals elevated him in 1534, Paul outfoxed his adversaries by ruling longer than any other pontiff in the sixteenth century. Laura's allusions to neatly paired, symmetrical passages from the Old and New Testaments (a strategy she repeats by linking David with Paul in her preface to the *Penitential Psalms*) seem to indicate that he was not only old but sick, like the bedridden Jerusalemites made whole by Peter's shadow or Hezekiah, whom heaven's "King" mercifully saved at death's very door. If so, this sonnet belongs to the brief period of his last illness, between November 2 and 10, 1549, when he passed away at the ripe age of eighty-two. What precipitated his death was his insistence on going out in the bitter cold to the Quirinal Palace, where he was enraged to hear news of a pet grandson's recalcitrance.

Anger and weather brought on a fever that shortly proved fatal.[25] If this was indeed the poem's occasion, the fact that Paul did not recover would help explain why it never enjoyed diffusion, even in manuscript at the Vatican court.

Some thirty years later, as Battiferra was compiling her third and final anthology of poetry, her *Rime*, she still cared enough for the sonnet to Pope Paul—which must have evoked fond memories of her youth, her father, and the elite social milieu in which he moved—to have these verses copied into its folios. The source of this single copy, never published, is the unfinished codex in which, under Laura's supervision, a Jesuit was transcribing her entire poetic corpus in a revised ordering that she intended for publication. Before that ambitious project could be finished, she died, and although her husband then tried to have it completed, his efforts, too, were cut short by death. The manuscript was to lie forgotten for the next four hundred years in the Biblioteca Casanatense, a repository for papers from the Jesuits' *Collegio Romano* after their order was suppressed in 1773.[26]

Had she succeeded in publishing her collected work, Laura Battiferra's afterlife might have been a happier one. As it was, almost all of her late production, entrusted to the Casanatense manuscript, never came to light—a trove of some one hundred spiritual sonnets, biblical narrative poems, and her incomplete epic on the Hebrew kings. Over the centuries, her place in a separate canon of women has immured her in a virtual matroneum, isolating her from the cultural mainstream where once she had thrived, a light among the brightest of her generation. She has managed to survive only as a marginal presence, but the same is true of the men who buoyed her reputation in the first place: Annibal Caro, Benedetto Varchi, Bernardo Tasso, Lodovico Domenichi—even the very visible Bronzino and Cellini, famous as artists but barely known as lyric writers. Owing to flukes of history, her husband has himself had an unfortunate *fortuna*. Unlike Vittoria Colonna, whose exemplary widowhood and attachment to such male luminaries as the divine Michelangelo and Pietro Bembo helped assure her momentum in historical memory, Laura Battiferra has been linked to a man whom Michelangelo himself cast into shadow. The mannerism that both Ammannati and Battiferra practiced in their respective art forms fell out of favor, as did her Petrarchismo. The Jesuits were suppressed in Italy. At least one-third of her corpus was never published, because she died before bringing it to light. Whereas in her midyears Battiferra aggressively sought recognition for her art, in later life she withdrew from public view, passing her days, as one historian reports, in the private chapel that Bartolomeo had had built for her at their villa in Camerata.[27] Ironically, she may herself have diminished the fame that she so aggressively pursued when younger by retreating into that more private life as a devout older woman, to meditate, to pray, and to compose spiritual poetry that never crossed the threshold of print.

❧ ❧ ❧

NOTES

1. Vettori's letter, in an Italian adaptation, prefaces Laura Battiferra's late incomplete collection, *Rime di Laura Battiferra* [Rhymes of Laura Battiferra], Rome, Biblioteca Casanatense, Ms. 3229, fols. 2r–5v. For the original Latin epistle, see *Petri Victorii epistolarum libri X. Orationes XIIII. et Liber de Ludibus Ioannae Austriacae* (Florence: Giunti, 1586). The English translation is mine, from the Italian version supplemented by the Latin. Benedetto Varchi (1504–65), scion of an old Florentine family, was a personage whose amazing intellectual energies carried him into virtually every branch of contemporary culture—lyrical, pastoral, and spiritual poetry, dramatic writing, Dante studies, history, philosophy, linguistic theory, esthetics, even alchemy and Pythagorean numerology. Titian painted his portrait, now in Vienna. He corresponded with countless contemporaries and mentored younger writers, among them Tullia d'Aragona and Laura Battiferra.

2. For an overview of Battiferra's life, see most recently Victoria Kirkham, "Creative Partners: The Marriage of Laura Battiferra and Bartolomeo Ammannati," *Renaissance Quarterly* 55 (2002): 498–558. Also useful, if by now somewhat dated, is Enzo Noè Girardi's entry, "Battiferri, Laura" in *Dizionario biografico degli Italiani* (Rome: Istituto dell'Enciclopedia, 1965), 7:242–44. The spelling of her family surname (always the feminine "Battiferra" in her signatures) is discussed by Kirkham, "Dante's Phantom, Petrarch's Specter: Bronzino's Portrait of the Poet Laura Battiferra," in *Visibile parlare: Dante and the Art of the Italian Renaissance*, ed. Deborah Parker, *Lectura Dantis* 22–23 (1998): 63–139, esp. 63–64. During her lifetime she published two books: *Il primo libro dell'opere toscane di m. Laura Battiferra degli Ammannati* [The first book of Tuscan works of Madonna Laura Battiferra degli Ammannati] (Florence: Giunti, 1560); and *I sette salmi penitentiali del santissimo profeta Davit. Tradotti in lingua Toscana da Madonna Laura Battiferra Degli Ammannati . . . insieme con alcuni suoi Sonetti spirituali* [The seven penitential psalms of the most holy prophet David, translated into the Tuscan language by Madonna Laura Battiferra degli Ammannati . . . together with some of her spiritual sonnets] (Florence: Giunti, 1564). The poems preserved today in the Casanatense Library (Ms. 3229), entitled simply *Rime*, were to have formed her third published collection, but she was unable to finish that book before she died. The *canzoniere* of 1560 has been republished with an introduction and minimal commentary as Laura Battiferri degli Ammannati, *Il primo libro delle opere toscane*, ed. Enrico Maria Guidi (Urbino: Accademia Raffaello, 2000). On Sappho's reputation for homosexuality see Mary R. Lefkowitz, *The Lives of the Greek Poets* (Baltimore: Johns Hopkins University Press, 1981), 36–37.

3. This fact is among the many thousands collected by the passionate local nineteenth-century historian known as Poligrafo Gargani and written on all sorts of paper scraps, now housed at the Biblioteca Nazionale in Florence. See Poligrafo Gargani, s.v. Ammannati, pacchetto 89, no. 96: "Laura Battiferra Ammannati, assistente nel 1565 [1566 modern style] nella Chiesa degli Angioli di Firenze, all'essequie del Varchi da

'una finestra serrata del piccolo Oratorio delle Donne'. Farulli, *Storia del Monastero degli Angioli*, pag. 81."

4. *Lettere di Laura Battiferri Ammannati a Benedetto Varchi*, ed. Carlo Gargiolli, Scelta di curiosità letterarie inedite o rare dal secolo XIII al XIX, Disp. 166 (1879; reprint, Bologna: Commissione per i testi di lingua, 1968). For Vettori's visit on July 20, 1561, see 45–46. Bronzino's stunning portrait of Laura is the subject of Kirkham, "Dante's Phantom, Petrarch's Specter." See also the rich essay by Carol Plazzotta, "Bronzino's Laura," *Burlington Magazine* 140, no. 1141 (1998): 251–63.

5. Piero Stufa, ed., *Componimenti latini, e toscani da diversi suoi amici composti nella morte di m. Benedetto Varchi* (n.p. [Florence?]: n. p. 1566). Three poems by Varchi appear in Battiferra's *Primo libro dell'opere toscane*. See Guidi's edition, 89–91. Battiferra and Varchi are prominently in dialogue in the funerary anthologies for the Medici duchess Eleonora and her sons, who all died suddenly late in 1562 of swamp fever. See Lodovico Domenichi, ed., *Poesie toscane, et latine di diversi eccel. ingegni, nella morte del S. D. Giovanni Cardinale, del Sig. Don Grazia de Medici, et della S. Donna Leonora di Toledo de Medici Duchessa di Fiorenza et di Siena* (Florence: L. Torrentino, 1563); and the closely related volume—perhaps Domenichi's source—*Rime di diversi eccellentissimi autori fatte nella morte dell'Illustriss. et Eccell. Duchessa di Fiorenza et Siena, et degli Illustriss.Signori suoi figliuoli* (Ferrara: Valente Panizza Mantovano, 1563). Bernardo Tasso's answer to a letter from Laura that does not survive indicates that she had asked him to contribute a sonnet to the Varchi commemorative volume. See Cesare Cimegotto, "Due lettere inedite di Bernardo Tasso," *Giornale Storico della Letteratura Italiana* 24 (1894): 388–98.

6. Luciano Bellosi called attention to the resemblance between Battiferra's profile and Dante's in "Il ritratto fiorentino nel Cinquecento," in *Firenze e la Toscana dei Medici nell'Europa nel Cinquecento. Il primato del disegno* (Florence, 1980), 39–46. For more detailed discussions of the portrait, which connects the poetess to both Dante and Petrarch, as well as reviews of the literature on the painting, see Kirkham, "Dante's Phantom, Petrarch's Specter"; Plazzotta, "Bronzino's Laura."

7. Laura writes about having heard that her sonnets had reached Madrid in her letter to Varchi of December 11, 1557 (Gargiolli, *Lettere di Laura Battiferri Ammannati*, 39–40). The translation by Pacheco (1571–1654) is mentioned in a note by C. L. Nicolay, "Francisco Pacheco and the Italians," *Modern Language Notes* 20, no. 7 (1905): 214–15.

8. "Mia moglie Laura Battiferri da Urbino, donna ornata di poesia è venuta qui molto visitata e acarezata da questi Academici, e vogliono che ela sia de una loro academia di quela che più si contenta de le tre. Cioè degli Intronati, de' Rozzi e de Desiosi. Penso si elegerà gli Intronati: e di già da di begli ingegni sono stati fatti di buoni sonetti. E cosi si passa il tempo." Cited by Adolfo Venturi, "Bartolomeo Ammannati," in *Storia dell'arte italiana*, vol. 10, pt. 2, *La scultura del Cinquecento* (Milan: Hoepli, 1936): 347–432, and for the passage quoted, 349. Laura's pseudonym is reported in two forms, but both define her as "graceful." It was "Aggratiata" according to L. Sbaragli, who lists her as the first woman enthroned, "'I tabelloni' degli Intronati," *Bullettino Senese di Storia Patria*, 3d ser., 1 (1942): 177–87. "Sgraziata" is the version given in antithesis by Guido Zaccagnani, "Lirici urbinati nel sec. XVI," *Le Marche* 3 (1903): 87–114. See esp. 99 and n. 1: Camillo Cieco Falconetti in a letter of December 3, 1559, writes the Urbino poet Antonio Gallo that Laura was admitted with the name "Sgratiata," the

first woman ever to be received into the Academy of the Intronati, and that her husband had become "dazed," too. On the history of the Accademia degli Intronati, see Michele Maylender, *Storia delle accademie d'Italia*, 5 vols. (1926–30; reprint, Bologna: Forni, 1976), 3:355–61. Its *impresa* is reproduced in F. Iacometti, "L'Accademia degli Intronati," *Bullettino Senese di Storia Patria*, n.s., 12 (1941): 189–98.

9. Dionigi refers to Laura as "this new Sappho of our times" in a note attached in his index to the first line of a sonnet by Annibal Caro. See also Dionigi Atanagi, ed., *Rime di diversi nobilissimi, et eccellentissimi autori, In morte della Signora IRENE delle Signore di Spilimbergo. Alle quali sono aggiunti versi Latini di diversi egregi Poeti, in morte della medesima signora* (Venice: Domenico and Giovanni Battista Guerera Fratelli, 1561), 117; on which see Anne Jacobson Schutte, "Irene di Spilimbergo: The Image of a Creative Woman in Late Renaissance Italy," *Renaissance Quarterly* 44 (1991): 42–61; and Antonio Corsaro, "Dionigi Atanagi e la silloge per Irene di Spilimbergo (Intorno alla formazione del giovane Tasso)," *Italica* 75, no. 1 (1998): 41–61.

10. For the full English text of the dedicatory letter, see Victoria Kirkham, ed., *Laura Battiferra and her Literary Circle*, forthcoming, University of Chicago Press. Italy, of course, had a strong tradition of female mystics, and Vittoria Colonna set an important precedent for spiritualized poetry with her *Rime spirituali* (see the essays by Maggi and Cox in this volume). Unlike the situation in England, however, few women actually tried their hand at translating the Bible or writing biblical commentary. One important exception was Chiara Matraini of Lucca, who in her later years composed *Meditazioni spirituali* [Spiritual meditations] (1581) and *Considerazioni sopra i sette salmi penitenziali del gran re e profeta Davit* [Considerations on the seven penitential psalms by the great king and prophet David] (1586). See Giovanna Rabitti, "Chiara Matraini," in *Italian Women Writers: A Bio-Bibliographical Sourcebook*, ed. Rinaldina Russell (Westport, Ct.: Greenwood Press, 1994), 243–52.

11. Laura Battiferra, *Rime*, Rome, Biblioteca Casanatense, Ms. 3229, fols. 67v–70r. Battiferra takes as her point of departure the biblical account of the birth of Samuel, whose father had two wives: Peninnah ("Fenenna") mothered many children, but Hannah ("Anna"), who suffered the taunts of her rival, was barren until she prayed to the Lord in the temple of Shiloh, and He opened her womb (1 Samuel 1.1–13). The story resembles other scriptural narratives of wives who conceive through divine favor—Sarah, Rebecca, Rachel, and Elizabeth. Perhaps the motif had personal resonance for the poet. Late in life, inspired by the spiritualism of Ignatius Loyola, Laura also composed a prose meditation on the Christmas creche, her *Oratione sopra il Natale di Nostro Signore*," now edited with an introduction by Victoria Kirkham, "La poetessa al Presepio: Una meditazione inedita di Laura Battiferra degli Ammannati," *Filologia e critica*, 27, no. 2 (2002): 258–76.

12. *I sette Salmi Penitentiali del Santissimo Profeta Davit. Tradotti in lingua Toscana, da Madonna Laura Battiferra degli Ammannati. . . . insieme con alcuni suoi Sonetti spirituali* (Florence: Giunti, 1564), A iir: "Io sarò forse Illustrissima, et Eccellentissima Signora ripresa da tutti quegli, i quali per avventura sapranno come io, che per lo piu sempre ho atteso all'humane lettere, sia hora stata ardita di tradurre i SALMI PENITENTIALI di Davit tanto divini, et misteriosi, senz'altra cognitione havere delle sagre scritture, et tanto piu havendo questi l'autorità del beato Girolamo. . . . Ma perche non dovrò io essere se non lodata certo scusata, se io non volendo far piu lunga dimora coi' Poeti, e coi' Filosofi (ancora che ne' loro libri si ritrovino infinite cose utili, et giovevoli al ben vivere) habbia voluto cominciare, con sincerità di cuore, a chiedere

gratia al signore IDDIO con le istesse preghiere del santissimo Poeta Ebreo? . . . ne Acchille appresso Homero, ne Enea appresso Virgilio si veggono armati, si come questo prudentissimo guerriero il quale con l'elmo della salute, con lo scudo della fede, et con la spada dello spirito, che è la parola d'Iddio, sempre consegui tante sue giuste, et honorate vettorie." Battiferra's *Psalms* soon appeared anthologized in a pocket edition (in 120): *Salmi penitenziali, di diversi eccellenti autori con alcune rime spirituali di diversi illust. cardinali, di Reverendissimi vescovi, & d'altre persone Ecclesiastiche. Scelti dal reverendo P. Francesco da Trivigi Carmelitano [Francesco Turchi] nuovamente da lui corretti et ristampati* (Venice: Gabriel Giolito de' Ferrari, 1568), reprinted in 1570 and 1572.

13. For her presence in anthologies of the period, see Benedetto Varchi, ed., *Cento sonetti sopra la morte di Luca Martini* (Florence. Biblioteca Nazionale), Ms. II, VIII, 140; *Esequie del divino Michelagnolo Buonarroti Celebrate in Firenze dall'Accademia de Pittori, Scultori, et Architettori. Nella Chiesa di S. Lorenzo il di 14 Luglio 1564* (Florence: Giunti, 1564). See also note 5, this essay. Among Bronzino's closest friends, she is conspicuous in his *canzoniere*, which Deborah Parker discusses, *Bronzino: Renaissance Painter as Poet* (Cambridge: Cambridge University Press, 2001), 40–79. Bronzino, Cellini, Caro, and Grazzini all contribute to her *First Book of Tuscan Works*. See note 5, this essay, for Cimegotto's announcement of letters to her from Bernardo Tasso. Victoria Kirkham documents her support of the Jesuits, "Laura Battiferra degli Ammannati benefattrice dei Gesuiti fiorentini," *Quaderni storici* 104, no. 2 (2000): 331–54. Giovan Maria Crescimbeni mentions the lost portrait by Hans van Aachen in *Dell'istoria della volgar poesia*, 6 vols. (Venice: Lorenzo Basegio, 1730), 4:95–96. See for the source Karel van Mander, *The Lives of the Illustrious Netherlandish and German Painters, from the first edition of the Schilder-boeck (1603–1604)*, 6 vols., ed. Hessel Miedema (Doornspijk: Davaco, 1994), 1:418: "Van Aken also went to Florence where he portrayed various great lords and ladies from life, as well as the illustrious Franciscus, duke of Florence. He portrayed there also a spirited versifier or poetess called Madonna Laura and he kept the copy of that face which is still in Amsterdam with his pupil Pieter Isaacksz."

14. Bernardo Tasso, *Amadigi* (Venice: Gabriel Giolito de' Ferrari, 1560), canto 100, stanza 19, gives her the epithet "onor d'Urbino." See Pietro Calzolai, *Historia monastica* (Florence: Lorenzo Torrentino, 1561), day 3, p. 4.

15. Giorgio Vasari, *Le vite dei più eccellenti pittori, scultori e architetti*, ed. Licia and Carlo L. Ragghianti, 4 vols. (Milan: Rizzoli, 1976), 3:159: "Ma certo in nessun'altra età s'è ciò meglio potuto conoscere che nella nostra; dove le donne hanno acquistato grandissima fama, non solamente nello studio delle lettere, com'ha fatto la signora Vittoria del Vasto [Vittoria Colonna], la signora Veronica Gambara, la signora Caterina Anguisola, la Schioppa, la Nugarola, Madonna Laura Battiferra, e cent'altre, sì nella volgare, come nella latina e nella greca lingua, dottissime; ma eziandio in tutte l'altre facultà." Several of these women are discussed in other essays in this volume. For Colonna and Gambara see Cox and Finotti; for Nogarola see Fenster. I can find no references to Caterina Anguissola. Vasari must have been thinking of Sofonisba Anguissola (1532–1625), whom he praises highly at the end of his life of Properzia de' Rossi. The first woman to gain international fame as a painter, she was especially renowned for her portraits, whose subjects range from her family members (she had five sisters) to Philip II of Spain. See, e.g., Ilya Sandra Perlingieri, *Sofonisba Anguissola: The First Great Woman Artist of the Renaissance* (Milan: Rizzoli, 1992). I am unable to identify "Schioppa."

16. The ladies of Scripture, thirty-five in all, run from Eve to Mary; the nine "unattractive" ones include Dalilah, Jezebel, and Herodias. See Tomaso Garzoni, *Le vite delle donne illustri della scrittura sacra. Con l'aggionta delle vite delle donne oscure e laide dell'uno e l'altro Testamento. E un Discorso in fine sopra la nobiltà delle donne*, ed. Beatrice Collina (Ravenna: Longo, 1994), 245: "Tacerò forse quelle che sono lumi della nostra era: Vittoria Colonna, Laura Terracina, Laura Battiferra, Tarquinia Molza, e mill'altre ch'empion della lor fama tutto l'universo?" Garzoni wrote several amazing encyclopedias, the most famous of which was a description of all the jobs in the world. He is the subject of an excellent Web site: <http://www.tomasogarzoni.org>. For a sample of verse by the prolific Neapolitan poet Laura Terracina (1519–ca. 1577), see Stuart Curran's essay in this volume. Tarquinia Molza (1542–1617) was a poet, composer, singer, and musician who distinguished herself at the court of Alfonso II d'Este of Ferrara and later was accorded perpetual honorary citizenship by the Roman senate. Glenda McCleod, *Virtue and Venom: Catalogs of Women from Antiquity to the Renaissance* (Ann Arbor: University of Michigan Press, 1991), surveys the tradition of listing famous women in a book that is useful for the references it assembles but otherwise is somewhat limited.

17. Bernardino Baldi, *Encomio della Patria* (Urbino: Angelo Ant. Monticelli, 1706), 119: "Non fù ella un'altra Corinna, un'altra Saffo? anzi di gran lunga migliore, perciocchè se quelle scrissero cose lascive, e profane, costei con molta sua lode trattò di cose Sacre." Crescimbeni, *Della volgare poesia*, 3:95–96: "Opere tutte nobilissime, e lavorate con ottimo gusto; e degne, che fossero lodate, anzi ammirate da i primi Letterati del secolo, . . : e Pietro Calzolai, il qual dice, *vive oggi con infinita gloria delle Donne, e di questi tempi, la dottissima e non mai bastevolmente celebrata* M. *Laura Battiferra*."

18. Girolamo Tiraboschi, *Storia della letteratura italiana*, 10 vols. (Naples: Giovanni Muccis, 1777–86), vol. 7 (1781), pt. 3, 44–45: "Laura Battiferra degli Ammanati figlia naturale, e poi legittimata, di Giannantonio Battiferri da Urbino, moglie del celebre Scultore e Architetto Bartolommeo degli Ammanati Fiorentino, e morta nel 1589, fu ella pure assai valorosa Poetessa, e secondando la rara pietà, di cui era adorna, esercitossi principalmente in argomenti sacri. Di lei ragiona il C. Mazzuchelli, e rammenta gli elogi, con cui ne parlarono il Caro, il Varchi, e più altri. A' quali un altro ancor più magnifico si può aggiugnere, che di essa fa Pier Vettori in una sua lettera a Mario Colonna, in cui narrando, che all'Orazion funebre, detta da Lionardo Salviati nell'esequie del Varchi, era intervenuta ancor Laura: *Cur enim*, dice, *non debuit femina illa locum eum visere, in quo virtus industriaque poetarum celebraretur? quae studio illo inflammata est, et quam praecipue Musae diligunt, ac saepe lepidum venustumque carmen scribentem adjuvant?* E siegue, dicendo gran lodi di Laura, e fralle altre cose afferma, che com'ella non è inferiore nell'arte, e nell'eleganza del verseggiare all'antica Saffo, così di molto la supera nell'onestà de' costumi."

19. Comba, Eugenio. *Donne illustri italiane proposte ad esempio alle Giovinette*, 6th ed. (Turin-Rome-Milan-Florence-Naples: Ditta G.B. Paravia e Comp., 1912), 226. Comba also wrote a *Compendium of Italian History* and a *Compendium of Theoretical and Practical Geography*. His *Illustrious Italian Women*, popular enough to enjoy multiple reprintings, was reissued again as late as 1935, a full half century after it had first appeared and during a fascist era that could still approve its patriotic spirit. A preface to the sixth edition (1912) carries readers back to ancient Athens, where, the saying went, woman was to be praised if no one spoke of her beyond the four walls of her home. But women, endowed with sensitivity and imagination, are sometimes more cre-

ative than men; hence it is no wonder, Comba understands, if some of them crossed the domestic threshold. Thank goodness, he smiles, that female education is being promoted today by Italy's government and local municipalities. Toward that effort, Comba contributes his model females, divided by an index into such categories of excellence as patriotism, philanthropy, science, fine arts, theater, and belles lettres.

20. Jolanda De Blasi, *Le scrittrici italiane dalle origini al 1800* (Florence: Casa Editrice "Nemi," 1930), 121–22. Lina Insana (see her essay in this volume) insightfully explains De Blasi's biases with reference to her fascist cultural milieu.

21. Benedetto Croce, *Poesia popolare e poesia d'arte. Studi sulla poesia italiana dal tre al cinquecento*, ed. Pietro Cudini (Naples: Bibliopolis, 1991), 361–62. Although Croce was an important pioneer in resurrecting some of the Italian Renaissance women poets, his esthetic reasons for doing so and his concomitant assumption that their lyrics should be read in an autobiographical key are now widely rejected. See, for example, the excellent new edition of Isabella Morra's *Rime* (Rome: Salerno, 2000) by Maria Antonietta Grignani, who puts Croce's views into historical perspective; see also the review of this edition by Victoria Kirkham, *Quaderni d'Italianistica* 22, no. 1 (2001): 161–64.

22. Her own poems total approximately four hundred; another one hundred sonnets were sent to her by correspondents in sonnet exchanges that also properly belong in her corpus. See Kirkham, "Creative Partners," for examples of Laura's identity today as a "pastoral" poet. This is precisely the epithet that Anthony Oldcorn uses to characterize her in his discussion of Italian lyric poetry in the recent *Cambridge History of Italian Literature*, ed. Peter Brand and Lino Pertile (Cambridge: Cambridge University Press, 1996), 264. Most of Battiferra's verse is more difficult than the so-called pastoral sonnets, and even they are not just simple effusions of sentiment but may turn on highly specific historical circumstances. See, for example, my discussion of "Alto monte, ima valle e dolce piano," in "Creative Partners." The sonnet confides her loneliness after being forced to move from Rome to Florence in 1555, an upheaval necessitated when her husband's papal patron died and he found new possibilities for work sponsored by Duke Cosimo I de' Medici.

23. Aggressively nepotistic in his designs, Paul appears as a shrewd old man in memorable portraits by Titian, one of which depicts him with the grandsons through whom he advanced his political ambitions. For the document of legitimation of the Battiferri children, signed by Paul III, see Archivio di Stato di Firenze, Conv. Soppr. da Leopoldo, *filza* 238, fols. 7r–8r. Giovan'Antonio Battiferri, an apostolic scriptor at the Vatican, fathered Laura and her brother Ascanio, probably older, by his concubine Maddalena Coccapani of Carpi; by another unmarried mother he had a third child, Giulio, who seems to have died young. See Kirkham, "Creative Partners," esp. 502.

24. Rome, Biblioteca Casanatense, Ms. 3229, *Rime di Laura Battiferra*, fol. 8v: "A Papa Paolo Terzo Farnese." In my transcription, I have eliminated the etymological "h," changed "et" to "e," and modernized punctuation.

25. See Ludwig Pastor, *The History of the Popes*, ed. Ralph Francis Kerr, 2d ed. 20 vols. (St. Louis: B. Herder Book Co., 1923), 11:10–25, for the election of Alessandro Farnese as Paul III and for his family connections; for his death, see 12:45–53.

26. Marginal notes with brief instructions to the printer in the Casanatense manuscript, entitled simply *Rime di Laura Battiferra* [Rhymes by Laura Battiferra], seem to be in Laura's hand as well as her husband's hand. From this and other evidence, it seems that Laura and her scribe were working on the project together in Florence,

where the Ammannati lived. The text itself is typical of Jesuit script of the very late sixteenth century, as I am informed by Isabella Ceccopieri, curator of manuscripts at the Casanatense Library. How the manuscript got from Florence to Rome is unclear, but one possibility is that it was sent to Rome so the transcription could be completed there in the *Collegio Romano* of the Jesuits. There is no evidence that a second scribe ever worked on it, so it must have simply been stored and would have passed into the Casanatense at the time the Jesuit order was suppressed. Ceccopieri refers to this period in the Casanatense history in "Il fondo manoscritti della Biblioteca Casanatense," *Accademie e biblioteche d'Italia* 56, no. 4 (1988): 22–42.

27. Filippo Baldinucci, *Notizie de' professori del disegno da Cimabue in qua*, ed. Ferdinando Ranalli, Decennale VI del secolo IV dal 1550 al 1560. Bartolommeo Ammannati scultore e architetto fiorentino (Florence: V. Batelli e Compagni, 1846), 3:365. In 1576 Bartolomeo Ammannati rented a villa in Camerata from the Camaldulensians, and Laura "stayed there most of the time, delighting in a new chapel that he had built there" [se ne stava 'l più del tempo deliziandosi in una Cappella fattavi dal medesimo fabbricare di nuovo].

BIBLIOGRAPHY

Atanagi, Dionigi, ed. *Rime di diversi nobilissimi, et eccellentissimi autori, In morte della Signora IRENE delle Signore di Spilimbergo. Alle quali sono aggiunti versi Latini di diversi egregi Poeti, in morte della medesima signora*. Venice: Domenico and Giovanni Battista Guerera Fratelli, 1561.

———, ed. *De le rime di diversi nobili poeti toscani*. Venice: Lodovico Avanzi, 1565.

Baldi, Bernardino. *Encomio della Patria*. Urbino: Angelo Ant. Monticelli, 1706.

Baldinucci, Filippo. *Notizie de' professori del disegno da Cimabue in qua*. Ed. Ferdinando Ranalli. 5 vols. Florence: V. Batelli e Compagni, 1845–47.

Battiferra degli Ammannati, Laura. *Il primo libro dell'opere toscane*. Florence: Giunti, 1560.

———. *I sette salmi penitentiali del santissimo profeta Davit. Tradotti in lingua Toscana da Madonna Laura Battiferra Degli Ammannati. Con gli argomenti sopra ciascuno di essi, composti dalla Medesima; insieme con alcuni suoi Sonetti spirituali*. Florence: Giunti, 1564.

———. *Rime*. Ms. 3229, Bibl. Casanatense, Rome.

———. *Oratione sopra il Natale di Nostro Signore*. Macerata, Biblioteca Comunale Mozzi-Borgetti, Ms. 137, 1590 ca., fols. 137r–141r.

———. *Il primo libro delle opere toscane*. Ed. Enrico Maria Guidi. Urbino: Accademia Raffaello, 2000.

Bellosi, Luciano. "Il ritratto fiorentino nel Cinquecento." In *Firenze e la Toscana dei Medici nell'Europa del Cinquecento. Il primato del disegno*, 39–46. Florence: Olschki, 1980.

De Blasi, Jolanda. *Le scrittrici italiane dalle origini al 1800*. Florence: Casa Editrice "Nemi," 1930.

Brand, Peter, and Lino Pertile, eds. *Cambridge History of Italian Literature*. Cambridge: Cambridge University Press, 1996.

Calzolai, Pietro. *Historia monastica*. Florence: Lorenzo Torrentino, 1561.

Ceccopieri, Isabella. "Il fondo manoscritti della Biblioteca Casanatense." *Accademie e biblioteche d'Italia* 56, no. 4 (1988): 22–42.

Cimegotto, Cesare. "Due lettere inedite di Bernardo Tasso." *Giornale Storico della Letteratura Italiana* 24 (1894): 388–98.

Comba, Eugenio. *Donne illustri italiane proposte ad esempio alle Giovinette*, 6th ed. Turin-Rome-Milan-Florence-Naples: Ditta G.B. Paravia e Comp., 1912.

Corsaro, Antonio. "Dionigi Atanagi e la silloge per Irene di Spilimbergo (Intorno alla formazione del giovane Tasso)." *Italica* 75, no. 1 (1998): 41–61.

Crescimbeni, Giovan Maria. *Dell'istoria della volgar poesia*, 6 vols. Venice: Lorenzo Basegio, 1730.

Croce, Benedetto. *Poesia popolare e poesia d'arte. Studi sulla poesia italiana dal tre al cinquecento*. 1933. Reprinted, ed. Pietro Cudini. Naples: Bibliopolis, 1991.

Domenichi, Lodovico, ed. *Poesie toscane, et latine di diversi eccel. ingegni, nella morte del S. D. Giovanni Cardinale, del Sig. Don Grazia de Medici, et della S. Donna Leonora di Toledo de Medici Duchessa di Fiorenza et di Siena*. Florence: L. Torrentino, 1563.

Esequie del divino Michelagnolo Buonarroti Celebrate in Firenze dall'Accademia de Pittori, Scultori, et Architettori. Nella Chiesa di S. Lorenzo il di 14 Luglio 1564. Florence: Giunti, 1564.

Gargiolli, Carlo, ed. *Lettere di Laura Battiferri Ammannati a Benedetto Varchi*. Scelta di Curiosità Letterarie Inedite o Rare dal Secolo XIII al XIX, Disp. 166. 1879. Reprint, Bologna: Commissione per i testi di lingua, 1968.

Garzoni, Tomaso. *Le vite delle donne illustri della scrittura sacra. Con l'aggionta delle vite delle donne oscure e laide dell'uno e l'altro Testamento. E un Discorso in fine sopra la nobiltà delle donne*. Ed. Beatrice Collina. Ravenna: Longo, 1994.

Iacometti, F. "L'Accademia degli Intronati." *Bullettino Senese di Storia Patria*, n.s., 12 (1941): 189–98.

Kirkham, Victoria. "Dante's Phantom, Petrarch's Specter: Bronzino's Portrait of the Poet Laura Battiferra." In *Visibile parlare: Dante and the Art of the Italian Renaissance*, ed. Deborah Parker. *Lectura Dantis* 22–23 (1998): 63–139.

———. "Laura Battiferra degli Ammannati benefattrice dei Gesuiti fiorentini." *Quaderni storici* 104, no. 2 (2000): 331–54.

———. "Creative Partners: The Marriage of Laura Battiferra and Bartolomeo Ammannati." *Renaissance Quarterly* 55 (2002): 498–558.

———. Review of Isabella Morra, *Rime*, ed. Maria Antonietta Grignani, and Isabella Morra, *Canzoniere. A Bi-lingual Edition*, trans. Irene Musillo Mitchell. *Quaderni d'Italianistica*. 22, no. 1 (2001): 161–64.

———. "La poetessa al Presepio: Una meditazione inedita di Laura Battiferra degli Ammannati." *Filologia e critica*. 27, no. 2 (2002): 258–76.

Lefkowitz, Mary R. *The Lives of the Greek Poets*. Baltimore: Johns Hopkins University Press, 1981.

Mander, Karel van. *The Lives of the Illustrious Netherlandish and German Painters, from the first edition of the Schilder-boeck (1603–1604)*. Ed. Hessel Miedema. 6 vols. Doornspijk: Davaco, 1994–99.

Maylender, Michele. *Storia delle accademie d'Italia*, 5 vols. 1926–30. Reprint, Bologna: Forni, 1976.

Mazzuchelli, Giammaria. *Gli scrittori d'Italia. Cioè notizie storiche e critiche intorno alle vite e agli scritti dei letterati italiani*. 2 vols. in 6. Brescia: Bossini, 1753–63.

McCleod, Glenda, *Virtue and Venom: Catalogs of Women from Antiquity to the Renaissance*. Ann Arbor: University of Michigan Press, 1991.

Morra, Isabella. *Canzoniere. A Bi-lingual Edition*. Trans. Irene Musillo Mitchell. Purdue, Ind.: Bordighera, 1998.

———. *Rime*. Ed. Maria Antonietta Grignani. Rome: Salerno, 2000.

Nicolay, C. L. "Francisco Pacheco and the Italians." *Modern Language Notes* 20, no. 7 (1905): 214–15.

Oldcorn, Anthony. "Lyric Poetry." In *Cambridge History of Italian Literature*, ed. Peter Brand and Lino Pertile, 251–76. Cambridge: Cambridge University Press, 1996.

Parker, Deborah. *Bronzino: Renaissance Painter as Poet*. Cambridge: Cambridge University Press, 2001.

Pastor, Ludwig. *The History of the Popes*. Ed. and trans. Ralph Francis Kerr. 2d ed. 20 vols. St. Louis: B. Herder Book Co., 1923.

Perlingieri, Ilya Sandra. *Sofonisba Anguissola: The First Great Woman Artist of the Renaissance*. Milan: Rizzoli, 1992.

Plazzotta, Carol. "Bronzino's Laura." *Burlington Magazine* 140, no. 1141 (1998): 251–63.

Poligrafo Gargani, s.v. Ammannati, Ms. Collection, Bibl. Nazionale, Florence.

Rabitti, Giovanna. "Chiara Matraini." In *Italian Women Writers: A Bio-Bibliographical Sourcebook*, ed. Rinaldina Russell, 243–52. Westport, Ct.: Greenwood Press, 1994.

Rime di diversi eccellentissimi autori fatte nella morte dell'Illustriss. et Eccell. Duchessa di Fiorenza et Siena, et degli Illustriss.Signori suoi figliuoli. Ferrara: Valente Panizza Mantovano, 1563.

Sbaragli, L. "'I tabelloni' degli Intronati." *Bullettino Senese di Storia Patria*, 3d ser., 1 (1942): 177–87.

Schutte, Anne Jacobson. "Irene di Spilimbergo: The Image of a Creative Woman in Late Renaissance Italy." *Renaissance Quarterly* 44 (1991): 42–61.

Stufa, Piero, ed. *Componimenti latini, e toscani da diversi suoi amici composti nella morte di m. Benedetto Varchi*. N.p. [Florence?]: n. p., 1566.

Tasso, Bernardo. *Amadigi*. Venice: Gabriel Giolito de' Ferrari, 1560.

Tiraboschi, Girolamo. *Storia della letteratura italiana*. 10 vols. Naples: Giovanni Muccis, 1777–86.

Turchi, Francesco, ed. *Salmi penitentiali, di diversi eccellenti autori con alcune rime spirituali di diversi illust. cardinali, di Reverendissimi vescovi, & d'altre persone Ecclesiastiche. Scelti dal reverendo P. Francesco da Trivigi Carmelitano [Francesco Turchi] nuovamente da lui corretti et ristampati*. Venice: Gabriel Giolito de' Ferrari, 1568; reprint 1570, 1572.

Varchi, Benedetto, ed. *Cento sonetti sopra la morte di Luca Martini*. Ms. II, VIII, 140. Biblio. Nazionale, Florence.

Vasari, Giorgio. *Le vite dei più eccellenti pittori, scultori e architetti*. Ed. Licia and Carlo L. Ragghianti. 4 vols. Milan: Rizzoli, 1976.

Venturi, Adolfo. "Bartolomeo Ammannati." In *Storia dell'arte italiana*, vol. 10, pt. 2, *La scultura del Cinquecento*, 347–432. Milan: Hoepli, 1936.

Vettori, Pietro. *Petri Victorii epistolarum libri X. Orationes XIIII. et Liber de Ludibus Ioannae Austriacae*. Florence: Giunti, 1586.

Zaccagnini, Guido. "Lirici urbinati nel sec. XVI." *Le Marche* 3 (1903): 87–114.

The Place of Female Mysticism in the Italian Literary Canon

Armando Maggi

Women writers have flourished historically in three major sectors of the Italian cultural tradition: the Renaissance, nineteenth- and twentieth-century literature, and Catholic mysticism. In sixteenth-century Italy a first important contingent of female poets arose within the otherwise all-male canon. Only in modern times, however, have women writers seemed to acquire an enduring presence in the history of Italian literature, enriching it with a wealth of influential novelists, essayists, and poets. Catholic mysticism, the third and final area in which women have offered a significant contribution, is not chronologically defined and is still the subject of a complex debate. Female mysticism is, in fact, a literary phenomenon that runs parallel to the entire lay tradition, from the Middle Ages to modernity. That fact that this tradition seems in ways to be outside the mainstream raises questions that this essay proposes to explore. Do women mystics belong in the canon of Italian literature, or do they pertain to an alternative heritage that we could call Catholic spirituality? Should we divide every national canon into specific and distinct subcanons?

Giovanni Pozzi and Claudio Leonardi's groundbreaking anthology of Italian women visionaries, *Scrittrici mistiche italiane* [Italian women mystics], is the most authoritative and accomplished attempt to establish the canon of

Italian female mysticism. The cultural prestige of this dense book, published in 1988, also derives from the fact that its two authors are senior scholars in the field of Italian literature and spirituality. Within this mystical canon, Angela of Foligno (1248–1309), Catherine of Siena (1347–80), Catherine Fieschi (1477–1510), Maria Maddalena de' Pazzi (1566–1604), Maria Domitilla Galluzzi (1573–1645), and Veronica Giuliani (1660–1727) would be its most important representatives, followed by a myriad of minor visionaries.[1] Much of this production, as Pozzi underscores in his introduction, is still disconnected from the mainstream of Italian language and literature. "Italian literary history," he points out, "has absorbed the religious production of the thirteenth and fourteenth centuries, but has glossed over the rest."[2] Pozzi contends that expressions of medieval spirituality have entered the lay canon only because they testify to the evolution of the Italian language, and not because they are perceived as valuable pieces of literature. Let us remember, argues Pozzi, that modern Italian culture is founded on a divorce between lay and Christian thought.[3]

Pozzi's argument is compelling but not completely accurate. It is a fact that modern histories of Italian literature fail to analyze the forms Italian women mystics used to express their religious experiences. Pozzi is right, too, in pointing out that women visionaries wrote "diaries, autobiographies, confession-letters" even before these "turned into distinct literary genres and became popular in lay environments."[4] Finally, Pozzi is correct in reminding us that religious literature disappears from the national canon with the beginning of the Renaissance. As we shall see in a later section of this essay, Pozzi's conclusive remark is of great relevance. What I find questionable is Pozzi's claim that medieval religious texts have become canonical only as linguistic specimens. The situation is in fact more complex and ambiguous.

For an analysis of the relationship between the lay canon and religious texts, we must first turn to the cultural conditions that in the second half of the nineteenth century led to the birth of the Italian state. If we examine the evolution of the Italian literary canon in light of the formation of the Italian nation, we cannot help but notice a crucial interplay between secular and religious texts. Italian intellectuals realized that the literary compilations published in the eighteenth and early nineteenth centuries failed to offer a synthesis of the Italian literary identity. Dedicating his important *Lezioni di letteratura italiana* [Lessons on Italian literature] (1869–72) to "young Italians," Luigi Settembrini (1813–76) writes that he doesn't intend "to narrate the history of our literature, but rather to consider our literature within our history."[5] Examining the production of the fourteenth century, a crucial period in the formation of Italian literature, Settembrini points out that "[t]he first monuments of modern art are Italian, because in Italy civilization was more advanced than anywhere else. These monuments are great because freedom was great and extensive."[6] Dante, Petrarca, and Boccaccio are "the representation of the Italian free spirit." However, the lay intellectual Settembrini is convinced that, to understand fully the "Italian free spirit," we must place those three authors within their contemporary cultural context. That is, we must relate them to other literary figures of the time.

The most striking aspect of Settembrini's analysis of medieval culture is his comparison between Francesco Petrarca and Catherine of Siena, the greatest Italian mystic. Catherine, we should remember, played a crucial role in fourteenth-century Italian politics. She worked actively to bring the papacy from Avignon back to Rome and strenuously supported a crusade against the Muslims. Settembrini describes Catherine as follows.

> Let us compare Francesco Petrarca to Saint Catherine of Siena, another solitary figure who lived in a constant ecstasy for thirty-three years. . . . Her letters, which she dictated to her secretaries, are one of the most beautiful monuments of our literature. . . . In them, we find the purity of Christianity. [In them], we find the Church as it should be. . . . [In them], we find a calm outrage against the unjust cardinals.[7]

Settembrini goes so far as to state that Catherine "saw what Petrarca couldn't see. . . . You may not believe in the miracles described [in the biography written by the friar Romualdo], but you must respect this woman for her historical greatness and read her works with reverential attention. . . . Her style and her language, along with her heart, can be admired, never imitated."[8]

According to Settembrini's concise analysis, the "young Italians" must remember Catherine because she is both a major writer and a fundamental historical figure. In Catherine, art and politics merge seamlessly. Writing during the period when Italy was constructing its independence, Settembrini portrays Catherine as the archetype of an artist who does not shun social intervention in favor of a solipsistic attention toward her writing but rather forges a literary language perfectly attuned to her political views, which he depicts as deeply anticlerical. Like the "young Italians" who fought against the State of the Church, which opposed the birth of the new Italy, Catherine pursued truth and freedom as the quintessential tenets of her mysticism.[9] In Settembrini's view, Catherine's literary expression is the highest example of Italy's original (medieval) longing for freedom and independence.

It is evident that at the foundations of the modern Italian canon lay an essential emphasis on the relationship between rhetoric, language, and social presence. The construction or retrieval of a national identity (a national soul) could only result from a remembrance of Italy's literary and historical past. This would be the meaning of a history of Italian literature.

Settembrini's ideology acquires a superior expression in Francesco De Sanctis's *Storia della letteratura italiana* [History of Italian literature], the most compelling analysis of the concept of literary history in the field of modern Italian studies.[10] Before publishing his *Storia*, whose first volume came out in 1870 (the year of Italian independence), De Sanctis tackles a fundamental issue concerning the composition of a national literary history in an essay on Settembrini's *Lezioni* [Lessons] (1869). De Sanctis is extremely critical of the surveys of the Italian literary tradition published in the late eighteenth and early nineteenth centuries and whose major representative is certainly Girolamo Tiraboschi's monumental *Storia della letteratura italiana* [History of Italian literature], a work of extreme value still today for its wealth of historical information.[11] De Sanctis believes that Settembrini's *Lezioni*, which he calls "a magical book . . . a work of art," represent a radically new approach toward the Italian literary heritage.[12] In a crucial passage on the challenges of the newly born Italian nation, De Sanctis writes:

> When will a literary history ever be possible? . . . Our current goal is not a history, but rather a monographic study. . . . Those who are impatient still give us syntheses and systems. These works are tired repetitions of no use. There is no life in them anymore. . . . A literary history presupposes a philosophy of art as it is generally perceived, an exact history of national life, of its thoughts, opinions, passions, costumes, characters, tendencies.[13]

According to De Sanctis, a literary history constructed as a mere compilation of facts fails to bring to the fore the "national life" in a given historical moment. We could say that he envisions a literary history as the biography of a nation. By studying the different historical stages of the Italian literary tradition, we should be able to reconstruct the identity or soul of the Italian people.

Like Settembrini, De Sanctis is convinced that the fourteenth century played a fundamental role in the formation of the Italian identity. In chapter 6 of the *Storia*, De Sanctis highlights the historical relevance of the Jubilee that Pope Boniface VIII organized for the year 1300. According to De Sanctis, this religious event

> offers an exhaustive portrait of what the literature in that century must have been. This literature received its matter, its instruments,

and its concept from the previous century, wonderfully manifested in the jubilee. But if in the thirteenth century that concept was still an intellectual and allegorical abstraction, . . . in the fourteenth century it acquired a full life, a perfect individualization and formation.[14]

For De Sanctis, Catherine of Siena is a perfect representative of the spirit of that century. She is indeed "the writer and painter of herself."[15] After abandoning her mother and her brothers to become a nun, De Sanctis synthesizes, Catherine "lives a life of ecstasies and visions, and writes in abstraction, or better yet, she dictates with a marvelous spiritual clarity."[16] She writes to popes and princes, kings and queens, De Sanctis continues, with the same direct style she uses to address her mother and brothers. With her simple and powerful literary style, she attains "a vision of what is abstract, and renders it as a body. She indeed makes the body into the light and face of that abstraction."[17]

In my view, De Sanctis's comments on Catherine of Siena's writing are among the most intense and beautiful pages ever written on this great mystic. For De Sanctis, Catherine is the living representative of the Italian soul in a pivotal historical moment. Catherine herself is the visible symbol (what De Sanctis calls "abstraction") resulting from her "visions and ecstasies," and which she accounts for in her letters and mystical treatise generally called *Il dialogo* [The dialogue]. In De Sanctis's view, Catherine of Siena embodies a literary and mystical quest in which a "body" (both the mystic's tormented life and her writings) acquires a "marvelous spiritual clarity." Catherine signifies the soul of fourteenth-century Italy.

As we have seen, at the birth of the Italian national identity, Catherine is viewed as a symbolic figure. Her writings are read as invaluable specimens of a mysticism that finds in political action its highest expression. In De Sanctis's *Storia*, no essential distinction exists between lay and mystical texts, because both exemplify the "soul" of a given historical moment. However, if we read how later generations of Italian critics appropriated and interpreted De Sanctis's highly influential views, we realize that Catherine of Siena's literary stature becomes more and more marginal and superfluous. Subsequent literary histories offer an ambiguous and contradictory portrait of this great medieval mystic.

In most literary histories written during the last years of the nineteenth century and most of the twentieth century, Catherine is portrayed as a powerful but untrained and emotional writer. Without knowing what to make of this mystic, critics offer vague and superficial analyses of her writings, which are often limited to her letters, with no reference to *Il dialogo*, her mystical treatise. Take, for instance, Attilio Momigliano's *Storia della letteratura ital-*

iana [History of the Italian literature] (1936). In the chapter "Minor Authors of the Fourteenth Century," this famous critic (1883–1952) writes that Catherine's letters "are not for everyone. One must get used to her unusual spiritual ascensions and to her intimate speech. . . . We must also consider that . . . her texts lack an artistic perfection, because Catherine did not have literary interests and was a woman of little culture. Not every letter is beautiful. Often one finds overwrought images due to the exceptional ardor of her feelings."[18] These are the typical remarks applied to every woman writer of the Italian canon. Catherine is still an author of an "exceptional ardor," but her inability to restrain her emotions taints her texts and consequently also her place within the canon.[19] What makes Catherine more questionable than every other woman writer is her "intimate speech," by which Momigliano means that Catherine's mystical discourse is foreign to him.

Distancing themselves from De Sanctis, modern generations of Italian literary historians shift Catherine to a subcategory, a sort of literary ghetto for medieval devotional books. The Italian literary canon, as it is reflected in all the surveys published in the twentieth century, is essentially made of a main list of classics with which every respectable and ambitious critic must confront himself, plus a series of scattered and superfluous presences gathered around some generic themes. I find clear evidence of this tendency in the 1972 *Letteratura Italiana. Storia e Testi* [Italian literature: History and texts] by Carlo Muscetta and Achille Tartaro. These renowned academics introduce Catherine as follows: "The work of Catherine of Siena is a fundamental moment in the history of fourteenth-century ethics and spirituality."[20] Not a real writer, Catherine is to be remembered for her moral message.

The publication of Pozzi and Leonardi's seminal *Scrittrici mistiche italiane* in 1988 represents a turning point in the perception of mystical literature.[21] As I pointed out at the beginning of this essay, thanks to Pozzi and Leonardi's academic authority, recent literary histories have expanded and enhanced their subsections on religious literature. Although women mystics are still perceived as "others" from the main canon, the chapters on their writings are of much greater critical accuracy.[22] The gulf between lay and religious production, however, is still wide open.

A fundamental question arises at this point. What is the meaning of a canon constructed as a set of oppositions between real and hypothetical presences, between living texts and dispensable fossils preserved in some sort of literary storehouse? The fact that a given author is listed in a literary survey doesn't necessarily mean that his or her works are the object of an academic debate. As Pamela Joseph Benson has stressed, we should distinguish between a canon of mere "names" and a canon of actual "works." In *The*

Western Canon, Harold Bloom contends that a national canon should resemble the Renaissance "art of memory."

> The Canon, once we view it as the relation of an individual reader and writer to what has been preserved out of what has been written, and forget the canon as a list of books for required study, will be seen as identical with the literary Art of Memory.[23]

Bloom alludes to early modern philosophical investigations on the unlimited power of remembrance, which finds its highest expression in Giordano Bruno, executed by the Catholic Church in 1600. For a sixteenth-century Neoplatonic philosopher like Bruno, to understand and dominate the creation means "to remember" its hidden and secret laws. In *De umbris idearum* [On the shadows of ideas], one of his most important treatises on the art of memory, Bruno contends that acts of memory are "shadows," echoes of a superior form of knowledge. These "shadows," Bruno writes, are reflections of the universal wisdom ruling over the creation.[24]

If, as Bloom says, the assumed goal of any history of a national literature is the promotion of a form of cultural remembrance, it is evident that the Italian canon suffers from a dangerous form of cultural oblivion.[25] We have seen that modern literary historians find themselves at odds with Catherine of Siena, who is paradoxically present in literary surveys more as a political figure than as a writer. How should we treat the other women mystics who lived a life of almost complete seclusion and had no intention of sharing their written texts, which they usually wrote to justify their mystical insights to their male superiors?

Let us examine first the stylistic components of these mystics' texts, one of their most puzzling aspects. How could one possibly posit, say, Angela of Foligno or Maria Maddalena de' Pazzi as authors if they haven't written their texts? I have chosen these two mystics because they represent two different forms of what we may call "literary alienation." Angela simply recounted her insights to a friar, who composed, edited, and interpreted her words, transferring Angela's spoken dialect into rather monotonous Latin. Maria Maddalena de' Pazzi is a similar case since her visions are monologues she delivered when she was "rapt in spirit," as her convent sisters say. If Angela consciously narrated what she had just seen to her confessor, Maria Maddalena speaks without being aware of her speech. The texts we read are what the mystic's sisters wrote while she was speaking. The case of de' Pazzi is particularly problematic not only because this sixteenth-century mystic objected to the transcriptions of her monologues by her sisters but also because she perceived the written word as a betrayal of her attempts to embody the Word in her oral expression. This raises the question of what we are actually reading when we read the seven volumes of "her" mystical communications.

Whether these women are "authors" is debatable from another essential standpoint. Is it possible to see the transcriptions of de' Pazzi's monologues as "works of art" if none of her possible authors (the mystic or her sisters) intended to trigger an aesthetic reaction in the reader?[26] In Bloom's words, the author's "aesthetic choice has always guided every secular aspect of canon formation."[27] If the obsessive journal of the seventeenth-century mystic Veronica Giuliani was meant to detail her daily visions and physical humiliations, is not any aesthetic interpretation of her writing a misconstruction?

So far I have been trying to avoid the question that has plagued Western culture since Kant, a necessary albeit impossible one: What makes a text "beautiful"? I cannot help but think that we still see art as an instance of "ecstatic knowledge" or, in Jean-Marie Schaeffer's words, as the revelation of final truths, or as a transcendental experience, or finally as the manifestation of what cannot be represented.[28] In other words, art is still the embodiment of De Sanctis's "abstraction," the visibility of an inner insight, a form, we may infer, of lay mysticism. Art as an act of disclosure, a communication beyond any form of verbal expression, a nonvisual sight. It is evident that, by using words such as *abstraction*, *intuition*, and *insight*, more than explaining what an artistic reaction actually is, we are conveying our inability to define this very experience. Does Veronica Giuliani's immense journal (thousands of handwritten pages) trigger an aesthetic appreciation? Are the transcriptions of Maria Maddalena de' Pazzi's raptures "beautiful" texts?

Although we are unable to define the essence of an aesthetic reaction, we know that beauty first of all results from the form of the text, from its rhetoric. In literature, "beautiful" is what is perceived as complete, as a rhetorical organism unfolding toward its completion. "Beautiful" is what envisions its own end as a foreseen closure. A text indeed becomes "beautiful" in its end. It is in the end that a text unveils its being a pleasurable unity, which opens in order to end, and in its foreshadowed end hypothesizes a possible new beginning, a renewed process of unfolding and closure. In recent times rereading has in fact become a topic of great interest.[29]

It is almost superfluous to remind the reader that the process of literary completion inevitably entails the presence of a rhetorical tradition, a referential, transcendental "form" lying behind the structure of a given text and affecting the possible response of its audience. The construction of a canon is thus based on a series of transcendental reflections (acts of memory), a dialectic process of unrelenting mirroring among forms. Consider, as a mere instance, the sonnet tradition. We all know what a sonnet is, where its construction comes from, what makes a sonnet a good or a mediocre sonnet. We know that a sonnet should develop as a succinct syllogism. We all know, finally, how essential its final line is, for it is in the last verse that the sonnet's meaning reveals its limit, its frame, and thus its beauty. From its formal structure we can also envision its thematic and stylistic deviations, its subdivisions and its possible evolutions. Genres are indeed constructed as variations, as linguistic risks taken within an established form.

Most texts written by women mystics certainly respond to a precedent religious tradition, but they often lack any "binding" connection with an existing literary form.[30] Who could possibly deny the essential influence exerted by the mysticism of Catherine of Siena? Aren't the most visible traits of her spirituality (such as her concept of "blood," her mystical marriage, and her stigmata) topoi of Italian female mysticism? After Catherine of Siena, the act of marrying the Word is a key moment for every woman mystic. According to her sisters' transcriptions, Maria Maddalena de' Pazzi married the divinity a number of times. Saint Catherine never failed to attend Maria Maddalena's mystical weddings. In one of the most dramatic episodes of her life, Maria Maddalena addressed her groom as follows: "Oh immense generosity [*silence*] when she saw the gift that Jesus wanted to give her, she rejoiced. . . . Oh Word, you too [*silence*] she meant: you too married Saint Catherine."[31]

Don't some of Veronica Giuliani's entries evoke the visions of Maria Maddalena de' Pazzi? Read, for instance, how Veronica recounts her repeated journeys through the regions of purgatory.[32] Maria Maddalena had narrated a similar experience in *Probatione* [Probation], in which she describes how her deceased brother begged her to alleviate his purifying pain. However, these thematic and even linguistic correspondences never become strict structural references, rhetorical procedures through which the writer, and thus the reader, recognizes a visible path toward a familiar (transcendental) end. The tradition of female mysticism is a sequence of loosely structured manuscripts.

How could we possibly explain, then, the undeniable attention that this nontradition is increasingly gaining among students of Italian culture and literature? I find in Rainer Rochlitz's recent *L'art au banc d'essai* a suitable answer to this question.[33] A first, essential element present in most contemporary analyses is the possible distinction between *oeuvre* [work] and *objet* [object], that is, between the work of art as a theoretical presence and its concrete manifestation, such as the difference between a play and its performance. Modern theoreticians, Rochlitz summarizes, envision a variety of different forms of interaction between a text and its performativity, for instance, between a play and its actual interpretation.[34] However, Rochlitz posits an additional, and much more fruitful, aesthetic procedure. For Rochlitz, a "reconstructive" aesthetic is founded on the critical relationship that apprehends the oeuvre as experience. According to this perspective, any aesthetic experience "is always inscribed in the context of critical debates, in which its heterogeneous nature summons an aesthetic reflection."[35]

We could say that the "revelation" brought about by a "reconstructive" approach is a dialogic process of sharing and debating with others; that is, it is an insight resulting from partial, subjective instances of aesthetic appropriation. Paul Ricoeur has defined the essential problem of subjective appropriation in a crucial article on the methodology of exegesis. According to Ricoeur,

> appropriation is the concept which is suitable for the actualization of meaning as addressed to someone. It takes the place of an answer in the dialogical situation, in the same way that "revelation" or "disclosure" takes the place of ostensive reference in the dialogical situation. The interpretation is complete when the reading releases something like an event, an event of discourse, an event in the present time. As appropriation, the interpretation becomes an event.[36]

The act of aesthetic appreciation is certainly an insight, a "revelation," but a revelation that exists insofar as the subject is able to verbalize his appropriation, that is, insofar as the subject addresses an insight to someone. "To appropriate" a text is an act of "liberation" from the strictures of any possible received interpretative formulation (for instance, mystical texts as exclusive expressions of Catholic dogmas). The text is what it does to me as a personal, private subjectivity, which receives the written page as a sudden "event." It is in shifting the focus from the text as a hypothetical and unchangeable idiom to the reader's appropriation that the text itself finds its final expression. This is when a literary work turns into a specimen of cultural retrieval (Bloom's "art of memory"). However, the subject's appropriation is not complete unless it becomes subject to a dialogic interaction with others. In other words, my insight is a critical exchange among various forms of subjective appropriations.[37] In my exchange with others, my "enlightenment" is clarified. This "reconstructive" aesthetic inevitably questions the authority of any established canon. By "canon" we should envision a dynamic and constantly renewed corpus of subjective "revelations." The term *revelation*, I believe, suits Bloom's concept of canon as an art of memory. Like Giordano

Bruno's "shadows," "canonical" texts conjure up a past that is ours even if we did not experience it and do not remember it. As Bruno would say, we are the shadows that visit us as remembrances.

❧ ❧ ❧

NOTES

1. Angela of Foligno didn't have a regular education but was able to read. Married with children, she experienced a first vision about 1285, during which she saw Francis of Assisi. The friar Arnaldo became her spiritual director and scribe. After the death of her family, Angela became a Franciscan tertiary. In 1291, she had a vision in the basilica of Saint Francis. From 1292 to 1296, she dictated her biographical *Liber* [Book], which is made up of her autobiography called *Memoriale* [Memoire] plus a group of other mystical texts. For the modern edition see *Il libro della beata Angela da Foligno* [The book by the blessed Angela of Foligno], ed. Ludger Their and Abele Calufetti (Grottaferrata: Editiones Collegii S. Bonaventurae, 1985).

Catherine of Siena is the greatest Italian mystic and a key figure of Italian medieval history. She had her first vision at the age of seven. About 1360, she became a tertiary of the Dominican order. When Florence was placed under an interdict by Pope Gregory XI in 1376, Catherine took public action to secure a double aim: peace within the church and in Italy and a crusade against the Muslims. She went as unofficial mediator to Avignon with her confessor, Raymond of Capua. She believed that the return of the pope to Rome was the only way to bring peace to Italy and to initiate a crusade against the infidels. In 1378, Catherine went to Rome, probably at the invitation of Pope Urban VI, whom she helped in reorganizing the church. Her writings include *Il dialogo* [The dialogue], about 380 letters, and 26 prayers. *Il dialogo* was published about 1475, and the letters in 1494 and 1500. Pope Paul VI proclaimed Catherine a doctor of the church in 1970. For *Il dialogo*, see Caterina da Siena, *Il libro*, ed. Umberto Meattini (Alba: Edizioni Paoline, 1975). Meattini has also published Catherine's letters: Caterina da Siena, *Le lettere*, ed. Umberto Meattini, 4th ed. (Alba: Edizioni Paoline, 1987). In 2001, the foundation Ezio Franceschini held the Seventh Annual Seminar on Catherine, by the title *Caterina. Testo, Contesto e Fortuna dell'Epistolario* (Certosa del Galluzzo, June 12, 2001), which examined the status of the critical edition of the epistolary. For a recent English translation of her mystical treatise, see Catherine of Siena, *The Dialogue*, trans. Suzanne Noffke (New York: Paulist Press, 1988).

Catherine Fieschi was born in Genoa and received a careful education. Although she wanted to take the veil, her family forced her to marry Giuliano Adorno. Her first mystical experience took place in 1473. She worked in a Genoese hospital for many years. The so-called *Corpus catherinianum* (first published posthumously in 1551) includes a famous treatise on purgatory and a dialogue between soul and body. The most recent Italian edition is *Trattato sul purgatorio e altri scritti*, ed. Tiziana Giuggia (Milan: Gribaudi, 1996). A recent English version is Catherine of Genoa, *Purgation and Purgatory*, trans. Serge Hughes (New York: Paulist Press, 1979).

Maria Maddalena de' Pazzi, one of the most original mystics of the Christian tradition, spent most of her life in the Carmelite convent of Santa Maria degli Angeli. Her visions have an oral nature. Her sisters slowly developed a complex system of faithful transcription of the words she uttered during her raptures. A first group of visions took place when she was eighteen (1584) and lasted forty days. They were called *Quaranta giorni* [Forty days]. A second set of visions is *I colloqui* [The dialogues], in which her sisters report the mystic's monologues and their subsequent questions to her. Another important group of visions is *Probatione* [Probation], which recounts the devil's temptations and her sense of distance from God. For the critical edition, see *Tutte le opere di Santa Maria Maddalena de' Pazzi dai manoscritti originali* (Florence: Nardini, 1960–66), and for discussion, see Armando Maggi, *Uttering the Word: The Mystical Performances of Maria Maddalena de' Pazzi* (Albany: State University of New York Press, 1998).

Domitilla Galluzzi was born into a very pious family. In 1615, she joined the Capuchin convent of Santa Franca in Pavia. Her extraordinary revelations, revolving around the Passion of Christ, began in 1619. Physical reactions (wounds, bleeding) accompanied these raptures. Her superiors humiliated her repeatedly. She was a prolific writer. Her most important text is her *Autobiografia* [Autobiography]. No critical edition is available. For more on the tradition of her writings, see the essay by Ann Matter in this volume.

Like Domitilla Galluzzi, Veronica Giuliani was a Capuchin. She entered the convent of Città di Castello in 1677. Her numerous confessors forced her to detail her daily mystical experiences. Like Domitilla, she was the object of repeated injustice and violence. Her journal opens in 1693 and consists of thousands of pages. Veronica is one of the most powerful mystics of the Italian tradition. For a modern edition of the mystic's journal and five autobiographies, see *Un tesoro nascosto, ossia Diario di S. Veronica Giuliani*, ed. Pietro Pizzicaria, 8 vols. (Prato, 1895–1905). Oreste Fiorucci has republished this edition in five volumes (Città di Castello: Monastero delle cappuccine, 1969–74). This is a very problematic work. The first editor deeply modified the syntax and lexicon of the original.

2. Giovanni Pozzi, "L'alfabeto delle sante," *Scrittrici mistiche italiane* (Genoa: Marietti, 1988), 25: "In Italia, la storia letteraria ha fatto pienamente sua la produzione religiosa volgare del due e trecento; ma ha trascurato il resto." Unless otherwise noted, all translations are mine.

3. Ibid., 26.

4. Ibid., 23: "[Le mistiche] hanno abbracciato d'istinto le forme letterarie prima che fossero delimitate in generi definiti e diffuse in ambito secolare: il diario, l'autobiografia, la lettera-confessione."

5. I quote from Luigi Settembrini, *Lezioni di letteratura italiana* (Naples: Morano, 1892), vii: "Io non intendo narrare la Storia della nostra Letteratura, ma considero la Letteratura nostra nella nostra Storia." On Settembrini's critical work, see Giorgio Baroni, *Storia della critica letteraria in Italia* (Turin: UTET, 1997), 414–15. Luigi Settembrini is one of the most important representatives of the Italian "Risorgimento," the intellectual and military movement that led to Italian independence. Born in Naples in 1813, Settembrini was persecuted and condemned to life imprisonment. When he returned to Naples, he became professor of Italian literature at the University of Naples (1861). Toward the end of his life, he composed the famous *Remembrances of My Life* [Ricordanze della mia vita].

6. Settembrini, *Lezioni di letteratura italiana*, 210: "I primi monumenti dell'arte moderna sono italiani, perché in Italia la civiltà era maggiore che altrove: sono grandi, perché grande e pienissima era la libertà."

7. Ibid., 217–18: "A Francesco Petrarca unite Santa Caterina da Siena, quest'al-

tra solitaria vissuta trentatré anni in un'estasi continua. . . . Le sue lettere, che ella dettava a segretari, rimangono come uno dei più belli monumenti della Letteratura nostra. In esse c'è tutta la purezza del Cristianesimo; c'è la Chiesa come dovrebbe essere. . . . C'è sdegno senz'ira contro i cardinali parteggianti."

8. Ibid., 218–20: "Ed ella vide ciò che il Petrarca non poté. . . . Voi potete non credere ai miracoli che si raccontano, ma dovete rispettare questa donna storicamente grande, e leggere le sue opere con reverente attenzione. . . . Il suo stile e la sua lingua, come il suo cuore, possono ammirarsi, non imitarsi mai."

9. Baroni underscores that it wouldn't be possible to understand the evolution of literary criticism in Italy without considering the historical events that led to the formation of the Italian nation. In Italy, modern criticism developed along with the evolution of a sense of national identity (*Storia della critica letteraria italiana*, 384–85).

10. De Sanctis was born in Morra Irpino in 1817 and died in Naples in 1883. He was arrested in 1850 for patriotic political activity and remained in prison for almost three years. Condemned to exile, he reached Turin, where he lived until 1856. He moved to Zurich, where he taught for four years. De Sanctis went back to Naples in 1860. Giuseppe Garibaldi, the leader of the Risorgimento, made him first governor of the province of Avellino and later director of public education. In 1869, De Sanctis wrote an important *Saggio su Petrarch* [Essay on Petrarch]. In 1870–71, the first two volumes of his *Storia della letteratura italiana* came out. In 1871, he became professor of comparative literatures at the University of Naples and in 1879 was elected minister of public education in Italy.

11. De Sanctis states: "Tiraboschi, Andres, Ginguené are syntheses of the past. Today, everything is new. A new world is arising in every field," in "Settembrini e i suoi critici," in *Saggi critici*, ed. Nino Cortese (Naples: Morano, 1932), 3:56. The Jesuit Girolamo Tiraboschi (1731–94) is the author of the monumental *Storia della letteratura italiana*. Tiraboschi, who makes his literary history extend from Etruscan times down to 1700, concerns himself with all matters of interest in belles lettres, philosophy, and history, accompanying the statement of his views with an abundance of precious documents. Tiraboschi's *Storia* appeared in its first edition between 1772 and 1782.

12. De Sanctis, "Settembrini e i suoi critici," 47.

13. Ibid., 57: "Quando una storia della letteratura sarà possibile? . . . Il lavoro di oggi non è la storia, ma è la monografia. . . . Gl'impazienti ci regalano ancora delle sintesi e de' sistemi: sono stanche ripetizioni, che non hanno più eco. . . . Una storia della letteratura presuppone una filosofia dell'arte, generalmente ammessa, una storia esatta della vita nazionale, pensieri, opinioni, passioni, costumi, caratteri, tendenze."

14. Francesco De Sanctis, *Storia della letteratura italiana* (Turin: Einaudi-Gallimard, 1996), 108: "Il giubileo ci dà un'immagine di quello che dovea essere la letteratura nel secolo decimoquarto. Ebbe dal secolo antecedente la sua materia, i suoi strumenti e il suo concetto, del quale il giubileo fu una così splendida manifestazione. Ma quel concetto rimaso nella sua astrazione intellettuale e allegorica . . . ebbe nel Trecento la sua vita, e venne a perfetta individuazione e formazione." For an English translation see Francesco De Sanctis, *History of Italian Literature*, trans. Joan Redfern, 2 vols. (New York: Harcourt, Brace, 1931).

15. De Sanctis, *Storia della letteratura italiana*, 112: "Ma ecco fra tante vite di santi il santo in persona, scrittore e pittore di sé medesimo, Caterina da Siena."

16. Ibid.: "[V]ive una vita di estasi e di visioni, e scrive in astrazione, anzi detta con una lucidità di spirito meravigliosa."

17. Ibid.: "Ha la visione dell'astratto, e lo rende come corpo, anzi fa del corpo la luce e la faccia di quello." For an introductory analysis of De Sanctis's critical language, see Guido Guglielmo, *Da De Sanctis a Gramsci: Il linguaggio della critica* (Milan: Il Mulino, 1976), 15–56. Guglielmo offers a clear explanation of De Sanctis's relationship with Hegel's philosophy.

18. Attilio Momiliano, *Storia della letteratura italiana* (Milan: Principato, 1936), 111: "Le sue lettere non sono accessibili a tutti: occorre abituarsi a quelle insolite altezze spirituali, a quel modo di parlare così intimo. . . . Si aggiungono a questo difficoltà dovute . . . a scarsa elaborazione del testo: poiché santa Caterina non aveva propositi letterari ed era donna di poca cultura. Non tutte le lettere sono belle; vi è anzi frequente un'esagerazione di immagini che non si può ben giustificare con l'ardore eccezionale del sentimento."

19. We find a similar attitude toward Catherine in many other literary histories of the nineteenth and twentieth centuries. For instance, Carlo Maria Tallarico, *Storia della letteratura italiana* (Naples: Morano, 1887), 468, holds that Catherine's letters have a "purity of language" that makes them one of the highest expressions of the fourteenth century. But Catherine's eloquence is "ruffled" [*scapigliata*] and shows "an overflowing emotion." In *Storia della letteratura italiana* (Turin: Unione tipografica torinese, 1930), pt. 2, 1:17, Giuseppe Zonta contends that "the soul of this mystic . . . is simple and ardent . . . but her style is prolix and monotonous, always too overflowing." According to Francesco Flora's *Storia della letteratura italiana* (Milan: Mondadori, 1940), 1:392, "Catherine was a saint and not a poet, not a great poet. Catherine belongs to the moral, political, and religious history of Italy. She has very little to do with poetry and philosophy." A subtler analysis of Catherine is in Emilio Cecchi and Natalino Sapegno's *Storia della letteratura italiana* (Milan: Garzanti, 1965), 2:660. Echoing De Sanctis, Cecchi and Sapegno stress that the mystic's letters shouldn't be judged in a superficial way, as mere historical documents. However, the two important critics believe that her texts exclusively belong in the history of mysticism.

20. Carlo Muscetta and Achille Tartaro, *La Letteratura Italiana. Storia e Testi. Il Trecento* (Bari: Laterza, 1972), 2:463: "Fondamentale nella storia dell'etica e della spiritualità trecentesche è l'opera di Caterina da Siena."

21. Among the innumerable works on women mystics, these are the most recent titles: E. Ann Matter and John Coakley, eds., *Creative Women in Medieval and Early Modern Italy: A Religious and Artistic Renaissance* (Philadelphia: University of Pennsylvania Press, 1994); Paul Lachance, *The Spiritual Journey of the Bd. Angela of Foligno* (Toronto: Peregrina, 1999); Bernard McGinn, *The Flowering of Mysticism: Men and Women in the New Mysticism, 1200–1350* (New York: Crossroad, 1998); Domenico Maffei and Paolo Nardi, eds., *Atti del Simposio internazionale cateriniano-bernardiniano, Siena, 17–20 aprile* 1980 (Siena: Accademia senese degli Intronati, 1982); Umile Bonzi, *Teologia mistica di Caterina da Genova,* 2 vols. (Genoa: Marietti, 1960–62); Armando Maggi, *Uttering the Word;* Monique Courbat, *Dico e ridico e non dico niente. Il fenomeno del diario sdoppiato in Santa Veronica Giuliani* (Siena: Edizioni Cantagalli, 1994); Armando Maggi, "When the O. Moves in the Heart: The Annunciation of the End in the *Journal* of Saint Veronica Giuliani," *Annali d'Italianistica* 18 (2000): 239–53. Volume 13 (1994) of the journal *Annali d'Italianistica* is entirely dedicated to Italian women mystics.

22. On Catherine of Siena, see for instance Enrico Malato, ed., *Storia della letteratura italiana* (Rome: Salerno editrice, 1995), 2:290–304.

23. Harold Bloom, *The Western Canon* (New York: Riverhead Books, 1994), 17. I quote Benson from the presentation she made at the conference "Strong Voices, Weak History?" See also volume introduction and n. 2.

24. *De umbris idearum* was published in Paris in 1582. I quote from Giordano Bruno, *De umbris idearum*, ed. Rita Sturlese (Florence: Olschki, 1991), 36–37.

25. Alberto Asor Rosa offers a brief analysis of this problem in "Letteratura, testo, società," *Letteratura italiana* (Turin: Einaudi, 1982), 18–20), 1:18–20.

26. Cf. Gerard Genette, *The Aesthetic Relation*, trans. G. M. Goshgarian (Ithaca: Cornell University Press, 1999), 3: "The difference between the 'ordinary' aesthetic relation and the artistic relation turns . . . on the presence or absence of an intentional factor, and on the various effects that factor inevitably produces."

27. Bloom, *Western Canon*, 21.

28. Jean-Marie Schaeffer, *L'art de l'âge moderne* (Paris: Gallimard, 1992), 15.

29. See, for instance, Matei Calinescu, *Rereading* (New Haven: Yale University Press, 1993). The idea of an artistic expression as a linguistic given that reveals its beauty in its being "framed" by its pending conclusion brings us back to the Renaissance conception of emblematic expression. According to numerous Italian theoreticians, an emblem or *impresa* was a hybrid, a datum made of words and figures but whose message resided neither in its verbal nor in its visual component but rather in the symbolic apprehension brought about in the viewer. An emblem was the synthesis arising in the mind, or again, a form of contemplation that identified with its "frame," with its being a communication harboring and sustaining its own end. A failed emblem was an artifact unable to summon a symbolic unity, an emotional "meaning" that could be reiterated at every new act of contemplation. I discuss this point in *Identità e impresa rinascimentale* (Ravenna: Longo, 1998).

30. This is the opinion expressed by Giovanni Pozzi in his seminal article on Veronica Giuliani: "Il parere' autobiografico di Veronica Giuliani," *Strumenti Critici* 54 (1987): 161–92.

31. De' Pazzi, *I colloqui*, in *Tutte le opere*, 2:17: "'O liberalità immensa' . . . Cominciando a vedere il dono che Jesu gli voleva dare, et cominciando a rallegrarsi grandemente disse . . . 'O Verbo anche tu' . . . Voleva dire anche tu sposasti Santa Caterina.'" I quote from my translation in *Uttering the Word*, 88. I explain that the transcribers of the mystic's speech meant "you married Saint Catherine too." But in my translation I was faithful to the original.

32. In 1701, Veronica visits a sister who had gone insane (*Un tesoro nascosto*, 2:921). When this sister dies, Veronica witnesses her fight with numerous devils who would like to drag her down with them. To save this sister's soul, Veronica accepts the pains she will suffer in purgatory (*Un tesoro nascosto*, 2:923). In 1718, during a mass, Veronica is told that she will have to suffer on behalf of sister Ottavia, a nun in Mercatello, who had died a few days before (*Un tesoro nascosto*, 3:1222). In 1722, Veronica helps a nun from the convent of Saint Maria Maddalena de' Pazzi to move from purgatory to heaven (*Un tesoro nascosto*, 4:590).

33. Rainer Rochlitz, *L'art au banc d'essai* (Paris: Gallimard, 1998), 57–70.

34. Ibid., 60.

35. Ibid., 61: "[L'] expérience est toujours inscrite dans le contexte de débats critiques, et c'est là que son hétérogénéité suscite une réflexion esthétique."

36. Paul Ricoeur, "Appropriation," in *A Ricoeur Reader: Reflection and Imagination*, ed. Mario J. Valdés (Toronto: Toronto University Press, 1991), 89.

37. Alberto Asor Rosa confirms this standpoint in his definition of Italian literature. The Italian critic contends that by "Italian literature" we must mean all the texts that our modern sensibility perceives as literary artifacts (in "Letteratura, testo, società," 21–22).

BIBLIOGRAPHY

Angela of Foligno. *Il libro della beata Angela da Foligno*. Ed. Ludger Their and Abele Calufetti. Grottaferrata: Editiones Collegii S. Bonaventurae, 1985.

Asor Rosa, Alberto. "Letteratura, testo, società." In *Letteratura italiana*, 1:5–29. Turin: Einaudi, 1982.

Baroni, Giorgio. *Storia della critica letteraria in Italia*. Turin: UTET, 1997.

Bloom, Harold. *The Western Canon*. New York: Riverhead Books, 1994.

Bonzi, Umile. *Teologia mistica di Caterina da Genova*. 2 vols. Genoa: Marietti, 1960–62.

Bruno, Giordano. *De umbris idearum*. Ed. Rita Sturlese. Florence: Olschki, 1991.

Calinescu, Matei. *Rereading*. New Haven: Yale University Press, 1993.

Catherine Fieschi [St. Catherina of Siena]. *Purgation and Purgatory*. Trans. Serge Hughes. New York: Paulist Press, 1979.

———. *Trattato sul purgatorio e altri scritti*. Ed. Tiziana Giuggia. Milan: Gribaudi, 1996.

Catherine of Siena. *Il libro della divina dottrina*. Ed. Umberto Meattini. Alba: Edizioni Paoline, 1975.

———. *Le lettere*. Ed. Umberto Meattini. 4th ed. Alba: Edizioni Paolini, 1987.

———. *The Dialogue*. Trans. Suzanne Noffke. New York: Paulist Press, 1988.

Cecchi, Emilio, and Natalino Sapegno. *Storia della letteratura italiana*. Vol. 2. Milan: Garzanti, 1965.

Courbat, Monique. *Dico e ridico e non dico niente. Il fenomeno del diario sdoppiato in Santa Veronica Giuliani*. Siena: Edizioni Cantagalli, 1994.

De' Pazzi, Maria Maddalena. *Tutte le opere di Santa Maria Maddalena de' Pazzi dai manoscritti originali*. Florence: Nardini, 1960–66.

———. *Selected Revelations*. Trans. Armando Maggi. New York: Paulist Press, 2000.

De Sanctis, Francesco. *History of Italian Literature*. Trans. Joan Redfern. 2 vols. New York: Harcourt, Brace, 1931.

———. "Settembrini e i suoi critici." In *Saggi critici*, ed. Nino Cortese, 3:33–59. Naples: Morano, 1932.

———. *Storia della letteratura italiana*. Turin: Einaudi-Gallimard, 1996.

Flora, Francesco. *Storia della letteratura italiana*. Milan: Mondadori, 1940.

Genette, Gerard. *The Aesthetic Relation*. Trans. G. M. Goshgarian. Ithaca: Cornell University Press, 1999.

Giuliani, Veronica. *Un tesoro nascosto, ossia Diario di S. Veronica Giuliani*. Ed. Pietro Pizzicaria. 8 vols. Prato, 1895–1905. Reprint, ed. Oreste Fiorucci. 5 vols. Città di Castello: Monastero delle Cappuccine, 1969–74.

Guglielmo, Guido. *Da De Sanctis a Gramsci: Il linguaggio della critica*. Milan: Il Mulino, 1976.

Lachance, Paul. *The Spiritual Journey of the Bd. Angela of Foligno*. Toronto: Peregrina, 1999.

Maffei, Domenico, and Paolo Nardi, eds. *Atti del Simposio internazionale cateriniano-bernardiniano, Siena, 17–20 aprile 1980*. Siena: Accademia senese degli Intronati, 1982.

Maggi, Armando. *Identità e impresa rinascimentale*. Ravenna: Longo, 1998.

———. *Uttering the Word: The Mystical Performances of Maria Maddalena de' Pazzi.* Albany: State University of New York Press, 1998.

———. "When the O. Moves in the Heart: The Annunciation of the End in the *Journal* of Saint Veronica Giuliani." *Annali d'Italianistica* 18 (2000): 239–53.

Malato, Enrico, ed. *Storia della letteratura italiana.* 14 vols. Rome: Salerno Editrice, 1995–.

Matter, E. Ann, and John Coakley, eds. *Creative Women in Medieval and Early Modern Italy: A Religious and Artistic Renaissance.* Philadelphia: University of Pennsylvania Press, 1994.

McGinn, Bernard. *The Flowering of Mysticism: Men and Women in the New Mysticism, 1200–1350.* New York: Crossroad, 1998.

Momiliano, Attilio. *Storia della letteratura italiana.* Milan: Principato, 1936.

Muscetta, Carlo, and Achille Tartaro. *La Letteratura Italiana. Storia e Testi. Il Trecento.* Vol. 2. Bari: Laterza, 1972.

Pozzi, Giovanni. "Il 'parere' autobiografico di Veronica Giuliani." *Strumenti Critici* 54 (1987): 161–92.

Pozzi, Giovanni, and Claudio Leonardi, eds. *Scrittrici mistiche italiane.* Genoa: Marietti, 1988.

Ricoeur, Paul. "Appropriation." In *A Ricoeur Reader: Reflection and Imagination*, ed. Mario J. Valdés, 86–98. Toronto: Toronto University Press, 1991.

Rochlitz, Rainer. *L'art au banc d'essai.* Paris: Gallimard, 1998.

Schaeffer, Jean-Marie. *L'art de l'âge moderne.* Paris: Gallimard, 1992.

Settembrini, Luigi. *Lezioni di letteratura italiana.* Naples: Morano, 1892.

Tallarico, Carlo Maria. *Storia della letteratura italiana.* Naples: Morano, 1887.

Zonta, Giuseppe. *Storia della letteratura italiana.* Turin: Unione Tipografica Torinese, 1930.

Thomas Bentley's Monument of Matrons

THE EARLIEST ANTHOLOGY OF ENGLISH WOMEN'S TEXTS

John N. King

Thomas Bentley's *Monument of Matrons: Containing Seven Several Lamps of Virginity* is the earliest printed collection of English women's writings.[1] It was published in London in 1582, at a time when intricate celebration of the perpetual virginity of Queen Elizabeth I was emerging. The editor contributes to this movement by gathering a massive collection of prayers and meditations written by the queen and her female contemporaries in addition to devotional texts constructed by men who wrote for a female audience. He contributes to the formation of a canon of female authors by treating their writings as contemporary fulfillments of writings about or deeds and speeches by notable women in the Bible. Organization of the collection into seven lamps (i.e., parts) fuses apocalyptic imagery related to the sevenfold visions of the Book of Revelation and Jesus' Parable of the Wise and Foolish Virgins (Matthew 25.1–13), whose number included five maidens who kept lamps filled with oil and another five who left theirs empty. Only the former are prepared for union with Christ, the mystic Bridegroom, and entry into the Kingdom of Heaven. The wise virgins function as female types for faith, constancy, and wisdom.

Although virginity in the title refers to divine "illumination" and spiritual readiness rather than maidenhood, strictly speaking, the *Monument of Matrons* pays homage to the Virgin Queen of England to whom Bentley dedicated the anthology. The date of publication coincided with the end of the queen's final round of marriage negotiations and the beginning of an esoteric cult that celebrated her steadfast virginity.[2] Bentley compiled the collection in support of a bid for patronage from the queen. A student of law at Gray's Inn at the time of publication, Bentley was appointed churchwarden of St. Andrew's Holborn through the offices of John Aylmer, bishop of London, in 1584.[3]

The *Monument of Matrons* prominently acknowledges the patronage of Bishop Aylmer (B1v). In its incessant application to Queen Elizabeth of scriptural precedents for governance by women—Deborah, Esther, and Judith—the collection follows precedents established by Aylmer's *An Harbor for Faithful and True Subjects, against the last blown Blast, concerning the government of women.* Published in London in 1559, at the outset of Elizabeth's reign, Aylmer's text attributes the virtues of Old Testament heroines to the young queen (B3v, D2v, E3v, o3r). Affording a foundation for queenly iconography at the beginning of the Elizabethan age, Aylmer compiled his defense of female government in order to refute John Knox's inflammatory attack on the capacity of women to govern as queens, *The First Blast of the Trumpet against the Monstrous Regiment of Women* (Geneva, 1558). In a masterpiece of bad timing, Knox's attack on governance by British queens—Mary I of England and Mary, Queen of Scots—was published soon after the death of the former, thus giving great offense to her successor, Elizabeth I.

The material production of the *Monument of Matrons* clarifies the nature of the readership to which Bentley appealed, over and beyond its potential coterie audience of Queen Elizabeth and Bishop Aylmer. Henry Denham, the assignee of William Seres for printing collections of private prayers, printed volumes 1 and 2 in their entirety but only quires A–B of volume 3. On behalf of Denham, Thomas Dawson printed the remainder of volume 3. Printing of this book in quarto format made each hefty volume an expensive commodity affordable only by an elite audience. Denham sold all three volumes, singly or as an ensemble, at the sign of the Star at Paternoster Row, a location at the north side of St. Paul's Cathedral and near the center of the London book trade.

Denham was no stranger to the production of illustrated books, because he had printed a string of them during the previous eighteen years.[4] Only the sections of the *Monument of Matrons* printed by Denham, rather than Dawson, contain the elaborate historiated woodcut borders and portrayal of Catherine Parr that he commissioned expressly for lamps 1–5. By contrast, Dawson employed worn-out, nonhistoriated compartments that circulated from one printing house to another on the title leaves for lamps 6 and 7.[5]

The densely symbolic title page of the entire collection elaborates upon its central concerns (fig. 1). With Queen Elizabeth's coat of arms at the top, the woodcut border associates her with the Spouse of the Song of Solomon (or Canticles), a figure allegorized by Jews or Christians as a type for Israel, the Church, or individual believers. She bears a seven-branched lamp stand and an open Bible in the lowest compartment of this border. The upper left medallion portrays the creation of Eve, a type for the Virgin Mary, while that at the upper right depicts the Annunciation to Mary, the second Eve. The lower medallions portray the Five Wise Virgins greeting Christ the Bridegroom at the left and in celestial flames at the right.

Succeeding title leaves develop Bentley's compliment by juxtaposing Queen Elizabeth with outstanding women from the Bible and recent history. The compartment for "The Second Lamp of Virginity" (fig. 2), which represents the principal focus of the present essay, affords an iconographical entryway into a gathering of "diverse godly meditations, and Christian prayers made by sundry virtuous Queens, and other devout and godly women in our time." Queen Hester (Esther) affords an Old Testament model for three contemporary queens: Elizabeth I; Catherine Parr, sixth wife of Henry VIII; and Marguerite d'Angoulême, consort of Henri II de Navarre. Each queen composed a pious devotional work included in lamp 2. They are portrayed on this title leaf not only because of their spirituality but because they expressed it in writing comparable to the devout speech of Queen Esther.

In a similar vein, the woodcut border for "The Third Lamp of Virginity, Containing sundry forms of divine meditations and Christian prayers" pays homage to Queen Elizabeth, portrayed in the medallion at the upper left, whose kneeling figure corresponds to those of three scriptural types for both the "true" church and queenly governance (fig. 3). In clockwise order, they are Bathsheba, Judith, and Deborah. Comparison of Elizabeth with Bathsheba is notable, given her adultery with King David prior to his murder of her husband, Uriah the Hittite. Nevertheless, scriptural commentators interpreted the Hebrew queen as a prefiguration of the union between Christ and his spouse, that is, the church. The compartment for lamp 4 likens Elizabeth I to Susanna, another type for the "true" church, and the prophetesses Huldah and Anne. The inclusion of St. Anne hints at an allusion to Anne Boleyn, whom Henry VIII executed during the infancy of their daughter, Princess Elizabeth. Protestant apologists such as John Aylmer and John Foxe rehabilitated Anne Boleyn in order to pay an indirect compliment to Queen Elizabeth and because of her mother's alleged friendship and support of their cause. The title leaf for lamp 5 includes Elizabeth among biblical women associated with spiritual renewal and resurrection: Martha, Abishag, and the Widow of Zarephath.

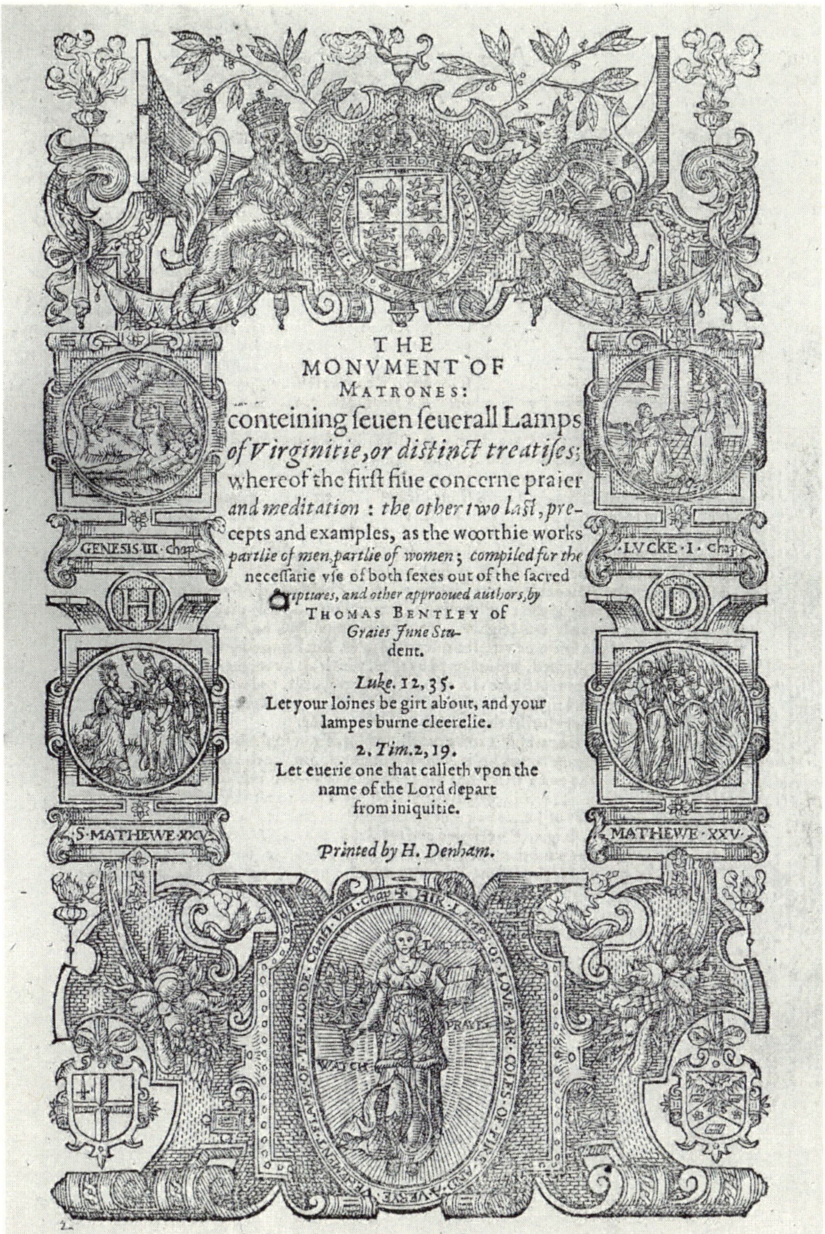

THE
MONVMENT OF
MATRONES:
conteining ſeuen ſeuerall Lamps
of Virginitie, or distinct treatiſes;
whereof the firſt fiue concerne praier
and meditation : the other two laſt, pre-
cepts and examples, as the woorthie works
partlie of men, partlie of women; compiled for the
neceſſarie vſe of both ſexes out of the ſacred
Scriptures, and other approoued authors, by
THOMAS BENTLEY of
Graies Inne Stu-
dent.

Luke. 12, 35.
Let your loines be girt about, and your
lampes burne cleerelie.

2. *Tim.* 2, 19.
Let euerie one that calleth vpon the
name of the Lord depart
from iniquitie.

Printed by H. Denham.

1. Title-page border, from Thomas Bentley, *The Monument of Matrons* (1582). (This item is reproduced by permission of the Huntington Library, San Marino, California.)

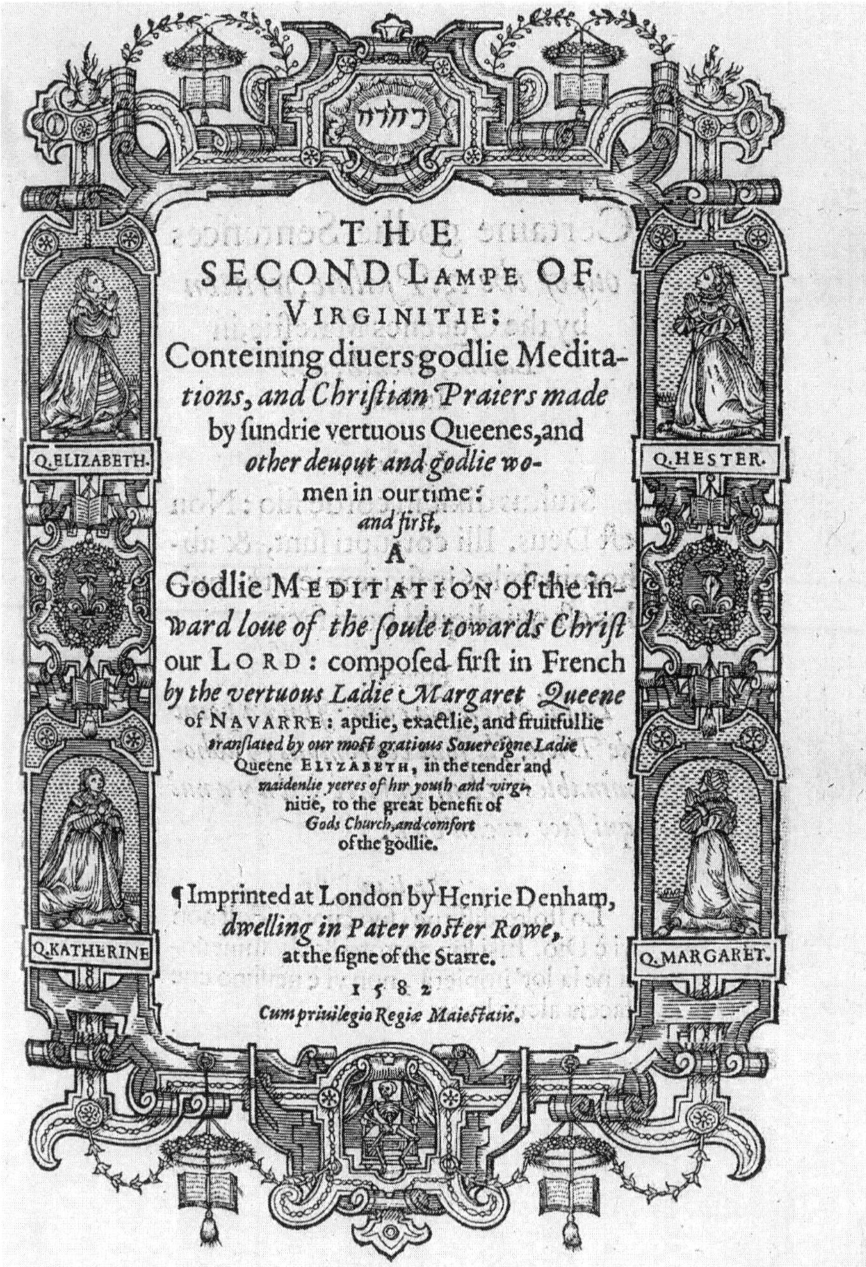

THE SECOND LAMPE OF VIRGINITIE:
Conteining diuers godlie Meditations, and *Christian Praiers made* by sundrie vertuous Queenes, and *other deuout and godlie women* in our time: *and first,*
A
Godlie MEDITATION of the *inward loue of the soule towards Christ* our LORD: composed first in French *by the vertuous Ladie Margaret Queene* of NAVARRE: aptlie, exactlie, and fruitfullie *translated by our most gratious Soueraigne Ladie* Queene ELIZABETH, in the tender and *maidenlie yeeres of hir youth and virginitie,* to the great benefit of *Gods Church, and comfort* of the godlie.

¶ Imprinted at London by Henrie Denham, *dwelling in Pater noster Rowe,* at the signe of the Starre.
1582
Cum priuilegio Regiæ Maiestatis.

2. "The Second Lamp of Virginity," from Thomas Bentley, *The Monument of Matrons* (1582). (This item is reproduced by permission of the Huntington Library, San Marino, California.)

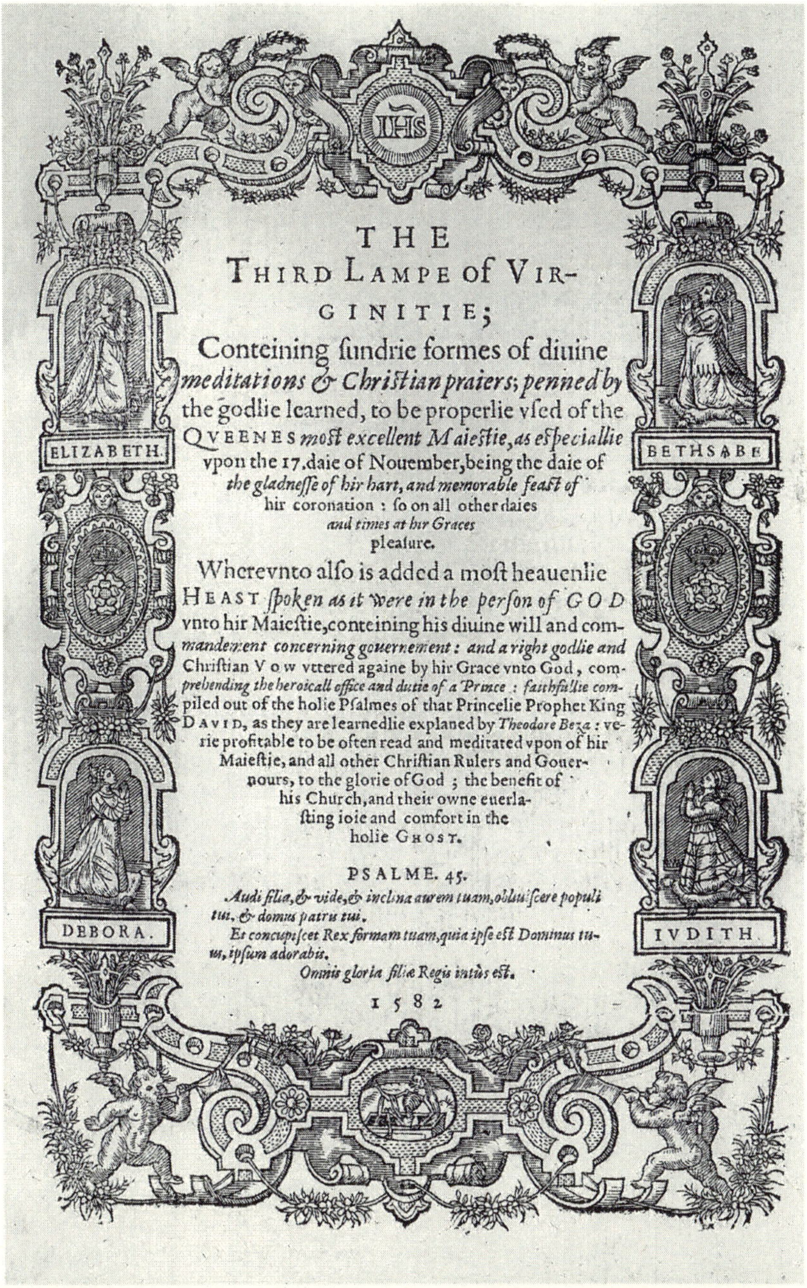

THE
THIRD LAMPE OF VIR-
GINITIE;

Conteining ſundrie formes of diuine *meditations & Chriſtian praiers; penned by* the godlie learned, to be properlie vſed of the QVEENES *moſt excellent Maieſtie, as eſpeciallie* vpon the 17. daie of Nouember, being the daie of *the gladneſſe of hir hart, and memorable feaſt of* hir coronation : ſo on all other daies *and times at hir Graces* pleaſure.

Whereunto alſo is added a moſt heauenlie HEAST *ſpoken as it were in the perſon of GOD* vnto hir Maieſtie, conteining his diuine will and com-*mandement concerning gouernement: and a right godlie and* Chriſtian VOW vttered againe by hir Grace vnto God, com-*prehending the heroicall office and dutie of a Prince : faithfullie com*-piled out of the holie Pſalmes of that Princelie Prophet King DAVID, as they are learnedlie explaned by *Theodore Beza* : ve-rie profitable to be often read and meditated vpon of hir Maieſtie, and all other Chriſtian Rulers and Gouer-nours, to the glorie of God ; the benefit of his Church, and their owne euerla-ſting ioie and comfort in the holie GHOST.

PSALME. 45.

Audi filia, & vide, & inclina aurem tuam, obliuiſcere populi tui, & domus patris tui.

Et concupiſcet Rex formam tuam, quia ipſe eſt Dominus tu-us, ipſum adorabis.

Omnis gloria filiæ Regis intùs eſt.

1582

3. "The Third Lamp of Virginity," from Thomas Bentley, *The Monument of Matrons* (1582). (This item is reproduced by permission of the Huntington Library, San Marino, California.)

Denham inserted a woodcut portrayal of Catherine Parr, the sixth wife and widow of Henry VIII, into lamps 3 and 4 (fig. 4; 2H2r, 3R6r, 4D4r). Not only does this illustration portray a learned queen who contributed writings to the *Monument of Matrons*, but it indirectly honors her stepdaughter, Queen Elizabeth. Surrounded by a strap-work frame portraying the four cardinal virtues personified as women—Justice, Prudence, Fortitude, and Temperance—the scene within the cartouche represents a fulfillment of the Parable of the Ten Virgins. It is surrounded with an oval frame bearing biblical texts: "BE THOU FAITHFUL UNTO THE DEATH" and "I WILL GIVE THEE A CROWN OF LIFE" (Revelation 2.10) and "WE MUST ALL APPEAR BEFORE THE JUDGMENT SEAT OF CHRIST" (Romans 14.10). The scene at the bottom constitutes a funerary portrait of Catherine Parr against a background of the Fall of Babylon symbolic of the demise of papal authority. At the top, Catherine receives a crown of glory as the Spouse of Christ while trumpeting angels and Wise Virgins salute her. Christ in Glory is surrounded by the seven lamps of the Book of Revelation and symbols of the Four Evangelists: winged ox, lion, cherub, and eagle. Flanking them at the left- and right-hand sides are King David and his son, King Solomon, who represent Old Testament types for Christian faith, wisdom, and kingship.

The lavish woodcut illustration of the *Monument of Matrons* affords one of many indications that Bentley and his publisher, Denham, designed the book primarily for an elite readership. In general, the commissioning of woodblocks involved considerable expenditure of capital. The added cost of illustration would have been all the more notable in this case, because the *Monument of Matrons* underwent publication only one time, and neither its compartments (as opposed to isolated headpieces or footpieces) nor its Catherine Parr woodcut underwent republication in any form. A higher than average price or a subsidy provided by a patron, presumably Bishop Aylmer, would have defrayed the cost of illustration. That the book catered to an elite clientage is suggested further by the prior publication of texts included in lamp 2 in the 16° and 32° editions.[6] These tiny formats were expressly geared for upper-class women, who concealed them in their garments or suspended them on chains from belts.

Containing close to half a million words, the *Monument of Matrons* is about half the length of the Bible. The three volumes collectively contain 816 leaves made by folding 204 large sheets of printed paper. Although booksellers might have sold a small number of ready-bound books, most bindings were commissioned by purchasers. Extant copies indicate that most owners preferred to read separately bound volumes, but some read multiple volumes bound together as a very thick book. When bound together, the three volumes are about as large as a hand-held book can be. Recognizing

4. "The Apotheosis of Catherine Parr," from Thomas Bentley, *The Monument of Matrons* (1582). (This item is reproduced by permission of the Huntington Library, San Marino, California.)

that purchasers or binders could opt to bind volumes separately, or omit one or two volumes altogether, Bentley and Denham planned the book with multiple indices at the end of volumes 1 (lamps 1–4) and 2 (lamp 5), in addition to yet another index at the end of lamp 3.

The physical construction of the *Monument of Matrons*, its contents, its illustrations, and its high price suggest that it was a luxury commodity used by a readership of well-to-do women (and some men). The inclusion of glosses on "the hardest places, for the better understanding and edifying of the unlearned reader" (C1r) indicates, however, that the editor and publisher had no desire to exclude more lowly readers despite the book's cost. At an approximate retail price of a halfpenny per sheet, an unbound copy of Bentley's *Monument of Matrons* would have cost approximately eight and one-half shillings (a sum equivalent to six weeks of wages for a skilled London shoemaker during 1589). A ready-bound copy with calfskin covers would have cost ten shillings more, but a specialty binding with gold tooling or embroidered covers might have raised the cost of the book closer to one pound.[7]

At the outset, *Monument of Matrons* invites the reader to assume the voice of a Wise Virgin in uttering a prayer that comments on the title page and the motto that it bears: "Take Heed. Watch. Pray." The prayer begins with a unique capital A illustrated with the royal emblem of the Tudor Rose surmounted by a crown imperial, flanked by the initials *ER* for *Elizabetha Regina*, and resting upon the queen's motto, *Semper Eadem* [always the same]. The prayer articulates the hope that Christ the Judge

> finding us heedful, watchful, praying, well occupied and ready, as those that have been very well content with our estates here for the time, and having our lamps filled brim full of the oil of his righteousness, grace, mercy, and merits, may (thereby only) escape the heavy judgment and direful doom of the dreadful day. (A1v)

In his prefatory epistle, Bentley comments on his editorial method of seeking out a diverse variety of profitable discourses written by and appropriate to reading or recitation by devout women of different ranks in society.

> Having myself taken no small comfort (good Christian reader) by the reading and perusing of diverse very godly, learned, and divine treatises, of meditations and prayer, made by sundry right famous queens, noble ladies, virtuous virgins, and godly gentlewoman of all ages, who to show themselves worthy patterns of all piety, godliness, and religion to their sex. (B1r)

He conceives of his anthology, "by some painful hand collected together," as a divinely inspired exercise in preserving "excellent and rare works" that are "dispersed unto several pamphlets, and in part something obscured and worn clean out of print, and so out of practice." He lodges an argument for the usefulness of these writings when he observes that women, and some men like himself, have worn out these books to the point that they are no longer read. His goal is to revive and restore these writings "to their former good and godly use in the church" by gathering them into "some apt treatise, or collection, to reduce these their manifold works into one entire volume . . . of good record, as perfect precedents of true piety and godliness in womankind to all posterity" (B1r).

The Bible supplies the essential model for the process of constructing a canon of texts written by female authors. In compiling his anthology, Bentley discovers an abundant array of female-authored texts in a very obvious location, the canon of canons, the Hebrew Bible, as well as the New Testament. Compilation of a collection of female authors of the Bible appears to lack precedent. In addition to the Bible, "many other good books as well of prayer as of other divine matter, such as from time to time have been penned by diverse godly learned men," provide anthology selections.

Bentley intends for these texts to function in an exemplary fashion by ensuring that "all godly and devout women readers might have in some measure [texts] wherewith to exercise their faith, to stir up their devotion, and to satisfy their godly desires." He explains that he gathers prayers and meditations in order to enhance the spirituality of individual women who "would either by prayer ask, by meditation ponder, by precepts learn, or by examples imitate, or avoid to their comfort and edification" (B1v). Exemplarity pervades this "domestical library plentifully stored and replenished both of the best approved precedents of Christian prayers and divine meditations made from time to time by many right godly authors, men and women of all ages, and also of the chosen sentences [i.e., maxims] or perfect precepts of holy scripture" (B2v). In order to facilitate application of these texts to the experience of women, he explains that he has "carefully digested the same into such a plain, easy, familiar, and certain method, order, and direction, both for matter and manner, as I could possibly devise, or was requisite to such a work, to make it profitable to the simple and unlearned reader" (B1v).

Bentley's concern for an elite audience is apparent in his view of feminine devotion as an all-encompassing pursuit that should occupy every hour of "day and night continually and incessantly, either silently in heart with Hannah, or openly in mouth with Mary, as they are bound, spend their whole life, and make it their whole work . . . to allow themselves apart from all company in prayer and meditation" (B1v). Methodical use of scores of prayers and meditations gathered by Bentley would have accorded with the strict piety of devout women such as Margaret Hoby, whose diary records how she governed each day by proceeding through a consuming cycle of introspective devotions. Her practice bears comparison with prayers and meditations in lamp 4, in particular, which begins with instances of "morning prayer before you arise," continues through prayers "in the mealtime," "at noontide," and other times during the day, before concluding with "evening prayers," including one for use "at midnight if you wake" (4D4v–8r).

After piously recording notes in a spiritual journal following her morning prayers, Hoby dedicated her day to intermingling Bible reading and prayer with domestic duties, reviewed a sermon heard on the previous Sunday, and applied herself to further self-examination and prayer both before and after dinner. A collection such as the *Monument of Matrons* would have been of great use to Hoby in a process of catechizing that enabled her to identify and repent for manifold failings.

> In the morning after private prayers and order taken for dinner I wrote some notes in my testament [i.e., diary] till ten o'clock; then I went to walk and after I returned home, I prayed privately, read a chapter of the Bible and wrought [i.e., did needlework] till dinner time. After, I walked awhile with Mr Rhodes and then I wrought and did some things about the house till 4. Then I wrote out the sermon into my book preached the day before and, when I had again gone about in the house and given order for supper and other things, I returned to examination and prayer. Then I walked till supper time and, after catechizing, meditated awhile of that I had heard, with mourning to God to pardon both of my omission and commission, wherein I found myself guilty for, I went to bed.[8]

The text of lamp 1 contains "divine prayers, hymns, or songs, made by sundry holy women in the scripture" (C1r). Examples include prayers by Hagar, Miriam, Naomi, Hannah, Abigail, Sara (the wife of Tobit), Judith, Esther, and Susanna, in addition to the song of Deborah, the complete text of the Song of Songs as a dialogue between the Bridegroom and the Spouse (that is, Christ and the Church), "The four lamentations of the daughters of Zion" (D4v–E3v), and the Magnificat delivered by the Virgin Mary.

According to Bentley's design, the writers of lamp 1 establish a precedent for the female authors and translators of writings in lamp 2. Although they may not have shared his belief, Bentley positions devotional translations and compositions by Elizabeth I, Catherine Parr, and Lady Jane Dudley (née Grey) as members of an evolving canon. Those whom he designates as "other devout and godly women of our time" include Lady Elizabeth Tyrwhit, who served as governess to Princess Elizabeth during Edward VI's reign; Frances Neville (née Manners), Lady Abergavenny, daughter of Thomas, earl of Rutland; and Mistress Dorcas Martin (née Ecclestone).

The contents of lamp 2 indicate that women and men collaborated in the construction of the canon of sixteenth-century texts written by women. Although the patronage and creation of manuscript writings in lamp 2 were the exclusive preserve of women, men edited and published printed editions from which Bentley drew his texts. William Cecil is a notable example, because he rose to the rank of Lord Burghley during service as the chief minister of Elizabeth I. He edited the original edition of Catherine Parr's *Lamentation of a Sinner* (1547) at the behest of Catherine Brandon, duchess of Suffolk. Prayers by Frances Neville and a few others went directly from manuscript into Bentley's anthology.

Writings by Lady Jane Grey and some other prayers in lamp 2 had already undergone canonization through inclusion in John Foxe's *Acts and Monuments of These Latter and Perilous Days* (1563), a quasi-official collection of Protestant martyrologies and other documents known from the beginning as the *Book of Martyrs*. Chained for public reading in guild halls, schools, and churches, Foxe's massive compilation was one of the best-known publications of its age.

Documents in lamp 2 illustrate the connectedness of women and their writings in Bentley's *Monument of Matrons*. This section includes writing by a stepmother who influenced her stepdaughter, a translation done by the stepdaughter for the stepmother, writings by a sister to a sister, by a mother to a daughter, and by a continental woman author with whom the mother of Elizabeth I, Anne Boleyn, had a familiar relationship.

Priority in lamp 2 goes to Princess Elizabeth's translation "in the tender and maidenly years of her youth and virginity" of the *Miroir de l'âme pécheresse* [Mirror of a sinful soul] (1531) by Marguerite d'Angoulême. Although Marguerite was not herself a Protestant, her evangelical piety fell under the influence of Jacques Lefèvre d'Étaples and other French humanists. As an eleven-year-old princess, Elizabeth Tudor translated Marguerite's meditations from French into English as a New Year gift for her stepmother, Catherine Parr. Under the title of "A Godly Meditation of the inward love of the soul toward Christ our Lord," Bentley incorporates a version of Elizabeth's translation published by John Bale in 1548.[9]

Of great interest are three prayers ascribed to Elizabeth as a princess in danger of death during the reign of her sister, Mary I, and as a young queen who attributed her accession to the throne to divine providence. The first two derive from Foxe's *Book of Martyrs*, a publication that begins with a dedication and well-known portrait of Elizabeth I. These prayers come from the "Miraculous Preservation of Lady Elizabeth,"[10] a narrative account of the princess's imprisonment when she was under suspicion of conspiracy against Queen Mary, her Roman Catholic sister.

Bentley's transcription of "The Christian prayer of our sovereign Lady Queen Elizabeth, which her grace made in the time of her trouble and imprisonment" transposes the following speech into a dramatic mode by divorcing it from the narrative in which Foxe embeds it. Upon her passage through Traitors' Gate at the Tower of London, she is said to have applied Jesus' Parable of the Two Houses (Matthew 7.24–27) to her own affliction.

> Help me now, O God, for I have none other friends but thee alone. And suffer me not (I beseech thee) to build my foundation upon the sands: but upon the rock, whereby all blasts of blustering weather may have no power against me. Amen.[11]

The second prayer, which Elizabeth uttered "when she was in great fear and doubt of death, by murder," invoked divine assistance at the time of her transfer from the Tower of London to house arrest at the Manor of Woodstock.

> Grant, O God, that the wicked may have no power to hurt or betray me; neither suffer any such treason and wickedness to proceed against me. For thou, O God, canst mollify all such tyrannous hearts, and disappoint all such cruel purposes. And I beseech thee to hear me thy creature which am thy servant, and at thy commandment, trusting by thy grace ever so to remain. Amen.[12]

Elizabeth uttered the third prayer at the outset of her reign, when she embarked from the Tower of London on her precoronation progress through the city of London on January 14, 1559. This text is a verbatim transcript from the scripted account of pageantry published by Richard Mulcaster in *The Queen's Majesty's Passage through the City of London to Westminster the Day before Her Coronation* (1559), which reports that the young queen lifted up her eyes when she entered her carriage and prayed:

> O Lord almighty, and everlasting God, I give thee most hearty thanks, that thou hast been so merciful unto me, as to spare me, to behold this joyful day. And I acknowledge that thou hast dealt as wonderfully with me, as thou didst with thy true and faithful servant Daniel the Prophet, whom thou deliveredst out of the den from the cruelty of the

> greedy raging lions: even so was I overwhelmed, and only by thee delivered. To thee therefore be only thanks, honor and praise for ever and ever. Amen.[13]

By comparing her deliverance to that of Daniel, she attributes her survival to govern after a period of duress to divine intervention.

Catherine Parr's enjoyment of a place of honor in lamp 2 affords a compliment to her stepdaughter, as do the woodcuts of the dowager queen's death and resurrection. She developed a reputation for devout learning through her *Lamentation or Complaint of a Sinner* and *Prayers or Meditations*, books originally published in 1547 and 1545. She designed the collection of biblical texts in the first book for devotional use by noble women. As a conversion narrative that affirms the doctrines of faith alone, grace alone, and Scripture alone, this work has a decidedly Protestant tenor. Derived from Thomas à Kempis's *Imitation of Christ*, the second text functions as a nondoctrinal supplement to Bible study.

Composed during imprisonment in the Tower of London, Lady Jane Grey's writings constitute the final queenly texts in lamp 2.[14] They derive from pietistic manuscripts compiled by an ill-fated figure who suffered execution following the failure of an effort to circumvent the line of royal succession and place her on the throne of England at the death of Edward VI. In her youth, she had received tutoring in Greek and Latin from Bentley's patron John Aylmer. Consisting of prayers on her forthcoming death, an exhortation to remain faithful addressed to her sister, and Latin verses inscribed in the form of pinpricks on paper, these texts attest to Jane's Protestant faith and antipathy toward Roman Catholic worship. Informed by scriptural tropes and figures, her style bears comparison with that of Catherine Parr and Anne Askew, who was burnt alive as a heretic at the end of Henry VIII's reign.[15] Just before her execution, Lady Jane recited Psalm 51 as the conventional sign to the headsman to strike off her head. Her recitation complements another section of lamp 2, "Certain prayers made by godly women martyrs," which include a preexecution prayer by Anne Askew and brief prayers by John Bradford's mother.

Lamp 2 continues with Lady Elizabeth Tyrwhit's "Morning and Evening prayers, with diverse Psalms, Hymns, and Meditations." Nearly one-third of lamp 2 consists of prayers by Frances Neville (née Manners), Lady Abergavenny, daughter of Thomas, earl of Rutland. At the hour of death, she conveyed them in manuscript to her only daughter, Lady Mary Fane, "as a Jewell of health for the soul, and a perfect path to Paradise, very profitable to be used of every faithful Christian man and woman." This segment concludes with acrostic prayers that spell out the names of both daughter and mother. Also containing Psalmic prayers "written by a godly hearted Gentlewoman," lamp 2 concludes with writings by Mistress Dorcas Martin (née Ecclestone), a notable Puritan who was wife to Richard Martin, Master of the Mint, and mother of a second Dorcas. She contributes a translation of a French catechism entitled "An instruction for Christians, containing a fruitful and godly exercise, as well in wholesome and fruitful prayers, as in reverend discerning of Gods holy Commandments and Sacraments"[16]; a prayer on mortification; and a "godly exhortation to move us to prayer, and to cause us to be in a continual readiness to wait on our Master Christ, when he shall come again to judge both the quick and the dead."

Lamp 3 brings the first volume of the *Monument of Matrons* to a conclusion with a panoply of prayers and meditations designed expressly for Queen Elizabeth's personal use. They include ingenious acrostic meditations that spell out ELIZABETH REGINA (2B8v–2C8v, 2D1r–3v) and prayers for the Seventeenth of November, Elizabeth's Accession Day, which zealous Protestant subjects celebrated as a national holiday in honor of her coronation as a deliverance from Roman Catholic tyranny.[17] The first Accession Day prayer accordingly styles the queen as a latter-day fulfillment of Old Testament heroes and heroines: "Yea, to be thy people's Joseph, their Moses, their Joshua, their David, their Josiah, their Samuel, and their Solomon: finally, to be their Deborah, their Jael, their Hester, their Judith, and their Elizabeth" (2A7v).

Bentley adapts scriptural language for the voice of Elizabeth I as another means of placing her within a canon of biblical writers. Dramatizing a line of spiritual descent from David and Solomon, the great kings of Israel and Judah, the editor constructs prayers for recitation by Elizabeth in which she repeatedly addresses the former as "my father David" (2A8r, 2B3v, 2E8v). Abstracting advice upon government from the Book of Psalms, as it is expounded by Theodore Beza, Bentley represents the succession to the throne of their purported author, David, as a prefiguration of Elizabeth's coronation. The compiler adapts Psalm 118, for example, to praise Elizabeth as a godly queen: "I beseech thee O Lord, preserve the Queen that is given us from heaven. I pray thee, I say, I pray thee O Lord give the Queen Elizabeth all prosperity" (2A6v). A petition for wisdom, which is to be delivered by Elizabeth in the guise of Solomon, the proverbially wise king, undergoes alteration that includes changes in gender from masculine to feminine and accommodation of Jewish practices to Christian circumstances.

> For I thy servant and *handmaid* am a feeble person, and of a short time, and yet less in the understanding of judgments and the laws. And though a man be never so perfect among the children of men; yet if

> thy wisdom be not with him, he shall be nothing regarded. Thou has chosen me to be a *Queen* unto thy people, and the judge of thy sons and daughters. Thou hast commanded me to *maintain thy Church, which from the beginning thou hast chosen*. (2B8r)

The italicized passages replace wording from the Bishops' Bible version of the Wisdom of Solomon 9.5–8, which refers to Solomon as "son of thy handmaiden" and "king," and to his construction of the temple in Jerusalem as "a temple upon the holy mount and an altar in the city wherein thou dwellest, a likeness of thy holy tabernacle, which thou hast prepared from the beginning."

Praise of Elizabeth as the Virgin Queen of England rises to a crescendo in "The King's [Be]hest, or God's familiar Speech to the Queen," a series of extracts from Beza's paraphrases on Psalms that style her as a divine daughter of whom God declares: "I have begotten thee, and espoused thee to thy king Christ, my Son; crowned thee with my gifts, and appointed thee Queen, to reign upon my Holy Mount Zion." This section functions as a *speculum principis* in claiming to articulate "divine will and commandment concerning government" (2A2r). As the Spouse of Christ, Elizabeth is "the mother, and the nurse of my people in Israel" (2D6r). As such, the new Israel of Elizabethan England stands in a covenantal relationship to God: "And I, O Queen, will surely perform my covenant (begun with thy father David that chosen man) unto thee also his daughter" (2D8v).

Also derived from Beza's Psalms, "The Queen's Vow, or Self-talk with God" represents Elizabeth as both a divine handmaid and a new Mary.[18] Bentley scripts responses that invest her prayers with Christological significance. For example, she is to address Christ in the manner of Mary Magdalene after the Resurrection (John 20.16): "Rabboni, my heart so boileth within me that I must needs burst forth that, which it hath conceived; even a magnifical vow of a Queen" (2E5r). As one "forsaken of all men" (2E7v) during the reign of her sister, Mary I, Elizabeth is akin to Christ as the sacrificial lamb, even though God chose "in thy secret wisdom to quicken me, that was *Tanquam ovis*, even as a silly sheep, or lamb led to be slain, to raise me up out of the dust and mire of persecution" (2B1v). Modeled on prophecies by Isaiah, this utterance conforms to speeches uttered by Elizabeth according to the account of her imprisonment in Foxe's *Book of Martyrs*. These examples therefore afford a complex case of imitation in which Bentley imitates her own voice in constructing prayers for the queen.

Consisting of lamps 1–3, the first volume of the *Monument of Matrons* contains the book's most significant and complicated selections. They include virtually all of the texts written or translated by women, notably those closely associated with Elizabeth when she was a princess, and the segments of the collection constructed for the queen's personal use. In contrast, lamp 4 consists of prayers and meditations *for men and women* during day and night, on Sunday, and on "other principal feasts, days, hours, times, and seasons of the year, privately both at home, and also in Church, at convenient times permitted" (2H1r). Lamp 4 juxtaposes prayers borrowed from the *Book of Common Prayer* with Bentley's own contributions on related subjects.[19] It branches off in directions high and low, which range from prayers for particular saints' days to meditation upon the washing of feet, when the reader is admonished to invoke Jesus, who "didst not disdain to wash the disciples' feet. . . . Wash thou, I say, not my feet only, O Lord, but my hands and head: yea my very heart, soul, and conscience also" (4C6r).

Bentley derives some prayers in lamp 4 from other collections. They include *Christian Prayers and Holy Meditations* (1570; 2d ed.) collected by Henry Bull, who collaborated with John Foxe in the construction of the *Book of Martyrs*. In counseling the reader to pray upon clothing herself, for example, Bentley reuses Bull's wording: "Clothe me, O Christ, with thine own self, that I may be so far from making provision for the flesh to fulfil the suits thereof; that I may clean put off all my carnal desires, and crucify the kingdom of the flesh in me."[20] In a prayer upon undressing, Bentley adapts a prayer by Bull to a feminine readership by systematically changing gender from masculine to feminine. Bentley transforms "first man" to "first woman Eve," "old corrupt Adam" to "old corrupt Eve," "transformeth himself" to "transformeth herself," and "the deceitful Eve" to "the deceitful serpent."

> Most gracious and merciful Savior Jesus Christ, thou knowest how we be born, clothed, and clogged with the grievous and heavy burden of the first woman Eve, who fell away into fleshliness, through disobedience; vouchsafe therefore, I beseech thee, to strip me of the old corrupt Eve, which being soaked in sin, transformeth herself to all encumbrances and diseases of the mind, that they may lead us away from thee. Rid me also quite and clean of that her tempter, the deceitful serpent, which turneth us away from the obedience of the father.[21]

By contrast to lamp 4, with its concern for female and male readers, Bentley designed lamp 5 for an exclusively female audience made up of "all degrees of women, in their several ages and callings: as namely, of virgins, wives, women with child, midwives, mothers, daughters, mistresses, maids, widows, and old women" (A1r). Composed for the most part by Bentley, these recitations also include contributions by Frances Neville and other women. Addressing virtually every aspect of woman's life, they include prayers on subjects that range from "silence, shamefastness, and chastity" to lamentation on "virginity or chastity, lost by fornication or adultery" to "prayer to be used of a virgin newly married together with her husband, the first night before they join together in the duty of marriage" to "chastity and purity in marriage" to weeping "in the time of bloody battle." The largest number of prayers concerns pregnancy and childbirth, including one meditation "for a Queen being with child." Among many petitions composed for midwives is one to be used "if the woman in sore travail or childbed lie in the pangs of death and be passing this life." Other invocations concern deliverance from childbed, the education of children, the plight of widows and orphans, a "prayer to be said generally for all women, that they may have in remembrance the fall of their grandmother Eve," and a "prayer made upon the similitude of the ten virgins" (A2r–N6v, passim).

The remainder of the *Monument of Matrons* shifts from prayer and meditation to Bentley's compilation of biblical precepts and examples for women (and sometimes men). Lamp 6 accordingly constitutes a "Mirror for Maidens and Matrons" that reflects the "several duties and office of all sorts of women in their vocation out of God's word, with their due praise and dispraise by the same" (A1r). It should come as no surprise to learn that the foremost entry concerns "Virginity, and the state of single life, together with the duty of Virgins, of Maids, or single Women" (A2r). Drawing its maxims from the Old and New Testaments, it cites Revelation 14.4 in defining "true" virginity with reference to those who "follow the lamb, whithersoever he goeth: these were redeemed from men, being the first fruits unto God, and to the lamb" (A6). Lamp 6 piles up scriptural texts concerning the duty of husbands to wives, commendation of marriage, prayer before the consummation of wedlock, abstention within marriage, adultery, the duty of wives to husbands, mothers to children, children to parents, servants to masters and dames, widowhood, remarriage of widows, dispraise of foolish women, harlotry, ungodly women, the Fall of Eve, and many other topics concerning family and social life.

Bringing the *Monument of Matrons* to a conclusion, lamp 7 lists "the acts and histories, lives and deaths, of all manner of women, good and bad, mentioned in the Holy Scripture" as a set of examples for "all womankind" in the "true imitation of virtue, and shunning of vice" (3K1r). The alphabetical series includes individuals already cited, who include Anna, Bathsheba, Deborah, and Judith, in addition to nameless figures such as the Witch of Endor, Potiphar's Wife, and Queen of Sheba. Under *H* for Harlot, the reader encounters the "description of the great whore or harlot of Babylon by St. John the Evangelist" (3S4v–5v; see Revelation 17). The contrasting figure of the Woman Clothed with the Sun is listed under *L* for Lamb's Wife: "The description of the woman called the Lamb's wife, or Church of Christ, persecuted by that dragon Antichrist: not unprofitable to be read of women in travail, to their comfort and edification, as a lesson in prayer" (3S7r–v; see Revelation 12). In the sixteenth century, these apocalyptic counterparts functioned respectively as types for conflict between allegedly "false" versus "true" churches or the individual choice between religious apostasy or fidelity.

The entry for the Wise and Foolish Virgins at the end of lamp 7 affords a fitting conclusion to the *Monument of Matrons* as a whole by bringing the reader full circle to the iconography of the elaborate title-page portrayal of the Wise and Foolish Virgins and the ensuing explication of its motto: "Take Heed. Watch. Pray." Applying the Parable of the Ten Virgins to individual spiritual experience, the conclusion provides an appropriate coda to the initial meditation of the entire collection.

> Our Savior Christ, to teach us that . . . we must continue and persevere unto the end without fainting or failing in the midway, and to the end he might warn every man to make provision in time, to watch for his sudden coming to judgment, put forth this similitude of ten virgins in the Gospel after St. Matthew, saying: "The kingdom of heaven shall be likened unto ten virgins."

According to Bentley's amplification of the scriptural text, the Groom condemns the Virgins who failed to keep their lamps filled with oil with these words: "Verily I say unto you, I know you not, watch therefore, and let your loins be girt about, and your lamps burning, yea take heed, watch, and pray, for ye know neither the year, day, time, nor hour, when the son of man will come to judgment: watch therefore I say, watch and pray" (U8v).

What may we conclude from the *Monument of Matrons* concerning the inclusion or exclusion of early modern English women from the canon of literary devotional texts? Despite the great lengths to which Bentley and Denham went in gathering texts and commissioning five expensive title-leaf borders, the collection never underwent republication. Despite the cachet attached to writings and translations by English queens by sixteenth-century and modern readers, most of the texts gathered into lamp 2 exist in no other printed form (Martin, Neville) or one (Tyrwhit), two (Grey), three (Parr's *Lamentation*), or four (Elizabeth's translation) editions published prior to the death of Queen Elizabeth in 1603. The only text to earn considerable attention from the reading public was the *Prayers or Meditations* of Catherine Parr, which went into thirteen editions between 1545 and 1575, plus a fourteenth in 1640. With the exception of that 32° book, which survives in a unique fragmentary copy, no early modern edition of the writings authored by women underwent publication after 1603.

The *Monument of Matrons* contributed to and reflected a unique moment, when grandiose celebration of the perpetual virginity of a regnant English queen was coming into existence. Reading and applying texts attributed to Elizabeth I and other women provided Elizabethan women and men with an important means of celebrating the Virgin Queen of England. Even then, it seems unlikely that the collection would have gone through the printing press without the patronage of a high-ranking member of the Elizabethan establishment, such as Bishop John Aylmer. It may be that texts in Bentley's collection will attract a greater readership during the twenty-first century than they did in the compiler's own age. After all, an edition of Elizabeth's translation of Marguerite d'Angoulême's *Miroir* has recently appeared,[22] an edition of the writings of Catherine Parr is in progress,[23] and the *Monument of Matrons* will soon appear in a facsimile edition.[24]

❧ ❧ ❧

NOTES

1. For discussions of the *Monument of Matrons*, see John N. King, *Tudor Royal Iconography: Literature and Art in an Age of Religious Crisis* (Princeton: Princeton University Press, 1989), 243–56; Patrick Collinson, "Windows in a Woman's Soul: Questions about the Religion of Queen Elizabeth I," in *Elizabethan Essays* (London: Hambledon Press, 1994), 104–8, 116–18; and Helen Hackett, *Virgin Mother, Maiden Queen: Elizabeth I and the Cult of the Virgin Mary* (New York: St. Martin's Press, 1995), 123–25. Unless otherwise noted, London is the place of publication and reference is to first editions. The abbreviation "sig." is omitted from signature references. Quotations are modernized. Italics supply added emphasis. I gratefully acknowledge sponsorship for research in the form of the Coca Cola Grant for the Study of Women and Gender administered by the Department of Women's Studies at the Ohio State University. I am also grateful for assistance in research rendered by Christopher E. Manion.

2. Roy Strong, *Gloriana: The Portraits of Queen Elizabeth I* (London: Thames and Hudson, 1987), 125; John N. King, "Queen Elizabeth I: Representations of the Virgin Queen," *Renaissance Quarterly* 43 (1990): 58–59.

3. I am indebted to Katherine Narveson for this information.

4. See Ruth Samson Luborsky and Elizabeth Ingram, eds., *A Guide to English Illustrated Books, 1536–1603* (Tempe: Medieval and Renaissance Texts and Studies, 1998), 2:186–87.

5. R. B. McKerrow and F. S. Ferguson, *Title-page Borders Used in England and Scotland, 1485–1640* (Oxford: Oxford University Press for the Bibliographical Society, 1932), nos. 174–78.

6. A.W. Pollard and G. R. Redgrave et al., eds., *A Short-Title Catalogue of Books Printed in England, Scotland, and Ireland, and of English Books Printed Abroad,*

1475–1640, 2d ed., 3 vols. (London: Bibliographical Society, 1976–91), nos. 4818.5, 4820, 4824, 4826, 4826.6, 4826.7, 24477.5.

7. Peter W. M. Blayney, *The First Folio of Shakespeare* (Washington, D.C.: Folger Library Publications, 1991), 25–26; Ann Jennalie Cook, *The Privileged Playgoers of Shakespeare's London, 1576–1642* (Princeton: Princeton University Press, 1981), 277; Philip Gaskell, *A New Introduction to Bibliography* (Oxford: Clarendon Press, 1972), 178. Price comparison is not adjusted for inflation.

8. Joel Hurstfield and A. G. R. Smith, eds., *Elizabethan People: State and Society* (London: Edward Arnold, 1972), 129.

9. See Anne Lake Prescott, "The Pearl of the Valois and Elizabeth I: Marguerite de Navarre's *Miroir* and Tudor England," in *Silent But for the Word: Tudor Women as Patrons, Translators, and Writers of Religious Works*, ed. Margaret Hannay (Kent, Ohio: Kent State University Press, 1985), 61–76.

10. See the version in John N. King, ed., *Voices of the English Reformation: A Sourcebook* (Philadelphia: University of Pennsylvania Press, 2004), no. 7.5.B.

11. Bentley, *Monument*, H4r–v. This wording expands Foxe's claim that Elizabeth struck an evangelical pose by calling "to her gentlewoman for her book [i.e., the Bible], desiring God not to suffer her to build her foundation upon the sands but upon the rock, whereby all blasts of blustering weather should have no power against her." Foxe, *Acts and Monuments of These Latter and Perilous Days* (London, 1563), 4N5r; hereafter cited as *A&M*.

12. Ibid., H4v. Foxe supplies the following wording: "'Well,' quod she, 'God grant it be so. For thou, O God, art the withdrawer and mollifier of all such tyrannous hearts and acts; and I beseech thee to hear me, thy creature which am thy servant, and at thy commandment trusting by thy grace ever so to remain'" (*A&M*, 4N6r–v).

13. Ibid., H4v. See Mulcaster, *Queen's Majesty's Passage*, C4r–v; in King, *Voices of the English Reformation*, no. 7.3.

14. See the version in King, ed., *Voices of the English Reformation*, no. 7.1.

15. On Anne Askew's use of scriptural tropes and figures, see essay by Beilin, this volume.

16. Micheline White identifies the translation as a reprint of a text no longer extant: *An Instruction for Christians, Containing a Fruitful and Godly Exercise, as well in wholesome and fruitful prayers as in reverent discerning of God's holy commandments and sacraments* (1581) in "A Biographical Sketch of Dorcas Martin: Elizabethan Translator, Stationer, and Godly Matron," *Sixteenth Century Journal* 30 (1999): 776.

17. David Cressy, *Bonfires and Bells: National Memory and the Protestant Calendar in Elizabethan and Stuart England* (Berkeley and Los Angeles: University of California Press, 1989), chap. 4; Roy Strong, *The Cult of Elizabeth: Elizabethan Portraiture and Pageantry* (London: Thames and Hudson, 1977), 117–28.

18. See Peter McClure and Robin Headlam Wells, "Elizabeth I as a Second Virgin Mary," *Renaissance Studies* 4 (1990): 43–44.

19. Bentley, *Monument*, 2O6v–2Q5r. Compare John E. Booty, ed., *The Book of Common Prayer 1559: The Elizabethan Prayer Book* (Charlottesville: University Press of Virginia for the Folger Shakespeare Library, 1976), 61–76.

20. Bull, *Christian Prayers*, H6v–7r; Bentley, *Monument*, 2I2r.

21. Bull, *Christian Prayers*, B3v–4r; Bentley, *Monument*, 2H5r–v.

22. Marc Shell, ed., *Elizabeth's Glass with "The Glasse of the Sinfull Soul" (1544) by Elizabeth I and "Epistle Dedicatory" and "Conclusion" (1548) by John Bale* (Lincoln: University of Nebraska Press, 1993).

23. Janel Mueller is completing this project.

24. Edited by Colin B. Atkinson and Jo Atkinson in the series *The Early Modern Englishwoman: A Facsimile Library of Essential Works—Essential Works Series III, Part One* (Ashgate: Aldershot, 2004).

BIBLIOGRAPHY

Aylmer, John. *An Harbor for Faithful and True Subjects*. Strasbourg (London), 1559.

Bentley, Thomas. *Monument of Matrons: Containing Seven Several Lamps of Virginity*. London, 1582.

———. *Monument of Matrones*. Edited by Colin B. Atkinson and Jo Atkinson. 3 Vols. *The Early Modern Englishwoman: A Facsimile Library of Essential Works—Essential Works Series III, Part One*. Ashgate: Aldershot, 2004.

Blayney, Peter W. M. *The First Folio of Shakespeare*. Washington, D.C.: Folger Library Publications, 1991.

Booty, John E., ed. *The Book of Common Prayer 1559: The Elizabethan Prayer Book*. Charlottesville: University Press of Virginia for the Folger Shakespeare Library, 1976.

Bull, Henry. *Christian Prayers and Holy Meditations*. With a preface by Miles Coverdale. 2d ed. London, 1570.

Collinson, Patrick. "Windows in a Woman's Soul: Questions about the Religion of Queen Elizabeth I." In *Elizabethan Essays*, 87–118. London: Hambledon Press, 1994.

Cook, Ann Jennalie. *The Privileged Playgoers of Shakespeare's London, 1576–1642*. Princeton: Princeton University Press, 1981.

Cressy, David. *Bonfires and Bells: National Memory and the Protestant Calendar in Elizabethan and Stuart England*. Berkeley and Los Angeles: University of California Press, 1989.

Foxe, John. *Acts and Monuments of These Latter and Perilous Days*. London, 1563.

Gaskell, Philip. *A New Introduction to Bibliography*. Oxford: Clarendon Press, 1972.

Hackett, Helen. *Virgin Mother, Maiden Queen: Elizabeth I and the Cult of the Virgin Mary*. New York: St. Martin's Press, 1995.

Hurstfield, Joel, and A. G. R. Smith, eds. *Elizabethan People: State and Society*. London: Edward Arnold, 1972.

King, John N. *Tudor Royal Iconography: Literature and Art in an Age of Religious Crisis*. Princeton Essays on the Arts. Princeton: Princeton University Press, 1989.

———. "Queen Elizabeth I: Representations of the Virgin Queen." *Renaissance Quarterly* 43 (1990): 30–74.

———, ed. *Voices of the English Reformation: A Sourcebook*. Philadelphia: University of Pennsylvania Press, 2004.

Knox, John. *The First Blast of the Trumpet against the Monstrous Regiment of Women*. Geneva, 1558.

Luborsky, Ruth Samson, and Elizabeth Ingram. *A Guide to English Illustrated Books, 1536–1603*. 2 vols. Tempe: Medieval and Renaissance Texts and Studies, 1998.

McClure, Peter, and Robin Headlam Wells. "Elizabeth I as a Second Virgin Mary." *Renaissance Studies* 4 (1990): 38–70.

McKerrow, R. B., and F. S. Ferguson. *Title-page Borders Used in England and Scotland, 1485–1640*. Oxford: Oxford University Press for the Bibliographical Society, 1932.

Mulcaster, Richard. *The Queen's Majesty's Passage through the City of London to Westminster the Day before Her Coronation*. London, 1559.

Pollard, A. W., G. R. Redgrave et al., eds. *A Short-Title Catalogue of Books Printed in England, Scotland, and Ireland, and of English Books Printed Abroad, 1475–1640*. 2d ed., 3 vols. London: Bibliographical Society, 1976–91.

Prescott, Anne Lake. "The Pearl of the Valois and Elizabeth I: Marguerite de Navarre's *Miroir* and Tudor England." In *Silent But for the Word: Tudor Women as Patrons, Translators, and Writers of Religious Works*, ed. Margaret P. Hannay, 61–76. Kent, Ohio: Kent State University Press, 1985.

Shell, Marc. *Elizabeth's Glass with "The Glasse of the Sinfull Soul" (1544) by Elizabeth I and "Epistle Dedicatory" and "Conclusion" (1548) by John Bale*. Lincoln: University of Nebraska Press, 1993.

Strong, Roy. *The Cult of Elizabeth: Elizabethan Portraiture and Pageantry*. Berkeley and Los Angeles: University of California Press, 1986.

———. *Gloriana: The Portraits of Queen Elizabeth I*. London: Thames and Hudson, 1987.

White, Micheline. "A Biographical Sketch of Dorcas Martin: Elizabethan Translator, Stationer, and Godly Matron." *Sixteenth Century Journal: Journal of Early Modern Studies* 30 (1999): 775–92.

The Collector's Cabinet

LODOVICO DOMENICHI'S GALLERY OF WOMEN

Deanna Shemek

The door to published authorship for women in Italy was opened by sixteenth-century presses, which embraced vernacular writings and especially contemporary Petrarchan verse in the middle decades of the sixteenth century. Because so much Petrarchan lyric took as its theme the male desire for a female figure imagined as both silent and absent, late-twentieth-century feminist criticism reflected extensively on early modern women poets' complex "renegotiation" of the speaking voice in this genre.[1] As those discussions show, many early modern women who took up writing understood themselves to be doing something new. Some of them wrote primarily on religious or moral themes (also in imitation of Petrarch), reflecting a social milieu in which religious writing, like sacred readings, was considered more fitting than secular literature for girls and women.[2] When they wrote love poetry, these poets often highlighted themes like the transgressive nature of their own appropriation of writing and speaking and the unpracticed and inferior quality of their poetic skills.

Whatever their difficulties may have been with its form and perspective, however, women took readily to Petrarchan poetry in the early years of print culture and tailored it to their own concerns. Beginning with the 1538 publication of Vittoria Colonna's *Rime*, women's lyric poetry trickled steadily through the Italian market for roughly two decades with little competition from other genres. In 1547 appeared both Tullia d'Aragona's poetry and the first of Laura Terracina's eight printed volumes of *Rime*. In 1554 were published the lyrics of Gaspara Stampa and of Veronica Gambara, followed in 1555 by those of Chiara Matraini.[3] To the modern eye these may appear as broadly spaced publication dates, but they were rapid and remarkable for the time. Important as these individual debut volumes were, however, in 1559 something potentially more significant happened, when Lodovico Domenichi published *Rime diverse d'alcune nobilissime et virtuosissime donne* [Assorted rhymes by some most noble and virtuous women], the first anthology of women's poetry ever to appear in print.[4]

Throughout the Cinquecento, Petrarchan lyric was, of course, widely produced by men as well, and one measure of both the genre's marketability and its increasing prestige was the phenomenon of the printed anthology. The first of these came from the Venetian presses of Gabriele Giolito, who published in 1545 *Rime diverse di molti eccellentiss. Auttori nuovamente raccolte*.[5] Part marketing gambit and part cultural statement, Giolito's multiauthored collection set off a chain of similar publications that quickly established the dominance of the Italian print industry by lyric anthologies for at least the next twenty years. Giolito was well known for his maverick publishing practices, which promoted contemporary Italian vernacular texts over the elegant printings of ancient classics and early Tuscan authors favored by his most celebrated humanist rival, Aldus Manutius. He was also closely watched by other printers, many of whom followed his modernist leadership in their own publishing decisions.[6] These editors' collective, unmitigated favoritism toward contemporary lyric helped establish Petrarchan poetry as the literary lingua franca across the European continent for at least the next century.[7]

In this context appeared Domenichi's anthology of women poets. Capitalizing in a single volume on the vogue for anthologies and the high profiles of a few female Petrarchists, Domenichi also integrated in this project several of his own long-standing interests. Domenichi was one of the famous *poligrafi* [polygraphs], the versatile intellectuals active in literary writing, book editing, and pamphlet journalism in the breathless early years of Italian printing. He began his career working as an editor and translator from 1543 to 1546 for Gabriele Giolito, with whom his many collaborations included that first *Rime diverse* anthology of 1545 as well as a collection of his own poems (1544).[8] He wrote the preface to Giolito's edition of Laura Terracina's *Rime* and entered into the fray of Italy's *querelle des femmes* by penning—or more precisely by purloining—*La nobiltà delle donne* [The nobility of women], a treatise largely plagiarized from the German Cornelius Agrippa and the Italian Galeazzo Flavio Capra.[9] Among his other writings, he later published a set of dialogues, including *Della stampa* [On printing], which militantly favored the proliferation of texts that resulted from the new technology of print and heroized pioneering editors of the sixteenth century, including Aldus Manutius and Gabriele Giolito.[10] In some sense, then, Domenichi's decision to publish a collection of poetry by contemporary women appears to follow logically from the combination of his Petrarchist writings, his editorial experience with anthologies, his contacts with women poets (a few of whom were already included in Giolito's earlier anthologies), and his attention to the debate on women that was contemporaneously appearing in print. Why, then, did this book brimming with women's lyric not contribute to a "strong history," to the continued presence of women poets in Italian print henceforth? Why instead would Carlo Dionisotti much later observe that neither before 1540 nor after 1560 did Italy see a coherent community of publishing women writers, but in this twenty-year period only?[11]

Dionisotti finds his answer in the literary classicism and Tridentine orthodoxy that together marked a growing Cinquecento anxiety about the broadening of cultural access. The vernacular's new legitimacy was opening literary markets not only to women but to all kinds of upstarts, and it had produced what Dionisotti terms a militant and experimental literature. But by 1560, he argues, this widening sphere was fostering a sense of political and cultural vertigo that prompted a conservative reorientation toward clear cultural patrimonies (the Aristotelian debates over the heroic poem are one example) and the remarginalization of nontraditional authors and forms. This oscillation provides my starting point for consideration of Domenichi's anthology, which seemed to bode for a rise of Italian female authorial community but which Italian literary history has cast as the brief and shining apex of women's lyric before a new decline. I will return to Dionisotti's assessment and the historical fortunes of Italian women's poetry later in my discussion. For now, let us turn to Domenichi's anthology.

The collection appears to be a conceptual breakthrough. In the eyes of posterity, Domenichi's decision is not simply to gather selected members of an existing category. The publishing category that interested Domenichi did not yet exist, and Domenichi *fabricated* it by assembling this book. Included in the volume are 330 poems, 316 authored by women and 14 by men in dialogue with women poets in the anthology. For literary history, his act would seem to carry profound significance. Since the poems gathered in Domenichi's volume coincide not merely in mode, and not at all in regional provenance (two common principles of organization for other lyric collections), but expressly in the sex of their authors, it stands as the first anthology of "women's poetry" ever to be published.[12] Certainly individual women wrote lyrics prior to Domenichi's editorial assembly, and some of them—as the present volume attests—wrote *as women*, conscious and articulate about their sex and gender difference. But Domenichi's book proposed women's poetry as a literary and bibliographical category, a gender turned genre. However long it has taken for this category to gain legitimacy as anything more than a novelty, Domenichi's feminine anthology of *Rime* acquires much of its significance today in the retrospective knowledge that women's literature is now a recognizable thing for purposes cultural, commercial, and pedagogical. But for roughly three centuries in Italy, this was not so: women's poetic history was weak in the terms posed by Pamela Benson and Victoria Kirkham in their introduction to this volume.

Factors like female literacy and women's lack of disposable independent income (both of which affected book marketing) clearly played a role in the uneven development of female authorship in Italy as elsewhere. Also important, however, were deeper, social and cultural attitudes toward women's writing as such, attitudes we can trace in the recorded reactions to women who did publish and that are discernible even between the lines of Domenichi's anthology.

One response to the appearance of women's poetry in print was diffidence: Gaspara Stampa was accused of plagiarism, for example.[13] Another reaction was open hostility and public slander: a penalty paid by Louise Labé and Veronica Franco for their writing. As Ann Rosalind Jones points out, the harshest criticism against women for writing often concerned their violation of class boundaries. When women of the middle class (like Labé in France) or from the ranks of the courtesans (like Franco in Italy) wrote lofty verses and attended salons, they appeared to many of their contemporaries not only as immodest but as outrageous social climbers.[14] The anxiety such mobility produced was verbalized in ways that cast the women poets' activities in gendered and moralizing terms. Veronica Franco as a courtesan was logically vulnerable to critics scandalized at her profession. But Natalie Zemon Davis notes that the bourgeoise Louise Labé endured similar slanders: "The books Louise read and wrote were lascivious; her salons an impure gathering of the sexes; and her literary feminism impudent. She was talked of in Geneva as a lewd female. . . . Calvin said she was a strumpet."[15]

The most common response to women's literary activity, however, and the one I will briefly explore here, was to regard female writers (or painters, or thinkers, or agents of almost any sort) as prodigies and curiosities. The moralist poet Laura Terracina, for example, was praised by her promoter Marcantonio Passero as a "mostro del sesso femminile" [a wonder of the female sex]. Similarly, at the end of the century Moderata Fonte's uncle appended to her treatise, *Il merito delle donne* [The worth of women], a minibiography of his niece to showcase her extraordinary achievements from childhood on, any of which would have been much less noteworthy in a male intellectual of the time.[16] The notion of women writers as curiosities continued to circulate in criticism and the market for hundreds of years; we know that, as late as the twentieth century, literary reviews and society pages referred to them as a category apart, with terms like "lady novelists" and "poets of the gentle sex." Some nineteenth- and early-twentieth-century women (like Mary Ann Evans, who became "George Eliot") adopted masculine or gender-neutral pen names in order to circumvent this condescending reception. All of these responses are efforts to contain anxiety about the perceived anomalous conjunction of femininity and literary creativity or discursive mastery. In the remarks that follow, I will consider Domenichi's act of anthology formation for women as another instance of such efforts at containment, one that draws on the logic of a burgeoning pastime among sixteenth-century Europeans: the hobby of collecting.

In Domenichi's dedication of the *Rime diverse* to Giannoto Castiglione, he paints himself not only as an editor and an advocate of women's excellence but also as a collector.

> It has now been many years since I turned my soul and my labors completely to celebrating to whatever extent I could the nobility and excellence of Women, and organized this material into a proper volume. My guiding thought at the same time was to gather what it seemed to me could procure their glory and honor. And so, aided by some of my loving friends whose fondness is great for Womanly merits, I collected from various sources a quite considerable number of rhymes composed by Women. These rhymes have up to now been kept by me in that condition in which the dearest and most precious things are usually held. And though when I began collecting them I was most determined to publish them to the world in the medium of print, so as to enlighten those who doubt the greatness of the female intellect, I was nonetheless never able to carry out my idea, for I was detained and prevented by one thing or another.[17]

If Domenichi's reference to delay refers to his 1549 publication of *La nobiltà delle donne* [The nobility of women], the text by Agrippa he translated and published as his own, then his wish to publish a women's anthology dates back at least ten years. At last, he says, he will fulfil his desire and make good on his *debito* [debt] by bringing the volume to light.

"To whom should this volume be dedicated?" Domenichi asks himself.

Admitting that some of his associates advised him to choose a female dedicatee for the anthology, he explains to Castiglione that "for good reasons" he decided not to follow such counsel. After naming six female candidates upon whom he might well have bestowed this honor (Lavinia Sanvitale; the Contessa Paola di Beccaria; her daughter Livia; Ottaviana Baiarda; Lucia Saoli; Lucia Bertana; and "many princesses and women of high rank, whose graces [he] might have hoped to win with such a noble gift"), he admits that he thought it much better to dedicate it to "un mio carissimo, & meritevole amico, & Signore, quale è la S.V." [a most dear and worthy friend of mine, and a Lord, such as Your Lordship is]. A crack in the editorial facade of feminist advocacy appears here, for despite Domenichi's insistence on women's merits, male social bonds preclude his squandering the opportunity to curry favor with a powerful man by dedicating his book to a female recipient.[18] Indeed the book itself instead becomes a metaphorical exchange of women "between men," men who presumably appreciate the wisdom of Domenichi's decision about his dedication.[19]

The volume Domenichi gives to Giannoto Castiglione publishes a few of the well-known female poets of the time, yet it emphasizes a broad network of privileged women, many of whom appear to be personally acquainted or interconnected. In 237 pages are printed 316 poems by 54 women (see appendix). The well-known Vittoria Colonna, Veronica Gambara, and Gaspara Stampa are present, but Domenichi's collection omits several of the most prominent (and presumably marketable) women poets of the day: Tullia d'Aragona, Laura Terracina, Chiara Matraini, and Laura Battiferra among them. Like Giolito's 1545 anthology and others that ensued, the collection showcases the high society of Domenichi's time. He places the obscure Silvia di Somma, countess of Bagno's two poems, the duchess of Amalfi Costanza d'Avalo's five poems, and Countess Isabella Pepoli de' Riarii's one poem, for example, on the same publishing plane with several celebrated poets of their generation.[20] More than half the women appearing in the volume contributed only one or two poems, while only ten appear with more than ten compositions. Many regions of the peninsula are represented, with a weighting, however, toward Tuscany and Siena in particular.[21]

Amedeo Quondam's landmark study of modern collections of Cinquecento poetry argues that anthologies by definition assert value, create relations, and set standards: they canonize.[22] As Quondam shows, moreover, the anthology's standardizing force—despite its collective premise—gravitates over time to restrict the number of poets and even the range of each poet's works to a set of obligatory and recognized exemplars, so that modern anthologies exhibit increasing conformity in their selection of poems. The anthology as institution, notes Quondam, rejects broad innovation and dwells safely in the conservative territory of the recognizable. Quondam finds that the same pattern holds true for feminine anthologies: once the broad category was established, its contents stabilized from the eighteenth through the twentieth centuries.

But are the sixteenth-century anthology editors already participating in the canonizing tradition Quondam identifies, or might their interests be different ones? The project of canon formation was surely under way by the mid-Cinquecento, in prestigious printings of early Tuscan works and in vigorous campaigns to publish single contemporary authors, including some women. But canonization was not the only editorial and cultural project of the Cinquecento. The organization of the large anthologies suggests that these volumes were not so much concerned with canonizing as with *assembling*. To take Domenichi at his word, for example, his anthology aimed not to argue the authority of the poets he included while excluding others thought to be unworthy but in effect to show that women all over Italy (at least in the upper classes) were expressing their intelligence (*genio*) in verse.

This sweeping inclusiveness suggests that Domenichi's anthology of women was participating in another widespread cultural practice of the period, that of collecting as such. Indeed, if we look at the larger context of lyric anthologizing in the Cinquecento, it becomes apparent that *all* of the large, early lyric anthologies reflect more a "culture of collecting" than one of canonization: they all contain many poets now virtually forgotten, and the claims their editors make are generally inclusive, not selective and canonizing. Particularly in light of the common regard for women writers as "curiosities," Domenichi's anthology may be viewed as a particularly charged, gendered, literary instance of early modern collecting culture.

As Paula Findlen observes in her study of early modern naturalist collecting, during the sixteenth and seventeenth centuries, "all of Europe seemed to be collecting," and she extends her view of this practice well beyond the museums of natural history to appreciate collecting as a kind of temperamental feature of the time.

> Collecting, in short, had become an activity of choice among the social and educated elite. It filled their leisure hours and for some seemed to encompass every waking moment of their lives. Through the possession of objects, one physically acquired knowledge, and through their display, one symbolically acquired the honor and reputation that all men of learning cultivated.[23]

Among the objects traditionally favored by collectors are, of course, books, which may or may not be read by their owners but which perform the important task of exhibiting knowledge and cultivation to which Findlen refers. The anthology is a particular version of this collecting practice, a version that performs its task not only for its owner but most spectacularly for its editor. The editor, after all, figures as the conceiver of the collection, as one who, in Domenichi's own words, gives birth to its authors as such; and he associates himself implicitly with each element in his collection, both because its presence suggests his acquaintance with the author and because he had the good taste to include it.[24] Domenichi's collection of poems by women thus carries personal, possibly even erotic, force, while at the same time it raises Domenichi's status as the possessor of such a large and widely ranging collection.

Jean Baudrillard has written suggestively on the erotic satisfactions of collecting.

> [T]he collector is pre-eminently the sultan of a secret seraglio. Ordinary human relationships, which are the site of the unique and the conflictual, never permit such a fusion of absolute singularity and indefinite seriality. This explains why ordinary relationships are such a conflictual source of anxiety: while the realm of objects, on the other hand, being the realm of successive and homologous terms, offers security.[25]

For Baudrillard, though a given collection is made up of a succession of terms, the final term must always be the person of the collector: "It is invariably oneself that one collects" (12). In this light, when Domenichi releases for publication the poems women (or their admirers) have given him over the years and that he has guarded as precious and intimate treasures, he begins to circulate an image of himself as the fortunate possessor of these feminine missives. He also makes a space within the anthology for his own reflection to shine out from the volume at intermittent moments, by including several poems addressed directly to him and appending to these the responses he wrote back.[26]

This mode of address is a distinguishing feature of the *Rime diverse* that extends well beyond Domenichi himself. The collection includes dedications to both men and women for seventy-eight poems, a textual feature that is rare if not altogether absent in the previous, male or mixed gender anthologies edited by Giolito and others.[27] Indeed, several poems that bear dedications in Domenichi's volume are reprints of compositions that included no dedication in their original published form.[28] Françoise Piejus remarks suggestively that Domenichi's framing of so many of the women's poems with dedications places these lyrics in a social and biographical context that may have been key to Domenichi's view of women's poetic activity: "The female poet more readily finds her place in the literary world if she is not presented alone, if she is supported by a social structure that guarantees and vindicates her."[29] This sort of social framing was, in fact, becoming all the rage for individual authors both male and female in the course of the sixteenth-century publishing boom, and Domenichi's adoption of it for the terrain of the large anthology appears as an especially astute move in the marketing of his volume.

One function of dedications is to draw lines of contact between writers and prominent persons with whom they would like to be associated or who might sponsor them in the future. The dedications also serve, however, to connect the women poets among themselves and to cast their writing as a form of correspondence or private conversation, a more limited and more socially acceptable framework for women's writing in the period. Some of the dedications are addressed to powerful public figures of the day; but others are directed at authors who also appear in the volume, including several men, whose appearance in this feminine lyric space is presumably motivated by their obligation to respond to the women poets or to provide context for responses written by the women.[30]

This sort of dialogue sets Domenichi's collection in motion, animating it with laudatory exchanges and offering exemplary instances of women's intelligence, modesty, courtesy, and poise as they volley gentle compliments back and forth among themselves or pay tribute to the accomplishments of other women. Gaspara Stampa, for example, who died in 1554 but is represented by five sonnets of her own, is also the posthumous recipient of this poem of mourning and celebration by Hippolita Mirtilla. Mirtilla clearly associates Stampa not only with Petrarch's Laura (postmortem) but with Dante's Beatrice, whose greeting in *Vita nuova* X and XI is endowed with miraculous effects.

O sola qui tra noi del ciel fenice,
Ch'alzata a volo il secol nostro oscura,
Et sovra lali al ciel passi sicura;
Si ch'a vederla a pena homai ne lice.
O sola a gli occhi miei vera beatrice,
In cui si mostra, quanto sà natura;
Bellezza immaculata, & vista pura,
Da far con picciol cenno ogni huom felice.
In Voi si mostra, quel che non comprende
Altro intelletto al mondo, se no'l mio,
Ch'Amor tanto alto il leva, quanto v'amai.

In Voi si mostra, quanto anchor s'accende
L'anima gloriosa nel desio,
Che per elettione a Dio la chiama.[31]

[Oh singular phoenix of the heavens among us, who rises in flight and dims our world as she wings her way safely to heaven so that now one may barely get a glimpse of her. Oh, one true beatrice in my eyes, in whom nature most aptly discloses immaculate beauty and pure vision, whose slightest nod delights every man. Visible in you is something no intellect in the world comprehends, if not perhaps mine, for mine rises as high as the love I bore you. In you one sees how brightly the glorious soul ignites, in the desire that elects to call it to God.]

In this instance, women exchange compliments at the same time as they show skills that themselves are worthy of praise. The dedicatory and dialogic features of the collection allow Domenichi's women also to lob sonnets into the world of men, only to have their discourse bounce reliably back on its own Petrarchan terms. As previously noted Domenichi himself is the recipient of several of these poems, which allow him both to display the elaborate arabesques of praise typical of courteous discourse and to bask in the admiration of the volume's contributors, who unfailingly declare their esteem for Domenichi and his intellectual endeavors. Livia Torniella Bonromea writes, for example:

Fiamma gentil, che da quel foco nasce,
Ch'accende il valor vostro in ogni core;
Cosi arde il mio, c'homai convien, che fore
Esca, & a Voi di se testimon lasce:
Onde con questo stil, che da le fasce
Meco rozzo portai scemo l'ardore:
Ma non scemi a Voi gloria, e splendore;
Pur de la cortesia vostra si pasce.
Et, se merto non hò meco, che vaglia,
DOMENICHI gentil, per farmi degna,
Che de la volgar schiera non m'habbiate;
Vagliami almen, ch'Io cosi in alto saglia,
Per quel poco, ch'in Me di spirto regna;
Ch'Io vi conosca honor di nostra etate.[32]

[Gentle flame, born of the fire that sparks your valor in every heart, mine so burns that now I must release it to testify before you. Whence I quell my

passion with the crude style I bring with me from the cradle. Let my style not dim your glory and splendor, though it feeds on your courtesy. And gentle DOMENICHI, *if I possess no merits to warrant your distinguishing me from the general crowd, let what little spirit reigns in me carry me high enough to praise you for the honor you bring our times.]*

Bonromea here adopts standard gestures of authorial modesty as she pays tribute to the influential Domenichi. At the same time, her poem implies that she has long been writing verses and now feels the urge to release a poem for circulation, at least to Domenichi if not to a wider audience. Bonromea's rhetoric for justifying this bold move is that of many of her contemporaries, male and female: she claims to burn with a desire to praise someone else, in this case Domenichi. He responds by raising the level of flattery still higher, while showcasing his lyric agility in recycling Bonromea's same rhymed words.

Dal vostro chiaro stil tanta in Me nasce
Luce, chel petto mi ralluma, e'l core,
che perche poco Io vaglia, assai di fuore
convien, che segno di valore Io lasce.
Voi ben portaste gia sin da le fasce
Non pur beltà, ch'altrui colma d'ardore,
Ma cortesia, bontà, senno, & splendore,
Ond'ogni alma gentil si nutre, & pasce.
Però con Voi, se non altro, mi vaglia
Lhumiltà, che vi si fa si d'honor degna,
chel mio cortese affecto in grado habbiate,
Si vedrem poi, quanto piu in alto saglia
chi piu s'inchina, & non chi altero regna,
E quanto speri in Noi la nostra etate.

[Your bright style begets so much light in me that it glows in my breast and my heart, and despite possessing little merit, from the outside I show signs of greatness. Surely you carried from your cradle not only a beauty that fills people with ardor but also courtesy, goodness, wisdom and splendor, which feed and nourish every gentle soul. And so, if nothing else, let that humility which does you such honor be a boon to me, that you might hold my courteous affection in esteem. And then we shall see how much higher rises the one who bows lower than one who rules proud, and how much our times might hope from us.]

In this exchange, typical Petrarchist and Dantean images of illumination, birth, nourishment, humility, honor, and genius allow the display of both Domenichi's support and the female poet's command of the lyric idiom. Domenichi insists (rather like the male dialogue participants in Castiglione's *Book of the Courtier*) that his performance is predicated on the inspiration he takes from his female interlocutor: that he only looks good thanks to her.[33] But Domenichi also turns his compliments into a competition in humility, suggesting in the rhetoric of courtly love that it is precisely Bonromea's self-effacement that constitutes her superiority to him, her placing herself lower that makes her higher. Running between the lines is of course the suggestion that Domenichi gave Bonromea a chance to distinguish herself from the "*volgar schiera*" [general crowd] by publishing her poem. However fleeting her fame, Domenichi here takes credit for it by printing her expression of gratitude.

Most importantly, perhaps, Domenichi's adoption of the dedication and the poetic exchange within this volume often turns the women's voices inward toward the collection itself. This device permits readers to overhear a society of women in conversation and to gaze upon these figures without being "looked back at" by feminine subjects engaged with the outside world. The women's poems and their dialogue are effectively contained, securely held within the covers of Domenichi's editing project, at the same time as his own figure is illuminated from within by their seemingly spontaneous praise.[34]

Domenichi's *Rime diverse* appears, like many curio collections, as a microcosm of the world, in this case a world of women's poetry constituted through the sheer accumulation of names and their participation in a ritual discourse. This little enclosed society, moreover, is arguably more audible and mobile on paper than it is in real life; for we find in Domenichi's anthology not a real society but a parasociety, a virtual community of women, many of whom may never have met but who appear, as an effect of the book's framing, to be in some sort of dialogue. At the same time, the anthology safely contains the women poets within authorized stanzas, where they appear captured for display but chaperoned by the men who speak intermittently throughout the volume.

Domenichi's first anthology of women may stand, finally, more as a curio collection for trade among men than as a crossing of women's poetic community into history. Indeed, we might view Domenichi's affinity for the framing devices I have described here as evidence of anxiety over his own militant gesture of facilitating women's entry into public and published discourse, even as he celebrated their authorship. The privileging of "firsts"—like the privileging of "mosts," "bests, " canons," and "influence"—pertains, as Margaret Ezell notes, to the narrative logic of male literary histories.[35] Women's writing, which has been less constant, less public, and less authorized, does not always reveal its historical significance within this competitive framework. Indeed, keeping in mind Quondam's notion of the anthology as a canonizing force and Susanne Woods's description of the canon as "the body of work that is both available to and read by" a determining reading public,[36] we must admit that Domenichi's anthology has had little canonizing effect. Even specialists in the field have heard of few of the poets represented therein; and those with whom we are familiar are known to us because they were published elsewhere. Quondam's magisterial analysis of the role anthologies play in a canonizing process may, it turns out, lead us astray if we assume its validity for the first large anthologies of Italian lyrics. As Franco Tomasi observes of these early collections:

> [T]he modern conception of the anthology as an organic and well planned map of a literary period effected through deliberate and precise selection of materials should not mislead us. [That model] cannot be mechanically superimposed on [Giolito's] *Libro primo*, nor perhaps on the later volumes, even those edited in the Fifties and Sixties by Dionigi Atanagi and Girolamo Ruscelli, though these were geared toward proposing more conscious historical frameworks.[37]

Against the model of the canonizing anthology, I have proposed here a somewhat playful, though not facetious, alternative: that of the collector's cabinet of curiosities and marvels. Such a model is both consonant with the developing sensibilities of the anthologies' reading public and consistent with contemporary attitudes about women's literary activities. It recognizes the early modern delight in acquisition, accumulation, assembly, and display that clearly played a role in the commercial success of lyric anthologies. And it gestures toward culturally broader, more figurative, and more adventurous frameworks that may help us to see better the historical patterns of women's writing and its reception.

Returning, for example, to Dionisotti's conclusions, we must note that, for all its brilliance, Dionisotti's analysis relies on a very partial picture of women's authorship, a picture that research devoted to women's literary history has tremendously expanded in the decades subsequent to his essay. It is not at all the case that women ceased to publish, to orient toward other women in their writing, or to innovate after 1560 only to reemerge as authors after the Risorgimento. Maddalena Campiglia's poems, *favole*, and discourses were published beginning in the 1580s. The plays, poetry, and letters of Isabella Andreini emerged in the 1590s and 1600s. Moderata Fonte's romance appeared in 1581, and her treatise defending women appeared in 1600. Lucrezia Marinella's heroic poems, her sacred lyrics, her biography of Catherine of Siena, her treatise defending women, and a range of her other writings all went to press beginning in 1595. Arcangela Tarabotti's indignant invective against forced convent life was printed in 1654. As this very partial list indicates, after 1560 women not only continued to publish, they also ventured ambitiously into production in literary genres besides Petrarchist lyric.[38] And all the while, reprints of women's poetic writings from the first half of the Cinquecento continued to roll off the presses.

What this discrepancy between literary and publishing history underscores is that the histories themselves must be examined as symptoms, even causes—and not as diagnoses—of the strong voices/weak histories problem. In terms of the present volume's concerns, the strong voice of the *Rime diverse* may still emanate today from the *poligrafo* Lodovico Domenichi, while the women writers it encloses remain audible, for the most part, in the decibels of weak history. We ourselves are engaged in the writing of an expanded history, however, and Domenichi's place in it as well as the significance of the poetry his anthology contains are yet to be determined.

❧ ❧ ❧

APPENDIX

Table of Names of the Women Described in This Book[39]

	Page	*Number of Poems*
Aurelia Petrucci	7	[2] 1
Anna Golfarina	54	[1]
Athalanta Sanese	77	[1]
Alda Torella Lunata	236	[1] 1
Berenice G.	11 (13)	[1]
Cassandra Petrucci	23	[14] 1
Clarice de Medici, & de gli Strozzi	13 (31)	[1]
Claudia dalla Rovere	32	[2]
Candida Gattesca de gli Alluminati	34	[1]
Cornelia Brunozzi de Villani	38	[3] 3
Catherina Pellegrina	41	[1] 1
Diamante Dolfi	42	[2]
Ermellina Arringhieri de Cerretani	(33)	[1]
Egeria da Canossa	46	[2]
Fiorenza G. Piemontese	35	[1]
Fausta Tacita	50	[4]
Francesca B. Sanese	234	[2]
Giulia Braccali de Ricciardi	37	[2]
Gentile Dotta	42	[1]

Gaspara Stampa	56	[5] 1
Suor Girolama Castellana	61	[10] 1
Gostanza Davala, Duchessa d'Amalfi	69	[5]
Honorata Pecci	72	[2]
Hortensia Scarpi	75	[2]
Hippolita Mirtilla	78	[11]
Isabella Riaria de Pepoli	55	[1]
Isabella di Morra	86	[13]
Livia Torniella Bonromea	229 (+12)	[7] 2
Laudomia da Sangallo	17	[2] 1
Lucretia Figliucci	19	[6] 1
Leonora Falletta da San Giorgio[40]	73. 218	[1] 1 [21] 1
Lucretia di Raimondo	100	[1]
Laudomia Forteguerri	102	[6]
Lisabetta da Cepperello	105	[5]
Livia Pia Poeti	109	[4] 1
Lucia Bertana	111	[11] 7
Maddalena Pallavicina de Marchesi di Ceva	31	[1]
Maria Langosca Solera	33	[1]
Maria Martelli de Panciatichi	39	[2] 3
Maria da Sangallo	59	[3]
Maria Spinola	119	[3]
Narda N. Fiorentina	121	[8]
Olimpia Malipiera	130	[33] 1
P.S.M.	44	[4]
Pia Bichi	75	[1] 2
Reina di Navarra	9 (11)	[2]
Silvia di Somma, Contessa di Bagno	8 (10)	[2] 1
Selvaggia Braccali de Bracciolini	40	[1]
Silvia Marchesa de Piccolomini	76	[1]
Virginia Gemma de Zuccheri	128	[2] 1
Veronica Gambara da Correggio	149	[22] 4
Virginia Martini de Salvi	162	[47] 1
Vittoria Colonna Marchesa di Pescara	206	[26] 4

NOTES

Special thanks for generous collaboration with this essay go to Victoria Kirkham, Fabio Finotti, Karen Bassi, and Julia L. Hairston. My thanks go also to the participants in Stanford University's conference "Working Texts: The Material Culture of the Book in Early Modern England and Europe" (April 2001), who responded to an earlier version of this essay.

1. Ann Rosalind Jones first proposed this terminology, borrowed from the work conducted at the Birmingham Center for Contemporary Cultural Studies, in *The Currency of Eros: Women's Love Lyric in Europe, 1540–1620* (Bloomington: Indiana University Press, 1990). See also Margaret F. Rosenthal, *The Honest Courtesan: Veronica*

Franco, Citizen and Writer in Sixteenth-Century Venice (Chicago: University of Chicago Press, 1992); Fiora A. Bassanese, *Gaspara Stampa* (Boston: Twayne, 1982); Deanna Shemek, "Getting a Word in Edgewise: Laura Terracina's *Discorsi* on the *Orlando Furioso*," in *Ladies Errant: Wayward Women and Social Order in Early Modern Italy* (Durham and London: Duke University Press, 1998), 126–57; and Victoria Kirkham, "Laura Battiferra degli Ammannati's 'First Book' of Poetry: A Renaissance Holograph Comes out of Hiding," *Rinascimento* 36 (1996): 351–91. On woman as figured in Petrarch's lyrics, see the fundamental essay of the period, Nancy Vickers, "Diana Described: Scattered Woman and Scattered Rhyme," in *Writing and Sexual Difference*, ed. Elizabeth Abel (Chicago: University of Chicago Press, 1982).

2. Regional and class differences account for significant variations in the education and reading habits of early modern women. A few women (e.g., Isabella d'Este, 1474–1539) benefited from instruction by top-notch progressive humanists. Others (e.g., Laura Terracina) received only a modest education yet became published poets. Poorer girls and peasants were often illiterate or barely literate. For fourteenth- and fifteenth-century views on female education, see Francesco da Barberino, "Reggimento e costumi di donna," ed. G. E. Sansone (Rome: Zauli, 1995); W. H. Woodward, ed., *Vittorino da Feltre and Other Humanist Educators* (Cambridge: Cambridge University Press, 1921); Leonardo Bruni, "De studis et literis," in *The Humanism of Leonardo Bruni: Selected Texts*, ed. Gordon Griffiths, James Hankins, and David Thompson (Binghamton: Medieval and Renaissance Texts and Studies, 1987), 235–50; Baldassarre Castiglione, *The Book of the Courtier*, trans. Charles S. Singleton, ed. Daniel Javitch (New York: Norton, 2002); Juan Luis Vives, *The Instruction of a Christian Woman* (1523; reprint, trans. and ed. Charles Fantazzi, Chicago: University of Chicago Press, 2000); and Giovanni Michele Bruto, *Institutione di una fanciulla nata nobilmente [1555]* (London: Adam Islip, 1598). For historical and critical perspectives, see Maria Lodovico Lenzi, *Donne e madonne. L'educazione femminile nel primo Rinascimento italiano* (Turin: Loescher, 1982); Anthony Grafton and Lisa Jardine, *From Humanism to the Humanities: Education and the Liberal Arts in Fifteenth- and Sixteenth-Century Europe* (London: Duckworth, 1986); Pamela Joseph Benson, *The Invention of the Renaissance Woman: The Challenge of Female Independence in the Literature and Thought of Italy and England* (University Park: Pennsylvania State University Press, 1992); and Brian Richardson, *Printing, Writers, and Readers in Renaissance Italy* (Cambridge: Cambridge University Press, 1999), esp. 110, 144–50.

3. Vittoria Colonna, *Rime de la Divina Vittoria Colonna Marchesa di Pescara, nuovamente stampate* [Rhymes of the divine Vittoria Colonna Marquise of Pescara, newly printed] (Parma: Viottis, 1538); Vittoria Colonna, *Rime*, ed. Alan Bullock (Bari: Laterza, 1982); Tullia d'Aragona, *Rime della Signora Tullia d'Aragona et di diversi a lei* [Rhymes of the lady Tullia d'Aragona and of assorted people to her] (Venice: Giolito, 1547); Aragona, *Rime*, ed. E. Celani (Bologna: 1891); Laura Terracina, *Rime della Signora Laura Terracina* [Rhymes of the lady Laura Terracina] (Venice: Giolito, 1548). The first (1547) edition of Terracina's poetry has been lost. Gaspara Stampa, *Rime di Madonna Gaspara Stampa* (Venice: Pietrasanta, 1554); *Rime: Gaspara Stampa e Veronica Franco*, ed. Abdelkader Salza (Bari: Laterza, 1913); Gaspara Stampa, *Selected Poems*, trans. Laura Anna Stortoni and Mary Prentice Lillie (New York: Italica, 1998); Girolamo Ruscelli, ed., *Rime di diversi eccellenti autori bresciani, nuovamente raccolte et mandate in luce da Girolamo Ruscelli, tra le quali sono le rime della Signora Veronica Gambara et di M. Pietro Barignano* [Rhymes of diverse excellent Brescian authors, newly gathered

and sent into print by Girolamo Ruscelli, among which are the rhymes of the lady Veronica Gambara and of messer Pietro Barignano] (Venice: P. Pietrasanta, 1554); Veronica Gambara, *Le rime*, ed. Alan Bullock (Florence and Perth: Olschki, 1995); Chiara Matraini, *Rime e Lettere*, ed. Giovanna Rabitti (Bologna: Commissione per i Testi di Lingua, 1989). For a useful chronology of women's early publishing, see Marina Zancan, ed., *Nel cerchio della luna. Figure di donna in alcuni testi del XVI secolo* (Venice: Marsilio, 1983). Translations from the Italian in this essay are mine.

4. Ludovico Domenichi, ed., *Rime diverse d'alcune nobilissime, et virtuosissime donne* (Lucca: Vincenzo Busdragho, 1559).

5. [Assorted rhymes by many most excellent authors, newly collected] See the reissued text, Franco Tomasi and Paolo Zaja, eds., *Rime diverse di molti eccellentissimi autori (Giolito 1545)* (Turin: RES, 2001). See also this reedition's informative "Introduzione," v–xlviii.

6. On Giolito see Daniel Javitch, *Proclaiming a Classic: The Canonization of Orlando Furioso* (Princeton: Princeton University Press, 1991); Louise George Clubb and William G. Clubb, "Building a Lyric Canon: Gabriel Giolito and the Rival Anthologists, 1545–1590," *Italica* 68, no. 3 (1991): 332–44; and Daniel Javitch, "La politica dei generi letterari nel tardo Cinquecento," *Studi italiani* 3, no. 2 (1991): 5–22.

7. Amedeo Quondam's pioneering work proposed shifting the study of Renaissance Petrarchan poetry away from individual lyric voices and toward a view of this corpus as a "colossal cultural macrotext." See his 1973 essay, "Dall'*abstinendum verbis* alla 'locuzione artificiosa.' Il petrarchismo come sistema linguistico della ripetizione," reprinted in Amedeo Quondam, *Il naso di Laura. Lingua e poesia lirica nella tradizione del Classicismo* (Modena: Panini, 1991), 181–99; see 185. See also Paolo Zaja, "Intorno alle antologie. Testi e paratesti in alcune raccolte di lirica cinquecentesche," in *I più vaghi e i più soavi fiori. Studi sulle antologie di lirica del Cinquecento*, ed. Monica Bianco and Elena Strada (Alessandria: Edizioni dell'Orso, 2001), 113–45.

8. Lodovico Domenichi, *Rime* (Venice: Giolito, 1544). For a brief overview of Domenichi's career, see A. Piscini, "Domenichi, Ludovico," in *Dizionario biografico degli italiani* (Rome: Istituto della Enciclopedia italiana, 1991), 40:595–600.

9. Lodovico Domenichi, *La nobiltà delle donne* (Venice: Giolito, 1549). On Domenichi's plagiarism, see Henricus Cornelius Agrippa, *Declamation on the Nobility and Preeminence of the Female Sex* (1529; trans. and ed. Albert Rabil Jr., Chicago: University of Chicago Press, 1996), 28.

10. Lodovico Domenichi, *Dialoghi di M. Lodovico Domenichi, cioè D'amore, De' rimedi d'Amore, Dell'Amor Fraterno, Della Fortuna, Della vera Nobiltà, Dell'Imprese, Della corte et Della Stampa* (Venice: G. Giolito de' Ferrari, 1562).

11. Dionisotti points to the academies (or salons) and to the publication of anthologies (both of letters and of poetry) as the clearest evidence of a new literary culture in Italy between 1540 and 1560. He writes, "La prova più vistosa di tale novità è naturalmente data, nelle condizioni di allora a non di allora soltanto, dal contributo delle donne. Certo è possibile, anche in Italia, disegnare una storia continuata della letteratura al femminile dalle origini ai giorni nostri. Una qualche donna che per irresistibile vocazione o per gioco o per disperazione scriva, si può sempre trovare. Ma storicamente, prescindendo dall'ultimo secolo, dal Risorgimento innanzi, il fenomeno è in Italia circoscritto. Soltanto nella letteratura del medio Cinquecento le donne fanno gruppo. Non prima né poi" [The most visible evidence of this novelty is naturally supplied, in that period and not only that period, by the contributions of women. Cer-

tainly it is possible in Italy, too, to trace a continuous history of women's literature from the origins (of Italian literature) up to our own day. We can always find some woman who writes, whether out of an irresistible sense of vocation, or for fun, or out of desperation. But historically, with the exception of the last century from the Risorgimento on, the phenomenon (of female writing) is a limited one in Italy. Only in the literature of the mid-sixteenth century do women constitute a group. Not before, nor after]. Carlo Dionisotti, "La letteratura italiana nell'età del concilio di Trento," in *Geografia e storia della letteratura italiana* (Turin: Einaudi, 1967), 227–54.

12. On the printing industry's attempts to capture new reader markets by specializing and focusing the successful genre of the anthology, see Francesco Erspamer, "L'industrializzazione della letteratura 8. Quantità e qualità della maniera: antologie ed esperimenti lirici fra Venezia e Napoli," in *Storia della civiltà letteraria italiana,* ed. Rinaldo Rinaldi (Turin: UTET, 1993), 1826–67. Among the most frequent subgenres Erspamer counts collections of *rime spirituali,* anthologies featuring geographically specialized authors, volumes in memory of deceased persons, and tribute collections of poems in honor of specific figures. See also Franco Tomasi, "Alcuni aspetti delle antologie liriche del secondo Cinquecento," in *I più vaghi e i più soavi fiori,* ed. Bianco and Strada, 77–111.

13. On Stampa, see Jones, *Currency of Eros,* 118–41; and Fiora A. Bassanese, *Gaspara Stampa* (Boston: Twayne, 1982). Still today, though perhaps for different reasons, the authenticity of female authorship in early modernity remains a constant question. This doubt often results from the paucity of clear documentation for women's writing. Other uncertainties derive from the historical accumulation of critical bias. In my ongoing work on the letters of Isabella d'Este, for example, I am regularly asked how Isabella's letters can really be "hers," since she dictated the vast majority of them. This question, valid as it is, has not to my knowledge been considered a serious problem regarding (for example) the letters of Lorenzo de' Medici, though Lorenzo's use of secretaries was as frequent as Isabella's. On secretarial mediation, see my "'Ci Ci' and 'Pa Pa': Script, Mimicry, and Mediation in Isabella d'Este's Letters," forthcoming in *Rinascimento.*

14. See Jones, *Currency of Eros,* 155–57; for Franco, see Rosenthal, *The Honest Courtesan.*

15. Natalie Zemon Davis, *Society and Culture in Early Modern France* (Stanford: Stanford University Press, 1975), 85–86.

16. On Terracina, see Shemek, "Getting a Word in Edgewise." On Fonte, see Paola Malpezzi Price, "A Woman's Discourse in the Italian Renaissance: Moderata Fonte's *Il merito delle donne,*" *Annali d'Italianistica* 7 (1989): 165–81; Price, *Moderata Fonte: Women and Life in Sixteenth-Century Venice* (Madison and Teaneck: Farleigh Dickinson University Press, 2003). See also Beatrice Collina, "Moderata Fonte e *Il merito delle donne,*" *Annali d'Italianistica* 7 (1989): 142–64. For Fonte's treatise, see Moderata [Modesta Pozzo de' Zorzi] Fonte, *Il merito delle donne. . . ove chiaramente si scuopre quanto siano elle più degne, e più perfette de gli huomini* (1600), ed. Adriana Chemello (Venice: Eiodos, 1988); Fonte, *The Worth of Women: Wherein Is Clearly Revealed Their Nobility and Their Superiority to Men,* trans. and ed. Virginia Cox (Chicago: University of Chicago Press, 1997).

17. "Sono gia molti anni passati, ch'essendo io con lanimo, & con lopere tutto volto a celebrare quanto per Me si poteva allhora, la nobiltà, & eccellentia delle Donne; laqual cosa io ridussi poi in un giusto volume; si come il pensier mi guidava, mi posi in un medesimo tempo raunare cio che mi pareua potere procurar loro gloria, e honore. Cosi con laiuto d'alcuni amorevoli miei, & grandemente affettionati al valor

Donnesco, raccolsi da piu parti assai ragionevole quantità di rime composte da Donne. Lequali rime sono poi state infino ad hora appresso di Me in quel grado tenute, che le piu care, & pretiose cose si soglion tenere. Et benche infino allhora, ch'io cominciai a raccorle, io fossi fermo di volere in ogni modo publicarle al mondo col mezo delle stampe, per chiarir coloro, iquali stanno in dubbio della grandezza dell'Ingegno feminile: nondimeno non ho potuto mai porre ad effetto tal mio pensiero, essendo quando da vno, & quando da vn'altro impedimento distornato" (3–4).

18. Zaja ("Intorno alle antologie," 116–17) comments that Domenichi's dedication to the Milanese Castiglione (a man with strong ties to the Spanish nobility) was an attempt to give his volume an international readership, while the publisher Busdragho's dedication of the same volume to the Lucchese Gerardo Spada aimed to connect with the local Tuscan market. Thus for Zaja, both dedications suggest ambitious marketing strategies. The rejection of female dedicatees in this light presumably indicates that no woman was in Domenichi's or Busdragho's mind capable of capturing the readership with which they hoped Castiglione and Gerardo would connect their innovative publication.

19. The phrase in quotes is borrowed from Eve Kosofsky Sedgwick, *Between Men: English Literature and Male Homosocial Desire* (New York: Columbia University Press, 1985).

20. This mixture of prominent with inconspicuous poets was a programmatic feature of the anthologies. Erspamer ("Quantità e qualità," 1828, 1834) underscores the purely commercial aims behind Giolito's inspiration to publish so many poets in a single anthology and his mingling of obscure with famous poets, both features that were quickly replicated by rival editors. See also Marie-Françoise Piejus, "La première anthologie de poèmes féminines: L'écriture filtrée et orientée," in *Le pouvoir et la plume. Incitations, contrôle et répression dans l'Italie du XVI siècle* (Paris: Université de la Sorbonne Nouvelle, 1982), 193–213.

21. The poets' cities are discernible not from the table of authors but from the more extended attributions that appear within the volume. Many poets' names are followed by their city of origin: Bagno, Navarre, Ceva, Vinovo (Piemonte), Pavia, Pistoia, Naples, Florence, Canossa, Sangallo, Ferrara, Amalfi, Siena, Orvieto, Correggio, Pescara, Monferrato.

22. Amedeo Quondam, *Petrarchismo mediato. Per una critica della forma "antologia"* (Rome: Bulzoni, 1974).

23. Paula Findlen, *Possessing Nature: Museums, Collecting, and Scientific Culture in Early Modern Italy* (Berkeley: University of California Press, 1994). See also Gigliola Fragnito, *In museo e in villa. Saggi sul Rinascimento perduto* (Venice: Arsenale, 1988).

24. Domenichi makes this claim for editorship in his treatise on printing, cited previously.

25. Jean Baudrillard, "The System of Collecting," in *The Cultures of Collecting*, ed. John Elsner and John Cardinal (Cambridge, Mass.: Harvard University Press, 1994), 7–24; 275–77.

26. Dedicated to Domenichi are poems by Laudomia da S. Gallo (17), Leonora B. da Giorgio (73), Lucia Bertana (111), Gostanza Castalda (118), Olimpia Malapiera (145), and Livia Torniella Bonromea (12; 229).

27. My count of seventy-eight includes the poems that function as part of exchanges, discussed subsequently. The phenomenon of poetic exchanges in print was probably inspired by contemporary single-authored volumes of verse, which make regular use of dedications and direct address for individual poems. But Piejus notes that it

was foreign to the large, multiauthored anthologies before Domenichi's 1559 women's volume. See Piejus, "La Première anthologie," n. 29, who observes that there are no dedications in Dolce's 1553 collection nor in that of Ruscelli (1558), with only rare instances in Domenichi's 1545 volume and in Giolito's anthology.

28. Piejus, "La Première anthologie," 202–3.

29. Ibid., 203: "La femme poète trouve plus aisément place dans le monde littéraire si elle ne s'y présente pas seule, si elle prend appui sur une structure sociale qui la cautionne, qui la justifie."

30. Not all poems addressed to men (or to women), however, are followed by responses.

31. Domenichi, *Rime diverse* 83.

32. This poem appears twice in the collection: once with Domenichi's reply appended on p. 12 and once alone on p. 229. Victoria Kirkham points out to me that the sonnet's opening appears also in compositions by Laura Battiferra, Tullia d'Aragona, and Galeazzo di Tarsia. It thus illustrates a range of mutual reading and borrowing among these poets that deserves further study.

33. See Castiglione's Book III, chapters 51, 52.

34. Piejus, "La premiére anthologie," 206–7, notes two other editorial choices by Domenichi that cohere with my argument about containment. The first is Domenichi's preference for religious lyric over other subject matter in his selection of the women's poems. The second is his aggressive reordering of Isabella di Morra's poems with respect to the two earlier instances of their publication. Morra was held prisoner by her brothers, who finally murdered her upon discovery of her correspondence (and suspected relationship) with a neighboring lord. They killed him, too. Eight sonnets and a canzone of Morra's had been published by Giolito in 1552, then reprinted in the fifth anthology in his series (1555). Three of her *canzoni* and two sonnets appeared in Giolito's volume 7 (1556). Domenichi united Morra's previously published poems for the first time, printing the thirteen in their entirety; but he also arranged them into a pseudo-biographical narrative implying Isabella's longing for marriage, her awaiting of her father's return from exile, her despair, and her ultimate turn to God. This order survives in most subsequent editions of Isabella di Morra's poems. See also the introduction to *Isabella Morra*, ed. Maria Antonietta Grignani (Rome: Salerno, 2000).

35. Margaret Ezell, *Writing Women's Literary History* (Baltimore: Johns Hopkins University Press, 1993).

36. Suzanne Woods made these remarks in the roundtable discussion at the conference that gave rise to this volume.

37. Tomasi, "Alcuni aspetti," 78. "Va subito detto che l'idea moderna dell'antologia, quella cioè di un'organica e ben progettata mappatura di un periodo letterario attuata grazie alla consapevole e precisa selezione dei materiali, non deve trarre in inganno, perché non è meccanicamente sovrapponibile al *Libro primo*, né forse ai volumi successivi, persino a quelli curati negli anni Cinquanta e Sessanta da Dionigi Atanagi e Girolamo Ruscelli, pur orientati a proporre un più avvertito quadro storiografico."

38. A few examples include Maddalena Campigli, *Flori. Favola boscareccia di Maddalena Campigli* [*Flori: A Pastoral Drama* by Maddalena Campigli] (Venice: Gl'heredi di Perin Libraro e T. Brunelli, 1588); *Calisa. Egloga* [Calisa. Eclogue] (Vicenza: G. Greco, 1589); *Il Fidamante. Poema eroico dell'Ill.mo Sign. Curtio Gonzaga . . . aggiuntivi gli Argomenti dell'Illustre e virtuosiss. Sign. Maddalena Campigli* [The true lover. Heroic poem by the most illustrious lord Curtio Gonzaga . . . with arguments added by the illustrious and most virtuous lady Maddalena Campigli] (Venice: Insegna del Leone, 1591);

Isabella Andreini, *Mirtilla pastorale d'Isabella Andreini comica gelosa* [Mirtilla, a pastoral play by Isabella Andreini comic (actress in the troupe of) "The Jealous Ones"] (Verona: S. Dalle Donne e C. Franceschini, 1588); *Rime di Isabella Andreini padovana, comica gelosa* [Rhymes of the Paduan Isabella Andreini, comic in the Gelosi (Milan: G. Bordoni and P. Locarni, 1601); *Lettere di Isabella Andreini. Comica gelosa e accademica Intenta, nominata l'Accesa.* [Letters of Isabella Andreini. Comic actress in the Gelosi and member of the Academy of the Intenti, nicknamed Lady Afire); Moderata Fonte, *Il merito delle donne* [The worth of women]; Fonte, *Tredici canti del Floridoro di Mad. Moderata Fonte* [Thirteen cantos of Floridoro by Madonna Moderata Fonte] (Venice: Eredi di F. Rampazzetto, 1581); Reprint, ed. Valeria Finucci (Modena: Mucchi, 1995); Lucrezia Marinella, *La colomba sacra. Poema eroico di Lucrezia Marinella* [The sacred dove. Heroic poem by Lucrezia Marinella] (Venice: G. B. Ciotti Senese, 1595); Marinella, *Amore innamorato ed impazzato. Poema di Lucrezia Marinella* [Love in love and driven mad. Epic by Lucrezia Marinella] (Venice: n.p., 1598); Marinella, *La nobiltà et eccellenza delle donne co' difetti et mancamenti de gli huomini* [The nobility and excellence of women with the defects and failings of men] (Venice: Ciotti Senese, 1621); Marinella, *De gesti heroici e della vita meravigliosa della serafica Santa Caterina da Siena. . .* [The heroic deeds and marvelous life of the seraphic Saint Catherina of Siena] [(Venice: B. Barezzi, 1624); Arcangela Tarabotti, *La semplicità ingannata* [Simplicity deceived] (Leida: G. Sambix, 1654). See the more comprehensive list in Zancan, *Nel cerchio*, 254–64.

39. "Tavola de nomi delle donne descritte in questo libro." Where page numbers printed in the table are not accurate, I add corrections in parentheses following Domenichi's numbers. Men whose poems appear in the anthology are Domenichi himself, Ottaviano della Ratta, Antonio Gaggi, Gio. Galeazzo Rosci, Gherardo Spini, Anton Francesco Rinieri, Lattantio Benucci, and Girolomo Popponi.

Numerals in brackets, added by me, indicate the number of poems printed for each author. Numerals following brackets indicate number of compositions addressed or dedicated to the same poet, including response poems.

40. Page 73 bears a sonnet to Domenichi by Signora Leonora B. da S. Giorgio. On p. 218 begins a series of twenty-one poems attributed to S. Leonora Falletta Sig. Di Melazzo in Monferrato. Domenichi's index appears to conflate the two names

BIBLIOGRAPHY

Agrippa, Henricus Cornelius. *Declamation on the Nobility and Preeminence of the Female Sex*. 1529. Reprint, trans. and ed. Albert Rabil Jr., Chicago: University of Chicago Press, 1996.

Andreini, Isabella. *Mirtilla pastorale d'Isabella Andreini comica gelosa*. Verona: S. Dalle Donne e C. Franceschini, 1588.

———. *Rime di Isabella Andreini padovana, comica gelosa*. Milan: G. Bordoni and P. Locarni, 1601.

———. *Lettere di Isabella Andreini padovana. Comica gelosa e accademica Intenta, nominata* 'Accesa.' Venice: M. A. Zaltieri, 1607.

———. *Mirtilla*. Trans. and ed. Laura Stortoni. Chicago: University of Chicago Press, 2002.

Aragona, Tullia d'. *Rime della Signora Tullia d'Aragona et di diversi a lei*. Venice: Giolito, 1547.

———. *Rime*. Ed. E. Celani. Bologna, 1891.

Barberino, Francesco da. *Reggimento e costumi di donna.* 1517. Reprint, ed. G. E. Sansone, Rome: Zauli, 1995.

Bassanese, Fiora A. *Gaspara Stampa.* Boston: Twayne, 1982.

Baudrillard, Jean. "The System of Collecting." In *The Cultures of Collecting,* ed. John Elsner and John Cardinal, 7–23, 275–77. Cambridge, Mass.: Harvard University Press, 1994.

Benson, Pamela Joseph. *The Invention of the Renaissance Woman: The Challenge of Female Independence in the Literature and Thought of Italy and England.* University Park: Pennsylvania State University Press, 1992.

Bruni, Leonardo. "De studis et literis." In *The Humanism of Leonardo Bruni: Selected Texts,* ed. Gordon Griffiths, James Hankins, and David Thompson, 235–50. Binghamton: Medieval and Renaissance Texts and Studies, 1987.

Bruto, Giovanni Michele. *Institutione di una fanciulla nata nobilmente [1555].* London: Adam Islip, 1598.

Campiglia, Maddalena. *Flori. Favola boscareccia di Maddalena Campiglia.* Venice: Gl'heredi di Perin Libraro e T. Brunelli, 1588.

———. *Calisa. Egloga.* Vicenza: G. Greco, 1589.

———. *Il Fidamante. Poema eroico dell'Ill.mo Sign. Curtio Gonzaga . . . aggiuntivi gli Argomenti dell'Illustre e virtuosiss. Sign. Maddalena Campiglia.* Venice: Insegna del Leone, 1591.

———. *Flori: A Pastoral Drama.* Ed. Lisa Sampson and Virginia Cox. Chicago: University of Chicago Press, 2004.

Castiglione, Baldassarre. *The Book of the Courtier.* Trans. Charles S. Singleton. Ed. Daniel Javitch. New York: Norton, 2002.

Clubb, Louise George, and William G. Clubb. "Building a Lyric Canon: Gabriel Giolito and the Rival Anthologists, 1545–1590." *Italica* 68, no. 3 (1991): 332–44.

Collina, Beatrice. "Moderata Fonte e *Il merito delle donne.*" *Annali d'Italianistica* 7 (1989): 142–64.

Colonna, Vittoria. *Rime de la Divina Vittoria Colonna Marchesa di Pescara, nuovamente stampate.* Parma: Viottis, 1538.

———. *Rime.* Ed. Alan Bullock. Bari: Laterza, 1982.

Davis, Natalie Zemon. *Society and Culture in Early Modern France.* Stanford: Stanford University Press, 1975.

Dionisotti, Carlo. "La letteratura italiana nell'età del concilio di Trento." In *Geografia e storia della letteratura italiana,* 227–54. Turin: Einaudi, 1967.

Domenichi, Lodovico. *Rime.* Venice: Giolito, 1544.

———. *La nobiltà delle donne.* Venice: Giolito, 1549.

———, ed. *Rime diverse d'alcune nobilissime, et virtuosissime donne.* Lucca: Vincenzo Busdragho, 1559.

———. *Dialoghi di M. Lodovico Domenichi, cioè D'amore, De' rimedi d'Amore, Dell'Amor Fraterno, Della Fortuna, Della vera Nobiltà, Dell'Imprese, Della corte et Della Stampa.* Venice: G. Giolito de' Ferrari, 1562.

Erspamer, Francesco. "L'industrializzazione della letteratura, 8. Quantità e qualità della maniera: antologie ed esperimenti lirici fra Venezia e Napoli." In *Storia della civiltà letteraria italiana,* ed. Rinaldo Rinaldi, 1826–67. Turin: UTET, 1993.

Ezell, Margaret. *Writing Women's Literary History.* Baltimore: Johns Hopkins University Press, 1993.

Findlen, Paula. *Possessing Nature: Museums, Collecting, and Scientific Culture in Early Modern Italy.* Berkeley: University of California Press, 1994.

Fonte, Moderata [Modesta Pozzo de' Zorzi]. *Tredici canti del Floridoro di Mad. Moderata Fonte*. Venice: Eredi di F. Rampazzetto, 1581. Reprint, ed. Valeria Finucci, Modena: Mucchi, 1995.

———. *Il merito delle donne . . . ove chiaramente si scuopre quanto siano elle più degne, e più perfette de gli huomini*. 1600. Reprint, ed. Adriana Chemello, Venice: Eiodos, 1988.

———. *The Worth of Women: Wherein Is Clearly Revealed Their Nobility and Their Superiority to* Men. Trans. and ed. Virginia Cox. Chicago: University of Chicago Press, 1997.

Fragnito, Gigliola. *In museo e in villa. Saggi sul Rinascimento perduto*. Venice: Arsenale, 1988.

Gambara, Veronica. *Le rime*. Ed. Alan Bullock. Florence and Perth: Olschki, 1995.

Grafton, Anthony, and Lisa Jardine. *From Humanism to the Humanities: Education and the Liberal Arts in Fifteenth- and Sixteenth-Century Europe*. London: Duckworth, 1986.

Javitch, Daniel. "La politica dei generi letterari nel tardo Cinquecento." *Studi italiani* 3, no. 2 (1991): 5–22.

———. *Proclaiming a Classic: The Canonization of Orlando Furioso*. Princeton: Princeton University Press, 1991.

Jones, Ann Rosalind. *The Currency of Eros: Women's Love Lyric in Europe, 1540–1620*. Bloomington: Indiana University Press, 1990.

Kirkham, Victoria. "Laura Battiferra degli Ammannati's *First Book* of Poetry: A Renaissance Holograph Comes out of Hiding." *Rinascimento* 36 (1996): 351–91.

Lenzi, Maria Lodovico. *Donne e madonne. L'educazione femminile nel primo Rinascimento italiano*. Turin: Loescher, 1982.

Marinella, Lucrezia. *La colomba sacra. Poema eroico di Lucrezia Marinella*. Venice: G. B. Ciotti Senese, 1595.

———. *Amore innamorato ed impazzato. Poema di Lucrezia Marinella*. Venice: n.p., 1598.

———. *La nobiltà et eccellenza delle donne co' difetti et mancamenti de gli huomini*. Venice: Ciotti Senese, 1621.

———. *De gesti heroici e della vita meravigliosa della serafica Santa Caterina da Siena . . .* Venice: B. Barezzi, 1624.

———. *The Nobility and Excellence of Women and the Defects and Vices of* Men. Ed. and trans. Anne Dunhill. Chicago: University of Chicago Press, 1999.

Matraini, Chiara. *Rime e Lettere*. Ed. Giovanna Rabitti. Bologna: Commissione per i testi di lingua, 1989.

Morra, Isabella. *Canzoniere: a bilingual edition*. Ed. and trans. Irene Musillo Mitchell. West Lafayette, IN: Bordighiera, 1998.

———. *Rime*. Ed. Maria Antonietta Grignani. Rome: Salerno, 2000.

Piejus, Marie-Françoise. "La première anthologie de poèmes féminins: L'écriture filtrée et orientée." In *Le pouvoir et la plume. Incitations, contrôle et répression dans l'Italie du XVI siècle*, 193–213. Paris: Université de la Sorbonne Nouvelle, 1982.

Piscini, A. "Domenichi, Ludovico." In *Dizionario biografico degli italiani*, 40:595–600. Rome: Istituto della Enciclopedia italiana, 1991.

Price, Paola Malpezzi. "A Woman's Discourse in the Italian Renaissance: Moderata Fonte's *Il merito delle donne*." *Annali d'Italianistica* 7 (1989): 165–81.

———. *Moderata Fonte: Women and Life in Sixteenth-Century Venice*. Madison and Teaneck: Farleigh Dickinson University Press, 2003.

Quondam, Amedeo. "Dall'*abstinendum verbis* alla 'locuzione artificiosa.' Il petrarchismo come sistema linguistico della ripetizione." 1973. Reprinted in Amedeo Quondam, *Il naso di Laura. Lingua e poesia lirica nella tradizione del Classicismo*, 181–99. Modena: Panini, 1991.

———. *Petrarchismo mediato. Per una critica della forma "antologia."* Rome: Bulzoni, 1974.

———. *Il naso di Laura. Lingua e poesia lirica nella tradizione del Classicismo*. Modena: Panini, 1991.

Richardson, Brian. *Printing, Writers, and Readers in Renaissance Italy*. Cambridge: Cambridge University Press, 1999.

Rosenthal, Margaret F. *The Honest Courtesan: Veronica Franco, Citizen and Writer in Sixteenth-Century Venice*. Chicago: University of Chicago Press, 1992.

Ruscelli, Girolamo, ed. *Rime di diversi eccellenti autori bresciani, nuovamente raccolte et mandate in luce da Girolamo Ruscelli, tra le quali sono le rime della Signora Veronica Gambara et di M. Pietro Barignano*. Venice: P. Pietrasanta, 1554.

Schiesari, Juliana. *The Gendering of Melancholia: Feminism, Psychoanalysis, and the Symbolics of Loss in Renaissance Literature*. Chicago: University of Chicago Press, 1991.

Sedgwick, Eve Kosofsky. *Between Men: English Literature and Male Homosocial Desire*. New York: Columbia University Press, 1985.

Shemek, Deanna. "Getting a Word in Edgewise: Laura Terracina's *Discorsi* on the *Orlando Furioso*." In *Ladies Errant: Wayward Women and Social Order in Early Modern Italy*, 126–57. Durham and London: Duke University Press, 1998.

———. "'Ci Ci' and 'Pa Pa': Script, Mimicry, and Mediation in Isabella d'Este's Letters." Forthcoming in *Rinsacimento*.

Stampa, Gaspara. Rime di Madonna Gaspara Stampa. Venice: Pietrasanta, 1554.

———. *Selected Poems*. Trans. Laura Anna Stortoni and Mary Prentice Lillie. New York: Italica, 1998.

Tarabotti, Arcangela. *La semplicità ingannata*. Leida: G. Sambix, 1654.

Terracina, Laura. *Rime della Signora Laura Terracina*. Venice: Giolito, 1548.

Tomasi, Franco. "Alcuni aspetti delle antologie liriche del secondo Cinquecento." In *I più vaghi e i più soavi fiori. Studi sulle antologie di lirica del Cinquecento*, ed. Monica Bianco and Elena Strada, 77–111. Alessandria: Edizioni dell'Orso, 2001.

Tomasi, Franco, and Paolo Zaja, eds. *Rime diverse di molti eccellentissimi autori (Giolito 1545)*. Turin: RES, 2001.

Vickers, Nancy. "Diana Described: Scattered Woman and Scattered Rhyme." In *Writing and Sexual Difference*, ed. Elizabeth Abel, 95–109. Chicago: University of Chicago Press, 1982.

Vives, Juan Luis. *The Instruction of a Christian Woman*. 1523. Reprint, trans. and ed. C. Fantazzi, Chicago: University of Chicago Press, 2000.

Woodward, W. H., ed. *Vittorino da Feltre and Other Humanist Educators*. Cambridge: Cambridge University Press, 1921.

Zaja, Paolo. "Intorno alle antologie. Testi e paratesti in alcune raccolte di lirica cinquecentesche." In *I più vaghi e i più soavi fiori. Studi sulle antologie di lirica del Cinquecento*, ed. Monica Bianco and Elena Strada, 113–45. Alessandria: Edizioni dell'Orso, 2001.

Zancan, Marina, ed. *Nel cerchio della luna. Figure di donna in alcuni testi del XVI secolo*. Venice: Marsilio, 1983.

Recollecting the Renaissance

LUISA BERGALLI'S *COMPONIMENTI POETICI* (1726)

Stuart Curran

Luisa Bergalli, who was born in Venice in 1703 and died there in 1779, led a long and, by any standards, productive life.[1] Although she came from humble origins—her father was a Piedmontese political exile who earned a modest living as a shoemaker—she was well educated, and through the connections of her tutors, most particularly the eminent man of the theater Apostolo Zeno, by the age of twenty-two she had begun to make a living as a dramatist, one of the few areas of literary endeavor traditionally accessible to an aspiring woman. We have it on the authority of Goldoni's rival Carlo Gozzi that she was so deeply committed to the literary life that she neglected both her household regulation and its finances in order to produce what he condemned as bad poetry, an estimate, given Italians' traditional veneration for authority, that seems to have occasioned Bergalli's general dismissal for a century and a half after her death. Even if we were not today likely to reverse the priorities Gozzi applied to a woman author, his judgment is highly suspect, since Bergalli was his older brother Gasparo's wife; and, moreover, she had been publicly deserted by him in 1756 and so was left in her early fifties, while her husband moved in with his mistress, to look after a household containing their five children on her own. It appears, then, that household management was in these circumstances something of an imperative, and Luisa fell back on organizational skills already long tested. Management, rather than having been her failing, seems instead to have been her metier, whether in the form of the theatrical companies with which she was involved over many years or in her single-handed efforts as a younger literary presence to reclaim monuments of the Italian female literary tradition, which is the subject of this essay. Her efforts in this line include a notable edition of the *Rime* of Gaspara Stampa printed in 1738, the year of her marriage to Gasparo—the similarity of the first names is surely worth contemplating—and, a decade before that, a remarkable anthology of 114 earlier women poets, *Componimenti poetici delle più illustri rimatrici d'ogni secolo* [Poetical compositions of the most illustrious women versifiers of every century], whose bland title conceals its radical gendered intensity, a work that was ostensibly intended as the first part of a series but never pursued beyond its first volume, whose scope ended in 1575. This she published in 1726, in only her twenty-third year.

Since Bergalli in her prefatory remarks "to the reader" [A chi legge] and in brief biographical entries for her authors at the volume's end goes to considerable length to detail where she found them, it is worth beginning with this formidable feat, which appears to have involved many private Venetian libraries as well as various ecclesiastical repositories. For, although she certainly attended to Lodovico Domenichi's groundbreaking 1559 anthology, *Rime diverse d'alcune nobilissime et virtuosissime donne* [Diverse poems of some of the noblest and most virtuous women], that volume contained only fifty-three authors, well under half the number Bergalli brought to light, and a careful comparison of the two volumes reveals that, if anything, Bergalli, rather than being derivative, went to extraordinary lengths to rethink Domenichi's choice of poets and the texts that were illustrative of their value. In some dozen cases where both Domenichi and Bergalli include only a couple of poems by a particular author, she conspicuously demonstrates her independent knowledge of the poet by changing at least one of the examples. Moreover, Domenichi's interest, it would seem, lies with poets almost exclusively of his own acquaintance. His earliest examples in his 1559 anthology are the by then famous Vittoria Colonna (1481–1547) and two other standbys of early Cinquecento verse, Marguerite of Valois, the queen of Navarre, and Veronica Gambara, all of whom came to prominence in the early to mid-1530s. All of Domenichi's other examples stem from the ensuing quarter century.

By contrast, nineteen of Bergalli's poets, comprising thirty-five pages, predate Domenichi's selections, and another twenty-four, accounting for some twenty-six pages at the end, represent the fifteen years succeeding the appearance of his volume. More than just comprehending a conspicuous expansion of range, Bergalli's selection testifies to a further and significant element in her independent perspective on the subject, her sense of a progressive historical development in the exfoliation of a woman's literary culture in the Cinquecento, which makes her take great care to establish an accurate, progressive chronology. There seems no like rationale for the organization of Domenichi's *Rime diverse d'alcune nobilissime et virtuosissime donne* beyond its representing his contemporaries (and even at that his exclusion of Laura Terracina, who seems to have fawned on him for patronage, suggests that an exclusiveness based on personal interests is a driving force behind his selections).[2] For Bergalli, on the other hand, this is a historical movement, one that on an initial scale demands that chronology dictate her inclusions and their order within the anthology.

If, however, she had looked for help from the principal contemporary anthology of historic Italian verse (and surely she must have at least glanced at it)—Agostino Gobbi's multivolume *Scelta di Sonetti, e Canzoni de' più eccellenti Rimatori d'ogni Secolo* [A selection of sonnets and songs by the most excellent poets of every century], which was originally issued in Bologna in 1709 and expanded several times thereafter—she would have been faced with something of a blank in terms of guidance. Specifically, she would have found the following, somewhat dismaying numbers of poets, whom Gobbi groups together by century: for the Trecento, 12 poets, 11 of whom were men, with Ortensia di Guglielmo accommodated among them by a single sonnet; for the Quattrocento, 14 exclusively male poets; for the first half of the Cinquecento 74 poets, including 4 women—Chiara Matraini, Tullia d'Aragona, Veronica Gambara, and Vittoria Colonna—and for the second half, another 77 poets of which but 2 are women: Laura Battiferra, with four sonnets, and Isabella Andreini, with another sonnet; for the Seicento, we encounter 33 solely male poets; and of the 110 poets anthologized from those living in 1709, only 7 are women. The total numbers—14 women among 320 poets—graphically testify to the extraordinary task faced by Luisa Bergalli in finding her way outside the enforced *patrimonio* of her established and truly immediate literary heritage.

Since the libraries to which Bergalli had access were of ancient origin, she clearly would have attended to the numerous contemporary anthologies by which the mid-sixteenth century organized and celebrated its remarkable outpouring of verse. Both to assess the scale of Bergalli's endeavor and for our own independent sense of the actual historical facts, it is well worth taking the time to contemplate the sort of presentation of evidence Bergalli would have encountered. To this end, I have consulted six of these anthologies: perhaps since all were published in Venice, they can be assumed to be the very same collections Bergalli searched through in the interests of further enlightening herself about the presence of literary mothers in the Renaissance. Of three issued by the enterprising press of Gabriel Giolito, she would have found the following results.[3] In *Rime diverse di molti eccellentissimi auttori nouvamente raccolte* [Diverse poems newly collected from many most excellent authors] (1545), likewise gathered by Domenichi as the first of seven successive anthologies of contemporary Italian poetry, 5 of the 85 poets are women: Francesca Baffa, Laodamia Forteguerri, Laura Terracina, Vittoria Colonna, and Veronica Gambara. This may not seem a minimal percentage, perhaps, yet in actuality the 5 women account for only 9 of its 374 pages. (We may begin perhaps to consider that Domenichi's anthology of women fourteen years later and after these several reprints of contemporary men, though we celebrate its uniqueness, reflects not so much his dedication to their welfare as a decent sense of remorse over that disproportion.) Seven years after it, in *Rime di diversi eccellenti autori* [Poems of diverse excellent authors] (1553), 2 female poets out of 65—Tullia d'Aragona, with a single sonnet, and Veronica Gambara, with another three—fill just 3 of the collection's 523 pages. Female fortunes do not improve with a more localized treatment: Giolito's *Rime di diversi illustri signori napoletani* [Poems of diverse illustrious Neapolitans] of 1552 includes only Isabella di Morra among its 56 Neapolitan poets, representing just over 6 pages among 414. If we shift compilers, the results do not change. Girolamo Ruscelli's similarly urban-centered *Rime di diversi eccellenti autori bresciani* [Poems of diverse excellent authors of Brescia] of 1554, perhaps because it is dedicated to, and therefore presumably subvened by, the Contessa Virginia Pallavicina Gambara of Brescia, devotes its first 19 pages to her relative Veronica Gambara, but thereafter the only other female presence among the 29 authors is the wraith-like (I say that because she is accorded less than a full poem) Lucia Albana Avogadra. In Ruscelli's larger poetic bouquet, *I fiori delle rime de' poeti illustri, nuovamente raccolti et ordinati* [Flowers of verse of illustrious poets, newly collected and arranged] (1558), 2 of the 38 authors are women—Veronica Gambara and Vittoria Colonna—and they account for just 12 of its 604 pages. Finally, I cite a different sort of anthology from 1555 in Venice: an elaborate example of the collected poetic tributes that are a staple of Italian verse production over many centuries (Bergalli herself contributed to a host of such volumes), including 295 poets writing in four tongues: *Del tempio alla Divina Signora Giovanna d'Aragona, fabricato da tutti i più gentili spiriti, & in tutte le lingue principali del mondo* [The temple to the divine lady Giovanna d'Aragona, created by all the most polite spirits, and in all the principal languages of the world]. Here 6 of the 208 Italian tributes are written by women, but even that small number turns out to constitute the totality, for there are no other women represented among the remaining poems, the 68 in Latin, 12 in Greek, or 7 in Spanish. I think, then, it is fair to conclude that, if Bergalli hoped to find a true estimate of the production of women in the Italian Renaissance, she would have to proceed on her own. It is also fair to conclude that what she took on was no easy task, for it was, in truth, a production largely occluded by her culture in the Renaissance and thereafter.

In anthologizing so many women poets, however, Luisa Bergalli, like her predecessors in the sixteenth century and Gobbi, her near-contemporary, was forced into a radical decontextualization of her sources.[4] The Cinquecento *canzoniere* is an elaborately formal and socialized form of poetic expression, constructed around verse dialogue among friends and fellow intellectual spirits and thus usually not limited only to the voice a volume purports to represent. Even in Domenichi's anthology of women, there occur a number of sonnet exchanges between him and the poets he anthologizes, and he is often careful to place women writing back and forth in proximity within the anthology itself.[5] Here and there in the *Componimenti poetici* one can detect traces of this original intertextuality, particularly with well-connected poets like Tullia d'Aragona (with sonnets addressed to Pietro Bembo and Benedetto Varchi) and Laura Battiferra (represented through a tribute to Lelio Capilupi, as well as poems to prominent Florentine and Roman women), but since there are no annotations beyond the brief bibliographical citations at the end, only the most erudite of readers will understand the interplay of voices thus implied through vocative allusion. Almost three centuries later, for us, such ungrounded referentiality is more than likely to breed confusion and uncertainty of critical focus. What is most particularly lost in this process are the dimensions of the dialogue undertaken by women with each other, which is a subject to which we will revert. In contrast, not only does Bergalli's edition of Gaspara Stampa of a dozen years later restore some of that earlier poetic dialogue—including eleven pages of tributes in prose "Testimonianze" (xxiv–xxxv) and another seven of "Rime di poeti antichi in lode di Gaspara Stampa" [Verses of early poets in praise of Gaspara Stampa] (xxxvi–xlii)—but she stresses there the important poetic collaboration between Stampa and her "most beloved" friend (xviii), Ippolita Mirtilla, and the role of Cassandra Stampa in bringing her sister's works to light. Moreover, following the rendition of Stampa's poetry, Bergalli adds poems by her lover, the count Collaltino di Collalto, his brother Vinciguerra, and her brother Baldassare and then turns to her own contemporaries for a further fifty pages of testimonial verses that at last include twelve of her own sonnets, many of which are written in dialogue with the descendant of Gaspara's lover's line, Antonio Rimbaldo de Collalto.[6] With the editor casting herself, then, as the legitimate inheritor of Gaspara Stampa's poetic legacy, Bergalli's Stampa edition is truly a baroque affair, exfoliating around the poet, her life, family, and friends and involving at last their collective influence on a literary circle of a full two centuries later that Bergalli, like her exemplar Stampa, organizes around herself.

Stampa, it is clear from the anthology, is already the young Bergalli's model woman poet: in *Componimenti poetici* she includes thirty-five of her poems, by far the highest number accorded any of the sixteenth-century women. There are, indeed, only twelve others who merit more than a handful of inclusions, and a list of these offers us an index to Bergalli's sense of literary value. After Stampa with thirty-five poems comes Vittoria Colonna (twenty-six) and Laura Battiferra (twenty-three). In the next set are ranked Veronica Gambara (eighteen), Tullia d'Aragona and Olimpia Malapiera (fourteen each), and Chiara Matraini and Laura Terracina (twelve each). The next smaller group involves Virginia Martini Salvi (eight), Gerolema Castellana (seven), and Lucia Bertani, Leonora Faletta, and Isabella di Morra (each with six). Since there are only 2 poets with five inclusions and another 4 who have four, we come to realize that Bergalli singles out fewer than 20 of 114 poets for any truly multiple treatment. On the one hand, this implies a commitment to absolute breadth, perhaps even a sense that this value must hold a priority in her attempt to restore prominence to women's voices after nearly two centuries of their occlusion. On the other hand, it also testifies to how many of her examples are derived not from single-author texts, even those modeled on a principle of dialogue, but from miscellanies with either a religious or celebratory intent or from sixteenth-century anthologies that may often preserve poems never otherwise published at all but instead circulated in manuscript. There are obviously manuscript sources of this sort yet to be unearthed, as Victoria Kirkham's important discovery of the holograph manuscript of Laura Battiferra's *First Book* of poetry in the Florence Biblioteca Nazionale makes strikingly clear.[7]

Although in the interests of space and inclusiveness, the preponderance of Bergalli's collection is of sonnets, that is of course likewise true of her sources in the Cinquecento, a century that in Italy spawned sonnets with abandon. Yet, there are a sufficiently large number of other forms and metrical styles in the collection to allow a modern reader to surmise that she was by no means bound by the constraints Gobbi observed in 1709, eschewing other forms beyond the sonnet and canzone, as he put it, limiting himself "solamente a quelle, le quali oggidì pajono le più usate" [only those that appear the most used today] (1:[a]5r), thus allowing contemporary standards of taste to dictate his selections from the past. In contrast, Bergalli prints a number of sestinas and other poems of high formal artifice. And it is to one of these that I wish to turn both to illustrate the polished artistry to be discerned in women's verse of the Cinqucento and to represent the editorial standards Bergalli applied to her recovery of women's verse: Laura Terracina's "Non posso più soffrir tanto tormento," originally published in Venice in her *Rime* of 1560.

Non posso piu soffrir tanto tormento,
Tanto dolor, & sparger tanti al uento
Sospiri, e certo in darno mi confido;
E 'ndarno io grido.
Indarno grido, ahi lasso, egli è palese,
Ch'Amor tien l'empie corde a l'arco tese,
Spesso porgendo offese al core, e al petto
In gran dispetto.
In gran sospetto io uiuo, in gran dolore
Ma colpa è stato sol di quel splendore,
Che passò il core, e per gli occhi hebbe uia
Per morte mia.
Per morte mia hebbe egli possanza,
Che schermo non giouò d'antica usanza;
Et con una speranza pur tiene
In uita e in pene.
In uita e in pene; & io fra questi monti,
Hauendo sempre gli occhi al pianto pronti,
Fatto gli ho fonti di perpetua uena,
Ch'ogn'hor è piena.
Ch'ogn'hor è piena, & bench'io pur m'ingegni,
Ch'ella conosca a mille chiari segni,
I miei penssieri degni; ella pur dura
Di me non cura;
Di me non cura questa mia nemica;
E quanto piu la cerco farmi amica,
Piu perdo la fatica, e piu uaneggio;
Hor, che far deggio?
Hor, che far deggio, s'ella uuol ch'io mora;
E con lei congiurato è'l cielo ancora,
Perch'io esca fuora di si trista uita
Altrui gradita.
Altrui gradita, a me certo noiosa,
Quanto esser possa piu spiaceuol cosa.
O' uita dolorosa, ch'io pur uiuo
Di speme priuo.
Di speme priuo mi nutrisco in foco:

E d'altrui, e di me, mi cal si poco,
Ch'io stimo gioco morte; e corro a lei,
Ch'io pur uorrei.
Ch'io pur uorrei, com'ella fugge in fretta
Poter sequirla,'a guisa di saetta.
E far d'amor uendetta, e di me stesso.
Dal duol oppresso.
Dal duol'oppresso ancor ch'io ritruoui
Senza haver cosa, che dilette, o gioui
Con pensier nuoui pur uado reggendo
Il peso horrendo;
Il peso horrendo è certo che mi preme
De la mia uita, giunta a l'hore estreme,
Che spera e teme; & uince ogni languire
Il mio martire.

Bergalli, Venezia, 1726:

Non posso più soffrir tanto tormento,
Tanto dolore, e sparger tanti al vento
Sospiri; e certo indarno mi confido,
E indarno io grido.
Indarno grido, ahi lasso, egli è palese,
Che Amor tien l'empie corde all'arco tese,
Spesso porgendo offese al core, e al petto,
In gran dispetto.
In gran dispetto io vivo, e in gran dolore,
Ma colpa è stato, sol di quel splendore,
Che passò al core, e per gl'occhi ebbe via,
Per morte mia.
Per morte mia, ebbe egli possanza,
Che schermo non giovò d'antica usanza,
E con una speranza pur mi tiene
In vita, e in pene.
In vita in pene, ed io fra questi monti,
Avendo sempre gl'occhi al pianto pronti,
Fatti gli hò fonti di perpetua vena,
Ch'ognor è piena.
Ch'ognor è piena, e benche io pur m'ingegni,
Ch'ella conosca a mille chiari segni
I miei pensieri degni, ella pur dura,

Di me non cura.
Di me non cura questa mia nemica
E quanto più la cerco farmi amica
Più perdo la fatica, e più vaneggio:
Or che far deggio?
Or che far deggio, s'ella vuol, ch'io mora,
E con lei congiurato è il Ciel ancora
Perch'io esca fuora di sì trista vita,
Altrui gradita.
Altrui gradita, a mè, certo noiosa,
Quant esser possa più spiacevol cosa.
O vita dolorosa, ch'io pur vivo,
Di speme privo.
Di speme privo mi nutrisco in foco,
E d'altrui, e di me, mi cal sì poco,
Ch'io stimo gioco morte, e corro a lei,
Ch'io pur vorrei.
Ch'io pur vorrei, com'ella fugge in fretta
Poter sequirla, a guisa di saetta.
E far d'amor vendetta, e di me stesso,
Dal duolo oppresso.
Dal duolo oppresso ancora ch'io ritrovi,
Senza aver cosa, che diletti, o giovi,
Con pensier novi pur vado reggendo
Il peso orrendo.
Il peso orrendo è certo che mi preme
Della mia vita giunta all'ore estreme,
Che spera, e teme, e vince ogni languire
Il mio martire.

[I can no longer suffer so much torment,
So much sorrow, scattering to the winds
So many sighs; surely in vain I look to myself,
And in vain I cry.
In vain I cry, alas, oh, it is clear
That Love has strung his dire bowstrings,
Intending frequent harm to heart and breast,
In great spite.
In great spite I live, and in great sorrow,
But at fault is only that splendor
That through my eyes struck at my heart

To cause my death.
To cause my death it had the power,
As my defenses did not protect me as once,
And with hope still kept me clinging
To life and suffering.
To life and suffering, and I on these mountains
With eyes always ready to weep,
Have made them unquenchable springs,
Ever full.
Ever full, and though yet I strive
To make her know by a thousand clear signs
My worthy thoughts, still she is hard,
Nor cares for me.
Nor cares for me this my enemy;
And however much I seek her friendship
The more I waste the effort, the more rave:
What now should I do?
What now should I do, if she wishes my death,
And heaven has yet conspired with her
To free me from so sad a life,
Pleasing to others.
Pleasing to others, but certainly hateful to me
So much so that nothing is more so,
O sorrowful existence that I continue in,
Devoid of hope.
Devoid of hope I feed on fire,
And of others and of me it matters so little
That I deem death a game and run to her
I so desire her still.
I so desire her still that as she flees in haste
I would follow her in the manner of an arrow
And take vengeance on love and on myself
Driven by grief.
Driven by grief, I find myself still
With nothing to delight or avail me,
With new thoughts I wander still supporting
The oppressive weight.
The oppressive weight surely squeezes
My life from me here in its last hours
So that what hopes, fears, and conquers all retreat
Is my suffering alone.]

This is a poem in a modified sapphic stanza, with quatrains consisting of three hendecayllables followed by a *quinario* (a line of five syllables), in which each short line recurs as the first distich of its successor. The quatrains are thus doubly linked by repetitions (derived from the old Provencal *coblas capfindas*, where the phrase closing a stanza is echoed at the beginning of the next stanza) and, within the reprise, by a *rima al mezzo* (internal rhyme), typical of the popular canzonetta form. Since it is the only such example of this difficult verse form in Bergalli's collection—indeed, only one of two, both by Terracina, I have found in surveying other anthologies and primary texts of the period—we can recognize how thoroughly its virtuoso display expresses its author's gifts as a poet. I cite it, then, as a model text not only for assessing Bergalli's editorial principles but for illustrating the high artistry that often distinguishes what has been an all but lost body of early modern literature. My translation follows Bergalli's text and has been rendered, with a few exceptions, in literal terms so as to emphasize the ways in which the poem deploys its repetitive structure, which is sometimes simply iterative but more often interlaces the repeated phrase of each stanza into a new grammatical unit or syntactic mode, typically transposing the predicate of one sentence into the subject of the next.

An obvious effort has been made by Bergalli to regularize punctuation and ellison in her source, so as to give it an immediate clarity: so, for instance, the removal of the ellision in line 4, even though she might expect that it would be naturally supplied in our reading. Such a modernization of the text is merely cosmetic, but that is not where Bergalli ceased her labors. She recognized what she saw as error in the original printing of line 9—"sospetto" for "dispetto"—and corrected it. Similarly two lines later, line 11, she saw that the early compositor had shifted the preposition "al" ("al core") to an article, "il," distorting the meaning. Both metrics and meaning similarly would appear to sanction her addition of the reflexive pronoun "mi" to line 15 ("E con una speranza pur mi tiene"). In line 19 she alters "fatto" to "fatti," to conform with more modern grammatical usage. Two lines earlier, in line 17, she drops an original conjunction—"In vita e in pene" but adds one in line 9—"In gran dispetto io vivo, e in gran dolore," though it should be noted that neither of these matters in the actual metrical scheme. In sum, if we take Terracina's poem as an epitome of the collection, we can conclude that Bergalli is an astute but not wholly reliable editor and that simply reprinting her collection, as useful—even crucial—as it might seem as a scholarly aim, can be only an interim step to the imperative of recovering and systematically editing the array of the originals from which she drew the *Componimenti poetici*.

Yet, it would not be fair either to her collection or to such a project to rest on such a narrowly pedantic notion. For the reason it is crucial to give this anthology a true currency among scholars of the early modern period is its unique perspective on the development of themes, tropes, mannerisms, and even (if you will) the predicaments among women writers of the Cinquecento, particularly of that astonishing middle decade. As Bergalli's dating indicates, fully forty-eight women, at the very least, can be enumerated as actively engaged in writing verse between 1550 and 1560, and clearly there is no single other primary source as useful as this anthology from which to bring order to such a diversity of voices and the history of that endeavor.[8] I am operating, it should be emphasized, on the hypothesis that Bergalli's anthology is a reasonably accurate representation of that diversity. First, the comparative numbers I noted earlier and the valorization of the earthy Gaspara Stampa suggest that Bergalli has a just sense of worth and is motivated by a youthful and unascetic ardor. Her inclusiveness of a multiplicity of representatives is likewise persuasive, as is the location of her research and publication. For, though the volume possesses the requisite church imprimatur and is even calculatedly dedicated to Cardinal Pietro Ottoboni, the republic of Venice—"La Serenissima" of fame—was in its eighteenth-century decadence a center of Enlightenment thought and relatively free of papal domination. Nowhere in the editorial apparatus is there the least suggestion of the obsequious tone taken by Gobbi when publishing in Bologna, that is, in the Papal States, who defines his abiding rule of selection as avoiding anything contrary to "buon costume . . . o contro le massime della Cristiana Religione troppo arditi" [contrary to good morals or too daring against the principles of the Christian religion] (I:[a8r]) and who asserts an identical paragraph protesting his adherence to Christian morals at the beginning of each of his volumes.

Now, it is obvious that Bergalli is defined in her culture by her youth and her maiden status, and we would therefore expect her to observe a certain propriety. But decorum should not be confused with sanctimoniousness. Surprisingly, only one-third of her authors—and it can be observed that the numbers diminish relatively as the volume moves forward—write within a conventional devotional framework, and even in this circumstance my own sense is that the preponderance of the twelve who pen prayers to the Virgin Mother are writing as much within a feminist as a religious ambience.[9] Even more so is this the case with poems addressed to the Muse, who is by nature a patroness always prepared to listen and to lend support to her female petitioners. On the other hand, beyond these contexts, since the anthology omits the dialogic structure that characterizes so much of the Petrarchan output, it is simply impossible for us from Bergalli's rendition to judge how originary or responsive in terms of tropes and themes are many of the poems we encounter. The ubiquity of Cupid's arrows, for instance, of the kind that Terracina invokes in the poem just cited, is not merely a conventional but is a necessary premise in the discourse of both men and women. On the other hand, when women introduce other presences from classical mythology, there may be subtly woven inner resonances. The many women poets who call on Apollo, we may assume, are speaking in the traditional language of male poets, but those who invoke Flora or especially Venus have shifted the terms of gendered discourse into a territory where men cannot readily follow them. Similarly, we may understand the frequent invocation of rivers to be a euphemism either for noble families who may be identified by property boundaries or particularly—with the Arno and Tebro (Tiber)—for a patriotic celebration of local communities, but we may find ourselves shocked out of these complacencies when women introduce the realities of war and politics, lamenting the fragmentation of Italy or the intrusions of other states, thus identifying themselves with the mother country and claiming to speak for the soul of Italy. Here, for instance, is a second production of Laura Terracina's, which, though on a theme conventional with men, strikingly eschews the decorum proper for a woman.

Veggio il Mondo fallir, veggio lo stolto,
E veggio la virtute in abbandono;
E che le Muse a vil tenute sono,
Talche l'ingegno mio quasi è sepolto.
Veggio in odio, ed invidia tutto volto
Il pensier degl'amici, e in falso tuono,
Veggio tradito il Malvagio dal buono,
E tutto a' nostri danni il Ciel rivolto.
Nessun al ben commun tien fermo segno,
Anzi al suo proprio ogn'un discorre seco,
Mentre hà di varj affetti il petto pregno.
Io veggo, e nel veder tengo odio meco;
Talche vorrei vedere per disdegno
O me senz' occhi, o tutto il Mondo cieco.

[I see the world fail, I see its folly,
And I see virtue abandoned;
And that the Muses are debased
So that my talents are almost buried.
I see that to hatred and envy are turned
My friends' minds, and their manners are false;
I see goodness betrayed into wickedness,

And all heaven turned against us. 8
To the common weal none hold firm,
But rather each is out for his own good,
While his breast teems with desires at odds. 11
I see this, and in doing so hate myself,
So much so that in my shame I wish I could see
Either myself without eyes, or all the world blind.] 14

What the *Componimenti poetici* illustrates with particular intensity, however, are the twin concerns of how women can participate in a dialogue in which they are implicitly cast in an inferior position, unable truly to share or voice large areas of male activity, and how they find a means to open secure arenas that will be acceptable at all levels of their culture. Even the comparatively open Gaspara Stampa, a Venetian courtesan poet, constructs the bulk of her sonnets from a distance, lamenting her separation from her lover when he is sent to France for several years. Though her poems sound an increasingly desperate tone over this period, the count's aristocratic marriage that subsequently ends their relationship is never explicitly mentioned. Thus, Stampa's sonnets are almost exactly modeled on Petrarch's to the inaccessible Laura, but Stampa's powerlessness to affect her situation, let alone control it, is the crucial difference, and, however universally her circumstances may in fact be known to her readers, by the nature of the culture they must be suppressed. It is because of this, perhaps, that Vittoria Colonna created what we might think of as the necrophiliac strategy, creating a sonnet cycle around her enduring love for the dead, why also it became over the subsequent generation, as Bergalli's anthology richly documents, the dominant mode for female Petrarchan poetry. The abiding trope is of the dead husband (lover) as the sun, the light of the woman's life, continuing its dominant role even when removed to circulate in a heavenly realm. Just as the sun/Son pun in the English Renaissance underlines all its devotional and not a little of its secular poetry, so does the pun of Sole (sun) and sole (the only one) in Italian, after Vittoria Colonna centers woman's poetic existence on the inaccessible husband to whom she is married for life. On the surface, this may appear to be radically demeaning, but in turn it opens an interesting avenue for women to move into realms—metaphysical, Neoplatonic—from which by education and practice they might otherwise be excluded and on which it is clear that many of them therefore set their sights. Still, when the price of love for women is not just the difficulty of its consummation—the normative condition of the Petrarchan sonnet—but the very impossibility of its physical manifestation, so dependent a conditional existence must give us pause. Yet again, however, conventions can operate as shields behind which a comparative freedom can be exercised. So, for a woman to set her eyes firmly on heaven at once testifies to her unassailable piety and allows ample space for the imagination to wander at will there. Bergalli preserves a number of sonnets in which it appears impossible to distinguish who is the referent for the "Sole," or particularly the "Signore," being invoked in passionate terms: God, a dead husband, or some other more mundane lord of the affections. So frequently is such a slippage apparent, indeed, that I would suggest that it constitutes an arena whose dimensions need remeasuring in light of a modern and comparative feminist scholarship that is attuned to the ways in which women find a means of skirting the societal restrictions within which they must operate.

A similar rethinking attends the final examples to which I call our attention. The sapphic stanzas of Laura Terracina, composed as a conventional male complaint to the hard-hearted woman he loves, are so formalized that one almost discounts the sorrow that is their burden. Still, however, her last line testifies to "Il mio martire," which can be a euphemism for mental torment or a tortured passion or can signify just plain martyrdom. The lament, of course, is the soul of Petrarchanism, but, as we witness with the sonnet revival in England during the late eighteenth century, when an entire generation of women invests its energies in writing what Charlotte Smith designated as "elegiac sonnets," something else, a shared psychological trauma within the culture or even a submerged rebellion, may be intimated. What, then, are we to make of poems like these two sonnets with which Bergalli concludes the short section given over to the productions of the honored but truly martyred Neapolitan Isabella Morra, who, it appears, was locked away and then murdered by her brothers?

> Ecco, che un altra volta, o valle inferma,
> O fiume alpestre, o rovinati sassi,
> O ignudi spirti di virtute cassi,
> Udrete il pianto, e la mia doglia eterna.
> Ogni monte udirammi, ogni caverna
> Ovunque arresti, ovunque io mova i passi;
> Che fortuna, che mai salda non stassi
> Cresce ognora il mio male, ognor l'eterna.
> Deh mentre, ch'io mi lagno, e giorno, e notte,
> O fere, o sassi, o orride rovine,
> O selve incolte, o solitarie grotte;
> Ulule, e voi del mal nostro indovine,
> Piangete meco, a voci alte interrotte
> Il mio più d'altro miserando fine.[10]

[Lo, yet one more time, o infernal valley,
O mountain streams, o stones fallen from ruins,
O destitute spirits stripped of virtue,
Listen to my cry, my eternal sorrow.
Listen to me, every mountain and cavern,
Wherever I pause or press on,
Since fortune, who never stands firm,
Ever increases my ills, ever makes them eternal.
Alas, while I complain, both day and night,
O savage beasts, o stones, o dreadful ruins,
O forest wildernesses, o solitary grottoes,
Night owls, and you whose cries are omens of evil,
Weep with me, in loud broken cries,
This fate of mine miserable beyond all others.]

Torbido Siri, del mio mal superbo,
Or, ch' io sento da presso il fine amaro;
Fa tu noto il mio duolo, al Padre caro,
Se mai quì il torna il suo destino acerbo.
Digli, come morendo disacerbo
L'aspra fortuna, e lo mio Fato avaro,
E con esempio miserando, e raro
Nome infelice, alle tue Onde serbo.
Tosto, ch' ei giunga alla sassosa riva,
(A che pensar m'adduci, o fiera stella)
Come d'ogni mio ben, son cassa, e priva;
Inqueta l'onde, con crudel procella,
E dì: me accrebber sì, mentre fu viva
Non gl' occhi nò, ma i fiumi d'Isabella.[11]

[Impetuous Siri, indifferent to my ills,
Now that I feel my bitter end is near,
Make known my sorrow to my dear father,
If ever his harsh destiny should return him here.
Tell him that, now dying, I find ease
From my bitter fortune and my stinted fate
And, with my pitiable and rare example,
I confide my sad name to your waves.
As soon as he reaches the rocky shore
(To what thoughts you provoke me, o cruel star,
How bereft I am and deprived of all well being!),

Rouse up your waves, with cruel passion,
And say: "I came to this flood, while she lived,
Not from Isabella's eyes, but her torrents."]

The operatic excess of these verses we could simply charge to the hyperbolic Italian character or a southern taste for emotional display or some other such convenient rubric by which we palliate or dismiss extreme behavior. Yet, if we take them seriously, these sonnets testify to a suicidal despondency, a sort of controlled hysteria, existing in an existential void beyond reason or rational cause. If no man would write in these timbres after two centuries of Petrarchan posturing, what does it say about the condition of a woman who does? Has she, perhaps, decided to take the Sapphic plunge, leaping off the pedestal on which she has been confined all those years, into the muddy waters of the Fiume Siri? Whatever her motivation, as Bergalli's brief biographical entry indicates, not only is Morra not treated as unhinged, a mad poetess under the influence of an undetermined afflatus, but her works are printed in dialogue with other women's.[12] It is clearly a conversation worth listening in on.

Finally, we come to the case of Rosa Levi, a converted Jew, represented in Bergalli's volume by one highly difficult but fascinating sonnet dating from 1571.

Non più desire omai l'alma vi cinga
Di cantar questa fral bellezza nostra,
Che non d'occhi splendor proprio mi mostra,
Ma lingua altrui convien, che vi dipinga.
Lasciate di cantar, che il cor vi stringa,
E se la faccia mia s'imperla, e innostra,
Quali ho le treccie, e gl'occhi; ma la vostra
Musa a maggiore soggetto omai si spinga.
Cantate la Vittoria, che Dio diede
Contro la Tracia invitta, e bellicosa
Ai veri adorator della sua fede.
Cio vi consiglia vergine amorosa;
Che al vostro altero stil più si richiede
D'una palma cantar, che d'una Rosa.[13]

[Let desire no longer besiege your soul
To sing about this frail beauty of ours,
For it reveals to me not my own eye's luster,
But another tongue is needed to portray you.

Leave off singing, no matter that your heart impel you,
Whether my face is empearled or enrouged
What my tresses are like, and my eyes; rather,
Your muse should be directed to a higher theme.
Sing then the Victory, that God,
Against the unconquered and warlike Thracians,
Gave to the true believers in his faith.
This a loving virgin counsels you;
For your lofty style is better suited
To sing of a palm than of a Rose.]

Converted or not, advertising as she does her religious orthodoxy, Levi is by birth as by name an outsider, who writes from the margin and offers a poem that very publicly positions itself against the Petrarchan tradition it so ornately invokes. Leaving aside the religious and political poems in Bergalli's volume, this is the only one she prints that seems directly to question the entire Petrarchan enterprise now two centuries old. I assume that Levi is Venetian and that she would not have been included in Bergalli's volume had she not been converted. Still, her voice testifies to an enduring alterity. We may likewise assume that, if Bergalli could retrieve her writings, other examples of them are preserved somewhere in the archives of her city.

Rosa Levi is but one of the other hundred or so women Bergalli intended never to be lost again. The more than two centuries that separate us from her learned endeavors as an editor make it necessary for a new generation to recover her erudition if we are ever to restore those silenced voices. It will be a daunting task involving many scholars. Yet, it should be undertaken by all of us in a sense of humble partnership with the young woman, yet just an adult, who began this process with such faith in its value in 1726.

✽ ✽ ✽

APPENDIX

Contents of the Bergalli Anthology

Louisa Bergalli, *Componimenti poetici delle più illustri rimatrici d'ogni secolo.* Parte prima, che contiene le Rimatrici Antiche fino all'Anno 1575. Venezia: Antonio Moro, 1726.

Maiden/Married Name | Page Number:Number of Poems | **D** (from Domenichi); **D+** (from Domenichi et al.)

1. Nina Ciciliana (1290) 1:1
2. Ricciarda de' Selvaggi (1308) 2:1
3. Giustina Lievi Parotti (1350) 2:1

4. Ortensia di Guglielmo (1350) 3:2
5. Giovanna Bianchetti (1358) 4:1
6. Leonora de' Conti / della Genca (1360) 4–5:2
7. Santa Caterina da Siena (1377) 5:1
8. Livia del Chiavello (1380) 6:2
9. Lisabetta Trebiani (1397) 7:1
10. Bartolomea da Matugliano (1406) 7–15:1
11. Battista da Monte Feltro / Malatesta (1430) 16–18:2
12. Santa Caterina Vegri (1450) 19–20:1
13. Lucrezia Tornabuoni / De' Medici (1450) 20–25:2
14. La Beata Battista Vorana (1591 [for 1491]) 25–29:2
15. La Beata Catterina / Fieschi Adorni 29:1
16. La Serafina (1500) 33:1
17. Isabella Capece (1500) 33:1
18. Barbara Torella Strozzi (1509) 33:1 **D**
19. Camilla Scarampa (1530) 34–35:4
20. Vittoria Colonna (1525) 36–54:26
21. Margherita di Valois (1530) 54–55:4
22. Veronica Gambera (1530) 56–65:18
23. Cornelia Brunozzi / de Villani (1535) 65:2 **D**
24. Lisabetta da Cepperello (1535) 66–68:2 **D**
25. Giulia Braccalli (1536) 68–69:2 **D**
26. Francesca Baffa (1540) 69–70:3
27. Aurelia Petrucci (1540) 71:1 **D**
28. Clarice Medici (1540) 71:1 **D**
29. Lugrezia di Raimondo (1540) 72:1
30. Maria Martelli / de' Panchiatichi (1540) 72:1 **D**
31. Selvaggia Braccalli (1540) 73:1 **D**
32. Silvia di Somma (1540) 73:1 **D**
33. Costanza d'Avalo (1545) 74–75:4
34. Laudomia Forteguerri (1545) 76:1
35. Liona Aldobrandina (1547) 77:1
36. Gaspara Stampa (1548) 76–100:35
37. Ippolita Mirtilla (1548) 101–3:2
38. Berenice G. (1548) 103–6:1 **D**
39. Gentile Dotta (1548) 107:1 **D**
40. Fiorenza [Piemontese] (1548) 107–8:1 **D**
41. Pia Bichi (1550) 109:1 **D**
42. Virginia Papa (1550) 109:1
43. Tullia D'Aragona (1550) 110–16:14
44. Gerolema Castellana (1550) 117–21:7
45. Maria Spinola (1550) 122–23:4
46. Sylvia Piccolomini (1550) 124:2 **D+**
47. Vittoria Corombana (1550) 125:1
48. Narda Fior (1550) 125–27:2 **D**
49. Cassandra Petrucci (1550) 127–29:5 **D**
50. Ermelma Aringhieri / de' Ceretani (1550) 130:1 **D**
51. Giulia Aragona (1550) 130:1

52. Faustina Vallentina (1550) 131:1
53. Olimpia Caraffa (1550) 131:1
54. Lugrezia Figliucci (1550) 132–33:2 **D+**
55. Maria Langosca (1550) 133:1
56. Ortensia Scarpi (1550) 134:1 **D**
57. Isabella di Morra (1550) 134–40:6
58. Virginia Gemma / de' Zuccheri 140–41:3 **D+**
59. Laura Terracina (1551) 142–51:12
60. Virginia Martini Salvi (1551) 152–61:8
61. Caterina Pellegrina (1552) 161–62:2
62. Atalanta [Sanese] (1554) 162–63:2 **D**
63. Livia Torinella / Boromea (1554) 163–64:3 **D**
64. Alda Torella Lunata (1555) 165:2 **D**
65. Anna Golfarini (1555) 166:1
66. Ersilia Cortese (1555) 166–67:2
67. Chiara Matraini (1555) 167–76:12
68. Isabella Pepoli / De' Riari (1555) 176–77:2
69. Onorata Peci (1556) 177–78:2
70. Gregoria [Gentildonna Romana] (1556) 178:1
71. Incerta (1558) 179:2 **D**
72. Ippolita Gonzaga (1558) 180:1 **D**
73. Claudia Della Rovere (1558) 180–81:2
74. Leonora Faletta (1559) 181–84:6 **D+**
75. Livia Pia Poeti (1559) 184–85:2 **D**
76. Lucia Bertana (1559) 185–88:6 **D+**
77. Maria de' Ferrari (1560) 188:1
78. Laura Serratone (1560) 189:1
79. Laura Battiferra (1560) 189–204:23
80. Egeria Canossa (1560) 204–8:2 **D**
81. Lucia Albana (1560) 208–9:2
82. Candida Gattesca (1560) 209:1 **D**
83. Maddalena Pallavicina (1560) 210:2 **D+**
84. Diamante Dolfi (1560) 211:12:3
85. Francesca B. [Sanese] (1560) 212:1
86. Fausta Tacita (1560) 213–14:2 **D**
87. Bianca Laura da Este (1560) 215:1
88. Olimpia Malapiera (1560) 215–22:14
89. Giulia Premarini (1560) 222:1
90. Fiametta Malaspina / Soderini (1562) 223–27:3
91. Dianora Sanseverina (1562) 227:1
92. Diana N. (1562) 227:1
93. Emilia Brembata (1563) 228:1
94. Incerta (1565) 228–29:2
95. Laudomia da San Gallo (1565) 229:1 **D**
96. Aurelia Roverella (1565) 230:1
97. Cassandra Giovia Magnacavallo (1565) 230:1
98. Cornelia Cotta (1565) 231:1
99. Giulia Cavalcanti (1565) 231:1

100. Leonora Maltaversa 232–34:1
101. Celia Romana (1565) 235:1
102. Laura Gabrielli degli Alciati (1570) 235:1
103. Ortensia Semolina de' Freschi (1570) 236:1
104. Nicoletta Celsa (1570) 236:1
105. Leonora Cibo / de' Vitelli (1570) 237:1
106. Isotta Grembata Grumella (1570) 237–41:2
107. Gianetta Tron (1571) 242:1
108. Rosa Levi (1571) 242:1
109. Ortensia Aliprandi (1571) 243–44:1
110. Beatrice Salvi (1571) 245–46:3
111. Incerta (1573) 246–49:1
112. Andromeda Felice (1575) 249:1
113. Bartolomea Costanza (1575) 249:1
114. Cintia dalla Fratta (1575) 249:1

NOTES

1. For biographical information, the reader may consult the entry on Bergalli by Pamela D. Stewart in Rinaldina Russell, *Italian Women Writers: A Bio-Bibliographical Sourcebook* (Westport, Conn.: Greenwood Press, 1994), 50–57, as well as Luisa Ricaldone's introduction (in Italian) to Bergalli's drama, *Le avventure del poeta* [The poet's adventures] (Rome: Vecchiarelli Editore, 1997).

2. This anthology has been surveyed and contextualized by Marie-Françoise Piéjus, "La première anthologie des poèmes féminines: l'écriture filtrée et orientée," 193–214, in *Le pouvoir et la plume. Incitations, contrôle et repression dans l'Italie du XVI siècle* (Paris: Université de la Sorbonne Nouvelle, 1982). See further the essay in this volume by Deanna Shemek. The exclusion of Terracina is all the more surprising since Domenichi had earlier published her first volume of poems in 1548. During her life Terracina amassed a sizable reputation: she can be read today only in a small edition of her last volume, prefaced with a brief biographical account: see Luigi Montella, *Una poetessa del Rinascimento: Laura Terracina, con le* None Rime *inedite* (Salerno: Episud, 1993). Domenichi likewise excludes two other women poets of considerable renown in his day, Tullia D'Aragona and Chiara Matraini.

3. On the endeavors of this publisher, see Louise George Clubb and William G. Clubb, "Building a Lyric Canon: Gabriel Giolito and the Rival Anthologists, 1545–1590," *Italica* 68, no. 3 (1991): 332–44.

4. For a valuable historical and theoretical meditation on the importance for early modern publication of grounding oneself in an accurate sense of originary context, see Margaret J. M. Ezell, *Writing Women's Literary History* (Baltimore and London: Johns Hopkins University Press, 1993).

5. There are twelve women in Domenichi's anthology writing poems to other women, nine of which are reprinted by Bergalli without the original designation of the addressee. Since much more work needs to be done on the formation of women's writerly communities, I will take the trouble to identify these poems exactly (with pages in the respective anthologies designated by **D** and **B**): (1) Margherita di Valois (Queen of Navarre), "alla Marchesa di Pescara [Vittoria Colonna] ("Felice voi")" (**D**

11, **B** 54); (2) Lugrezia Figliucci, "a Mad. Cassandra Petrucci ('Quella chiara virtu')" (**D** 19, **B** 132)—Petrucci's immediate "risposta" or response ("Quanto delici in Voi sieno i lieti anni") is not included among the poems by her that Bergalli anthologizes; (3) Giulia Braccalli, "a Madona Cornelia Villani ('Veggio coperte sotto un chiaro velo')" (**D** 37, **B** 68); (4) Cornelia Brunozzi de' Villani, "a M. Maria Maria [*sic*] Martelli de' Panciatichi ('Hor si vedra')" (**D** 38, **B** 65), followed by a second poem to the same associate that elicits this ensuing response; (5) Panciatichi, "a M. Cornelia Villani ('Per quelle dolci rime')" (**D** 39, **B** 72), with yet another poem "Cornelia mia" (**D** 40, not in **B**); (6) Selvaggia Braccalli de' Bracciolini, "a M. Maria Martelli de Panciatichi ('Ben ti puoi dir felice')" (**D** 40, **B** 73); (7) Egeria Canossa, "alla Signora Lucia Bertana ('Donna, la cui alma bellezza')" (**D** 50, **B** 206); (8) Ortensia Scarpi, "a Mad. Pia [Bichi] ('Vaga angeletta')" (**D** 76, **B** 134); (9) Virginia Martini di Salvi, "alla Reina di Francia [to the Queen of France] ('Affliti, e mesti intorno')" (**D** 197, **B** 155–56). In addition, there are three other poems written to women in the Domenichi volume that are not reproduced by Bergalli: number 8 in the enumeration is actually a more complicated example, since "Vaga angeletta" is itself the second of two responses to Pia Bichi's "O di lagrime mie fida fontana" (the first is "Da due bei colli una chiara Fontana," **D** 75). Domenichi also reprints Silvia di Somma's "alla S. Lavinia Colonna ('Salda Colonna a Noi')" (**D** 10) and Laodamia Forteguerri's "a Alda Torelli Lunata ('Il maggior don, che Dio, e la Natura / donasse')" (**D** 104).

6. *Rime di Madonna Gaspara Stampa; con alcune altre di Collatino, e di Vinceguerra Conti di Collalto: e di Baldassare Stampa* (Venice: Francesco Piacentini, 1738).

7. For a valuable preliminary exposition of an ongoing resuscitation of Battiferra, see "Laura Battiferra degli Ammannati's *First Book* of Poetry: A Renaissance Holograph Comes out of Hiding," *Rinascimento* 36 (1996): 351–91.

8. The classic essay concentrating on the flowering of women authors during these years is Carlo Dionisotti's "La letteratura italiana nell'età del concilio di Trento," 227–54, in *Geografiia e storia della letteratura italiana* (1967; reprint, Turin: Einaudi, 1999).

9. I had originally thought that the number was thirteen, but comparison with Domenichi's *Rime diverse d'alcune nobilissime et virtuosissime donne* underscores just how tricky can be the ground where the original contexts are removed in Bergalli's reprinting of these poems. Specifically, number 6 in note 5, Selvaggia Bracalli's "a M. Maria Martelli de Panciatichi," a sonnet that ends "Del sesso femminil gloria, ed onore—glory and honor of the feminine sex" and that includes a vocative invocation of "Maria" in line 3, suggests how very easy it would be to transcendentalize a poem that only pays tribute to mundane female friendship. And it is likewise possible that the spur to such poems to the Virgin is less devotional models than the last of Petrarch's *Canzoniere*, "Vergine bella, che di sol vestita—Beautiful virgin, clothed in the sun," which would make them more of a piece with the overwhelmingly Petrarchan cast of the poems Bergalli reprints.

10. Bergalli makes several errors in her representation of the Morra sonnets. Citing the now standard edition by Maria Antonietta Grignani of Isabella Morra's *Rime* (Rome: Salerno Editrice, 2000), I note these substantive corrections: v. 1: "o valle inferna"; v. 2: "o ruinati sassi"; v. 3: "spirti di virtute e cassi"; v. 6: "ovunqu'io arresti"; v. 10: "orride ruine." (Bergalli's substitution of "rovine" for "ruine," and "rovinati" for "ruinati" could testify, like certain of her emendations to Terracina's sapphic, to a desire to make her texts correspond to a modern usage.)

11. Here, too, Bergalli either relies on a corrupt text or is inaccurate in her transcription of the sonnet. Substantive corrections are the following: v. 7: "e, con esempio miserando"; v. 11: "priva!), i.e., the closing parenthesis is at the end of this line, not line 10.

12. This is Bergalli's brief biographical entry: "Isabella di Morra, una delle più colte Rimatrici del buon secolo. Napoli fu sua patria, e le sue Rime vanno impresse con quelle di Veronica Gambara, e di Lucrezia Marinella" (261). [Isabella di Morra, one of the most learned poets of the good century. Naples was her homeland, and her poems were printed with those of Veronica Gambara and Lucrezia Marinella]. A contextualization of her endeavors within those of associated women poets can be found in Isabella Morra, *Canzoniere: A Bilingual Edition*, ed. and trans. Irene Musillo Mitchell (West Lafayette, IN: Bordighera Press, 1998).

13. I have corrected Bergalli's text at two points. She places a question mark at the end of the first quatrain, but I prefer to understand it as a hortatory rather than an interrogative mode. In line 7, context surely dictates emending "traccie" to "treccie."

BIBLIOGRAPHY

Bergalli, Luisa. *Componimenti poetici delle più illustri rimatrici d'ogni secolo*. Venice: Antonia Mora, 1726.

———. *Le avventure del poeta*. Ed. Luisa Ricaldone. Rome: Vecchiarelli Editore, 1997.

———. ed. *Rime di Madonna Gaspara Stampa; con alcune altre di Collatino, e di Vinceguerra Conti di Collalto: e di Baldassare Stampa*. Venice: Francesco Piacentini, 1738.

Clubb, Louise George, and William G. Clubb. "Building a Lyric Canon: Gabriel Giolito and the Rival Anthologists, 1545–1590." *Italica* 68, no. 3 (1991): 332–44.

Dionisotti, Carlo. "La letteratura italiana nell'età del concilio di Trento." In *Geografiia e storia della letteratura italiana*, 227–54. 1967. Reprint, Turin: Einaudi, 1999.

Domenichi, Lodovico, ed. *Rime diverse di molti eccellentissimi auttori nouvamente raccolte*. Venice: Gabriel Giolito, 1545.

———. *Rime diverse d'alcune nobilissime et virtuosissime donne*. Lucca: Vincenzo Busdragho, 1559.

Ezell, Margaret J. M. *Writing Women's Literary History*. Baltimore: Johns Hopkins University Press, 1993.

Giolito, Gabriel, ed. *Rime di diversi illustri signori napoletani*. Venice: Giolito, 1552.

———, ed. *Rime di diversi eccellenti autori*. Venice: Giolito, 1553.

Gobbi, Agostino, ed. *Scelta di Sonetti, e Canzoni de' più eccellenti Rimatori d'ogni Secolo*. 4 vols. in 3. Bologna: Costantino Pisarri, 1709.

Kirkham, Victoria. "Laura Battiferra degli Ammannati's *First Book* of Poetry: A Renaissance Holograph Comes out of Hiding." *Rinascimento* 36 (1996): 351–91.

Montella, Luigi. *Una poetessa del Rinacimento: Laura Terracina, con le* None Rime *inedite*. Salerno: Episud, 1993.

Morra, Isabella. *Canzoniere: A Bilingual Edition*. Ed. and trans. Irene Musillo Mitchell. West Lafayette, IN: Bordighera Press, 1998.

———. *Rime*. Ed. Maria Antonietta Grignani. Rome: Salerno Editrice, 2000.

Piéjus, Marie-Françoise. "La première anthologie des poèmes féminines: l'écriture filtrée et orientée." In *Le pouvoir et la plume. Incitations, contrôle et repression dans l'Italie du XVI siècle*, 193–213. Paris: Université de la Sorbonne Nouvelle, 1982.

Ruscelli, Girolamo. ed. *Rime di diversi eccellenti autori bresciani*. Venice: Plinio Pietrasanta, 1554.

———. *Del tempio alla Divina Signora Giovanna d'Aragona, fabricato da tutti i più gentili spiriti, & in tutte le lingue principali del mondo*. Venice: Plinio Pietrasanta, 1555.

———. *I fiori delle rime de' poeti illustri, nuovamente raccolti et ordinati*. Venice: Plinio Pietrasanta, 1558.

Russell, Rinaldina. *Italian Women Writers: A Bio-Bibliographical Sourcebook*. Westport, Conn.: Greenwood Press, 1994.

Terracina, Laura. *Rime Della S. Laura Terracina*. Venice: Domenico Farri, 1560.

Bad Press

MODERN EDITORS VERSUS EARLY MODERN WOMEN POETS (TULLIA D'ARAGONA, GASPARA STAMPA, VERONICA FRANCO)

Ann Rosalind Jones

In this decade of new editions of the work of early modern women writers, in paperback and on-line, I am going to cast a gloomy look backward at certain processes of decorous reconstruction through which three Italian poets were represented by their late-nineteenth- and early-twentieth-century editors.[1] These male scholars' judgments of what was an acceptable sequence of poems by a woman writer led them to provide early-twentieth-century readers with reordered, censored, and falsely expanded texts by (or, rather, not by) Tullia d'Aragona, Gaspara Stampa, and Veronica Franco. These editors also argued for art-historically dubious portraits of each writer that corresponded to their own definition of the canonizable *poetessa* as an idealized, isolated, and penitential figure, a fantasy female who had almost nothing in common with the women writers under study.

The three editor-critics in question—Enrico Celani, Abdelkader Salza, and Arturo Graf—interest me not because I want to denounce bad old misogynist archivists. On the contrary, all three of these editors were interested enough in a woman poet to help put her back on the map of Italian literary history. Yet the ways in which they did so represent a problematic kind of progress. I will suggest here that the best editions now need to go backward to the most transparent possible reproduction of original editions. More broadly, these histories of textual revision interest me because they reveal the historically gendered assumptions on which the canonization of early modern European women poets has proceeded—the insistent narratives, we may find, that have shaped the treatment of women writing in other times and places as well.

Tullia d'Aragona as Chilly Salome: Enrico Celani, Guido Biagi, and Moretto

Tullia d'Aragona published her *Rime* in Venice in 1547, after living as a courtesan in Rome, Venice, Ferrara, and Siena.[2] Soon after she arrived in Florence in 1546, she was brought before the city magistrates for refusing to observe Cosimo de' Medici's new sumptuary law requiring prostitutes to wear a yellow-bordered veil. But she was exempted from the law because of her reputation as a poet, which had preceded her. Cosimo himself wrote on her petition, "Fasseli grazia come poetessa" [Pardon her, as a woman poet], and a notice in the Florentine state archives explains the basis for this judgment as "la rara scientia di poesia e filosofia" [The rare knowledge of poetry and philosophy] for which she was famous.[3] In what may well be genuine gratitude as well as canny courtship of her new patrons, Tullia celebrates the Medici clan in many of the first poems in her collection.

The full title of her book is *Le Rime della Signora Tullia d'Aragona; et di diversi a lei* [Sonnets by Tullia d'Aragona; and from various men to her], and this is an accurate description of the collection, which includes a majority of poems written to Tullia by men (67 out of 116).[4] The first section contains 38 poems by Tullia, most addressed to a variety of interlocutors; the second section, "Sonetti della Signora Tullia, con le risposte" [Sonnets by Signora Tullia, with replies], contains five pairs of sonnets, each of which begins with a sonnet by Tullia, below which is set a man's sonnet written in response. The third section, "Sonetti di diversi alla Sig. Tullia, con le risposte di lei," contains six pairs of sonnets, each beginning with a man's *proposta,* followed by Tullia's *risposta.* After a long eclogue by Girolamo Muzio, a Roman writer of poems and tales, dedicated to Tullia, "La Tirrhenia," a fifth and final section consists of 55 poems written by men in praise of Tullia. As a whole, the collection has a highly public, conversational quality. Very few of its poems are written in the solitary meditative mode typical of Romantic poetry; rather, its emphasis on multiple authors and, in the central sections of paired sonnets, on sonnets written as dialogues dramatizes Tullia's engagement as a poet with a wide world of courtiers, scholars, and public men.

This autograph-book aspect of poetic collections was typical of the time. When Tullia's 1547 publisher, Giolito de' Ferrari, added titles to each of

Tullia's sonnets, identifying in capital letters the person she addressed, he was following the practice of his fellow editors when they published the poems of male poets such as Benedetto Varchi, whose Florentine publisher, Lorenzo Torrentini, headed each of Varchi's *Rime* (1555) with the capitalized names of the persons to whom they were addressed or who had written poems to him, set *proposte* and *risposte* on the same page, and even began the book with an index of the men and women to whom Varchi addressed his poems. Giolito, Tullia's publisher, followed a similar typographical pattern in his edition of the *Rime* of Girolamo Muzio, entitling each sonnet with the name of the person to whom Muzio wrote it or with the name of each writer whose poem to Muzio he printed. Setting *proposte/risposte* sonnets on the same page, Giolito emphasizes, at one point, the fact that Muzio's response to a sonnet by the marchese del Vasto uses the same rhyme words as the marchese by entitling the sonnet "Una altra risposta per le medesime parole."[5] It was common in such collections to see the poet address international royalty, military heroes, and local nobility as well as fellow poets. To the extent that Varchi and Muzio produce a self-portrait in their *Rime*, it consists as much of records of their relationships to famous public figures as of love poems to a private mistress.

Similarly, many of the names foregrounded in Tullia's *Rime* belong to Cosimo's Spanish relatives and courtiers and to well-known humanists and scholars whom Tullia had met throughout her career (such as Pietro Bembo, who ended up as a cardinal in Rome; Benedetto Varchi, a Florentine poet and tragedian; and Girolamo Muzio). In the two central sections of the collection, Giolito systematically set a poem that Tullia wrote to each man on the same page as the one the man wrote in response, placing the poem written by the initiator of the duet above the poem composed in answer. A typical pairing from this first edition, from the third section, is a compliment to Tullia's eloquence written by the young humanist (and later bishop of Glandeva) Ugolino Martelli, followed by her rejection of his praise. The publisher capitalizes and prints each poet's name above the sonnet and, within each sonnet, capitalizes the name of the poet addressed (line 8 in Martelli, line 13 in Tullia). This parallel uppercasing, like the placement of the second poem in the pair directly under the first on the page, insists on the greeting-response performance they enact and calls attention to Tullia's continuation of Martelli's rhyme scheme throughout her sonnet.

VGOLINO MARTELLI

Se lodando di uoi quel che palese
Di fuor si mostra a le piu strane genti,
Rare bellezze, e disusati accenti,

Degne parole a cio mi son contese;
Com'esser ui potrà larga, e cortese
La lingua a dir, che non tema o pauenti
Di tante ascoste in uoi uirtuti ardenti,
TVLLIA, ch'amor diuino al cor u'accese?
Bontà, senno, ualor, e cortesia
Con l'altre mille insieme in uoi cosparte
Rozamente contar forse potria;
Ma come rara, e eccellente sia
Ciascuna d'esse in uoi con mille carte
Mantoua, e Smirna a dir non basteria.

LA TVLLIA
Ben sono in me d'ogni uirtute accese
Le uoglie tutte, et gli spirti alto intenti,
Ma'l poter, et l'oprar si freddi, et spenti,
Ch'io mi ueggo hauer l'hore indarno spese.
Onde non lodi, no; ma graui offese
Mi son le rime uostre; et però tenti
Vostr'alto stil fra tante, et si eccellenti
Mille di lui cantar piu degne imprese.
Ben puo celar il uer finta bugia:
A qualche tempo, o'n qualche loco, o parte:
Ma non si ch'ei non uinca, e'n sella stia.
Dunque per piu secura, et corta uia
Rivolgete VGOLIN tanta vostra arte,
Ch'in altrui molto, in me poco saria.

(sig. C3, p. 19)

[Martelli
If, to praise what in you clearly appears
Outwardly to people farthest away—
Your rare beauty and unusual rhythms—
Adequate words fail me,
How can my tongue be eloquent and polished enough
Not to feel fear and terror
At so many brilliant virtues revealed in you,
TULLIA, which divine love lit up in your heart?
The kindness, good sense, valor and courtesy
bestowed on you, with a thousand other qualities,
It could, perhaps, clumsily recount;
But to declare how rare and admirable each is

Both Mantua and Smyrna, and a thousand pages
Devoted to you, would not be enough.

Tullia
All my intentions are fired with high ambition
And my spirit is focused on high,
But my skill and composing are so cold and weary
That I see I've spent my time in vain.
So your verses seem not praises, no, but sharp attacks
to me; challenge your high style, then,
Among a thousand greater and finer subjects,
With one more worthy of being sung.
A lying falsehood may well hide the truth,
For a certain time, or in a certain place,
But truth never fails to win and take the saddle again.
Accordingly, to a safer and shorter route,
Redirect, UGOLINO, that great art of yours,
Which can do great things for others, but little for me.]

The positioning of Martelli's poem above Tullia's, as the first of the only two texts on the page, emphasizes the great difference in their tones. His ecstatic praise (moving quickly from her beauty to emphasize her moral goodness and her poetic skill, which he underlines allusively by mentioning Mantua, Virgil's city, and Smyrna, thought by many to be Homer's birthplace) reads as the enthusiasm of a young writer when it is confronted by her melancholy humility. Claiming poetic fatigue, she speaks as a corrector of the younger poet, warning him about the ephemeral quality of false praise and exhorting him to other themes, from a moral high ground. Both poems, in fact, are about poetry—its difficulty, its early practitioners, its proper topics—and the printer's treatment of the two poems invites readers to recognize the technical virtuosity in Tullia's response, allowing us to see how each of her lines rhymes with the corresponding line in Martelli's sonnet. The contrasting characters of the paired writers and their shared facility in rhyme, as demonstrated here, are equally evident in the eleven other pairs of juxtaposed sonnets in the collection.

When Enrico Celani edited Tullia's poems for Romagnoli Dall'Acqua in 1891, he dissolved the organization of the original edition, in which these *proposte/risposte* sonnets were printed in pairs. Celani split Tullia's poems off from the texts of the men to whom she responded or who responded to her by dividing all the poems into two new sections: poems by Tullia and poems to Tullia. This order gives pride of place to Tullia as author-poet, but it obscures her on-the-page engagement with many cooperative humanists throughout Italy. Celani's splitting up of poems originally set in dialogue also obscures the virtuosity with which Tullia and the writers she knew echoed and played off one another's rhyme schemes and conceits.

In addition to suppressing the lively interchange of *carte* (letter-poems) that the readers of Tullia and the poets associated with her saw in the original edition of the *Rime*, republished four times in the same form before the end of the sixteenth century, Celani introduces Tullia as a courtesan who hypocritically concealed her real profession and was redeemed only by the "sincere" poems she wrote as an unrequited lover to the young Piero Manelli.[6] But it was Celani who defined eight sonnets by Tullia as a series written to this one man. In the original edition, only one sonnet, in the section of poems written entirely by Tullia, bears the title "A Piero Manelli," a title reemphasized by her use of "Manel" in her fourth line and "Piero" in her ninth (sig. B1v, p. 9v).[7] And Tullia's poem to Manelli is more about poetry than love: God has given her the same "desio d'onore" (desire for poetic skill and fame, she goes on to specify) as to Manelli, and she, too, hopes to turn her amorous suffering into an enduring reputation: "lasciar del mio nome in terra fama" (line 11) [to leave my name famous on earth]. Nowhere in the sonnet does she suggest that her amorous passion is directed toward Manelli; rather, she insists that her desire to be a successful poet equals his. The following seven poems, in the original edition, are untitled; most do indeed explore the pains of unrequited love, and in one, "Qual vaga Philomena," [Like lovely Philomel],Tullia declares that she now endures a second, unexpected passion. But none of these love sonnets contains the name Manelli, although Tullia's few other untitled poems usually do name their addressee internally. Celani, without any evidence, added the title "Allo Stesso" [To the same man] to all seven of Tullia's poems following the one in which she names Manelli as her addressee, corralling all eight sonnets into a history of Tullia's devotion to one man. To elevate her into a heroine capable of suffering from unrequited love, he himself framed a set of poems to suggest a long-term fixation on a single man.

Yet in his introduction to the *Rime*, Celani judged Tullia in general as typifying the promiscuous "fawning courtiership" [la strisciante cortigianeria] of Renaissance courts and described her as a celebrity-seeking, "cold" Petrarchist, in contrast to the frankly erotic Veronica Franco (xvi, lii–liii). This sort of characterization of Tullia as beautiful but cold was also the basis on which Tullia's earlier biographer, Guido Biagi, claimed in his 1886 book that a painting by the Brescian painter Alessandro Bonvicino, nicknamed Il Moretto, was a portrait of Tullia (fig. 1).[8] This painting presents a slim, regal young woman holding a scepter, coiffed in pearls and dressed in a modest

5. Alessandro Bonvicino (Il Moretto), oil on canvas, *Salome*. Pinacoteca Tosio Martinengo, Brescia. (With permission of the City Museums of Art and History of Brescia.)

high-necked robe, a fur cape, and a striped veil. The Latin inscription carved in the tablet to the lower right identifies her as Salome: "Quae sacru[m] Ioanis caput saltando obtinuit" [she who obtained the sacred head of John by dancing]. Biagi justified his identification of Il Moretto's sitter as Tullia by referring vaguely to a longstanding tradition and also to the fact that when an engraving of the painting was hung in the Academy of Arts in Milan in 1823, a poem displayed with it alluded not to Salome but to Tullia (who claimed to be related to the royal family of Aragon): "The golden scepter shows what was my cradle, / The growing laurels what my talent is."[9]

Biagi dismissed the Latin inscription by claiming that the painting had belonged to a convent and that before the embarrassed nuns sold it to the collector Tosio Martinengo, they had a painter later than Moretto add the marble shelf and the inscription, to give the image a pious meaning. Art historians have firmly rejected this claim, however: Moretto typically included just such marble surfaces for inscriptions in his paintings; there is no underpainting to suggest an earlier version; and Salome as a fantasized Old Testament princess could easily have been represented with a headpiece of pearls and a scepter.[10] In addition, the kind of striped, finely woven shoulder veil this figure wears often appears in Cinquecento painting as a textile signifying the Middle East. Biagi's main motive for this attribution was romantic: he thought the painting corresponded to the praises of Tullia's fine hair and eyes by the male poets included in her *Rime*.[11] But at least he took seriously the likely link between these printed compliments and a visual representation of Tullia's public persona.

In contrast, to the extent that Celani admires the poet he edits, he removes her from the network of mutually profitable social and literary relations recorded in *Le Rime*, through which she and the men whose poems she had collected aimed for shared recognition. He praises Tullia as the lover of Manelli rather than the interlocutor of a range of literary mentors and colleagues; indeed, he deprecates her letter-poems as a symptom of her "mania di passare ai posteriori insieme ai letterati che ella canta" (liii) [fixation on descending to posterity along with the literary men of whom she sings]. For Celani, as for other post-Romantic editors of the nineteenth century, admirable poetry, particularly by a woman, is private and passionate. Hence his creation of Tullia as the long-term lover of Manelli. This attitude not only mistakes the historical specificity of Renaissance writing among the elite, even the discourses of love, which were always linked to public processes of patronage seeking and group identity building in courts, coteries, and academies; Celani also overlooks the particular problem Tullia faced as a woman and a courtesan attempting to represent herself not as a passionate lover of one man but as a socially recognized intellectual and poet. In addition, by focusing his textual analysis exclusively on Tullia's sonnets, Celani downplays the series of texts in ascending genres through which she aspired to canonical status on the model of men's poetic careers: lyric (*Le Rime*), philosophical dialogue (*Dell'Infinità di amore*, also 1547), and epic (*Il Meschino Guerrino*, 1560). In his introduction to the *Rime*, he quotes an earlier critic, Giovanni Crescimbeni, who dismisses Tullia's dialogue as a composition largely inspired by Varchi, and he mocks Tullia's preface to her epic, which she advertises as inspiring and noncorrupting reading for young women, as a risible mask for her own status and a misrepresentation of the poem itself (lvi–lviii).

Celani, then, reworks Tullia's sequence of poems according to an ideology of Romantic individualism. The poet is split off from her worldly connections, praised for poems recording a passionate one-to-one love, and condemned for her calculating search for fame—a search that, in fact, corresponded to the practice of most male intellectuals of the Cinquecento. This privatized representation of the poet engaged in an inaccurately lengthened amorous soliloquy is the only form in which Tulia's poems are readily accessible today. There is no post-Celani edition of *Le Rime* (though Julia Hairston is preparing one for the Other Voice series published by the University of Chicago Press).

Gaspara Stampa Converted and Kidnapped for the Collaltini: Abdelkader Salza, Luisa Bergalli, and Guercino da Canto

Gaspara Stampa's *Rime*, first published by Pietrasanta in Venice in 1554, were edited by Abdelkader Salza for Laterza's Scrittori d'Italia in 1913.[12] Stampa, who grew up in Padua and moved to Venice after the death of her wealthy merchant father in 1531, wrote close to 250 poems on the subject of her three-year love affair with a nobleman of the mainland north of Venice, Collaltino di Collalto, as well as poems to royalty, fellow poets, and female friends.[13] Stampa died suddenly in 1554 at the age of about thirty; the count married a woman of his own rank some years later. Stampa's poems, which she had reworked and revised for three years between 1551, when she broke off with Collaltino, and her death, were gathered together by her sister Cassandra, with the help of Giorgio Benzone, a poet who had edited other books for Pietrasanta.

In this 1554 edition, Stampa's poems (unnumbered) are ordered according to genre, in sections emphasized with illustrated headings: "Rime," "Capitoli," "Madrigali." The "Rime" include four sets of sonnets, most, though not all, on her love for Collalto. These four sets end, respectively, with a canzone, a sestina, a second sestina, and a ballata. Next, she addresses three sonnets to French royalty (one to Henri II of France and two to Catherine de' Medici) and three to fellow poets. These are followed by a canzone in which she praises a recently dead nun and four elegaic sonnets on the same woman. Then follow forty-one sonnets to friends and fellow poets, including one to an "Amica, dolce ed honorata schiera" [a beloved, sweet, and distinguished group], probably the poets and scholars whom Stampa saw at meetings of the Venetian Accademia dei Dubbiosi.[14] Nine religious sonnets follow, in which Stampa prays to be delivered from earthly obsessions; in two sonnets following these she directs her muse to sing of her beloved's spirit and wisdom rather than the beauty of his eyes or face—"Canta tu Musa mia non più questo volto" (151) [You, my Muse, sing no longer of this face]. The *capitoli,* six long poems in terza rima, follow. Five focus on the count, and the sixth laments the illness of her friend, the poet Ippolita Mirtilla. The collection ends with nineteen madrigals, mostly on unrequited love. One result of this arrangement is that *Rime* comes across as a poet's workbook, the history of her use of a variety of lyric forms and of her involvement not only with the inaccessible count but with a range of friends and poet-colleagues, male and female.[15] It is impossible to know whether this organization was the one intended by Gaspara Stampa. But the three years she lived on after the end of her relationship with Collalto and the collaboration between her sister and Benzone (whose appreciative preliminary sonnets emphasize the beauty of her verse as well as her person) make this order seem reasonably trustworthy.

Stampa takes a startlingly un-Petrarchan direction at the end of the fourth set of sonnets: in sixteen poems, she explores her love for a second man, whom she identifies as Bartolomeo Zen, member of a long-standing patrician family in Venice, in the acrostic of Sonnet 111 in the series.[16] In the seventh of her sonnets on this "foco eguale al primo foco" [fire equal to the first fire of love], Stampa makes a witty, even scandalous use of Christian doctrine to convince the new beloved to return her love.[17]

Dove volete voi, ed in qual parte
Voltar speme, e disio che più convenga,
Se volete Signor far cosa degna
Di quell'amor, ch'io vo spiegando in carte?
Forse à Dio? Già da Dio non si diparte
Chi d'Amor segue la felice insegna:
Ei di sua bocca propria pur c'insegna
Ad amar lui e'l prossimo in disparte;

Hor se devete amar non è via meglio
        Amar me, che v'adoro e che ho fatto
        Del vostro vago viso tempio, e speglio?
Dunque amate, e servate amando il patto
        C'ha fatto Cristo; ed amando io vi sveglio
        Che amiate cor, che ad amar voi sia atto.

[Where, to what more fitting place,
        Do you want me to shift my hope and desire,
        My lord, to do what is required
        By this love, which I describe in verse?
To God, perhaps? But whoever loves
        Does not abandon Love's blessed banner:
        God, indeed, from his own mouth, teaches us
        To love Him and our neighbor as well.
So, if you must love, is it not better by far
        To love me, since I adore you and have built
        A temple and a mirror of your lovely face?
Love, then, and fulfill, by loving, the promise
        Christ made with us; and by loving, I awaken you
        To love a heart that will be worthy to love you.]

Elsewhere, Stampa writes more seriously on religious themes, for example, in the canzone in which she praises the pure life of a deceased nun ("Alma celeste, e pura," [Soul, heavenly and pure], lines 22–24), followed by four sonnets presumably to the same nun. Among her nine religious sonnets, the fourth ends with a plea for salvation.

Mesta e pentita de' miei gravi errori,
        E del mio vaneggiar tanto, e si lieve,
        E d'haver speso questo tempo breve,
        De la vita fugace in vani amori,
A te, Signor, ch'intenerisci i cori,
        E rendi calda la gelata neve;
        E fai soave ogn'aspro peso, e greve
        A chiunque accendi di tuoi santi ardori,
Ricorro; e prego, che mi porghi mano
        A trarmi fuor del pelago, onde uscire,
        S'io tentassi da me, sarebbe vano.
Tu volesti per noi Signor morire,

Tu ricomprasti tutto il seme humano;
Dolce Signor non mi lasciar perire.

(148)

[Sad, and repenting my grievous errors,
And my wild wanderings, so many and so vain,
And having spent this brief interval
Of fleeting life in pointless loves,
To you, Lord, who softens hearts,
And warms even frozen snow,
And lightens every heavy burden
For those you enflame with your holy fire,
I turn; and I beg you to hold out your hand
To pull me from these depths, which,
On my own, I would try to escape in vain.
You were willing, Lord, to die for us,
You redeemed the entire human race;
Dear lord, do not let me perish.]

But Stampa shifts her focus to the varieties of poetic convention in the two sonnets that follow this poem, which announce Collalto's intellectual rather than bodily beauty as a new theme. And the following six *capitoli* and the madrigals, which vary from eight to ten lines, leave the reader impressed by the skill with which she manages long and short poetic forms.

Abdelkader Salza, however, editing Stampa for republication in 1913, rearranged her poems radically. The rearrangement was the consequence of his obsessive research over a fifteen-year period to prove that Stampa was not a *virtuosa,* a musical performer (as has been suggested since), but a courtesan corrupted by the loose morals of the Cinquecento.[18] He reordered the 1554 edition in many ways. Most broadly, he set up a new first section, "Rime d'amore," from which he eliminated all poems not clearly linked to Collaltino. He then established a second new section, "Rime varie," which he concluded by putting together thirteen religious poems gathered from throughout the original edition. He opened this gathering of religious poems with a *capitolo* in praise of the monastic life ("Felice in questa et più ne l'altra vita" [Happy in this and in the life to come])—a poem not present in the original edition. In fact, as he acknowledges, this *capitolo* was printed five years after Stampa's death, in a collection of lyrics by various hands published by the Genoese Cristoforo Zabata in 1559. The eighteenth-century dramatist and anthologizer Luisa Bergalli, to whom I will return, first included it in her 1738 edition of Stampa's poems. Salza himself admits that

Zabata's identification of the writer as "la Signora Gaspara Stampa" suggests another, married woman and caused him to doubt the poem's authenticity.[19] In fact, it has a generalizing, moralistic tone quite unlike Stampa's other religious lyrics. But Salza included "Felice in questa et più ne l'altra vita" anyway, giving it the title "Esaltazione dello stato monastico" [Praise for the life of a nun] because of its address to a young nun. Evidently, he added this poem of dubious authorship in order to reinforce the story of Stampa's final conversion. His edition builds up to and concludes with the penitential sonnet "Mesta e pentita de' miei gravi errori," in contrast to the original edition, in which it was followed by Stampa's sonnets promising a new Neoplatonic focus and by the set of amorous madrigals. Moreover, Salza adds an exclamation point to the final line ("Dolce Signor, non mi lasciar perire!"), a revision that creates a note of desperation absent from the original.

Salza justified this reordering as a "più esatta interpretazione psicologica del canzoniere della nostra poetessa" [a more accurate psychological interpretation of the poetic sequence of our poetess] (372). But he defines this "exactness" through a distorting moralistic lens. His reordering is based on an assumption contradicted by the actual ending of Stampa's collection: the fitting and inevitable end of a courtesan's life is that she should reject her past and turn away from the world in which she has sinned and suffered. Stampa's poems to women, including her elegy for a dead nun (the canzone "Alma celeste e pura") and her long epistolary address to the poet Ippolita Mirtilla, are extremely interesting, and the placement in the original edition of the *capitolo* to Ippolita as the last long poem ends this penultimate section on a surprising note of professional regard and intense affection between women. But Salza repositions this poem, setting it before his conversion series. As he orders the *capitoli*, they no longer conclude with Stampa's wish for Ippolita's recovery from fever and for a poem from her, as a female colleague whose *carte* she values as much as or more than those she seeks from men: "le carte tue care e gioconde, / Mirtilla mia . . . / . . . le amiche carte, / de la memoria tua perpetuo segno" [your beloved and merry letters, my Mirtilla, friendly letters, an everlasting memorial to you (166–67, lines 25–26, 38–39)]. Rather, Salza positions the religious *capitolo* and *canzone* before the religious sonnets in a way that suggests that the example of the nun set Stampa on the path leading to the final sonnet in which she appeals to Christ to protect and save her.

Salza also added to his edition thirty-four poems by Stampa's brother Baldassare and set up an appendix composed of eighteen poems by Count Collaltino and his brother Vinciguerra—texts that most critics concur in dismissing as mediocre or worse. These poems had been gathered by Luisa Bergalli and Apostolo Zeno for their 1738 edition of Stampa's poems, assembled and expanded at the request of Collalto's descendant Antonio Rambaldo di Collalto. This edition was the first to change Stampa's order, ending it with "Felice in questa et più ne l'altra vita," the *capitolo* of dubious authorship to the nun. So not only did Salza present Stampa as a spiritual convert rather than the rejuvenated lover of a second man, but he resituated her, following Bergalli and Zeno, in an invented family coterie, among poems composed by several generations of men in the aristocratic clan that would, in fact, have firmly refused her as a public companion to Collaltino.

This Collaltine framing is reinforced by two engravings that open the Rambaldo/Bergalli edition, one of Stampa and one of Count Collaltino (figs. 2 and 3).[20] Collaltino's portrait may well have been engraved from a family painting (it includes a coat of arms and a Latin inscription containing the family motto). But the image of Stampa, though Rambaldo claimed it was engraved from a portrait painted by Guercino da Canto, is purely fanciful: Guercino was born in 1591, almost forty years after Stampa herself died at about thirty, so he couldn't have painted a portrait of her from life.[21] And the conventional, neoclassical features and loose-cut robe given to the poetess in the engraving suggest an eighteenth-century ideal rather than a living sixteenth-century model. Salza's edition as a whole, then, not only reorchestrates Stampa's second love affair as the lead-up to a conversion; it also repeats her absorption into a textual theater choreographed by Collalto, his brother, their artists, her brother, and the eighteenth-century editor who carried out Rambaldo's design.

The unreality of this portrait of Stampa offers a visual analogue to the unreality of the sequence as it was reordered by Salza as editor. And there are two particularly acute ironies in Stampa's case: that the least conventional feature of her *canzoniere,* the turn to another man, was played down by Salza's editing and that the independence she finally claimed from the Collalto clan is effaced by the way she was captured in Rambaldo's family album. Again, as in the case of Tullia, the woman poet is domesticated, captured in a private realm that diminishes her active engagement with contemporary scholars and writers. And she is presented in a way that obscures her departure from the "respectable" pattern of one love followed by a final conversion.

Here, I would argue, we have a canonization of the Mary Magdalene variety. Stampa can be saved, made part of literary history, only if her challenge to the conversion myth—the sexual sinner who turns to Christ—is made to disappear. "She loved much," Salza says of her; so she can be forgiven much.[22] But what if the sequence were left in its original order, centralizing the final drama in which Stampa herself records frankly, even triumphantly, that she loved twice? Would such nonconformity to Catholic female deco-

6. *Portrait of Collatino Collalto*, engraving (1737). (By permission of the Hougton Library, Harvard University.)

7. Supposed *Portrait of Gaspara Stampa*, engraving (1738). (By permission of the Houghton Library, Harvard University.)

rum make her uncanonizable? This imposed repentance exposes another double standard in canon formation: the male poet is expected to have ripened, gained breadth, through a range of experience—emotional, geographical, professional. Even Dante, in *La Vita nuova,* courts a screen lady. But the woman poet who oversteps the one-love, one-apologia model has to be returned to a more acceptable order of things. Petrarch, struggling to turn away from the physical Laura, is admired for the complexity and difficulty of that struggle, incomplete even at the end of *Il Canzoniere*. But Stampa's *canzoniere* as first published was intolerable to her early-twentieth-century editor. And so far his revision of it has prevailed. Both Maria Bellonci's 1976 *Rime* and Stampa's *Selected Poems*, edited by Laura Stortoni in 1994, repeat Salza's order.[23]

Veronica Franco as the Savior of Courtesans: Arturo Graf, Abdelkader Salza, and Benedetto Caliari

Abdelkader Salza also edited Veronica Franco's *Terze Rime* for Laterza, this time without altering the order of the poems.[24] So we read her twenty-five *capitoli* in the order they were first published in Venice in 1575, beginning with a set of highly erotic poems from and to Venetian men she had known as a courtesan and ending with a long pastoral poem celebrating Marcantonio della Torre's country villa as the summit of sensual and intellectual pleasures. But when it came to the end of Franco's life, Salza wanted a narrative like the one he constructed for Stampa, so he constructed a new conclusion for the sequence. Using the discovery by an earlier Venetian scholar, Emmanuele Cicogna, of an anonymous penitential sonnet in a miscellany in the Biblioteca dei Serviti to prove Franco's change of heart as she approached death, he set this poem next to last among fifteen sonnets verifiably written by Franco.[25] He added to the sonnet the title "Elevazione e conversione" [Uplift and Conversion].

> Ite, pensier fallaci e vana spene,
> ciechi ingordi desir, acerbe voglie;
> ite, sospir ardenti, amare doglie,
> compagni sempre alle mie eterne pene.
> Ite, memorie dolci, aspre catene
> al cor, che alfin da voi pur si discioglie,
> e'l fren de la ragion tutto raccoglie,
> smarrito un tempo, e in libertà pur viene.
> E tu, pura alma, in tanti affanni involta,
> slègati omai, e al tuo Signor divino

leggiadramente i tuoi pensier rivolta:
sforza animosamente il tuo destino,
e i lacci rompi e poi leggiadra e sciolta,
drizza i tuoi passi a più sicur cammino.[26]

[Go, lying thoughts and empty hope,
blind, greedy desires, bitter longing;
go, burning sighs and biting grief,
constant companions to my endless pain.
Go, sweet memories, heavy chains
on my heart, so that it may finally escape you,
gather up again wholly the reins of reason,
lost for a time, and come at last to freedom.
And you, pure soul, trapped in such agonies,
free yourself henceforth, and to your heavenly Lord
joyfully turn your thoughts again.
With a brave spirit master your fate,
break your bonds, and then, light and free,
step upward to a safer path.]

In attributing this sonnet to Franco, Salza was following the outlines of Arturo Graf's 1888 biography of Franco, "Una Cortigiana fra mille," in which Graf imagines Franco's last days as a pure performance of the conventional conversion ritual. Graf writes:

> Franco's loss of health . . . in 1580 must have disposed and attracted her to the conversion with which, like Tullia d'Aragona and many other famous courtesans, she ended her career, intensifying her religious feeling and her fatigue and disgust with the courtesan's life. . . . Reconciled with God, forgotten perhaps by her former friends, but blessed by the misfortunes which had shown her the road to salvation and opened up an asylum of pardon and peace, poor Veronica died still in the bloom of youth.[27]

This conjectural conversion narrative is as misleading as Salza's addition of the conversion sonnet to Franco's *Rime*. Graf himself was following earlier biographers' claims, based on a 1577 letter addressed to the Venetian senate in which Franco proposed that she be put in charge of a *casa di soccorso* [shelter for ex-prostitutes];[28] Graf claimed that she both founded and spent her final days in such a shelter. Benedetto Croce, however, in the course of research for his 1949 edition of Franco's letters, recognized that the sonnet "Ite, pensier fallaci" was in fact written by Veronica Gambara, a noblewoman of Correggio.[29] He also pointed out that when such a *casa di soccorso* was begun in 1580, Franco was on the point of publishing her *Letters*, which show no signs whatsoever of a repentant end to her career as courtesan or writer.[30] And Margaret Rosenthal has since pointed out that Franco's letter exists only as a draft; there is no evidence that it was ever sent to the senate. What's more, Franco in fact died in the Venetian palazzo of Andrea Tron, the father of her sons, not in the house of convertites in which Salza imagined her writing "Ite, pensier fallaci."[31]

The mentality revealed in Graf and Salza's edifying version of Franco's end also had a visual outcome. Both accepted the identification by Cicogna (the discoverer of the penitential sonnet Salza added to Franco's sequence) of a figure in an altarpiece painted for the Casa di Soccorso as Franco.[32] In the church begun for the Casa in 1593, Benedetto Caliari, the brother of Paolo Caliari (Veronese), painted a middle-aged woman soberly dressed in black; this figure intercedes with Mary Magdalene and the Virgin Mary on behalf of two courtesans kneeling behind her (fig. 4). Commenting on this painting in the 1830s, Cicogna identified the figure in black as Franco herself, painted from life in her duty as director of the Casa of leading other courtesans to salvation.[33] This identification, too, is false. Caliari painted the altarpiece sometime during the building of the church, from 1593 to 1609, but Franco had died in 1591. Equally important, the city fathers of Venice would never have appointed her or any other courtesan as director of the Casa; this sort of position was reserved for Venetian noblewomen of impeccable reputation. The woman in black has since been identified as Laura Caravella, the patrician wife appointed as first prioress of the Casa.[34] But to Cicogna and Graf, the image of the repentant prostitute, chastely clothed and interceding with the Virgin via Mary Magdalene, made sense. To them, an unrepentant whore would have been unthinkable in such a painting and in such a life story. Hence their eagerness to interpret any text or image as evidence for Franco's turn to a religious life.

Croce's colleague Angiolo Tursi finally found a clearly identified portrait of Franco in the Biblioteca Marciana, on an engraved title page designed for her 1575 *Rime* (fig. 5).[35] Here Franco is stylishly coiffed and dressed, but in a much less spectacular way than courtesans in contemporary prints, who were famous for their high lace collars, ropes of pearls, high double-peaked hairdos, and bare breasts. Franco wears a very pared-down version of the courtesans' two-pointed coiffure and a small standing collar, and a partlet (shoulder veil) covers her corsage (as one does in Bronzino's portrait of Laura

8. Benedetto Caliari, oil on canvas, *The Founding of the Casa del Soccorso* (ca. 1597). Gallerie dell'Accademia, Venice. (Reproduced by permission of the Minister per i Beni Culturali e Ambientali, Venice/Italy.)

Battiferri). The inscription gives Franco's age as twenty-three, but she was actually thirty when her poems were published. Croce conjectures that this discrepancy explains why the title page was not used.

In any case, these two incompatible portraits of Franco—the austere mother superior backed by gloriously dressed, if repentant, temptresses versus the quietly modish, serious courtesan as author—sum up the problem of canonization I have been discussing. Nineteenth- and early-twentieth-century editors of Italian women poets have wanted the same drama, according to which the heroine turns from the whore to the saint, and when they have not found this conventional plot, they have invented it. But conversion stories have not been required of men writing during the Cinquecento (think of

9. *Portrait of Veronica Franco,* engraved frontispiece (ca. 1575). (Reproduced by permission of the Ministero per i Beni e le Attività Culturali; Biblioteca Nazionale Marciana.)

the legend of Aretino, dying of laughter after a night of drinking and joking with his neighbors).[36] To the extent that a woman poet's self-representation in words dramatizes her ambitious, successful, and ongoing connection with powerful men rather than her stricken withdrawal from social and sexual contacts, the story has had to be reworked: reordered, fictitiously expanded, "chastened," to use Stephanie Jed's term, in whatever way possible.[37] Recent history in Franco's case is brighter, however, and points the way toward better editions of Tullia d'Aragona and Gaspara Stampa: Stefano Bianchi's 1995 *Rime* omits Salza's Sonetto 15 and is admirable in other ways as well.[38]

Conclusion: How Not to Canonize a Woman Poet

Joanna Russ, in her 1983 book *How to Suppress Women's Writing,* lists a variety of ways in which women's texts, if women manage to produce them at all in the face of the great cultural odds confronting them, have been discredited once they are published. Although Russ concentrates on texts by women in the nineteenth and twentieth centuries, she identifies several assumptions equally operative in critical responses to early modern women writers: denial of agency (she didn't really write it, a man did); pollution of agency (she did write it, but she shouldn't have); demeaning categorization (she did write it, so it's trivial); and isolation (she did write it, but she never wrote anything else).[39]

But I have been analyzing an even more radical procedure: the editorial *revision* of Renaissance women's texts. One of Russ's categories for the dismissal of women writers, to repeat, is "pollution of agency." If the critic cannot deny a woman's authorship, he decries it: yes, she wrote it, but she shouldn't have. I have been analyzing, rather, "purification of agency." One way to deny what a woman wrote is to transform it to fit a definition of acceptable feminine authorship—for example, Romantic isolation followed by expiatory repentance.

But what happens when this powerful legend is sought—or created—with such regularity in the work of early modern women poets? Originality, in the Renaissance sense of intelligent reworking of previous and contemporary models, is invoked to justify the canonization of male writers, but it becomes invisible in women's texts to the extent that their writings are treated as spontaneous, unworldly confessions of the turn to a conventional path, be it amorous or spiritual. The double standard whereby men are appreciated as rebels against convention while women are judged according to their conformity to sexual norms produces a focus on decency in the private realm that leads critics to overlook more complex patterns in women's engagement with the lyric discourses of their time and the appeal for public recognition in their lyric—and also to downplay women's work in genres other than love poetry, thereby excluding them from the map of poetic progress according to which male writers have been canonized.

So what is an ideal edition? I have defined it negatively: one that preserves the sequence of the original publication, one that preserves the poet's engagement in the social world recorded in her addressees and *risposte*, one that ends as the first edition ended. Let modern editors allow the same construction of a public persona, risky convention breaking, and unresolved conclusions to women poets as to men. A few years ago, I asked Elizabeth Hageman, who had been working on a new edition of Katherine Philips, whether her research had changed her impression of Philips. "Oh, yes," she said. "I've realized what a public person she was, how many people she was in contact with throughout her life." Not one lover and then God, but a range of acquaintances, collaborators, friends, lovers, and enemies. Now that is an edition I look forward to reading!

✻ ✻ ✻

NOTES

Unless otherwise stated, all translations in this essay are mine.

1. For a detailed study of the ideological bases on which nineteenth-century editors judged, selected, and printed the love poetry of a range of sixteenth-century poets, see Amedeo Quondam, *Petrarchismo mediato: Per una critica della forma "antologia"* (Rome: Bulzoni, 1974).

2. For Tullia's biography, see Guido Biagi, *Tullia d'Aragona: Un etèra romana* (Florence: Roberto Paggi, 1897). First published as "Un Etèra romana: Tullia d'Aragona," *Nuova antologia di scienze, lettere ed arti*, 3d ser., 4, no. 6 (August 16, 1886): 655–711. A more recent, popular account is Georgina Masson, *Courtesans of the Italian Renaissance* (New York: St. Martin's Press, 1975), chap. 5. In an excellent recent article, Julia L. Hairston identifies four of Tullia's addressees, and, citing Victoria Kirkham, uses the term "choral anthology" to identify the genre of Tullia's collection. See "Out of the Archive: Four Newly-Identified Figures in Tullia d'Aragona's *Rime della Signora Tullia di Aragona et di diversi a lei* (1547)," *Modern Language Notes* 118 (2003): 257–60.

3. For Cosimo's response and the archival record, see Salvatore Bongi, "Il velo giallo di Tullia d'Aragona," *Rivista critica della letteratura italiana* 3.3 (March 1886): 85–95. Translations are mine. See also Masson, *Courtesans*, 119–20.

4. Tullia d'Aragona, *Le Rime della Signora Tullia di Aragona; et di diversi a lei* (Venice: Gabriel Giolito de' Ferrari, 1547). All quotations are from this edition unless otherwise noted. All translations are mine.

5. Girolamo Mutio, *Rime* (Venice: Giolito de' Ferrari, 1551), 58. Muzio is the modern spelling of the author's name. Giolito follows the same procedure in the *Rime* of Bernardo Tasso (Venice: Giolito de' Ferrari, 1560), capitalizing titles such as "A Tiziano Pittore" and first names within sonnets. This socially inclusive pattern contrasts with the earlier *Rime* of Pietro Bembo (Venice: Giovanni Antonio and Fratelli

da Sabbio, 1530–31), a model in many ways for these later poets but whose lyrics are addressed almost exclusively to his beloved lady, with an index to first lines rather than the names of addressees.

6. Enrico Celani, ed., Studio in *Le Rime di Tullia d'Aragona, cortigiana del secolo XVI* (1891; reprint, Bologna: Commissione per i testi di lingua, 1968), xvi, liii.

7. For a new translation of this sonnet and of "Qual vaga Philomena," see Elizabeth Pallitto, "A Selection of Poems of Tullia d'Aragona," *Forum Italicum* 36 (spring 2002): 179–89.

8. Alessandro Bonvicino [Il Moretto], *Salome*, Pinacoteca Tosio Martinengo, Brescia. For a good color reproduction of the painting, see Pier Virgilio Begni Redona, *Alessandro Bonvicino, Il Moretto* (Brescia: La Scuola, 1988), 355.

9. Biagi, *Tullia d'Aragona*, 3–5.

10. Redona summarizes arguments against Biagi's claim that the *Salome* painting is a portrait of Tullia in *Il Moretto*, 354–56.

11. Biagi, *Tullia d'Aragona*, 5.

12. Gaspara Stampa, *Rime*, in Gaspara Stampa and Veronica Franco, *Rime*, ed. Abdelkader Salza, Scrittori d'Italia 52 (Bari: Laterza, 1913).

13. For a biography and thoughtful study of Stampa in English, see Fiora Bassanese, *Gaspara Stampa* (Boston: G. K. Hall, 1982).

14. On Stampa's membership in the Accademia dei Dubbiosi, see Elisa Innocente Greggio, "In difesa di Gaspara Stampa," *L'Ateneo Veneto* 38, nos. 1–2 (1915): 28–31.

15. For a strong argument that the original arrangement of the poems themselves and the wording of Cassandra Stampa's dedication emphasize Stampa's writing as poetic composition rather than spontaneous outpouring of emotion, see Bassanese, *Gaspara Stampa*, 37–44.

16. Gaspara Stampa, *Le Rime di Madonna Gaspara Stampa*, ed. Cassandra Stampa and Giorgio Benzone (Venice: Plinio Pietrasanta, 1554), 113. All quotations are from this edition unless otherwise noted. All translations are mine.

17. Ibid., 110. For discussion of the "distorted evangelism" of this and other sonnets to Zen, see Bassanese, *Gaspara Stampa*, 119–20.

18. Salza published his arguments for Stampa as a courtesan in two installments: "Madonna Gasparina Stampa secondo nuove indagini," *Giornale storico della letteratura italiana* 62 (1913): 1–101, and "Madonna Gasparina Stampa e la società veneziana del suo tempo," *Giornale storico della letteratura italiana* 70 (1917): 1–60, 281–99. The argument that Stampa was a musical performer was first made by Gioachino Brognoligo in "Gaspara Stampa," *Giornale storico della letteratura italiana* 76 (1920): 134–45.

19. Abdelkader Salza, ed., Nota to *Rime* by Gaspara Stampa and Veronica Franco, Scrittori d'Italia 52 (Bari: Laterza, 1913), 371–72.

20. Engravings of Gaspara Stampa and Collaltino di Collalto, preceding the title page of *Rime di Madonna Gaspara Stampa con alcune altre di Collaltino e di Vinciguerra conti di Collalto, e di Baldassare Stampa*, ed. Luisa Bergalli and Apostolo Zeno (Venice: Piacentini, 1738).

21. For a discussion of the engravings, including Guercino's dates, see Maria Bellonci's introduction to her edition of *Le Rime di Gaspara Stampa* (Milan: Rizzoli, 1976), 64–65.

22. Salza writes: "l'eterna storia d'amore trova in [il suo canzoniere], per opera di una donna che molto amò e dell'amore godette senza misura tutti i gaudi . . . un'espressione. . . . E la poesia riabilita agli occhi nostri madonna Gasparina dai molti

amori." [The eternal story of love is expressed in her *canzoniere*, through the work of a woman who loved greatly and enjoyed the pleasures of love without restraint. . . . And (her) poetry excuses, in our eyes, little madonna Gaspara for her many loves.] (Nota to *Rime*, 366).

23. For Bellonci, see note 21; Laura Stortoni, ed. *Selected Poems/Gaspara Stampa*, trans. Laura Stortoni and Mary Prentice Lillie (New York: Italica Press, 1994).

24. Veronica Franco, *Rime*, in Gaspara Stampa and Veronica Franco, *Rime*, ed. Abdelkader Salza, Scrittori d'Italia 52 (Bari: Laterza, 1913). All quotations are from this edition unless otherwise noted. All translations are mine.

25. Salza cites Emmanuele Cicogna, editor of a series of volumes of Venetian writings, as his source for the sonnet in his Nota in *Rime*, 385.

26. Franco, *Rime*, ed. Salza, 360.

27. Arturo Graf, "Una Cortigiana fra mille: Veronica Franco," in *Attraverso il Cinquecento* (Rome: Loescher, 1888), 276 (my translation).

28. One of Graf's sources for this argument was Bartolomeo Gamba, in his *Alcuni ritratti di dame illustrati delle provincie venetiane* (Venice: Alvisopoli, 1826).

29. Benedetto Croce, Proemio to *Le Lettere* by Veronica Franco (Naples, Ricciardi, 1949), xxx.

30. Croce, Appendice to *Le Lettere* by Veronica Franco, 76.

31. Margaret F. Rosenthal, *The Honest Courtesan: Veronica Franco, Citizen and Writer in Sixteenth-Century Venice* (Chicago: University of Chicago Press, 1992), 131, 315–16 nn. 43 and 44.

32. This painting is reproduced, in black and white, in the exhibition catalogue *Le Cortigiane di Venezia dal Trecento al Settecento*, Casinò di Venezia (Milan: Berenice, 1990), 181.

33. Cited in Salza, ed., Nota in *Rime* by Veronica Franco.

34. For the identification of Caravella and a summary of recent art historians' debunking of the identification of Franco in this painting, see Entry 119, "Benedetto Caliari, 'L'istituzione del Soccorso,'" in *Cortigiane di Venezia*, 180, and the essay by Giuseppe Ellero, "I Luoghi della redenzione," in the same volume, 60.

35. For the history of Tursi's discovery and a reproduction of the title-page engraving, see Croce, "Sulla Iconografia di Veronica Franco," Appendix in *Le Lettere* by Veronica Franco, 75–76.

36. For an account of this nonmoralized end of a man's life, see Thomas Caldecot Chubb, *Aretino, Scourge of Princes* (New York: Reynal and Hitchcock, 1940), 448. On Petrarch and later editorial attempts to "chasten" his *Canzoniere*, see Teodolinda Barolini, "The Making of a Lyric Sequence: Time and Narrative in Petrarch's *Rerum vulgarum fragmenta*," *Modern Language Notes* 104.1 (1989): 1–38. But no interpreter of Petrarch rearranged or revised his poems to the extent that the editors I discuss here transformed the sequences of women poets.

37. I refer here to Stephanie Jed's analysis of how female figures such as the Roman Lucretia were used to reinforce masculine authority in the public sphere, in *Chaste Thinking: The Rape of Lucretia and the Birth of Humanism* (Bloomington: Indiana University Press, 1983).

38. Stefano Bianchi, ed., *Le Rime di Veronica Franco* (Florence: Mursia, 1995).

39. Joanna Russ, *How to Suppress Women's Writing* (Austin: University of Texas Press, 1983), chap. 4.

BIBLIOGRAPHY

Aragona, Tullia d'. *Le Rime della Signora Tullia d'Aragona; et di diversi a lei.* Venice: Gabriel Giolito de' Ferrari, 1547.

Barolini, Teodolinda. "The Making of a Lyric Sequence: Time and Narrative in Petrarch's *Rerum vulgarum fragmenta.*" *Modern Language Notes* 104.1 (1989): 1–38.

Bassanese, Fiora. *Gaspara Stampa.* Boston: G. K. Hall, 1982.

Bellonci, Maria, ed. *Rime di Gaspara Stampa.* Milan: Rizzoli, 1976.

Bembo, Pietro. *Rime.* Venice: Giovanni Antonio and Fratelli da Sabbio, 1530–31.

Bergalli, Luisa, and Apostolo Zeno, eds. *Rime di Madonna Gaspara Stampa con alcune altre di Collaltino e di Vinciguerra conti di Collalto, e di Baldassare Stampa.* Venice: Piacentini, 1738.

Biagi, Guido. *Tullia d'Aragona: Un etèra romana.* Florence: Roberto Paggi, 1897. First published as "Un Etèra romana: Tullia d'Aragona," *Nuova antologia di scienze, lettere ed arti,* 3d ser., 4, no. 6 (August 16, 1886): 655–711.

Bianchi, Stefano, ed. *Le Rime di Veronica Franco.* Florence: Mursia, 1995.

Bongi, Salvatore. "Il velo giallo di Tullia d'Aragona." *Rivista critica della letteratura italiana* 3 (March 1886): 85–95.

Brognoligo, Gioachino. "Gaspara Stampa." *Giornale storico della letteratura italiana* 76 (1920): 134–45.

Celani, Enrico, ed. *Le Rime di Tullia d'Aragona, cortigiana del secolo XVI.* 1891. Reprint, Bologna: Commissione per i testi di lingua, 1968.

Chubb, Thomas Caldecot. *Aretino, Scourge of Princes.* New York: Reynal and Hitchcock, 1940.

Le Cortigiane di Venezia dal Trecento al Settecento. Exhibit catalogue, Casinò di Venezia. Milan: Berenice, 1990.

Croce, Benedetto ed. *Veronica Franco: Le Lettere.* Naples: Ricciardi, 1949.

Ellero, Giuseppe. "I Luoghi della redenzione." In *Le Cortigiane di Venezia dal Trecento al Settecento,* 178–82. Milan: Berenice, 1990.

Franco, Veronica. *Terze Rime.* Venice: n.p., 1575.

Gamba, Bartolomeo. *Alcuni ritratti di dame illustrati delle provincie venetiane.* Venice: Alvisopoli, 1826.

Graf, Arturo. "Una Cortigiana fra mille: Veronica Franco." In *Attraverso il Cinquecento.* Rome: Loescher, 1888.

Greggio, Elisa Innocente. "In difesa di Gaspara Stampa." *L'Ateneo Veneto* 38, nos. 1–2 (1915): 28–31.

Hairston, Julia L. "Out of the Archive: Four Newly-Identified Figures in Tullia d' Aragona's *Rime della Signora Tullia di Aragona et di diversi a lei* (1547)." *Modern Language Notes* 118 (2003): 257–60.

Jed, Stephanie. *Chaste Thinking: The Rape of Lucretia and the Birth of Humanism.* Bloomington: Indiana University Press, 1983.

Masson, Georgina. *Courtesans of the Italian Renaissance.* New York: St. Martin's Press, 1975.

Mutio, Girolamo. *Rime.* Venice: Giolito de' Ferrari, 1551.

Pallitto, Elizabeth, trans. "A Selection of Poems of Tullia d'Aragona." *Forum Italicum* 36, no. 1 (spring 2002): 179–89.

Quondam, Amedeo. *Petrarchismo mediato: Per una critica della forma "antologia."* Rome: Bulzoni, 1974.

Redona, Pier Virgilio Begni. *Alessandro Bonvicino, Il Moretto*. Brescia: La Scuola, 1988.
Rosenthal, Margaret F. *The Honest Courtesan: Veronica Franco, Citizen and Writer in Sixteenth-Century Venice*. Chicago: University of Chicago Press, 1992.
Russ, Joanna. *How to Suppress Women's Writing*. Austin: University of Texas Press, 1983.
Salza, Abdelkader. "Madonna Gasparina Stampa secondo nuove indagini." *Giornale storico della letteratura italiana* 62 (1913): 1–101.
———. "Madonna Gasparina Stampa e la società veneziana del suo tempo." *Giornale storico della letteratura italiana* 70 (1917): 1–60, 281–99.
———, ed. *Rime*, by Gaspara Stampa and Veronica Franco. Scrittori d'Italia 52. Bari: Laterza, 1913.
Stampa, Gaspara. *Le Rime di Madonna Gaspara Stampa*. Ed. Cassandra Stampa and Giorgio Benzone. Venice: Plinio Pietrasanta, 1554.
Stortoni, Laura, ed. *Selected Poems/Gaspara Stampa*. Trans. Laura Stortoni and Mary Prentice Lillie. New York: Italica Press, 1994.
Tasso, Bernardo. *Rime*. Venice: Giolito de' Ferrari, 1560.

Fascist Appropriations

THE CASE OF JOLANDA DE BLASI'S *LE SCRITTRICI ITALIANE*

Lina Insana

With the publication of her *Le scrittrici italiane dalle origini al 1800* in 1930, Jolanda De Blasi broke new ground in the field of Italian women's writing and its criticism: her two volumes (a literary history and an anthology with bibliographic and editorial information) represented the most comprehensive collection and criticism of women's writing in Italy to date. This was an accomplishment of which she was clearly aware. Outlining in her preface the form and structure of her critical and anthological work, De Blasi herself states that her "anthology . . . is completely new in its fullness, variety and scope of inquiry. An exhaustive document that one could subtract from or add to marginally, without increasing or decreasing the value of its conclusions."[1]

Propagandistic tone aside, De Blasi had truly tapped into an underexplored sector of Italian literary production. Prior to her *Scrittrici italiane*, the majority of critical and anthological projects focusing on women writers consisted of monographs (mostly devoted to the best-known and prolific women writers, such as Vittoria Colonna, Gaspara Stampa, and Veronica Gambara), genre- and epoch-specific works (such as those concentrating exclusively on the *poetesse* of the 1500s), and studies that sought to place women in their specific geopolitical or sociohistorical contexts (such as those that grouped women writers according to their origins in the Veneto).

Despite De Blasi's claims regarding her work's exhaustive nature, she also seems to have been inspired by another kind of lack in prior scholarship, judging from her complaints not only of its inferior quantitative breadth but of its weak critical quality. As she declares in the very first sentence of her preface,

> [a] literary history of Italian women does not exist, or else they [the existing histories] are chivalrous digressions by courteous scholars who have brought a flower and a smile from the field, paying eternal homage—even here—to the eternal feminine. . . . [These] short accounts in general literary histories, and monographs devoted to those few female writers on whom tradition has focused . . . are inadequate tools for arriving at an accurate and exact conception [of the field]: the former are too superficial, inexact, and incomplete, while the latter are biased both in terms of their selection and in terms of their passion.[2]

De Blasi's interest in literary and cultural issues was by no means limited to the publication of *Le scrittrici italiane* and its accompanying anthology. The archives of the Vieusseux literary circle of Florence show that the "writer Jolanda De Blasi" joined that group in 1903;[3] furthermore, De Blasi's studies at the Istituto di Studi Superiori di Firenze brought her into close contact with many of the leading cultural figures of her day.[4] As her impressive list of publications shows (see appendix), De Blasi maintained an active research agenda well into the 1950s, writing books on the Jubilee, St. Peter's Basilica in Rome, and Italian saints as well as publishing her own translations of the *Iliad* and the *Odyssey*. But De Blasi's most prolific and well-documented work was done under the auspices of the Lyceum Club di Firenze, a women's cultural organization founded in 1909 that was, according to Victoria De Grazia, an important site of "the . . . struggle to articulate a new woman's culture." She goes on to note that "the venerable old Lyceum['s] . . . 'numerous, choice public' was presided over by the Princess of Piedmont" and that the club's public consisted of the "cultivated genteel ladies and worthy professional women" of Florence.[5] As president of the Lyceum's section on literature—other sections included painting, sculpture and industrial arts, international relations, music, science, teaching, and philanthropy—Jolanda De Blasi held sway over the club's cultural program for more than a decade, organizing, contributing to, editing, and publishing the Lyceum's yearly lecture series from 1932 through 1943. As Simona Maionchi has discovered in her study of the Lyceum archives, the level of intellectual and star power during these years was significant.

> Among the handwritten documents [of the archive] we should note three notebooks containing autographs and dedications left by the various figures who passed through the Lyceum, either as formal presenters or participants in informal conversations at afternoon tea. To understand the caliber of these figures, we could cite the presence of autographs such as that of Luigi Pirandello in 1926, or Guglielmo Marconi in 1934. The regular presence of Princess Maria of Piedmont—who left her signature on four occasions from 1933 through 1941—underscores the Club's steady loyalty to the monarchy, and its equally strong support of Mussolini's regime.[6]

A cursory look at the indexes of the Lyceum's publications during this period not only supports Maionchi's assertions regarding the club's status in Florentine cultural life but also attests to the personal and professional prestige of De Blasi herself. Most of the volumes that resulted from the Lyceum's lecture series included an introduction authored and delivered by De Blasi to inaugurate the proceedings and a contributing lecture, usually the last of the series. Moreover, the participants and coeditors who collaborated with De Blasi on her projects were of a particularly high political caliber, revealing De Blasi's ties with various important members of the Fascist regime, particularly in the Ministry of Education. Giovanni Gentile (1875–1944), professor, philosopher, Fascist minister of public instruction from 1922 to 1924, and president of the *Enciclopedia Italiana,* contributed to at least two of the Lyceum's lecture series (on Leopardi and on *Romanità e germanesimo* [Romanism and Germanity]) and was to have contributed to at least one other (in the "Visioni spirituali dell'Italia" series). Another notable academic collaboration was that with Giuseppe Bottai (1895–1959), futurist and Fascist minister of education from 1936 to 1943, with whom De Blasi organized and edited the series on *Romanità e germanesimo* in 1941 and who was slated to contribute a talk on Giovanni Pascoli's political thought to the Lyceum's series on Pascoli but was held away by commitments related to the Ethiopian war effort.[7]

The project of the 1930 *Le scrittrici italiane* is, in many ways, a precursor to the fusion of cultural and political agendas that was exemplified by De Blasi's later relationship with the Lyceum di Firenze. Though it did not boast the same collaborations with high-profile members of the regime, we will see that its aims—literary "analysis" in the service of Fascist cultural politics—were quite similar.

Despite the fact that De Blasi's introduction to the literary historical volume makes mention of a second volume (of both components) covering the period 1800–1930, no other indication of this volume's existence is to be found. The anthology of the period dating from the thirteenth to the eighteenth centuries runs to 564 pages and assembles the poetry and prose of no fewer than 111 women writers, including La Compiuta Donzella, Catherine of Siena, and Lucrezia Tornabuoni de' Medici, and significant sections on Veronica Gambara, Vittoria Colonna, and Gaspara Stampa. When compared to other modern anthologies the De Blasi volume presents no clear omissions in terms of the writers represented—indeed, in purely numerical terms her collection is more extensive than those of other anthologies. However, qualitative differences do exist, such as De Blasi's emphasis on Veronica Franco's poetry on amorous and diplomatic topics to the exclusion of her personal letters, such as that, translated in the Stortoni and Lillie anthology, discouraging young women from the life of a courtesan.[8]

The literary historical text is arranged chronologically, with each chapter covering an entire century of women's literary production. De Blasi's survey of the material is nothing if not complete; the chapter on the women writers of the 1600s, for example, takes up almost one hundred pages of text and mentions 162 writers by name. Typically, De Blasi gives biographical and historical information about each writer and attempts to situate the physical woman in terms of her family or husband. When there is little documentation to support the writer's existence (this is particularly true of the earlier writers), De Blasi turns to literary or literary historical references (Dante's and Petrarch's poetry, for example). Often, as is the case with Nina Siciliana and Gaia da Camino, De Blasi comes to the conclusion that most of these women are literary inventions, their poems having been attributed erroneously to male-constructed female personae. De Blasi's interest in biography and historiography is indicative of her approach to the texts, which centers, as we shall see, more on private life than on public written expression or on the creation of a literary persona. She often employs a thematic approach (for example, her discussion of Catherine of Siena's use of binary opposites such as good and evil) and a vaguely psychological one (her reading of written texts closely follows her "reading" of the women themselves). Her use of *explication de texte* is sporadic and brief, showing De Blasi to be more concerned with larger, meta-literary and meta-historical matters such as reception (she devotes a full page to prior interpretations of Catherine's writing vis-à-vis her literary and philosophical predecessors) and criticism; whether she is refuting or building on canonical interpretations of a writer, De Blasi's vast familiarity with primary and critical texts is her most striking tool. Ultimately, though, as we shall see, De Blasi's critical approach consists of a constant and methodical comparison of biographical and poetic accomplishments. Even in her laudatory discussion of Catherine, the focus of her analysis is not the stylistic, or even the political, force of her words but rather the purely mimetic relationship between Catherine's words and her historical reality: "her words' narrative covers its reality like a piece of clear glass."[9]

De Blasi's attempt to redress what she saw as a lack in the historiography of Italian women's literature was a worthy and natural project, especially in the context of an Italian cultural landscape in which both the Fascist state and its female citizens were struggling to define and crystallize women's roles. In this sense, women and women's issues played a vital, albeit ambiguous, role in Fascist ideology. As the propagator of the race and keystone of the all-important basic unit of Fascist society—the nuclear family—the Fascist woman was entrusted with the central functions of generational continuity and social stability. Gentile—who in addition to his governmental posts and contributions to De Blasi's Lyceum series was author of the 1925 "Manifesto degli Intellettuali Fascisti" [Manifesto of fascist intellectuals] and of the 1934 "La donna nella coscienza moderna" [Woman in modern consciousness]—maintained that "[e]very healthy and well-ordered society . . . has at its core the family and religion, and it is the woman who acts as the principal agent and guarantor of the ethics and sanctity of the family,"[10] even as he theorized that "the female self is but the completion of the male, and . . . woman exists only as the other of man."[11]

As Gentile's words reveal, much of Fascist social philosophy centered on misogynist, conservative principles that simultaneously made women its society's most central and most marginalized members.[12] In the words of Victoria De Grazia,

> Official propaganda exalted women as mythic figures—"the bearers of numerous children," "the mothers of soldiers," "the procreators of the race." At the same time, antifeminist ideologies provoked the petty despotic behaviors that in authoritarian regimes are commonly turned against society's most vulnerable members. Where both state and church, official publicist and priest confessor, united in upholding the cult of maternity, a woman whose husband's notion of virility was satisfied only when she repeatedly bore him children had no public recourse.[13]

Given the importance of women in Fascist ideology, then, it is not at all surprising that the largest chapter in De Blasi's literary historical volume is devoted to the fifteenth and sixteenth centuries, the only other periods in Italian history in which the "questione della donna" was so prominent—and so ambiguous—in social and literary agendas. And if the great number of very public and successful female literary figures, political decision makers, and *matresfamilias* is not strong enough testament to the prominence of women in the Renaissance, we should consider Juliana Schiesari's assertion that the literary fashion of writing histories and treatises on the virtues of women is an important index of the woman's place in this culture and society.

> [T]he question of women and their place in Renaissance Italy—and elsewhere in Europe—was very much alive and very much a problem for the men who shaped the dominant discourses and for those women who, necessarily situated by them, strived to understand, outwit or resist that hegemony. Indeed, the very flurry of writing about domestic life is itself a sign that the patriarchal forces needed to redefine the parameters of propriety and regulate anew the paradigms of familial behavior.[14]

Though Schiesari's comments are intended to bear directly on the period of her inquiry—the Italian Renaissance—her analysis of the significance of public definitions of private, domestic situations is certainly relevant for our examination of De Blasi's work. Just as the increased attention given to women in the Renaissance period was an indication of the importance of women in that period, so was the spate of legislative, cultural, and social activity centered around women and women's issues reflective of the male order's need to define the role of women in—and for the survival of—the Fascist state. As Robin Pickering-Iazzi notes in her introduction to the volume *Mothers of Invention: Women, Italian Fascism, and Culture*,

> Reflecting the general concern about the increasing ambiguity of gender roles, the writings by male intellectuals [such as Camillo Pellizzi and Giuseppe Ravegnani] of the 1920s and 1930s demonstrate a preoccupation with the ongoing changes in female practices of everyday life and culture. Indeed, in the interwar period, communities of Italian women fashioned female models of their own devising, expanding the sites and ways of their engagement with cultural life.[15]

As an educated woman clearly entrenched in the institutions and issues of her time, Jolanda De Blasi had a strong interest in participating in this process of definition, despite, or perhaps because of, the ideological conflicts that may have arisen as a result. Gramsci's notion of "contradictory consciousness," which De Grazia briefly applies to her discussion of women's negotiation of elements of the regime's hegemonic ideology in arriving at their own system of practical and theoretical response,[16] might be a fruitful theoretical starting point in exploring De Blasi's position vis-à-vis the institutions and ideals of the Fascist regime. In Gramsci's terms, a contradictory consciousness arises from the disjoint between hegemonic ideologies and the real-life situation of a subaltern group and from the attempts of that group's members to find compromises between the two.[17] For this reason, if we are to understand the question of canon formation from the perspective of the age in which it takes place, the literary historical volume of De Blasi's work is an even more fruitful object of study than the anthology itself. In its attempt to define women's roles, De Blasi's commentary in effect exposes an inherent weakness in the dominant discourses on gender; that is, when she is forced to address female activity according to the parameters that the regime itself had created, the result is a problematic and contradictory portrait of woman: essential, yet inferior. When the two components of her work (anthology and literary historical text) are read dynamically and in dialogue, it becomes clear that De Blasi's project is undercut by a central tension: while its literary historical component harshly disparages the female poetic production of the fifteenth and sixteenth centuries (and, indeed, most of the women's literary tradition), the anthology presents and reproduces it in a more comprehensive way than ever before. Though the ample space given to these centuries is natural, given the prominence of women writers in the Renaissance, we must ask ourselves why the project was undertaken at all, if De Blasi found women's literary production as a whole to be so inferior. We shall see that Fascism's practice of placing a disempowered and marginalized woman at the heart of its social policy informs De Blasi's contradictory duality in many ways and sheds light on the central conflict of her work: the need to define women's—including, indeed, her own—roles in a cultural and political atmosphere in which women were being legislated into a central role that was nonetheless emptied of any personal or political power.

A second and related tension inherent to the work emerges if we consider that De Blasi denies most of the *poetesse* in question any objective literary analysis. One of the ways in which she accomplishes this is by claiming that their work is so devoid of literary worth that only biographical details remain to be discussed. On rare occasions, De Blasi does grant some of the Renaissance *poetesse* some degree of "*diligenza*," even if it is at the cost of any "*originalità*." Laura Battiferra degli Ammannati's descriptive sonnets of Rome, Florence, and Venice, for example, are "flashes, sudden bursts of light that [her] mannerism quickly cools and flattens."[18] De Blasi's assessment of the poetry of Gaspara Stampa—whom, according to Stortoni and Lillie, "modern criticism . . . generally acknowledges . . . as the greatest and most original of the three [most famous Italian women poets] as well as possibly the greatest Italian woman poet ever"[19]—is even harsher.

> I have said that the public appreciated the eager, sugary sweet femininity of Gaspara Stampa's amorous *Rime* more than the spiritual poetry of Vittoria Colonna. But we must not get carried away even in this. An unsuspecting reader would find himself yawning by the tenth of more than two hundred and twenty sonnets that make up [Stampa's] *canzoniere*.[20]

Since De Blasi is unable to accept most of the *poetesse*'s work on its literary merits, her main litmus test for valuable poetry seems to be biographical: did the woman lead an interesting life? Did her "real" life contain any conflicts or problems to be reflected in her literary production? Was she someone for whom the personal intersected with the historical? Did she influence her contemporary world? As closer examination of her work will reveal, De Blasi valorizes a certain sort of public literary or political activity, but only when this activity falls within certain definitions, stereotypes, and roles. Not coincidentally, these roles also happen to be in line with "official" Fascist cultural and social theories being developed and implemented at the time.

We can advance at least two hypotheses as to the relationship between De Blasi's criteria for the evaluation of the women writers in her critical text and the Fascist regime that, by 1930, had already had eight years to consolidate and solidify its ideology and policies and three to enact its decidedly pronatalist, pro-marriage demographic campaign.[21] First, given Gentile's formulation of a definition of woman that is "the completion of man"[22] and therefore completely dependent on man for her material, moral, and social identities, De Blasi's insistence on the "real-life" biographical information of her *scrittrici* can be interpreted as an attempt to judge these women according to their relationship to a male hegemonic order. Even in the attempts of so-called Fascist feminists to come to compromise between Fascist ideology and feminist goals, and to free women from the biologically based determinism and inferiority of Fascist thinkers like Gentile, women were defined in socially constructed (and male-dominated) terms of marriage and family.[23] As we will see, the work of writers whose private lives and literary careers were carried on largely outside of the family- and state-oriented constructs approved of by the Fascist regime (such as Veronica Franco and Tullia d'Aragona) is entirely discredited by De Blasi. Conversely, women who fulfilled their role as *matresfamilias* and otherwise within paternalistic structures of church and state, notably Catherine of Siena, Lucrezia Tornabuoni de' Medici, and Vittoria Colonna, are singled out as role models in literary and moral spheres so intertwined that it is often impossible to disentangle them.

Second, De Blasi's use of Fascist, male-dominated social and cultural norms as criteria for assessing the value of these women's poetry resulted in a striking confusion between the private and public spheres. By judging the *poetesse*'s publicly distributed poetic production according to the standards of their private lives, De Blasi abandons any pretense of rigorous critical methodology and dedicates her unique "scope of inquiry," instead, to the task of attributing "inferior" poetry to "inferior" morality.

This tendency to blur the lines between public and private was also a hallmark of Fascist policies and legislation. With the passage of 1926 and 1931 penal codes that codified everything from adultery to rape, from orphanages to charitable aid organizations, the Fascist state, in "legislating around issues of family morality and honor, inclined to treat the family as a public rather than private institution."[24] As such, the ideal of the Fascist family—numerous, traditional, and in the service of the state—was institutionally installed as the basic unit of Italian politics and society.[25] Such a pro-family configuration of the Fascist state allowed it to enter the private sphere of its citizens, both women and men, in order to regulate and legislate "normal" sexuality, pronatalist policies, and "appropriate" gender roles. In Victoria De Grazia's words,

> Mussolini's government sought to nationalize Italian women, much as during the previous century, in Italy and elsewhere, bourgeois governments sought to nationalize men. . . . As it turned out, the "nationalization" of women in Italy occurred under authoritarian, not liberal, terms. . . . Every aspect of being female was thus held up to the measure of the state's interest and interpreted in light of the dictatorship's strategies of state building.[26]

Under the Fascist regime, women enjoyed rights and freedoms only to the extent that they allowed them to contribute more productively to the goals of this particular totalitarian state. State incentives to raise large families by taxing single men, increasing family-based fertility, and providing institutionalized support for pre- and neonatal education took the form of organizations like Opera Nazionale Maternità ed Infanzia (OMNI) [National agency for maternity and childhood], whose paradoxical aims were emblematic of much Fascist-era policy.[27] These brief examples indicate the extent to which the realm of the private—that to which women had been historically relegated—was being legislated, addressed, and defined—in short, made public. But what De Grazia's sociological, legislative study also brings to light is the manner in which the public—politics, economics, foreign policy—was also being transferred into the private sphere, through the demands of autarchy and of competing interests between the Fascist state and the family unit that was supposed to be its most basic element.[28] In the aftermath of the League of Nations sanctions against Italy in 1935, demands for fiscal discipline quickly became transplanted onto domestic terrain as women were asked to buy Italian in the management of their own homes. On a more symbolic level, the now legendary wedding ring donation ceremony of March 7, 1936, gave Italian women the semblance of power and free participation in the war effort and in the domestic struggle against League of Nations sanctions, but as De Grazia points out, the very gesture of trading gold wedding rings for metal substitutes put women's loyalties in conflict with one another and "cast uncertainty on whether a woman's first obligation was to the Duce, fascism, and the nation, or to her spouse, children, and kin as decreed by custom, sacred church vows, and pronatalist sloganeering."[29]

Fascist policies and ideologies, then, transgressed in both directions the boundaries between private and public by legislating the sexuality and gender roles of its citizens in the interest of the state and by imposing state economic policies on the family unit and the woman who had been entrusted with its survival. Furthermore, this program created a situation for women that, even while placing them at the center of Fascist society, isolated and marginalized them by overlegislating their restrictive maternal role.

Jolanda De Blasi and her work are telling links between the Fascist and Renaissance eras. As such, her commentary on women's writing from its origins up through the sixteenth century is also an unconscious one on the Fascist era itself, reflecting its biases, ideals, and policies toward women. I hope to illustrate this with the aid of four examples from De Blasi's critical volume, specific cases wherein the author's ideological bent is illustrated by her "analysis" of particular *poetesse* or groups of them. In De Blasi's treatment of Saint Catherine of Siena, Lucrezia de' Medici, Tullia d'Aragona, and Veronica Franco, we shall see that the Fascist ideology identified previously is in fact the litmus test used to evaluate the "poetic" merits of early modern *scrittrici italiane*.

After providing a brief introduction to the troubadour origins of Italian female writing, De Blasi begins a century-by-century analysis of female writing. Her assessment of the Trecento—and, we discover, of the whole of Italian female literary production—is dominated by the "flashing star"[30] of Catherine of Siena; after Catherine, in the opinion of De Blasi, "at least in the space of our first volume—there are no close seconds."[31] This mystic saint is presented as the most important of all the women discussed and as the precursor of the great themes of Romanticism: "she started out, incredibly alone, on the road for which the romantics would dictate the itinerary

500 years later: *God, country, sacrifice and love*. The romantics—which is tantamount to saying . . . the moderns."[32]

Notable in De Blasi's exuberant assessment of Catherine of Siena's place in the Italian literary landscape is her attachment to Romanticism, a stance shared by both Italian Fascism and German National Socialism. Both regimes, in putting personal sacrifice [*dolore*] and the fatherland [*patria*] at the top of their ideological agendas, drew heavily on the themes of nineteenth-century Romantic movements. These movements, which were also closely connected to both countries' unification, were thus especially convenient in terms of the rhetoric of nationalism and imperialism and of the founding myths of two countries who defensively saw themselves as latecomers to the international political and colonial scenes.

Consistent with her methodology throughout the critical volume, De Blasi quickly turns from Catherine's literary style to biographical details: "Not confined in a cloister, but orating and working, she assembled around her a flock of disciples—prelates, magistrates, painters, poets—and political matters, which is to say, at that time, matters that spanned all aspects of social and civil life, led her to serious undertakings and courageous endeavors."[33]

Catherine's spiritual mysticism—whose irrational, spontaneous aspects were exemplary of Romantic ideals—in the context of an engaged political existence provides a "double example"[34] of contemplation and activity, which De Blasi likens to a Dantean ideal. Because this brand of contemplation is decidedly spiritual, irrational, and inspirational, the kind of activity that it inspires—unquestionably subjected to the ideals and exigencies of the all-important and male-dominated *patria*—is thus in line with Fascism's antirationalistic bent. Furthermore, just as Catherine's role in service to the papal empire represented a conflation of spiritual and political aims, so does it blur the lines between private devotion and public action, and it is privileged in just those terms by De Blasi: "The commitment with which she strove to return Christianity to a state of peace diminished more and more her constitution, already weakened by fasting and penance."[35] The foggy boundary between public and private is now a zone of self-sacrifice, whose very private nature has attained clearly public implications.

Catherine's negation of self-interest (and thus the subjective self) in favor of the needs of the state and church is a model against which De Blasi negatively compares other women writers whom she anthologizes, Giustina Levi Perotti and [E]Leonora della Genga, for example.[36] These two *poetesse* are linked by a common theme in the one poem each that De Blasi reproduces: the right of women to write poetry and to be active in otherwise "masculine" spheres. Della Genga's sonnet "Tacete, o maschi, a dir che la Natura" and De Blasi's analysis of it are particularly representative of this theme's treatment on the whole.

Tacete, o maschi, a dir che la Natura
a far il maschio solamente intenda,
e per formar la femmina non prenda
se non contra sua voglia alcuna cura.
    Qual'invidia per tal, qual nube oscura
fa che la mente vostra non comprenda
com'ella in farlo ogni sua forza spenda,
onda la Gloria lor la vostra oscura?
    Sanno le donne maneggiar le spade,
sanno regger gl'imperi, e sanno ancòra
trovar il cammin dritto in Elicona.
    In ogni cosa il valor vostro cade,
uomini, appresso loro. Uomo non fôra
mai per tôrne di man pregio o corona.

[Stop saying, you men, that Nature
makes man—and man alone—by her design,
and in making woman does not take
any pains if not against her will.
    What envy of woman, what dark cloud
prevents your mind from understanding
that she exhausts herself in her creation,
whence their glory darkens yours.
    Women know how to wield the sword,
how to rule empires, and they, too, know
how to find the straight path to Helicon.
    Your valor fails in every way,
men, next to them. Never could man
rob her of her merit or her crown.][37]

Typically, De Blasi criticizes this sonnet and others like it on purely thematic—and not stylistic—grounds, comparing their ostentatious, attention-hungry subjects to Catherine's desubjectivized stance, indicating that her standards are more informed by ideology and a perception of appropriate gender morality than by any real aesthetic concerns.

> But what a difference between these scatterbrains on whom intrudes an applause-seeking "I," and the declaration made so often by Cather-

> ine [of Siena] on her own behalf, "servant and slave of the servants of Jesus Christ," Catherine who admonished: "Know that nothing can be seen or known of me if not the highest misery; ignorant and with little capacity for understanding."[38]

Saint Catherine's Christian subservience to her Lord is thus set up as a standard for the secular poet, a comparison of unlike terms if there ever was one. Implicit in De Blasi's statement is a negative evaluation of *poetesse* who openly assert their rights in male spheres, refuse to maintain an inferior position in the male-dominated order, and dare to do so in terms of the male-dominated realm of rhetoric and poetry.

This scenario is easily translated into Fascist terms, if we consider the regime's strict regimentation of gender roles and attributes. Given Fascism's theorization and legislation of a biological determination of sex and gender (as opposed to a culturally constructed one), women were assigned to the roles of mother and wife, educator of tradition, guarantor of continuity and stability of the family unit, and moral guide to a life of pain and sacrifice in the service of the *patria*. These roles were also public and political insofar as they were in the interest of the state, but the primacy of the state was always maintained, and any attempt to use the advances afforded to women—as instruments of the state—for individual, private aims was clearly unwelcome.

If Saint Catherine of Siena is De Blasi's positive example of feminine subservience to the needs of the state and church, her models for the role of woman as *matresfamilias* are Lucrezia Tornabuoni de' Medici and Alessandra Macinghi Strozzi.[39] Here, the *patria stupenda* is Florence, and for De Blasi, these women's literary productions were not their most noteworthy attribute; their integral support of the Florentine *patria* was a far more noble achievement.

> [T]he Medicis of the Quattrocento were Florentines to the marrow of their bones, to the last hair on their heads. Imagine if their women or those that worked industriously in their homes would have been able to stand the thought of shutting themselves up in libraries, only to emerge stale smelling and long-faced, eagerly participating in useless gatherings.[40]

Lucrezia garners particular mention from De Blasi for her inspirational power over the men that surrounded her at the Medici court—and for accepting her literary place behind that of her men.

> Now we would not exchange for the lucubrous and sterile meditations of [other women poets,] one smile of Madonna Lucrezia, mother of Lorenzo Magnifico, one of those smiles—thoughtful and affectionate, witty and astute—that repaid Poliziano's labors, turned from his classical studies to Italian poetry, with maternal candor, that inspired and guided Luigi Pulci's *Morgante* cantos. . . . *We should be more grateful to her for this than for her versifying of little religious canzoni and of biblical octaves, to which she accorded only relative importance—intimate and domestic—, consoling herself with her grandchildren's beautiful recitations of her poetry.*[41]

Tornabuoni modern editor objects to this approach because "Lucrezia's soft light has been obscured by the great figures that were close to her, and as a result she is hastily reduced to 'Poliziano's and Pulci's friend,' or 'muse of the *Morgante*.'"[42] De Blasi, however, finds Lucrezia Tornabuoni's import to lie almost entirely in the maternal (read: supportive and supporting) role that she played for the great cultural and literary figures surrounding her at court. If her literary production can be awarded any merit of its own, it is due to its value as a religious didactic tool in the "intimate and domestic" confines of the home, as a tool of moral instruction across generations. In no uncertain terms, De Blasi gives us a definition of the parameters of acceptable *attività femminile* for Fascist Italy: it is self-deprecating, supportive, edifying, private in its realization, and public in its aims.

Conversely, the figure of the courtesan poet is negatively portrayed by De Blasi. In addressing their moral character, she refers to the courtesans variously as "great sinners" and "hired procurers" and discusses their biographical details and physical attributes far more exhaustively than their literary merits.[43] Of Tullia d'Aragona, author of a collection of *Rime* and the *Dialogo della infinità dell'amore*, De Blasi cites only a line and a half[44] drawn from a poem dedicated to the man who was "the most enflamed and tortured passion of Tullia's maturity"[45] and then judges that "it is not very good, especially in the tiring and discordant meeting of ill-chosen syllables that in the second quatrain give the verses an unbearable bitterness. Let the reader judge the rest from this."[46]

Veronica Franco is given the most extensive treatment among the courtesan poets discussed by De Blasi. Though she is introduced in similarly disdainful terms—"Veronica Franco, public sinner of Venice, was not ashamed to be what she was. . . . [O]ne understands immediately—and she does not care to hide it—with whom one is dealing"[47]—the particulars of her private life are at first less central to De Blasi's assessment than in other cases. De

Blasi hints at some positive elements in Franco's writing style; she speaks of "the natural expression that is not rare in the *Rime*,"[48] but she ultimately determines that the poems are raw and undeveloped. Finally, though, biography dominates De Blasi's analysis of Franco, and her section on her ends on a note of moral redemption and reformation. Though De Blasi imaginatively attributes to the *poetessa* a litter of scattered children fathered by many men, she then describes a *contrapasso*-like turn at the end of her life that seems to have redeemed Franco to some extent in De Blasi's eyes.

> What happened to her husband? He was a physician, and we know nothing else except that he did not live very long with that exuberant wife of his. What about her children? Also about them—*and she must have had many of them by many men—the chronicles are silent*. We know much of her, however: and not only the product of her studies—the *Rime* and *Lettere famigliari a diversi*—and the spectacle of her hedonistic lifestyle; but we also know that in her last years she went from dissolute living to a life of piety, with a fervor so efficacious and sincere that it continues to bear fruit even today: the Hospice of Santa Maria del Soccorso for abandoned children in Venice traces its origin from its foundation by the convert Veronica Franco.[49]

What is it about the courtesans that makes them the antithesis of De Blasi's—and the Fascist regime's—ideal woman? First, they represent none of the devotion to family and state that we see in the lives and works of other, more favorably judged female writers. Furthermore, they resist both popular definitions of sexuality and gender, the biologically based theory favored by doctrinal Fascist thinkers as well as the culturally oriented view devised by Fascist feminists as a compromise between loyalty to the regime and feminist goals. The former, as we have discussed, sees women as being defined by their biological procreative functions. This definition results in both the inevitable relegation to the role of mother to the exclusion of all other possible and competing roles and the resulting institutionalization of essential difference between men and women. And although the recognition of sexual difference is one of the main tenets of modern feminist thought, when it is defined and legislated by a male hegemonic order such as Fascism, it is rarely favorably articulated, and the *donna-madre* becomes the marginalized other who completes the male subject, as is the case in Gentile's thought, but is herself denied subject-hood. The Renaissance courtesan defies this definition by refusing her traditional role of mother and wife and by staking her ground as an independent poetic and cultural subject whose identity lies outside of all traditional male-dominated orders.

The latter culturally based view, as expounded by Fascist feminist Teresa Labriola, is a response to misogynistic state ideology that attempts to turn the Fascist logic on itself, as is suggested by Barbara Spackman in her "Fascist Women and the Rhetoric of Virility." In her view, Labriola's position forces her to "use the rhetoric of virility in defense rather than scorn of women," in this case to defend women against the rhetoric of biological determinism. By rejecting the biological and physical definition of woman as "Bolshevik," Labriola pits one aspect of Fascist doctrine squarely against another: on the one hand, its institutionalization of a biologically based difference that is not necessarily congruent with the pro-family Fascist agenda (and, indeed, may in fact be more in line with the "Bolshevik" disintegration of bourgeois social structures); and on the other, its imposition of cultural roles that must dictate this agenda when biology deviates from it.[50] Labriola comes down firmly on the side of culturally and legislatively constructed gender roles, while remaining firmly within the pro-family ideology of doctrinal Fascism. Spackman summarizes Labriola's argument in the following way:

> [M]others have rights and duties insofar as they occupy a juridical position, claims Labriola, not insofar as they may have physically given birth; faithful to Roman law, that juridical position is dependent upon marriage. *In fact, Labriola's Fascist mother appears to be a revival of the social fiction that was Roman motherhood, in which maternity was limited to motherhood within marriage and the materfamilias was such not because she had children but because she was the wife of a paterfamilias*.[51]

To return once again to the Renaissance *poetesse*, Labriola's amalgam of Fascism and feminism is reflected in De Blasi's assessment of courtesans like Veronica Franco and indeed might reflect De Blasi's own attempts to reconcile the competing pulls of faith in feminism and adherence to the Fascist regime. The biological motherhood that De Blasi attributes to Franco—unfounded though it may be—lies decidedly outside the strong nuclear family structure that the Fascist state saw as its microcosm and basic unit. As such, physically based definitions of sexuality and gender roles do not necessitate the cultural roles of wife and *materfamilias*; indeed, they often exclude them, as is the case with both the Renaissance courtesans and Labriola's unwed Bolshevik *genetrix*.

We have seen, through De Blasi's analysis of these women writers and their lives, that her methodology is much less a poetics or an aesthetics than a culturally specific moral assessment. This allows us to say that De Blasi's approach, that of delimiting appropriate female roles, participates in the Fascist program of gender delineation. Furthermore, given the very public and political ramifications of the functions that Renaissance women are expected to carry out, De Blasi's mixture of public and private mirrors that deployed by the Fascist state, an assertion that is borne out textually, as we shall see.

This is illustrated principally in three points that Jolanda De Blasi makes in the course of her analysis: that the private life of a female writer is almost always more intriguing than her poetry and as such must be a factor in evaluating that poetry; that biographical and/or historical events necessarily influence a female writer's art and vice versa; and that the most esteemed figures of the period are those for whom public history and private life commingle and intersect. The first point is made explicit early in De Blasi's literary historical volume. Despite her noble earlier stated claim to want to "summarize, through a reserved and minute study, the value it [female intellectual activity] may have for us, and its nature and degree,"[52] De Blasi soon realizes that intellectual activity might not really be at the center of her analysis.

> From this point on, there is no longer any need to search high and low for these female writers: indeed, as we proceed, we will stumble upon them . . . fidgeting about in situations that are sometimes honorable, and sometimes not, in such a way as to be able to point out, if not exactly any literary excellence, at least *a moral* and even physical *portrait*. . . . This is not a very encouraging beginning, if we consider that *we are here to discuss the quality of art and artistic talent*, and already we must admit that the central focus of our attention will be for many female writers drawn by other—and even completely different—factors than by illustrious poetic virtue.[53]

A discussion of these writers' moral characteristics and private lives, then, is a suitable replacement for an analysis of their public literary achievements. But we see elsewhere that not only do moral criteria replace poetic ones, but they are often confused and conflated, as is the case with Veronica Gambara. Gambara's style is criticized for being "ornate and sterile . . . lacking intimacy" despite the fact that her poetry, admittedly, "in sum, is not lacking in any regard." The very stylistic quality that De Blasi praises as *limatura* [refinement] when speaking of Petrarch is here assessed as personal coldness: "if we had to reconstruct the woman from the poet, we would absolutely not know where to find a heart to put into her chest." This accusation of Gambara's "distance" reveals an attempt to brand the genetic woman with attributes that belong to the *poetessa* and to blur the distinction between the two. A poet whose "reflective and meditated" poetry (this is De

Blasi's citation of Pietro Bembo) defies De Blasi's attempts either to ignore her talent or to judge her work in terms of her life, Gambara's life is thus judged in terms of her work, a transgression of public and private all the same.[54]

No less problematic is De Blasi's discussion of the fifteenth century figure of Alessandra di Messer Bartolomeo Scala, who is seen as actively intermingling her "erudition" and private life. According to De Blasi, Alessandra's performance of the part of the title character of *Electra* won her the heart of none other than Poliziano, who happened to be present for her performance. It was also her great learning and passion that resulted in her marriage to the poet Marullo when their "conversations . . . turned from idyll to matrimony." This exemplary conflation of public art and private life is even more noteworthy considering the very public and performative nature of Alessandra's artistic identity: recitation and conversation. Even this sort of public activity is clearly acceptable and positive in De Blasi's view, insofar as it leads, ultimately, to Alessandra's future role as a faithful wife and Christian servant: "as honest as she was beautiful, when a tragic death took her husband from her, Alessandra ended up, still a very young woman, a Benedictine sister in the convent of San Pier Maggiore."[55]

Ultimately, in summarizing the importance of Vittoria Colonna, De Blasi will abandon the pretense of art as criterion altogether. Colonna is described as "a specimen without exemplum,"[56] and, not surprisingly, her exemplary life and support of military causes and ideals are treated much more extensively than her poetic production. But the scarce attention it gets is rather contradictory: though De Blasi claims Colonna's to be "the only high female poetry of the century," she immediately levels the same criticism against Colonna that she has leveled against so many others: "she lacks the flame that entrances; and this—the sentence passed on the other woman poets—is also the sentence on the poet Vittoria Colonna."[57] In the end, Colonna's poetry is placed on the same level as that of the other *poetesse,* with their cold imitation of Petrarchan techniques and themes; rather, we find that it is Vittoria Colonna's *life* that is exemplary. Although this *poetessa* did not fit the mold of Lucrezia Tornabuoni de' Medici—*materfamilias* and inspiration to literary achievement—Colonna is privileged for her unselfish support of military action and her central position in her world. And although she did not directly affect history in the way her husband-soldier did, Vittoria Colonna is portrayed by De Blasi as the perfect marriage between moral exemplum and public history; she is the private life behind public, political, and military greatness; she is proof that, for Jolanda De Blasi regarding the female poets of the fourteenth, fifteenth, and sixteenth centuries, the private has value on public terms: "and so the day in which a change in her life took place, the march of history also followed, and she, *whatever the judgment of her verses may be,* will forever be the outstanding woman who leaps forward from mediocrity in name and spirit."[58]

In literary terms, all three of these points effectively erase the possibility of the poetic persona and conflate author with writer, genetic female with literary self-creation. Translated into other terms, the erasure of the poetic persona is nothing less than the elimination of the subjective self, for if the female writer cannot creatively and independently inscribe herself as subject into traditional and public literary structures, she is once again marginalized, relegated to the domestic "real-life" roles that her biography—and as such the Fascist state—determines. Jolanda De Blasi's work—both in her foundational anthology and in her expansive literary historical volume—achieves this by confusing private roles with public ones and by using moral and regime-specific ideological criteria to judge the appropriateness and merits of poetic production. In this sense, she participates in the overall cultural program of Fascism, which was to place its ideal woman at the center of a profamily, pronatalist society—all the while legislating her private life and morality—asserting its right to legislate the private in the interests of the public.

❧ ❧ ❧

APPENDIX

Bibliography of Jolanda De Blasi's Published Works

Books, Articles, and Collections of Critical Essays Published by De Blasi

Pietro Cossa e la tragedia italiana. Firenze: Tip. Galileiana, 1911.
Laura Minali-Comparetti (contributor). Firenze: G. C. Ariani, 1913.
Il re allo specchio. Romanzo. Firenze: Vallecchi, 1923.
L'Italia e gli italiani del secolo XIX (editor and contributor). Firenze: G. C. Sansoni, 1930.
Antologia delle scrittrici italiane dalle origini al 1800 (editor). Firenze: Nemi, 1930.
Le scrittrici italiane dalle origini al 1800. Firenze: Nemi, 1930.
Itinerarii amorosi d'Italia (published in the "Visioni spirituali dell'Italia" series). Firenze: Nemi, 1932.
Giovanni Pascoli (editor and preface, published in the "Letture pascoliane" series). Firenze: G. C. Sansoni, 1937.
Giacomo Leopardi (editor and contributor). Firenze: G. C. Sansoni, 1938.
Gabriele D'Annunzio (editor and contributor). Firenze: G. C. Sansoni, 1939.
I Savoia dalle origini al 1900 (editor). Firenze: G. C. Sansoni, 1940.
Romanità e germanesimo (with Giuseppe Bottai). Firenze: G. C. Sansoni, 1941.
Italiani nel mondo. Firenze: G. C. Sansoni, 1942.
Firenze (editor). Firenze: G. C. Sansoni, 1943.

Memorie autobiografiche di Giuseppe Garibaldi (editor and preface). Firenze: Cya, 1944.
Firenze (editor and contributor). Firenze: G. C. Sansoni, 1944.
Santi Italiani. Firenze: G. C. Sansoni, 1947.
Le 4 basiliche patriarcali dell'anno santo. Firenze: Del Turco, 1949.
Il giubileo, racconto di sei secoli e mezzo. Firenze: Del Turco, 1950.
La basilica di San Pietro in Roma. Roma: Del Turco, 1957.
St. Peter's in Rome (translator). Roma: Edizioni del Drago, 1959.

Works by Other Authors Edited by De Blasi

Garbasso, Antonio Giorgio. *Scienza e poesia*. Pref. Benito Mussolini. Firenze: F. Le Monnier, 1934.
D'Annunzio, Gabriele. *Solus ad solam* (preface). Firenze: G. C. Sansoni, 1939.

Translations

Homer. *L'Illiade di Omero*. Firenze: G. C. Sansoni, 1944.
Homer. *L'Odissea di Omero*. Firenze: G. C. Sansoni, 1944.

Series Edited

"Visioni spirituali dell'Italia." Firenze: Nemi.
Fotta, Salvator. *Il Canavese*. 1931.
Lipparini, Giuseppe. *L'appennino pistoiese*. 1931.
Marpicati, Arturo. *Fiume*. 1931.
Stanghellini, Arturo. *Toscana minore*. 1931.
Viani, Lorenzo. *Versilia*. 1931.
Milanesi, Guido. *Mari d'Italia, l'immersione profonda*. 1931.
De Blasi, Jolanda. *Itinerarii amorosi d'Italia*. 1932.
Muratori, Santi. *Ravenna*. 1932.
Ferretti, Lando. *Il volto dell'Italia virile*. 1934.
Meano, Cesare. *Torino novecento*. 1934.

"Letture pascoliane." Firenze: G. C. Sansoni.
Pasquali, Giorgio. *Poesia latina di Pascoli*. 1937.
Galletti, Alfredo. *L'arte poetica di Pascoli*. 1937.
Briganti, Gabriele. *Testimonianze e valutazioni pascoliane*. 1937.
De Blasi, Jolanda, ed. *Giovanni Pascoli*. 1937.

NOTES

1. "A ciascuna delle due parti si confronta un'antologia: che, posso ben dirlo, è cosa assolutamente nuova per ampiezza, varietà, e curiosità: documento esauriente a cui si potrà togliere e aggiungere, ma in margine, e non aumentarne né diminuirne il valore probativo." Jolanda De Blasi, ed., *Le scrittrici italiane dalle origini al 1800* (Florence: Nemi, 1930), 1:10. This and all translations of De Blasi's text are mine.

2. "Una storia letteraria delle donne italiane non esiste, oppure sono cavalleresche scorribande di studiosi cortesi che dal campo han riportato un fiore e un sorriso, eterno omaggio—anche qui—all'eterno femminino. . . . Non restano che i cenni nelle storie letterarie generali, e le monografie consacrate alle poche scrittrici su cui la tradizione ha fatto centro. Ma sono, quei cenni e queste monografie, strumenti non

bastevoli a raggiungere una visione giusta ed esatta: gli uni troppo sbrigativi approssimativi ed incompleti; le altre troppo parziali così nel senso dell'economia come in quello della passione." De Blasi, *Le scrittrici*, 1:9.

3. Gabinetto Scientifico Letterario G. C. Vieusseux, <http://www.vieusseux.fi.it> (June 19, 2002), Cenni Storici.

4. The Web site of the Fondo Michelstaedter, maintained by the Civic Library of Gorizia, reports a brief romantic relationship between De Blasi and the Italian philosopher in 1906–7 and, indeed, lists a number of letters to De Blasi dating from that period among its holdings. Fondo Michelstaedter, <http://www.michelstaedter.it> (June 19, 2002), Lettere.

5. Victoria De Grazia, *How Fascism Ruled Women: Italy, 1922–1945* (Berkeley: University of California Press, 1992), 257.

6. "Tra i documenti manoscritti si devono rammentare tre quaderni di firme autografe e dediche lasciate dai vari personaggi di passaggio al Lyceum, sia che si fossero esibiti sia che si fossero intrattenuti in una conversazione informale per il tè del pomeriggio. Per comprendere il calibro dei personaggi si può citare l'autografo di Luigi Pirandello del 1926 o quello di Guglielmo Marconi del 1934. Presenza ricorrente in quattro occasioni dal 1933 al 1941, la firma di Maria Principessa di Piemonte, a sottolineare la costante fedeltà monarchica del Club e il suo altrettanto tenace sostegno al regime mussoliniano." Simona Maionchi, "Lyceum Club Internazionale di Firenze—circolo culturale femminile. Ricognizione storica dai documenti manoscritti del 1908 ai bollettini a stampa," March 5, 2001, <http://www.archiviodistato.firenze.it/memoriadonne/materiali_donne/maionchi.pdf> (June 19, 2002), 4.

7. There is much to note about this particular volume, starting with its publication in the year 1941. Though Italy formed its "Pact of Steel" with Germany in May 1939 and solidified its military support of the Nazi program by declaring war on the French in June 1940, it was not until Italy's almost failed invasion of Greece in October that Italy's absolute weakness with regard to Germany's military and political power was revealed. When Yugoslavia, early in 1941, installed an anti-Nazi government to respond to gestures of Italian aggression, Germany invaded both Greece and Yugoslavia to salvage the weak Italian position. See Alexander J. De Grand, *Italian Fascism: Its Origins and Development* (Lincoln: University of Nebraska Press, 1978), 123–24. Given the precarious state of Italian-German relations at this time and the prominence of Bottai in the Fascist educational apparatus, the publication of a volume on the interrelatedness of the two cultures' imperial pasts points to an Italian program that was attempting to redress its military and political weaknesses through cultural means, placing the Italians and their German allies on equal footing, if not giving Italy the cultural advantage outright. As De Blasi states in her inaugural comments, "This lecture series and the book that will result from it . . . propose to clearly illustrate the contribution of Roman and Germanic elements to the strengths and expressions indicated by the themes [of the conference], noting their similarities and highlighting their differences, in order to indicate the balance and complementarity that have allowed the two peoples to sow the spiritual and political seeds of the Middle Ages and of the dawning modern age." Published as Premessa [Introduction] to *Romanità e germanesimo* (Florence: G. C. Sansoni, 1941), x. [Questo Corso di conferenze e il conseguente libro "Romanità e germanesimo" . . . si propongono di illustrare a lume sereno l'apporto dei due elementi Romano e Germanico nelle forze e nelle espressioni indicate dai temi, notandone le confluenze e mettendone in rilievo le differenze, per segnare il punto di

equilibrio e di complemento che già permise ai due popoli di dare i fermenti spirituali e politici al mondo del Medioevo e dell'albeggiante età moderna]. Other publications are just as overt in their support of Fascist policies and enterprises. Giovanni Pascoli, for example, is hailed as the poet of colonial expansion in De Blasi's introduction to that particular lecture series. Here, she points to the relevance of the Lyceum's celebration of Pascoli's poetry in 1937, in light of his protoimperial support of the Libyan campaign of 1912 and in the wake of Italy's successful invasion of Ethiopia. Jolanda De Blasi, Premessa [Introduction] to *Giovanni Pascoli* (Florence: G. C. Sansoni, 1937), x–xi.

8. Veronica Franco, "Letter to a mother who wanted her daughter to become a courtesan," in *Women Poets of the Italian Renaissance: Courtly Ladies and Courtesans*, ed. Laura Anna Stortoni and trans. Laura Anna Stortoni and Mary Prentice Lillie (New York: Italica Press, 1996), 174–79.

9. "[L]a trama delle parole sta sul fatto come un vetro trasparente." De Blasi, *Le scrittrici*, 1:44.

10. Quoted in Lucia Re, "Fascist Theories of 'Woman' and the Construction of Gender," in *Mothers of Invention: Women, Italian Fascism, and Culture*, ed. Robin Pickering-Iazzi (Minneapolis: University of Minnesota Press, 1996), 85.

11. Re, "Fascist Theories," 90.

12. Gentile's ideas on the family and his program for educational reform essentially laid the foundation for most legislation centering around women and the family enacted during the Fascist era. As "founder and president of the Italian Institute of Fascist Culture and . . . the major arbiter of Fascist cultural politics in the 1920s," Lucia Re rightly calls him "the official thinker of the regime." Ibid., 81.

13. De Grazia, *How Fascism Ruled Women*, 73.

14. Juliana Schiesari, "In Praise of Virtuous Women? For a Genealogy of Gender Morals in Renaissance Italy," *Annali d'Italianistica* 7 (1989): 68.

15. Robin Pickering-Iazzi, ed., Introduction to *Mothers of Invention: Women, Italian Fascism, and Culture* (Minneapolis: University of Minnesota Press, 1995), x.

16. De Grazia, *How Fascism Ruled Women*, 14.

17. See Gramsci's essays on "The Modern Prince" in *The Modern Prince and Other Writings*, trans. Louis Marks (New York: International Publishers, 1959), and also Joseph V. Femia, *Gramsci's Political Thought: Hegemony, Consciousness, and the Revolutionary Process* (Oxford: Clarendon Press, 1981).

18. "[S]ono lampi, illuminazioni subitanee che il manierismo s'affretta a raffreddare e appiattire." De Blasi, *Le scrittrici*, 1:123.

19. Laura Anna Stortoni, ed., Introduction to *Women Poets of the Italian Renaissance*, xviii.

20. "Ho detto che più della poesia spirituale . . . espressa da Vittoria Colonna . . . gradisse al pubblico la smaniosa dolcissima femineità delle *Rime* amorose di Gaspara Stampa. Ma non bisogna esagerare nemmeno in questo. Un lettore non avvertito sbadiglierebbe al decimo dei duecentoventi e più sonetti che formano il canzoniere amoroso." De Blasi, *Le scrittrici*, 1:149.

21. Most historians trace the beginning of this program to Mussolini's speech of May 26, 1927 (the *Discorso dell'Ascenzione*).

22. Giovanni Gentile, "La donna nella coscienza moderna," in *Preliminari allo studio del fanciullo*, vol. 42 of *Opere Complete di Giovanni Gentile* (Sansoni: Firenze, 1969), 85.

23. See Re, "Fascist Theories," for a discussion of the rhetoric of Gentile's argument in "La donna nella coscienza moderna" and a comparison with the more radical theories of Cesare Lombroso. For a treatment of the feminist writings of Teresa Labriola and her compromises on the matter of essentialism versus culturally constructed identity, see Barbara Spackman, "Fascist Women and the Rhetoric of Virility," in *Mothers of Invention*, ed. Pickering-Iazzi, 100–120.

24. De Grazia, *How Fascism Ruled Women*, 88.

25. On this matter, see Lesley Caldwell's synthetic review of Fascist-era legislation on family and women's issues in "Reproducers of the Nation: Women and the Family in Fascist Policy," in *Rethinking Italian Fascism: Capitalism, Populism and Culture*, ed. David Forgacs (Lawrence and Wishart: London, 1986). According to Caldwell, Fascism attempted to project ideal images of woman and mother (which became synonymous under the regime) through both rhetorical means and legislative policies, largely bolstered by a close relationship between the regime and the Catholic Church. This agenda touched virtually all areas of women's lives: moral welfare, ideal physical shape, fashion choices, labor, and demographic controls. This latter is particularly noteworthy for our purposes, as the Fascist demographic campaign's attempts to bring population to ideal levels resulted in the legislation of matrimonial and procreative decisions. Concerns over the *difesa della stirpe* [defense of the race] led to a legislative program of infant health care aid, marriage loans, tax concessions for large families, birth and marriage premiums, and rulings against contraception and abortion. In the workplace, women were excluded from large areas of the educational and governmental sectors from 1923, even as deceptively generous working mother laws were passed that had the effect of making women (and especially mothers) "undesirable" in some sectors and that had no effect whatsoever in others (notably domestic and agricultural, the largest employers of women in the 1930s). Also of interest is Caldwell's treatment of OMNI (Opera Nazionale Maternità ed Infanzia) [National agency for maternity and childhood] and its symbolic and rhetorical strategies for promoting large families and the cult of the mother, such as La Giornata della Madre e del Fanciullo [Mother and child day]. An equally informative, if profoundly theoretical, discussion of the range of Fascist ideas of gender can be found in Re, "Fascist Theories."

26. De Grazia, *How Fascism Ruled Women*, 6–7.

27. "[W]hile propaganda insisted that, by nature, women were fulfilled only in motherhood, government social services cast doubt on whether women were naturally the better nurturers, especially when the women were unwed, delinquent, or simply impoverished. And while propagandists idealized biological destiny, medical professionals and social workers silently undercut the control traditionally exercised by female kinship and community networks over childbirth and infant nurturing." Ibid., 60. For a complete discussion of the legislation of motherhood under Fascism, see ibid., chap. 3.

28. Autarchy was imposed on the "Italian Empire" in the form of League of Nations sanctions after its 1935 invasion of Ethiopia and was then appropriated by Mussolini and the regime as a badge of honor. Many of the calls for personal and national sacrifice made after the militarization of the regime were made in the name of autarchy, which was added to already existing elements of Italy's imperial myth. For further reading on this aspect of Italian economic and cultural life under Fascism, see Giuseppe Carlo Marion, *Autarchia della cultura: Intellettuali e fascismo negli anni trenta* (Roma: Riuniti, 1983); Jeffrey Schnapp, "The Fabric of Modern Times," *Critical Inquiry*

24 (1997): 191–245; and Barbara Spackman, "Shopping for Autarchy: Fascism and Reproductive Fantasy in Mario Camerini's *Grandi magazzini*," in *Re-viewing Fascism: Italian Cinema, 1922–1943*, ed. Jacqueline Reich and Piero Garofalo (Bloomington: Indiana University Press, 2002), 276–92.

29. De Grazia, *How Fascism Ruled Women*, 78.

30. De Blasi, *Le scrittrici*, 1:45.

31. "[A]lmeno per lo spazio del nostro primo volume—il conto si ferma." De Blasi, *Le scrittrici*, 1:51.

32. "[S]'avviò, stupendamente sola, per la strada di cui, cinquecent'anni dopo, i romantici detteranno gli itinerarii: *Dio, patria, dolore, e amore*. I romantici. Che è quanto dire . . . i moderni." De Blasi, *Le scrittrici*, 1:12–13. Emphasis mine.

33. "Non reclusa in un chiostro, ma orante ed oprante, le s'accolse intorno uno stuolo di discepoli—prelati, magistrati, pittori, poeti—, e le cose della politica, che è quanto dire, a quel tempo, le cose di tutta la vita sociale e civile, la trassero a gravi imprese e a coraggiose proposte." Ibid., 1:33.

34. Ibid., 1:36.

35. "L'impegno con cui si adoperò per ridar la pace alla cristianità affievolì sempre più la sua fibra già indebolita dai digiuni e dalle penitenze." Ibid., 1:34.

36. Leonora della Genga, member of the noble della Genga family, is best known for the Petrarchan sonnet discussed by De Blasi. The dearth of biographical information on Giustina Levi-Perotti caused De Blasi to call her the "pseudo-Perotti," though she is generally acknowledged by modern scholars to have been contemporary with Petrarch and to have inspired one of his sonnets with one of her own.

37. Translation mine.

38. "Ma che differenza tra queste frasche in cui fa capolino l'io che cerca i battimani, e la dichiarazione che Caterina ripete di sè, 'serva e schiava de' servi di Gesù Cristo,' Caterina che ammoniva: 'Sappiate che di me non si può vedere nè contare altro che somma miseria; ignorante e di basso intendimento.'" De Blasi, *Le scrittrici*, 1:46.

39. Lucrezia Tornabuoni de' Medici (1425–82) was the author of forty-nine extant private letters to family members, nine lauds, and five long sacred poems in ottava or terza rima based on biblical stories. She was the wife of Piero de' Medici, mother of Lorenzo the Magnificent and Giuliano de' Medici, and was the generous benefactress of orphaned girls. Alessandra Macinghi Strozzi, Florentine, wife of Matteo Strozzi, engaged in extensive correspondence with two of her eight children who were exiled as a result of their family's political conflicts with the Medicis and working far from home. For information on Strozzi and for the text of the letters, see the bilingual edition, *Selected Letters of Alessandra Strozzi*, trans. and annotated by Heather Gregory (Berkeley: University of California Press, 1997).

40. "[I] Medici del quattrocento erano fiorentini fin nel midollo delle ossa, fin sulla cima dei capelli. Figurarsi se le loro donne o quelle che trafficavano per le loro case avrebbero potuto soffrire di rinchiudersi nelle biblioteche per uscirne con un puzzo di stantio addosso a immusonirsi e a prendersi sul serio in radunanze che lasciavano il tempo che trovavano!" De Blasi, *Le scrittrici*, 1:64.

41. "Ora noi non cambieremmo le elucubrate e sterili meditazioni di Cassandra Fedele . . . con un sorriso di Madonna Lucrezia, madre del Magnifico Lorenzo, un di que' sorrisi pensosi e affettuosi, arguti e avveduti che ripagarono con candore materno le fatiche del Poliziano volte dagli studii classici alla poesia italiana, che ispirarono e

guidarono i canti del Morgante di Luigi Pulci. . . . *Più dobbiamo esserle grati di questo, che del suo un'importanza relativa—intima e domestica —, consolandosi del bel recitare che ne facevano i suoi nipotini nelle ville di Fiesole e di Careggi*." Ibid., 1:65. Emphasis mine.

42. "[I]l tenue splendore di Lucrezia è stato oscurato dai grandi personaggi a lei vicini, per cui spicciamente ella diviene 'amica del Poliziano e del Pulci,' oppure 'ispiratrice del *Morgante*.'" Fulvio Pezzarossa, ed., Introduction to *I Poemetti Sacri di Lucrezia Tornabuoni* (Firenze: Olschki, 1978), 9. Translation mine.

43. De Blasi, *Le scrittrici*, 1:86–87.

44. The line quoted is "Qual vaga Filomena, che fuggita / è da la odiata gabbia." Ibid., 1:93. The translation is "Like the lovely Philomela, fleeing / Her hateful prison," quoted in Ann Rosalind Jones, *The Currency of Eros: Women's Love Lyric in Europe, 1540–1620*, Women of Letters (Bloomington: Indiana University Press, 1990), 116.

45. "la più accesa e torturante passione della maturità di Tullia." De Blasi, *Le scrittrici*, 1:93.

46. "[E] non è gran che, specie nell'incontro faticoso e disarmonico di sillabe male assortite che nella seconda quartina danno ai versi un'asprezza insostenibile. Si giudichi da questo il rimanente." Ibid., 1:93. Belittling tone aside, De Blasi does devote a significant portion of the anthology to D'Aragona, reproducing eleven poems and the beginning and concluding sections of her "Dialogo della infinità dell'amore."

47. "Veronica Franco, pubblica peccatrice veneziana, non si vergognava di essere ciò che era, e . . . si capisce subito, e lei non ci tiene a nasconderlo, con chi s'ha da fare." Ibid., 1:97.

48. "il piglio disinvolto che non è raro nelle *Rime*." Ibid., 1:98.

49. "Che ne fu del marito? Era un medico, e null'altro sappiamo se non che convisse poco tempo con quella esuberantissima moglie. *Che ne fu dei figliuoli? Anche di loro, e dovette averne parecchi e da parecchi, le cronache tacciono*. Ben si sa di lei, invece: e non solo il prodotto de' suoi studii—le *Rime* e le *Lettere familgiari a diversi*—e i fasti della sua vita gaudente; ma anche si sa che negli anni più tardi passò dalla dissipazione alla pietà, con un fervore così operante e sincero che a tutt'oggi ne durano i frutti: l'Ospizio di Santa Maria del Soccorso per le fanciulle abbandonate, a Venezia, trae infatti le sue origini dalla fondazione della convertita Veronica Franco." Ibid., 1:99. Emphasis mine.

50. Spackman, "Fascist Women," 106, 112.

51. Ibid., 113. Emphasis mine.

52. "reipiloga[re], attraverso un esame sereno e minuzioso, che valore essa [l'attività intellettuale femminile] abbia presso di noi, e quale e quanta essa sia." De Blasi, *Le scrittrici*, 1:9–10.

53. "Da ora in avanti non c'è più, le scrittrici, da andare a cercarle col lanternino: anzi, via via che procederemo, le sentiremo . . . agitarsi in fatti talvolta onorevoli e talvolta no in maniera da poter di talune segnalare, se non proprio l'eccellenza letteraria, certo *i ritratti morali* e anche fisici. . . . Preambolo poco incoraggiante, se si pensa che *dobbiamo dissertare di qualità d'arte e d'ingegno artistico*, e già confessiamo che il fuoco centrale dell'attenzione sarà per molte scrittrici richiamato da altro e forse da tutt'altro che da preclare virtù poetiche." Ibid., 1:48. Emphasis mine.

54. "ornato e nitido . . . senza intimità," "insomma non manca nulla," ibid., 1:127; "se dovessimo ricostruire la donna dalla poetessa, il cuore da metterle in petto non sapremmo proprio dove andarlo a scovare," 1:126–27; "riflesso e meditato," 1:126.

55. "[O]nesta non meno che bella, quando una morte tragica le tolse il marito,

Alessandra finì, giovanissima, monaca benedettina nel convento di San Pier Maggiore." Ibid., 1:61.

56. "un esemplare senza esemplo." Ibid., 1:131.

57. "unica alta poesia femminile del secolo"; "le manca il fuoco che rapisce; ed è questa, con la condanna delle altre rimatrici, anche la condanna di Vittoria Colonna poetessa." Ibid., 1:45.

58. "[I]nsomma il giorno in cui si compiva un mutamento nella vita di lei, anche il cammino della storia procedeva, ed ella, *qualunque sia il giudizio da darsi alle sue rime*, è pur sempre la donna insigne che balza fuori della mediocrità col nome e con l'animo." Ibid., 1:147. Emphasis mine.

BIBLIOGRAPHY

Bergalli, Luisa, ed. *Componimenti delle più illustri rimatrici di ogni secolo*. Venice: Morra, 1726.

Caldwell, Lesley. "Reproducers of the Nation: Women and the Family in Fascist Policy." In *Rethinking Italian Fascism: Capitalism, Populism, Culture*, ed. David Forgacs. Lawrence and Wishart: London, 1986.

De Blasi, Jolanda, ed. *Le scrittrici italiane dalle origini al 1800*. 2 vols. Florence: Nemi, 1930.

———. Premessa [Introduction] to *Giovanni Pascoli*. Florence: G. C. Sansoni, 1937.

———. Premessa [Introduction] to *Romanità e germanesimo*. Florence: G. C. Sansoni, 1941.

De Grand, Alexander J. *Italian Fascism: Its Origins and Development*. Lincoln: University of Nebraska Press, 1978.

De Grazia, Victoria. *How Fascism Ruled Women: Italy, 1922–1945*. Berkeley: University of California Press, 1992.

Femia, Joseph V. *Gramsci's Political Thought: Hegemony, Consciousness, and the Revolutionary Process*. Oxford: Clarendon Press, 1981.

Fondo Michelstaedter. <http://www.michelstaedter.it>. June 19, 2002. Lettere.

Gabinetto Scientifico Letterario G. C. Vieusseux. <http://www.vieusseux.fi.it>. June 19, 2002. Cenni Storici.

Gentile, Giovanni. "La donna nella coscienza moderna." In *Preliminari allo studio del fanciullo*, 81–99. Vol. 42 of *Opere Complete di Giovanni Gentile*. Sansoni: Firenze, 1969.

Gramsci, Antonio. *The Modern Prince and Other Writings*. Trans. Louis Marks. New York: International Publishers, 1959.

Graziosi, Mariolina. "Gender Struggle and the Social Manipulation and Ideological Use of Gender Identity in the Interwar Years." In *Mothers of Invention: Women, Italian Fascism, and Culture*, ed. Robin Pickering-Iazzi, 26–51. Minneapolis: University of Minnesota Press, 1996.

Jones, Ann Rosalind. *The Currency of Eros: Women's Love Lyric in Europe, 1540–1620*. Women of Letters. Bloomington: Indiana University Press, 1990.

Lyttleton, Adrian, ed. *Italian Fascisms*. New York: Harper and Row, 1973.

Maionchi, Simona. "Lyceum Club Internazionale di Firenze—circolo culturale femminile. Ricognizione storica dai documenti manoscritti del 1908 ai bollettini a stampa." Archivio di Stato di Firenze, March 5, 2001. <http://www.archiviodistato.firenze.it/memoriadonne/materiali_donne/maionchi.pdf>. June 19, 2002.

Marion, Giuseppe Carlo. *Autarchia della cultura: Intellettuali e fascismo negli anni trenta*. Roma: Riuniti, 1983.

Nolte, Ernst. *Three Faces of Fascism*. Trans. Leila Vennewitz. New York: Holt, Rinehart, and Winston, 1965.

Orban, Clara. "Women, Futurism, and Fascism." In *Mothers of Invention: Women, Italian Fascism, and Culture*, ed. Robin Pickering-Iazzi, 52–75. Minneapolis: University of Minnesota Press, 1996.

Pezzarossa, Fulvio, ed. Introduction to *I Poemetti Sacri di Lucrezia Tornabuoni*. Florence: Olschki, 1978.

Pickering-Iazzi, Robin, ed. *Mothers of Invention: Women, Italian Fascism, and Culture*. Minneapolis: University of Minnesota Press, 1995.

Re, Lucia. "Futurism and Feminism." *Annali d'Italianistica* 7 (1989): 253–71.

———. "Fascist Theories of 'Woman' and the Construction of Gender." In *Mothers of Invention: Women, Italian Fascism, and Culture*, ed. Robin Pickering-Iazzi, 76–99. Minneapolis: University of Minnesota Press, 1996.

Salvemini, Gaetano. *The Origins of Fascism in Italy*. New York: Harper and Row, 1973.

Schiesari, Juliana. "In Praise of Virtuous Women? For a Genealogy of Gender Morals in Renaissance Italy." *Annali d'Italianistica* 7 (1989): 66–85.

Schnapp, Jeffrey. "The Fabric of Modern Times." *Critical Inquiry* 24 (1997): 191–245.

Spackman, Barbara. *Fascist Virilities: Rhetoric, Ideology, and Social Fantasy in Italy*. Minneapolis: University of Minnesota Press, 1996.

———. "Fascist Women and the Rhetoric of Virility." In *Mothers of Invention: Women, Italian Fascism, and Culture*, ed. Robin Pickering-Iazzi, 100–120. Minneapolis: University of Minnesota Press, 1996.

———. "Shopping for Autarchy: Fascism and Reproductive Fantasy in Mario Camerini's *Grandi magazzini*." In *Re-viewing Fascism: Italian Cinema, 1922–1943*, ed. Jacqueline Reich and Piero Garofalo. Bloomington: Indiana University Press, 2002.

Stortoni, Laura Anna, ed. Introduction to *Women Poets of the Italian Renaissance: Courtly Ladies and Courtesans*. Trans. Laura Anna Stortoni and Mary Prentice Lillie. New York: Italica Press, 1996.

Strozzi, Alessandra. *Selected Letters of Alessandra Strozzi*. Trans. and annotated by Heather Gregory. Berkeley: University of California Press, 1997.

West, Rebecca. "'A voce piena': An Introduction to Women's Voices in Italian Literature." *Annali d'Italianistica* 7 (1989): 4–15.

A Woman for All Seasons

THE REINVENTION OF ANNE ASKEW

Elaine V. Beilin

A smiling young woman in a bright yellow gown with a Tudor headdress and long brunette hair arrives at the court of Henry VIII in the spring of 1545. Soon, the voice-over tells us, she will be "trapped in the Tower's nightmare world, the victim of cruel torture." On the television screen Anne Askew appears in her most recent cultural configuration as the subject of an episode of The Learning Channel's *Tales from the Tower* (1998). Askew looks out from a portrait frame as the voice-over continues: "Forced to marry a man she did not love, independent and headstrong, she rebelled against the abusive marriage and sued for divorce. . . . To make things worse, her husband accused her of heresy for challenging the church's teachings." Askew's cause is supported by a number of "powerful women" at court, including Queen Katherine Parr, who befriends "Anne"; the friendship is dangerous, however, because belief in the doctrines of the Reformation is heresy, and Anne must do battle with bishops, government officials, and Henry VIII himself to defend her Protestant views. But the reason for Askew's inclusion in these *Tales* appears to be less the drama of her confrontation with the authorities and more, as the episode lead-in makes clear, because she was tortured on the rack in the "notorious secret basement room" of the Tower.[1]

In that room, we finally hear a voice-over of Askew's own words, spoken from her "own testimony."

> Then they did put me on the racke, bycause I confessed no ladyes nor gentyllwomen to be of my opynyon, and theron they kepte me a long tyme. And bycause I laye styll and ded not crye, my lorde Chauncellour . . . toke peynes to racke me [with] . . . [his] owne handes, tyll I was nygh dead.[2]
>
> *[Then they put me on the rack because I confessed no ladies or gentlewomen to be of my opinion, and they kept me on the rack for a long time. And because I lay still and did not cry, my lord Chancellor . . . took pains to rack me with his own hands until I was nearly dead.]*

Indeed, this is the only point in the episode when we do hear Askew's exact words from *The firste examinacyon* (1546) and *The lattre examinacyon* (1547), her own account of her imprisonment for the sacramentarian heresy and her interrogations by officials of church and state in the last days of Henry VIII. In *The Examinations*, in spare, compelling language, Askew records her arrests and her questioning, continually using scriptural allusion, irony, and understatement to represent powerfully dramatic confrontations with her inquisitors and to articulate her fervent Protestant faith.

Askew is almost completely silent, however, about the details of her own biography, giving no information about her background or any court connections she may have had. In her account of the interrogation leading up to her torture in the Tower, she does record that her questioners show an interest in her acquaintance with court ladies, but she writes only that "Then they asked me of my ladye of Sothfolke, my ladye of Sussex, my ladye of Hertforde, my ladye Dennye, and my ladye Fizwyllyams. I sayd, if I shuld pronounce anye thynge agaynst them, that I were not hable to prove it" (121–22).

Her answer is a good example of the ways in which Askew continually subverts the interrogation itself: she shifts authority to herself by informing her interrogators that any answer she makes will be meaningless because it lacks evidence. Certainly, as this essay will show, her self-representation as a woman of faith engaged in religious debate is often quite different from her representation by other writers.[3] Unlike many early modern women writers, Askew has been a continuous presence over the centuries, but more often as a canonized martyr rather than as a canonized writer. It appears that her very martyrdom has occluded her authorship: rather than becoming a "sacred" text, Askew's *Examinations* has been fragmented and fished for the parts needed to shape the reinvention of Anne Askew as required for hagiography, ballad, sermon, novel—or television episode.

After Askew was executed for heresy in July 1546, her manuscript came into the hands of the Protestant polemicist John Bale, then living in exile on the continent; he published *The firste examinacyon* in November 1546 and *The lattre examinacyon* in January 1547, probably in Wesel in the duchy of Cleves. Apparently deciding that Askew's text would assist the Reformers' campaign against English Catholicism, Bale wrote a preface and an "Elucidation" to demonstrate Askew's place in providential history and to interpret her life and work as part of the anti-Catholic struggle. During the reign of the Protestant King Edward VI, Askew's *Examinations* appeared in three editions: in 1547 with Bale's "Elucidation" and in 1548 and around 1550 without Bale's commentary. In Elizabeth I's reign, *The Examinations* were published around 1560, again without Bale's commentary. John Foxe, the Protestant historian and martyrologist, published a Latin translation of Askew's *Examinations* in his history of the Reformation, *Rerum in Ecclesia Gestarum . . . Commentarii* (1559), and also her English text in his *Actes and Monuments* (1563). Thus, from the beginning, Askew's work was widely available, although published within the contexts that her editors or publishers chose for her work.[4]

But the creators of *Tales from the Tower* do not direct our attention to Askew the writer of Protestant polemics. Part of the purpose of the episode is to show Askew stretched on the rack in the Tower, and yet even there the focus soon shifts to her torturers. Probably drawing on a narrative added to the second edition of Foxe's *Actes and Monuments* (1570), this reenactment of the torture scene shows the lieutenant of the Tower entering suddenly, reacting in horror when he sees the lord chancellor racking Askew, and deciding to notify the king immediately. Opening out the scene and freely inventing details, the episode presents, complete with maps, a race between Lord Chancellor Wriothsley on horseback and the lieutenant in a boat on the River Thames as each strives to reach Henry VIII at Whitehall first. The lieutenant wins and tells Henry about Askew's racking, so that when Wriothsley arrives he is "met with a brutal reception" as Henry slaps his face for offending the king's honor. I can only speculate that because Askew's racking is represented with some restraint, perhaps with an eye to a family or school audience, her torture had only limited dramatic possibilities, whereas the action of the race to the king and the shock of the slap provide some additional conflict and visual interest. The final shot of the scene at Whitehall, a close-up of a smirkingly triumphant Katherine Parr, adds a juicy hint of royal gossip.

As the episode continues, Askew is once more the center of attention because she is again in trouble for "her radical views on religion," and when "she preached in public, her celebrity drew large crowds." No evidence from the time confirms what would have been Askew's illegal public preaching; whatever celebrity she actually possessed appears to have derived from her martyrdom and from the subsequent dissemination of her *Examinations*. The episode concludes with Askew's burning at Smithfield, the execution grounds outside of London Wall, and focuses largely on the "merciful" bag of gunpowder placed around her neck to "blow her head off" before she burns to death. Here, a violent detail delineates Askew's horrific death, replacing, for instance, Askew's own words, like these in her response to a letter from her coreligionist, John Lascelles, in which she writes movingly of the strong faith in God's providence that gives her courage to face death.

> Oh frynde most derelye beloved in God. I marvele not a lyttle, what shuld move yow, to judge in me so slendre a faythe, as to feare deathe, whych is the ende of all myserye. In the lorde I desyre yow, not to beleve of me soch wykednesse. For I doubt it not, but God wyll performe hys worke in me, lyke as he hath begonne. (133)
>
> *[Oh friend most dearly beloved in God. I marvel not a little what moves you to judge so slender a faith in me as that I should fear death, which is the end of all misery. In the Lord, I desire you not to believe such wickedness of me. For I do not doubt but that God will perform his work in me, just as he has begun.]*

Similarly, the television show does not dramatize Askew's refusal to recant despite the urgings of Nicholas Shaxton, the former bishop of Salisbury, who "counselled me to recant as he had done. Then I sayd to hym, that it had bene good for hym, never to have bene borne with many other lyke wordes" (119). In *The Examinations*, Askew places herself within a scriptural context, invoking as a model the death of St. Stephen, the first martyr, who is represented in Acts 7 as historian, resister of corrupt government, preacher, teacher, and imitator of Christ.[5]

In *Tales from the Tower*, however, Askew assumes little of this significance; instead, she appears almost entirely as a victim. Students with whom I discussed the episode remarked that the spiritual drama that Askew creates from her interrogations was replaced by the visually more horrifying racking and then the "exciting" race between horse and boat with the climactic slap in the face. In her most recent reinvention, then, Askew has been shaped to fit the generic requirements of an episode of purportedly sensational "tales" for television.[6] In this genre, except for her comparatively restrained account of her racking, there is little room for Askew's own words, especially the uncomfortable severity of her theological arguments or her incessant allusion to Scripture. She is incorrectly described but, significantly, not shown as a preacher who drew "large crowds"; she is not represented as a writer. Once Askew's body is displayed on the rack and on the pyre, her purpose for *Tales from the Tower* is concluded. A reconfigured narrative about Anne Askew takes precedence over her text, a version of her life over her work—but it is a life in which Askew's agency is erased by emphasis on external forces. This is, of course, not an inevitable strategy in the reinventing of a martyr; although they were working in a radically different medium, the writers of *Tales from the Tower* appear to take the opposite tack to the one Robert Bolt chose in his account of the most famous Henrician martyr, Thomas More.

In his 1960 preface to *A Man for All Seasons*, Bolt characterizes More as a man "with an adamantine sense of his own self," as a Christian who "found something in himself without which life was valueless."[7] Bolt's profound admiration for the humanist More results in an idealized portrait of a noble patriarch. Drawing much material from More's letters and thus recognizing More as an author and polemicist, Bolt creates the wise, ironic, courageous character whom at least two generations of scholars have been working to make more nuanced and complex in the public imagination. In an interview, Fred Zinnemann, the director of the 1966 movie based on Bolt's stage play, explains his interest in More: "Thomas More standing up for what he believes in, until he gets his head cut off—which in his defeat is really a victory—is to me a celebration of the human spirit."[8] Notably, then, More's "self" is everywhere in evidence; Bolt's strong emphasis on dialogue and language in both stage play and film means that he can shape More's character in a dynamic relationship with his antagonists. By contrast, the pressing visual requirements, narrative voice-over, and sensationalism of *Tales from the Tower* obfuscate the "historical" Askew and her language. Nevertheless, television is not entirely to blame, for this treatment is a paradigm for what continually happens to this particular woman writer—a "self," as constructed by her own words, is subsumed by the "story" of her life, a story that is cut and shaped by pressures created at the intersection of genre, gender, and religion.

Remarkably, Askew's text has always been available. After the initial six separate editions, it was included in every edition of Foxe's *Actes and Monuments*, meaning that Askew's *Examinations* have never been out of print; however, there appear to have been no further separate editions of *The Examinations* until the mid-nineteenth century, when they were published by the Religious Tract Society in London (1831, 1836, 1840, 186?) and in Philadelphia by the Presbyterian Board of Publication in 1842. In 1849, *The Examinations* were included in an edition of her first editor's works, *The Select*

Works of John Bale . . . Containing the Examinations of Lord Cobham, William Thorpe, and Anne Askewe and the Image of both Churches, edited by the Reverend Henry Christmas for the Parker Society. Founded by Evangelicals in 1840, the Parker Society's mission was to counter Tractarian editions of the fathers and "to republish the classics of the English Reformation."[9] The society intended, of course, to publish John Bale's work, which, luckily, included his edition of Askew's *Examinations*. After this edition, there were no further separate editions until the 1990s, when two editions appeared in series intended to recover significant women writers: a facsimile of the first edition, published by Ashgate, and a lightly edited version based on the first edition, published in the Women Writers in English series by Oxford University Press.[10] Before these editions, then, the publication of Askew's text was partly serendipitous and partly the result of a religious mandate. But until recently, religious texts by women have lacked full or wide appreciation.

In *Writing Women's Literary History*, Margaret Ezell argues that it has proved difficult to write religious women writers into literary history because of generic priorities, ahistorical assumptions about the oppressive role of religion for women, and preconceptions about what constituted acceptable or interesting female authorship, personae, positions, and emotions.[11] With the notable exception of Ruth Hughey's groundbreaking 1932 Cornell dissertation, "Cultural Interests of Women in England from 1524–1640," this situation long affected Askew's reception. Treating Askew—among others—as a writer, Hughey remarks on the importance of her use of the "dialogue device" and comments on "the penetration of her thinking and upon her knowledge of the technical [i.e., theological] points under discussion."[12] Not until the 1980s was Askew's significance as a writer again recognized, beginning with Betty Travitsky's anthology, *The Paradise of Women* (1981), and John King's analysis in *English Reformation Literature* (1982).[13] Recent textual and cultural studies have brought Askew the writer to the foreground, revising considerably the sole emphasis on the martyr's story. Within the last few years, new scholarship has most cogently demonstrated how Askew's text operates. Thomas Betteridge shows how Askew incorporates three kinds of discourse to create her "performance" as the handmaid of God; and Theresa Kemp argues that Askew's text represents the bids for power of Henrician conservatives, Reformers, and Askew herself.[14]

We may wonder, then, whether Askew the religious writer has finally "arrived." The growing scholarship on Askew indeed seems to be a beachhead in the academy or a toehold in the canon. However, *Tales from the Tower* tells us that a cultural representation of Askew the woman martyr, the nonwriter, still lives, accruing ever-new details. This distinction should instruct us because it helps us to see why Askew the martyr and Askew the writer have often been mutually exclusive. As I examine a few of the many representations of Askew over the last 450 years, I will argue that the religious genres in which she appears actually require subordinating, or erasing, Askew's authorial self. In a variety of texts, Askew has become a female hero, but one who habitually speaks from a script other than her own.

Askew's first publisher, John Bale, bears some responsibility for beginning the process of Askew's "deauthorization."[15] To write his history of the Reformed church, Bale literally surrounds Askew's text with commentary written to expose the crimes of the Catholic hierarchy and to explain how his "yonge, dayntye, and tender" (7) subject is an important representation of St. Paul's text, "The strength of God is here made perfyght by weaknesse" (13). Many readers of *The Examinations* have distinguished between Askew's self-representation as a theological controversialist and opponent of the Anglo-Catholic court faction and the Askew created by Bale, her self-styled "elucidator." His violently anti-Catholic commentary uses Askew's text as evidence that the battle with the Antichrist—the Catholic Church—was at hand and that Askew's trial and execution demonstrated God's providential strengthening of the weak—a young woman who becomes a martyr for the True Church. For Bale, and later for John Foxe, Askew is an exemplum, a "gentylwoman . . . borne of a verye auncyent and noble stocke" (9) who rejected a life of privilege for her faith.

At the beginning of Askew's *Lattre examinacyon*, Bale provides a brief biographical note about Askew's background before she became known in London as a Reformer or heretic. Glossing Askew's account of her examination by the Privy Council during which she refused to talk about her husband, Thomas Kyme, Bale writes:

> Concernynge mastre Kyme, thys *shuld seme* to be the matter. Her Father Sir Wyllyam Askewe knyght and hys father olde mastre Kyme,were sumtyme of famylyaryte and neybers within the countye of Lyncolne shyre. Wherupon the seyd Sir Wyllyam, covenaunted wyth hym for lucre, to have hys eldest doughter marryed with hys sonne and heyre (as an ungodlye maner it is in Englande moch used amonge noble men). And as it was her chaunce to dye afore the tyme of marryage, to save the moneye he constrayned thys to supplye her rowme. So that in the ende she was compelled agaynst her wyll or fre consent to marrye with hym. Notwithstandynge the marryage ones past, she demeaned her selfe lyke a Christen wyfe, and had by hym (*as I am infourmed*) ii. chyldren. In processe of tyme by oft readynge of the sacred Bible, she fell clerelye from all olde superstycyons of papystrye, to a perfyght beleve in Jhesus Christ. Wherby she so offended the

prestes (as is to be seane afore) that he at their suggestion, vyolentlye drove her oute of hys howse. Wherupon she thought her selfe free from that uncomelye kynde of coacted marryage, by thys doctryne of S. Paule 1.Cor.7. If a faytfull woman have an unbelevynge husbande, whych wyll not tarrye with her, she may leave hym. For a brother or syster is not in subjeccyon to soch, specyallye where as the marryage afore is unlawfull. Upon thys occasyon *(I heare saye)* she sought of the law a dyvorcement from hym, namelye and above all, bycause he so cruellye drove her out of hys howse in despyght of Christes veryte. She *coulde not thynke* hym worthye of her marryage whych so spyghtfullye hated God the chefe autor of marryage. Of thys matter was she first examyned *(I thynke)* at hys instaunt laboure and sute. (92–93; emphasis mine)

[Concerning Master Kyme, this seemed to be the matter. Her father, Sir William Askew, knight, and his father, old Master Kyme, were at one time friendly and neighbors in the county of Lincolnshire. Whereupon, the said Sir William contracted with him to marry his eldest daughter to his son and heir for profit (according to an ungodly custom practiced in England among noble men). And as it chanced that she [the eldest daughter] died before the time of the marriage, to save the money, he forced this [daughter, i.e., Anne Askew] to take her place. So that in the end, she was compelled against her will or free consent to marry him. Notwithstanding, once the marriage was performed, she conducted herself like a Christian wife, and had by him (as I am informed) two children. In course of time, by often reading the sacred Bible, she fell clearly from all old superstitions of papistry to a perfect belief in Jesus Christ. Whereby she so offended the priests (as is to be seen above) that at their suggestion, he violently drove her out of his house. Whereupon she thought her self free from that unseemly kind of forced marriage, by this doctrine of Saint Paul, 1. Corinthians 7: If a faithful woman has an unbelieving husband who will not stay with her, she may leave him. For a brother or sister is not in subjection to such, especially whereas the marriage is unlawful before. Upon this occasion (I hear say) she sought from the law a divorce from him, namely and above all, because he so cruelly drove her out of his house in spite of Christ's truth. She could not think him worthy of marriage to her who so spitefully hated God, the chief author of marriage. She was first examined about this matter (I think) as a result of his importunate efforts and suit.]

To his credit, Bale hedges his account with "this shuld seme," "as I am infourmed," "I heare saye," "she coulde not thynke," and "I thynke." Elsewhere in the text, he does identify his sources for other information as "duche merchants," but here Bale does not or cannot name sources, and so he implicitly acknowledges his suppositions. Perhaps Bale hesitates because he has no sources and because he is responding to a significant generic pressure. His own earlier life as a priest and his violent, satiric attack on Catholic saints in *Actes of Englysh Votaryes* (1546) indicate that Bale knew Catholic hagiography inside out. He knew the importance of the saint's life as exemplum, and he recognized that details of the life were essential to show how the saint conquers the material world, finds the path to faith, and dedicates her life to God. In casting Askew as a female Protestant martyr, Bale places her deviance from "good womanhood" in the familiar context of the female saint's life, which characteristically celebrates the ways in which the saint dedicates her life to God, breaking the rules and challenging authority particularly in regard to conventional gender roles. The lives of Saint Lucy, Saint Agnes, Saint Margaret, and Saint Cecilia are familiar examples. Indeed, Bale explicitly mentions Cecilia in his preface, comparing Askew to the "holye mayde Cecilia," who carried "the Gospell of Christ . . . in her harte . . . and never after ceased from the stodye therof, nor from godlye communycacyon and prayer, tyll she was clerlye by most cruell tormentes, taken from thys wretched worlde" (9). *[The holy maid Cecilia (who carried) . . . the Gospel of Christ . . . in her heart . . . and never after ceased the study thereof, nor godly communication and prayer, until she was clearly by most cruel torments taken from this wretched world.]* This passage is very close to the depiction of the saint in *The Golden Legend:* "She always carried the Gospel of Christ hidden in her bosom, and ceased not, day or night, from prayer and converse with God."[16] Countering, however, the insistence of the Catholic saint's life on the subject's virginity, Bale writes of Askew that "the marryage ones past, she demeaned her selfe lyke a Christen wyfe, and had by hym (as I am infourmed) ii. chyldren." No other contemporary sources record the existence of those two children.[17] Considering the importance that Protestantism attached to marriage, we may even wonder whether Bale himself creates the children as part of the reinvention of Askew as a married female Protestant martyr who would replace the Catholic virgin saints.

Bale appears to have construed Askew's text as the guided writing of a medium more than as the work of a writer. For Bale also turns Askew's story, particularly her execution, into a miraculous demonstration of providential signs and wonders. In his account of her burning with three others, he writes,

> Credyblye am I infourmed by dyverse duche merchauntes whych were there present, that in the tyme of their sufferynges, the skye abhorrynge so wycked an acte, sodenlye altered coloure, and the cloudes

> from above gave a thonder clappe, not all unlyke to that is written, Psalm 76. The elementes both declared therin the hygh dyspleasure of God for so tyrannouse a murther of innocents.[18] (154)
>
> *[Credibly am I informed by various Dutch merchants who were present there, that in the time of their sufferings, the sky, abhorring so wicked an act, suddenly altered color, and the clouds from above gave a thunder clap, not at all unlike the one written in Psalm 76. The elements both declared therein the high displeasure of God for so tyrannous a murder of innocents.]*

According to Bale, Askew's death created converts and harmed the Catholic cause in England, for "Manye a wone sayth yet both in Englande and Duchelande, also, O that woman that woman O those men those men" (154–55). [*Many say yet both in England and also in Holland, O that woman that woman; O those men those men.*]

Like Bale, Foxe has a particular view of Askew's life, death, and work.[19] In his epitaph, which appeared at the end of Askew's *Examinations* in *Rerum in Ecclesia Gestarum . . . Commentarii*, Foxe emphasizes the brutal execution and Askew's calm fortitude.

> Artubus luxis resoluta cedunt
> Ossa iuncturis, nihil in pudico
> Corpore infractum est. Superat tyrannos
> Pars tamen una.
> Sola enim nullis potuit moveri
> Lingua rupturis: socias periclo
> Dum suo solvit, iubet & quietam
> Stertere in aurem.[20]
>
> *[Her limbs are forced apart; her bones are broken, severed*
> *from their joints; nothing in that chaste body is left intact.*
> *Still one part of her defeats the tyrants.*
> *For her tongue alone could not be moved by any suffering:*
> *in rescuing her companions from her own peril, she bids*
> *them slumber with untroubled ears.]*[21]

Embedded here is another remnant of the saint's life, the episode showing that no amount of torture or continued attempts to kill the saint can prevent her speech. Saint Lucy, for example, keeps speaking, even though a sword is plunged in her throat. In Foxe's epitaph, the initial discourse of violation is succeeded by Askew's own maternal language as she speaks to comfort her fellow martyrs, to bid them "slumber with untroubled ears." Foxe may have remembered Bale's comparison of Askew to the second-century martyr Blandina, whose burning converted many: "Though Blandina were yonge, yet was she called the mother of martyrs. Manye men have supposed Anne Askewe. for her Christen constancye to be no lesse" (12). Foxe writes: "Shaxton . . . began his Sermon. Anne Askew hearing, and answering againe unto hym, where he sayde well, confirmed the same: where he sayd amysse, there sayd she, he misseth, and speaketh without the booke."[22] Foxe may be using an eyewitness report, as he often did; in either case, he contributes to Askew's martyrology the portrait of a supremely calm and confident believer citing the Bible even as she was tied to the stake.[23]

Bale and Foxe create frames for Askew's work that essentially initiates her martyrology; they signal the manner in which inspirational stories about Askew will increasingly divert attention from Askew's own controversialist text and suppress her authorship. As these narratives, shaped by the discourses of faith, become attached to Askew the female martyr, she becomes a vessel and an exemplum rather than an agent or an author. Her text is absorbed or overwritten in narratives with generic requirements different from the polemic in which she was engaged.

But it is actually a contemporary of Foxe, John Louth, archdeacon of Nottingham, who appears to be responsible for several stories about Askew that survive to be published in the eighteenth and nineteenth centuries. In his "Reminiscences" of Askew's life, Louth recounts how Askew was spied on when she came to London, how she was examined by the lord mayor, and how she was executed. Louth names one Wadloe, a "great papiste" who spies on Askew from the house next door but finds only that she prays all night and is the "devouteste and godliest woman" he has ever known.[24] But Louth claims to have been an actual eyewitness only at the public execution in Smithfield. On that day, he says, "she hadd an angels countenance, and a smylyng face," and he bears witness to a miracle: "And afore God, at the fyrst puttyng-to of the fyar, theyre felle a lytle dewe or a few pleasante droppes apon us that stode by and a pleasant crackyng from heaven."[25] [*And before God, at the first placing of the fire, there fell a little dew or a few pleasant drops upon us that stood by, and a pleasant cracking from heaven*.] Rather than Bale's thunderclap from an angry God, Louth describes God's grace descending on those present at the making of a martyr. Louth offered his "Reminiscences" to Foxe as source material, but for reasons unknown, Foxe did not incorporate any of this material into *Actes and Monuments*; he may have doubted its veracity or its usefulness for his own particular emphasis on the martyrs' suffering or on Askew's "invincible constancie" as she comforted them (Askew 192).

From a radically different perspective, another near-contemporary commentator, Robert Parsons, the Jesuit writer, *agent provocateur,* and educator, attacks such martyrology as a clear spiritual and social danger. In a 1604 treatise written to discredit Protestant "saints" or martyrs, particularly those glorified by Foxe, Parsons took Foxe's treatment of Askew as an opportunity to attack both Foxe and Bale. Parsons tells the counterheroic narrative, and just as Bale needed Askew's youth and gender to argue his ideological position for the Reformation, Parsons needs them to compromise her credibility and inveigh against it. He complains about the freedom with which Askew travels around: that after leaving her husband she "did follow the liberty of the new ghospell, going up and downe at her pleasure" until King Henry "restrayned her by imprisonment."[26] In Parsons's version, Askew is released because she recants, but she is arrested the next year because "she did in secrett seeke to corrupt diuers people, but especially weomen with whome she had conversed; and that she had found meanes to enter with the principall of the land, namely with *Q. Catherine Parre herselfe*." [*She did in secret seek to corrupt various people, but especially women with whom she had conversed; and she had found means to associate with the principal [people] of the land, namely with Queen Catherine Parr herself.*] Parsons reserves particular contempt for the very idea that Askew is a writer, misrepresenting her text and mocking Bale, who places "her among the famous wryters of her age for that perhapps she wrote some 4. or 5. sheets of paper in priuate letters, which yow may see set downe in Foxe" (494). Representing Askew as a woman who defies all injunctions to obedience, silence, chastity, and domesticity, and using the tactics of many misogynist writers, Parsons claims that her speech implies not her Christian heroism but her uncontrolled sexuality: "for that she was a coy dame, and of very evill fame for wantonnesse: in that she left the company of her husband *Maister Kyme,* to gad up and downe the countrey a ghospelling and ghossipinge where she might, & ought not" (495). Here, Parsons represents Askew as the unruly woman who threatens to undermine social order; as David Underdown documents, such fears were widely expressed in the early seventeenth century in vigorous attacks on and repression of independent and outspoken women.[27] For Parsons, then, the best way to discredit Protestant martyrology and the Reformation itself is to represent the Protestant martyr as a woman of unrestrained speech and sexuality roaming the countryside.

In later texts, sympathetic tellers of Askew's story erase Parsons's disapproval yet retain some of his "information," for instance, that Askew, with Joan of Kent, was the supplier of heretical books to the court. In his magisterial history, *Ecclesiastical Memorials* (1721), John Strype collects his materials from Parsons as well as from Foxe and Louth to compose an influential version of Askew's story that will be the acknowledged source of most accounts of Askew's life for the next two centuries. Most notably, despite its earlier rejection by Foxe, Strype enshrines Archdeacon Louth's account of Askew's examination by the lord mayor of London, effectively erasing Askew's version. A comparison of the lord mayor's interrogation in Askew's original text with its later redactions will demonstrate how radically even her supporters modify Askew's persona.

Here, first, is Askew's version of part of her interrogation.

> Besydes thys my lorde mayre layed one thynge unto my charge, which was never spoken of me, but of them. And that was, whether a mouse eatynge the hoste, receyved God or no? Thys questyon ded I never aske, but in dede they asked it of me, wherunto I made them no answere, but smyled. (27)
>
> *[Besides this my lord mayor charged me with one thing, which was never spoken by me, but by them. And that was, whether a mouse eating the Host received God or not. I never did ask this question, but indeed, they asked it of me, to which I made them no answer, but smiled.]*

That smile may signal another instance of Askew's continual identification with scriptural resisters of authority.[28] She may be following the prophet Daniel, whom she quotes in *The lattre examinacyon* when he confronts the idol-worshiping King Cyrus: "O kynge (sayth Daniel) be not deceyved Daniel 14" (106). Verse 5, from which her quotation comes, begins, "Then Daniel smiled." Here, then, Askew represents herself refusing to engage in an argument with idolaters or on the lord mayor's terms, and she withdraws from the dangers of heretical statements, insisting that *she* does not introduce this topic into the debate.[29] Similarly, when asked a direct question about the "Sacrament of the aultre," Askew says that she had indeed asked the priest "to hold me excused concernynge that matter" (24). This statement is consistent with Askew's restrained style and apparent position in 1545 that she did not want overtly to incriminate herself by denying transubstantiation.

Here is Louth's version, one that is replicated in narratives about Askew for the next few centuries.[30]

> My Lord Mayre, Sir M. Bowes, syttyng with the cownsell, as moste meetest for hir wysdome, and seeing hur standyng apon lyff and dethe, "I pray yow (quod he,) my lordes, gyve me leave to talke with this woman." Leave was granted. Lord Maiore. Thou folyshe woman, sayest thow—that the prestes can not make the body of Chryste? A.

Askowghe. I say so, my lorde, for I have redd—that God mayd man; but that man can make God, I never yet redd, nor I suppose ever shall red yt. L. Maior. No? yow folyshe woman: after the worde of consecratione ys it not the Lordes body? A. Askowghe. No, it ys bot consecrated bredd, or Sacramentale bredd. L. Maior. What, yf a mowse eate yt after the consecratione, what shalbecome of the mowse? What sayeste thow, thow folyshe woman? A. Askowghe. What shall become of hur, say yow, my lorde? L. Maior. I say—that that mowse is damned. A. Askew. Alacke poore mowse! By this tyme—the lordes had ynowghe of my lorde maiores divinitie, and perceavyng that some cowld not keap in theyr lawghyng, proceeded to the botchery and slawter that they entended afore thei came thither."[31]

[My Lord Mayor, Sir M. Bowes, sitting with the council, as most fitting for their wisdom, and seeing her on terms of life and death, "I pray you (said he,) my lords, give me permission to talk with this woman." Permission was granted. Lord Mayor: You foolish woman, do you say that the priests cannot make the body of Christ? A. Askew: I say so, my lord, for I have read that God made man, but that man can make God, I never yet read, nor I suppose ever shall read it. Lord Mayor: No? you foolish woman: after the word of consecration, is it not the Lord's body? A. Askew: No, it is but consecrated bread or sacramental bread. Lord Mayor: What if a mouse eat it after the consecration? What will become of the mouse? What do you say, you foolish woman? A. Askew: What do you say will become of her, my lord? Lord Mayor: I say that that mouse is damned. A. Askew: Alack, poor mouse! By this time the lords had enough of my Lord Mayor's divinity, and perceiving that some could not keep their laughter in, proceeded to the butchery and slaughter that they intended before they came there.]

The Askew represented in this scene participates in a lively, dramatic dialogue that develops the folly and brutality of her enemies and builds to Askew's broadly humorous punch line. While retaining the character of a woman versed in the Bible—at least in Genesis—and articulating standard Reformation doctrine, Louth's Askew shows none of the strategic caution of the original, nor her subtle identifications with persecuted prophets.[32] Since Louth was not present at any of Askew's interrogations, his so-called reminiscences just possibly derive from an account of the interrogation different from Askew's. But the more likely scenarios are that Louth actually revises Askew's text or that he recollects an oral version that had made the rounds; in either case Askew's character is transformed into a stereotype, the witty woman familiar from jest books, and her representation of herself as following in the footsteps of Daniel or St. Stephen disappears.[33]

In the mid-nineteenth century, the mouse story was still circulating and still erasing Askew's own text, particularly in religious contexts. One of the texts in which it reappears is a sermon on Anne Askew preached twice by the Evangelical minister Reverend Benjamin Oswald Sharp, once on November 11, 1868 at the church of St James Clerkenwell, and again on January 6, 1869 at the mission church on the site of a proposed Smithfield Martyrs Memorial Church. The sermon was printed in 1869.[34] Askew is, says Sharp, "the heroine of my story of to-night,"[35] a story directed with particular virulence against Roman Catholics and with particular enthusiasm to the women in his congregation, because, Sharp says, women have gained the most from the Reformation. His premise that "The highest and noblest life for woman is the domestic life" (8) seems an unlikely fit for Anne Askew—who left her husband and perhaps those ghostly children—but he continues to embellish the Protestant romance: she is an example of those "pure, noble, wise, gentle, and lovely women, pre-eminent for every gift and grace that could adorn humanity." He cites Lord Campbell's opinion that she was "a lady of great beauty, of gentle manners, and warm imagination."[36] When Sharp turns to the events covered in Askew's own *Examinations*, he paraphrases her text, using quotation marks, as if he were a novelist writing a dramatic dialogue: "'Please inform me why Stephen was stoned?' Like the Pharisees he answered, 'I cannot tell'" (10). "Her woman's wit stood her in good stead," Sharp says, and he cites Louth's mouse dialogue; after Askew says, "Alack! Poor mouse!" Sharp writes, "the cat played yet awhile with the poor mouse," thus emphasizing Askew's victimization and taking the anecdote one bathetic step further away from Askew's own text. But Askew, the "fair young creature, delicately nurtured, so unused to hardship—this mother of two little children—this sweet young Christian—this wise and noble lady," horribly racked and tortured, but triumphant in her faith, is an example to his congregation: "You can do here in Clerkenwell even as Anne Askew did at Smithfield" (16). Barely able to contain Askew in the confines of the mid-Victorian domestic ideal he has summoned, and standing eerily near to the place where she was burned, Sharp struggles with the didactic urge to make Askew into a religious model for middle-class women and yet to keep her from "gadding" out of bounds.

Sharp's reinvention of Askew joins a number of nineteenth-century texts, some of them histories of the Reformation, in which the shaping of Askew as a Protestant "heroine" continues not only as Protestant hagiography but also as a Protestant romance: Askew appears as the clever, suffering, doomed heroine betrayed by father and husband, dying tragically, the victim of the foolish and evil authorities of church and state. Bale himself had outlined the romance plot of the miseries of enforced marriage, and over the years it gathers more details, as in Anne Manning's *The Lincolnshire Tragedy* (1866), the first historical novel about Askew.[37] But it is finally another, later fiction, a second novel about Askew, that fully restores the figure of Anne Askew as an author and theological debater. Accomplishing what religious histories could not, Alison Macleod's 1965 novel, *The Heretics*, creates a historical context to illuminate the significance of Askew's text and actions. As Macleod knowingly writes in her author's note, "Historians can only guess, and the novelist's guess may be as good as theirs."[38] When I recently interviewed Macleod, she provided remarkable information about her writing of this clever, vivid, and politically engaged narrative. Interestingly, Macleod remembered her own aversion to Bolt's portrait of Thomas More when she saw the play *A Man for All Seasons*. She thought More was "much too simple" a hero since Bolt neglects to mention that "he was a passionate and determined persecutor of Protestants, and he was not . . . simply a martyr. . . . he had supported the king in all his tyrannical acts as long as he possibly could. So it was a much more complex and interesting situation than Robert Bolt made up."[39] Reacting against the idealized "great man" view of history, Macleod wrote a novel that is resolutely populist and feminist, rooted alike in the 1540s, in postwar England, and in her own political and professional experience. The narrator is Askew's maid, christened "Nancy Scarlett," who has returned to Lincolnshire after Askew's execution; with the help of Askew's brother, Francis, she has set up a school. John Foxe comes to interview her, and in a flashback she tells Askew's and her own story. With considerable energy, this novel treats such themes as disillusionment with authority; forced marriage; underground resisters to government persecution; the bonding of women that cuts across class lines; women's careers, particularly as scholars and teachers; and the unbridgeable divide between intellectually ambitious women and their husbands or lovers who want them to give up their careers to look after the house and children. Macleod's achievement here is to bring Askew's authorship—and authority—into the foreground by quoting *The Examinations* at length. Nancy Scarlett's task of circulating Askew's "pamphlets" after her death is of central importance to the plot and characterization. Even though the novel freely invents a close relationship with Katherine Parr, an audience with Henry VIII, and the heartbreaking death of those two little children in infancy, Macleod is always clear about Askew's agency. Interestingly for those scholars who see the Reformation as an important moment for the modern state, the reasons for Macleod's perspective appear to derive from her reading of the 1540s as a historical analogue to the 1950s.

In her account of the writing of her novel, Macleod explains how her own politics shaped her creation of Henry VIII's England. As a member of the British Communist party from 1939 to 1957 and as a subeditor of the *Daily Worker* from 1944 to 1957, Macleod once shared the idealistic hope of many party members that the Soviet Union would be the model for a new economic and social order. Refusing to credit the evidence of Soviet totalitarianism and of Stalin's horrific crimes well into the mid-1950s, Macleod did not leave the party until April 1957. For years after that, she looked for a way to explain how Soviet propaganda could have succeeded in co-opting so many intelligent, dedicated party members—and in converting their idealism into unblinking obedience to Soviet lies and mythmaking. In Macleod's own honest words, they had been "willing accomplices."[40] Feeling that the scale of Stalin's brutality was too recent and too overwhelming to represent in fiction, and that both her co-option and her disillusionment needed a smaller stage and a more focused vehicle, Macleod claims that "Henry VIII took hold of my imagination." Looking back into history for parallels to Stalin's regime, she found a workable analogy in "Henry VIII, whom a lot of very decent people supported because he was breaking away from the Pope, making England independent of Rome. And these people struggled to find excuses for him as long as they possibly could."[41] She imagined Henrician rule as a tyranny in which self-interest, fear, and the desire to survive turned subjects into willing puppets. Katherine Parr herself is depicted as a survivor who compromises her own ideals in obedience to her husband. In contrast to such expediency, Anne Askew stands out as the courageous individual who cannot bend to circumstance or tailor her faith to authoritarian requirements. At the same time, Macleod's Askew is hot-tempered, rash, even foolish in her single-mindedness, to the point of endangering others. But it is in Askew's total commitment to her faith that Macleod found her analogy for an unshakeable twentieth-century political conscience. As Sir William Parr is made to say, "You hot gospellers talk religion, but you mean politics. Democracy! Do you really think that's possible?"[42] Askew does indeed, believing in the rights of the individual—and of the individual woman—to speak out, to write, and even to defy the king himself on matters of conscience.

By emphasizing Askew's spoken, written, and performed resistance to the tyranny of Henrician rule, *The Heretics* demonstrates that recognizing the significance of Askew the religious writer means writing narratives that do not represent her either as a victim or as an uncomprehending onlooker at her own conflict with authority.[43] Macleod's fictional narrative "elucidates" Askew by imagining her simultaneous political, religious, and linguistic agency. By contrast, Bale implicitly undermines Askew's text by "elucidating" every sentence of his "young, dainty, and tender" subject's work and by providing details that make her words simply providential; Archdeacon Louth erases her scriptural allusiveness and her ironic discomfiture of her interrogators; Reverend Sharp substitutes a model Victorian heroine; and *Tales from the Tower* provides a victim of torture. Repeatedly, the problem appears to be in representing her as a writer, a woman, and a martyr all at the same time. Each version mentioned here reshapes *The Examinations* and Anne Askew herself in response to these intersecting—and historically contingent—elements of genre, gender, and faith. As work on Askew proceeds in dissertations, essays, and fictional narratives, it is my hope that the connections among these elements will be researched, theorized, and explored so that Askew's strong voice will always be represented by a culturally complex, strong history.

❧ ❧ ❧

NOTES

1. Ardent Productions with Eyemark Entertainment for The Learning Channel.

2. *The Examinations of Anne Askew*, ed. Elaine V. Beilin (Oxford: Oxford University Press, 1996), 127. In the absence of a television script, I provide Askew's words from her own text. All subsequent references to Askew's *Examinations* are to this edition. My modernized version follows long quotations.

3. For an extended discussion of Askew's self-representation as "a defender of the faith and teacher," see Elaine V. Beilin, *Redeeming Eve: Women Writers of the English Renaissance* (Princeton: Princeton University Press, 1987), chap. 2.

4. Bale's "Elucidation" makes explicit his reading of Askew's work; for an account of Foxe's less obvious, but arguably just as intrusive and ideologically motivated, editing, see Thomas S. Freeman and Sarah Elizabeth Wall, "Racking the Body, Shaping the Text: The Account of Anne Askew in Foxe's 'Book of Martyrs'," *Renaissance Quarterly* 54 (2001): 1165–96.

5. See Elaine V. Beilin, "Anne Askew's Journey to Lincoln" (paper presented at the Sixteenth Century Studies Conference, 1998). The material is now included in "Anne Askew: A Cultural History," in progress.

6. I'm grateful to students in my seminar "Prose and Poetry of the Renaissance" for their insights: Diala Alkhalil, James Brolin, Katherine Kellett, Sarah Lesselbaum, Vincent Livoti, Jennifer Redden, Aja Signor, and Allison Szewczyk.

7. Robert Bolt, preface to *A Man for All Seasons* (1960; reprint, New York: Vintage, 1990), xii–xiii.

8. Arthur Nolletti Jr., "Conversation with Fred Zinneman," in *The Films of Fred Zinneman*, ed. Arthur Nolletti Jr. (Albany: State University of New York Press, 1999), 11. See also Joel L. Super, "Fred Zinneman, *A Man for All Seasons* (1966) and Documentary Fiction," in *The Films of Fred Zinneman*, ed. Nolletti, 157–78. Super argues

that the film, like Zinneman's "documentary fictions," explores "how the protagonists are affected by political actions or events beyond their control" (161) and that Zinneman "far from seeing politics as eliminating the possibility of an individual narrative, sees it as providing both the impetus and the context for such a narrative" (175).

9. Owen Chadwick, *The Victorian Church* (New York: Oxford University Press, 1966), 1:450.

10. Anne Askew, *The First Examinacyon and The Lattre Examinacyon*, ed. John King (Aldershot, Hants: Ashgate, 1996); Askew, *The Examinations*.

11. Margaret Ezell, *Writing Women's Literary History* (Baltimore: Johns Hopkins University Press, 1993), chap. 1.

12. Ruth Willard Hughey, "Cultural Interests of Women in England from 1524–1640. Indicated in the Writings of the Women. A Survey" (Ph.D. diss., Cornell University, 1932), 26.

13. Betty Travitsky, ed., *The Paradise of Women: Writings by Englishwomen of the Renaissance* (1981; reprint, New York: Columbia University Press, 1989), 167–86; John King, *English Reformation Literature: The Tudor Origins of the Protestant Tradition* (Princeton: Princeton University Press, 1982), chap. 1 and passim. My own work places *The Examinations* within the contexts of local history and the religious, political, and gender polemics of the 1540s; see Beilin, "Anne Askew's Self-Portrait in *The Examinations*," in *Silent but for the Word: Tudor Women as Patrons, Translators, and Writers of Religious Works*, ed. Margaret Hannay (Kent, Ohio: The Kent State University Press, 1985), 77–91, and *Redeeming Eve*, chap. 2.

14. Thomas Betteridge, *Tudor Histories of the English Reformations, 1530–83* (Aldershot, Hants; Brookfield, Vt: Ashgate, 1999), 80–119; Theresa D. Kemp, "Translating (Anne) Askew: The Textual Remains of a Sixteenth-Century Heretic and Saint," *Renaissance Quarterly* 52 (1999): 1021–45.

15. Although Bale does include Askew in his catalog of British writers, *Illustrium maioris Britanniae scriptorum summarium* (Wesel, 1548), he continues to emphasize her youth and her resemblance to early Christian martyrs resisting idolatrous tyrants rather than her text.

16. Jacobus de Voragine, *The Golden Legend*, trans. Granger Ryan and Helmut Ripperger (New York: Arno, 1969), 690.

17. In his fictionalized history, *A Tudor Tapestry: Men, Women, and Society in Reformation England*, Derek Wilson writes, "Local legend says that Thomas and Anne had two children and that Anne neglected them in order to go 'gospelling' around the shire" (163–64), but he provides no source, written or oral, for this "local legend." Notably, the Privy Council record mentions no children when Askew and Kyme are summoned to appear on June 19, 1546: "Thomas Keyme of Lincolnshire, who had married one Anne Ascue, called hither, and likewise his wiffe, who refused him to be her hosbande—without any honeste allegacion—was appointed to return to his countrey tyll he shoulde be eftesoones sent for: and for that shee was very obstynate and headdy in reasonyng of matters of relygeone, wherein she shewed herselfe to be of a naughty oppinyon seeinge no perswasione of good reason could take place, she was sent to Newgate, to remaine there to answere to the lawe." *Narratives of the Days of the Reformation, Chiefly from the Manuscripts of John Foxe the Martyrologist*, ed. John Gough Nichols (London: Camden Society, 1859), appendix, 301. No later genealogies show two children. Other writers who mention them acknowledge Bale as their source. As recently as 1999, Susan James wrote, "Anne dutifully bore Kyme two children but her spirit was irrepressible. With no sanctioned social outlet for her abilities, Anne's temper turned

to religious zealotry. She became outspoken to the point that the much tried Thomas Kyme threw her out of his house for insulting the priests." *Kateryn Parr: The Making of a Queen* (Aldershot, Hants: Ashgate, 1999), 270.

18. The Psalm reference reads: Thou hast with thine arm redeemed thy people, the son of Jacob and Joseph. Selah. . . . The voice of thy thunder was in the heaven: the lightnings lightened the world: the earth trembled and shook (Psalm 77.15, 18, King James Version).

19. Freeman and Wall argue that Foxe's layout, particularly the paragraphing, heightens "the rhetorical power" of Askew's story ("Racking the Body," 1178). Their main claim, however, is that through "marginal notes, additional stories and documents, omissions and the arrangement of his narrative . . . Foxe ensured that the potentially subversive figure of Anne Askew was transformed into an effective icon for the causes he cherished" (1191); these causes included "the horrible consequences of royal and magisterial indifference to religious reform" (1190).

20. "In Annae Askevae Constantissimae feminae & martyris bustum, Epitaphium Sapphicum, I.F," in John Foxe, *Rerum in Ecclesia Gestarum Commentarii* (Basel, 1559; reprinted in Beilin, ed., *The Examinations*, 193).

21. John Foxe, "Epitaph in Sapphic Verse," trans. G. P. Goold, in Beilin, ed., *The Examinations*, 194.

22. John Foxe, *Actes and Monuments* (London: John Daye, 1570), 1420.

23. Freeman and Wall find that Francis Russell, the second earl of Bedford, was probably one of Foxe's sources and may have given Foxe information about his father's attendance at Askew's execution ("Racking the Body," 1185).

24. John Louth, "Reminiscences," in *Narratives of the Days of the Reformation*, 40.

25. Ibid., 42, 45–46.

26. Robert Parsons, the third part of *A Treatise: of Three Conversions of England*, [by N.D.] (1604), 491–92. The modernized version in square brackets is mine.

27. See Lynda Boose's work on scolds: "For Tudor-Stuart England, in village and town, an obsessive energy was invested in exerting control over the unruly woman—the woman who was exercising either her sexuality or her tongue under her own control rather than under the rule of a man. As illogical as it may seem, the two crimes—being a scold and being a so-called whore—were frequently conflated." "Scolding Brides and Bridling Scolds: Taming the Woman's Unruly Member," *Shakespeare Quarterly* 42 (1991): 195. See David Underdown, *Revel, Riot, and Rebellion: Popular Politics and Culture in England, 1603–1660* (Oxford and New York: Oxford University Press, 1985), 36–40; and "The Taming of the Scold: The Enforcement of Patriarchal Authority in Early Modern England," in *Order and Disorder in Early Modern England*, ed. Anthony Fletcher and John Stevenson (Cambridge: Cambridge University Press, 1985), 116–36.

28. See Elaine V. Beilin, "'The World reproov'd': Writing Faith and History in England," in *Culture and Change: Attending to Early Modern Women*, ed. Margaret Mikesell and Adele Seeff (Newark: University of Delaware Press, 2003).

29. Bale makes a similar point but makes it more vociferously: "No wyse man wyll thynke, that Christ wyll dwell in a mouse, nor yet that a mouse can dwell in Christ." Beilin, ed., *The Examinations*, 29.

30. See Reverend Benjamin Oswald Sharp, "Ann Askew—Martyr, A. D. 1545" (London: S. W. Partridge, 1869), 3; see also "Anne Askewe, The Lincolnshire Martyr," in *Religious Tracts* (London, [1870?]), 2; Mary E. T. Stirling, *Anne Askew: Her Life and Martyrdom* (London: Thynne, 1930), 11; Anthony Martienssen, *Queen Katherine Parr* (New York: McGraw-Hill, 1973), 191–92.

31. Louth, "Reminiscences," 41. The modernized version in square brackets is mine.

32. In something of the same vein, Susan James comments on Askew that Bishop Gardiner "mocked her steadfastness and told her that 'she was a parrot', quoting theology that she did not and could not understand." *Kateryn Parr*, 271.

33. Pamela Brown suggested the excellent point about jest books, and I gratefully include it.

34. The Smithfield Martyrs Memorial Church was built at the corner of St. John's Street and Wyclif Street in the old parish of St Peter's; the church was heavily damaged during World War II and was demolished in 1955. Today there is a large memorial in St James Clerkenwell to all the Smithfield martyrs, copying the names that were on the wall of the Smithfield Martyrs Memorial Church. I am grateful to Ben Walker, the verger of St James Clerkenwell, for his responses to my questions.

35. Sharp, "Ann Askew," 3.

36. Ibid, 9. Lord Campbell, of strong Presbyterian upbringing, was a leading Protestant parliamentarian.

37. Anne Manning, *The Lincolnshire Tragedy* (London: Bentley, 1866); also published as *Passages in the Life of the Faire Gospeller, Mistress Anne Askew* (New York: Dodd, 1866). I analyze these texts in "Anne Askew: A Cultural History," in progress.

38. Alison Macleod, *The Heretics* (London: Hodder and Stoughton, 1965; Boston: Houghton Mifflin, 1966), 6.

39. Interview by author, June 26, 2000.

40. Alison Macleod, *The Death of Uncle Joe* (Rendlesham, Woodbridge: Merlin Press, 1997), 12.

41. Of Henry's 1541 visit to Lincolnshire, the narrator writes: "When the King himself appeared, on his great warhorse, he towered above the dust. There was a sort of wave that rolled before him—the movement of the people, sinking on to their knees. It was impossible for us not to kneel. Not because everyone else was doing it, but because of the splendour of the King's look. . . . Nowadays when the young people ask me how this man could make brothers betray their sisters, wives their husbands—how a whole nation could leave the faith of their fathers, and put their faith only in him—I cannot explain it. I can only say: 'You never saw King Harry smile.' I was not blinded. . . . But . . . the secret of his power, perhaps, was this; he looked at us, the people, as if he loved us" (Macleod, *The Heretics*, 80).

42. Macleod, *The Heretics*, 122.

43. See, by contrast, Alison Plowden's version in *Tudor Women: Queens and Commoners* (New York: Atheneum, 1979): "Anne Askew is an interesting example of an educated, highly-intelligent, passionate woman destined to become the victim of the society in which she lived—a woman who could not accept her circumstances but fought an angry, hopeless battle against them. She was unquestionably sincere in her religious convictions—to what extent she also used them unconsciously to sublimate tensions and frustrations which might otherwise have been unbearable, we can only speculate" (112).

BIBLIOGRAPHY

"Anne Askewe, The Lincolnshire Martyr." In *Religious Tracts*. London, [1870?].

Askew, Anne. *The First Examinacyon of Anne Askewe*. [Wesel: Dirik van der Straten], 1546.

———. *The Lattre Examinacyon of Anne Askewe*. [Wesel: Dirik van der Straten], 1547.

———. *The First Examinacion. The latter examynacyon.* [London: Nicholas Hill?, 1547].

———. *The first Examinacion. The latter Examination.* [London: William Hill?, 1548?].

———. *The fyrst Exawinacion* [sic]. *The latter Examinacion.* [London: William Copland? c. 1550].

———. *Prima examinatio. Secunda Examinatio.* In John Foxe, *Rerum in Ecclesia Gestarum Commentarii.* Basel, 1559.

———. *The First Examination. The Latter Examinacion.* [London, c. 1560?].

———. *The Two Examinations.* In John Foxe, *Actes and Monuments.* London: John Daye, 1563. (Note: *The Examinations* appeared in all subsequent editions of *Actes and Monuments*)

———. *The First Examination of the Worthy Servant of God, Mystresse Anne Askew.* London: Robert Waldegrave [1585].

———. *Writings of Edward the Sixth, William Hugh, Queen Catherine Parr, Anne Askew, Lady Jane Grey, Hamilton and Balnaves.* London: Religious Tract Society, n.d. Rpt. 1831, 1836, 1840, 186?. Republished in *British Reformers.* Philadelphia: Presbyterian Board of Publication, 1842. Vol. 3.

———. *The Account of the Sufferings of Anne Askew.* London: Francis & John Rivington, 1849.

———. *The First Examination. The Latter Examination.* In *Select Works of John Bale . . . Containing the Examinations of Lord Cobham, William Thorpe, and Anne Askewe.* Ed. Reverend Henry Christmas. The Parker Society. Cambridge: Cambridge University Press, 1849. Rpt. New York: Johnson Reprint Corp., 1968.

———. *The Examinations of Anne Askew.* Ed. Elaine V. Beilin. Oxford: Oxford University Press, 1996.

———. *The First Examinacyon and The Lattre Examinacyon.* Ed. John King. *The Early Modern Englishwoman 1500–1700,* Part 1, Vol. 1. Aldershot, Hants: Ashgate, 1996.

Bale, John. *The Actes of English Votaryes.* Antwerp, 1546.

———. *Illustrium maioris Britanniae scriptorum summarium.* Wesel: Dirik van der Straten, 1548.

Beilin, Elaine V. "Anne Askew's Self-Portrait in *The Examinations.*" In *Silent but for the Word: Tudor Women as Patrons, Translators, and Writers of Religious Works,* ed. Margaret Hannay, 77–91. Kent, Ohio: The Kent State University Press, 1985.

———. *Redeeming Eve: Women Writers of the English Renaissance.* Princeton: Princeton University Press, 1987.

———. "'The World reproov'd': Writing Faith and History in England." In *Culture and Change: Attending to Early Modern Women,* ed. Margaret Mikesell and Adele Seeff. Newark: University of Delaware Press, 2003.

Betteridge, Thomas. *Tudor Histories of the English Reformations, 1530–83.* St. Andrews Studies in Reformation History. Aldershot, Hants, and Brookfield, Vt: Ashgate, 1999.

Bolt, Robert. Preface to *A Man for All Seasons.* 1960. Reprint, New York: Vintage, 1990.

Boose, Lynda E. "Scolding Brides and Bridling Scolds: Taming the Woman's Unruly Member." *Shakespeare Quarterly* 42 (1991): 179–213.

Chadwick, Owen. *The Victorian Church.* Vol. 1. New York: Oxford University Press, 1966.

Ezell, Margaret. *Writing Women's Literary History*. Baltimore: Johns Hopkins University Press, 1993.

Foxe, John. *Actes and Monuments*. London: John Daye, 1570.

———. "In Annae Askevae Constantissimae feminae & martyris bustum, Epitaphium Sapphicum, I.F." In *Rerum in Ecclesia Gestarum . . . Commentarii*. Basel, 1559. Reprinted in *The Examinations of Anne Askew*, ed. Elaine V. Beilin. Oxford: Oxford University Press, 1996.

Freeman, Thomas S., and Sarah Elizabeth Wall. "Racking the Body, Shaping the Text: The Account of Anne Askew in Foxe's 'Book of Martyrs'." *Renaissance Quarterly* 54 (2001): 1165–96.

Hughey, Ruth Willard. "Cultural Interests of Women in England from 1524–1640. Indicated in the Writings of the Women. A Survey." Ph.D. diss., Cornell University, 1932.

James, Susan. *Kateryn Parr: The Making of a Queen*. Aldershot, Hants: Ashgate, 1999.

Kemp, Theresa D. "Translating (Anne) Askew: The Textual Remains of a Sixteenth-Century Heretic and Saint." *Renaissance Quarterly* 52 (1999): 1021–45.

King, John. *English Reformation Literature: The Tudor Origins of the Protestant Tradition*. Princeton: Princeton University Press, 1982.

Louth, John. "Reminiscences." In *Narratives of the Days of the Reformation, Chiefly from the Manuscripts of John Foxe the Martyrologist*, ed. John Gough Nichols. London: Camden Society, 1859.

Macleod, Alison. *The Heretics*. London: Hodder and Stoughton, 1965; Boston: Houghton Mifflin, 1966.

———. *The Death of Uncle Joe*. Rendlesham, Woodbridge: Merlin Press, 1997.

———. Interview by author. June 26, 2000.

Manning, Anne. *The Lincolnshire Tragedy*. London: Bentley, 1866. Also published as *Passages in the Life of the Faire Gospeller, Mistress Anne Askew*. New York: Dodd, 1866.

Martienssen, Anthony. *Queen Katherine Parr*. New York: McGraw-Hill, 1973.

Narratives of the Days of the Reformation, Chiefly from the Manuscripts of John Foxe the Martyrologist. Ed. John Gough Nichols. London: Camden Society, 1859.

Nolletti, Arthur, Jr. "Conversation with Fred Zinneman." In *The Films of Fred Zinneman*, ed. Arthur Nolletti Jr. Albany: State University of New York Press, 1999.

Parsons, Robert. *The Third Part of A Treatise, Intituled: of three Conversions of England*. [By N.D.] 1604.

Plowden, Alison. *Tudor Women: Queens and Commoners*. New York: Atheneum, 1979.

Sharp, Reverend Benjamin Oswald. "Ann Askew—Martyr, A. D. 1545." London: S. W. Partridge, 1869.

Stirling, Mary E. T. *Anne Askew: Her Life and Martyrdom*. London: Thynne, 1930.

Strype, John. *Ecclesiastical Memorials*. 3 vols. London: John Wyat, 1721. Vol. 1.

Super, Joel L. "Fred Zinneman, *A Man for All Seasons* (1966) and Documentary Fiction." In *The Films of Fred Zinneman*, ed. Arthur Nolletti Jr., 157–78. Albany: State University of New York Press, 1999.

Tales from the Tower. Ardent Productions with Eyemark Entertainment for The Learning Channel.

Travitsky, Betty, ed. *The Paradise of Women: Writings by Englishwomen of the Renaissance*. 1981. Reprint, New York: Columbia University Press, 1989.

Underdown, David. *Revel, Riot, and Rebellion: Popular Politics and Culture in England, 1603–1660*. Oxford and New York: Oxford University Press, 1985.

———. "The Taming of the Scold: The Enforcement of Patriarchal Authority in Early Modern England." In *Order and Disorder in Early Modern England*, ed. Anthony Fletcher and John Stevenson, 116–36. Cambridge: Cambridge University Press, 1985.

Voragine, Jacobus de. *The Golden Legend*. Trans. Granger Ryan and Helmut Ripperger. New York: Arno, 1969.

Wilson, Derek. *A Tudor Tapestry: Men, Women, and Society in Reformation England*. London: William Heineman, 1972.

Further Reading

Dolan, Frances E. "'Gentlemen, I Have One Thing More to Say': Women on Scaffolds in England, 1563–1680." *Modern Philology* 92 (1994): 157–78.

Kendall, Ritchie D. *The Drama of Dissent: The Radical Poetics of Nonconformity, 1380–1590*. Chapel Hill and London: University of North Carolina Press, 1986.

Kennedy, Gwynne. *Just Anger: Representing Women's Anger in Early Modern England*. Carbondale and Edwardsville: Southern Illinois University Press, 2000.

Knott, John R. *Discourses of Martyrdom in English Literature, 1563–1694*. Cambridge: Cambridge University Press, 1993.

Linton, Joan Pong. "The Plural Voices of Anne Askew." In *Write or Be Written: Early Modern Women Poets and Cultural Constraints*, ed. Barbara Smith and Ursula Appelt, 137–51. Aldershot, Hants, and Burlington Vt.: Ashgate, 2001.

Mazzola, Elizabeth. "Expert Witnesses and Secret Subjects: Anne Askew's *Examinations* and Renaissance Self Incrimination." In *Political Rhetoric, Power, and Renaissance Women*, ed. Carole Levin and Patricia A. Sullivan. Albany, N.Y.: State University of New York, 1995.

McQuade, Paula. "'Except that they had offended the Lawe': Gender and Jurisprudence in *The Examinations of Anne Askew*." *Literature and History*, 3d ser., 3 (1994):1–14.

Mueller, Janel. "A Tudor Queen Finds Voice: Katherine Parr's Lamentation of a Sinner." In *The Historical Renaissance: New Essays on Tudor and Stuart Literature and Culture*, ed. Heather Dubrow and Richard Strier, 15–47. Chicago and London: University of Chicago Press, 1988.

Watt, Diane. *Secretaries of God: Women Prophets in Late Medieval and Early Modern England*. Cambridge: D. S. Brewer, 1997.

Contributors

Elaine V. Beilin is professor of English at Framingham State College. She is the author of *Redeeming Eve: Women Writers of the English Renaissance* (Princeton: Princeton University Press, 1987) and numerous articles on early modern women writers and the editor of *The Examinations of Anne Askew* (New York: Oxford University Press, 1996). She is currently working on a cultural history of Anne Askew.

Pamela Joseph Benson is professor of English at Rhode Island College. She is the author of *The Invention of the Renaissance Woman: The Challenge of Female Independence in the Literature and Thought of Italy and England* (University Park: The Pennsylvania State University Press, 1992) and numerous articles on women and literature in the late Middle Ages and Renaissance and editor of *Italian Tales from the Age of Shakespeare* (London: J. M. Dent; Vermont: Charles E. Tuttle, Everyman, 1996). She is currently working on a book on Aemilia Lanyer in English and Italian literary and cultural contexts.

Kevin Brownlee is professor of Romance languages at the University of Pennsylvania, specializing in medieval French and Italian literature. His work in French ranges from Chretién de Troyes to François Villon. His most recent book is *Discourses of the Self: Autobiography and Literary Models in Christine de Pizan* (forthcoming). His coedited volumes include *The New Medievalism* with Marina S. Brownlee and Stephen G. Nichols (Baltimore: John Hopkins University Press, 1991); *Rethinking the "Romance of the Rose": Text, Image, Reception* with Sylvia Huot (Philadelphia: University of Pennsylvania Press, 1992); and *Generation and Degeneration: Tropes of Reproduction from Antiquity through Early Modern Europe*, Valeria Finucci (Durham [N.C.]: Duke University Press, 2001). His primary research focus in Italian is Dante, centering on authority and the authorial self, on literary genealogies, and on Dante's use of Classic models. He is currently writing a book on cultural authority and genealogy in medieval France and Italy, including the dynamic of Franco-Italian literary interaction in Brunetto, the *Fiore*, Dante, and Petrarch.

Virginia Cox is professor of Italian at New York University; author of *The Renaissance Dialogue: Literary Dialogue in Its Social and Political Contexts, Castiglione to Galileo* (Cambridge and New York: Cambridge University Press, 1992); translator and editor of *The*

Worth of Women by Moderata Fonte (Chicago: University of Chicago Press, 1997); and editor of Castiglione's *Courtier* (London: J. M. Dent; Vermont: Charles E. Tuttle, Everyman, 1994). Her essay "The Single Self: Feminist Thought and the Marriage Market in Early Modern Venice" [*Renaissance Quarterly* 48 (1995): 513–81] won that journal's prize for best article published there in 1995.

Stuart Curran is Vartan Gregorian Professor of English and served for a decade as the director of the Center for Italian Studies at the University of Pennsylvania. A founding member of the Brown University Women Writers Project, he has been actively involved in the recovery of British women writers of the eighteenth and nineteenth centuries. Along with authoring numerous critical essays, he has edited the poems of Charlotte Smith (New York: Oxford University Press, 1993) and Mary Shelley's novel set in medieval Tuscany, *Valperga* (New York: Oxford University Press, 1997).

Thelma S. Fenster is professor of French at Fordham University, New York, where she has also directed the Medieval Studies Program. Her publications include editions and translations of Christine de Pizan's narrative poetry, including the *Epistre au dieu d'Amours*, the *Dit de la Rose*, and the *Livre du duc des vrais amans*, as well as several articles on Christine. With Clare A. Lees, she edited *Gender in Debate from the Early Middle Ages to the Renaissance* (New York: Palgrave, 2002). She also writes on Arthurian subjects.

Fabio Finotti is tenured professor of history of Italian language at the University of Trieste and of history of Italian literature in Portogruaro (Trieste-Padova). He also teaches at the Fondazione Giorgio Cini in Venice. He is secretary of Antonio Fogazzaro's "National Edition," is a member of the Venice Petrarca Committee, and serves on the National Committee for the "Lingua Italiana nel Mondo." He has edited Tommaseo, Carducci, D'Annunzio (Einaudi), and Fogazzaro (Accademia Olimpica). He has written and contributed to books on subjects ranging from Petrarch and the Renaissance to Leopardi to the contemporary novel and poetry. In 1993 he won the Mario di Nola Prize of the Accademia Nazionale dei Lincei.

Lina Insana is assistant professor of Italian at the University of Pittsburgh. Her interests include Italian and French Holocaust literature, the literature of Fascism and World War II, the modern Italian detective novel, women under Fascism, and political and economic approaches to literature of all periods and genres. She has published on Fenoglio, Levi, and Boccaccio and is currently revising for publication her dissertation, which looks at the metaphor and practice of translation in Primo Levi's Holocaust works.

Ann Rosalind Jones is Esther Cloudman Dunn Professor of Comparative Literature at Smith College. Her publications include *The Currency of Eros: Women's Love Lyric in Europe, 1540–1620* (Bloomington: University of Indiana Press, 1990), a translation of *The Poems and Selected Letters of Veronica Franco* with Margaret Rosenthal (Chicago: University of Chicago Press, 1998), and *Renaissance Clothing and the Materials of Memory* with Peter Stallybrass (Cambridge: Cambridge University Press, 2000). Her next projects are a translation and study of Cesare Vecellio's costume books (Venice, 1590 and 1598) and a comparison of women's dialogues in the French, Italian, and English *querelle des femmes*.

John N. King is Humanities Distinguished Professor of English and of Religious Studies and Distinguished University Professor at The Ohio State University. His books include *English Reformation Literature: The Tudor Origins of the Protestant Tradition* (Princeton: Princeton University Press, 1982); *Tudor Royal Iconography: Literature and Art in an Age of Religious Crisis* (Princeton: Princeton University Press, 1989); *Spenser's Poetry and the Reformation Tradition* (Princeton: Princeton University Press, 1990); and *Milton and Religious Controversy: Satire and Polemic in Paradise Lost* (Cambridge and New York: Cambridge University Press, 2000). His research and teaching interests include sixteenth-century English nondramatic literature; Reformation cultural studies; writings by John Foxe, Edmund Spenser, and John Milton; Tudor and Stuart iconography; religious writing by and for early modern women; and late medieval and early modern manuscript and print culture. He serves as an editor of *Literature and History*, *Reformation*, and the British Academy project to edit John Foxe's *Acts and Monuments of the Christian Martyrs*. In addition to the Lilly Foundation Fellowship in Religion and the Humanities at the National Humanities Center, he has received four long-term National Endowment for the Humanities Fellowships, including residential fellowships at Brown University, the Huntington Library, and the Folger Shakespeare Library. He has directed three National Endowment for the Humanities Summer Seminars for College and University Teachers.

Victoria Kirkham is professor of Romance languages at the University of Pennsylvania. She is coauthor with Anthony K. Cassell of *Diana's Hunt. Caccia di Diana. Boccaccio's First Work* (Philadelphia: University of Pennsylvania Press, 1991) and author of *The Sign of Reason in Boccaccio's Fiction* (Florence: Leo S. Olschki, 1993) and *Fabulous Vernacular: Boccaccio's Filocolo and the Art of Medieval Fiction* (Ann Arbor: University of Michigan Press, 2001), winner of the Modern Language Association's Scaglione Manuscript Prize for 2000. She has published half a dozen articles on Laura Battiferra, including "Creative Partners: The Marriage of Laura Battiferra and Bartolomeo Ammannati" (*Renaissance Quarterly* 55, no. 2 [2002]), the nucleus of a book in progress. She is currently preparing an anthology of selected writings by Battiferra with translation and commentary for "The Other Voice" series at the University of Chicago Press.

Armando Maggi is an associate professor in the Department of Romance Languages at the University of Chicago. He is author of *Uttering the Word: The Mystical Performances of Maria Maddalena de' Pazzi, a Renaissance Visionary* (Albany: State University of New York Press, 1998) and *Identità e impresa rinascimentale* (Ravenna: Longo, 1998). He has most recently published *Satan's Rhetoric: A Study of Renaissance Demonology* (Chicago: University of Chicago Press, 2001). Editor of three Renaissance treatises, he has also written many essays on the Renaissance philosophy of love and female mysticism. His areas of work are Italian and Portuguese Renaissance literature and philosophy, Renaissance mysticism, religious studies, and contemporary Italian and Portuguese literature.

E. Ann Matter is professor and chair of religious studies at the University of Pennsylvania. She has published on medieval and early modern Christian literature and culture, especially concentrating on themes of biblical interpretation, mysticism and spirituality, and women's experience. She is currently writing a book on Maria Domitilla Galluzzi.

Deanna Shemek is associate professor of Italian in the Literature Department of the University of California, Santa Cruz. Her publications include *Ladies Errant: Wayward Women and Social Order in Early Modern Italy* (Durham [N.C.]: Duke University Press, 1998), with essays on Ariosto, Bandello, Laura Terracina, and the role of women in early modern festivals. She is cotranslator and editor of Adriana Cavarero's *Stately Bodies* (Ann Arbor: University of Michigan Press, 2002), a feminist examination of the metaphor of the body politic in ancient, Renaissance, and modern political and literary thought; and coeditor with Dennis Looney of *Phaeton's Children: The Este Court and Its Culture in Early Modern Italy* (Medieval & Renaissance Texts & Studies, forthcoming). Her current book projects include a selection of Isabella d'Este's letters translated into English and a critical monograph on Isabella d'Este.

Janet Levarie Smarr is a professor in the Department of Theater and Dance and in the Italian Studies Program at the University of California, San Diego. Her publications include *Boccaccio and Fiammetta: The Narrator as Lover* (Urbana: University of Illinois Press, 1986), translations of Boccaccio's *Eclogues* and of Italian Renaissance tales, and an edited volume on *Historical Criticism and the Challenge of Theory* (Urbana: University of Illinois Press, 1993), along with articles on Dante, Petrarch, Boccaccio, and Renaissance women writers, including Gaspara Stampa, Moderata Fonte, and Tullia d'Aragona. Her new book, *Joining the Conversation: Dialogues by Renaissance Women*, is being published by the University of Michigan Press. Smarr has also coedited with Daria Valentini *Italian Women and the City*. (Madison, N.J.: Fairleigh Dickinson University Press; London and Cranbury, N.J.: Associated University Presses, 2003).

Index

Note: This index does not include literary critics and theorists from the mid–twentieth century and later. These names appear in the bibliographies that follow the essays.